JAZZ

A HISTORY

SECOND EDITION

FRANK TIRRO

Yale University

W. W. NORTON & COMPANY

NEW YORK   LONDON

Copyright © 1993, 1977 by W. W. Norton & Company, Inc.

The text of this book is composed in Caslon
with the display set in Gill Sans Bold & Arcadia
Composition by Vail
Manufacturing by Courier, Westford
Book design by Maura Fadden Rosenthal

Library of Congress Cataloging-in-Publication Data:

Tirro, Frank.
    Jazz : a history / by Frank Tirro. — 2nd ed.
        p.   cm.
    Discography:
    Includes bibliographical references and index.
    1. Jazz—History and criticism. I. Title.
    ML3506.T57   1993
    781.65'09—dc20   92-32682
                                                          CIP
                                                          MN

ISBN 0-393-96187-7 (cl)   ISBN 0-393-96363-2 (pkgd with disk)
ISBN 0-393-96368-3 (pa)   ISBN 0-393-99734-0 (compact disk)

W.W. Norton & Company, Inc., 500 Fifth Avenue, New York,
N.Y. 10110
W.W. Norton & Company Ltd., 10 Coptic Street, London WC1A
1PU

1 2 3 4 5 6 7 8 9 0

To the Memory of

FRANK TIRRO, SR.

He played his way to America,
gigged with a ragtime band, and
gave me my first clarinet lesson.

CONTENTS

4

5

6

7

8

A PROLIFERATION OF STYLES ● 330
FROM THE '40S THROUGH THE '50S

Overview. Cool Jazz. Third Stream. West Coast Jazz. Funky and Hard Bop. Something Old and Something New. Sonny Rollins. Something Borrowed. Modal Jazz—Miles Davis and Kind of Blue. Social Cause and Musical Effect. Summing Up the '50s.

9

SOCIAL AND MUSICAL REVOLUTION ● 371
THE 1960S

Introduction. Free Jazz—Ornette Coleman. Musical Reactions. A Central Figure—John Coltrane. Out in Front—Miles Davis in the '60s and '70s. The New Groups. The AACM. One More Time.

10

CONFUSION AND FUSION ● 406
FROM THE '70S TO THE '80S

Introduction. Ornette Coleman. Miles Davis Again. Cecil Taylor. The Keyboard Players—Bill Evans, Herbie Hancock, Chick Corea, Keith Jarrett, Joe Zawinul. Weather Report. The Mahavishnu Orchestra. The AACM and the Art Ensemble of Chicago. Rehearsal and Recording Bands. The Decade in Review.

11

A PLURALITY OF STYLES ● 438
THROUGH THE '80S AND INTO THE '90S

Introduction. Fusion and Miles Davis. Neoclassicism and Modern Bebop. Wynton Marsalis. Other Neoclassicists. Free Jazz of the '80s—George Lewis. Jazz Composition in the 1980s—Anthony Davis. Postmodernism and Jazz—Jane Ira Bloom. New Sounds, New Wave, New Age, and Good Old-Fashioned Jazz. Ray Anderson. Today and Tomorrow.

APPENDICES

LISTENING GUIDES • 3*

TRANSCRIPTIONS • 61*

SYNOPTIC TABLE ● 89*

ANNOTATED BIBLIOGRAPHY ● 103*

General Bibliography. Dictionaries and Encyclopedias. Histories and Chronologies. Bibliographies. Discographies. Indices of Music. Periodicals. Indices to Periodical Literature. Jazz Archives. African Music. Music of the U.S. in the Late Nineteenth Century. Ragtime. The Blues. Early Jazz. Swing. Modern Jazz. Women in Jazz. Miscellaneous—Literature, Philosophy, Interviews, Rock, Gospel, Recordings, etc.

SELECTED DISCOGRAPHY ● 127*

INDICES TO THE RECORD COLLECTIONS ● 131*

GLOSSARY ● 169*

LIST OF ILLUSTRATIONS

PREFACE

Jazz is a *democratic* music in the best sense of the word, for it is the collective achievement of a people. It is not the diversion of an elite aristocracy—it emerged from humble beginnings to be shared by rich and poor alike. It is a participative music, a communal event of listeners and performers, and its proponents and practitioners come from every walk of life. The performance and enjoyment of jazz embodies those principles of equality of rights, access of opportunity, and fair treatment that are taken for granted by all people of a free society. Its language is direct and expressive, can be both simple or eloquent, and requires an interaction between player and listener where even the listener must participate actively.

Every live performance of a jazz work is new, exciting, and challenging, and the classic recorded performances can help us develop discriminating taste and increase our enjoyment through informed, repeated, attentive listening. This book is intended to serve as a guide to the music and as an interpretation of the historical interaction that has taken place among jazz musicians, the music, and society. It is a survey of the historical development of this music from its African precursors to its current living exponents. To profit from this book, the reader must become a serious listener and pay careful attention to the music. Fortunately, doing that is not a burden but an immense pleasure.

Jazz is a beautiful music, an American music, an art form that has influenced creative thought throughout the world. The peoples of Great Britain, Europe, the former Soviet Union, Africa, the Near and Far East, Australia, and all of North and South America are now participants in its story. They have made important contributions to the music, to its roster of important musicians, and to its history, but jazz is an American phenomenon. It was born here in the United States, and it has not renounced its citizenship. It was first performed by black Americans newly released from bondage who expressed their God-given talents and their beliefs about freedom, identity, and art through their music. Jazz is still a profound manifestation of freedom, talent, achievement, and identity.

This book is not a recounting of anecdotes nor a simple chronology of musical events, but a history. It evaluates the gathered evidence and draws conclusions. Its narrative and summaries are based on repeated careful listenings to thousands of recordings, on the reports of musicians who witnessed and experienced many of the crucial events and created some of the masterworks, and on the fresh research and insightful thought of hundreds of serious scholars who love and respect this music. Because the student needs ready access to important samples of jazz from all periods, the text frequently refers to a new collection, The *Norton Anthology of Jazz (NAJ)*, and recorded examples collected in two widely available anthologies, *The Smithsonian Collection of Classic Jazz (SCCJ)* and the New World Records *Recorded Anthology of American Music (NW)*. Virtually every college music library owns both collections, and the two sets remain available for purchase.* Also, the recordings of *SCCJ* and *NW* have accompanying critical notes that are insightful, instructive, and accurate, including important discographical information. The discussions in this text are by no means limited to the several hundred examples preserved in these three anthologies, but a judicious use of these selections and the acquisition of a handful of important modern recordings (jazz of the '70s and '80s) will provide the reader with a second resource of prime examples and acknowledged masterworks on which to build a lifetime of rewarding listening. To ease the initial task of finding specific examples in these anthologies, appendices at the back of this book cross-reference the *NAJ*, *SCCJ*, and *NW* editions, indicate title locations within the available formats (LP, cassette, or CD), and combine the three lists to show the complete spectrum of available offerings chronologically and alphabetically (by leader or group).

Since jazz history, that is, the story of the music and the musicians, is inextricably tied to American social history, I have attempted to describe and interpret the relationship between jazz and American culture in general. Throughout the narrative, I have highlighted specific links between individ-

---

*The *Norton Anthology of Jazz* as well as the complete set of *The Smithsonian Collection of Classic Jazz* may be ordered at a special educational rate in any of three forms (LPs, cassettes, or CDs) from W. W. Norton, 500 Fifth Avenue, New York, NY 10110 (tel. 800/223-2584). Individual recordings of the *New World* series may be ordered from New World Records, 701 Seventh Avenue, New York, NY 10036 (tel. 212/302-0460).

ual compositions, stylistic movements, or particular musicians and the unfolding history of twentieth-century America. At the back of the book, readers will also find a synoptic table to help correlate significant events in other fields with those in jazz.

This book is organized into almost a dozen chapters, each of which embraces a chronological and musical span. Clearly, musical styles do not conform to arbitrary time designations, but there is a logical developmental scheme in the history of this music that unfolds in a rather orderly fashion. Jazz has its eclectic elements, but each generation of new musicians builds upon the explorations and accomplishments of its musical ancestors. In this book both the process and the product are described.

Today, jazz appears in a multiplicity of styles that could never have been imagined forty or fifty years ago. Also, today we revere the past in a manner completely different from the way it was viewed in those days. There were no "History of Jazz" courses in college and there was no New York Jazz Repertory Company or Louisiana Repertory Jazz Ensemble to re-create the excitement of historical performances (the former group includes some of the original soloists, leaders, and composers, and the latter employs authentic instruments, makes use of scholarly research, performs stylistically correct solos, and in general pays meticulous attention to performance practices of earlier times). We not only luxuriate in the present, we savor the past and eagerly await the future.

In writing—and now revising—this book, I have attempted to integrate recent research in the field with relevant scholarship from allied areas: sociology, cultural anthropology, and American history. Also, I have written what follows with the assumption that a greater interest in and awareness of jazz will develop inevitably from understanding specific monuments of the art, so the reader will find analyses of important solos and recognized works rather than an encyclopedic listing of names, dates, works, and places. Regrettably, many extraordinary musicians have been excluded in order to maintain interpretive balance and restrict the size of the volume, but an abundance of factual detail remains. Still, one should not expect to find out the name of every trumpet player in the December 1936 Benny Goodman orchestra without going to the bibliography for outside references. The high quality and remarkable quantity of serious jazz research in recent years has enlarged the bibliography. It might have been shorter and more selective, but then it would not have served its intended purpose. It stands at the end of this book to help readers explore beyond the limits of these pages.

During the fifteen years between editions, I have rethought many of my views. Most remain firm; a few have been modified, and I have heard much new music of the last two decades. The chapters spanning 1960 to the present are almost entirely new. They deal with the complex interactions of younger musicians and recent events, with much new material on Miles Davis, John Coltrane, Ornette Coleman, the Association for the Advancement of Creative Musicians (AACM), and the musicians associated with these catalytic personalities and agents. Wynton Marsalis and his generation are covered as well, even though writing about music so recent sometimes feels more prophetic than historical. The earlier chapters have also been modified, to incorporate new research on old masters. Especially noticeable will be the extensive revisions and additions to the sections dedicated to Duke Ellington and Charlie Parker. However, one cannot simply add new material to a one-volume work, so the opening of the book has been revamped and restructured to move the narrative more directly from African precursors to ragtime, blues, and early jazz.

My debts to the ideas and work of other writers and scholars of jazz are numerous, and I hope they are obvious from the references in the text. The writings of Leonard Feather, Gunther Schuller, Dan Morgenstern, André Hodeir, Samuel Charters, Eileen Southern, and many others are the seminal studies upon which this volume has been constructed, but the essence of my writing is the verbal distillation of what I have actually heard live or on record. Also, I have learned so much through my cordial association over the years with Gerry Mulligan, George Wein, Mary Lou Williams, Benny Goodman, Lionel Hampton, Jane Ira Bloom, Willie Ruff, Bunky Green, Patrick Williams, and especially Richard Wang, that I can never fully repay this debt. I feel the same about what I have learned from my students. Claire Brook, Vice President and Music Editor of W. W. Norton, made this book possible. I will be eternally grateful to her for her understanding, honesty, patience, and impartiality.

The magnificent resources of Yale University's libraries were especially useful during this period of revision. The skill and generosity of Richard Warren, Jr., Curator of the Historical Sound Recordings Collection; Patricia Willis, Curator of the James Weldon Johnson Collection of the Beinecke Rare Book and Manuscript Library; Harold E. Samuel, Librarian, and Kendall Crilly, Public Services Librarian, of the John Herrick Jackson Music Library (Benny Goodman, Stanley Dance, and Fred Plaut Collections); and Vivian Perlis, Director of the Oral History, American Music Archive (the Duke Ellington Collection), are gratefully acknowledged. In preparing the first edition, I received assistance from several quarters and am still grateful to the Duke University Research Council for financial support to visit archives, collect material, and acquire some editorial assistance. Particular thanks are due Professor Richard Wright of the University of Kansas who made his enormous collection of recordings available to me and taped many examples

I needed for my course work as well as for this book. He and Dean Warrick L. Carter of the Berklee College of Music, Professor Thom David Mason of the University of Southern California, and Professor Charles Blancq of the University of New Orleans all gave critical readings to the manuscript, and their comments helped me focus my ideas, reevaluate some conclusions, and correct factual errors. Those faults which remain are mine, but many of the improvements are theirs. Christopher White, fine bassist and former Director of the Rutgers Institute of Jazz Studies, generously opened the doors of the Institute and the drawers of the files. Many libraries and librarians were always ready to provide one more document, and a few that were particularly helpful were those of the University of Chicago, New York Public Library, Library of Congress, Duke University Libraries, Chicago Public Library, New Orleans Jazz Museum, Kansas City Public Library, Newberry Library, University of Kansas Libraries, Tulane University Library, and University of North Carolina Libraries. Gary M. Shivers, Station Director of Station KMUW-FM at Wichita State University, and David Baker, Professor of Music at the University of Indiana, read the first draft of the manuscript and many others have reviewed portions of subsequent versions. Marilyn Bliss prepared the fine index that multiplies the utility and reference value of this book.

I am grateful to Michael Ochs, the new music editor at W. W. Norton, for his enthusiasm for this project and for keeping it moving smoothly through many obstacles. Barry Feldman of Sony, a musician and true jazz expert, meticulously cared for the production of the new *Norton Anthology of Jazz* on compact disc, which accompanies this revision. And most important, I thank my wife Charlene who, from the moment of the book's inception to the present, steadfastly believed in this project and my ability to complete it. She allowed stacks of 78s to clutter our basement; suffered tapes, CDs, and LPs all over the house and in two offices; agreed to the purchase of books and music far in excess of a reasonable budget; endured instruments, computers, equipment, and trips; and made available to me that most precious gift of all, time.

Drum on your drums, batter on your banjos,
sob on the long cool winding saxophones.
Go to it, O jazzmen.

—*Carl Sandburg, from* Smoke and Steel *(1920)*

JAZZ: A HISTORY

𝒥NTRODUCTION

——— AMERICA'S CLASSICAL MUSIC ——

Jazz is an American art form, a music that came into being in the United States toward the end of the nineteenth century. This music is no longer new or experimental; it has endured the test of time. Like all classical music, it conforms to established standards of form and complexity, contains a large repertoire of recognized masterworks, and requires standards of musical literacy of both its artists and its listeners. The embryonic music developed from the traditions of West African, European, and American music as they were brought together by African Americans in the southern United States. It continued to evolve from the marriage of African-American sacred and secular music with American band traditions and instruments as well as with European harmonies and forms. Improvisation is a crucial feature of jazz, and the spontaneous creation of new works within its stylistic parameters is the key to jazz performance. The post–Civil War American black musician was the most prominent creator of jazz; still, this new art form does not owe its existence entirely to any one culture or race, for many disparate elements fused to make a new sound, one never before heard in Africa, Europe, or America. Today, all the countries of Europe, Great Britain, the former Soviet Union, Japan, Africa, Canada, and several South American countries can claim musicians on the roster of significant jazz artists. Jazz is becoming a world music.

When the scholar William W. Austin viewed the music of the twentieth century from the vantage point of the 1960s, he concluded that the West had produced four outstanding styles, three European and one American: those of Schoenberg, Bartók, and Stravinsky, and that of jazz. Of jazz, he writes:

It is . . . profoundly continuous with older music; its continuity with the past may be more important than its obvious novelty. . . .

The new styles also, to be sure, are both alike and different. The differences among them, when scrutinized with sympathy, prove to be more important than any similarity. . . . But the similarity, however superficial, is important in a broad historical perspective.[1]

PRECURSORS

Although black slaves were brought to America from many regions of Africa, most were torn from clans and tribes that populated the west coast of the African continent south of the Sahara. This region, variously called the Ivory Coast, the Gold Coast, and the Slave Coast, is populated by such tribes as the Yoruba, Ibo, Fanti, Ashanti, Susu, Ewe, and others. Since these are, for the most part, oral societies, written evidence from these cultures does not exist from as far back as the sixteenth, seventeenth, and eighteenth centuries—the worst years of the slave trade, when most African blacks were imported to the Americas. Except where foreign visitors—missionaries, colonizers, adventurers, and the slave traders themselves—wrote down their observations in journals, letters, ledgers, and the like, we have little documentary proof about the customs of these men and women. However, current research by anthropologists, ethnomusicologists, and Africanists has provided a wealth of information about most of these societies. Even where written evidence is lacking, Africa's strong oral tradition has enabled these cultures to preserve their past.

When blues scholar Paul Oliver visited northern Ghana in 1964, in the area near the upper Volta River and south of the Sahara, he recorded Fra-Fra musicians playing and singing an ancient Yarum Praise Song. In this performance we can note some arresting parallels—musical, literary, cultural, and formal—with music found in North America among many black communities. Very similar music has been performed on the Georgia Sea Islands, and we can compare the two styles. Sea Island music is American music with pronounced African retentions, reflecting the widespread phenomenon of black American customs retaining African characteristics. The ritual use of insult in humor, the use of dance and musical improvisation in worship services, and the incorporation of thousands of words and names from African languages in "Black English" are but a few of many examples.

[1] William W. Austin, *Music in the 20th Century from Debussy through Stravinsky*, p. 178 f. [NOTE: Complete bibliographic information for items cited briefly in footnotes may be found in the bibliography.]

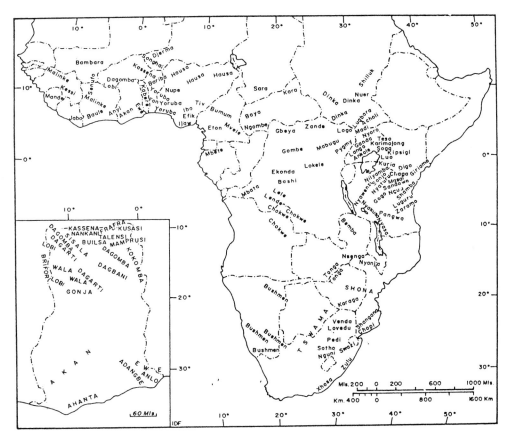

Ethnic-group map of south of the Sahara. Africa

New Orleans holds a special place in the history of jazz: it was the most important center of jazz in the early days of its history, and the city is usually considered the fountainhead of this new music. In most areas of the South, specific legislation outlawed drumming, so black slaves substituted hand clapping and foot stomping in their own private gatherings. African rhythms could thus be practiced and perpetuated without offense to the white masters. One important exception to the drumming ban was the Place Congo, a square in New Orleans known today as "Congo Square." There, until the Civil War, slaves were allowed to gather to dance, sing, and play percussion instruments. Instruments of all kinds were heard there, including several types of drums, pebble-filled gourds, jew's-harps, jawbones, thumb pianos (African sansa), and the four-string banjo.

Dancing the *bamboula* in Place Congo.

Through the first half of the nineteenth century, black musical traditions in America included voodoo dancing and ritual. They encompassed ring-shout, ceremonial dancing, and singing; music of the banjo, drums, fifes, fiddles, and other instruments; dancing to the patting of juba; singing of work songs; and a vast repertoire of spirituals. Certain elements were common to many of these activities while others were not. Some elements transferred to the post–Civil War period, others did not. Some of these many traditions readily incorporated Western music and proceeded with a rapid transformation, while others lingered on in an unchanging, basically African mode. The drummers of Place Congo were not jazz drummers, and the singers of the cotton fields were not jazz singers. Still, their heritage profoundly influenced music in America at the turn of the twentieth century, and jazz did emerge.

It is interesting and instructive to observe the process of transportation, translation, and transformation that African and African-American music underwent in locales far from New Orleans, the traditional birthplace of jazz. We can find evidence for this metamorphosis in many locations, and a clear example may be heard in the music of black Americans isolated on the Georgia Sea Islands.[2]

Along the eastern seaboard of the United States, from Maryland to Florida, there are a series of islands separated from the mainland by rivers and

[2]The following description is taken from the author's study, "Music of the American Dream: Brass Traditions and Golden Visions" in Josephine Wright, ed., *New Perspectives on Music: Essays in Honor of Eileen Southern* (Warren, MI: Harmonie Park Press, 1992).

swamps. Many are fertile and were once the sites of large cotton plantations worked by slaves. The islands are inhabited by Gullahs (sometimes called Geechies), descendants of ex-slaves who spoke a black-English dialect called Gullah and who were among the last group of blacks brought to this country in bondage from West Africa. Even today, these islands maintain many African customs and a spoken dialect that blends African languages and English.

In anecdotal reports, James P. Johnson, Willie "the Lion" Smith, and others on the New York scene (p. 107) attest to the connection of Gullah customs and music to jazz. Gullah music is related to the development of "shout" stride piano as well as ragtime and blues. Its connection to the music and customs of tribal West Africa is also clear, and we can observe some of these direct ties.

The black residents of St. Simons Island, a remote and isolated area off the Atlantic coast of Georgia, maintained many African traditions well into the twentieth century and preserved both African and slave song repertoires—shout songs, fiddle songs, the ring-shout dance, the buzzard lope (a solo dance), and more.

When Lydia Parrish began her investigation of these people and their music in 1912, many of the freed slaves were still alive. She discovered them to be secretive, and that—in addition to their having been left alone, for the

The slave's dance was often a test of physical endurance. From an engraving c. 1800, artist unknown.

most part, by post–Civil War whites—accounted for a remarkable environment in which they were able to develop and preserve their own life styles. To a certain degree, the same is true today, but the situation is changing:

> Such is the precarious position in which the slave music finds itself today (1942). While it is not hopeless, it is none too encouraging. Jaunts up and down the coast of South Carolina and Georgia, to the out islands of the Bahamas, and to Haiti, in search of African art survivals of all kinds give proof that they still exist, but the white man's drive against illiteracy is enabling the Negro school-teachers to make a drive, at the same time, against all things African.[3]

Their relatively self-sufficient circumstances allowed these people an opportunity to nourish and preserve African cultural survivals in the New World. A musical tie to West Africa is certain, but it is partly speculation that links the music of Fra-Fra tribesmen of Ghana directly to music of black Americans living on St. Simons Island, Georgia. Still, it is true that the blacks on St. Simons Island are the most recent descendants of tribal Africans brought to America as slaves from the same general area in Africa, both cultures employ Praise Songs as part of their musical tradition, and Praise Songs from the two cultures have striking similarities, as exemplified by the Yarum Praise Song[4] and its counterpart, *Daniel* (*NW* 278, I/5),[5] sung by Willis Proctor and seven companions.

The Yarum Praise Song is performed by two Fra-Fra musicians, one a player of a gourd rattle and the other a player of a bowed, two-string fiddle. Both performers sing while creating their own accompaniment, the gourd player establishing the beat, and the fiddle player sounding a complex ostinato. These African musicians are singing traditional verses of praise for their chief, although at one point they interpolate an improvised jibe at white people who pay them for making music.

> *In the village they call me a fool when I sing,*
> *But the white man gives me money to hear my music.*[6]

[3] Lydia Parrish, *Slave Songs of the Georgia Sea Islands*, music transcribed by Creighton Churchill and Robert MacGimsey (New York: Creative Age Press, 1942), p. 11.

[4] *The Story of the Blues* (Columbia Records CG30008), side 1, band 1, *Yarum Praise Songs*. Some recorded examples are necessary to illustrate the discussion but are not available on either the old or the revised releases of the *Smithsonian Collection of Classic Jazz*. Where possible, recordings have been selected that are commonly found in college libraries and are likely to remain available by special order from the manufacturer (although such availability cannot be guaranteed). Transcriptions in the text cite the source performances.

[5] *Georgia Sea Island Songs* (New World Records *NW* 278), side 1, band 5, *Daniel*.

[6] Quoted by Paul Oliver on the liner notes of *The Story of the Blues* (Columbia Records CG 30008).

This African fiddler both sings and improvises on his instrument.

The primary literary tradition of West Africa is not written but preserved in memory and transmitted orally through the griot, an official poet-historian whose mission is to preserve and pass on the tribal heritage of history, epic, myths, tales, riddles, proverbs, and lyric poetry. The most common and widespread genre in West Africa is the praise poem, and with it the musician will extol kings, courtiers, important personages, and the gods. The musical storyteller, who is always a male, would often begin with several verses establishing his own credentials as a son of a master of eloquence descended from a long line of men who were the repositories of secrets of royal houses many centuries old, and so on. Then, after assuring the listeners that his words are true, he would begin to unfold an elaborate and fanciful tale of the exploits and powers of great men, beasts, and gods. Much of the performance would be traditional, but there would also be spontaneity and a sense of community among the singers and the other participants gathered around.

In America, black slaves fused many of their West African traditions to the newly imposed Protestant Christianity and surrounding European-American music—Jesus replaced king, prophet replaced courtier, the lining of Psalms replaced leader-chorus responsorial patterns, and so on. Ezekiel and the "dry bones" or Daniel and the lions' den served in the New World where "Maghan Sundiata, Lion of Mali, against whom sorcery could avail nothing," served as story material in Africa. Lawrence W. Levine, in his study of *Black Culture and Black Consciousness*,[7] lists several factors that were important in this fusion process:

1.   the rich West African musical tradition common to almost all of the specific cultures from which the slaves came;

2.   the comparative cultural isolation in which large numbers of slaves lived;

3.   the tolerance and even encouragement which their white masters accorded to many of their musical activities;

4.   the fact that, for all the divergences in rhythm, harmony, and performance style, nothing in the European musical tradition with which the slaves came into contact in America was totally alien to their own traditions while a number of important features, such as the diatonic scale, were held in common and a number of practices . . . were analogous.

He concludes,

All of these conditions were conducive to a situation which allowed the slaves to retain a good deal of the integrity of their own musical heritage while fusing

[7]Page 24.

An African griot (praise singer) collects passersby as an American blues artist might on payday.

to it compatible elements of Euro-American music. The result was a hybrid with a strong African base.[8]

Black Americans singing praises of Daniel have created just such a hybrid. The identification of the black slave in the American South with Daniel in the lions' den is one example from the slave song repertory of black Americans' sense of identification with the Children of Israel—an example of the persistent image of the chosen people during a time of affliction. It was Daniel's faith that preserved him from the beasts, and it would be their faith too that would preserve African Americans during a period of suffering and suppression.

LEADER (Willis Proctor)	REFRAIN (Chorus)
Walk, believer, walk.	O Daniel!
Walk, I tell you, walk.	O Daniel!
Shout, believer, shout.	O Daniel!
Give me the kneebone bend.	O Daniel!
On the eagle wing.	O Daniel!
Fly, I tell you, fly.	O Daniel!
Fly, believer, fly.	O Daniel!
Rock, believer, rock.	O Daniel!
Etc.	

Many aspects of this music could be studied in greater depth, but our primary concerns are the musical relationships of American to African music and slave song to jazz. For example, the Yarum Praise Song has a steady, unwavering pulse that underlies the entire performance and measures the time so that irregular patterns and syncopations can be added and perceived. The sound of the gourd shaker establishes and slightly embellishes the beat.

The actual rhythm of the gourd is closer to:

Rhythm of Gourd

[8] Ibid.

Triplets, however, are clumsy to notate and more difficult to read in a complex score or during performance. Also, they are seldom used in notated jazz music. The convention for jazz arrangers and composers is to notate even eighth-notes or dotted figures and allow performers the freedom to divide the beat unevenly in a manner suitable to the tempo.

Convention

Approximate Performance

An accurate transcription of this recorded excerpt is virtually impossible to achieve, but the following score of the opening measures will serve as a useful guide.

Yarum Praise Song

During this portion of the piece, recurring patterns seem to divide the stream of music into four-beat patterns, so a 4/4 time signature was chosen for convenience in the transcription. But this, along with all other conventional signs of Western musical notation, must be accepted with skepticism when used to represent a performance of non-Western music. The above notation is an approximation and a guide for study only; it is not a performance score! The same is true of the following score for *Daniel*. Rhythms and pitches are only approximate. In fact, the performance is a quarter-tone off our standard pitch, and G minor, rather than F♯ minor, was selected mainly to facilitate comparisons with the Yarum praise song.

Daniel, Sung by Willis Proctor and Companions

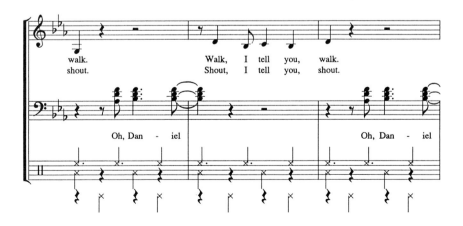

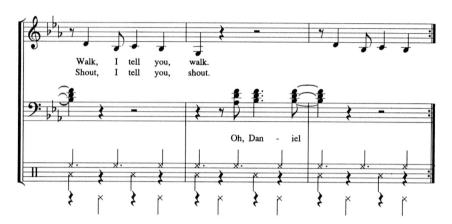

Both patterns skip the second step of the scale. The Fra-Fra pattern stresses the G and C while Willis Proctor stresses the G and D, but both praise songs are unified by a similar ostinato and identical modal configuration.

Scale of Ostinato

Fra-Fra Fiddle

Willis Proctor

Both pieces move to a similar beat (a pulse in the metronome range of 220–232 beats per minute). They both display syncopations and complex rhythms, the latter often resulting from the leader's insertion of extra text syllables.

Important differences should be noted too: ostinato accompaniment versus ostinato lead; distant refrains versus regular choral interruptions; even gourd performance versus syncopated clapping; and so on. One outstanding and significant difference is the use of harmony in the Georgia excerpt, and another is the challenge to the G-minor mode of Willis Proctor's lead posed by the B♭-major chord of his singers. These pieces are different but clearly related. Both share elements with music in the jazz tradition, the Georgia

Sea Island song more so than the African piece. Some of these elements are: metronomic underlying pulse, syncopated melodies, rhythmic instrument accompaniment (gourd and hands), a performer-composer aesthetic, performance techniques common to jazz (such as glissandos and special vocal articulations), and reliance on a melodic mode that is compatible with, if not identical to, a blues scale.

Melodic Mode

Neither performance offers much in the way of musical improvisation, although no two performances of these pieces, even by the same musicians, would be completely identical. It is important to note that the melodic and rhythmic patterns are fairly inflexible. Also, where the African piece employs no harmony, the Georgia Sea Island Praise Song uses but a single repeated chord.[9]

Another step in the transitional process can be seen if we observe the music of a black church meeting recorded in New York in 1926.[10] The Reverend J. M. Gates leads his congregation with a sermon that moves from speech to chant to song. As he intones the message, a soprano in the congregation begins to sing an improvised descant melody. One man, and then another, join in quietly while the Reverend Gates continues with a chanted patter that both sets the mode and almost establishes a beat. Gradually, the congregation tunes up in anticipation of the change from recitative to song, and the Reverend does not disappoint them. He sings:

Music at a Black Church Meeting, 1926

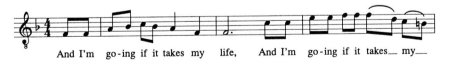

[9] Alan Lomax pairs a Louisiana work holler with a field song from Senegal on *Roots of the Blues* (New World Records *NW* 252). This is but another example showing African-American musical relationships.

[10] *History of Classic Jazz* (Riverside SDP 11), side 1, band 4, *I'm Going to Heaven if it Takes My Life* (originally recorded on Gennett 6034).

life. And   if I die   on the   bat-tle - field,__ I'm   go-ing if it takes my   life.

and the sermon and singing continue. Like the Georgia Sea Island singers, Reverend Gates's congregation improvises a simple harmony; and notice that it too consists of only one chord! However, this simple tune can be seen as transitional and closer to the harmonic idiom of the day, for the eight-measure **AABA** form[11] cries out for a I–IV–V progression at the end of the second **A** section to make the transition to the "bridge" or **B** section. As in the Sea Island praise song, the flow of the leader's narration is interrupted by periodic ejaculations from the other participants (the congregation); and like its Georgia counterpart, it avoids the second tone of the scale and toys with a tendency tone (the seventh scale step):

Scale

1   2   3   4   5   6   7   8

Even the soprano obbligato, which is sung two different times, sets out the scale minus the second step.

Soprano obbligato

Ah   loo_____   Oh   loo_____

The singer plays with the gap between scale steps 3 and 1 by sliding a glissando across it for the final two notes. Here the mode is major; in the first example it was minor, and in the second it was minor with a major accompaniment. This interplay of major and minor, this teasing of pitch up and down, are all part of the melodic and harmonic art exploited and developed by jazz artists. None of these samples is jazz, but all have their affinities with the style and serve as mileposts along the road of development.

[11] **AABA** (A musical idea is stated twice, followed by a contrasting phrase and concluding with a restatement of the original theme) is often called "popular-song form," because of its widespread use in American popular music. Pop-song form and blues form are the two most widely used formal structures in jazz.

RAGTIME

INTRODUCTION

Ragtime was the first black music ever to achieve widespread popularity and commercial distribution. It not only profoundly affected American music, it had a worldwide influence on classical composers even while it was still in its own infancy. Charles Ives composed a ragtime dance and thirteen ragtime pieces for theater orchestra between 1902 and 1904; Claude Debussy composed *Golliwog's Cakewalk* as part of his *Children's Corner Suite* during the years 1906 to 1908; and the list of major composers who listened to ragtime and composed music either in the style or incorporating elements of the style includes Erik Satie, Igor Stravinsky, Darius Milhaud, Arthur Honegger, and Paul Hindemith.

During the years 1895–1915, ragtime was available to the public in published piano scores, on piano rolls, and in live performances by resident and itinerant ragtime pianists. Also, classic ragtime—"which may be defined very simply as the piano rags of Scott Joplin, James Scott, Joseph Lamb, and their immediate collaborators, students, and followers"[1]—was adapted for use by instrumental ensembles, minstrel companies, and vaudeville groups, and the names of Tom Turpin and Scott Joplin, as well as many others, became household words in America.

The piano was the principal performing instrument of ragtime, but the style, since it was also suitable for other combinations, was frequently adopted for brass band music, solo banjo performance, and vocal solos with accompaniment.

[1] William J. Schafer and Johannes Riedel, *The Art of Ragtime*, p. 49.

A SOUTHERN RAG

Prior to 1900, many different types of dance music flourished among the Southern black communities. Weekend frolics and barn dances often took the form of square dances in eight-or sixteen-hand sets or circle dances, and these were accompanied most frequently by a few favorite instruments—banjo, fiddle, fife—instruments with prototypes brought to this country from Africa. Bones, rhythm sticks, spoons, clapping, and slapping often provided rhythmic accompaniment. The accordion was introduced, and the guitar replaced the banjo as the most popular instrument during the last decades of the nineteenth century. Intricately picked rags accompanied both set dances and buckdances, solo strutting pieces frequently performed between sets while the dancers rested. The repertory of reels and rags is not entirely clear, for it was not written down, and instrumental blues were sometimes called "rags," especially in the Piedmont of the Carolinas. Still, an instrumental ragtime dance form was present and was later preserved on recordings of itinerant black guitar players.

Able-bodied black men had to accomplish hard physical labor, first for their masters and later to earn a living. There were exceptions, of course, but during the late nineteenth and early twentieth centuries, most able-bodied black musicians were amateurs, men who performed in the evenings and on weekends when their work was finished. Not too surprisingly, a class of professional musicians developed among the handicapped, who, when talented enough, found that playing and singing was an excellent way to earn a living. Many of the male folk music virtuosos from the black community during the '20s and '30s (when this music was first recorded) were disabled: "Blind Boy" Fuller, "Blind" Gary, "Blind" Sonny Terry, "Brownie" McGhee (crippled), and "Blind Lemon" Jefferson. One virtuoso who recorded guitar rags and had a strong influence on the blues was "Blind" Blake, a consummate guitar picker and self-deprecating blues singer.

> *Because wild women live in Detroit,*
> *that's all I want to see.*
> *Wild woman and bad whiskey*
> *will make a fool out of me.*[2]

"Blind" Arthur Blake, who was probably born in Florida, traveled extensively in the South—especially Georgia, Tennessee, and the Carolinas—and

[2] From *Detroit Bound Blues* (Paramount 12657).

more or less settled in Chicago during the 1920s where he recorded *Southern Rag* in 1927.[3] Unlike the published classic rags for piano, this music does not have a fixed compositional structure and contrasting key levels. Instead, it consists of a series of four- and eight-measure phrases that can be extended indefinitely to accompany a dance. There is little melodic interest, and our attention is drawn to the harmonies, the dance beat, the syncopations, the fluent playing, and the words, a combination of entertainer patter and dance instructions. Unlike the "bottleneck" guitar playing of Robert Johnson on *Preachin' Blues*,[4] an emotional blues performance with irregular patterns and changing beat, Blake's music is perfect for dance accompaniment. When he says, "Now we going all do Southerners' Rag," he means a dance that is well known among blacks from Georgia and the Carolinas. When he calls out, "Do the Gandie Roll now, do the Geechie Down," and later, "Now we gonna do the Downtown—we call it the Geechie Down," he is talking about a specific dance: steps, body motion, and music. In this *Southerners' Rag*, we hear the most lively syncopations after Blake announces, "Now I'm gonna do some music they call the Geechie Music now." People familiar with James P. Johnson's composition, *The Charleston* (1923), will immediately recognize the similarity of the opening progression—C–E[7]–A–Dm–G[7]—and rhythm patterns. Both of these musicians can trace their ragtime to Geechie music.

Harmonically, Blake essentially alternates two simple patterns throughout:

Southern Rag, Harmonic Pattern

a. First 8 measures

b. Second 8 measures

Recognizing and following the pattern is fairly easy, an important consideration for a dancer, and one observes that the patterns can be repeated, alternated, and varied *ad infinitum* to satisfy the needs of a real dance.

[3] Paramount 12565-B.
[4] Columbia CL 1654. See page 61–64 for a discussion of *Preachin' Blues*.

Southern Rag, Formal Structure

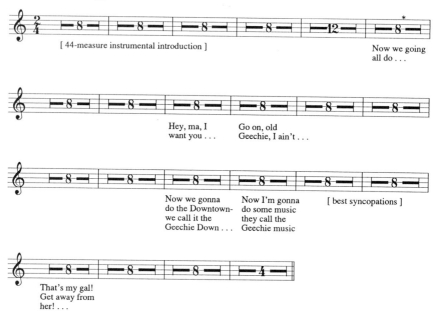

[44-measure instrumental introduction]

Now we going
all do . . .

Hey, ma, I
want you . . .

Go on, old
Geechie, I ain't . . .

Now we gonna
do the Downtown-
we call it the
Geechie Down . . .

Now I'm gonna
do some music
they call the
Geechie music

[best syncopations]

That's my gal!
Get away from
her! . . .

* Blake inserts an extra beat, making this phrase 8 1/2 measures long.

STYLE CHARACTERISTICS _____

The chief stylistic characteristics of this music are its duple meter (2/4 or 4/4, but almost invariably written in the former); functional diatonic harmony stressing tonic, dominant, subdominant, and applied dominants in a major tonality; compounded song-form structures with sixteen- or thirty-two-measure periods and shorter introductions, vamps,[5] and codas; a syncopated treble melody that operates in opposition to a harmonic and nonsyncopated bass line; and a bass line that moves approximately at half the speed of the melody. The chief ragtime syncopations occur on the second and fourth eighth notes in a 4/4 measure (second and fourth sixteenth notes in a 2/4 measure), while accented melody notes often, but not always, reinforce beats 3 and 4 (fifth and seventh eighth notes in a 4/4 measure).

[5]A short, connecting passage, usually four or eight measures long, connecting two sections of music that lie at different harmonic levels by modulating (changing key). Sometimes no modulation takes place and a simple chord pattern is repeated as a "filler" between sections.

Ragtime Characteristics

a. Meter   [occasionally]   [very rarely]

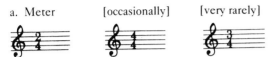

b. Harmony: Common Progressions

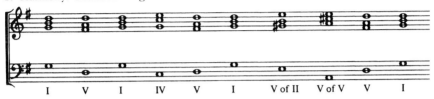

I   V   I   IV   V   I   V of II   V of V   V   I

c. Form: Typical Structural Outline

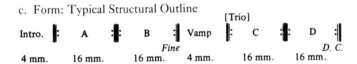

Thus it can be seen that ragtime typically contains two layers of rhythmic activity, a fast-moving treble melody that strongly cross-accents the regularly accented progression of the bass.

Ragtime, when played by solo piano, normally calls for the pianist's left hand to "stride" up and down; that is, the performer uses the left hand in a downbeat-upbeat manner (an oom-pah, oom-pah rhythm) in which beats 1 and 3 (in 4/4) are heavily accented single notes, octaves, or tenths, and beats 2 and 4 are unaccented triads. The characteristic syncopated melodies of the right hand have rhythmic figures like the following:

Rhythms of Melodic Motives

a. Charles Hunter, *Tickled to Death Ragtime March* (1899), mm. 17–18

b. Scott Joplin, *Maple Leaf Rag* (1899), mm. 1–2

c. James Scott, *Frog Legs Rag* (1906), mm. 1–2

d. Joseph F. Lamb, *American Beauty Rag* (1913), mm. 1–4

The authentic ragtime pianist's touch was percussive, and it seems that the pedal was used very sparingly, even for legato effects.[6] Occasionally, the feet (or foot) would be called upon to add a rhythmic effect to the performance of the work. Scott Joplin, in the introduction to his *Stoptime Rag* (1910), advises the performer that "to get the desired effect of 'Stoptime' the pianist should stamp the heel of one foot heavily upon the floor, wherever the word 'Stamp' appears in the music."[7] Strangely enough, the indication is to stamp twice in each measure, once on each beat of the piece in 2/4 time. Although the foot-stomp instruction is rare in the works of this composer,[8] many of his rags begin with the warning "Do not play this piece fast. It is never right to play 'Ragtime' fast."

While syncopation is the chief characteristic of ragtime melodies, these syncopes were generally placed in simple proportion to the beat (usually in a ratio of 2 : 1). Rhythms of more complex proportions, although they do occur, are exceptional. These configurations tend to appear in the music of the later ragtime performers, such as Jelly Roll Morton and James P. Johnson, whom some would view as transitional figures from ragtime to jazz. However, it has been pointed out that first-hand experience with the performances of ragtime pianists of recent vintage—e.g., Willie "The Lion" Smith

[6] Most published ragtime compositions have no pedal indications, but a few by Joplin, such as *Eugenia*, do indicate pedaling. However, its employment there is sparse, and there are passages notated legato in which the pedal is not used.

[7] Scott Joplin, *The Collected Works of Scott Joplin*, ed. Vera Brodsky Lawrence, I, p. 215 ff.

[8] In the composition *The Ragtime Dance* (1905), which has the subtitle *A Stoptime Two-Step*, he gives a stamp instruction as before, but adds to it, "Do not raise the toe from the floor while stamping." The same piece provides, in the third measure of the trio, one variation from stamping only on the beat.

(1897–1973)—"suggests that, as with most dance music of any era, the rags in print tend to be a simplified form of the music as performed."[9]

The first composition entitled "rag" was not published until January 27, 1897, when there was a publisher's race to copyright ragtime pieces.[10] William H. Krell, a successful Chicago bandleader who toured through the Mississippi area, won the honor of being the very first composer to publish a ragtime composition, *The Mississippi Rag*. It was followed three days later by Warren Beebe's *Ragtime March*, and the next month by R. J. Hamilton's *Ragtime Patrol*. Others followed throughout the year, and on December 17, 1897, the first rag by a black composer was copyrighted: Tom Turpin's *Harlem Rag*.

The word "rag" seems to have come from black clog dancing, which was called "ragging." The division of the melody into syncopated patterns is traceable to patting juba, a procedure that produces dance music by clapping hands, stamping feet, and slapping thighs. Fred Stone published a song called *Ma Ragtime Baby* in 1893, and, interestingly enough, *Turkey in the Straw* (1896) was subtitled *Ragtime Fantasie*. However, most critics would term these compositions primitive ragtime, because they lack the characteristic syncopations in the melody. It becomes quite clear that ragtime must have been widespread in the early 1890s, for if in a single year so many white composers could have published composed music in ragtime style, the music, by whatever name it was called, had to be present in abundance as the form that had been developed by black performers.

───── PIANO RAGS ─────────

The big three of the classic ragtime world are Scott Joplin (1868–1917) and his two disciples, James Scott (1886–1938) and Joseph Lamb (1887–1960), the latter a white ragtime composer who most closely approximates the classicism of Scott Joplin. During the heyday of ragtime, many lesser names composed and published excellent rags, among them the black composers Tom Turpin, Louis Chauvin (1883–1908), Arthur Marshall (1881–1956), and Scott Hayden (1882–1915); and the white composers Charles Hunter (1878–1907) and Charles Johnson (1876–1950).

Thomas Million Turpin (c. 1873–1922) was born in Savannah, Georgia, and raised in St. Louis, Missouri, where as a boy he worked in his father's saloon. Turpin, a self-taught pianist, was a big man, over six feet tall, and, in his later years, about 300 pounds in weight. After an excursion to the

[9] H. Wiley Hitchcock, *Music in the United States: A Historical Introduction*, p. 123.
[10] Rudi Blesh and Harriet Janis, *They All Played Ragtime*, p. 100.

Nevada gold mines around 1890, he eventually returned to St. Louis where, with his brother, he opened his own saloon, The Rosebud, at 2220 Market Street, in the Tenderloin. His saloon became a ragtime center, and it was at The Rosebud that he wrote his music. His *Harlem Rag*, the first published black rag, had a catchy tune, characteristic syncopations, and a relative simplicity that made it performable by less-than-professional talent.

Harlem Rag (1897; arr. by D. S. DeLisle)

Turpin's first work follows an **ABA** song form. The sixteen-measure **A** section in the key of C contains an eight-measure antecedent-consequent phrase that is repeated. The **B** section is divided in three, each subsection being thirty-two measures long. Consequently, the bulk of the piece, in the key of G, seems to be framed by two shorter sections in the key of C. In each of the three subsections of the middle, Turpin composes but one eight-measure theme for each. Then he invariably uses the same developmental pattern: the theme is repeated, after which the entire sixteen-measure section undergoes a written repeat in which the melody is ragged with more syncopation and is thickened by a fuller chording in the right hand. In the last of these middle sections, Turpin slows the rhythm of the right hand to equal that of the left. The characteristic layer effect of ragtime is absent here. However, this passage effectively closes off the section in G and sets up the return to the key of C. Turpin employs no introductions or vamps, but the opening of each section follows smoothly from the close of the previous one.[11]

His published music displays many characteristics one might expect in the work of a self-trained musician: simple forms, simple keys, regular phrase structure, and uncomplicated harmonies. This is certainly true of *Bowery Buck* (1899), *Rag-Time Nightmare* (1900), and *St. Louis Rag* (1903). All three are in the key of C, the first having an **ABC** structure with thirty-two-measure sections, each section being formed from an eight-measure phrase that

[11]The music of Tom Turpin and others is available in *Classic Piano Rags*, selected by Rudi Blesh.

The cover of Tom Turpin's *Harlem Rag.*

is repeated. *Rag-Time Nightmare* is a little different: it has a four-measure introduction followed by an **ABCB** form that employs four-measure phrases in the **C** section. But still, simplicity can be seen as Turpin's chief hallmark. All of his works have a naive charm that emanates both from the characteristic rags and from an innate melodic skill. The *St. Louis Rag* is slightly more complex. The piece, whose form may be outlined as Intro-**ABA**, moves to the subdominant key, F, in the **B** section. But this is no great musical surprise.

However, in Turpin's last published rag, *Buffalo Rag* (1904), a new harmonic activity is displayed. It is generally acknowledged that the profusion of new ideas that appear in this later rag resulted partially from Turpin's association with Scott Joplin in St. Louis. In the introduction, we can see a rapid modulation of barbershop harmonies and the employment of a diminished chord in the first full measure, a vertical structure common in this piece but unusual in his earlier efforts.

Buffalo Rag

In the introduction we can see a harmonic progression that changes chords on every beat: $F-G\sharp^{dim}-F_4^6-D^7-G^7-C^7-F$; in the first eight-measure phrase there is a similar rapid progression, and in the fourth measure of the first phrase, a particularly rich vertical sound, the superimposition of a $G\sharp^{dim7}$ over a D-minor triad on the second beat. The rattle of $G\sharp-A-B$ was not at all unusual for symphonic composers of this period, but for Turpin this piece marks a high point of harmonic sophistication. Tom Turpin, his music, and his St. Louis establishment provided both an influence and an impetus for all Midwestern ragtime composers.

SCOTT JOPLIN

Scott Joplin was born on November 24, 1868, in Texarkana, Texas, and was raised in a musical atmosphere. His father, an ex-slave, played the violin; his mother sang and played the banjo; his brothers played the guitar, sang, and composed. Joplin's first instruments were the guitar and bugle, and when an eight-year-old, he became fascinated with a neighbor's piano. He was improvising well enough by the age of eleven to impress the local music teacher, and he received free lessons in piano, sight reading, and harmony. When his mother died in 1882 (Joplin was fourteen at the time), his father tried to force him to learn a trade, so Joplin left home. He traveled throughout the Mississippi Valley in these very formative years, and it is generally assumed that the music he came in contact with during his peregrinations served as a source of melodic and rhythmic inspiration. He arrived in the St. Louis-Sedalia area in 1885 and worked with other ragtime pioneers, including Tom Turpin, Arthur Marshall, and Louis Chauvin. The first pieces Joplin published were songs, *A Picture of Her Face* and *Please Say You Will*, in 1895, and he published his first ragtime piece, *Original Rags*, in 1899. Earlier, in 1893, Joplin formed a small orchestra and, doubling on piano and cornet, he went to the World's Columbian Exposition in Chicago. Pianists from all over the central United States gathered on the midway as well as in the Chicago red-light district, and a comparison of styles and ideas took place both informally and in the many ragtime contests. This was the first time the general public had an opportunity to hear the new ragtime music.

Scott Joplin (1868–1917).

Joplin returned to St. Louis and Sedalia to play and later publish. In the same year that *Original Rags* appeared, 1899, he published his most famous work, *The Maple Leaf Rag* (*SCCJ* 1), a composition that sold hundreds of thousands of copies and allowed him to free himself from the duties of a honky-tonk pianist. Between 1895 and 1917, Joplin wrote fifty-three pieces for piano, including six instructional exercises for teaching ragtime, as well as ten songs, a ragtime ballet, and two operas. Joplin was not interested in haphazard ragtime improvisation. His dream was to develop a classic ragtime that would compare with serious European music and would be used in the larger, traditional forms such as operas and symphonies. In 1902 he composed a twenty-minute work, the *Ragtime Dance*, a ballet based on black social dances of the time with added narration. In it there are a clean-up dance, jennie cooler dance, slow drag, World's Fair, buckstep prance, dude's walk, Sedalia walk, town talk, and stoptime dance. Partly because of its length, this composition did not sell well and proved a major disappointment to the composer. John Stark was Joplin's publisher, and although the success of *Maple Leaf Rag* set him up in the printing business, he could not afford to publish compositions that did not sell. Consequently, after the financial disaster of *Ragtime Dance*, Stark refused to publish Joplin's first opera, *A Guest of Honor*, when it was finished in 1903. It was performed once in St. Louis; a card for the work dated February 18, 1903, is on file in the copyright office in Washington, but no copy of the music has been found.

Joplin's rags used many meters: 2/4, 4/4, 6/8, and 3/4. Although there is much variety in his works, most rags have four themes of sixteen measures, each repeated, with an introduction and a modulatory passage before the third theme. Sometimes the first theme is repeated before the third, and this form is the same as that standardized by the march composers of the time. Except that it lacks an introduction, *The Maple Leaf Rag* exactly parallels march form: first strain (sixteen measures, repeated), second strain (sixteen measures, repeated), first strain again, trio or third strain (sixteen measures, repeated) in the subdominant, and a fourth strain (sixteen measures, repeated) in the tonic. Joplin's trios are usually in the subdominant, although he sometimes uses a contrasting minor theme or a more remote key.

In 1906 Joplin moved from St. Louis to Chicago and then to New York, where his publisher, John Stark, had relocated. He went on a series of vaudeville tours in 1907, and in 1909 he settled in New York to devote himself to teaching and composition. He began writing his opera, *Treemonisha*, at this time. The socially oriented plot tells the story of Treemonisha, a black baby, who was found under a tree by a childless couple. They raised her and provided an education. Treemonisha fights superstition, black conjurers, and voodoo magic. She becomes a leader of her people and begins to show them the way to freedom and equality through education. Joplin spent years of his life on this work and began seeking a publisher as early as 1908. John Stark refused the opera, and Joplin finally financed its publication himself in 1911. The three-act opera was written for eleven voices and piano accompaniment; it contains twenty-seven complete musical numbers, including an overture and a prelude to Act III. He could find no sponsors for a performance so he undertook the project himself, rehearsing the cast and playing the piano. There was one performance in 1915 without scenery, and the middle-class black audience, which resented the reminder of their not-too-distant past, was less than receptive. Joplin became depressed, and it was not long before he began to lose his physical coordination as well as his mental faculties. In 1916, gravely ill with "dementia paralytica cerebral" caused by syphilis, he was committed to the Manhattan State Hospital on Ward's Island, New York, where he died on April 1, 1917.[12] Scott Joplin is generally acknowledged as the consummate genius of ragtime. "He was the central figure and prime creative spirit of ragtime, a composer from whom a large segment of twentieth-century American music derived its shape and spirit."[13]

The rags of Scott Joplin are meant to be reproduced from the score with accuracy and metrical precision. A significant factor in his life and philosophy was his musical training. Unlike the pioneers of the country blues and many

[12] Rudi Blesh, "Scott Joplin: Black-American Classicist," in *The Collected Works of Scott Joplin*, I, p. xxxix.

[13] Ibid., p. xiii.

of his contemporary honky-tonk piano players, Joplin had a thorough musical education, at least as thorough as was available for black musicians at that time in American history. He received his first formal instruction in Texarkana, Texas, from a German music teacher who included harmony, in the traditional European sense, as part of Joplin's piano instruction. The same teacher also, apparently, spoke about opera and other traditional large forms and impressed the youthful Joplin with the significance of concepts like tradition, composition, masterpieces, and large-scale works. When Joplin moved to Sedalia, he attended George Smith College for Negroes and took advanced courses in harmony and composition, which provided him with the technical facility he needed to notate the syncopations that seemed to baffle others interested in scoring the new music. Certainly his education was decisive in establishing a framework for classic ragtime, a composed music to be played under exacting performance standards.

Joplin's preoccupation with classical music is most clearly seen in his systematic attention to matters of balanced form employing closely related keys, for example:

Maple Leaf Rag	AA BB A CC DD	with A, B, and D in the tonic, and C in the subdominant
Original Rags	I AA BB CC V A DD EE*	With A, B, and E in the tonic, C in the subdominant, and D in the dominant
The Easy Winners	I AA BB A V CC DD	with A and B in the tonic, and C and D in the subdominant
Peacherine Rag	I AA BB A CC DD	with A in the tonic, B in the dominant, and C and D in the subdominant
The Chrysanthemum	I AA BB A CC DD C	with A in the tonic, B in the dominant, and C and D in the subdominant
Reflection Rag	I AA BB CC DD EE	With A, B, and C in the tonic, and D and E in the subdominant

*In formal schemes, I represents an introduction and V a vamp.

Joplin displays great talent in his melodic invention, for beneath the broken, arpeggiated, and ragged sounds, a catchy tune resides. In graceful patterns up and down, Joplin's melodies tend to follow the classic antecedent-consequent phrase pattern in which an eight-measure melody is broken into two related halves. The first is similar to the second but leaves the listener at a point where, musically, the melody cannot end; the second half takes up the material from the former but closes out the phrase comfortably. If Joplin's classic rag has typically four "tunes," the opening phrase of each is played at least four times, providing a musical experience that is easily remembered by the most unsophisticated listener.

Although it is Scott Joplin's classic rags that earned him lasting popularity, they have a significant shortcoming that would have prevented him from achieving the kind of stature as a composer to which he aspired: an absence of developmental passages. Within the confines of eight-measure phrases and sixteen-measure sections, there was no room for creative expansion. In spite of their perfection within the norms of the style, the predictable regularity of the form, phrase length, and harmonic patterns are limiting factors. Still, each rag is a gem.

Joplin had grander ambitions, and, to a certain degree, he was able to achieve his goals in two other kinds of composition: an occasional experimental rag, like *Euphonic Sounds*, and his large-scale work *Treemonisha*, an opera in three acts. In *Euphonic Sounds*, Joplin explores harmonic relationships not at all common in popular music of the period.

Euphonic Sounds

a. First Strain

In the second strain of *Euphonic Sounds*, Joplin moves without modulation from the key of B♭ to F♯ to B minor, climaxing with a diminished-seventh chord on which he pivots back to the original key.

b. Second Strain

On the third strain, he abandons the regular oom-pah ragtime left hand and employs harmonic devices that may have been commonplace with Continental composers, but were quite striking within the context of an American popular piece.

c. Third Strain

Treemonisha is much more an opera than a ragtime composition, even though the syncopated features characteristic of rag permeate the music. Arias, such as *The Sacred Tree* (No. 6), in triple meter, are spun-out sentimental ballads. And yet, if the naiveté is one of its major faults, it is also one of its strongest features. Just as a Grandma Moses painting is able to capture the essence of simple country life, so do the language, melodies, harmonies, and rhythms of this Joplin opera bring to life the characters and emotions of the simple people portrayed in the drama. A thoroughly modern device is Joplin's employment of *Sprechstimme*, a kind of stylized declamation wherein the vocalist neither sings nor sustains a steady pitch, but creates a speech-melody to heighten the dramatic action. The device was not unique to Joplin: Charles Ives used it in his *Soliloquy, or A Study in Sevenths and Other Things* (composed in 1907 but unpublished until 1933), and it appears in Schoenberg's *Pierrot Lunaire* of 1912, two works that Joplin could not possibly have heard before he completed *Treemonisha* in 1911.

Two other facets of Joplin must receive comment before we move on—Joplin the piano player, and Joplin the collaborator. Although there is not general agreement about the quality of Joplin's piano technique, it must

A scene from the Houston Grand Opera's 1975 production of Scott Joplin's *Treemonisha*.

have been prodigious. Legend has it that he always fared exceedingly well in formal or informal competition, and the technique necessary for the correct performance of his own music is sufficient to mark him as an accomplished professional pianist. However, we have no direct evidence about his playing. At least thirty-three piano-roll recordings bear his name, but recent research has ascertained that only piano rolls made in late 1915 or early 1916 can be positively attributed to Joplin's fingers. As one authority points out, "made in the culminating period of his illness, they are more evidence of his fading powers than of his playing style at its earlier best."[14]

Not all of Scott Joplin's works bear the name of a single composer. Although some of his songs indicate that Joplin wrote both words and music, Henry Jackson, Louis Armstrong Bristol, Sidney Brown, and others frequently sup-

---

[14] Blesh and Janis, *They All Played Ragtime*, first unnumbered page before p. 1.

plied his lyrics. At least seven rags were collaborations: *Swipesy* and *Lilly Queen* with Arthur Marshall; *Sunflower Slow Drag, Something Doing, Felicity Rag,* and *Kismet Rag* with Scott Hayden; and *Heliotrope Bouquet* with Louis Chauvin. Also, one work, *Sensation,* was written by Joseph F. Lamb but arranged by Scott Joplin. It was not uncommon for ragtime composers to collaborate, and the same Arthur Marshall is responsible for completing the last known rag composition by Tom Turpin, *Pan-Am Rag,* registered in 1914 but not published until its inclusion in *They All Played Ragtime.*[15]

JAMES SCOTT

The music of James Scott (1886–1938) is considered closest to that of Scott Joplin and of enough consequence to earn him a position of prominence in the history of ragtime. Born in Neosho, Missouri, Scott moved to Ottawa, Kansas, at the age of thirteen or fourteen. He was basically self-taught in music, although an older black pianist in Neosho, John Coleman, gave the boy lessons in piano and sightreading. He moved to Carthage, Kansas, in 1900, and at the age of seventeen published his first composition, *A Summer Breeze.* He continued working at Dumars Music Store in Carthage until around 1914, when he moved to St. Louis. There, on an earlier visit, he had met Scott Joplin. Probably through Joplin's good offices, he had made contact with John Stark, who eventually published many of his ragtime compositions. In St. Louis, Scott supported himself at first by giving piano lessons, house to house, and later by working for the Panama Theater as organist and musical arranger. He moved again in 1919 to Kansas City and continued publishing until 1922, when his *Broadway Rag* appeared, although by then ragtime had been eclipsed by the newer form called jazz. He continued teaching until well into the 1930s, during which he also led an eight-piece dance band. After his wife died, he moved across the river to Kansas City, Kansas, to live with a cousin. He remained active in composition until shortly before his death in 1938.

The rags of James Scott are consistent to a flaw. He was not an experimental composer, but a craftsman who turned out remarkably regular works in standard form. *Frog Legs Rag,* although one of his earliest (1906), is one of his best. The balance between stride left hand and melodic right hand gives it a rhythmic suppleness sometimes lacking in his other works. Scott was satisfied to work within the restrictions of standard rag form, both in melodic design and harmonic scheme. Invariably, the harmonic level moved up to the subdominant in the second half. Occasionally he would begin his rags in

[15] Following p. 209.

James Scott (1886–1938).

the minor mode—for example, the opening theme of his *Rag Sentimental* (1918)—but he quickly moved back to the major at the appearance of the second theme. Parallel thirds are one of Scott's favorite sounds; they appear at the opening of *Evergreen Rag* (1915)

Evergreen Rag

and in the second strain of *Kansas City Rag* (1907).

Kansas City Rag

A favorite melodic device Scott employed is a rocking pattern in the right hand that produces both syncopation and alternation of chords with single notes.

Hilarity Rag (1910)

Ragtime Oreole (1911)

Paramount Rag (1917)

Rag Sentimental (1918)

Experts have seen in the music of James Scott "an impression of charm and directness closer to folk style than to a finished art form" and point out that "Scott shared with Joplin a belief in the dignity and value of his music, the idea that this music labeled 'ragtime' was an art music developing under a wholly new aesthetic. Since Scott worked with Joplin, studied his compositions, and delved into the same regional folk background, it is not remarkable that their rags should be so similar. Yet while Scott has existed in Joplin's shadow, he is clearly a composer of great genius, with a talent as large as Joplin's."[16]

——— JOSEPH F. LAMB ————————————

The last of the ragtime giants is Joseph F. Lamb, a white man born in Montclair, New Jersey, in 1887. Until meeting Scott Joplin in 1907, he was totally unfamiliar with blacks, black culture, and black-American music, except what he may have been able to learn from ragtime sheet-music publications. Without being intentionally derivative, Lamb wrote rags that connoisseurs describe as characteristic of the black-American style, substantiating the contention that classical ragtime had become an American, not an ethnic, music. Lamb attended college in Berlin (Kitchener), Canada, and later passed his entrance examinations in engineering for Stevens Institute. However, after finding a job in New York he decided not to matriculate. Although two of his sisters were classically trained pianists, he took no lessons and was self-taught both as a composer and pianist. He had already composed several rags before meeting Joplin, who took an interest in the younger musician and helped him both with his composition and with publication. Lamb's first ragtime publication with John Stark, *Sensation Rag* (1908), bears the name of Joplin as arranger, but Lamb later recalled that Joplin agreed to add his name only to help sell the rag and had not in fact arranged any of the music.

Joseph Lamb disappeared from public notice when the ragtime vogue

[16] Schafer and Riedel, *The Art of Ragtime*, p. 79 f.

passed after the First World War. The quality of his rags gave rise to the theory that Joseph F. Lamb was but a Scott Joplin pseudonym! Lamb continued to publish rags with Stark until 1919, and although another publisher, Mills, accepted a few works after that date, they were never issued. Most ragtime followers assumed that Lamb was black, until Blesh and Janis found him thirty years later, living modestly in Brooklyn, New York, and working in the import business. Until his rediscovery he had stopped composing, and in the years before his death he completed several unpublished rags and made some recordings. He published twelve rags between 1908 and 1919, and when he died in 1960 another two dozen were found, unpublished. In addition, he composed songs, four of which were published between 1908 and 1913; an additional fifty-one are known but unpublished.

In his ragtime compositions, Lamb borrowed and transformed material from other compositions and also invented completely new material. For example, his *Sensation Rag, American Beauty Rag*, and *Patricia Rag* all have motives that derive from Scott Joplin's *Maple Leaf Rag. Patricia Rag* also borrows from Joplin's *Gladeolus Rag*, and three of his compositions, *Cleopatra*

Joseph F. Lamb (1887–1960).

Rag, Champagne Rag, and *Reindeer Rag,* share motivic material.[17] Lamb's rags display a harmonic sure-footedness that does not exclude chromaticism or key signatures with many flats. *Excelsior Rag* (1909) and *Ethiopia Rag* (1909), both in D♭, have trios in G♭, necessitating occasional double flats as accidentals. The fact that these works were bought in large numbers suggests that the typical American family before the First World War, with its square piano in the living room, was fairly proficient in home music making. Lamb's rags tend not to be as consistently syncopated as those of Joplin and Turpin. The Trio of Lamb's *Ethiopia Rag* has only two syncopations in the first four measures. The opening section of his *Ragtime Nightingale* (1915), with the title and tempo indication deleted, could easily be mistaken for a Romantic character piece so popular among the classical piano composers of that generation.

Ethiopia Rag

Ragtime Nightingale

[17] Ibid., p. 80 ff.

Lamb, like Turpin, Joplin, Marshall, and the other composers of classic ragtime pieces, was locked into the formulas of the style in that all of his pieces are divisible in half, each half being separated by key and divisible into sections, usually two, of sixteen measures each. However, he had a tendency to interpret these formal restrictions loosely and to insert a little developmental material within the confines of the structure. His *Champagne Rag* (1910) is an excellent example of the integrated and developmental nature of his compositional thinking. It takes the form **I AA BB' A—CC' DA' DA'**, with the introduction borrowing material from the first **A** phrase. The second **B** is not a direct repeat but a version written at the octave, so that it has at least some developmental characteristics. The same is true of the two **C**s. The last strain, which has two themes, the second of which is a transposition and variation of the opening theme, rounds out the form and marks this rag as an unusually integrated work within the style.

Champagne Rag: March and Two-Step

Form:

                                   Trio
I ‖ :A: ‖ B │ B′ │ A ‖ C │ C′ ‖ :DA′: ‖
4   16   16   16   16   16   16   32

Thematic redundancy: each pattern is eight measures long, except the first (introduction), which is four measures long.

[A] A A A A B B B′ B′ A A C C C′ C′ D D A′ A′ D D A′ A′

Themes:

Scott Hayden (1882–1915), Louis Chauvin (1883–1908), and Arthur Marshall (1881–1956) are three of the important early pioneers of ragtime who traveled in the same circles as Scott Joplin. But piano players were legion during the heyday of ragtime. Alfred Wilson and Charlie Warfield won the ragtime contest at the Louisiana Purchase Exposition in 1904; Tony Jackson, Plunk Henry, Ed Hardin, "Old Man" Sam Moore, Robert Hampton, Charles Hunter, Artie Matthews, and Percy Wenrich are all names known to the connoisseur of this music.

To the classic ragtime buff, the name of Ferdinand "Jelly Roll" Morton (1890–1941) denotes not a ragtime player but a jazz pianist and composer. His career and music will be discussed below in Chapter 5, but now might be an appropriate time to compare the two versions of *Maple Leaf Rag* recorded in the *Smithsonian Collection* (*SCCJ* 1,2) to observe the significant differences that appear in these two performances of the same work. Scott Joplin recorded his *Maple Leaf Rag* but a year before his death and only a few months before his hospital commitment in 1916, and it is truly remarkable that he played as well as he did. Clearly the variations from the score, such as the left-hand flourishes that occur on the last half beat of measures 2, 8, 12, 16, and elsewhere, were intentional. Occasionally Joplin embellished the first beat of a measure, as in the second ending of the trio. In one instance, measure 14 of the trio, he rewrote the left hand by playing the octave on the first beat, inserting rests in the middle of the bar, and playing a crush of four thirty-second notes and an eighth note on the second half of the second beat. Perhaps Joplin was playing from memory, perhaps he was reading from a score at a time when his vision was impaired; but, no matter, the changes are only minor decorations of a written composition. In the treble part, he occasionally misses octaves. Often the performance lacks the precision and cleanliness we might hope for, but for someone critically ill, this recording is a remarkable testament to Joplin's pianistic prowess. His performance shows us that, essentially, ragtime rhythms are played exactly as written, that is, time is measured in ratios of two to one. Four sixteenth notes in a row are all equal in length, quarter notes are twice as long as eighth notes, and dotted figures balance three-fourths of the whole with one-fourth.

RAGTIME JAZZ

Jelly Roll Morton's performance of Scott Joplin's piece is instructive about jazz performance in general. It clearly illustrates what most jazz musicians consider to be the essence of jazz and, in this case, the distinction between jazz and ragtime: a sophisticated sense of swing. This characteristic combines a propelling sense of drive and forward motion with a relaxed, rolling syncopation, and Morton and other New Orleans musicians were noted for their ability to perform and improvise in this manner. The timing of the harmonies remains faithful to the original, regardless of all other rhythmic and melodic variation that Morton introduced. However, the time relationships between individual notes are no longer limited to the two-to-one ratio, but include three-to-one as the most commonly recurring element in the rhythmic patterns. In ragtime, a brace of two equal eighth notes is performed with each note receiving equal time; in jazz, at mid-range tempos, two notated eighth notes are performed as a triplet figure: a quarter note followed by an eighth, all squeezed into the time allotted for one beat. This smooths off the ragged edges of the ragtime syncopation, and this must have been what James Scott had in mind when he named his ragtime composition of 1921 *Don't Jazz Me Rag—I'm Music*. The jazz age was under way, and the neat metrical divisions scored by composers such as Scott were being ignored by the jazz players, who played their pieces in the new style. Although Morton's recorded performance of *Maple Leaf Rag* (*SCCJ* 2) was made twenty-two years after Joplin's (*SCCJ* 1), we can assume that his later performance, by which time jazz performing styles had changed radically, reflects a continuous tradition. The comparison of the two is enlightening.

Maple Leaf Rag

a. Notated

b. As Played by Scott Joplin (*SCCJ* 1)

c. As Played by Jelly Roll Morton (*SCCJ* 2)

d. Same as "c"

Morton's performance is not ragtime at all, but jazz. The notes Joplin composed for the right hand are heard only in Morton's imagination, if at all. All that remains of Joplin's piece is the harmonic progression, the form (although Morton ignores repeats in the first two sections and adds an introduction), and the references to the essential elements of the melody that Morton chooses to throw in from time to time.

Melodic Rhythm (Moderate tempo)

A common rhythmic cliché that Morton employs with relative frequency in this performance is the following:

It should be noted that duplets are inserted into the pattern to provide the ragtime syncopations at the end of beat 3 of the first measure and beat 2 of the second measure. This is one of the elements jazz borrowed from ragtime. Morton offers the listener a very subtle harmonic shift at the end of his eight-measure introduction. The meter of the first five measures of the introduction is very clear: Morton begins with three pickups and then strongly accents the first beat of each measure. The sixth measure begins as expected, but the downbeat of measure 7 does not get the anticipated stress, and Morton inserts the rhythmic cliché illustrated above on the second beat of the measure, forcing a new accent where none is expected. The normal reaction of the untrained listener is to hear this pattern as a mistake, where a beat is either lost or gained. But, in fact, Morton changed measure 6 to a five-beat measure, kept measure 7 as a four-beat measure beginning where the old second beat was, and shortened the eighth measure to three beats. One can see the rhythm of the notes in the last two measures of *Maple Leaf Rag* as played by Jelly Roll Morton:

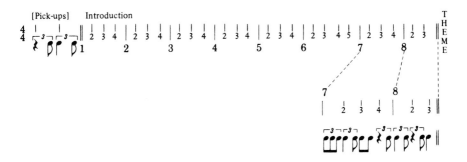

As Martin Williams points out, "Morton's music also reflects the changes that had taken place in New Orleans, and at this point these changes are perhaps best understood as rhythmic changes. To go back for a moment . . . [ragtime] melodies had more syncopations than were heard in the cakewalk. In New Orleans, when the form of ragtime came together with the soul of the blues, even more rhythmic variety and complexity were introduced."[18]

Piano ragtime virtually came to an end with the close of the First World War, New Orleans ragtime bands developed into the jazz bands of the '20s, and Harlem ragtime was partly responsible for the development of swing in the '30s. The stride pianists of New York in the '20s trained both Fletcher Henderson and Duke Ellington, and the young Count Basie was at home playing stride left hand. Their groups were to become the leaders in the evolution of the big bands. Whether ragtime is jazz, whether it is peripherally related to jazz, or whether it is a totally isolated, independent form are moot questions whose resolution leaves little profit for the debater. The music is interesting of and by itself, its derivation from American and black American music is plain, and its influence upon American and black American music, as well as popular and classical music in Europe, is undeniable.

Remarkably enough, ragtime, like classic jazz, has undergone a revival, and today a new generation of composers such as Max Morath, Robert R. Darch, Donald Ashwander, Thomas W. Shea, and William Bolcom are composing new music in the old style. Hundreds of new recordings of ragtime have been issued since the 1950s; books, periodicals, and reprinted sheet music are pouring forth in a steady stream. The old music has found a new audience, both popular and scholarly. In the words of Treemonisha and Lucy:

> *Marching onward, marching onward,*
> *Marching to that lovely tune;*
> *Marching onward, marching onward,*
> *Happy as a bird in June.*
> *Sliding onward, sliding onward,*
> *Listen to that rag.*
> *Hop and skip, now do that slow,*
> *Do that slow drag.*[19]

---

[18] *SCCJ* liner notes, p. 6.
[19] *The Collected Works of Scott Joplin*, II, pp. 221–34.

THE BLUES

Rats in my kitchen. Got so many in my kitchen—
  Order me a Model T cat.
The way they stolen my groceries,
  You know it's tough like that.
That's blues.

> —Sleepy John Estes, from an interview
> by Glenn D. Hinson and Bruce S. Babski,
> November 1973

INTRODUCTION

The blues is a personal statement made in musical terms which is nevertheless valid for all members of a society. There are many instances in literature, as well as folklore, of the word's use to describe a disconsolate or depressed emotional state. In a letter to Peter Garrick, written on the 11th of July, 1741, the British tragedian David Garrick wrote:

> The Town is exceeding hot & Sultry & I am far from being quite well, tho not troubled wth ye Blews as I have been.[1]

At the very beginning of the nineteenth century, Washington Irving wrote:

> My friend Launcelot concluded his harangue with a sigh, and as I saw he was still under the influence of a whole legion of the blues, and just on the point of sinking into one of his whimsical, and unreasonable fits of melancholy abstraction, I proposed a walk . . .[2]

[1] David Garrick, *Letters*, ed. David M. Little and George M. Kahr, I (Cambridge, Mass.: Harvard University Press, 1963), p. 26.
[2] Washington Irving, *Salmagundi*, No. 15 (New York: David Longworth, 1807), p. 310.

The blues can differ in mood, theme, approach, or style of delivery. Blues are not intrinsically pessimistic even though they often tell of defeat and downheartedness, for in expressing the problems of poverty, migration, family disputes, and oppression, the blues provides a catharsis that enables the participants to return to their environment with resignation, if not optimism. There is an expressive sensuality in the blues that is almost exultant in its affirmation of life, and the music eases the pain, providing an outlet for the frustration, hurt, and anger that blues singers and their audiences feel. In their natural setting, whether rural or urban, blues singers maintain a feeling of kinship with their audience. Their statements, describing their own states of mind, are generalized by the audience when they recall the same or similar experiences.

The advent of recording was not necessary to sustain the blues, for country blues have thrived in rural America as a living tradition within a society often so impoverished that recordings were not available to them. But recordings preserved a poverty-stricken folk art and spread the genre first throughout the nation and later throughout the world. Down home, in the ghetto or on the farm, the blues has a social importance that disappears in the popularized, re-performed versions. Personal feelings are verbalized and serve to call community attention to one's predicament and misfortune. The expression of criticism and complaint, the verbalization of these plights, provides the needed catharsis—an antidote to the problem. Within the black community, the words are usually direct, sometimes laced with disguised meaning, but always full of real-life experience.

Innuendo and double meanings are important aspects of blues lyrics. This practice may be traced to the pre-abolition period, when slaves needed a system of secret communication while they were still within earshot of their masters.[3] This custom of double-entendre, intentional ambiguity through the use of words with two meanings, which was strong in the African literary tradition as well,[4] was incorporated naturally and smoothly into the lyrics of the blues. Racial protest as well as sexual feelings are often hidden in humor or metaphor. Two examples are Victoria Spivey's *Handyman:*

> *He shakes my ashes, freezes my griddle,*
> *Churns my butter, stokes my pillow,*
> *My man is such a handyman.*

[3] See Eileen Southern, "The Underground Railroad," *The Music of Black Americans: A History,* 2nd ed., p. 142 ff.

[4] See Henry Louis Gates, Jr., *The Signifying Monkey: A Theory of Afro-American Literary Criticism.*

He threads my needle, gleans my wheat,
Heats my heater, chops my meat,
My man is such a handyman.[5]

and Lonnie Johnson's *Hard Times Ain't Gone Nowhere:*

People is raisin' 'bout hard times,
Tell me what it's all about,
People is hollerin' 'bout hard times,
Tell me what it's all about,
Hard times don't worry me,
I was broke when it first started out.

Friends, it could be worser,
You don't seem to understand,
Friends, it could be worser,
You don't seem to understand,
Some is cryin' with a sack of gold under each arm
And a loaf of bread in each hand.

People ravin' 'bout hard times,
I don't know why they should,
People ravin' 'bout hard times,
I don't know why they should,
If some people was like me,
They didn't have no money when times was good.[6]

Although metaphors, puns, and other methods of expressing double meaning have traditionally been a part of the blues, the most blatant expressions of sexual imagery and racial protest were reserved solely for the ears of the black community. The record companies acted as censors, although not always rigorous enforcers, in order to make recorded blues inoffensive to the sensibilities of the white customer. But vocal blues are essentially racial, and the language employed is shot through with words particular to the subculture. It has been pointed out that:

> The existence of a strong tradition of black music which has continued to the present is in part due to the isolation of blacks from the mainstream of American life. Though Gellert [author of *Negro Songs of Protest*] accurately stressed the presence of protest in black music, it is also separated from white ears by

[5] Paul Oliver, *Aspects of the Blues Tradition*, p. 209.
[6] Paul Oliver, *The Meaning of the Blues*, p. 58 f.

"Red Willie" Smith in York, Alabama.

factors such as style and the language used in verses. Few whites would be familiar with voodoo terms such as "black cat bone" and "John the Conqueror root" which are found in many blues tunes. In effect, the language of blues is a cultural code, in the sense that few whites would grasp its sexual and racial levels of meaning. Terms such as "jazz" and more recently "nitty gritty" have been assimilated by popular white culture, but scholars suggest their meanings are considerably altered from their original usage.[7]

Had it not been for the phonograph, the blues artists of the 1920s and '30s would be virtually unknown to us today, and until 1920 no recordings were made of this folk art. Beginning in the 1930s and '40s, field recordings were made of prisoners on work gangs in prison farms and penitentiaries and of Southern rural laborers, chiefly through the pioneering efforts of Alan Lomax. Although these recordings are useful in ascertaining the musical antecedents of the blues, it is important to note that they were made relatively late. Also, Paul Oliver points out that we have no way of determining whether recorded blues give an accurate picture of the genre, for there is an almost total absence of contemporaneous research and notated blues music.[8] Using a convenient, tripartite division of the blues—country blues, classic or city blues, and urban blues—we might examine each category briefly to observe those characteristics salient to our study of jazz.

BLUES FORM

"Blues" refers to a style of music, a type of performance, a musical form, and a state of mind. Structurally, the chief characteristic of the musical form is a repeated harmonic pattern of twelve measures' duration in 4/4 time. This twelve-measure period is divided equally into three four-measure phrases, the first in the tonic, the second in the subdominant and tonic, and the last in the dominant and tonic (frequently, the dominant slips back to the subdominant before resolving to the tonic in this final phrase).

A.

measure	1	2	3	4	5	6	7	8	9	10	11	12
harmony	I————				IV——I——				V———I——			
									(IV)			

B.

measure	1	2	3	4	5	6	7	8	9	10	11	12
harmony	I	V^7	I	I^{b7}	IV	II	III♯	VI	II^7	V^7	I——	

[7] William Ferris, *Blues from the Delta*, p. 100.
[8] Oliver, *Meaning of the Blues*, p. 29.

C.

measure	1	2	3	4	5	6	7	8	9	10	11	12
harmony	B♭	F♯m⁷	BM⁷ Em⁷	A⁷ Dm⁷ Bm⁷ E⁷	E♭⁷	B♭⁰ A⁷ B♭ Cm⁷	Dm⁷ G⁷		Cm⁷	F⁷	B♭ G⁷	Cm⁷ F⁷
	(I)				(IV)		(I)		(II⁷)	(V⁷)	(I)	

Example A represents the simplest harmonic plan, whereas B and C show embellished and more harmonically complicated schemata. Vocal blues most often overlaid an **AAB** text and melody on an **ABC** harmonic structure— that is, the singer's first phrase was repeated, but the harmonies continued to move on. In the classic blues phase, instruments would play background music for the first two measures while the singer would carry the text and tune. The melody instruments would then fill in with a break during the following two measures. This call-and-response pattern between singer and instrumental soloist can be seen graphically as follows:

Typical Blues Pattern

Measure	1	2	3	4	5	6	7	8	9	10	11	12
Singer	a————————rest				a————————rest				b————————rest			
Instruments	back————break————				back————break————				back————break————			
Harmony	A				B				C			
	I————————————				IV————I————				V——IV—I————			

Blues harmony, although appearing to be a major-mode phenomenon upon first inspection, is actually neither major nor minor, for the characteristic blues sound results from the simultaneous use of major and minor tonalities and nontempered scale intervals. The blues scale, in the key of C, often admitted A♭ as well as E♭ and B♭. These are the minor thirds of the major I, IV, and V harmonies. Although any chromatic note could be admitted, the flatted fifth, G♭, was also commonly stressed. In performance, all of these notes were unstable in intonation and function, and this quality was an important characteristic of the blues. Also, since blues stems from a vocal, rather than an instrumental, tradition, portamentos, "falloffs," nonstandard vibratos, and nontempered tuning were all part of the melodic style.

The Blues Scale

a. In the Key of C

1	2	3♭ (blue) 3♮	4	$\frac{1}{5}$	$\frac{2}{6}$	3♭ (blue) 3♮ / 7♭ 7♮	4 8

b. Transposed to the Key of A♭

c. A blues in A♭ (*Chi Chi,* by Charlie Parker) with flat and sharp thirds and sevenths (to an A♭ harmony [tonic chord]) marked with asterisks.

Chi Chi, Take 1

[The asterisks, in order - 3♮ , 7♮ , 7♭ , 3♭]

More complete transcriptions of *Chi Chi* and other original tunes by Charlie Parker may be found in *Charlie Parker Omnibooks: 60 Recorded Solos,* available in E♭, C, B♭, and Bass Cleff, and *Charlie Parker for Piano: 15 Piano Solos Based on His Recordings,* vols. 1–3, arranged by Paul Smith, and Morris Feldman (Hollywood: Criterion Music Corporation).

The lowered third and seventh scale steps are commonly called "blue notes," a phenomenon that has been variously described by writers on jazz. One describes the blues scale as two disjunct tetrachords with a variable third, and labels the result a purely negroid scale.[9] Another expert accepts this reconstructed jazz scale, but explains the blue notes as "neutral thirds," pitches that sound flat to a classical musician expecting a major third.[10] He, too, ties these sounds to an African tradition and explains that a noted British Africanist, A. M. Jones, says he has never heard an African sing the exact third or seventh of our tempered scale. A third authority, reviewing the work of the first, correctly observes, "[He] could not have found the full blues scale in African recordings, since indeed it does not exist in that form in

[9]Winthrop W. Sargeant, *Jazz, Hot and Hybrid,* pp. 132–44.
[10]Marshall W. Stearns, *The Story of Jazz,* pp. 276–80.

Africa, but developed out of melodic-harmonic practices peculiar to African music only, as we have shown, upon contact with European harmony."[11] Supporting this view, a fourth writes:

> A frequently mentioned characteristic of U.S. Negro songs is the so-called "blue note," the flatted or slightly lowered third and seventh degrees in a major scale. The origin of this phenomenon is not known, but it probably cannot be traced to Africa. Here is a musical trait which may, possibly, have come into folk music from the practices of American Negro popular and jazz musicians.[12]

Referring to the paired tetrachords mentioned above, another commentator states, "This, in fact, is the blues scale. It is, as we said, a scale that constitutes the common denominator of all American Negro folk music; but while all other American Negro idioms may occasionally take recourse to it, the blues is the only one that makes exclusive use of it."[13]

In sum, there are African scales that contain an untempered third and seventh degree, but the blues scale is a composite sound that developed in the United States when the African melodic idiom was tempered by European harmony. The question of whether or not the blues scale is part of the essence of jazz is moot and need not be settled here. The most commonly held view is that the blues' melodic material is part and parcel of jazz. The blues approach to jazz allows for constant embellishment and variation, in addition to encouraging individualized performances, a kaleidoscope that multiplies the lights of auditory delight.

Rhythmically, blues offer an interesting contrast to ragtime. Whereas the regular rhythmic line of ragtime, the standard against which a melody might syncopate, was an alternation of strong and weak pulses, the regular rhythmic line of blues was a steady stream of strong pulses. Whether the text falls into an iambic pentameter scheme or any other, stretching syllables improvisationally for musical, as well as textual, reasons makes the beat placement in blues performances unpredictable. The ragtime performer syncopated by accenting midway between beats or on weaker beats; the blues performer often syncopated by missing, rather than hitting, a particular accent. This improvisatory rhythmic style allows for great flexibility.

In contrast, the unpredictable nature of rhythmic performance in country blues is nowhere better illustrated than in Robert Johnson's *Hell Hound on My Trail* (*SCCJ* 3). Johnson's performance involves four stanzas of blues lyrics. In a standardized version by a blues composer such as W. C. Handy we

---

[11] Gunther Schuller, *Early Jazz*, p. 47.

[12] Bruno Nettl, *Folk and Traditional Music of the Western Continents* (Englewood Cliffs, NJ: Prentice-Hall, 1973), p. 185.

[13] Ernest Borneman, "Black Light and White Shadow," *Jazzforschung*, 2 (1970), p. 57.

would expect to find each stanza twelve measures long in 4/4 time. The introduction would be two, four, or eight measures long. Johnson's performance only approximates this concept, especially in the placement of the blues harmonies at the structural points of each verse. But careful inspection of this performance will show that the introduction has only fourteen beats; a regular four-measure introduction would have sixteen. In the first stanza there are three phrases consisting of 22 beats, 20 beats, and 24 beats; or, 5½ measures, 5 measures, and 6 measures of four beats each. Subsequent verses are of slightly different proportions: 20, 16, 21; 17, 18, 20; 22, 18, 21.

The general characteristics of the blues are ever present: the I–IV–I–V–I harmonies in each stanza, the repeated first line answered by a second and different line; a melodic statement that takes approximately half of the first phrase and is answered by an instrumental statement in the second half; and so on. However, the 253 beats of this particular piece are irregularly divided according to Robert Johnson's own personal style. The performer's freedom to insert words or melismas[14] into the melodic line can be seen, for example, in the second line of the third stanza.

Hell Hound on My Trail (Verse 3)

Only three relative time-values are used in the example to approximate free-flowing speech rhythm (short equals eighth note, middle equals quarter note, and long equals half note), but even with this lack of precision, one can readily perceive how Johnson creates irregular groupings in his melodic line. In some blues and jazz performances, the combination of five or seven notes in one part overlapping two or three beats in another part, with no points of coincidence for that brief duration, is not exceptional. It is just part of the style, part of the rhythmic freedom introduced to jazz through the blues.

[14] A melisma is an ornamentation slipped into a melodic line. The word was originally used to describe a method of singing in which several different pitches are used for a single syllable of text.

COUNTRY BLUES

The country blues, sometimes called Southern blues, folk blues, or Delta blues, is a rural folk expression usually performed by a male singer. If it is accompanied, the singer usually plays the accompaniment himself on a simple folk instrument, like the fiddle, banjo, or guitar.

Country blues most assuredly existed before jazz but its origins are lost in the past, before the days of sound recordings. However, it persists to the present day and is still performed in a manner virtually unchanged from that preserved in the earliest recordings. A few rural blues singers have achieved some degree of national prominence, probably more through chance than through artistic achievement. The colorful and folksy nicknames taken by Huddie Ledbetter ("Leadbelly"), Son House, Blind Lemon Jefferson, and "Sleepy" John Estes have an earthy quality that seems to signal that the music is an expression of a society, not necessarily the achievement of art and artifice. By definition, folk music is that body of ethnic or traditional music that stems from a particular part of the world where urban, professionalized, and cultivated classical music have also developed.[15]

Country blues is such a folk music, for it is perpetuated by oral tradition. Songs are passed on by word of mouth, and performance tradition is learned by watching and hearing. It is a functional aspect of the culture of the people from which it stems, and it reflects their vision and their values. When the people change, so must the music; and if country blues have remained essentially stable over the last seventy or so years, it is because one can still find areas in rural America where farm life and culture for black Americans have changed little since the turn of the century. If we cannot investigate the history of country blues, we can at least survey some of the well-known figures and their music.

"PAPA" CHARLIE JACKSON

In July 1924, Paramount Records of Chicago produced the first country blues record, *Papa's Lawdy Lawdy Blues*, by "Papa" Charlie Jackson. Born around 1890 in New Orleans, he made his way to Chicago via a couple of minstrel shows. Between his first record in 1924 and his last in April 1935, Papa Charlie cut seventy-seven works. In 1928 he recorded two duets with Ma Rainey, *Ma and Pa Poorhouse Blues* and *Big Feeling Blues*. During his career, he worked

---

[15] Nettl, *Folk and Traditional Music*, p. 1.

with Ida Cox and Big Bill Broonzy as well as Ma Rainey. In 1925, singing to a fast banjo accompaniment, Papa Charlie recorded *Shave 'em Dry*. (The suggestive title has more than one layer of meaning; as a sexual reference, it connotes intercourse without preliminary lovemaking.) The bawdy song, in folk tradition, celebrates physical love and smiles at the triangle situation.

> *Why don't you run here mama, lay back in my arms,*
> *If your man catches you I don't mean no harm,*
> *Mama let me holler, daddy let me shave 'em dry.*[16]

This work preserves the archaic eight-bar blues form, as well as the original harmonic and poetic structure. Jackson was not the first to record *Shave 'em Dry;* Ma Rainey sang this blues for the same company in August 1924,[17] so it is possible he either learned the song from her or taught it to her. Jackson's records sold well, and he continued to record for Paramount for the next four years. He was unable to read or write, and during recording sessions someone would sit behind him whispering the words into his ear.

Papa Charlie continued to work the vaudeville circuit, and his early recording *Salty Dog Blues*,[18] the second he did for Paramount, was always associated with him. He rerecorded the number with Freddie Keppard's Jazz Cardinals in 1926.

> *Funniest thing I ever saw in my life*
> *Uncle Bud came home and caught me kissin' his wife.*
> *Salty Dog, oh, yes, you Salty Dog.*

——— BLIND LEMON JEFFERSON ———

Perhaps the best-known rural blues singer of the 1920s was Blind Lemon Jefferson. Born blind in Couchman, Texas, in 1897, he began singing for money in Wortham, Texas, in 1911 or 1912. He went to Dallas around 1917, and was fairly successful working the red-light district. There he met Leadbelly (Huddie Ledbetter), another important country blues singer, who was in prison most of the time that Blind Lemon was working in Dallas. Jefferson seems to have traveled as far east as Mississippi and Alabama, and some of the older bluesmen tell stories of him in towns like Jackson, Mississippi, and

---

[16]Paramount 12264, recorded February 1925.
[17]Paramount 12222.
[18]Paramount 12236.

Memphis, Tennessee. Blind Lemon traveled to Chicago in 1925 and began recording there in 1926. He cut his last disc in 1929 and died in Chicago in 1930. One song associated particularly with Blind Lemon was *The Black Snake Moan*. When it was recorded originally by Victoria Spivey in 1926, the *Black Snake Blues* may have had no sexual overtones. It may have simply described a rustic scene where a young girl came upon a black snake in her cabin. But Lemon transformed it into a sexual lament in 1927, recording a second version the same year and a third black snake piece in 1929. In the second version, recorded for Paramount around 1927, he sings

> *I aint got no mama now,*
> *I aint got no mama now,*
> *She told me late last night you don't need no mama nohow.*
>
> *Black snake crawlin' in my room,*
> *Black snake crawlin' in my room,*
> *And some pretty mama had better come in and get this black snake soon.*
>
> *. . . Well, I wonder where this black snake's gone?*
> *Well, I wonder where this black snake's gone?*
> *Lord, that black snake, mama, done run my darlin' home.*[19]

This recording, available in a modern reissue, is particularly interesting from a musical standpoint. It retains all the typical characteristics of the blues except that which is usually considered of foremost importance, the harmony. It has an **AAB** melodic structure and an **AAB** text structure; it has a call-and-response pattern dividing each phrase between voice and guitar; and, in spite of the rubato tempo, it maintains a twelve-measure structure. However, although the first four measures are in the tonic, as is traditional, the second four measures do not change to subdominant, but remain at the tonic level. The third phrase, which traditionally moves directly to the dominant, places the harmonic emphasis instead on the submediant (VI) and only implies the dominant harmony when you imagine it as the fifth above the root in the tonic chord.

The flexibility and unpredictability of the country blues is one of its most enduring charms and most important features. A soloist singing to his own accompaniment may wax eloquent and rhapsodize over an interesting word or a catchy melodic figure. Until recently, sex as a topic for song lyrics was held in low esteem by middle-class white America, but it has been argued that there was a social and psychological need for obscenity in black Ameri-

---

[19]Paramount 12407, reissued Folkways FP 55.

can singing. The unrelenting hard work and oppression which were their lot created the need for a "safety valve of ribald laughter [rather] than a neurotic stimulant and breaker of Puritan inhibitions."[20] Since the early blues were primarily "race" songs, they could flourish without the imposition of white middle-class morals. Still, Victoria Spivey resented the fact that Blind Lemon changed her *Black Snake Blues* to a sex song.

When Blind Lemon recorded *Shuckin' Sugar Blues* in 1926,[21] the standard blues harmonies were more apparent, but liberties were taken with the length of the final line of each stanza. When Jefferson recorded *Risin' High Water Blues* in 1927,[22] he was accompanied by George Perkins on piano. Here the traditional twelve-measure form was played in its standardized version. The topic of these lyrics is one of the typical rural subjects commonly found in country blues. Events that affect the lives of poor black country folk recur as persistent phenomena: *When the Levee Breaks, The Flood Blues, The Mississippi Flood Blues, Mississippi Heavy Water Blues,* and many others. Spoiled crops, ruined homes, death, and separation are all subjects for the storytelling country-blues singer.

HUDDIE LEDBETTER

Leadbelly (Huddie Ledbetter) acknowledged the influence of Blind Lemon Jefferson upon his development and recalled hearing him as early as 1917 in the bordellos of Dallas, Texas. Ledbetter, born in Morringsport, Louisiana, in 1885, grew up in Texas, where as a boy he learned work songs as well as blues and other folk songs. He received long jail sentences from several Texas and Louisiana prisons for violent crimes. It was at the Angola Prison Farm, Louisiana, that he was "discovered" by John and Alan Lomax and first recorded the prison songs for their collection, now preserved in the Music Division of the Library of Congress. Leadbelly led the life of a farmhand, both inside and out of prison, and as a participant in work gangs he frequently acted as lead singer in the work songs. He made a living as a professional folk singer, accompanying himself on the guitar in almost three hundred recordings. Although he was co-composer with John Lomax of a popular song, *Good Night, Irene*, he died in 1949 before the tune was transformed into a commercial hit with orchestral accompaniment and cover singers. During his last years he received recognition as a folk singer; he gave concerts and entertained in clubs on the West Coast.

[20] Alain Locke, *The Negro and His Music*, p. 88.
[21] Paramount 12454, reissued Riverside SDP II.
[22] Paramount 12487, reissued Riverside SDP II.

Huddie "Leadbelly" Ledbetter (1885–1949).

Juliana Johnson and *John Henry*,[23] two work songs recorded by Leadbelly, are ballads from the pre-blues tradition, the former setting a rhythm for ax cutting and the latter for hammering with a sledge. One of the characteristics that distinguishes these songs from the blues is the importance of the verse sequence in the total composition. These work songs exist as an entity, are committed to memory, and are passed on orally as a unit. They may change through errors in the process of transmission, but essentially they retain their identity. Since the blues are all based on the same simple structure, the individuality of any particular blues results from the remodeling of the same basic material by individual singers according to their talents and personal needs. Improvisation is an essential element of the blues, where it is only incidental in the transmission of folk ballads.

Typical blues performances by Leadbelly can be heard on two recordings he made for the Library of Congress in 1938, *The Bourgeois Blues* and *De Kalb Woman*.[24] His style of guitar playing differs from that of Blind Lemon Jeffer-

[23] Folkways FP 53.
[24] Electra EKL 301–2, reissued Sine Qua Non SQN 103.

son in that his four-beat strumming submits to a variety of rhythmic fills. In *Bourgeois Blues* he often strums·bass strings as a drone to create a pedal point beneath the changing blues harmonies. Blind Lemon Jefferson, in a sound more akin to country-western guitar playing, accompanies his singing with a boom-chuck or oom-pah bass, one similar to the left-hand pattern of ragtime piano. Also, Blind Lemon's enunciation is clear and fairly understandable to whites unaccustomed to a black dialect, whereas the lyrics of Leadbelly are thrown out in the thick drawl of the black rural South.

Lines of demarcation between country-blues singers, classic-blues singers, popular singers, and jazz singers are not easily drawn, and in the workings of Papa Charlie Jackson and Leadbelly we can see several areas of overlap. If Ma Rainey is a classic-blues singer, then is Papa Charlie Jackson one as well when he sings *Ma and Pa Poorhouse Blues* with her? If Freddie Keppard and Johnny Dodds are jazz-ensemble musicians, is Papa Charlie a jazz singer when he sings a blues to the accompaniment of Freddie Keppard's group? At what point in its history does *Good Night, Irene* make a transition from folk music to popular music? When Mike Leadbitter and Neil Slaven published their blues discography, they footnoted the entry of Leadbelly as follows: "As this artist has mainly recorded in the true folk vein, only sessions thought to be of interest to blues collectors are listed."[25] Still, they list *Good Night, Irene* in more than one take, and here we have a work that is clearly not blues and only peripherally of folk derivation.

ROBERT JOHNSON

One of the most influential bluesmen from the Mississippi Delta was Robert Johnson, who, as a little boy, started playing harmonica and listened to the music of "Son" House and Willie Brown. He died in his mid-twenties, recorded only twenty-nine songs (all for the Vocalion label in 1936 and 1937),[26] but still influenced a host of followers, including Muddy Waters, Howling Wolf, Sonny Boy Williamson, Junior Parker, and even the Rolling Stones. Although his recorded music is highly personal, his work is characteristic of Delta Blues from the 1930s and forms one of the many links between the country blues of the Delta and the urban blues of Chicago.[27] Johnson's *Preachin' Blues*, which had antecedents in *Preachin' the Blues* of James McCoy and Son House,

[25] Mike Leadbitter and Neil Slaven, *Blues Records, 1943–1966*, I, p. 189.

[26] The complete recordings of Robert Johnson are now available on compact disc (CBS 22190).

[27] Important studies are William Ferris, *Blues from the Delta;* Giles Oakley, *The Devil's Music: A History of the Blues* (New York: Harcourt Brace Jovanovich, 1976); Paul Oliver, *The Blues Tradition;* and Charles Keil, *Urban Blues* (Chicago: University of Chicago Press, 1966). The author gratefully acknowledges the assistance of Stephen C. LaVere in ensuring the accuracy of the information about Robert Johnson contained in this volume.

Robert Johnson (1898–1937) is represented in this drawing in a makeshift recording studio set up in a San Antonio hotel room in November 1936.

is part of a long tradition of Preaching Blues that has little or no connection to religion or to preaching in church. For the most part, all denominations of the African-American Christian churches avoided the blues and the blues singer, referring to the larger blues tradition as "the devil's music." Johnson, in this work, personifies the blues, and makes him out to be the devil incarnate.

Mmm, I's up this mornin', ah, blues walkin' like a man.
I's up this mornin', ah, blues walkin' like a man.
Worried blues, give me your right hand.

And the blues fell, mama's child, tore me all upside down.
Blues fell mama's child, and it tore me all upside down.
Travel on, poor Bob, just cain't turn you 'round.

The blues is a low-down shakin' chill. (Yes, preach 'em now.)
Mmm, is a low-down shakin' chill.
You ain't never had 'em, I hope you never will.

Well, the blues is an achin' old heart disease.
  (Do it now. You gon' do it? Tell me all about it.)
Let the blues is a low-down achin' heart disease.
Like consumption, killing me by degrees.

I can study rain, oh oh, drive, oh, oh, drive my blues.
I been studyin' the rain and I'm gon' drive my blues away.
Goin' to the 'stil'ry, stay out there all day.

Johnson plays his guitar with a fierce intensity—irregular rhythms, broken patterns, shakes and slides, and a driving, propulsive beat. Despite the overall simplicity of the formal scheme, the harmonic progression, and the poetic form, Johnson's music is so complex and irregular that it defies even approximate transcription into Western notation. The following sketch is a guide to the opening and shows the lowered seventh and contrasting major and minor thirds, but it does not even approach the subtleties of pitch, timbre, and rhythm employed by Johnson in the actual performance.

Preachin' Blues (Up Jumped the Devil)

This piece shares many characteristics with the Yarum Praise Song and the Georgia Sea Island song *Daniel*, discussed in chapter one: repeated ostinato pattern (bottleneck guitar riff[28]), rhythmic accompaniment (lower-string strumming), melodic scale that avoids the second tone, and melodic use that stresses the lowered seventh and the interplay of major and minor third (the blue notes).

Preachin' Blues (Up Jumped the Devil), Melodic Scale

Actually, a pentatonic scale with "blue" third would suffice to notate this blues.

Preachin' Blues (Up Jumped the Devil), Pentatonic Scale

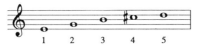

The **AAB** pattern of each three-line stanza of text is a regular characteristic of the blues, although Johnson varies the number of beats within and between the phrases as he sees fit. Overall, the patterns are regular, but close examination reveals a jagged, asymmetrical patchwork that is common among the works of the country blues musicians.

The Mississippi Delta has produced many country-blues singers of note—Charlie Patton, Son House, Skip James, Robert Johnson, and Booker T. Washington "Bukka" White. The Delta is a rich alluvial plain extending from Vicksburg, Mississippi, to Memphis, Tennessee, defined by the Mississippi River on the west and the Yazoo River on the east. It is an agricultural region and contains the densest black population of the state, blacks outnumbering whites by more than a two-to-one ratio. Racial pride is still felt by Delta blacks toward blues singers, who have become the musical representatives for the black communities. Although the oral tradition is strong, the area has not proved impregnable to outside musical interests, and white country music with fiddle and banjo has also become a part of the culture. Robert Johnson has been called "King of the Delta Blues." He was born May 8, 1911, in Hazelhurst, Mississippi, and was raised by his mother, half-sisters, and two stepfathers. His early years were spent in Memphis, Tennessee, and Commerce, a north Mississippi farming community near Robinsonville. He played harmonica as a youth and took up the guitar sometime around 1930. At first tutored by Ike Zinnerman, a local favorite at country

---

[28] When a guitar's strings are tuned to a chord rather than the "normal" E–A–D–G–B–E, the player may lay a jackknife or the neck of a soda bottle across all the strings and change the chords by merely running the "bottleneck" up and down the fingerboard.

suppers and fish fries, Johnson soon chose the life of an itinerant bluesman, performing mainly in the tri-state area but traveling as far as Ontario, Canada, Brooklyn, New York, and as far west as Texas, where he made his now famous recordings. He died in Greenwood, Mississippi, on August 16, 1938, probably from poison administered by the unsuspecting female accomplice of a jealous husband. A portion of his blues repertoire suggests that he had a premonition of a violent, sinful, love-related death. His lyrics deal with three recurring themes: the impermanence of human relationships, incessant wandering, and irrational terrors. His blues are shot through with dark foreboding, saying there is no home for him anywhere, not even a place for his body after death. His *Me and the Devil Blues*, recorded in Dallas in 1937, is an example:

> *Early this morning when you knocked upon my door,*
> *Early this morning when you knocked upon my door,*
> *And I said, "Hello Satan, I believe it's time to go."*
>
> *Me and the devil was walking side by side,*
> *Me and the devil was walking side by side,*
> *And I'm going to beat my woman until I get satisfied.*
>
> *You may bury my body down by the highwayside,*
> > *(I don't care where you bury my body when I'm dead and gone.)*
> *You may bury my body down by the highwayside,*
> *So my old evil spirit can get a Greyhound bus and ride.*[29]

In *Stones in My Passway*, Johnson sings again of trouble, death, and travel:

> *I got stones in my passway and my road seems dark at night,*
> *I got stones in my passway and my road seems dark at night,*
> *I have pains in my heart, they have taken my appetite.*
>
> *. . . Now you tryin' to take my life, and all my lovin' too,*
> *You laid a passway for me, now what are you tryin' to do?*[30]

His insistent, droning bottleneck slide guitar complements his slightly nasal, intense, and passionate voice. His rhythm is always nervous; the irregularities of phrase structure are sometimes matched by an irregularity in beat. But together, the accompaniment and the lyrics provide a powerful musical force capable of expressing an apocalyptic vision. Johnson's *Hell Hound on My Trail* (*SCCJ* 3) has been evaluated as

one of the most personal and expressive moments in blues poetry. . . . All of the images, the blues falling down like rain on him, the leaves on the trees

[29] Vocalion 0418.
[30] Columbia CL 1654.

over his head shaking with the wind, intensified the desperation he felt at the thought of the hellhound trailing through the day . . . the feeling of the immediate in the first verse, however, still hung over the song like a low line of clouds over the levees along the Yazoo River, and it was one of his most effective performances.[31]

Robert Johnson was an itinerant musician who for several years worked the Mississippi Delta from a home base in Helena, Arkansas. On the road, he would usually take up with a local woman, live at her place, and play his music at an area road house called a "jook joint." Though he avoided the tough "working girls," he could not evade the problems of casual relationships and jealous boyfriends. He encapsulated this experience in his poignant 1936 recording, "I Believe I'll Dust My Broom" (NAJ 1). In it one notices the reference to West Helena and nearby East Monroe, the artful injection of humor into an otherwise pathetic situation, and the unusual repeat of the first verse as a form of recapitulation near the end. In his singing and playing, Johnson displays his introspective style and character, a fascinating boogie-woogie-beat accompaniment to his singing, and a solo guitar response to each vocal call of the blues poetry. (See Listening Guide 1.)

Taking the repertoire of country blues preserved and recorded by our older bluesmen and extrapolating backward, we can surmise that blues form was originally variable and stretched from eight to sixteen measures in length, but that a predominant form emerged: the twelve-measure stanza of three lines, each accompanied by simple chordal harmony of tonic, subdominant, and dominant. By the time blues were taken over by improvising instrumental jazz ensembles, the twelve-measure blues form had become standard.

In country blues, with vocal lines approximately two measures long, the singer was able to play instrumental "breaks" between phrases, and this pattern is commonly cited as the tie between American blues and African call-and-response singing. Bruno Nettl has pointed out that

> African and Western music are by their nature compatible; that is, important elements of each are structurally capable of being accommodated by the other. . . . the way the voice is used and the kinds of sound produced by the singer . . . is one of the ways in which the musics of the world differ most obviously and consistently. A musical culture may change its songs, scales, and rhythms, but it will tend to keep its singing style unchanged even over many centuries; it appears to be the musical element most resistant to change.[32]

[31] Samuel Charters, *The Bluesmen,* p. 91 f.
[32] Bruno Nettl, "The Western Impact on World Music: Africa and the American Indians," in *Contemporary Music and Music Cultures,* by Charles Hamm, Bruno Nettl, and Ronald Byrnside, pp. 112, 119.

The country blues gave jazz not only one of its most important forms, but also a mode of performance, with all its concomitant sounds and attitudes.

The names of other country-blues singers are as colorful as they are numerous: Peg Leg Howell, Sleepy John Estes, Blind Willie Johnson, Washboard Sam, Big Bill, "Ragtime Texas" Henry Thomas, and more. They created and preserved one of the richest repertoires of native American music. The blues tradition continued to change. Just as the country blues was preceded by other folk types, it was followed, although not superseded, by classic blues, urban blues, rhythm and blues, and the more contemporary sounds of Motown, hip-hop and rap, and soul music. To the listener raised on the concert-hall or recording-studio sounds, country blues may seem coarse and perhaps even unimaginative at first hearing. To the connoisseur trained to detect the subtle nuance of double-entendre and to accept the unexpurgated feelings of an agrarian people sympathetically, country blues offers a musical art form consonant with earthy values.

THE CLASSIC BLUES

Classic blues, often sung by women, bridged the gap between folk music and the entertainment world. Developed in minstrel shows and black theaters, the city blues gave voice to the more callous aspects of ghetto life and attitudes.

GERTRUDE "MA" RAINEY

Gertrude "Ma" Rainey was one of the first black female vocalists who performed classic blues to the accompaniment of jazz band or piano. Born in Columbus, Georgia, in 1886, she was married at fourteen and toured with her husband, Will Rainey, in The Rabbit Foot Minstrels. Her performances brought a degree of professionalism, of polished and consistent artistry, to the genre, and her work is preserved in recordings that span the years 1923 to 1929. She was not the first blues singer to record, and the recordings she made (when she was nearly forty) show us the formally standardized, instrumentally accompanied form of city blues.

Ma Rainey was one of the most influential blues singers of the age. She earned the title "Mother of the Blues" both as a leading early figure and as the mentor of the "Empress of the Blues," Bessie Smith. Her earliest recordings of 1923, *Bo Weevil Blues* and *Southern Blues*, depict situations from black American life closely allied to country blues. In *Southern Blues*, she sings of typical African-American homes:

"Ma" Rainey with her Georgia Jazz Band, 1925.

If your house catches on fire and there aint
no water around,
If your house catches on fire and there aint
no water around,
Throw your trunk out the window and let that
shack burn down.[33]

She was backed by Lovie Austin's Blues Serenaders, a group which, on this occasion, consisted of cornet, clarinet, piano, and violin. By the time she had finished recording in 1929, she had cut almost one hundred sides in her simple, direct blues style. She was the first to record *Shave 'em Dry*, and, as was mentioned earlier, she and Papa Charlie Jackson both recorded this number for Paramount within a year of each other. The work, incidentally, is most archaic in its structure, in that it is eight measures long rather than twelve.

It becomes apparent that in the mid-1920s "the blues" referred not only to a standardized instrumental piece twelve measures long, but to a style of singing and a type of subject matter. When Ma Rainey recorded *Titanic Man Blues* in 1926,[34] she departed from the standardized blues form with a six-

[33] Paramount 12083.
[34] Paramount 12374, reissued Riverside RLP 12-113.

teen-measure strophic piece divided in half into two similar phrases. The first ends with an open cadence, II^7–V, and the second finishes with a closed cadence, V^7–I. In other words, each strophe, or stanza, of the song consists of antecedent and consequent phrases. Further, each phrase is divided in three, as though it were a blues piece eight measures long. The last portion of each half carries the characteristic refrain "Fare thee well," but were the word "blues" not part of the title, we would certainly doubt its authenticity today.

Titanic Man Blues

The four-measure introduction serves as a coda at the end, and its harmonic pattern follows a circle of fifths (I–VI–II–V–I) derived from the last four measures of the sixteen-measure phrase. The accompaniment is played by the Georgia Jazz Band, with Joe Smith (trumpet), Charlie Green (trombone), and Buster Bailey (clarinet) in the front line; and Fletcher Henderson (piano), Charlie Dixon (banjo), and Coleman Hawkins (bass saxophone) for a rhythm section. Although the front-line instruments perform polyphonically, the trumpet frequently interacts heterophonically with the voice.

Before her recording career ended in 1929, Ma Rainey performed with many notables of the jazz world: Don Redman, Louis Armstrong, Kid Ory, and others already mentioned. Her popularity dwindled after 1930; and she retired from music in 1933. She was virtually unknown when she died in 1939, but her strong voice and straightforward style of projecting the words made her one of the most influential singers of the period.

W. C. HANDY

The distribution of recorded performances of the blues helped standardize the form, but published music also played a significant role. One man largely responsible for the spread and popularity of the blues as we know it today was William Christopher Handy, a black composer, cornetist, and bandleader, who designated himself the "Father of the Blues." Born in Florence, Alabama, in 1873, he traveled throughout the United States, Canada, Mexico, and Cuba as bandmaster of the Mahara Minstrels. He not only composed

W. C. Handy and the band of the Teachers' Agriculture and Mechanical College, Huntsville, Alabama, 1900.

music, he collected traditional African-American themes, which he incorporated in his own music. The first blues tune ever to be published was one of Handy's own compositions, *The Memphis Blues*. It was originally written as a campaign song during the 1909 election for a Memphis mayor. Handy's band was hired to help promote Edward H. Crump, who was running on a strict reform platform. Since Boss Crump wanted to attract votes from the Beale Street area, which was full of dancehalls and barrelhouses, he needed a gimmick to please the sporting crowd. The result was an extremely popular song titled *Mr. Crump*, and it was later published, in 1912, as *The Memphis Blues*.[35]

BESSIE SMITH

Handy's most famous composition was the *St. Louis Blues*, written in 1914 and given a classic performance in 1925 by the "Empress of the Blues," Bessie Smith, and the great jazz cornet and trumpet player, Louis Armstrong (*SCCJ* 4). Born in Chattanooga in 1894,[36] Bessie Smith went on the road as an entertainer while still in her teens. For years she worked in traveling tent shows, honky-tonks, and carnivals. She was discovered by Frank Walker, recording director for Columbia Records, singing in a club in Selma, Alabama, in 1917. Everything about Bessie Smith was big: her imposing person, her moving voice, and the quantities of alcohol she consumed. As a full-grown adult, she stood five feet nine inches tall and weighed in at 210 pounds. The volume of her voice was extraordinary, and it is perhaps for this reason that she was able to record so successfully on the primitive recording apparatus of the early '20s.

Bessie Smith combined a remarkable sense of rhythm with an extremely sensitive feeling for pitch and a crisp diction, all of which allowed her to convey the meaning of the words to a large audience. Her articulation of words and notes, delivered with a variety of tonal and rhythmic attacks, gave her interpretations a sense of poise as well as an improvisatory feeling. Smith's first recording, *Downhearted Blues*,[37] made in New York in February 1923, has great historical significance because of its early date, but is not considered one of her most musical achievements. She was obviously nervous, she was not singing one of her standard songs, and she had had no previous experience in a recording studio.

Bessie Smith soon reached a high degree of sophistication in *Jailhouse Blues*,[38] which she recorded in September 1923. In a sense, this recording marks the beginning of the classic-blues style, a method of performance that

[35] Also see discussion of *Memphis Blues* in chapter four.
[36] John Chilton gives 1895 and Paul Oliver 1898 as her birth year.
[37] Columbia A3844, reissued Columbia GP 33.
[38] Reissued Columbia CL-855.

differs significantly from the previous traditional blues performances. By 1925, Smith had achieved the maturity of style that marked her as the major recording artist of the era in this genre.

Her rendering of *St. Louis Blues* (*SCCJ* 4) is the epitome of the classic-blues performance, and the balance between the vocal and cornet solo work is extraordinary. The similarity of inflection, phrasing, and accent contribute the essential characteristics of tension and release that Bessie Smith and Louis Armstrong inject into this performance and that mark this recording as one of the landmark performances of both blues and jazz. When Smith recorded the work again a few years later with James P. Johnson at the piano, the Hall Johnson Choir, and members of the Fletcher Henderson Orchestra for the soundtrack of a movie short,[39] the powerful singing and professional certainty of a well-known vocalist are present, but the sensitive interworking of two jazz giants is not.

Throughout the '20s and well into the '30s, the twelve-bar blues as a standard form became more entrenched, but did not totally eclipse the many blues variants, even among performances by classic-blues singers. Bessie Smith's *St. Louis Blues* is an excellent example of a piece constructed with a twelve-bar blues at the beginning, a bridge in between, and a second twelve-bar blues at the end. Her recording of *Blue Blue* for Columbia in 1931[40] begins with a twelve-measure phrase that is blueslike, for it has three four-measure sections. But the pattern is **ABB** rather than **AAB**. It is followed by a sixteen-measure bridge that repeats the same four-measure phrase—**CCCC**. Then Smith sings a regular twelve-measure blues, once, and this is followed by two instrumental performances of the same twelve-measure phrase. The piece closes with a repeat of the initial **ABB** pattern, and when the overall structure of *Blue Blue* is gathered together, we have **ABCA,** where **C** indicates three repetitions of a regular twelve-bar blues. The recording by Smith of *Shipwreck Blues*[41] at the same session displays a regular twelve-bar blues, but she inserts no words into the third phrase of the first two patterns, where one would normally find the refrain.

Bessie Smith's recording of *Lost Your Head Blues* (*SCCJ* 5) exemplifies the blues in its most elemental and most comprehensible form (see examples on pages 51–53). Fletcher Henderson's piano playing in this recording is in the so-called boogie-woogie style, the left hand performing an eight-notes-to-the-measure ostinato (that is, repeating the short bass riff again and again throughout the number).

Bessie Smith's singing, which combined the flexibility and sophistication

[39] Riverside RLP 12-113.
[40] Columbia 14611, reissued Columbia GP 33.
[41] Columbia 14663, reissued Columbia GP 33.

Bessie Smith (1894–1937).

of jazz with the elemental appeal of country blues, made her a special favorite with the black public of the 1920s. Her records sold well; she made a short movie in 1929, *St. Louis Blues;* and she was a headline vaudeville star. Unfortunately, she became an alcoholic and began to disintegrate both professionally and personally during the latter part of the 1920s. She continued to record until 1933, but her last recording was more an affectionate token from John Hammond than a professional session made for profit. She made her last public appearance while touring the Memphis area in 1937 and died in September of that year in an automobile accident. Controversy still shrouds the circumstances of her death. It was reported, and later dramatized,[42] that she was denied emergency treatment at a Mississippi hospital for whites and died from loss of blood and shock while being rushed to the nearest hospital for blacks.

She worked and recorded with the most important musical figures of the day: Sidney Bechet, Fletcher Henderson, Coleman Hawkins, Don Redman, Louis Armstrong, Jack Teagarden, Benny Goodman, and many others. Her influence was felt by all contemporary blues singers, and the vocal tradition she established is still with us today. Gunther Schuller sees her as

> one of the great tragic figures, not only of jazz, but of her period, and she more than any other expressed the hopes and sorrows of her generation of jazz musicians. If that were all, we would have reason enough to eulogize her. But Bessie Smith was a supreme artist, and as such her art transcends the particulars of life that informed that art.[43]

IDA COX

A leading contemporary of Bessie Smith's was Ida Cox, born in Knoxville, Tennessee, in 1889. She too toured with her own tent show in the South. One of the most successful blues recording artists, she began recording for Paramount in 1923. In 1925 she made *Rambling Blues*[44] with her husband, Jesse Crump, at the piano and a New Orleans–born cornetist, Tommy Ladnier. In many ways this is an archetypal blues, for it not only presents the standard blues form and offers the text in the simplest pattern, it deals with the state of mind most commonly accepted as that of the blues.

> *Early this morning the blues came walkin' in my room,*
> *Early this morning the blues came walkin' in my room,*

[42] By Edward Albee in his play, *The Death of Bessie Smith* (1959).
[43] Schuller, *Early Jazz*, p. 241.
[44] Paramount 12318.

A rare photograph of Ida Cox (1889–1967).

> *I said, 'Blues, please tell me what you're doin'*
> *makin' me feel so blue."*

Another side, probably recorded at the same time, *Coffin Blues*,[45] is a lament to a dead lover.

> *Daddy, oh Daddy, won't you answer me please?*
> *Daddy, oh Daddy, won't you answer me please?*
> *All day I stood by your coffin tryin' to give my*
> *poor heart ease.*

Like other singers of the day, not everything Ida Cox recorded with the word "blues" in the title was in fact a blues. Her recording of *I've Got the Blues for Rampart Street*[46] is not a blues at all but a piece in the ragtime-Dixieland style. Eight-measure phrases with chromatic harmonies moving around the circle of fifths form the basis of this piece in contrast to the four-measure phrases and slower-moving harmonies of the blues.

Ida Cox was rediscovered in 1939 by John Hammond and brought to New York for a "From Spirituals to Swing" concert. She recorded *Hard Times Blues*, *Take Him Off My Mind*, and *Last Mill Blues* at that time. She continued to work regularly until she suffered a stroke in Buffalo, New York, in 1945, and eventually retired to her home in Knoxville in 1949. She came out of retirement to record once more, in 1961, before she died in 1967. In some

---

[45] Ibid.

ways, Ida Cox more truly typified the singers of the 1920s than Bessie Smith did. Smith's artistry towered over the rest, making her performances individual and unique, while Cox represents the legion of singers whose work met high professional standards but was uninspired. She had a good voice, a professional demeanor, and accurate rhythm and pitch, but her recordings are more regular and predictable than subtle and emotional.

——— BERTHA "CHIPPIE" HILL ———

Bertha "Chippie" Hill, on the other hand, a talent equal to that of Bessie Smith, has for one reason or another not been accorded the fame she deserves. Born in Charleston, South Carolina, in 1905, she, like Smith, toured with Ma Rainey's show, first as a dancer and later as a singer. Also like Smith, she went through a period of obscurity that lasted from about 1930 to the mid-1940s and, uncannily, also died in an auto accident. At her best, Chippie Hill was the equal of any blues singer, past or present. The melodramatic and comic solution of *Trouble in Mind*[47] blues was to lay her head on a railroad track, and this song, composed by Richard M. Jones and recorded by Hill in 1926, was to become the best-known of all her blues performances. When she was rediscovered, working in a bakery in 1946, by Rudi Blesh, she began recording once again. Her musical powers had not diminished, and her comeback was an exciting historical event. Her recording of *Around the Clock Blues*[48] was made with an authentic group of early New Orleans jazz musicians: Lovie Austin, piano; John Lindsay, bass; and Baby Dodds, drums. It is interesting to note that at so late a date, 1946, a sixteen-bar blues was still being recorded. In form, it resembles a popular song—**AABA**—but the phrases are only four measures long; the second **A** repeats the text of the first; and the short sixteen-measure piece is strophic. *Around the Clock Blues* is a variant of *My Daddy Rocks Me*, recorded by May Alix with Jimmy Noone and his Orchestra in 1929.[49] The forty-six-year-old Chippie Hill belts out the celebration of physical love in the best blues style of the 1920s:

> *Now my baby rocks me with one steady roll,*
> *Now my baby rocks me with words untol',*
> *Now I look at the clock, the clock struck one,*
> *me and my baby havin' such fun,*

[46] Paramount 12063, reissued Riverside RLP 12-113.
[47] OKeh 8273, reissued Folkways FP 59.
[48] Circle J1013, reissued Riverside RLP 12-113.
[49] Vocalion 2779.

*I say keep on rockin' me baby with your good old
    steady roll.*

*Now my baby rocks me with one steady roll,
Now there's no lovin' until he takes hol',
Now I looked at the clock, and the clock struck two,
    let's see what he intends to do
Before rubbin' me, baby, with that good old steady
    roll.*

MAMIE SMITH

A name almost forgotten today because her records have disappeared from general circulation is Mamie Smith, "First Lady of the Blues." On August 10, 1920, she recorded Perry Bradford's *Crazy Blues*,[50] the first vocal recording with choruses based on a twelve-measure structure. A few months earlier, she had cut the first disc to be made by a black singer, and because of

Mamie Smith (1890–1946).

[50] OKeh 4169, reissued Columbia C3L-33.

its success, she was called back to the studios for what inaugurated the history of recorded blues. According to the composer, 800,000 copies of Mamie Smith's performance of *Crazy Blues* were eventually sold. Her recording career lasted from 1920 through 1931, but whereas the entire Bessie Smith oeuvre has been reissued on long-playing records, not a single LP or CD of Mamie Smith's works has been issued on a major American label. Her only modern recorded appearances are in two anthologies, *Women of the Blues* and *The Sounds of Harlem*.[51] A fair evaluation of her singing style is not really possible from this small sample.

The song that brought Mamie Smith to the recording studios for a Victor test recording with piano in January of 1920 was Perry Bradford's *That Thing Called Love*,[52] which she was asked to record in place of the popular white singer Sophie Tucker. Shortly thereafter she recorded it again with the Rega Orchestra, a group consisting of trumpet, trombone, clarinet, violin, and piano (Willie "The Lion" Smith was at the keyboard). Although it is not a blues, the text is in the blues tradition.

> *I'm worried in my mind,*
> *I'm worried all the time,*
> *My friend he told me today,*
> *That he was going away to stay,*
> *Now I love him deep down in my heart,*
> *But the best of friends must part . . .*[53]

LOUIS ARMSTRONG

A common fallacy held by many jazz buffs is that classic blues were sung only by women; but even as early as the 1920s, men were recording the same repertoire. A list of leading blues singers of the 1920s always includes Ma Rainey, Bessie Smith, Ida Cox, Chippie Hill, and others, such as Sarah Martin, Clara Smith, Victoria Spivey, Mamie Smith, Sippie Wallace, and Trixie Smith, but it hardly ever lists Louis Armstrong, Big Joe Williams, Jimmy Rushing, and Jack Teagarden, who all sang the classic blues. It is true that Louis Armstrong did not specialize in blues singing as did most of the women singers, but his performance of *Gully Low Blues*,[54] recorded in May 1927, is a classic blues in form, delivery, and text.

> *Now mama, why do you treat me so?*
> *Oh mama, why do you treat me so?*

[51] Victor LPV-539 and Columbia C3L-33.
[52] OKeh 4113.

> *I know why you treat me so bad, you treat me mean,*
> *baby, just because I'm gully low.*
>
> *Now if you listen baby, I'll tell you somethin' you*
> *don't know.*
> *If you just listen to me honey, I'll tell you*
> *somethin' you don't know.*
> *If you just give me a break and take me back,*
> *I won't be gully no more.*

The preceding day, Armstrong recorded the same blues but used a different verse in his vocal chorus. As a result, it received a different title, *S.O.L. Blues.*[55]

> *Now I'm with you sweet mama as long as you have the*
> *bucks (I mean money, mama).*
> *I'm with you sweet mama as long as you have bucks.*
> *When the bucks run out, sweet mama, I mean you*
> *are out of luck.*

Two years earlier, Armstrong recorded *I'm Not Rough,*[56] and although this version lacks successive verses and fails to pair the first two lines, he still sings the sophisticated classic blues.

> *Now I aint rough, and I don't bite,*
> *but the woman that gets me gots to treat me right.*
> *Cause I'm crazy 'bout my lovin',*
> *and I must have it all the time.*
> *It takes a brown-skinned woman to satisfy my mind.*

Perhaps the most poignant vocal performance by Louis Armstrong is his 1929 recording of *What Did I Do to Be So Black and Blue?*[57] Although this song is in thirty-two-measure, pop-song form (**AABA),** both its lyrics and style of performance place it among the monuments of classic blues. At the peak

[53] Quoted by Paul Oliver, *The Meaning of the Blues,* p. 21.
[54] Columbia CL-852.
[55] Columbia CL-851.
[56] Ibid.
[57] Columbia CL-854. *Black and Blue* was composed for the 1929 stage show *Hot Chocolates,* by Andy Razaf, Thomas "Fats" Waller, and Harry Brooks.

of commercial success, and at the height of his mature solo style, Armstrong let slip for a moment the smiling mask of the black stage personality and revealed a bit of the desolation that crowded his inner being.

> Old empty bed, springs hard as lead,
>   feel like "Ol Ned," wish I were dead.
> All my life through I been so Black and blue.
>
> Even a mouse, ran from my house,
>   they laugh at you, and scorn you too.
> What did I do to be so Black and blue?
>
> Oh, I'm white inside, but that don't help my case,
> 'Cause I can't hide what is on my face.
>
> How will it end, aint got a friend,
>   my only sin is in my skin.
> What did I do to be so Black and blue?

ETHEL WATERS

Although Ethel Waters (born in Chester, Pennsylvania, in 1896, and died in California in 1977) lacked the musical virtuosity with which Louis Armstrong imbued his performance, she laid out the text even more melodramatically in her recorded version of the same song.

> (Intro)   Out in the street, shufflin' feet, couples
>   passing two by two.
>   And here am I, left high and dry, Black,
>   and cause I'm Black, I'm blue.
>   All the race fellows crave "high yellow,"
>   gentlemen prefer them light.
>   I'm just another spade who can't make the grade,
>   Looks like there's nothin' but dark days in sight.
>
> (Verse one) With a cold empty bed, springs hard as lead,
>   pains in my head and I feel like "Ol Ned,"
>   What did I do to be so Black and blue?
>
>   No joys for me, no company
>   even the mouse, ran from my house,
>   All my life through I been so Black and blue.
>
>   I'm white, but it's inside,
>   so that don't help my case,
>   Cause I can't hide just what is on my face.

**Ethel Waters
(1896–1977).**

Oh, sad and forlorn, life's just a thorn,
  my heart is torn, oh why was I born?
What did I do to be so Black and blue?

(Verse two)   *Just cause you're Black, boys think you lack,*
  they laugh at you and scorn you, too.
What did I do to be so Black and blue?

When I draw near, they laugh and sneer,
  I'm set aside, always denied.
All my life through I been so Black and blue.

How sad I am, and each day
  the situation gets worse.
My mark of Ham seems to be a curse.

Oh, how will it end, can't get a boyfriend,
  yet my only sin lies in my skin.
What did I do to be so Black and blue?[58]

In Waters's performance, we can clearly see how this thirty-two-measure piece relates to the blues tradition. It is strophic not only in having two verses, but in matching each phrase against the next as a constant embellishment of the blues' theme, "What did I do to be so Black and blue?" Each eight-measure phrase, except that of the bridge, pairs two lines of commentary as preparation for the refrain answer. In its musical structure, *Black and*

[58] Columbia Archive Series C3L-35.

Blue lacks both the twelve-measure pattern and the characteristic harmonic sequence, but as we have seen in recorded examples of other classic-blues singers, the notion that the repertoire consisted only of standardized twelve-measure blues pieces is not substantiated in fact.

JIMMY RUSHING

James Andrew Rushing, born in Oklahoma in 1903, is best known as a blues singer in the Kansas City style of Count Basie. He went to New York City with Basie's band in 1936 and worked as a blues singer with Basie until 1950 (*NW* 295, I/2). He began working in California in 1923 or 1924 at the Jump Steady Club, where he was occasionally accompanied by Jelly Roll Morton. In 1927–28 he sang with Walter Page's Blue Devils, and in 1929 he was the vocalist for Bennie Moten's band. There are no recordings by Jimmy Rushing from this period, but if his singing style resembled what he recorded later, he was singing the classic blues in the 1920s.

Blues singing and jazz singing have been continuous from the earliest appearance of the genre until the present day, and a single line of development can be traced from Mamie Smith and Ma Rainey to Bessie Smith and Chippie Hill, and on to Billie Holiday, Ella Fitzgerald, and Janis Joplin. Once recording and radio made the music of star vocalists available to the country at large, it was no longer necessary to have a direct master-apprentice relationship. Similarly, connecting a historical line from early jazz and blues singers like Louis Armstrong and Jimmy Rushing to Nat King Cole, Billy Eckstine, and Frank Sinatra is made possible for the same reason. The interchange of musicians between bands, the path-crossing on the vaudeville, club, and concert circuits, and the personal meetings that naturally brought musicians in contact with each other in the large metropolitan areas provided an artistic exchange that had an extraordinary effect on musical activity in America.

URBAN BLUES

The country blues continue to the present day, just as do the city blues. Once a new music appears, if it has validity and gains a following, it may have phases of prominence and obscurity, but it rarely disappears totally. During the mid-and late-1930s, a new blues type made its appearance. It was characterized by the introduction of big-band riff accompaniments, arrangements, a greater importance of saxophone as a characteristic accompanying and solo sound, the absence of harmonicas, and freer vocal phrasing. It has been labeled "urban blues,"[59] and its first great exponents were shout-

[59] Keil, *Urban Blues*.

ing blues vocalists with the Kansas City and Southwest territory bands, men such as "Hot Lips" Page, Jimmy Rushing, and Joe Turner. Rushing's driving rhythmic interplay with the Count Basie orchestra in his 1938 recording, *Sent for You Yesterday and Here You Come Today*,[60] provides a classic example of a blues singer's ability to electrify the band and charge the audience with a propulsive excitement that few bands have ever been able to duplicate.

After World War II, Memphis became a blues center, as was Chicago, which featured the music of B. B. King, Bobby Bland, and Jr. Walker. As blues scholar Charles Keil explains:

> The refinements leading to urban blues are best viewed in terms of three phases: the period from 1925 to 1942 chronicled by Driggs[61]—that is, the time when big bands of eight pieces and larger toured the Southwest playing blues in arranged form, an era culminating in the Kansas City fluorescence; the period from 1942 to 1952 when similar bands toured the same terrain usually featuring a blues singer, electric guitar, saxophone solos, and an even stronger emphasis on rhythm and blues; and what might be called the Memphis synthesis, or the foundation of today's urban blues.[62]

Following on the heels of the Memphis synthesis, Otis Rush, Earl Hooker, and others spearheaded what is labeled, by Keil, the "Industrial" phase, a music in which everything is electrically amplified and the typical blues ensemble consists of two or three guitars, drums, and possibly a tenor saxophone.

Many young jazz musicians got their first professional experience playing with rhythm-and-blues bands. Eddie "Cleanhead" Vinson, leader, alto saxophonist, and blues singer, who in 1950 recorded his swinging *My Big Brass Bed Is Gone*,[63] was partly responsible for changing his young sideman, John Coltrane, from alto to tenor saxophone. Ornette Coleman worked with Pee Wee Crayton's rhythm-and-blues band in Texas and California, and many other jazz musicians starting their careers in the '40s and '50s gained both apprenticeship experience and a deep-rooted feeling for the blues through their schooling on the road with R & B bands. Also, rhythm-and-blues of the 1940s served as an important transition to rock 'n' roll, which emerged at the end of the decade. Saxophonist Louis Jordan (1908–75) left the Chick Webb band in 1938 to form his own band in New York. Like the Kansas City bands, his too was blues-based and featured horn-riff accompaniments, but

[60] Decca 1880.

[61] Franklin S. Driggs, "Kansas City and the Southwest," in *Jazz*, eds. Nat Hentoff and Albert J. McCarthy, pp. 190–230.

[62] Keil, *Urban Blues*, p. 61.

[63] King 4381.

it centered its beat around the eight-to-the-bar boogie-woogie pattern, which became the foundation beat of rock 'n' roll. In his music, which was extremely popular in Harlem, he combined a real flair for showmanship with his singing, strutting, and saxophone playing. In 1946 he recorded a million-record-sale hit, *Choo Choo Ch'Boogie* (*NW* 261, I/6),[64] and began to influence a wider market. Big Mama Thornton (1926–84), daughter of a Montgomery, Alabama, minister, moved from the gospel music of her father's church to blues singing in Montgomery as a teenager. After several years of touring the South during the 1940s, she joined the Johnny Otis Rhythm and Blues Caravan in 1951. The following year, she recorded *Hound Dog* (*NW* 261, II/4),[65] the song that would play a crucial role in the development of rock 'n' roll as the dominant American popular music. It reached number one on the rhythm-and-blues charts by 1955, but it was the 1956 "cover"[66] recording by Elvis Presley that captured the market and catapulted rock 'n' roll to phenomenal heights.[67] As Presley skyrocketed, Big Mama Thornton faded, only to emerge again during the blues revival of the 1960s.

The blues has a history that is largely independent from that of jazz, but its central role in the creation and early development of jazz is undeniable. Blues' musical form, scale, and performance practices are a part of all jazz and are crucial to its understanding. The blues' continuous intertwining with jazz and American popular music throughout the jazz era elevate this once simple, rural expression to a level of significance that can be matched by few other forms of music. It has an intrinsic merit and beauty all its own, but it also holds a place of prominence in the history of jazz.

INSTRUMENTAL BLUES

One kind of 1920s music called blues has no vocal lyrics or vocal line. The twelve-measure form that employs three chords (tonic, subdominant, and dominant) served as the basis for countless instrumental compositions and improvisations in jazz. The twelve-bar blues became standard with instrumental ensemble musicians during the 1920s. No further instruction was necessary once an experienced jazz musician was told "Blues in B♭" or "Blues

---

[64] Decca 23610.

[65] Peacock 1612.

[66] The term "cover" is used by the popular recording industry for a recording of a particular song by performers other than those originally responsible. During the 1950s, many international hits were cover versions by established white performers of songs originally recorded by blacks on small regional labels.

[67] RCA 47-6604.

in three" (three flats, or, key of E♭). Although they were capable of performing blues outside the standardized schema, this structure, with its set harmonic pattern, became the norm.

——— JOE "KING" OLIVER ———————

Dippermouth Blues (*SCCJ* 6) as played by Joe Oliver and his Creole Jazz Band in 1923 is but one of thousands of similar performances of the B♭ blues. The four-measure introduction and the two-measure ending obviously had been worked out in advance. In its formal outline, the piece consists of a four-measure introduction, nine improved blues choruses of twelve measures each, and a two-measure tag. The remainder of the performance is improvised, except for the stoptime chords of choruses 3 and 4, which accompany the clarinet solo of Johnny Dodds. It is also typical that two ensemble choruses of the blues begin the piece, for the twelve-measure form at a moderate-to-fast tempo is too brief to establish the sound of the particular piece in the listener's ear.

Dippermouth Blues

Intro	I Blues	II Blues	III Blues	IV Blues	V Blues	VI Blues	VII Blues	VIII Blues	IX Blues	Tag
4 mm.	12 mm.	12 mm.	12 mm.	12 mm.	12 mm.	12 mm.	12 mm.	12 mm.	12 mm.	2 mm.
Comp.*	Impro.† Ensemb.‡	Impro. Ensemb.	Impro.	Impro.	Impro. Ensemb.	Impro.	Impro.	Impro. Ensemb.	Impro. Ensemb.	Comp.
			Dodds clarinet (stop-time)	Dodds clarinet (stop-time)		Oliver cornet	Oliver cornet		"Oh play that thing"	

* Composed
† Improvised
‡ Ensemble

The solo by King Oliver that begins in the sixth chorus and continues for the seventh is a classic cornet riff[68] that was imitated by hosts of other trumpet players who admired both the style of the music and the details of this performance.

[68] A "riff" usually signifies a short, repeated melodic figure, but here it is used to indicate a blues melody (e.g., Charlie Parker's *Bird Feathers* or *Big Foot* refer to blues melodies known and performed by other jazz musicians).

Dippermouth Blues, Oliver Solo on Choruses 6 and 7 (OKeh 4918)[69]

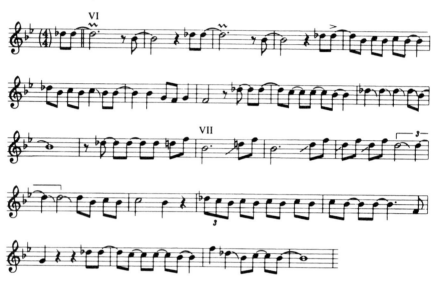

The way Oliver bends his minor third against the major harmonies of the accompaniment (D♭ against a B♭-major chord; chorus 6, mm. 1 and 3); the way he inflects notes both upward and downward (chorus 6, m. 10, and chorus 7, mm. 2 and 3); and the tantalizing manner in which he stretches the solo rhythm patterns off the beat in contrast to the regular pulse of the accompaniment (chorus 7, mm. 3 and 4) are some of the elements in this performance that help make it an outstanding jazz solo of the 1920s. Motivically, too, it has great structural integrity, as Oliver plays with the minor and major third intervals B♭–D♭ and B♭–D♮. At one point he stretches the sound up to F (the end of chorus 6) and lets it melt back from D to B♭ (chorus 7, mm. 3 to 4).

Sound recording in 1923 was not perfected to the point where it could reproduce, distinctly, all the sounds of the instruments in ensemble. Consequently, it is difficult to show exactly what each instrument is playing at any one moment. The counterpoint does not have the smooth, balanced quality of classic polyphony, where dissonances are carefully introduced and

[69]The revised edition of the *Smithsonian Collection of Classic Jazz* replaced the OKeh version of *Dippermouth Blues* (OKeh 4918, Chicago, June 23, 1923) with the earlier recording for Gennett (Gennett 5132, Richmond, Indiana, April 6, 1923). The Oliver solos are similar, but my transcription is from the OKeh performance, which is to my mind superior.

just as carefully resolved. Rather, it displays the happy, free flow of lines that remain distinct by virtue of their contrasting timbre, difference in range, and diversity of rhythmic values. In this example, the speed of notes for the clarinet line does not differ from that of either of the cornet lines, but this is a small sample. The layerlike separation between the speeds of the soprano instruments and the trombone is more obvious.

The blues is omnipresent in the repertoire of instrumental jazz, and this sample can serve as a prototype of the typical jazz performance blues pattern of introduction, ensemble, solos, ensemble, and out. Derived from a vocal form that never achieved any real uniformity, even as late as the mid-1930s, the blues pattern in instrumental jazz was a *forme fixe*, a set form, by the time this recording was made.

Gunther Schuller, commenting on "Oliver's own justly famous solo on both *Dippermouth Blues* recordings," sums up the effect of this performance and the significance of the year in which they were recorded:

> Here the OKeh performance especially has a remarkably dense and well-balanced texture, perfectly captured by the engineers; and its great swing must have had an overwhelming effect in person in 1923.
>
> Since that year jazz has experienced a prodigious development in terms of instrumental virtuosity, dynamic and timbrel variety. It is, therefore, all the more amazing that we can still listen with interest to the Creole Jazz Band, since these features are virtually nonexistent on its recordings.[70]

The blues is many things—the music of people, a style of music, a type of performance, a despondent state of mind, and a musical form. As all of these things, the blues has contributed to jazz. Within the formal concept of continuous improvisation over a constantly recurring harmonic framework, the blues has given jazz its most significant element.

---

[70] Schuller, *Early Jazz*, p. 85.

4.

JAZZ IN ITS INFANCY

HISTORICAL OVERVIEW: FROM THE BEGINNING TO WORLD WAR I

1917 was a landmark for jazz because it marks the date of the first recording by any musical group in which the word "jazz" is used as a descriptive qualifier,[1] and it is the year in which the word "jazz" first begins to appear regularly in print. The first occurrence thus far uncovered was in the March 6, 1913 issue of the San Francisco *Bulletin*, where it is written:

> The team which speeded into town this morning comes pretty close to representing the pick of the army. Its members have trained on ragtime and 'jazz.'[2]

Damon Runyon, in his regular column, "Th' Mornin's Mornin'," which appeared in all the Hearst papers, wrote on January 21, 1917:

> The Old Jaz Band

> New York. Jan. 20.—A Broad way cafe announces, as something new to the big Bright Aisle, the importation from the West of a syncopated riot known as a Jaz Band.[3]

[1] The Original Dixieland Jazz Band made a New York recording in January 1917.
[2] San Francisco Bulletin, March 6, 1913, p. 16. The 'team' referred to is a baseball team.
[3] I am indebted to J. R. Taylor, who called this article to my attention.

Walter Kingsley, writing for the *New York Sun* on August 5, 1917, offered his readers a little musical history following the headline, "Whence comes jass? Facts from the great authority on the subject":

> Variously spelled Jas, Jass, Jaz, Jasz, and Jascz. The word is African in origin. It is common on the Gold Coast of Africa and in the hinterland of Cape Coast Castle . . . Jazz is based on the savage musician's wonderful gift for progressive retarding and acceleration guided by his sense of 'swing.'

Unquestionably, the new music called "jazz" did not begin in 1917, it simply gained immediate prominence and widespread recognition with the issue of the Original Dixieland Jazz Band's (ODJB) recordings and the publication of several written accounts of the new music. Also, we should note that the publication of the blues in sheet music form, which preceded this date, was widespread geographically. Although blues and jazz are not equivalent or interchangeable, their relationship is close and will be examined further. For the time being, however, it is of note that *Baby Seals Blues* had been published in St. Louis on August 3, 1912. How widespread the genre had become by that time is documented by two other publications in the same year: one in Oklahoma City on September 6, 1912, of the *Dallas Blues*, and the other in Memphis, Tennessee, on September 23, 1912, of W. C. Handy's *Memphis Blues*. This much publishing activity over so large a geographical area suggests the possibility of a well-established market, a mature tradition, and a supply of musicians associated with the field.

Undoubtedly, some early ragtime performance must be considered jazz, for although the published ragtime tradition was close to the European composed tradition, early jazz groups and soloists included ragtime pieces in their repertoires. While recognizing a distinction between composed syncopated music—ragtime—and improvised syncopated music—jazz—we cannot definitively separate the two. Both new musics were developing side by side in the same venues and often with the same musicians, and some of the early jazz musicians loosely referred to their music as ragtime. So, if we count some early ragtime as jazz, and there seems to be no stylistic reason for not doing so, then we can find an even older publishing history. Chicago takes the honors for the first ragtime publication: in 1897 bandleader William H. Krell saw his *Mississippi Rag* come off the press. Later that same year, Tom Turpin's *Harlem Rag* was published in St. Louis, Missouri, thus becoming the first rag by a black composer to achieve publication. In 1899, Scott Joplin's *Original Rags* appeared from Kansas City, Missouri. It was followed later that year by his first major ragtime success, the *Maple Leaf Rag*, published in Sedalia, Missouri, in March 1899.

Charles J. Harris, retired Professor of Music at Alabama Agricultural and

Mechanical College in Normal, Alabama, was a black pianist whose experiences in music date back to the turn of the century. The following lengthy excerpt from an interview recorded in his home on August 4, 1975, allows us to gain the perceptions of a musician who worked in America during the formative years of jazz.

I was born in Augusta, Georgia, . . . on the "Hill" [Summerville]. I was born there July the 2nd, 1885, in kind of a large family. My mother was quite young when she married—I think she may have been sixteen. My daddy was ten years older. And during my mother's childhood, she had a grandfather who was a sexton at a white Episcopal church. And the colored people went to the Sunday School. Back in those days, they had their separate Sunday School, and the whites had their separate Sunday School. . . .

When I was a child, I pumped the old-fashioned pipe organ in a white Episcopal church. I did it for about nine years at the great salary of 50 cents a week. [That was the] Church of the Good Shepherd. It's still flourishing. I saw the rector about two, three years ago, and he told me they had a $5 million building program. . . . I hope to go down there again this fall and maybe make a little music for them. They have me to come down once in a while, and I talk about Scott Joplin. And so they may have me come down and play some for them. You know, I was ninety last month. . . .

I studied about two years before I left Augusta. I attended Atlanta University one school year. I would have liked to have stayed there until I got through college, but, you know, money. [I studied] piano, just piano [with Charles Driscol], and of course we went to classes in solfeggio. When I went to Atlanta, there was a German who taught privately in town named Krueger, E. H. Krueger, and I took a few lessons from him before I went to Boston. I got to Boston in 1906, and I left there in '17. When I first got there, I worked in hotels, bellman and waiter. I was a much better bellman than waiter! . . .

Beginning my second year, I began to play for dances. That was in 1907. . . . When I began to play for dances and eating in restaurants, I began to go down, way down, down, down [in weight and health]. If I hadn't seen an ad that gave me some inspiration, I think I would have died before I was 35 years of age. I was just going downhill. I'd sleep two hours a night . . . and not another wink. . . . Uncle Charlie is still hanging on. I still walk the streets like a young man. Hope to make it another ten years, though I don't know.

[Back in 1907 when I started playing dance jobs, there were] five men—piano, trombone, trumpet, drums, and violin. . . . The most robust man in the group, Joe Bonner, drummer, he died early. The violinist, Raymond Jefferson, he was from South Carolina, Columbia. The lawyer, Charles Wilson, was the trombone player, and Henry Dixon was the trumpet player. Henry was the brother of a man who became famous at the turn of the century, George Dixon, featherweight champion. . . . We played by note [not by ear]. Ragtime, I think, was the most popular at that time. 'Course the waltzes, we played. Two-steps, some of them were modern; some of them were written about that time. The violinist owned the music. He'd bought it right down at the music stores. There were a good many men who arranged this music. I never learned [studied] to play ragtime. I presume if I had been playing [ragtime previously] they might have let me go ahead [improvise]. But this man held me down to just play what was on the page, see? And there was one crack player among colored men at that time—maybe more than one, but I remember one—a fellow named Pat Toy. He was a small man, about 5′5″. Oh, but Pat could play that ragtime! He joined the navy during the First World War, and the captain of the ship on which he sailed put a piano in there. And all Pat had to do was entertain the captain. But Pat took with the flu and died at sea. . . .

[The way to play ragtime] once in a while you may give you[rself] some little measure with a shot of it [decoration], but most times you just play chords in the bass, you know. And the same way about waltzes. Once in a while you might have a little something here or there to play, but they [my group] stuck mostly to letting the other instruments do the decorative work. . . . There were some fellows who played by ear. They gave more satisfaction than those who played by note, of course. And there were some groups who played by ear. I played for about four years, and then this man changed to a regular ragtime player. When I first got to Boston, this same piano player was playing violin. I accompanied him on a little concert here and there, but after a while he gave up the violin and began to play the piano. And he got to be so good that Ziegfeld Follies had him to build a band and play behind the scenes. His name was Walter Johnson. . . . See, I played four years, and this orchestra kept going. Of course they had additional men, because the trombone player (the lawyer) went on to Chicago, and some of the other—[pause]. That's a pretty hard life, all those late hours, and fellows get to drinking, too much running around, and most of those fellows are in the cemetery.

So Walter Johnson, and there was another fellow, a very thin fellow—they called him "Skinny" [Johnson]—"Skinny" was much more refined. . . . So all those men with whom I made music and was acquainted, they've all crossed over Jordan. But they were excellent. Those fellows got to be so good, Yale and Harvard and those places had them to come out to play for dances, especially after the First World War. [The group] I played with [was] Jefferson's Five. His name was Raymond Jefferson and the Jefferson Five. When we played for a big ball, he would add about fifteen men—twenty men for a big ball. . . .

[After I left this band] I taught a little privately, piano, and occasionally I'd

The Original Fisk Jubilee Singers, London, 1873.

work a banquet. It was around 1911, and Roland Hayes[4] came to Boston, and we associated very early. He came there with a group from Fisk University of Nashville, and they sang in a big hall there . . . [that was] the Jubilee Singers. Roland had been in school down there at Fisk three or four years, but they had a falling out, and he had gone to Louisville, Kentucky. And he was waiting table and singing in a big white club called the Pendennis. Roland had a big fine voice to start with, and there was a man who was a guest there one night from Boston, and this man heard Roland sing, of course. So he told Roland, "If you ever come to Boston, look me up." So in about a couple of years it was, Roland went there, and this man was named [Henry H.] Putnam. He paid for Roland's lessons for about three years, and then Roland began to pay for his own. And Roland began to travel, go to Chicago, St. Louis, and California, and South, and sing in concerts. And so I think it must have been about 1919 or early 1920 that Roland went to Europe. He took an accompanist with him, and they did fairly well, but they were having a pretty tough time. And Roland told me he was kind of sick in bed [one day], and his accompanist was out trying to find something to eat. And Roland had sung for some well-known

[4] Noted black tenor. For more information, see Eileen Southern, *The Music of Black Americans*, 2nd ed., p. 400 f.

singers. There was an Australian soprano, Nellie Melba, and Nellie knew King George V very well and his family. So in conversation with him, she inquired if the king had heard the black tenor from the United States, and the king said he hadn't. So he sent a command in for Roland to sing that afternoon. And Roland said he got up out of that bed—wouldn't lose this opportunity—and went and sang for King George and his family. And they talked to him about his mother and his early life and all. Roland was pretty sharp, and he sent that information right back to the United States—ROLAND HAYES SINGS FOR KING GEORGE AND HIS FAMILY! And then Roland came over and did a concert in Boston and one in Washington. And the Symphony Hall people there, Boston, got themselves together and did something they had never done. They arranged forty concerts for Roland the next season beginning in the fall of the year. And that was 1923, and Roland was a sensation, see?

[During this time] I had come South. I came South in '17 and began to teach in schools. I taught in Nashville first to a little school there under the M[ethodist] E[piscopal] Church. It was part of the Meharry Medical School at that time. I worked there two months, and I got a call for a job paying a little more money at a college in Augusta. . . . Then I went to Paine [College], and I stayed two and a half years. Then I went to Holly Springs, Mississippi. The war, America was still in the war, and there was a camp in Augusta. . . . I'd go up to the camp, and I'd take a violinist. We'd play for dances among the soldiers and in and around the town. . . . [At Holly Springs] white folks learned that I played the piano, just alone, you know, played the piano fairly well, and they would hire me to come out two or three times a week and play for them to dance. I'd usually play for them from about 7:00 or 8:00 to about 11:00 or 12:00 o'clock. I was slightly embarrassed one day though, in the square of this town. . . . These young men had come and got me in a car, and they stopped the car and hollered to some of their comrades, "Go and get the girls, we got the nigger!" . . .

[When I played these dances in the evening] I played ragtime. I got one of the pieces here . . . [plays *Twelfth Street Rag*, M.M. = 104, rounded eighth-notes, heavy-handed, steady beat, a little inaccurate, but he was 91 years old at the time].

I just practiced and observed the other fellows. Pat [Toy] was my real choice. I never did hear none of those fellows around New York play, but I did hear Eubie Blake play in Atlantic City one summer I was up there for a while . . . this was in 1920. Blake is in his 90s now. He must be 93 or '4, somewhere around there. . . . Pat Toy was my favorite of the men I heard. Pat was something else. And most of the fellows who played by ear were much more satisfying than the fellows who read the notes. . . .

I was teaching public school music, that is solfeggio, and a little history, and then piano. And I had some good vocal students even though I can't do anything myself. In fact, I got a degree in singing, not in piano playing. . . . I've often wished that I had grown up on a farm. Didn't grow up on a farm, grew up in a village. My daddy was a house servant; my mother sewed. Never could do back in those days. . . .

I'm not certain of the year, I think it was about 1913 or '14 in Boston. I met him [Scott Joplin] on the street. He was standing there talking to some young men, and they knew me, and they introduced me to him. Well the other boys went away and left Mr. Joplin with me, so I took him to where I was staying, and he played his *Maple Leaf Rag* for me. And he said that people play his music too rapidly, but it seems to me that there is more to life if you give it a little more pickup. But he was a small man, about 5'5½", something like that. And Joplin [was] a very serious man. I guess you may have read, he wrote an opera called *Treemonisha*. . . . He talked mostly about his music, and he told me about where he—see, he earned his living mostly—see, he spent most of his time in Missouri playing around barrooms, I guess around what they call "Sporting Emporiums." Anywhere he could pick up a dollar. Stark, I think Stark Music Publishers, was the main music publisher of his music, and I understand that Stark Company wasn't doing any too well, just ordinary. But they began to publish Joplin's music and began to make money. The man was able to take his family on trips to Europe and around. But Joplin eventually went to New York. I guess he was living in New York then, when I met him. Unfortunately for the poor man, he picked up a disease. It ate away his brains. . . . Oh, yes, he was clearheaded then [around 1913 or '14]. He died in '17. I don't know whether the disease had taken a hold to him at that time, or not, but his mind was clear, and he dressed neatly. . . . He played accurately, but I heard other persons play that I enjoyed much more. Now that *Maple Leaf Rag*, I never did hear Pat Toy play it, but I heard other players, you know. And as I said, the persons who did not read music, who learned to play very well, they would seem to get more out of it than the persons who used the notes. I heard both young men and young women just play that *Maple Leaf Rag*. . . . He [Joplin] didn't seem to have much vigor, but he played very accurately, of course. . . .

I think he published this *Maple Leaf Rag* in 1899, and I guess maybe it was the beginning of "Rag." I do not know. . . . You know, dance music has styles. This for a while. I forget, which came after ragtime. I know they were doing the one-step, and James Reese Europe, a black man, took a band to Europe during the First World War with the 92nd Division. [James Reese] Europe had had lots of experience in New York before he went over there, but there was a white man named [Vernon] Castle and his wife named Irene, and they first began this one-step. I guess you never did see the dance called the one-step.

. . . It's a dance that's nearly walking, but you'd go round the hall two or three times with a lady. Then you might otherwise be slower in getting around, but it was just a step. And that took on in the latter part of the teens. . . . When Europe came back from the First World War, he had several bands, and these colored bands supplanted the white bands way back there for a while with this lively one-step music. . . .

There was a hotel . . . down in Kentucky, they had all colored help—chamber maids, bellboys, and waiters. And this proprietor thought so much of his help that he had Paul Whiteman to come down from New York and play for this dance among colored people. This man got the finest dance hall in Louisville, and the whites went as spectators. And you know, it was a revelation among a lot of those white folks down there to see so much refinement among Negroes. They hadn't ever seen that, you know. They had been around among their servants, and all that, and mostly they had heard about the rough and tumble. But these boys, the waiters and the bellmen, invited the cream of the colored race, and they were dressed well, and they ported themselves just as well as anybody, you see. And it was a revelation to those people there. . . .

Now when I was a boy before I left home, there was a hotel in Augusta called the Bonne Aire. It was a very good winter resort, and during the season, two or three times, they had the colored waiters and colored maids and colored bellboys—and two or three times, I say, in the dining room, which was quite spacious, they would move all the tables back, and these waiters and bellmen would do this cakewalk. . . . more of a prance, throwing your head back, and dressed in all kind of clothing, sometimes full dress and otherwise. And they would do that for the entertainment of the guests.

The syncopated rhythm of the cakewalk was part of every American minstrel show, which carried this popular dance from hamlet to city in its travels across the country. By the end of the century, contests for cakewalking and ragtime piano playing were the rage, and pianists were given an allotted amount of time in which to demonstrate their improvisational ability in ragtime style. "Coon songs" in the new syncopated style became popular in the 1880s, and J. S. Putnam's *New Coon in Town*, published in 1883, became a popular addition to the new ragtime school.[5] As Samuel B. Charters and Leonard Kunstadt point out in their history of jazz in New York: "In a 1903 minstrel recording, 'The Cakewalk in Coontown,' the 'dancing' is accompanied by a five-piece band—two clarinets, cornet, trombone, and piano, playing an unmistakably jazz style."[6] That minstrelsy and syncopated coon

[5] "Coon," probably from "racoon," is a pejorative slang expression used by American whites to label and degrade African-Americans.
[6] *Jazz: A History of the New York Scene*, p. 14.

songs were popular as far west as San Francisco is attested to by the characteristic ragtime rhythms of *There's No Coon That's One Half So Warm.*[7] With
blues and rag publications in Missouri, Oklahoma, Tennessee, Illinois; with
ragtime "combo" recordings in New York; and with "Ethiopian Minstrelsy"
traveling from coast to coast, it is clear that the story of jazz begins neither
with the origin of the word nor with the magic of a single creative genius in
a specific, isolated locale.

Jazz developed in America during the last decades of the nineteenth century with a kind of spontaneous combustion that singed both coasts. Two
distinct varieties, ragtime and blues, seemed to develop side by side, with
many variant forms within each category. Coon songs, ragtime vocal solos,
piano rags, and ragtime bands developed the "hot" rhythms and angular
melodic styles. The blues, which came from spirituals, field hollers, and
work songs, were sung solo, accompanied by a guitar or other simple folk
instrument, and were eventually played by instruments alone.

The word "blues" had currency as early as 1853, when a Boston newspaper recommended light reading "to all who are afflicted with the blues, or
ennui."[8] An even earlier use of the word as an abbreviation for "blue devils,"
a phrase meaning despondency or depression of spirits, can be found in
Washington Irving's colorful observations of America, *Salmagundi* (1807). The
first definite association between the word "blues" and the music known as
"the blues" appears in a 1903 report of archaeologist Charles Peabody,[9] who
describes the singing and guitar playing of his black workers in Mississippi.
His analysis of the formal structure, melodic style, and mode of performance
of one class of songs unquestionably describes the blues. Writing in 1941,
W. C. Handy recollects his first contacts with the folk blues in Mississippi at
about the same time that Peabody made his observations,[10] but this distinctive musical genre must surely have had an unrecorded history before these
accounts. However, as William Ferris points out,

> Blues probably developed after the Civil War when black musicians were free
> to travel throughout the South and develop their repertoires. W. C. Handy and
> Big Bill Broonzy mention that the music was sung before 1900 and since the
> mobility so important to blues performers in this century was not possible before
> the Civil War, we can speculate that the music developed as a separate musical

[7] *A San Francisco Songster 1849–1939*, ed. Cornel Lengyel. History of Music in San Francisco, 2 (San Francisco: W.P.A., 1939), p. 106 f.

[8] Samuel B. Charters, *The Country Blues*, p. 34.

[9] Charles Peabody, "Notes on Negro Music," *Journal of American Folk-Lore*, 16 (1903), pp.
148–52.

[10] William Christopher Handy, *Father of the Blues: An Autobiography*, especially pp. 16 and 74.

genre when the South moved from plantation to sharecropping economy. Certainly the instrument most commonly associated with the blues—the guitar—is never seen in pre–Civil War illustrations, and unlike most early slave songs and hymns, blues are performed by solo musicians.[11]

Also, as Eileen Southern wisely suggests, plantation dance music, performed by black musicians, certainly contributed to the making of jazz and may in fact be a primary link to the development of the jazz combo. She observes that plantation dance music

> was functional, intended only for accompanying the dance; it was instrumental, showing a preference for certain instruments; and it had a distinctive performance practice. . . . The sources indicate the basic dance-music combination . . . on the plantation to be a three-piece group consisting of fiddle, banjo, and small percussion. . . .
>
> By the 1890s prototypes clearly had been established for the jazz dance bands that would emerge in the twentieth century in the plantation combos consisting of fiddle, banjo, string bass (or cello), straight trumpet or cornet, and small percussion. At some time during the early twentieth century the fiddle disappeared, its melodic function taken over by the cornet or trumpet; the trombone became a regular member of the combo; clarinets were added as new members; and the guitar replaced the banjo, but very gradually, for banjos lingered on in jazz combos into the 1920s and even later in some groups.[12]

Jazz, or its immediate antecedent, was actively being performed across the country in the years before 1917. The name seems to have come into common use in the years 1913–15, according to jazz musicians of that period, although the exact derivation of the word "jazz" is unclear. It may have been used originally as a minstrel or vaudeville term, but it may also have had African or Arabic origins. That it was possibly associated with the sex act, for which the word is used in slang as a synonym, has been suggested by a number of writers. A particularly intriguing possibility, because of the French culture of New Orleans, is a derivation from the French verb *jaser*, which may be translated as "to chatter or have an animated conversation among diverse people." Scholars have systematically examined all the suggestions and viewpoints advanced in the literature from 1917 through 1958. The resulting study, although fascinating, settles nothing and leaves the reader

[11] William Ferris, *Blues from the Delta*, p. 31.
[12] Eileen Southern, "A Study in Jazz Historiography: *The New Grove Dictionary of Jazz*," *College Music Symposium*, 29 (1989), p. 126 f.

stranded with: ". . . the need for linguistic and philological research although we are not at all sure that the origin of jazz, the word, can ever be found."[13]

Ragtime and blues as performed before 1917 had certain musical characteristics in common, such as melodic improvisation to a harmonic scheme, special timbres, scales, and intonations, syncopated rhythms applied to a basic unwavering pulse, and other features peculiar to jazz. The diffusion and more-or-less simultaneous emergence of the two genres across the country are phenomena worth viewing, so before we undertake the actual study of the music itself, we will survey briefly some of this activity in several different locales.

A major problem of jazz historiography is the lack of agreement on a working definition—a musical, stylistic definition—of jazz. Rudi Blesh, a leading historian of ragtime and author of an important text, separates jazz from ragtime and blues, counting the latter—along with work songs, spirituals, the music of the marching bands, the French dances, and the rhythms and tunes of Spanish America and the Caribbean—as elements that all lie outside the sphere of jazz. He also excludes the new jazz of the 1930s, swing:

> The dilution and deformation of jazz took place from 1920 on because of the influences of commercialism, white playing, and sophistication of the Negroes themselves. . . . Swing, which is not jazz, is a type of European music with transplanted Negroid characteristics.[14]

This point of view, while conveniently limiting the subject to an easily circumscribed area, does not meet any rigorous musical or historical criteria. Blesh and others who hold this view would limit jazz to the improvisational instrumental music typical of the New Orleans jazz bands from about 1900 to 1920. All groups with a rhythm section and a front line of three instruments—clarinet, cornet, and trombone—employing black personnel and playing in a group improvisational manner are easily categorized as exponents of "classic jazz," sometimes referred to as "traditional jazz" ("trad jazz"), or New Orleans jazz. Musically, this approach runs aground on the sandbars of stylistic analysis. Jelly Roll Morton's Red Hot Peppers was a ragtime band, or at least, Jelly Roll Morton was a ragtime pianist. If a ragtime band plays the same music in the same style as a classic New Orleans jazz band, such as King Oliver's Creole Jazz Band, and if the music of one is jazz, then the music of the other must be too. Likewise, if the blues singing of Bertha

---

[13] Alan P. Merriam and Fradley H. Garner, "Jazz—The Word," *Ethnomusicology*, v. 12 (1968), pp. 373–96.

[14] Rudi Blesh, *Shining Trumpets: A History of Jazz*, 4th ed., pp. 3, 6.

"Chippie" Hill and Mamie Smith is included in the corpus of jazz, then where does one draw the line separating blues folk singing from blues jazz singing?

From a purely historical, nonmusical point of view, the historian is obliged to look back at the music that is considered jazz by its performers and its audiences and accept their decision as final. The incongruities fostered by the purists who maintain that classic jazz is the only jazz become apparent when we observe that for most of the history of that music the word "jazz" was never uttered. In contrast, the music of the swing era was called jazz, and it was common knowledge in America that organizations such as the Duke Ellington Orchestra, the Count Basie Band, and the Charlie Parker Quintet, as well as the New Orleans–style ensembles led by Louis Armstrong and others, were jazz bands.

JAZZ— A MUSICAL DEFINITION

The exact time when country blues made the musical transition to jazz has not been determined, nor has the stylistic cleavage been charted between ragtime compositions and performances that are clearly jazz and those that do not qualify. Therefore, this book will cover the broad spectrum of all those musics popularly categorized as jazz. Readers may eliminate any portions they choose, but all those musics that have survived in the repertoire or significantly influenced its development will at least be touched upon and given a place in this history. As a working definition, we will consider jazz to be the music that came into being through the African-American experience in the southern part of the United States during the late nineteenth century and first blossomed in the vicinity of New Orleans at the turn of the twentieth century. This music, which has undergone many stylistic changes, may be considered to include ragtime, blues, classic jazz, Chicago-style jazz, swing, boogie-woogie, Kansas City–style jazz, bebop, progressive jazz, free jazz, and fusion-jazz, as well as others. Certain musical elements are common to all, and the musical sound produced in combination is usually recognizable as jazz even by the untrained listener. These elements may be present in varying proportions, depending upon the style, the performers, and sometimes accidental circumstances, but the common features usually are:

1. improvisation, both group and solo;

2. rhythm sections in ensembles (usually drums, bass, and chordal instrument such as piano, banjo, or guitar);

3.   metronomical underlying pulse to which syncopated melodies and rhythmic figures are added (in this regard, additive rhythm[15] is frequently employed);

4.   reliance on popular song form and blues form in most performances;

5.   tonal harmonic organization with frequent use of the blues scale for melodic material;

6.   timbral features, both vocal and instrumental, and other performance-practice techniques that are characteristic of particular jazz substyles, such as vibratos, glissandi, articulations, etc.; and

7.   performer or performer-composer aesthetic rather than a composer-centered orientation.

In any particular jazz performance, one or more of these elements may be absent. For example, some big-band arrangements of the swing era allowed for no improvisation, and others limited improvised solos to one or two short instrumental breaks. Duke Ellington and his music represent a jazz composer's world much more than that of the jazz performer. Buddy DeFranco's clarinet sound is closely akin to symphonic clarinet timbre, while Johnny

---

[15] Additive rhythm and divisive rhythm are terms used to explain, in contrasting ways, the organization of beats or pulses into regular groupings. The former organizes quick beats into larger units, and the latter subdivides slow pulses and large groupings into smaller units. For example, a measure in 4/4 meter may be notated as follows to indicate a basic "rhumba" beat:

The traditional method for drummers schooled in the African-derived genres to play this pattern is to organize the lowest common denominator, the eighth note (♪), into two groups of threes and one group of twos:

This method of thinking, organizing smaller units of the hierarchy into larger units, is called additive rhythm. The traditional method for drummers who are schooled in the European tradition to play this pattern is to subdivide larger beats, the quarter notes (♩), in half, and accent the offbeat of beat two as well as the onbeat of beat four, a normally unaccented beat, thereby producing an equivalent rhythmic pattern.

The difference, in this instance, is subtle—a succession of irregularly spaced downbeats as opposed to suppressed downbeats and accented afterbeats, but one method, additive rhythm, provides the means by which African drummers and jazz musicians create complex, polyrhythmic ensembles.

Dodds's sound has a roughness, imperfection, and charm typical of classic jazz. Likewise, it is important to note that these features are not exclusive to jazz. Improvisation is not limited entirely to jazz musicians, and we may see it in the work of European organists and many avant-garde ensembles today. Furthermore, it was a major practice in music of the Baroque, the Renaissance, and other great periods of Western classical music. A metronomic pulse can be observed in marches and classical symphonies, and additive rhythms may be observed in French secular music of the late fourteenth century as well as in African drumming. It is the employment of several of these features in combination that is unique to jazz and that characterizes its distinctive sound and spiritual essence.

THE EAST

The "gay nineties" and the first decade of the twentieth century in America saw young people dancing to a new kind of syncopated music. American minstrelsy had disseminated the coon song and cakewalk, and ragtime piano playing had become popular. The latter proliferated from the saloons, whorehouses, and riverboats to a larger audience, and composers were taking the new syncopated sounds seriously. Ragtime gained worldwide distribution as keyboard music and in orchestral transcription, and its impact on American music was felt through classic jazz, popular music, and vaudeville. In 1881, when Tony Pastor moved his Music Hall to East 14th Street, he advertised his new house as "the first specialty vaudeville theater of America, catering to polite tastes, aiming to amuse, and fully up to current times and topics."[16] Vaudeville acts spread out in ever-widening circles and carried their songs and dances on a circuit that touched every major American city and many smaller ones. They spurred public interest in the purchase of sheet music and made the latest musical sounds familiar. Some of the places where performances were held had only a piano, others used a small ensemble, and only a few employed full-sized orchestras. Ragtime, like other popular music, was adaptable to the circumstances, and improvisation was the cheapest and most practical way of filling out an arrangement with the forces available.

Just as New York City was the center for vaudeville, it was also a center for syncopated dance music in the East. As Eileen Southern points out, the center of fashionable black life in New York was "Black Bohemia," on the West Side of Manhattan.[17] One of the most successful and influential musicians and band directors was Will Dixon, who led a group called the Nash-

---

[16] David Ewen, *The Life and Death of Tin Pan Alley*, p. 27.
[17] Eileen Southern, *The Music of Black Americans*, 2nd ed., p. 343.

An Orpheum Circuit vaudeville tour that was scheduled for 1914 but that never materialized brought together in rehearsal: (standing, left to right) Clarence Williams, John Lindsay, Jimmy Noone, Bebe Ridgley; (seated, left to right) Oscar Celestin, Tom Benton, Johnny St. Cyr. The snare drummer (left front) is Ernest Trepagnier; the violinist (center front) is Armand J. Piron.

ville Students (including no one from Nashville nor any students) that was comprised of banjos, mandolins, guitars, saxophones, drums, a violin, a couple of brasses, and a bass. They played at a vaudeville theater, Hammerstein's Victoria, and on the Roof Garden for dancing at night. Probably the most influential black musician in New York was James Reese Europe, who organized a black musician's union called the Clef Club in 1910, and developed an orchestra of mandolins, banjos, guitars, saxophones, and drums. For an exceptional concert at Carnegie Hall in May 1912, Europe directed an orchestra of 145, including mandolins, bandoras, harp-guitars, banjos, violins, saxophone, tuba, cellos, clarinets, baritones, trombones, cornets, tympani, drums, basses, and ten pianos. They played and sang in syncopated style, and although professional criticism was mixed, they seem to have had a dynamic impact upon their audience.

A remarkable performance that illustrates a transitional step from blues and ragtime to jazz is heard on a recording of W. C. Handy's *Memphis Blues* by Lieutenant James Reese Europe's 369th Infantry "Hellfighters" Band in 1919 (*NW* 269, I/3). In New York, a month after their return from Europe following their service during the First World War, they recorded *Memphis*

James Reese Europe conducting the Hellfighters Band at an army hospital in Paris during World War I.

Blues, interestingly subtitled *A Southern Rag.*[18] In the southeastern United States, "blues" was used as a generic term for black secular music—"Devil Songs"—and blues included dance music as well as vocal performances. Blues

---

[18]The original subtitle of the 1912 edition reads, *Better known as Mister Crump,* referring to its original use as a campaign song in the 1909 election of "Boss" Crump. Handy published it himself, in Memphis, first in 1912, and later added the subtitle *A Southern Rag* to some early editions.

musicians, especially guitar players, would refer to their music as "rags," particularly those syncopated pieces with a lively beat.[19] *Memphis Blues* is an obvious combination of blues and ragtime, with similarities to "Blind" Blake's *Southern Rag*[20] and Robert Johnson's *Preachin' Blues*.[21] One can even hear small outcroppings of jazz features in Europe's recorded performance, though the piece as a whole can hardly be classified as jazz.

W. C. Handy, *Memphis Blues (A Southern Rag)*

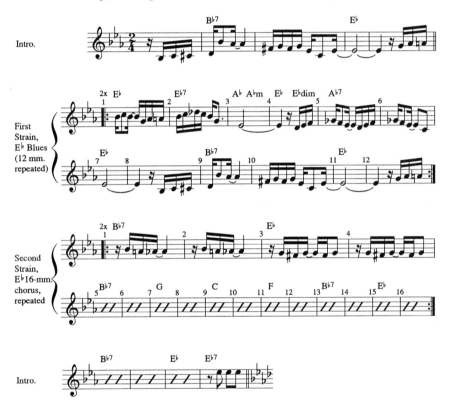

[19] In 1977 and 1978, both Mary Lou Williams (b. 1910) and "Guitar Slim" (James Stephens, b. 1915) played blues for the author and called them "rags." Much attention has been given to the vocal blues, but there is virtually nothing in the literature about traditional blues in their function as dance music. Giles Oakley touches on it in his study, *The Devil's Music: A History of the Blues*, pp. 31–33, but the entire repertoire of early instrumental blues deserves deeper exploration and full treatment.

[20] Paramount 12565-B.

[21] Columbia CL 1654.

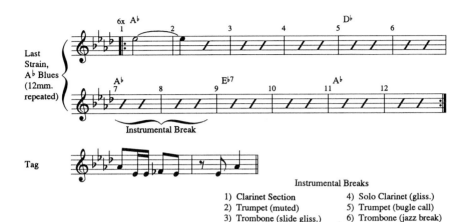

Last Strain, Aᵇ Blues (12mm. repeated)

Instrumental Break

Tag

Instrumental Breaks
1) Clarinet Section
2) Trumpet (muted)
3) Trombone (slide gliss.)
4) Solo Clarinet (gliss.)
5) Trumpet (bugle call)
6) Trombone (jazz break)

A four-measure introduction is followed by a twelve-measure blues in Eᵇ, which is repeated. The introductory phrase serves also as the last four measures of the blues and as a transition to the last strain. The exact number of players in the recording studio is uncertain, but the ensemble is large and has military band instrumentation. Although the performance is "loose" or relaxed, very little is played that is not part of the arrangement or orchestration. This is not an improvised performance, but a band performance of a written composition.

The last strain is a twelve-measure blues too, in Aᵇ, and a two-bar "break," or instrumental filler, is featured in the performance at measures 7 and 8 of this chorus. All the "breaks" are a bit "jazzy," but only the last rings true as an interesting bit of improvisation. How then, does this piece fit into the mosaic of roadstones that progresses gradually and perceptibly toward a clearly defined new music, jazz?

Formally, the first and last strains are regularizations of the same blues formal scheme developed and exploited by country blues artists such as Blind Lemon Jefferson and Robert Johnson. These twelve-measure choruses, partly through the efforts of W. C. Handy, are now seen in a standardized format—three four-measure phrases with a standard chord progression: I–IV–I–V–I.

Blues Progressions in Eᵇ and Aᵇ

	I	IV	I	V	I
First Strain	Eᵇ	Aᵇ	Eᵇ	Bᵇ	Eᵇ
Last Strain	Aᵇ	Dᵇ	Aᵇ	Eᵇ	Aᵇ

The melodic material uses and emphasizes blue notes, but the melodic substance has now been transformed into an instrumental idiom that uses the entire diatonic scale and chromatic alterations as well.

Notes Used in the Melody of the First Strain, Key of E♭

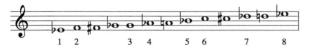

The notes numbered 1 through 8 are those pitches that belong to the E♭-major diatonic scale. The notes between pitches 2 and 3 (F♯ and G♭) represent the "blue third"—a G♭ with a lowered third feeling and an F♯ with a raised "leading tone" function. On a well-tempered (normally tuned) piano, these notes are identical, but in wind, string, and vocal performances they are often not. The pitches between notes 6 and 7, the "blue seventh" notes, function similarly: the flattened note with a melodic tendency down and the sharpened note with a melodic tendency up. The A♭ between notes 4 and 5 should more properly be notated B♭♭ (B double flat), for it is operating in this melody as a flatted fifth, another of the blues sounds traceable in the old African-American tradition. So, in the first chorus of *Memphis Blues* we see an amalgamation of the old blues characteristics and the new instrumental blues features.

The second strain of *Memphis Blues* is not a blues at all, that is, not in the formal sense of the twelve-bar blues structure. It is a sixteen-measure ragtime chorus that could fit neatly into the middle of any popular ragtime piece of the day. Like Blake's *Southern Rag*, it could be repeated indefinitely to accompany a dance (here it is used twice), and it employs secondary dominants, a harmonic progression commonly used in most ragtime compositions. The chord progression beginning in measure 5 of this strain takes the piece temporarily out of the key of E♭ and circles through G, C, F, and B♭ before returning again to the home key at the final cadence of the strain.

Memphis Blues, Second Strain, Secondary Dominants

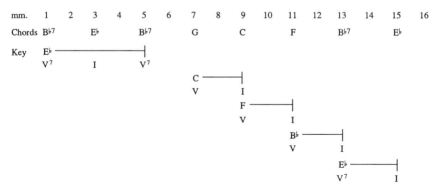

The harmonic journey begins with the irregular resolution of the dominant-seventh chord in measure 5.

Throughout the entire composition we find ragtime rhythms,

and in the last strain we hear primitive jazz breaks that relate to the African call-and-response patterns and the blues break. These fill the second half of each of the three four-measure phrases of the classic blues. Europe did not record this piece until 1919, but he had recorded *Castle House Rag*[22] as early as 1914 with an exciting jazz drum improvisation for a climax. During these years, the line between jazz and ragtime was very indistinct, and James Reese Europe walked that line with his various instrumental ensembles.

Dixon and Europe were not the only performers propagating jazz sounds in New York before 1917. Ragtime pianists abounded there: Jess Pickett, Sam Gordon, "Jack the Bear," William Turk, Eubie Blake, "One-Leg" Willie Joseph, and James P. Johnson are almost legendary names of the stride piano school (see p. 23). They improvised, syncopated, and occasionally published. Eubie Blake was one of the first Eastern black ragtimers to get his instrumental pieces published, but he was not the only one.

A fascinating African tradition persisted in New York at least until 1950, when it was claimed that the ringshout "is still danced in some of the churches of Harlem, the most sophisticated of all American Negro communities."[23] The ringshout is an African dance that features a group of singers circling counterclockwise around the leader of the religious chant. Ragtime pianist Willie "The Lion" Smith relates New York–style ragtime directly to the ringshout.

[S]houts are stride piano—when James P. [Johnson] and Fats [Waller] and I would get a romp-down shout going, that was playing rocky, just like the Bap-

---

[22] See illustration, p. 109.
[23] Rudi Blesh and Harriet Janis, *They All Played Ragtime*, 4th ed., p. 187.

tist people sing. You don't just play a chord to that—you got to move it and the piano-players do the same thing in the churches, and there's ragtime in the preaching.[24]

The blues were also in New York, first, perhaps, as a part of the ragtime, popular-piano style repertoire. Jess Pickett's *The Dream* (also called *Lady's Dream*, *Bowdigger's Dream*, and *Digah's Dream*) was performed "first fast and then slow-drag with blues."[25] W. C. Handy's blues circulated freely in New York, and "so many blues were being written on Twenty-eighth Street and its environs that by 1917 one of the songs to come out of the Alley was called 'Everybody's Crazy 'bout the Blues!' "[26]

Handy, being the first to write a blues composition, did, in effect, initiate a genre we have come to call the city blues, a standardized twelve-measure form sung to an instrumental accompaniment. However, his real fame lies in having popularized a portion of American folk music that had been around much longer in the the rural areas of America, especially the South: the country blues. Handy did not begin his career in New York, but when he got there in 1917, there was a large group of black songwriters there already writing blues hits: Perry Bradford, Joe Jordan, Clarence Williams, Noble Sissle, and two ragtime pianists we have already mentioned, James P. Johnson and Eubie Blake. Two white New Yorkers, Irene and Vernon Castle, became the first successful dance team to anticipate the moods and attitudes of the jazz age. They joined Jim Europe's orchestra and, in a sense, became patrons of New York's early jazz style. Europe's *Castle House Rag*, pictured right, and the *Castle Walk* became popular among the New York elite; both compositions were recorded in 1914 by Europe's Society Orchestra.[27] The instrumentation of violins, cello, cornet, clarinet, and two pianos, a typical society band combination, is augmented by banjos, mandolins, and Buddy Gilmore on drums. His solo break on the last chorus of *Castle House Rag* is one of the most exciting glimpses we have of early improvised jazz-like performances, and it certainly demonstrates that the information preserved and communicated by means of notated sheet music only vaguely resembles the sound of the actual music. Black syncopated music became fashionable in New York. White musicians there took a serious interest in learning the new styles, and two of the more successful songwriters composing blues were Irving Berlin and Gus Kahn. But the real leaders and innovators were the blacks. They felt they were playing their own music, and indeed they were.

[24] Ibid., p. 188.
[25] Ibid., p. 191.
[26] David Ewen, *The Life and Death of Tin Pan Alley*, p. 192 f.
[27] Originally issued on Victor 35372 and 17553.

Vernon and Irene Castle were the first dance team to adopt the moods and attitudes of the Jazz Age.

Eubie Blake had been playing professionally since around 1899 and had moved to New York soon after the turn of the century. Rudi Blesh relates an amusing anecdote:

> I picked up ragtime by ear. I first heard it when I was about eleven or twelve. It had no name. It just swung and made me feel good. It was my baby. Goodbye, Beethoven. . . . I didn't hear ragtime until a little later [after starting piano lessons around the age of six], but I heard syncopation in the Negro bands coming back from the funerals and, of course, in the shouting in the church. That was all right, it seems, but not at home. I'm in there ragging hell out of *Traumerei* on the organ and my mother opened the door and laid down the law, 'Take that ragtime out of my house.' That was the first time I ever heard the word.[28]

THE MIDWEST

When did the raggedy sounds hit Chicago? In 1893, for the World's Fair. The Chicago midway hosted the World's Columbian Exposition and the catchy new raggedy music was present, even if the name "ragtime" was not. This exposition, like the others that followed, brought Americans from every corner of the nation to view and hear the newest and latest. The Chicago Expo-

[28] Rudi Blesh, *Combo, U.S.A.: Eight Lives in Jazz*, pp. 188, 190.

sition was followed by the Trans-Mississippi Exposition at Omaha, Nebraska, in 1899; the Pan-American Exposition at Buffalo, New York, in 1901; and the Louisiana Purchase Exposition at St. Louis, Missouri, in 1904. Before 1897, when the word "ragtime" first appeared on published music, ragtime piano was called "jig piano," and the syncopated bands were called "jig bands." Jig piano, syncopated coon songs, and the stage entertainment of vaudeville and minstrel shows were current in the Midwest before the turn of the century.

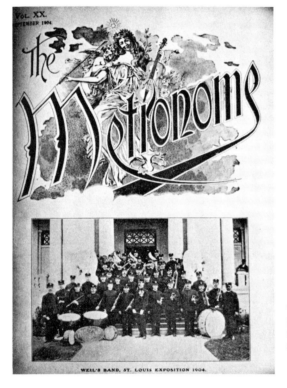

The cover of Metronome Magazine in September 1904, featured Weil's Band, playing at the St. Louis Exposition.

In Toledo, Ohio, the Tuxedo Club Minstrels were organized in 1897, and in their early performances their repertoire included the new ragtime hit *All Coons Look Alike to Me*.[29] This song and its brethren helped foster bigoted

[29] Marion S. Revett, *A Minstrel Town* (New York: Pageant Press, 1955), p. 74. The cover of the sheet music of *All Coons Look Alike to Me*, as well as many other coon song covers, can be found in William J. Schafer and Johannes Riedel, *The Art of Ragtime*, pp. 170–75. Also, excerpts from *All Coons Look Alike to Me* by Ernest Hogan appear in Southern, *Music of Black Americans*, p. 315.

attitudes in America, and one puzzles over the motivations of the black song-writer, Ernest Hogan, who exploited the clichés and superstitions of white America seemingly for the sake of financial profit and fame.

The chorus expounds what is clearly a white attitude (all black people look alike and therefore are alike, all inferior, lacking individuality or distinctive human souls); but it puts the sentiment in the mouth of a black persona. The song, then, is doubly damning, for it makes "black" people say exactly what a white racist would want them to admit:

> *All Coons look alike to me,*
> *I've got another beau, you see,*
> *And he's just as good to me*
> *As you, nig! ever tried to be.*
>
> *He spends his money free,*
> *I know we can't agree,*
> *So I don't like you no how,*
> *All Coons look alike to me.*

The black woman purportedly singing this satisfies complex demands of the devious racist mind. She is promiscuous, going from one "beau" to another; she is stupid (only a stupid person could not identify members of her own race); she is avaricious, looking only for a free-spender; and she says precisely what all racists want to hear, that there really are no differences between black individuals, that they lack the nobility and intelligence of real human beings.[30]

The psychology and sociology of the song text offer areas of investigation for longer serious studies, but for our purposes, the text represents a large number of musical pieces in the coon song fad of the day: it is a syncopated ragtime piece that had currency in the heartland of America.

If ragtime traveled north to Chicago, Toledo, and Omaha, it certainly was well known in Missouri, the home of Scott Joplin and the seat of the early ragtime publications. If ragtime, minstrel shows, gospel songs, and American band music were well known in Missouri at this time, so were the country blues. Missouri had a large black population, and George Morrison, black violinist and bandleader, reports of his early days in Fayette, Missouri:

My father was a musician. In fact, as far back as you can trace the Morrison family, the men were all fiddlers—in those days instead of violinists they called them fiddlers. . . . they couldn't read a note—never knew what a note looked

---

[30] Schafer and Riedel, *The Art of Ragtime*, p. 26.

like—played everything by ear. . . . I first heard the word jazz way back around 1911. Yes, when I married, that word was coming in then.[31]

Sedalia, Missouri, the town that figured so prominently in the early history of ragtime, was a railroad center in the middle of Missouri that attracted large numbers of blacks to work in the shops and yards after the Civil War. Newly emancipated blacks were also attracted to St. Louis by the jobs that the riverboat trade provided. The levees of St. Louis and the farmland around Sedalia were populated by rural blacks, who carried their blues tradition with them.

THE SOUTHWEST

Some of the musicians who settled in Sedalia had traveled a long way. One was the ragtime pianist Scott Joplin, who arrived in 1896 after a long, roundabout trip from his home town of Texarkana, Texas. A slave state before the war, Texas has a continuous, well-documented work-song and blues tradition from slave days through the 1930s. At that time, two great scholars of black music in America, John and Alan Lomax, recorded in prison camps along the Brazos River. They found that the prisoners still sang the slow rhymed choral songs that had almost disappeared everywhere else in the South. Perhaps the most exciting blues singer of all was Blind Lemon Jefferson, born in a small farmhouse near Wortham, Texas, in 1897. His success eventually carried him to Chicago, where he died at the age of thirty-three. He recorded for only four years, but of the eighty-one blues he left for posterity, we learn:

> It was a beautifully moving and sensitive group of blues. Many of them were
> direct reworkings of old field cries and work songs. He shouted the melody in
> a long, free rhythmic pattern, and the guitar sang behind the voice in a subtle
> counterpoint. Many of the songs were from the Texas prisons.[32]

The blues tradition was strong in Texas, and Jefferson passed it on to Sam "Lightnin' " Hopkins, who has been called "perhaps the last of the great blues singers" (*NW* 261, II / 2).[33] The rural country blues was present everywhere in the twenty or so years that preceded jazz recording, and if we single out Jefferson and Hopkins as two of the representatives from the Southwest, we must realize that they do not represent isolated phenomena. The thousands of players who never left their farms, their small towns, their black

---

[31] Gunther Schuller, *Early Jazz*, pp. 359, 362.
[32] Charters, *The Country Blues*, p. 67.
[33] Ibid., p. 254.

"suburbs," were the main force in this style—a style that depended less on the great and famous players than on its thoroughly permeating and saturating the society.

The country blues was a spontaneous music expressing a wide range of thought and mood as well as a great diversity of subject matter. Where the city or urban blues tended to concentrate on love and sex, the country blues continued to reflect the work songs, the religious pieces, and the general life and environment of the rural black. Because no expensive instruments or formal training were required of the country blues singer, an abundance of country blues was present wherever large numbers of blacks congregated during the early years of the twentieth century. In Texas and Sedalia they farmed, in New Orleans and St. Louis they worked on the levees; and the texts and the music were fluid and highly personal.

If blues was to be found in Texas, so was ragtime, for the greatest composer of all, Scott Joplin, stemmed from there. Born in 1868 in the northeast corner of the state, he wandered all over Texas, Louisiana, and the Mississippi Valley, and as far north as Chicago in 1893 for the World's Columbian Exposition before returning to St. Louis and its Tenderloin district. The itinerant nature of the black musicians of this period was more typical than exceptional, and as they traveled and worked, listened, and played, they created and spread a blues and ragtime culture that was omnipresent in American society.

The leading question that grows out of this introductory discussion is: At what point in the history of American music did an identifiable sound emerge that can be classified as the new American jazz? Can any portions of ragtime and blues be considered jazz, or were these merely its predecessors? The older histories would have us believe that jazz was laid at the doorstep of New Orleans in the form of a fully developed infant with a loud voice and keen rhythm.

The same confusion exists among students of ragtime. Scholars have identified at least three types of pianists who play ragtime: pseudo-ragtime (honky-tonk) pianists, jazz stylists, and classic ragtime pianists.[34] The distinction between ragtime and its earlier and later styles is more than academic—it borders on the pedantic. The evidence in hand clearly shows that the composers, the performers, and the knowledgeable listeners of the day clearly identified all of this music as ragtime. If we can regard minstrelsy and jazz as part of the total repertoire known as ragtime, then ragtime and the blues were just as plainly part of the total repertoire we now know as jazz.

In the years before 1917 and the first jazz recording, a living, dynamic music took hold in all of the United States. Here we indeed sense the birth

---

[34] Schafer and Riedel, *The Art of Ragtime,* p. 176.

of jazz. It was not an isolated event that took place at a particular time in the city of New Orleans, but a widespread cultural development that was taking place over a number of years throughout the land. The strongest concentrations of improvising ensembles collected in the Delta; the major heartbeats of ragtime and jazz piano playing were felt in the metropolitan areas and entertainment centers of the East Coast, the Mississippi River, and the Great Lakes; and the blues emerged from every field and back alley where African-Americans lived and worked.

——— THE SOUTH ————————————

Most of the musical considerations that permeate the historical discussions of jazz music before 1917 are close to pure speculation, for what most people now call jazz was unrecorded in any form that can be accurately brought back to life. The best musical record of that period is the piano-roll archives, and even here we can see that the great classic ragtime composers and players, such as Scott Joplin, added embellishment and did not play their music literally from the published scores, as our conservatory-trained pianists of today would do. Still, using the best evidence available, we can reconstruct a fairly accurate musical picture of the improvising New Orleans ensemble in the years before the Original Dixieland Jazz Band. Gunther Schuller underscores the difficulty of determining the real sound of early jazz by pointing out the many contradictions that writers and musicians face when they discuss early jazz, ragtime, novelty, minstrel, and blues. He wisely states:

> In those years of vast changes, as several musical styles coalesced into the one that finally came to be known as jazz, the only tributary source of jazz that seemed to remain constant was the blues. It is unlikely that the blues changed basically between the 1880's and the early 1920's. And one can be sure that when Bunk Johnson says that as a kid he "used to play nothin' but the blues" in New Orleans barrelhouses, he was playing essentially the same instrumental blues that spread like wildfire in the 1920's race recordings, or—going back in time—that he had heard Buddy Bolden play in the 1890's.[35]

Who was Buddy Bolden? According to *The New Edition of the Encyclopedia of Jazz*,[36] he is the almost legendary cornet player and bandleader who is said to have been the first or one of the first New Orleans musicians to play in the style subsequently called jazz. Charles "Buddy" Bolden was born in New Orleans in 1868 and died there in 1931. He was a barber by trade and sup-

[35] Schuller, *Early Jazz*, p. 64 f.
[36] Ed. Leonard Feather, p. 139.

posedly led several early jazz bands. Bunk Johnson, who claimed to have played with him from 1895 to 1899, was one of the chief witnesses to the existence of Bolden and his music. Bolden was reputed to be one of the world's loudest cornet players, and his sound was said to carry to a distance of one to five miles. There seems to be some truth to this claim. At the turn of the century, there were two amusement parks in New Orleans, Johnson and Lincoln parks. Legend has it that Buddy Bolden, when playing in Johnson Park, would stick his horn through a hole in the park fence and play a call that people would recognize as a signal to leave Lincoln Park for Johnson Park and the entertainment of the Buddy Bolden Band.

Probably the only known picture of the legendary **Buddy Bolden** (standing, second from left), taken sometime before 1895. Two other members of his band are recognizable in this photograph: trombonist **Willie Cornish** (at Bolden's left) and clarinetist **Frank Lewis** (seated).

The memory of a senior musician may not be the most reliable witness to
events that occurred when he was five years old, but the authority of a Louis
Armstrong is not something to dismiss lightly. Armstrong spoke of Buddy
Bolden this way:

> I remember the time in New Orleans when I was a little youngster, you know,
> after I left Jane Alley—back of town, they called it—in New Orleans, you
> know. I remember the time when it had the good old street parades, you know,
> and brass bands, and every one of 'em was great. They'd all congregate in front
> of the Eagle Saloon at Rampart and Perdido. . . .
>
> I could go on for hours about them good old cats like Manny Perez, Joe
> Oliver, Freddy Keppard, Bunk Johnson, and Big Eyed Louis. Buddy Bolden,
> one of the early masters, see. I remember hearing Buddy Bolden when I was
> five years old. In those days he used to play back in the Funky Butt Hall, see.
> They'd play a half hour in front of the Hall, you know, outside, and then
> they'd go in and play. . . . When they played that half, we kids could, on the
> other side—you know, it's sidewalk now, but it was banquette then—we kids
> on the side of the banquette, and we'd dance, and I was in my little old dress,
> you know, and I'd be wailin' and havin' a ball. Well, when they'd go inside,
> we had to go to bed, see, 'cause they played from 8:00 to 4:00 in the morning.
> And that's my first time of hearin' Buddy Bolden. And he used to blow awful
> hard.

William J. Schafer attempts to separate fact from fiction and concludes,
"We have been asking 'Who was the man who first played jazz?' when we
should ask 'Who were the *people* who first played jazz?' The second question
can be answered in elaborate detail.[37] Among the members of the Bolden
bands were Willie Warner, clarinet; Frank Lewis, clarinet; Frank Keely,
valve trombone; Willie Cornish, trombone; Willie "Bunk" Johnson, cornet;
Bob Lyons, bass; Albert Glenny, bass; Bebe Mitchell, bass; and Frankie
Dusen, the trombone player who finally took over the band. Bolden played
all over New Orleans, and, with extra musicians, he marched in the streets
of the city. For funerals the band would improvise Baptist hymns like *What
a Friend We Have in Jesus* and lead the people away from the cemetery to the
traditional *Oh Didn't He Ramble*. They marched for Mardi Gras and for whatever occasion a little festive music was appropriate, and they marched through
the red-light district so frequently that the "working girls," according to legend, would recognize the band by its theme song, the second strain of *Sen-*

---

[37] William J. Schafer, "Thoughts on Jazz Historiography: 'Buddy Bolden's Blues' versus
'Buddy Bottley's Balloon,' " *Journal of Jazz Studies*, 2 (1974), p. 13.

sation Rag.[38] Bolden's heavy drinking and syphilis led to symptoms of insanity beginning around 1906, and the last job he is known to have held was as a cornetist in the Allen Brass Band in the spring of 1907. He was committed to a state institution in June of that year and died there in 1931.

NEW ORLEANS

Two types of orchestras were at work in New Orleans at this time, "sit down" orchestras from downtown and improvising bands from uptown. This was so because New Orleans in the nineteenth century was really two cities: an American city west of Canal Street (uptown), and a French city east of Canal Street (downtown). The east side contained the French Opera, chamber ensembles, polished dance orchestras, and all the paraphernalia that accompanies the social and cultural values of the upper class. French New Orleans was peopled with whites, black servants, and Creoles of color—families of mixed blood which, while not accepted socially, were successful in business and became prominent in the cultural and economic life of the section.

Uptown presented an enormous contrast. It was populated by newly freed blacks who were poor, uneducated, and lacking in all the cultural and economic advantages available to the Creoles of color. The musical standards of the downtown orchestras were very high—most of these musicians were conservatory trained, played at the Opera House, and prided themselves on their ability, knowledge, propriety, and general refinement. A well-known orchestra leader, John Robichaux, hired the best musicians and took over most of the city's best jobs. In contrast, very few of the uptown musicians could read music, and until 1894 they frequently studied with their opposite numbers from across Canal Street. In that year, a restrictive racial segregation code, enacted throughout the city, included the Creoles among those to be segregated. The Creoles found themselves forced to live on the other side of the tracks, and they began a passionate struggle to maintain status in a hostile atmosphere. Where there had been a tendency for black music on both sides of Canal Street to move toward a common polished goal, no such attempt was made after the odious law was passed. The uptown musicians reacted by playing as loudly as possible, because the Creoles prided themselves on their soft, delicate tone. Even the uptown musicians who could read music, and it was reported that Buddy Bolden had been trained in the solfeggio method of sight reading, reacted by emphasizing the attributes of the musically illiterate. Memorization and nascent improvisation were characteristic of the uptown bands; sight reading and correct performance were characteristic of the Creole bands.

[38] Note that rags formed part of the repertoire of an acknowledged early jazz band.

A few years later, in 1897, the city council passed another ordinance that would have a profound effect on music in New Orleans. The city fathers legislated to move all the prostitutes from the city brothels into a thirty-eight-block area that became known as Storyville, the Crescent City's legendary red-light district. There were actually two Storyvilles, one white and the other black. White Storyville, which ran several blocks deep, was bordered by Canal, Basin, and North Robertson Streets. Black Storyville (Uptown or 'Back o' Town), on the west side of Canal Street, was bordered by Perdido, Gravier, Locust, and Franklin Streets. The lines were drawn. Lewd women were not permitted to occupy any house, room, or closet outside Storyville. At the height of its activity, Storyville had between 1,500 and 2,200 registered prostitutes. The sporting houses employed everything from string trios to ragtime pianists and brass bands. Storyville brought black and tan musicians together, and one of the local activities was the brass bands' uptown-downtown cutting (carving) contests in the streets and at picnics. The atmosphere has been described as follows:

> The 1890's had been an especially tough period for middle class and poor people in the Crescent City. The younger Creoles of color, whose parents had struggled for almost two generations, reached out for economic stability wherever they could find it. Storyville was there. For most, the pay was small, but anything was a gain. Young Creoles like Sidney Bechet often worked the District without their proud relatives' knowledge, because, for many Creoles of color, playing in Storyville meant a loss of status within their own community. Jelly Roll Morton's grandmother kicked him out of the house when he was 15 for playing in Storyville. She loved music, but said people who played in such places were bums, and she didn't want him to be a bad influence on his sisters. Many of the "dark" Negroes, though, "didn't give a damn" if it was a whorehouse they were playing in. They had an opportunity to play the music they loved and get paid for doing it.[39]

Among the early bandleaders working the district, in addition to Buddy Bolden and his follower Frankie Dusen, were Joe "King" Oliver, Freddie Keppard, and, somewhat later, Manuel Perez, Pops Foster, George Baquet, and Sidney Bechet. What these musicians played and how well they played it is almost entirely speculation based on the friendly recollections of interested parties. The repertoire included polite social dances by string orchestras, instrumental blues, ragtime on the piano and in combination, and every variety of entertainment music appropriate for the patrons of a red-light district.

The influence of Storyville on New Orleans jazz performers, especially

[39] Jack V. Buerkle and Danny Barker, *Bourbon Street Black*, p. 20.

Canal Street, the main thoroughfare in New Orleans, ca. 1910.

black musicians, was profound, but one should not forget that similar music was also played in the cabarets and dance halls surrounding the district, at the resort areas around Lake Pontchartrain, on the riverboats, in the French Quarter, and in the cafes and hotels scattered all over town.

At least one music historian has argued that no jazz was being played anywhere before 1916[40] (but what can anyone say with certainty about an improvised music that was never recorded?). The weight of the evidence leans heavily the other way, and even if Buddy Bolden was not playing jazz around 1895, some other black musician in the New Orleans area probably was.

It is less likely that the New Orleans Creole groups were playing jazz in the early days, but one technical innovation, introduced by the Creole musician John Robichaux in 1894 or 1895, profoundly influenced its development. Robichaux's drummer, Dee Dee Chandler, built a crude wooden pedal for a bass drum so that he might play it with his foot while playing a trap drum with sticks in his hands. His invention proved to be a sensation and was widely imitated. Chandler helped establish Robichaux's reputation as the first person to add traps to the orchestra.

[40] Harry O. Brunn, *The Story of the Original Dixieland Jazz Band*, p. v.

THE JAZZ COMBO

One of the key elements in the emerging jazz ensemble was the rhythm section, a group of musicians within the larger ensemble who had a nonmelodic function in the band. Eventually, the rhythm section became standardized with three players: piano, bass, and trap drums. All of these performers had to develop the ensemble style of playing characteristic of a well-functioning rhythm section; even the piano player had to adapt the ragtime piano style to the jazz-ensemble piano style. Where the ragtime pianist basically operates as a self-contained unit, performing all the melodic, harmonic, and rhythmic elements of the piece, the jazz-ensemble pianist specializes in but two of these three functions: the harmonic framework and the motor-pulse rhythm. By using two hands to play what the ragtime pianist normally plays with his left hand alone, the ensemble pianist carries the harmonies of the piece (roots on the strong beat in the left hand and complete triads in the right hand) and the steady eighth-note pulse at the same time.[41] The steady pulse of the African rhythm ensembles on which additive rhythmic figures are superimposed by other percussion instruments has its parallel in the jazz rhythm section. The steady eighth-note pulse of the piano player supplies the common denominator for additive groupings while presenting a basis for syncopations by others and paralleling the strong beat–weak beat grouping of Western meters. When Dee Dee Chandler added the foot-activated bass-drum pedal and attached a trap drum to the larger bass drum, he developed a purely percussive instrument operable by one person. The drummer could synchronize with the motor-pulse of the piano player (the foot pedal would strike simultaneously with the left hand of the piano) and also add a grouping of smaller-value rhythmic figures—some in conjunction with the rhythm of the piano and some syncopated against it—through the employment of sticks in both hands. The drummer's speed and dexterity of sticks on a trap drum gave life, excitement, and syncopation to the early ensembles.

The early ensembles often featured a brass bass, since the groups frequently derived from brass bands. Functionally, the bass added nothing to the music beyond what was played by the left hand of the piano, but it was louder, it was portable, and it provided a more compatible envelope of sound. Also, early rhythm sections were not standard, and frequently a banjo or a guitar might sound in place of the piano.[42] When this happened, the left-

---

[41]Quarter-note pulse in 4/4 or eighth-note pulse in 2/4. Rags were notated most frequently in 2/4.

[42]The original Superior Orchestra (c. 1908–13) with Bunk Johnson on cornet used violin, clarinet, cornet, trombone, guitar, string bass, and drums. The only photograph extant of the Bolden band reveals two clarinets, cornet, valve trombone, bass, and guitar.

hand function of the piano was absent, for although these plucked string instruments could carry the offbeat chords that the piano might have played in the right hand, they were not capable of laying down the harmonic root with power on the strong beats. Consequently, bass, banjo, and drums; or piano and drums; or bass, piano, and drums; or bass and piano; or some other similar combination was considered necessary to provide a satisfactory harmonic and rhythmic framework for the music called jazz.

The other members of the early jazz ensembles were grouped in what is familiarly called the "front line." The melodic instruments of the classic jazz band, frequently clarinet, cornet, and trombone, would often stand in front of the rhythm section, and their musical functions, different from those of the rhythm section, comprised the portion of the improvising jazz ensemble that was primarily melodic and syncopated. The function of the Dixieland trombonist, however, was not as clear-cut as that of the two higher melody instruments. Except for an occasional rhythmic break, solo, or characteristic rhythmic trombone figure, the trombone frequently functioned as the bass of the rhythm section. Consequently, many early jazz ensembles had trombone or bass, but not both. When both were present, the opportunity for the trombone to be freed from the normal bass functions presented itself, but a new role, as harmonic filler and secondary melodic instrument, took years to develop.

The trumpet or cornet was the key melodic instrument of the ensemble, and basically played melodies in ragtime style, that is, ragged or syncopated the tune. The clarinet was responsible for adding a high-speed, high-pitched obbligato to whatever else was going on in the ensemble and occasionally played parallel harmonies with the trumpet or cornet, but its chief function during the group-improvisation passages was to add another layer of fast-moving melodic and rhythmic groupings.

Group improvisation was facilitated by the tacit understanding among the musicians that each had a specific musical role to perform as determined by the instrument. The trumpet played "lead," the clarinet created the obbligato, and the trombone customarily played what has come to be described as the "tailgate trombone" part,[43] a melodic-harmonic line deriving from the harmonic structure of the piece but acting as a countermelody to the trumpet. The Dixieland piano reinforced the harmonic structure by playing triads on the offbeats with the right hand, while the left hand, the brass bass, and the foot of the bass drum established the two-beat ragtime rhythm by emphasizing the strong beats in 2/4 time. The hands of the drummer were

---

[43] "Tailgate trombone," or New Orleans–style trombone playing, is said to derive its name from the customary location of the trombonist on a horse-drawn parade cart. Because of the freedom of movement necessary to operate a trombone slide, the open tailgate was the favored seat of most trombonists.

free to use sticks on a variety of percussion instruments in a free and ornamental manner. The Dixieland band's repertoire was heterogeneous, for
anything could be molded into its style by the improvising musicians.

EARLY JAZZ MUSICIANS
AND THEIR MUSIC

Among the early great musicians who played authentic jazz before the 1920s
were King Oliver, Freddie Keppard, Louis Armstrong, Jelly Roll Morton,
Sidney Bechet, and, of course, Buddy Bolden. Also, some groups that did
not use a leader's name for identification were probably playing the new
improvised music at an early date. The Excelsior Brass Band, a group of ten
to twelve pieces organized before 1885 and active until 1931; the Onward
Brass Band, a group of the same size, organized before 1889 and active until
about 1925; the Alliance Brass Band; the Big Four String Band; the Excelsior
String Band; and many other novelty groups and orchestras were active at
this time.

An important trumpet player who functioned as a kind of transition between
Buddy Bolden and Louis Armstrong was Joseph "King" Oliver. Born in 1885,
he was but a young man when he first played in the Melrose Brass Band in
1907. Oliver worked with several brass bands before leaving New Orleans,
among them the Olympia Band under A. J. Piron, the Eagle Brass Band, the
Onward Brass Band, and the Magnolia Brass Band. He also played with
trombonist Kid Ory's group and, in 1915, led his own band with Sidney
Bechet on clarinet as a sideman. Exactly what and how these musicians played
at that time is anyone's guess, but as Martin Williams points out:

> There seems greater emotional range and depth in [classic] jazz [than in normal
> ragtime] (an infusion of the feeling of the blues is the answer here). It also
> seems different, more varied, rhythmically. It *is*—and that is why the layman
> had to get a new name for it. *Jazz* became that name.[44]

When King Oliver recorded with his Creole Jazz Band in Chicago in the
1920s, he brought New Orleans musicians with him. Perhaps the music played
then was considerably different from what came before, but the most likely
possibility is that his recordings from that time closely approximate original
New Orleans jazz and are, therefore, the most authentic classic jazz recordings we have available to us today.

[44] Liner notes to *The Smithsonian Collection of Classic Jazz*, selected and annotated by Martin
Williams (Washington, DC: The Smithsonian Institute, 1973), p. 5 f.

What are the characteristics of King Oliver's *Dippermouth Blues*, which he recorded in Chicago in June 1923, with Louis Armstrong as second cornet, Johnny Dodds on clarinet, Honoré Dutrey on trombone, Lil Hardin (later to become Mrs. Louis Armstrong) on piano, Bud Scott on banjo, and Baby Dodds (the brother of Johnny Dodds) on drums (*SCCJ* 6)? What is there about this recording that is most likely to convey a real sense of New Orleans classic jazz music? Let's examine some of the problems that stand in the way of a completely accurate reconstruction.

When ethnomusicologists make field records of non-Western music, they assume that the music they are hearing is historically correct if the tradition was passed down from master to apprentice and if other musical influences do not seem to have affected the culture. In other words, a recent recording of an unchanged musical tradition probably represents fairly well what might have been recorded years earlier had such recording equipment been available. In early jazz, the only valid comparison is the guild-system method of training musicians. If the master Buddy Bolden passed his skills on to apprentice Joe Oliver, and if Joe "King" Oliver passed his skills on to apprentice Louis Armstrong, then supposedly what the mature Louis Armstrong played would represent, with a fair degree of accuracy, the music Buddy Bolden played, in an unchanging tradition.

The guild system was present, but the tradition was not. Jazz was not only evolving at this time, it was changing rapidly. Indeed, it had no history. Edmond Souchon acts as an interested and educated informant with regard to this question. Born in New Orleans, Souchon first heard Joe Oliver play around 1901–02, when he was four or five and the musician was sixteen or seventeen. From approximately 1907 through 1917, Souchon listened to Joe Oliver play fairly regularly. He picked up on him again in 1924 in Chicago, when Oliver had acquired the title "King" and was leading the Creole Jazz Band. At this time, Souchon reports, "He was now 'King,' the most important personage in the jazz world, surrounded by his own handpicked galaxy of sidemen." Souchon claims that even before Oliver left for Chicago "he had acquired a technique that was much more smooth, and that his band was adapting itself to the white dances more and more." Souchon continues, "By the time Oliver had reached Chicago and the peak of his popularity, his sound was not the same. It was a different band, a different and more polished Oliver, an Oliver who had completely lost his New Orleans sound."[45] We have no way of measuring the accuracy of Souchon's statements, but he was an interested participant, a member of the jazz community of both New Orleans and Chicago.

[45] Edmond Souchon, "King Oliver: A Very Personal Memoir," in *Jazz Panorama*, ed. Martin Williams (New York: Collier, 1964), pp. 27, 28, 29.

Joseph "King" Oliver's Dixie Syncopators, Plantation Cafe, Chicago 1925. (Front row, left to right) Bud Scott, banjo; Darnell Howard, Albert Nicholas, and Barney Bigard, reeds. (Back row, left to right) Bert Cobbs, bass; Paul Barbarin, drums; King Oliver, cornet; George Field, trombone; Bob Schoffner, trumpet; Luis Russell, piano.

If Souchon's observations are correct, and Oliver's sound in Chicago was a distortion of the New Orleans jazz-ensemble sound, then we can imagine how much further the evidence is distorted by the poor recording techniques of the early 1920s. Larry Gushee, when reviewing a recent remastering of the April 1923 recordings of the Creole Jazz Band (Riverside RLP 12-122), comments on the uncertainty of determining the real sound of the band, explaining that some of the reissued sides must have been "cut in marsh-mallow—with Johnny Dodds crouched inside the recording horn." To his ear, good reproduction shows that the "clarinet is toned down, cornets are strong, with the second part actually being heard, the piano chording does not run together in an amorphous droning, and the bass line is generally clearer."[46]

[46] Larry Gushee, "King Oliver," in *Jazz Panorama*, p. 40.

If the original recording distorted an already changed sound, then our newly mastered track of the June 1923 recording of the same piece piles insult upon abuse. The original performance in 1923 was played in the key of B♭; the new 33⅓ rpm disc reproduces the piece in the key of B. How significant is this change? The same reviewer makes the following observation about tempo in New Orleans style:

> Whether the tempos, so often felicitous, were Joe Oliver's independent choice, or determined by prevailing dance style, I cannot know. The fact remains that the Creole Band (and the New Orleans Rhythm Kings) played a good deal slower than bands like the Wolverines and the Bucktown 5, which recorded only a year later. The tempos they chose never exceeded their technical limitations, while, for instance, the Wolverines and, especially, the later Chicagoans often played too fast for comfort (theirs and ours). I am sure that this accounts for much of the superb swing of the Creole Band.[47]

John Mehegan stresses the critical nature of tempo in the total mix of jazz: "Tempo in jazz has always been a primary consideration for the performer in choosing the pulsation best suited for 'swing' and urgency."[48] He then goes on to chart tempo differences between New Orleans groups and Chicago groups, saying that the former work with a quarter-note span of 104–248 per minute, the average being 166.7; Chicago groups span 108–264 per minute, for an average pulse of 179. This seemingly innocent mistake at the re-recording level has completely transformed one of the most important stylistic elements of New Orleans jazz, tempo. The original performance in B♭ moved at 186 beats per minute—fast enough—the "new" performance travels at 200 beats per minute!

To a certain extent, the relative tempos of New Orleans and Chicago groups is based on intuition, for all the recordings of the early New Orleans groups were made in Chicago while the musicians were working there for Chicago audiences. We have no way of proving that Chicago jazz was indeed faster than New Orleans jazz; the suggestion is logical and probable, but not conclusive. The purpose of these introductory remarks is not to prove one case or the other, but to show how little we know with certainty about classic New Orleans jazz.

The next step in our "scientific" investigation will be to discover as much as we can about the music preserved for us on the 1923 recordings. Using the modern master (*SCCJ* 6) as our original source, what can we actually hear

---

[47] Ibid., p. 41.
[48] *Jazz Improvisation*, II (New York: Watson-Guptill, 1962), p. 22 ff.

the individual musicians doing? If we slow the recording down to a key of B♭ with a 440 A (it is probable that the A of the 1920s was closer to 435 vibrations per second), we can listen to Baby Dodds on drums. His work is virtually inaudible except during the stoptime chorus, when the tone of a wood block cuts through the timbre of the percussive chords. At times, one can imagine that he is playing the trap drum on beats 2, 3, and 4, or beats 2 and 4, but this sound blends so well with the attack of the banjo and piano that the ear cannot be certain whether that is, in fact, what Baby Dodds is playing. The sound of the bass drum is not heard. Indeed, Baby Dodds was probably not playing any instrument except wood blocks at this recording session. The powerful sounds of a trap drummer could not be accommodated by the recording instruments of the time. W. C. Handy describes his first recording session in 1917 as follows:

> Our clarinetist sat in the corner on a six-foot stool and played into a megaphone near the ceiling. There were stools of varying heights for the other players. The three violinists stood directly in front of the recording apparatus and played

Warren "Baby" Dodds (1892–1940).

into megaphones there. The saxophonists were seated on the side and played into their own megaphones. Cornet and trombone played into one in the rear. The cellist occupied another corner and another megaphone. But the poor drummer was a dead goose where the record was concerned. While they played as hard as ever in life, the drums and basses could not be recorded in those days. All megaphones emptied into one recording horn. . . .

To my way of thinking the records were not up to scratch.[49]

In live performance, Baby Dodds played differently from the way he did in the studio—normally, the trap drummer is almost omnipresent in a jazz group.

Little definition exists between the sounds of piano and banjo. Lil Hardin's left hand makes little impression, and the four-beat strumming of banjo melts with the right-hand chording of the piano. Likewise, Louis Armstrong's second cornet playing in ensemble can be identified only by the connoisseur-specialist. What remains of the earliest recordings of a genuine New Orleans black jazz ensemble are the melodies of the principal three of the front line: clarinet, cornet, and trombone. We have already been told by a great connoisseur of King Oliver, Edmond Souchon, that the Chicago sound of King Oliver had already changed from the New Orleans sound he heard as a young man, and our simple observations of this one recording help confirm his conclusion that "those records even miss conveying the way that Oliver was playing in Chicago when I heard him."[50]

So what was jazz like in New Orleans in the years before the first jazz recordings? We simply don't know. The best we can do is recall the names, look at the photographs, interview the old-timers, and make an educated guess. As one thoughtful commentator has observed:

The study of jazz differs from the study of concert music. The chief documents of its history are the performances on phonograph records, which were very rare before 1923, and nonexistent before 1917. How the style arose and what it was really like before many examples of it were recorded we can never know as surely and thoroughly as we might wish. Hence, legends are rife, and opinions differ. Opinions and even legends based on personal recollections are invaluable, although of course they need to be critically compared with each other and with all other evidence.[51]

The characteristics of jazz before the name "jazz" emerged that seem to inspire general agreement are these: Jazz was the music played by perform-

[49] W. C. Handy, *Father of the Blues: An Autobiography*, p. 173 f.
[50] Souchon, "King Oliver," p. 30.
[51] William Austin, *Music in the 20th Century*, p. 182.

ers such as Louis Armstrong, Lil Hardin, King Oliver, Buddy Bolden, Nick La Rocca, Jelly Roll Morton, Kid Ory, Honoré Dutrey, Johnny Dodds, Baby Dodds, and Jimmy Noone, and sung by artists such as Ma Rainey and Bessie Smith. It is possible that the music played by pianists for example—Scott Joplin and Eubie Blake, should also be included, as well as the music of thousands of others who played or sang ragtime, blues, novelty, jazz, and so on. The most common instrumental groups had a front line of clarinet, cornet, and trombone, and a back line of rhythm section that included piano, drums, bass, and banjo, all together or in any combination.

The rhythm of the New Orleans group, like that of most jazz styles to follow, operated on three levels of time: the quarter-note pulse, the half-note harmonic unit, and the eighth-note melodic or ornamental unit. New Orleans tempos were probably slower than those commonly used by the groups recording in Chicago and New York in the later years, and the volume level of New Orleans groups probably far exceeded that used elsewhere. The improvised polyphony of the front line consisted of ornamentation, obbligato playing, and countermelody invention. The lead cornet would rag an identifiable melody and superimpose a rhythmic configuration upon the basic structure laid down by the rhythm section—quarter notes syncopated by the addition of eighth-note values. The clarinet obbligato moved primarily at eighth-note speeds or faster, and the trombone moved at the slow half-note or whole-note harmonic-rhythm speed. However, when the trombone played countermelodies, it moved at approximately the same speed as the lead cornet. When the lead cornet broke the melody at the end of a phrase to take a breath, the trombone or clarinet picked up the slack with an improvised "fill," and this is a procedure that most writers on early jazz like to compare with the call-and-response patterns of African tribal music. The bass drum and piano would usually play a nondifferentiated 4/4 pulse, while the piano and snare drum, sometimes aided by a bass instrument such as the tuba, would tend to superimpose a 2/4 structure over the continuous 4/4 pulse. Blues form, ragtime forms, and popular-song form were all employed, and we will investigate these as we analyze other specific pieces of music.

Kansas City Stomp (1928)

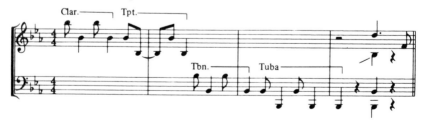

New Orleans jazz was very closely tied to social functions in that it provided music for funerals, weddings, and dances, and as background in the whorehouses. As we shall observe in subsequent recorded examples, classic jazz employed the diatonic system of harmony and kept triadic extensions limited to the minor seventh. Some claim that dominant preparation in the New Orleans style was restricted to a secondary dominant constructed by altering the natural triad built on the second scale step. Without any music surviving from the period, this supposition seems a bit presumptive. It is possible that New Orleans jazz limited the trombone to a purely harmonic role, and it is thought by some that the evolution to a melodic-harmonic function took place during the Chicago period. In addition to the regular use of the instruments, the New Orleans jazz musicians employed mutes of various kinds for the brass, and they altered the attacks, vibratos, and regular pitches by lipping, half-holing, and sliding.

Stoptime and the New Orleans stomp are two common rhythmic characteristics. They differ in that stoptime produces homophony, while stomp patterns are polyphonic. These are characteristics the classic-jazz buff looks for in New Orleans jazz performances. Stomping, the process of taking a rhythmic figure, placing it into a melodic line, and repeating it in an ostinato or riff pattern, leads to a polyphonic accentuation that produces strong rhythmic momentum within the improvising polyphony. Rudi Blesh explains the process thus:

> The stomp pattern, which forces the melody into a rhythmic design, derives indirectly from the polyrhythmic drum patterns of West Africa; these were transmitted through the functional figures of the work-songs and play patterns of the children's songs, then revived in guitar and banjo strumming. . . .
>
> In stomping [by a jazz band], the regular beat or pulse is maintained by the full rhythm section. The lead, one or two cornets or trumpets, plays the melody fitted into the stomp pattern. The clarinet plays a free melody of many notes around the lead, placing the accents to correspond with the stomp pattern.[52]

The early jazz of New Orleans and elsewhere was probably primitive in the sense that virtuoso solo playing had not been developed. Here, however, there are conflicting reports, and one cannot tell whether or not the big names of New Orleans were great soloists in the early days. At any rate, New Orleans mothered the infant music until 1917. Then the Navy stepped in and closed Storyville:

> Early in August [1917], Secretary of War Newton D. Baker issued an order forbidding open prostitution within five miles of an army cantonment, and a similar ruling was made by Josephus Daniels, Secretary of the Navy, respecting naval establishments . . . on September 24, and again on October 1 [1917], he [Mayor Martin Behrman] was notified by Secretary Daniels that unless the red-light district was closed by the city it would be closed by the Army and the Navy. . . . After midnight of November 12, 1917, it would be unlawful to operate a brothel or assignation house anywhere in New Orleans.
>
> The exodus from Storyville had begun two weeks before November 12. . . . As late as midnight of the 12th, there was a stream of harlots and their servants, laden with property, leaving the segregated area. . . . The next day [November 15] many leading churchwomen, and members of the Louisiana Federation of Women's Clubs, held a meeting and appointed a committee to

[52] Blesh, *Shining Trumpets*, p. 188 f.

help the prostitutes. But none applied for succor. Few, in fact, needed it. They had simply moved from Storyville into various business and residential sections of New Orleans and were doing very well.[53]

When the red-light district, the great patron of jazz in New Orleans, went out of business, black musicians began to look for work elsewhere. Some went to New York, some went to Chicago, and some stayed home. But jazz would have spread like wildfire whether Storyville closed or not. Nick La Rocca's Original Dixieland Jazz Band, which had been playing in New Orleans under various names from 1908 on, was about to record in New York. Subsequently, Victor released a sales catalog of new recordings on March 17, 1917, and on the front cover it advertised the world's first jazz phonograph record:

> The Original Dixieland Jass Band
>
> Spell it Jass, Jas, Jaz, or Jazz—nothing can spoil a jass band. Some say the jass band originated in Chicago. Chicago says it comes from San Francisco—San Francisco being a way off across the continent. Anyway, a jass band is the newest thing in the cabarets, adding greatly to the hilarity thereof.
>
> They say the first instrument of the first jass band was an empty lard can, by humming into which, sounds were produced resembling those of saxophone with the croup. Since then the jass band has grown in size and ferocity.[54]

During the first decade and a half of the twentieth century, in the years before sound recording, there were at least twenty-three Creole and black dance orchestras and brass bands working in New Orleans for which we have sufficient documentation to reconstruct, rather accurately, their organization and their music. Among these, the better-known groups are the Excelsior Brass Band, The Olympia Orchestra, the Tuxedo Brass Band, the Silver Leaf Orchestra, and the Onward Brass Band. Employment was plentiful for qualified musicians, and many establishments in the red-light district, the river steamers, and the black fraternal organizations provided employment on a regular basis for professional musicians. Thousands of people were employed in the lively port entertaining the travelers and visitors with ready money. In Storyville, bars, sporting houses, dance halls, and other nighttime

---

[53] Herbert Asbury, *The French Quarter* (New York, 1936), quoted in Blesh, *Shining Trumpets*, p. 202 f.

[54] Brunn, *Story of the Original Dixieland Jazz Band*, fourth unnumbered illustration after p. 92.

The Onward Brass Band in 1905. (Left to right) Manuel Perez, Andrew Kimball, Peter Bocage, Lorenzo Tio, Jr., Adolphe Alexander, Sr., Bebe Matthews, Dandy Lewis, Isidore Barbarin, Buddy Johnson, Vic Gaspard, Eddie Atkins, and Eddie Jackson.

establishments flourished, and it quickly became the principal tourist attraction in New Orleans. Tom Anderson, a bar owner in the area, published the *Blue Book—An Illustrated Directory and Gentleman's Guide to the Sporting District.* Elegantly bound in pale blue, with harps and flowers on the cover, it enumerated the various Storyville houses in detail, to the extent of describing the "beautiful girls" within.

RAGTIME JAZZ BANDS

If a pleasure palace did not support an entire orchestra, it maintained, at the least, a piano player from evening to dawn. An entry in the New Orleans *Daily Picayune* of March 25, 1913, informs us that

the Tuxedo, a model of the dance halls which make up a good part of the Tenderloin, occupies a berth on North Franklin. . . . Here a Negro band holds forth and from about 8 o'clock at night until 4 o'clock in the morning plays varied rags, conspicuous for being the latest in popular music, interspersed with compositions by the musicians themselves. The band has a leader who grotesquely prompts the various pieces, which generally constitute several brass pieces, a violin, guitar, piccolo, and a piano.[55]

Even without sound recordings, we can reconstruct the music of these ragtime bands with a fair degree of accuracy, for ragtime orchestrations are extant from this period. Also, photographs of some of the early bands show us the precise instrumentation of the performing ensembles. A photograph of the Superior Orchestra, a dance ensemble active from 1910 to 1913, reveals cornet, clarinet, trombone, violin, guitar, string bass, and drums (one player for snare and bass).[56] A photograph of the Imperial Band from the same period shows exactly the same instrumentation.[57] The Onward Brass Band, pictured about 1913, has twelve members: clarinet, three cornets, two horns, baritone, two trombones, bass, snare drum, and bass drum.[58] All of these groups had only black or Creole musicians, but white musicians did play in the area at the same time. The all-white Reliance Brass Band, photographed in 1910 before the "Big Show" tent of Laine's Greater Majestic Minstrels that was pitched behind a car barn at Canal and White Streets, is pictured with a group of seven musicians: clarinet, cornet, trombone, baritone, bass, snare drum, and bass drum and cymbal.[59] The pictures, written reports, and notated music all help explain the relationship of ragtime to early hot jazz. For example, *Knock Out Drops Rag*, by F. Henri Klickmann, arranged by the famous bandmaster Harry L. Alford, could have been purchased and adapted to the various musical combinations present in New Orleans and elsewhere at that time. In this typical four-strain rag with introduction, Alford assigned the ragged melody to the solo cornet most of the time, worked a counter melody into the baritone part (a common practice in many marches), and left the oom-pah of the ragtime pianist's left hand to the bass and horns. The performance direction for the second strain of the trio is "Noisy," as New Orleans jazz was, and these rags were the newest, most modern thing at that time.

Many of the musicians who later acquired fame as recording jazz stars belonged to these ensembles: Jimmy Noone, John Lindsay, and Johnny St. Cyr played in Oscar "Papa" Celestin's Tuxedo Band; Willie "Bunk" Johnson played for the original Superior Orchestra; and Alcide "Yellow" Nunez, of the Original Dixieland Jazz Band, was a member of the Reliance Brass Band. White musicians were in the minority, but they occupied a significant place

[55] Quoted in Samuel B. Charters, *Jazz: New Orleans 1885–1963*, p. 17.

[56] Orin Keepnews and Bill Grauer, Jr., *A Pictorial History of Jazz* (New York: Crown, 1955), p. 7.

[57] Ibid.

[58] Al Rose and Edmond Souchon, *New Orleans Jazz: A Family Album*, p. 193.

[59] Ibid., p. 185.

KNOCK OUT DROPS

Rag
A Trombone Jag

F HENRI KLICKMANN
Arr. by Harry L. Alford.

Solo B♭ Cornet.

Knock Out Drops Rag: Trio, Second Strain

in the musical picture of those early days. Jack "Papa" Laine, sometimes described as the "Father of White Jazz," was a disciple of Buddy Bolden and formed successful bands of his own in New Orleans. His Reliance Brass Band was eventually renamed Jack Laine's Ragtime Band.

Another important white musician from New Orleans was Tom Brown, a trombonist who was the first to bring a Dixieland band to Chicago in 1915. A hot jazz group, the Louisiana Five, led by Alcide "Yellow" Nunez, played at Bustanoby's Restaurant in New York in 1915, and although he missed out on the first recording sessions with the Original Dixieland Jazz Band, he was later to become a member of the group.

The music of this era included many novelty tunes, and not only were non-standard instruments such as jugs and homemade horns used, but new ways of playing the old instruments were developed. Burt Kelly, leader of Frisco's Jazz Band, reported in a newspaper interview of 1919 that Ray Lopez was the first cornet player to use a derby mute and Tom Brown the first trombonist to use a hat over his bell.

Most of the influential early jazz musicians were black, and they came from a community that has been called "Bourbon Street Black." Within the larger black community there was

> a semi-community in New Orleans of musicians, their relatives, peers, friends, and general supporters whose style of life is built around the fundamental assumption that the production and nurture of music for people, in general, is good.[60]

From 1897 to 1917, members of this community filled the major houses of Storyville with music. In the early 1910s, the Eagle Band was at Globe Hall, Celestin was at the Tuxedo, Perez was at Rice's, King Oliver was at Huntz's. Freddie Keppard, Bunk Johnson, and others worked the remainder of the houses. Outside the district, the musicians played for society dances, parades, and funerals. The Excelsior and Onward were probably the best brass bands in the city, but Papa Celestin's Tuxedo Brass Band, by playing the more up-to-date music, began taking jobs away from the older bands.

THOUGHTS ON THE HISTORY OF JAZZ

No definitive history of jazz before the years labeled by F. Scott Fitzgerald as "The Jazz Age" will ever be written. The primary source material is lacking, and the existing documentation, although copious, is spotty and often

[60] J. V. Buerkle and D. Barker, *Bourbon Street Black*, p. 41.

contradictory. Still, there is no question that Americans living in the years before the First World War heard an exciting new music played by some of the most creative musicians America has ever produced. Although we lack sound recordings, we are beginning to acquire a new wealth of historical information that is just as stimulating, albeit in a different way. The recent interest in music of black Americans has stimulated research and uncovered gold mines of historical evidence that is available and accessible and is, to a large degree, presented in a language understandable by modern Americans. Until very recently, some of the jazz pioneers were still alive, and oral evidence concerning most of the important historical events has been obtained from many people who observed and participated in the events themselves. As a result, we know a great deal about what we cannot hear.

Jazz was not the only style to emerge just before World War I; the music of Schoenberg, Bartók, and Stravinsky was in its formative stages too. But jazz was the American music of the early twentieth century, the product of a democracy, the work of a group of talented, predominantly black, obscure American musicians. It was a collective effort, just as collective improvisation was its principal feature.

The chief documents of its history were still to be produced, but the infant recording business was growing in tandem with the infant music. It was not until 1909 that popular songs were recorded. The first of these, made on cylinders, proved impractical. Columbia and Edison were the pioneers, and they were joined in 1901 by Victor. The 78-rpm record developed in these early years was used, with some improvements, until about 1950. The significance of the role played by sound recording in the development of jazz cannot be emphasized too strongly. Records provided improvising jazz musicians a means by which they could sell their product to a widespread audience. The ragtime composer had access to the printing industry, but jazz musicians, whose only product were the performances themselves, could reach only those people with whom they came in personal contact. Records provided not only an avenue to employment, but, more important, a forum for the exchange of musical ideas among professionals.

Radio became available to the general public only on a limited scale in 1922, and the first radios, crystal sets with earphones, allowed only one person to listen at a time. Broadcasting and recording developed hand in hand, and the first electrical records appeared in the mid-twenties, contemporaneously with the earliest radios. Before that date, the acoustical recording process was the only means of preserving sound on cylinder or disc. Until about 1925, the horn of the acoustical recorder collected sound waves, which vibrated a diaphragm attached mechanically to the stylus. To achieve any fidelity or volume at all, performers had to shout or produce instrumental sounds loudly and directly into the horn. Even a small, five-piece jazz group

In 1937, several of the members of the Original Dixieland Jazz Band recreated a 1917 recording session for the March of Time.

of cornet, clarinet, trombone, piano, and drums had enormous difficulty fitting into the open end of a horn, and one must take into account these restrictions when evaluating the performances themselves. Documentary recording, that is, recording live in the natural environment of the musicians, was not possible, and the music played for the early records had to be modified from an all-night brothel performance to a three-minute studio session. In turn, the new format began to reshape the music itself, for economics dictated that a good three-minute performance on a best-selling record was "better" than a ten-minute improvisation at a local engagement. Not until the advent of the long-playing record after World War II was it possible to record a typical jazz performance and play it back in one continuous, uninterrupted sitting. The existence of any musical spontaneity at all in the early recordings is remarkable; it is also a credit to the dedication and talent of the musicians.

When black blues singer Mamie Smith recorded *That Thing Called Love* and *You Can't Keep a Good Man Down* in 1920 for the OKeh Record Company,[61] the instantaneous success of this record led other companies to rush into the market. Pace Phonograph Corporation, later renamed the Black Swan Phonograph Company, was the first black recording company to open its doors in 1921, and before the end of the decade the term "race record" was

[61] OKeh 4113.

coined by the industry to designate black music. Advertising and distribution of race records was primarily aimed toward a black market, and although whites had access to these recordings, segregationist practice fostered a performance style so rooted in the black tradition that it was virtually inaccessible to large numbers of middle-class white Americans. Thus, we can see that both the technology and the commercial interests of the recording industry affected the music itself and served as important dynamic forces in shaping its destiny.

Another influence made its appearance at about this time, although with much less force than either radio or recording: the infant film industry. In 1925, Columbia and Victor began producing electrical recordings; 1926 saw NBC Radio, the first nationwide network, enter into the scene; and 1927 marked the production of the first talking picture, *The Jazz Singer*, featuring Al Jolson. The dissemination of jazz before World War I was widespread—we have seen that blues singers, vaudeville musicians, minstrel shows, ragtime pianists, and jazz musicians circulated freely throughout the United States. The First World War expanded the boundaries to Europe and permitted a musical infiltration of American sounds into the Continental culture at a more intense rate. Sound recordings acted as an additional catalyst, and electrical recordings and radio further stimulated an eager market.

Not until 1947 were there any new technological breakthroughs in the recording industry. The shellac, ten-inch, 78-rpm disc recorded by electrical means was the standard medium for jazz from the mid-twenties to the mid-forties. Consequently there were accepted limits within which the music operated, developed, and flourished. Although live performance between the First and Second World Wars was far more important than broadcast or recorded performance in terms of what actually was happening in America, the history of jazz has largely become the history of jazz recording. Again, since jazz is primarily a performer's art, recordings became the sole means of preserving the music. Consequently, our historical investigation from this point forward will be devoted almost entirely to analyzing and understanding the significant and representative recordings that document the progress of the art.

THE JAZZ AGE—
FROM WORLD WAR I
THROUGH THE
ROARING TWENTIES

JAZZ AND MORALITY

The Victorian, pro-prohibition majority of white Americans automatically associated the music played by New Orleans musicians with the lifestyles they led, so in spite of its immediate popularity, jazz was met by impassioned opposition. Just as Storyville had its public, it also had its enemies, and there is no question that the business of prostitution also brought with it drug addiction, alcoholism, venereal disease, gambling, and the syndicate. Jazz became the symbol of crime, feeble-mindedness, insanity, and sex, and was subjected to constant attack by the press from the early 1920s on. It was seen as a symptom of general cultural decay. Karl Engel, writing in the *Atlantic Monthly*, urged his readers not to become alarmed because "almost every race and every age have known social conditions which result in an unloosing of instincts that nature wisely has taught us to hold well in check, but which, every now and then, from cryptic reasons, are allowed to break the bonds of civilization."[1] *The New York Times* ran an article in April 1922:

> Musician is Driven to Suicide by Jazz;
> Wouldn't Play It, Couldn't Get Employment

[1] "Jazz: A Musical Discussion," *Atlantic Monthly*, 130 (August 1922), p. 182.

His fellow-lodgers at 124 East Thirty-first Street said yesterday that jazz was responsible for the death of Melville M. Wilson. . . . Then came jazz. The old man revolted. He wouldn't insult his 'cello, he said, nor the old melodies he had played so long and loved so well. . . . Jazz was everywhere and no one seemed to have any use for Wilson and his cello.[2]

The 1916 election campaign that preceded the closing of Storyville included a major push by the "drys" to secure legislation prohibiting the sale and advertisement of liquor. At that time there were nineteen prohibition states. Jazz, along with ragtime, which seemed to be an accessory of whorehouses and saloons, was spreading across the country at the same time that the Puritan tradition in the form of prohibition was moving toward its moment of triumph. While women were campaigning for prohibition and the vote, jazz was extolling fun, excitement, and the pleasures of youth.

> *Beer is bad,*
> *Whisky's worse;*
> *We drink water—*
> *Safety first.*
>
> *We can't vote,*
> *Neither can Ma.*
> *If Nebraska goes wet—*
> *Blame it on Pa.*[3]

One commentator has noted:

The degree to which jazz served as a symbol of culturally defined evil in the United States, and in other countries as well, may seem incredible to us today, but it was a real fact in the 1920's and 1930's. It is an extremely clear illustration of how music, and in this case not individual sounds but an entire body of sound, can be used symbolically on the level of affective ascribed cultural meaning.[4]

Jazz was, and is, a powerful cultural force, and it is ironic that we preserve, study, and enjoy a music today that was felt to be insidious and lascivious only yesterday.

Following the successful conclusion of the First World War, girls' skirts

[2] *New York Times,* April 7, 1922, section 1, page 1.
[3] *Nebraska Campaign Songs* (Lincoln: Nebraska Dry Federation, 1916), p. 14.
[4] Alan P. Merriam, *The Anthropology of Music* (Evanston: Northwestern University Press, 1964), p. 244.

moved high above the knees, women were seen smoking and drinking in public, and sex became an acceptable topic for discussion. Those who were incapable of coping with the rapid changes they saw taking place around them turned on dancing and the music that accompanied it, declaring the music not merely a symptom but a cause of moral decay. Another newspaper article ran:

Jazz Ruining Girls, Declare Reformers

Chicago, Jan. 21—Moral disaster is coming to hundreds of young American girls through the pathological, nerve-irritating, sex-exciting music of jazz orchestras, according to the Illinois Vigilance Association.

In Chicago alone the association's representatives have traced the fall of 1,000 girls in the last two years to jazz music.

Girls in small towns, as well as the big cities, in poor homes and rich homes, are victims of the weird, insidious, neurotic music that accompanies modern dancing.

The degrading music is common not only to disorderly places, but often to high school affairs, to expensive hotels and so-called society circles.[5]

The teens and twenties of this century were without question a time of ferment in the United States. The First World War, prohibition, the closing of Storyville, and the invention of sound recording were all elements that had a profound effect on the development of the new music. World War I brought American popular music, including jazz, to Europe. It had lured thousands of young American men away from home and placed them in an environment that made them receptive to jazz and all its implications. When the war and prohibition served as an excuse to close Storyville, the criminal syndicates opened similar establishments elsewhere, most notably, of course, in Chicago. The riverboats had already carried Dixieland jazz to St. Louis and Kansas City, and when New Orleans musicians were left without any place to play, they began a further exodus to New York and Chicago.

But even before the first recording, several musicians had achieved prominence as leading jazz performers, and several numbers of what was to become the standard repertoire had already been developed. *Tiger Rag* and *Oh Didn't He Ramble* were played long before the first jazz recording, and the names of Buddy Bolden, Jelly Roll Morton, Bunk Johnson, Papa Celestin, Sidney Bechet, King Oliver, Freddie Keppard, Kid Ory, and Papa Laine were already well known to the jazz community.

[5] *New York American*, June 22, 1922.

BUNK JOHNSON, PAPA CELESTIN, AND SIDNEY BECHET

Willie Geary "Bunk" Johnson was a leading figure in the days of early Dixieland jazz in New Orleans. His association with Buddy Bolden in the earliest period of New Orleans jazz was the turning point in his musical career. He achieved more recognition among his fellow musicians than he did from the listening public, for his playing did not resemble that of the popular Bolden, Keppard, and Oliver. He was acknowledged for his ability to swing a band in a conservative, restrained manner. Born in 1879, he began playing second cornet in Bolden's band as a teenager. He has recounted this experience:

> Here is the thing that made King Bolden's Band be the first band that played jazz. It was because it did not Read at all. I could fake like 500 myself; so you tell them that Bunk and King Bolden's Band was the first ones that started jazz in the City or any place else.[6]

He played with other bands during this period, including the Excelsior, and traveled to New York City in 1903 with a minstrel show, Holecamp's Georgia Smart Set. He traveled to Dallas and San Francisco, and returned to New Orleans in 1910 to join the Superior Orchestra. Between 1911 and 1914, Johnson, with Sidney Bechet, was a member of Frankie Dusen's Eagle Band, playing and marching at the many occasions that called for music. He left New Orleans permanently in 1914 and worked on and off with innumerable vaudeville, minstrel-show, and club bands. He was with Evan Thomas's Black Eagle Band in Crowley, Louisiana, when the leader was murdered on the bandstand and Johnson's horn was destroyed in a fight. Johnson worked less and less as a musician in the ensuing years. When he was rediscovered in 1937, he was hauling sugarcane in the fields. The remainder of his musical life is a part of the New Orleans revival (NW 235, I/7), but his work is mentioned here because of its significance in the years before recording.

Johnson serves as a useful example of both the problems and the blessings that surface when one tries to reconstruct history on the basis of information supplied by "knowledgeable" informants. Although Bunk Johnson, without doubt, was a performing musician in New Orleans during the early years of

---

[6] Quoted by Rex Harris, *Jazz*, p. 82.

William Geary "Bunk" Johnson (1879–1949).

this century, much of the information he furnished about early jazz is questionable. For example, it would seem that he, better than anyone else, could settle the question of which of Buddy Bolden's bands he played in. However, we still do not know whether he played in the Olympia Band or in one of the others that Bolden was leading at the same time. Johnson claimed to have been Louis Armstrong's teacher and influence, but Armstrong denied this, saying King Oliver was his only teacher and that he merely admired Johnson's tone. Just as Jelly Roll Morton once claimed to have "invented" jazz, Johnson also claimed a thing or two that has been contradicted by his contemporaries. As a spokesman for early jazz, he did, however, provide us with some insights into the music from the viewpoint of a Dixieland jazz musician.

Johnson was, without doubt, a fundamental participant in the history of early jazz. His relationships with Buddy Bolden and Frankie Dusen's Eagle Band were intertwined with the roots of Dixieland improvisation. Although he remained unrecognized in the annals of jazz until after the New Orleans revival around 1942, it was evident even at such a late stage in life that he was a jazz musician of high calibre. His style and attitudes toward jazz seem more representative than unique, and he acted as a leading figure in the reconstruction of traditional jazz.

A popular bandleader in New Orleans for forty-four years, Oscar "Papa" Celestin formed the Original Tuxedo Orchestra in 1910 and the Tuxedo Brass Band in 1911. For most of his career, Celestin was one of the most popular musicians in the city, and to a certain degree, he owed his success to his colorful mannerisms rather than to any extraordinary musical abilities. He was a strong cornet player and is usually regarded as a pioneer jazz musician. He was not a good reading musician, and often used a second cornet player to handle the hot solos. Born in Napoleonville, Louisiana, in 1884, he moved to New Orleans in 1906. His orchestra opened the Tuxedo Dance Hall in Storyville in 1910, and after a gun fight at the Tuxedo Bar in 1913 during which five men were shot to death, he and his orchestra were out of work. In New Orleans, he worked with many of the leading musicians, including Clarence Williams, A. J. Piron, Jimmy Noone, Johnny St. Cyr, Peter Bocage, and Louis Armstrong. He recorded for OKeh in 1925,[7] and unlike the Armstrong recordings from the same period, the performances are noted more for their polish in ensemble than for exciting improvisational flights. His recording group, which he still called Celestin's Original Tuxedo Jazz Orchestra, included one or two trumpets, a trombone, two or three reeds, piano, banjo, bass, and drums. During his last years, Celestin was honored as one of the greats of New Orleans music. He died in 1954, and four thousand people marched in his funeral procession.

Sidney Bechet, the first jazz performer to achieve fame on the soprano saxophone, was active in Paris as a professional for almost as many years as Papa Celestin played in New Orleans. Born in New Orleans in 1897, he played clarinet and was introduced to the famous Eagle Band of New Orleans by Bunk Johnson around 1912. He left the Crescent City in 1914, touring with Clarence Williams and Louis Wade, and returned in 1916, when he worked with King Oliver's Olympia Band. In 1917 he traveled to Chicago and two years later moved to New York, where he joined Will Marion Cook's Southern Syncopated Orchestra. This organization took him to Europe, where Bechet became the first jazz musician to receive serious consideration by a distinguished classical musician when Ernest Ansermet became interested in Cook's orchestra and Bechet's playing. Bechet remained in Europe, primarily in Paris, until 1921, when he returned to New York City and made his first records with Clarence Williams's Blue Five. It was here that he

[7]OKeh 8215, reissued Columbia C3L-30.

A photograph taken in 1918 of Sidney Bechet (1897–1959).

played sessions with Mamie Smith and other blues singers, and worked briefly, during 1924, with Duke Ellington. For the next fifteen years, he worked in Europe and America with various artists, including Noble Sissle, Tommy Ladnier, and Willie "The Lion" Smith. He returned to jobbing in New York and appeared with Eddie Condon in many Town Hall concerts in the early 1940s (*SCCJ* 12). After shuttling back and forth between Europe and America from the late 1940s on, he died in Paris in May of 1959.

Bechet's solo work in *Texas Moaner Blues*,[8] recorded with Clarence Williams and Louis Armstrong in 1924, exhibits most of the characteristics associated with his playing throughout the years: a facile and liquid technique, a melodic line heavily shaded by blue notes and blues intonation, and a large and rapid vibrato. Bechet thought of his instrument as a medium by which he might dramatize and communicate his own personal feelings to sensitive listeners. As a result, his recorded solo work is generally considered in extra-musical terms as dignified, empathic, and so on. On a purely musical level, his solos have great structural integrity. Decorated with an occasional virtuosic flight, musical ideas proceed with logic and rational order. His thirty-two-measure solo on *I've Found a New Baby*,[9] recorded in 1932 with Tommy Ladnier, is a classic example of developmental technique in jazz improvisation. The first of the four phrases states a musical idea of a descending melodic motive. Each of the following three phrases amplifies the same idea, the last phrase stating it most clearly and rounding it off with a melodic turning figure that provides a passageway to the next solo.

Bechet achieved great public success in France, not only for his musical powers, but also for his position as a vaudeville figure, an entertainer, and a personality. Because of his self-imposed expatriation, he had less influence on the course of American jazz than he would probably have had, had he remained in America to pursue his musical career. His style and sound were highly personal and seemed to have inspired few followers. Still, he won the respect of leading jazz musicians and must be counted as one of the important personalities of early jazz. Perhaps more than any other single figure, Bechet was responsible for introducing jazz elements into French classical composition of the early twentieth century.

THE NEW ORLEANS SOUND

The musical characteristics of jazz before 1917 will always remain something of a mystery, but descriptions of the early sound based on photographic evidence, verbal recounting, notated music, and the earliest sound recordings

[8] OKeh 8171, reissued Columbia C3L-30.
[9] RCA Victor LPV-535.

have considerable value, even if they are not one-hundred percent correct. Some suppositions, however, may be safely made. The tempo of early jazz probably ranged between moderate and moderately fast. With the possible exception of early piano players, instrumental virtuosity does not seem to have been highly developed by 1917. Still, liveliness and excitement are the feelings most commonly expressed about the music by people who first encountered jazz.

Whether early New Orleans jazz was two-beat, four-beat, or a mixture is an unsettled question. The New Orleans revival of the 1940s would have one believe that true New Orleans jazz was two-beat, and the four-beat rhythm section was a result of Chicago and swing. Still, the majority of the earliest recordings exhibit an insistent strumming pattern of guitar or banjo. Beneath the four-beat chording of the banjo, the drums most often seem to play four-beat with the sticks and two-beat with the pedal. The same mixed performance occurs with ensemble piano playing. Sometimes the left and right hands alternate beats, but just as often the left hand plays either a walking-bass pattern or a boogie-woogie configuration. The dances that developed in conjunction with early jazz do not help, for their performance is equally successful in two-beat and four-beat subdivisions. (We might note here that the instrumental breaks in many of the early pieces corresponded to dancers' trick steps.) In general, it is safe to say that early jazz displayed a democratization of the rhythm-section activity, that is, it brought the weak beats up to the level of the strong beats.

The front line of the various ensembles created a rhythmic layer of syncopation, polyrhythms, cross rhythms, and call-and-response patterns. The static insistence of the rhythm section was balanced by the flexibility and unpredictability of the front line. Unison playing in early jazz was totally absent. On occasion, when a band accompanied a singer, the cornet wove a countermelody. But two instruments in unison are unheard of in classic jazz. On some of the early recordings, two or three instruments play in harmony; however, this seems to be a later development resulting from the influence of the society bands of New York and Chicago. Individual responsibility within the front line is the norm in classic jazz.

The repertoire of early jazz consists of a collection of thirty-two-measure, four-phrase, **AABA** popular-song-form tunes; four-strain, two-key, ragtime tunes; and twelve-measure instrumental blues. The harmonic rhythm of the ragtime pieces tends to move more quickly than it does in the other two categories. The harmonic rhythm of the blues, by definition, moves most slowly; and in compensation, the solo lines of blues pieces tend to have more inflections, a greater variety of attacks, and more pitch variation. Of course there are exceptions, and many songs of the early repertoire have the word "blues" in their title although they were clearly in popular-song or some

The New Orleans Rhythm Masters in 1926. (Front row, left to right) Jack Teagarden, trombone; Red Bolman, trumpet; Sidney Arodin, clarinet; Charlie Cordilla, sax and clarinet; Amos Ayala, drums. (Back row, left to right) Terry Shand, piano; George Shaw, vocals; Jerry Fresno, bass.

other related form. By and large, the word "blues," as we have already seen, was just as likely to denote an emotional state as a form.

The instrumentation of the early ensembles tends to call for an average of eight players. This means that the accepted stereotype of the New Orleans jazz ensemble was in fact usually augmented by two instruments. Sometimes an extra cornet and extra rhythm-section instrument are added; sometimes a violin is used as a lead instrument in the ensemble. The orchestras of Armand J. Piron (1888–1943) and Peter Bocage (1887–1967) were important early jazz groups that featured the violin as a lead instrument.

Another characteristic of early New Orleans jazz, and perhaps its most important, is group improvisation. The members improvise in ensembles, not merely as soloists. The spontaneous give and take of all participants in the ensemble, limited only by a framework of chord progressions, was a new sound instantly recognizable to any listener in the early years of the twentieth century as the music called "jazz." In a sense, this feature was at the heart of all the other musical characteristics attributed to early classic jazz. One of the most fascinating aspects of group improvisation is that the members of an ensemble both compete and collaborate, both respect and ignore the limits imposed upon them, one and all.

KING OLIVER, KID ORY, AND FRIENDS

A bandleader of great significance was Joseph "King" Oliver (1885–1938), cornet player, mentor of Louis Armstrong, and musical director of the Creole Jazz Band, the finest jazz ensemble of its day. The group included the best black jazz musicians in the business: Johnny and Baby Dodds, Jimmy Noone, Lil Hardin, Kid Ory, Barney Bigard, Honoré Dutrey, and Louis Armstrong. In spite of the fame and popularity he achieved during his peak years of 1915 to 1928, Oliver was found to be near starvation just before his death in 1938. Born on a plantation near Abend, Louisiana, in 1885, he was blinded in one eye as a child. He began playing with the Melrose Brass Band in 1907 and

King Oliver's Creole Jazz Band (1923). (Left to right) Honoré Dutrey, trombone; Baby Dodds, drums; King Oliver, cornet; Louis Armstrong, slide trumpet; Lil Hardin (later Armstrong), piano; Bill Johnson, banjo; Johnny Dodds, clarinet.

the Olympia Band in 1912. He formed his own band at the "25" cabaret with Sidney Bechet and Peter Bocage as sidemen. It is reported that Oliver played seated in a chair that leaned against the wall, a derby tilted over one eye to hide a scar. He is also reported to have been the first cornet player to play with mutes, cups, and bottles, and brought to jazz a polished, collectively improvising ensemble. He moved to Chicago in 1918 and sent for Louis Armstrong in 1922. His series of recordings made in 1923 represents the state of the art of black jazz to that date (see pages 85–87, *SCCJ* 6).

One of Oliver's sidemen was a bandleader in his own right. Kid Ory was the most famous of the New Orleans tailgate trombone players and seems to have been the trombonist who first used the instrument consistently for fills, glissandi, rhythmic effects, and the other jazz devices. Although King Oliver's Creole Jazz Band was the first black ensemble to record a series of jazz pieces—forty-two numbers in 1923 alone—Kid Ory cut the first records ever made by a black New Orleans band. The 1922 recordings of Kid Ory's Sunshine Orchestra, although less musically interesting than the series produced by King Oliver's group, is of historical moment, for it marks the beginning of the recorded black jazz tradition (*NW* 269, I/7 and 8).

Edward "Kid" Ory was born in La Place, Louisiana, in 1886[10] and organized his own four-piece skiffle band[11] as a youngster. He brought his own band to New Orleans in 1913 and led one group or another until he left the city permanently in 1919. His sidemen included some of the most notable musicians of New Orleans—Johnny Dodds, Jimmy Noone, King Oliver, and Louis Armstrong. He moved to Los Angeles in 1919, then to Chicago, where he joined King Oliver's Dixie Syncopators in 1924. His recorded performances of 1926–27 with King Oliver display a limited repertoire and technique on his solo improvisations, but as the harmonic and rhythmic instrument of the front line, his playing is the epitome of the New Orleans tailgate-trombone style. Ory later worked with Louis's Hot Five and returned to Los Angeles in 1929. He retired from music during the thirties, but gradually began working again in the forties when the New Orleans revival resurrected the old music. His own composition, *Muskrat Ramble*,[12] which he originally recorded with Louis Armstrong in 1926, was set to words in 1954 and became very popular. He remained musically active on the West Coast, appearing in movies, at Disneyland, and on television. His second recording career, beginning in the 1940s, grew to sizable proportions in the 1950s.

[10] Al Rose and Edmond Souchon, *New Orleans Jazz*, p. 94, and Leonard Feather, *The New Edition of the Encyclopedia of Jazz*, p. 373, cite 1886 as Ory's birth date. Samuel Charters, *Jazz: New Orleans*, p. 43, cites 1889.

[11] A skiffle band is a novelty orchestra that depends largely on showmanship, slapstick, and extramusical effects for audience appeal.

[12] Also known as *Muskat Ramble*.

Edward "Kid" Ory's Original Creole Jazz Band, c. 1922, probably in San Francisco or Oakland, California. (Left to right) Baby Dodds, Ory, "Mutt" Carey, Ed Garland, and Wade Whaley.

It is unfortunate that many of the fabulous New Orleans musicians either never recorded at all or did so when they were past their primes. Another legendary cornet player from New Orleans was Freddie Keppard. "King" or "Whalemouth" Keppard was born in New Orleans in 1889 and acquired a reputation as a performer of extraordinary power. Power seems to be a recurrent theme in the descriptions of the early New Orleans brass players and jazz ensembles, so we must assume that under normal conditions these groups played very loudly. His reputation stems from the period before the First World War, but, since he was an alcoholic, the recorded evidence of his work from his Chicago days in the mid-twenties suggests, but does not demonstrate, that his playing was aggressive and exciting. He died from alcoholism in Chicago in 1933.

Only six black bands were recorded in New Orleans during the twenties—Davey Jones and Lee Collins's Astoria Hot Eight, Sam Morgan's Jazz Band (*NW* 269, II/1 and 2), Armand Piron's New Orleans Orchestra (*NW* 269, II/3), Oscar "Papa" Celestin's Original Tuxedo Jazz Orchestra, Fate

Marable's Society Syncopators, and Louis Dumaine's Jazzola Eight—but these recordings, of poor quality and late date, probably present a distorted picture of the sound of the earlier days. The other New Orleans bands recorded in other cities where outside influences left their mark on the musicians as soon as they arrived. The reconstructed sound of New Orleans during this crucial period is at best fragmentary, and may at the very worst misrepresent what actually took place.

THE ORIGINAL DIXIELAND JAZZ BAND

White musicians unquestionably played a role in the development of jazz in New Orleans before the advent of recording. When Nick La Rocca brought his white New Orleans musicians to New York and recorded in January of 1917, they displayed a fully developed Dixieland style, a Dixieland repertoire, and all the musical characteristics necessary to satisfy the contention that they were the first musicians to record in the idiom. La Rocca's claim to have been the founder of jazz has as much truth in it as Jelly Roll Morton's claim to have been the inventor of jazz, but due honor should attend La Rocca as the primogenitor of jazz recording.

Dominic J. "Nick" La Rocca was a white, left-handed cornet player born in New Orleans in 1889. He first played with Papa Laine and later formed the Original Dixieland Jazz Band, which he took to New York during World War I. The band remained active until 1925, and their early recordings display ensemble work of the highest quality in the Dixieland idiom. The band did not boast outstanding soloists, but La Rocca played a clear, precise lead. Larry Shields, the clarinetist, commanded a smooth technique and liquid sound, and Eddie Edwards, the trombonist, played rhythmically, in tune, and with the ornamental grace of a skilled tailgate trombonist. The repertoire of the ODJB consisted of ragtime and early dance music played in the jazz idiom. Still, their performances were convincing and authentic, and the criticism leveled against their animal-sound performance of *Livery Stable Blues* is unfair—all the bands, including the black ensembles, employed a variety of squeaks and squawks derived from the skiffle bands and their repertoire. In fact, Freddie Keppard had a reputation for earning tips by neighing like a horse with his trumpet. The flip side of the record, *Dixie Jass Band One-Step*,[13] is an original composition that is still performed today by musicians who keep the old style alive.

---

[13] Victor 18255. Some copies are labeled with the piece's better known and more frequently used name, *Dixieland Jass Band One-Step*.

The Original Dixieland Jazz Band in London, c. 1920. (Left to right) Anthony Sbarbaro (Spargo), drums; Emile Christian, trombone; Dominic James "Nick" La Rocca, cornet; Larry Shields, clarinet; and Billy Jones, piano.

The group's ensemble performance of *At the Darktown Strutters' Ball*,[14] recorded at a single session in January 1917, is excellent in every way. The rhythm section's steady beat is overlaid with the three lines of the lead instruments. The group swings along nicely as the members fill the spaces according to their individual functions. Had the personnel roster included a great soloist or two, this recording would be a monument on musical as well as historical grounds. Strangely enough, the polish of the ODJB's performances is frequently criticized by purists who insist that "the tone quality is considerably more pure—more of a 'white' tone—than vocal in the Negroid way."[15] Some of the criticism may derive more from a preference for black ensembles than from an objective evaluation of the performance itself. The following statement, written by an eminent historian of ragtime and early jazz, is simply not consistent with the recorded facts:

> While the playing of the Original Dixieland Jazz Band does not equal the fine
> Negro playing of classic jazz, or even that of the more average bands, like Sam

[14]Columbia 2297, reissued Columbia C3L-30.
[15]Rudi Blesh, *Shining Trumpets*, p. 211.

Morgan's Jazz Band, or Louis Dumaine's Jazzola Eight, it must be considered a form of jazz. With all its faults of rhythm, tone, and polyphony, it is fairly well integrated and had much more variety in actual performance than it shows on its records. Only one of these men, Larry Shields, was an outstanding musician. Edwards was a good, but by no means a great player. La Rocca was merely adequate as were the others, although Ragas may have been a good ragtime player.[16]

While outstanding solo playing may be lacking, the group's rhythm, tone, and polyphony are not. Their sound was exciting to their contemporaries, it was enthusiastically accepted by the public at its first introduction, and it influenced other important jazz musicians, most notably, Bix Beiderbecke.

In 1936 La Rocca reformed the Original Dixieland Jazz Band and re-recorded some of his earlier hits. He continued in music primarily as an avocation from 1938 until 1958, when he retired from the building business and devoted his time to writing songs. He died in New Orleans in 1961 after donating his memorabilia to the archives at Tulane University. La Rocca never moved into the limelight as a leading jazz musician. Had he not been the first to record jazz, he may have been totally forgotten among the thousands of names that passed unnoted through the history of jazz.

JELLY ROLL MORTON

The fame of Jelly Roll Morton is primarily a story of the 1920s, but his participation in jazz and contributions to it in the first decades of this century are both large and important. Ferdinand Joseph Lamothe "Jelly Roll" Morton was the best, if not the first, of the classic-jazz pianists. In his playing he merged the elements of ragtime, blues, and brass-band music. His style of playing is orchestral in concept, ragtime-centered in form and harmonies, and blues-based in its melodic lines and crush dissonances. Born in 1890, he was a second liner before the turn of the century and digested the sounds of the brass bands as they paraded the streets of New Orleans. He played with Bunk Johnson and Jim Packer at Frankie Spano's in the early 1900s, and continued as a Storyville "Professor" until he left town permanently in 1907. Despite the voluminous documentation we have about his life, the result of hours of interviews recorded by Alan Lomax at the Library of Congress in 1938, it is difficult to piece together an account of his career before 1922, when he settled for a while in Chicago. Bunk Johnson recalls seeing him in Gulfport, Mississippi, around 1903 and 1904; James P. Johnson remembers

[16]Blesh, *Shining Trumpets*, p. 212.

Jelly Roll Morton's Red Hot Peppers, Chicago, 1926. (Left to right) Andrew Hilaire, drums; Kid Ory, trombone; George Mitchell, trumpet; John Lindsay, bass; Jelly Roll Morton, piano; Johnny St. Cyr, banjo; Omer Simeon, clarinet.

him in New York in 1911; Reb Spikes, Morton's publisher, met him in Tulsa, Oklahoma, in 1912; he is known to have joined a touring show in Memphis, Tennessee, around 1909; and between that time and 1915, when he went to San Francisco to appear at the Exposition, he worked in St. Louis, Kansas City, and Chicago. He returned to Chicago later that year and played a solo-piano engagement at the Fairfax Hotel in Detroit. He came back to California around 1917, and by the time he went to Chicago again in 1923, where he recorded with the New Orleans Rhythm Kings, he had made appearances in Alaska, Wyoming, Colorado, Mexico, and California.

The activities of his life are as varied as his travels. He was not only a remarkable pianist, he was the first great jazz composer, a pool shark, a pimp, a comedian, and, according to himself, the "inventor of jazz." Many of his works have become jazz standards, and the dates he composed some of his works lend credence to his claim of having invented jazz and affirm his significance as a major jazz musician of the early years of the twentieth century.

A late photograph of Ferdinand Joseph Lamothe "Jelly Roll" Morton (1890–1941).

New Orleans Blues (1902 or 1903), *King Porter Stomp* (1905), *Jelly Roll Blues* (1905), and *Wolverines* (1906, renamed *Wolverine Blues* by a publisher)—these compositions bear the design and hallmark of ragtime compositions but display in performance (recorded as piano solos in 1923–24) jazz feel, blues phrasing, and virtuosic improvisation. His recording of *Maple Leaf Rag* for Alan Lomax in 1938 (*SCCJ* 2) transforms another ragtime composition into a New Orleans-style jazz performance.

Morton claims credit for transforming a French quadrille that was performed in different meters into *Tiger Rag*,[17] but experts have proven that *Tiger Rag* was worked out by the Jack Carey Band, a group that developed many of the standard tunes that were recorded by the Original Dixieland Jazz Band.[18] The work was known as *Jack Carey* by the black musicians of the city and as *Nigger #2* by the white musicians. It was compiled when Jack's brother Thomas, "Papa Mutt," pulled the first strain from a book of quadrilles. The band evolved the second and third strains in order to show off the clarinetist, George Boyd, and the final strain ("Hold that tiger" section) was worked out by Jack, a trombonist, and the cornet player, Punch Miller.

The circumstances surrounding the composition (or compilation) of *Tiger Rag* and the checkered career and far-flung travels of Jelly Roll Morton serve to demonstrate that jazz had widespread currency in the public domain before the proliferation of sound recording. That New Orleans was a hotbed of activity, both musical and otherwise, goes without saying; but it would be foolhardy to suppose that Morton was not playing jazz in New York in 1911 or in California in 1915. Also, the existence of compositions like Morton's *Wolverine Blues* and Kid Ory's *Muskrat Ramble* undermines arguments that jazz is a performer's, and not a composer's, art. Admittedly, compositions incorrectly played do not represent any genre accurately, be it jazz or classical. To play ragtime, jazz, Debussy, or Beethoven correctly, one must know the performance tradition and acquire the necessary technical facility. Beyond that, great performances in any style require creativity, ability, dedication, and sincerity.

THE JAZZ EXPLOSION

Jazz began to achieve widespread popular recognition when the Original Dixieland Jazz Band made its debut in New York City at Reisenweber's Cabaret on the evening of January 26, 1917. They were in the right place at the right time, and their first jazz recordings, issued on Victor's popular lists, sold in the millions. All the musicians were from New Orleans, but three of

[17] Ibid., p. 191 ff.
[18] Charters, *Jazz: New Orleans*, p. 24.

the group, Nick La Rocca, Eddie Edwards, and Henry Ragas, were fresh from a visit to Chicago, where they had been playing with Stein's Dixie Jass Band at Schiller's Café. Their first recording sessions in January and February of 1917 produced *Dixieland Jass Band One-Step* / *Livery Stable Blues*[19] and *Darktown Strutters' Ball* / *Indiana*.[20] In the same year, W. C. Handy's Orchestra recorded *That Jazz Dance* / *Livery Stable Blues*,[21] but the front line of the musical onslaught was held by the members of the ODJB.

The *Dixieland Jass Band One-Step*, zinging along at 252 beats per minute, captivated the public by showing the band off at its best. The three men from Chicago, together with Larry Shields, clarinet, and Tony Sbarbaro, drums, formed a cooperative, profit-sharing organization, designating La Rocca as the musical leader. The *Dixieland Jass Band One-Step* (originally called *Mutt and Jeff*) is a work in the ragtime-jazz tradition in which two sixteen-measure themes are repeated before a modulation to a "trio" theme for a close. Through the veil of the acoustic recording, one can hear the noodling obbligato of Shield's clarinet floating high above the glissando-filled part of Daddy Edwards's tailgate trombone. The ensemble is tight, and the well-rehearsed group cut a ragged path through the grooves of the original jazz disc.

The *Livery Stable Blues*, which Nick La Rocca claimed to have composed by himself in 1912,[22] is more a novelty number than a jazz piece. It achieved immediate popularity and even became the subject of copyright litigation when Alcide "Yellow" Nunez, former clarinetist of the Original Dixieland Jazz Band, and Ray Lopez, a cornet player with Burt Kelly's Band, wrote out the music, published it in 1917, and credited themselves on the published copies with being members of the ODJB. Judge Carpenter, on October 12, 1917, found that neither the plaintiff nor the defendant was entitled to a copyright, stating that neither conceived the idea of the melody, and stating further that "no living human being could listen to that result on the phonograph and discover anything musical in it, although there is a wonderful rhythm, something which will carry you along, especially if you are young and a dancer."[23]

As the five members of the Original Dixieland Jazz Band were skyrocketing to success in 1917, Scott Joplin died unnoticed in the same city, for public taste had changed dramatically from ragtime to jazz. Storyville had closed that year, and some of the musicians began seeking work elsewhere.

[19] Victor 18253.

[20] Columbia A-2297.

[21] Columbia A-2419.

[22] George Brunies, trombonist, counters, "They were tunes originated by the Negro boys of New Orleans."

[23] H. O. Brunn, *The Story of the Original Dixieland Jazz Band*, p. 85.

Piron and Williams Orchestra, c. 1915. (Standing:) Jimmy Noone, William Ridgley, Oscar Celestin, John Lindsay; (seated:) Ernest (Ninesse) Trepagnier, A. J. Piron, Tom Benton (probably mandolin-banjo), John A. St. Cyr; (seated on floor:) Clarence Williams.

Armand Piron teamed up with Peter Bocage and began working at Tranchina's Restaurant at Spanish Fort on Lake Pontchartrain in 1918. A. J. Piron and His Novelty Orchestra, a Creole ensemble of trumpet, trombone, alto sax, clarinet and tenor sax, piano, banjo, drums, and violin, remained in New Orleans and played at Tranchina's from 1918 to 1928.[24] Jelly Roll Morton had left New Orleans, and although he traveled considerably from 1917 to 1922, he spent most of his time in California. Kid Ory worked actively in Los Angeles between 1919 and 1924. Sidney Bechet had already gone to Europe, and was playing in London in 1919 when Ernest Ansermet first heard him and admired his work. Alcide "Yellow" Nunez, who had played clarinet with members of the Original Dixieland Jazz Band in New Orleans and again in Chicago in 1916, chose to remain in the Windy City. After La Rocca, Edwards, and Ragas left for New York, he teamed up with four other musicians to form the Louisiana Five in 1919 and maintained the continuity of white Dixieland music in Chicago.[25] Although the Original Dixieland Jazz Band had stolen the limelight, New York jazz was continuously in session

---

[24] In 1923, this group recorded *Bouncing Around* and *West Indies Blues* (OKeh 40021 and Columbia 14007-D, reissued Columbia C3L-30).

[25] *I Ain't-en Got-en No Time to Have the Blues*, recorded in New York City in June 1919 (Columbia A-2775, reissued Columbia C3L-30).

through these years. James P. Johnson was fronting a band at the Clef Club at the end of World War I. After that, he played solo piano engagements and vaudeville shows, and made player-piano rolls for the Aeolian Company. Two years earlier, in 1915, Eubie Blake had joined forces with Noble Sissle to form a vaudeville team that lasted successfully for many years. They wrote musicals, and one of their lasting hits was *I'm Just Wild about Harry*.

Around 1917 in New Orleans, Joe Oliver began billing himself as "King." With the demise of Storyville, he moved to Chicago in 1918, working as a sideman until 1919, when he formed his own band. The year 1922 was the fateful one when Oliver sent for the young Louis Armstrong to play cornet in his band. The resulting Creole Jazz Band, led by King Oliver, was an inspirational force that began to reshape the tradition by blending in the latest Chicago jazz sounds.[26]

[26] *Aunt Hagar's Blues* by King Oliver's Dixie Syncopators, September 10, 1928 (MCA Records MCA 2-4061).

One of the bands proliferating in 1917 called itself the Original New Orleans Jazz Band when it played at the Alamo Cafe in New York City. Its members (left to right) were Johnny Stein, Achille Bacquet, Jimmy Durante, Frank Christian, and Frank L'Hotag.

Shortly before this, a group of white New Orleans musicians literally traveled the riverboat north and settled in Chicago. Tom Brown, a trombonist, was the first white musician to bring New Orleans jazz to Chicago. Stein's Dixie Jass Band with Nick La Rocca followed a year later. The New Orleans Rhythm Kings, NORK (*NW* 269, II/4), began playing at Friar's Inn as the Friar's Society Orchestra in 1921. Before that, during the summer of 1920, Paul Mares and George Brunies were playing a riverboat on the Mississippi. At Davenport, Iowa, they took on Leon Rappolo, a clarinetist, who introduced them to a young local cornet player, Bix Beiderbecke. The group that eventually formed the Friar's Society Orchestra—Paul Mares (cornet), George Brunies, (trombone), Leon Rappolo (clarinet), Elmer Schoebel (from Illinois, piano), Louis Black (banjo), Frank Snyder (drums), and Arnold Loyocano (bass)—later renamed themselves the New Orleans Rhythm Kings and worked in the Chicago area.[27]

The criminal world took advantage of American naiveté by capitalizing on prohibition, and the clubs of Chicago and New York, especially the former, became entertainment centers to rival the halcyon days of Storyville. Audiences for hot jazz were in great supply during the postwar boom years, and all the young jazz musicians were able to support themselves rather handsomely during the 1920s. Jelly Roll Morton returned to the Midwest in 1923 to record some solo piano works in Richmond, Indiana.[28] Kid Ory came to Chicago about the same time and played with many groups.[29] He worked with Louis Armstrong's Hot Five only when they recorded, but these sides, made in Chicago in the mid-1920s, are perhaps the most extraordinary monuments of classic jazz to have survived. Their closest rivals, and perhaps equals, are the recordings of Jelly Roll Morton's Red Hot Peppers made in Chicago and New York from 1926 to 1930.

After the initial recordings for Columbia and Victor, the Original Dixieland Jazz Band recorded twelve tunes for the Aeolian Company during the remainder of the year. The company released only four records,[30] but the next year the band was back with Victor and placed five more records on the market during 1918 and 1919. The repertoire of the group included the standards of New Orleans, such as *Tiger Rag* and *Barnyard Blues*, plus some originals: *Reisenweber Rag* and *Fidgety Feet*. The last, a fast one-step, displays La Rocca at his best—a lead trumpet player who can also whip off a snappy break. In 1919, the Louisiana Five made three recordings for Columbia.[31]

---

[27] An apocryphal recreation in 1934 of the 1923 version of *Tin Roof Blues* by New Orleans Rhythm Kings is available on MCA 2-4061.

[28] *King Porter Stomp* by Jelly Roll Morton, ibid. (April 1926).

[29] *Wild Man Blues*, recorded in 1927 by Johnny Dodd's Black Bottom Stompers, ibid.

[30] Aeolian 1205, 1206, 1207, and 1242.

[31] Columbia A-2742, A-2768, and A-2775.

Once again, the musicians were white, for the Louisiana Five was the Tom Brown band from Chicago rechristened. By 1919, the ODJB had traveled to England and recorded there for Columbia until 1920. Some selections were old favorites, such as *Tiger Rag* and *Barnyard Blues*, and some were completely removed from the jazz vein, for example, *I'm Forever Blowing Bubbles* and *Alice Blue Gown*.[32] By this time, Emile Christian had replaced Eddie Edwards on trombone and J. Russel Robinson and Billy Jones played piano with the group.

By 1921, jazz had stirred up an emotional furor in America that can hardly be rivaled in either intensity or imbecility. Still, the pejorative press could hardly slow a tidal wave, and in 1921 and 1922, more and more jazz recordings hit the market. The most noteworthy of these were James P. Johnson's first recordings for OKeh,[33] Ladd's Black Aces recordings for Gennett,[34] The Original Memphis Five recordings for Banner and Paramount,[35] more from the Original Dixieland Jazz Band, and the first recordings of Mamie Smith: *Lonesome Mama Blues*, *New Orleans*, *You Can Have Him*, and *Wish that I Could but I Can't*.[36]

THE NEW YORK SCHOOL

Four Eastern ragtime pianists achieved significance both for their playing and for their published compositions: James Hubert "Eubie" (or "Hubie") Blake (1883–1983), Charles Luckeyeth "Luckey" Roberts (1895–1965), James Price Johnson (1894–1955), and Thomas "Fats" Waller (1904–43).

Eubie Blake was playing in the red-light district of Baltimore as a ragtime pianist at the age of fifteen, and was one of the first Eastern black ragtime composers to see his works in print—*Chevy Chase* and *Fizz Water* (both 1914). He joined forces with Noble Sissle in 1915, and the Sissle and Blake composing-and-writing team began turning out successful Broadway musicals in 1921 (*Shuffle Along; NW* 260, I). More renowned as a composer of popular songs than of ragtime compositions, Eubie Blake is best known for his tunes *I'm Just Wild About Harry* (1921) and *Memories of You* (1930).

Luckey Roberts, a giant of a man, was born a Quaker in Philadelphia. His huge hands were comfortable playing tenths and twelfths in the ragtime basses. His first published piece, *Junk Man Rag* (1913), was immediately successful and he published another, *Pork and Beans*, the same year and two more the next, *Music Box Rag* and *Palm Beach*. He maintained a successful career as a

[32] Columbia 735, 736, 748, 759, 804, 805, 815, 824, and 829.
[33] OKeh 4495 and 4504.
[34] Gennett 4762 and 4794.
[35] Banner 1062 and 1082, and Paramount 20161.
[36] OKeh 4630, 4670, and 4689.

bandleader and pianist in New York, gave a well-received concert in Carnegie Hall in 1931 and gave another at Town Hall in 1941. He was a friend of—and influence on—many Harlem pianists, including Duke Ellington and James P. Johnson.

James P. Johnson, like Scott Joplin, entertained the same dream of concert ragtime in larger forms. Born in New Brunswick, New Jersey, he moved to San Juan Hill in New York City as a child, where he received a solid musical education from an Italian music teacher, a Professor Giannini. His lessons included harmony, counterpoint, and opera, as well as classical piano. His first rag was published in 1914 *(Caprice Rag)*, and he continued writing in this style for most of his life. A larger work, *Rhythm Drums*, is scored for flutes, oboes, English horns, bassoons, French horns, trumpets, trombones, etc., and his *Jazzmen (Jazz-o-Mine) Concerto* is for piano and full orchestra. His *Harlem Symphony* (1932) has been played at Carnegie Hall, the Brooklyn Academy of Music, and elsewhere. He composed a musical comedy, *Sugar Hill*, which opened in Hollywood in 1948, but in spite of favorable reviews it ran for only three months.

Fats Waller was born in New York and died in Kansas City at the height of his fame. Son of a middle-class black family, he received excellent instruction in classical keyboard performance, and was only twenty years old when he recorded his first solos on the OKeh label in 1924. When he died nineteen years later, he had recorded almost five hundred pieces, as well as a large number of player-piano rolls, and he had copyrighted over four hundred musical compositions! A nimble stride pianist and an influential jazz performer, Waller composed many popular songs that have become standards in the jazz repertoire—*Ain't Misbehavin, Honeysuckle Rose,* and *I've Got a Feeling I'm Falling* (all in 1929). He was a well-known public figure and even made a number of movie shorts.

Another musician to be reckoned with during this period is, of course, William Christopher Handy. In 1917 Handy was already almost forty-five years old, an established composer and bandleader. We can attribute the failure of his first Columbia recordings, intended to compete with the Original Dixieland Jazz Band, to the "pickup" musicians he used to make his recordings in New York. His own band was located in Memphis, and could not make the trip. Many of Handy's compositions were featured by the early bands, and the black bandleader Lieutenant James Reese Europe was successful in Europe during World War I playing Handy's music. But for all his contributions to music in America, especially African-American music, W. C. Handy played only a minor role in the history of jazz. He was, after all, not an outstanding performer, and jazz has always chosen its leaders from among the virtuoso instrumentalists.

Willie "The Lion" Smith (1897–1973) and Thomas "Fats" Waller (1904–43).

JAMES P. JOHNSON

James P. Johnson's earliest recordings were made on piano rolls in 1916 when he was twenty-two years old. His recorded legacy of popular songs, ragtime pieces, and blues, cut in New York and nearby New Jersey, provide insights into both the extraordinary technique of this remarkable pianist and the state of ragtime and jazz in New York at an early date.[37] Johnson's first release, *After Tonight*,[38] a piano duet with William A. Farrell, was quickly followed by two solo ragtime numbers, *Caprice Rag* and *Steeple-chase Rag*.[39] The first features triplet figures and complex right-hand syncopations against a steady left hand; the second uses an intricate rhythmic pattern of chords in the right hand during the third strain as its chief motivic feature.

Johnson's first recordings of his famous stride piano composition, *Carolina Shout*, were released in 1918 and 1921 on piano rolls,[40] and on October 18, 1921, he recorded it (*SCCJ* 13) for the OKeh label of the General Phonograph Corporation. *Carolina Shout*,[41] a remarkable bit of piano playing, demonstrates New York jazz at its best. Although it retains a few of the basic ragtime characteristics in its formal structure, harmonic speed, sixteen-measure phrases, and oom-pah left hand, even these features are modified far beyond the norm of ragtime piano. The basic form, in its simplest terms, is Intro **A** **B** Coda, but where the ragtime composition normally divides **A** in half, with each half repeated, and **B** in half, with each half also repeated, and **B** is usually in the subdominant key, *Carolina Shout* is laid out as follows:

	‖ Intro ‖			A				B			‖ Coda ‖
	‖ Intro ‖	‖: a	:‖	b	‖:	c	:‖	d	e	d	‖ Coda ‖
mm.	4	16		16		16		16	16	16	4

The entire piece is in the key of G, but in the middle of the second half (section **e**), a feeling of subdominant is implied with the IV-I progression (in the key of C) that opens the phrase. However, through a series of chromatic modulations, the phrase returns to the key of G, as all the others do.

[37] Scott E. Brown's excellent study, *James P. Johnson: A Case of Mistaken Identity*, contains a complete Johnson discography, 1917–50, compiled by Robert Hilbert. Especially interesting is Brown's research relating Johnson's playing to "shout dances" and "ring-shout" (pp. 12–22).

[38] Universal 2191; on LP, Biograph BLP 1009Q. The exact recording dates are not known, but Johnson made two rolls a month for Aeolean and other companies beginning in 1916. They were published, or released to the public beginning in May 1917.

[39] Metro Art 203176 and Universal 203179; both are on LP, Biograph BLP 1009Q (*Steeple-chase Rag = Over the Bars*).

[40] Artempo 12975 and QRS (Quality Reigns Supreme) 100999; on LP, Biograph BLP 1003Q and Riverside RLP 1046.

[41] OKeh 4495. The reverse side, *Keep Off the Grass*, is reissued on Columbia C3L-33.

James Price Johnson (1894–1955).

The various phrases are not readily identifiable by the melodic lines only. Instead, each phrase has a distinctive opening harmonic progression that sets it apart from all others, and listening for the form is facilitated by a chord chart rather than a melodic chart. In studying this invariable characteristic, one finds the tap root of jazz, for the blues-based practice of improvising to a given harmonic scheme carries over to jazz from the ragtime repertoire, the pop-song repertoire, and all other sources. Another blues-derived feature that is immediately apparent in the introduction are the crushed dissonances played by the right hand, a cluster of two notes a half step apart, which most jazz scholars attribute to the pianist's need for representing the neutral third of the blues scale. By striking both the minor and major third at the same time, a blues cluster is produced. The same effect is used by pianists on the seventh scale step.

Carolina Shout

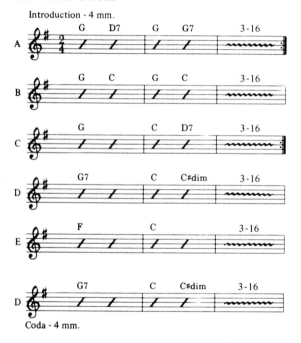

The rhythmic treatment of both hands also differs from the common practice of ragtime piano players. The right hand is syncopated, but mixes eighth-note syncopations with ternary subdivisions of the beat, thus producing a richer collection of rhythmic activity. The two-beat feel of the left hand is constantly interrupted by a walking eighth-note pattern, which totally blends the two-beat and four-beat concepts.

It should be noted that a repeat in jazz is not an invitation to play the same notes, it indicates only that the same harmony is to be used. Listening to James P. Johnson's left hand through the sixteen measures of the first phrase and its repeat, measures 17–32, one can hear the rhythmic variations as well as some harmonic passing chords that were added to the basic harmonic scheme.

The chord structure supporting these measures is:

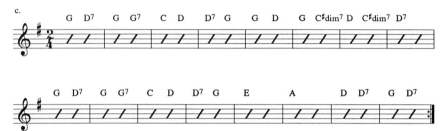

The last four measures of the piece reveal a typical cliché of the player-piano style: treble and bass moving in contrary motion just before the final chords. In spite of the rhythmic variety imposed upon the left-hand patterns by the right-hand syncopations and ternary figures, Johnson's metronomic sense of beat is infallible. The layer effect of rhythm section and front line can easily be equated to left hand and right hand. The rhythmic drive of Johnson's playing with ten fingers constantly filling all available space produces both vitality and swing, those indefinable qualities with which great jazz musicians are able to invest their performances. Gunther Schuller points out that

> *Carolina Shout* also contains in the third strain James P.'s keyboard version of a "shout," in turn the Negroes' extemporized and intensified elaboration of European-American hymn tunes. It is at the same time a call-and-response chorus in the old preacher-to-congregation relationship. In its full-voiced, brass-like chords it is a close relative to the famous last chorus of Morton's *King Porter Stomp*.[42]

LOUIS ARMSTRONG

Louis "Satchmo" Armstrong was a legend in his own time, and some would even say that he is the single greatest figure in the Jazz Hall of Fame. Born on August 4, 1901,[43] in the abject poverty of black, uptown New Orleans, Daniel Louis Armstrong was the child of an illiterate turpentine factory worker, Willie Armstrong, and his wife, Mary, later called Mayann. Born in a shack off Jane Alley in the stifling heat of a Louisiana summer with only the assis-

[42] Gunther Schuller, *Early Jazz*, p. 219.
[43] Facsimiles of the documents, baptismal register and census report, are reproduced in Gary Giddins, *Satchmo* (New York: Doubleday, 1988), p. 48 f. I am indebted to Professor Charles C. Blancq of the University of New Orleans for alerting me to this find.

Daniel Louis "Satchmo" Armstrong (1901–71).

tance of a midwife, this black baby grew up to earn the international recognition that was heaped upon him in the decade before his death. When he died in 1971, headlines throughout the world announced his death and front-page obituaries paid tribute and lamented his loss. Everything this landmark musician achieved he gained through fortitude, skill, and devotion. Even during his last years, at the triumphant height of a successful career, he was forced to experience the hardships of prejudice and segregation in the country that so proudly boasted his name as one of its own. His achievements were more than personal and more than musical, for in his striving, he became a symbol of the creativity of the black American. The writers who claim that Armstrong was born in the right place at the right time, the most wretched ghetto of New Orleans at the turn of the century, are either sadistic or naive, for his early years as a street urchin in the Storyville district are hardly to be recommended as a part of the Great American Dream.

Armstrong's parents separated when he was five years old, and he lived with his mother at Liberty and Perdido Streets in the Third Ward. He had no musical training until he was arrested at the age of thirteen and sent to the Colored Waifs Home in New Orleans. In the reformatory, he was taught music by two amateur musicians, "Captain" Joseph Jones, director of the Home, and the warden, Professor Peter Davis. The latter instructed him in fundamentals, the former in the cornet. He was released after one year and worked at various day jobs selling coal, delivering milk, unloading banana boats, and the like. He made no real progress on his instrument until 1918, when Joe "King" Oliver befriended him, encouraged and tutored him, and eventually recommended that Armstrong replace him during the summer of 1918 or early in 1919 as cornetist in Kid Ory's Band. He played various engagements during the next four years, including Streckfus Steamer jobs with Fate Marable. In 1922 he received the call from Joe Oliver in Chicago to join him as second cornetist. His days with Oliver's Creole Jazz Band marked the beginning of Armstrong's most creative and influential period. During the 1920s, he acquired the technique that allowed him to become the leading jazz virtuoso of the day. His fame among jazz musicians in Chicago is legendary—the anecdotes describe local musicians flocking to hear him performing in order to learn the secrets of hot jazz. Armstrong's inconspicuous role in the Creole Jazz Band recordings of 1923 (*SCCJ* 6) changed quickly, for by the end of 1924 he was known as the most powerful, creative soloist on the jazz recordings promoted by pianist Clarence Williams.

Clarence Williams was a capable early-jazz pianist and combo leader who assumed the musical direction for OKeh race records in 1923 and was responsible for their catalogue through 1928. The list of jazz artists he recorded during that period is impressive, and the recording of *Cakewalking Babies* made in New York in December 1924 for Gennett with Louis Armstrong and Sidney Bechet represents the very latest musical ideas in the pop-jazz field at that time.

From July 1922 to October 1924, Armstrong worked in Chicago, first with King Oliver and then with Ollie Powers. It was during this period that he met Lillian Hardin, Oliver's pianist, whom he married in February 1924. Armstrong was one black New Orleans musician who was impressed by the "sweet" band sounds, especially those of Guy Lombardo and His Royal Canadians. His exposure to Lombardo's music came after he received a call from black bandleader Fletcher Henderson in New York. Armstrong said,

> Now you dig that *Sweethearts*. . . . It reminds you of Lombardo. . . . When we were at the Savoy in Chicago in 1928, every Saturday night we'd catch the Owl Club, with Guy Lombardo, and as long as he played we'd sit right there. . . . We didn't go nowhere until after Lombardo signed off. That went on for months.[44]

Henderson, who was successful and influential in the East, did not run a New Orleans–style band, but rather one that depended on arrangements and ensemble. Armstrong joined the Henderson band at the Roseland Ballroom in New York on September 29, 1924. There he became impressed with the importance of sight-reading skills, a facet of his playing that had not concerned him seriously until then. It was also there that he developed his abiding respect for the ensemble playing that emanated from the music of the reading bands. The *Cakewalking Babies* recording displays a blend of elements from the New Orleans tradition and society music, the sweet sound of New York's Fletcher Henderson and Guy Lombardo. (*SCCJ* 11) The instrumentation is New Orleans style, with single instruments rather than sections fulfilling the various musical functions. But the ensemble playing, from the beginning through the vocal choruses, is constricted, inhibited, clean, and predictable. Armstrong plays an accurate but unimaginative lead, and Bechet's arpeggios, on soprano saxophone rather than the New Orleans–style clarinet, are virtuosic but regular. The vocal chorus is typical of the white, pop-jazz style of the day, which became epitomized in the megaphone solos of Rudy Vallée. However, the jazz choruses that follow the vocal performance are in the best polyphonic, jazz-ensemble, Dixieland style. Although Bechet's sound predominates, it is Armstrong's rhythmic drive that gives the group its forward impetus. Armstrong has no opportunity for solo

---

[44]Quoted in John Chilton and Max Jones, *Louis: The Louis Armstrong Story 1900–1971*, p. 111.

display here, but the recording shows the stage of development at which he had arrived during his days with Fletcher Henderson.

Armstrong's return to Chicago in the summer of 1925, when he joined Lil's Band at the Dreamland Ballroom, marks the beginning of his meteoric rise to the summit of the jazz world. When he subsequently organized a recording band for OKeh records with Clarence Williams's approval, the jazz world began to receive recorded music under Louis Armstrong's own name. Time has memorialized these discs as the classic recordings of the period. The series began with *Gut Bucket Blues*,[45] an introductory piece in two senses: first, Armstrong introduces each of the performers by name, and second, the music is still strongly reminiscent of the sound of the King Oliver ensemble. During the same year, 1925, three other recordings were released by other musicians that show the state of ferment in which jazz found itself. Bennie Moten, leader of the Kansas City band that would eventually become the Count Basie Orchestra, recorded *18th Street Blues* and *South Street Blues* for OKeh;[46] Fletcher Henderson released *Money Blues, Sugar Foot Stomp*, and *Carolina Stomp*;[47] and a white, twenty-two-year-old star of the Chicago-based Wolverines, Bix Beiderbecke, recorded and issued a hometown lament, *Davenport Blues*.[48]

The year 1925 is a good one to exemplify the jazz activity omnipresent in the United States. In addition to Armstrong, Beiderbecke, Henderson, and Moten, dozens of lesser organizations were recording an extended jazz repertoire: Creath's Jazzomaniacs recorded Morton's *King Porter Stomp*;[49] Sonny Clay, *Bogaloosa Blues*;[50] Jack Gardner, *The Camelwalk*;[51] Halfway House Orchestra, *Maple Leaf Rag*;[52] Original Memphis Five, *Bass Ale Blues*;[53] Original Indiana Five, *Indiana Stomp*;[54] New Orleans Owls, *Stompoff Let's Go*;[55] and Tennessee Tooters, *Milenberg Joys*.[56] Paul Whiteman, whose claim to the title "King of Jazz" does not go undisputed among jazz connoisseurs, had been recording popular music since 1920 (*NW* 215, I/4 and 260, I/7). That year he issued *Wang Wang Blues*,[57] and before the decade was over his

[45] OKeh 8261, reissued Columbia CL-851.
[46] OKeh 8242 and 8255.
[47] Columbia 383-D, 395-D, and 509-D.
[48] Gennett 5654.
[49] OKeh 8210.
[50] Vocalion 15078.
[51] OKeh 40518.
[52] Columbia 476-D.
[53] Victor 19805.
[54] Gennett 3112.
[55] Columbia 489-D.
[56] Vocalion 15068.
[57] Victor 18694.

The Hot Five: (Left to right) Louis Armstrong, Johnny St. Cyr, Johnny Dodds, Kid Ory, and Lil Hardin Armstrong.

band included sidemen such as Bix Beiderbecke, Frankie Trumbauer, Jimmy Dorsey, Tommy Dorsey, and Joe Venuti. The year 1925 also marked the publication of Hoagy Carmichael's *Washboard Blues* (Mitchell Parrish and Fred Callahan, lyricists). All in all, the issuance of the first Hot Five recordings by Louis Armstrong should not be seen as an oasis in a desert, but rather as the tallest trees of a forest. By 1925 live jazz was available everywhere, and its leading exponents of both races were cutting recordings with abandon.

The Hot Five was a remarkable group, for all of the front line were the best of the New Orleans–style instrumental soloists. Johnny Dodds was without peer among clarinetists, both in his solo work and ensemble performance. Kid Ory was a well-known bandleader in New Orleans before the closing of Storyville, and Armstrong had once played in Ory's Brownskin Band. Yet for all their brilliance, Ory and Dodds played second fiddle to Armstrong. When he finally broke loose as a soloist in *Cornet Chop Suey*,[58] (*NAJ* 2) there was no other jazz soloist on any wind instrument to rival him.

[58] OKeh 8320.

His 1926 release of *Heebie Jeebies*[59] marks the introduction of the now-famous Louis Armstrong style of "scat singing," an instrumental solo performed by the voice to vocables, or nonsense syllables. The same year that OKeh issued *Heebie Jeebies* and *Cornet Chop Suey* (1926), [See Listening Guide 2] the firm also issued a milestone record, *Big Butter and Egg Man (SCCJ* 14),[60] one of the most inventive cornet solos ever recorded. The consistency, quality, and quantity of superlative jazz recordings issued by the Hot Five and Hot Seven earned for Louis Armstrong the historic position he enjoys. Where Bix Beiderbecke went generally unnoticed among the public, Armstrong was both a household word with amateurs and a name of significance among professionals. Martin Williams's summation is exactly correct: "Armstrong's story on records between 1923 and 1932 is one of almost continuous sweeping growth—and after that is frequently one of entrenched excellence."[61]

Struttin' With Some Barbecue (SCCJ 17) is an interesting combination of sweet-band and hot-jazz sounds. The "cornball" ending lacked only the cymbal sound of a typical Guy Lombardo Mickey ending—a stereotyped closing pattern that was used in the music of the Mickey Mouse cartoons:

The backing chords of the offbeat stoptime choruses, beginning with Kid Ory's solo and continuing through Armstrong's, are typical of a band arrangement whether or not the notes are actually written out or taught by rote. The rhythm of *Struttin'* is clearly two-beat, and that two-beat/four-beat ambiguity of New Orleans jazz is not present here. The piece, composed by Armstrong's wife, Lil Hardin, has a striking melodic shape at the opening. The ascending octave outlining the major-seventh chord is clearly a modern innovation in jazz pieces of the day. Dodds's and Ory's solos, both excellent in their own ways, are totally eclipsed by the driving, forceful cornet solo, which spans the total compass of the instrument in melodic flights that embellish a germinal idea developed from the initial theme itself (see Transcription 2). The ragtime grouping of eighth notes into patterns of three, which Armstrong inserts into the last phrase of his solo, plays tricks with the steady rhythm of the accompaniment, which lacks the strong beats. The complete performance embodies both the old and the new, and in the new we find

[59] OKeh 8300.
[60] OKeh 8423.
[61] *SCCJ* liner notes, p. 20.

the elements of hot jazz and, in places, some "sweet" sounds from the repertoire of the white popular bands.

S.O.L. Blues[62] (*SCCJ* 15) is a piece that can be studied in two versions, for
Gully Low Blues was meant as a re-recording of a partially unsatisfactory first
take.[63] Armstrong's solo on *S.O.L. Blues*, containing five descending phrases,
each starting on high C (concert B♭), displays the developmental logic this
musician was able to incorporate in the best of his solos (see Transcription
1). Each succeeding phrase modifies the initial idea and lays out a pattern
that directs the listener's attention inevitably to a musical goal at the end of
the blues pattern. The almost extramusical insertion of the Lombardo ending, complete with vibrato chords and cymbal crash, jars the modern listener's sensibilities. But within the musical context of the '20s, it was a
cliché that added class and respectability to a music that had suffered considerable abuse.

The *Potato Head Blues* (*SCCJ* 16) is not a twelve-measure blues, in spite
of the name, but a thirty-two-measure structure. The chords of Armstrong's
bravura stoptime solo are played, not on the offbeat as in *Struttin' With Some
Barbecue*, but on the first beat of every other measure. In other words, seven
out of every eight temporal spaces are blank except for the solo line of the
cornet. Armstrong's melodic pattern is, once again, more than virtuosic, it is
developmental in a melodic progression that leads to a climax at the *rip* (upward
glissando) to the D above high C. The carefully structured nature of the solo
is revealed in the rhythmic treatment as well, for the first two measures,
which receive regular accentual treatment with respect to meter, are offset
rhythmically in the following two measures when Armstrong shifts his accents
to the offbeat. Gunther Schuller points out the strong probability that Hoagy
Carmichael was familiar with this solo, for his opening to *Stardust*, written in
1927, is almost a twin to Armstrong's solo line at measure 25. Given the
relationship of Carmichael to Bix Beiderbecke, an Armstrong disciple, the
similarities between *Potato Head Blues* and *Stardust* are especially striking.
Once again, note the insidious society-band cliché at the ending. Beiderbecke looked to Armstrong for inspiration, but, strangely, Armstrong in this
case looked to Lombardo.

Hotter Than That, by Lil Hardin (*SCCJ* 18), is a composition based on a
thirty-two-measure harmonic pattern that divides in half, each half receiving
a two-measure first or second ending. The thirty-two-measure stanza is
repeated three times, is interrupted by an out-of-time vocal and guitar call-
and-response duet, and ends with a final thirty-two-measure chorus. A four-

[62] In the Smithsonian booklet, *Potato Head Blues* precedes *S.O.L. Blues*. The record label,
with the reverse order, is correct.

[63] Both versions, complete, are available on Columbia CL-852.

measure piano vamp reestablishes the rhythm at the end of the vocal and
guitar duet, and an eight-measure introduction precedes the piece. The harmonies for the introduction are derived from the last eight measures of the
piece. At the very end, two two-measure cadenzas by cornet and guitar com-
prise the closing coda. Every first and second ending is filled by an instrumental break, the vocal scat singing being considered instrumental.

Hotter Than That

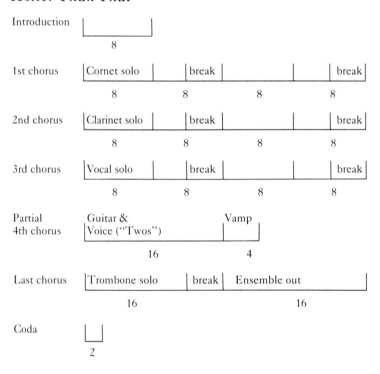

The overall scheme and the instrumental breaks are not new in concept,
but a few features of the piece are extraordinary and herald ideas to be developed by other groups in later years. The last sixteen measures of the final
chorus is an ensemble "out" that is accompanied by Armstrong's cornet riff
on beats four and one. This pattern, which was to become a cliché of the
1930s swing bands, transforms the old New Orleans stomp to a brass-ensem-
ble arrangement. The work does not close with a typical Mickey ending, but
rests instead on an unresolved diminished chord built on the submediant.
This incongruous harmony is but a clue to one of the most important developments in the piece. William Austin sensed the significance of Armstrong's

solo work in this performance and offers not only a successful analysis of many of the subtleties that distinguish it from other improvisations, but also a brief justification for the analysis itself:

A study of these few phrases [the last eight measures of the tune in each of its five appearances—see next page] can show not only the characteristic details of syncopation and phrasing . . . but also the sweeping progression of melody that gives Armstrong's performance as a whole its cumulative power. The bracketed motif with repeated notes is the outstanding idea of the introduction, where it brings a mild unexpected accent that welds the whole phrase together, as suggested by the metrical signs above the notes; the motif serves at once, slightly varied, to make the cadence. In the first full chorus, Armstrong shifts this motif very subtly, anticipating and consolidating it. In the vocal chorus he simplifies it, and then drastically changes the cadence in order to dovetail with the interlude, by way of the most expressive blue note in the whole piece. In the final chorus he brings the motif to a real development, starting four measures ahead, rising to the top note of the piece and overriding the caesura that had preceded the motif in each earlier chorus, so that the final, expected appearance of the motif is now late and the cadence is a quick blur of blue notes. A sympathetic listener can enjoy all this intricate melodic thought without benefit of verbal or graphic analysis, just as Armstrong composed it entirely in his imagination of sounds; but analysis can contribute to greater enjoyment, and it can open the way to new enjoyment for some music-lovers who have formerly allowed the melodic intricacy to be overshadowed by the harmonic and rhythmic simplicity of the accompaniment. The accompaniment supports this kind of melody, eggs it on, and gives it freedom. Such melodies seem to be invented only when the accompaniment is giving the right kind of support. Moreover, they probably grow out of the experience of contrapuntal music—Armstrong's single line often seems to be incorporating fragmentary antiphonal answers to its own leading ideas. But the one rich melody is now the proper focus of interest.

The harmonic relation between Armstrong's melody and the band's accompaniment is subtle. Whereas Dodd's melody is composed mainly of broken chords and simple ornaments, Armstrong's is more independent, more long-breathed, bolder in its dissonances—notably in the cross-relations marked by asterisks. Yet Armstrong's melody does harmonize convincingly, and its drive to the cadence is the Bach-like drive of a melody in counterpoint against a melodic bass. This harmonic subtlety is neglected in most accounts of Armstrong's style. It is what distinguishes him and his best colleagues from their routine imitators. It is also what points ahead most distinctly to the best work of younger men, like Charlie Parker.[64]

[64] William Austin, *Music in the 20th Century*, p. 281 ff.

Armstrong, *Hotter Than That,* variants of last phrase

West End Blues is another example of the musical excitement generated by Louis Armstrong's extraordinary improvisatory skills (see Transcription 3). Fred Robinson's trombone solo is lifeless, and Zutty Singleton's drum accompaniment to the trombone solo is inept. But we hear in the solo piano a newly developed style that is beginning to lose its ragtime roots. Fatha Hines's solo, the fourth full chorus (*SCCJ* 19), employs a right-hand technique that substitutes flowing rapid-note passages for the old-fashioned ragged syncopations. The accompanying left hand, although it begins in oompah style, quickly shifts to walking parallels that project a 4/4 meter in undifferentiated quarter notes. Armstrong's ad lib introduction rapidly descends an octave and a third in the first two measures, only to ascend just as rapidly to a climactic high D above high C. It then falls gracefully to a second climactic low note with a facility and instinctive selection of correct notes that leaves the listener breathless. The rhythmic activity of his solo work is no longer regular, as mixtures of duplets, triplets, quadruplets, quintuplets, and other irrational values are incorporated in a scheme that is uncanny in its musical logic. The end of his first twelve-measure solo can be found, almost note for note, in the third and fourth measures of the introduction. The descent from his climactic high note in the introduction is carried a step further in his descent from the held opening high note of his last chorus.[65]

West End Blues

Intro
(ad lib)

9

Trumpet solo	Trombone solo

12   12

Vocal solo with clarinet lead	Piano solo

12   12

Trumpet solo piano	Tag

12   (8 plus 4)   2

———— JELLY ROLL MORTON ————

Louis Armstrong was not the only hot band leader playing at this time. The three examples of Jelly Roll Morton's ensemble work, *Black Bottom Stomp*, *Dead Man Blues*, and *Grandpa's Spells*,[66] were all recorded toward the end of 1926. *Black Bottom Stomp* (*SCCJ* 7) is a superlative tour de force of New Orleans jazz, and one can see that there is a certain overlap of personnel among the groups recording at that time. Kid Ory on trombone and Johnny St. Cyr on banjo were also part of the Armstrong ensembles. Where Morton's group lacked the outstanding trumpet player of the day, it more than compensated by featuring the greatest jazz composer and one of the outstanding piano virtuosos of the period, Jelly Roll Morton himself. The clarinetist, Omer Simeon, displays facility, tonguing, phrasing, tone, and improvisational ingenuity that are unmatched by any other clarinetist in jazz at that time. Neither Sidney Bechet nor Johnny Dodds had the technical mastery of the instrument that Simeon displays on this recording. The pure energy

[65] A transcription of Armstrong's trumpet solo from *West End Blues* can be found in John Mehegan, *Jazz Improvisation*, 2 (New York: Watson-Guptill, 1962), pp. 64–65. A similar transcription in a more complex rhythmic notation but in the wrong key, B♭ instead of E♭, can be found in Schuller, *Early Jazz*, pp. 116–19. The Schuller transcription is instructive insofar as it demonstrates the difficulty of notating jazz rhythms accurately, but the incorrect key relationship makes difficult an understanding of the harmonic subtleties of the Armstrong solo.

[66] *SCCJ* 7, 8, and 9, respectively. The recordings are listed in chronological order.

of the final chorus, the ensemble close, seems to reach a level of hysteria, and yet the group remains in control at all times.

Certain features of this performance are typical of Morton, but one is unusual in the recorded jazz at this date. The stoptime phrases, the rhythmetized melodic patterns (stomps), the continuous eighth-note obbligato, and the exciting breaks that gain effectiveness through well-rehearsed ensemble practice are all typical of the Jelly Roll Morton ensembles. The novel feature is John Lindsay's pizzicato string-bass playing. This instrument in the rhythm section became a standard during the swing era, and here we have an early recorded example of the bass used properly to supply the rhythmic life and harmonic ground so essential in the developing idiom.

Where *Black Bottom Stomp* (*SCCJ* 7) achieves great heights, *Dead Man Blues* (*SCCJ* 8) hardly lifts itself off the floor. The solos of Simeon and Mitchell are sophomoric; the trombone obbligato solo to the riff-like accompaniment of the clarinets is simple-minded; and the continuity of the piece is such that one more or one less chorus would hardly be noticed. Still, to understand a music, we must have some knowledge of the ordinary and the failures as well as the masterpieces. Just as a study of the Rocky Mountains would be inadequate if it were limited to peaks above 14,000 feet, a survey of jazz of the '20s is misrepresented if we sip only the distilled nectar of the ten best performances. *Dead Man Blues* typifies the music produced by bands called upon to entertain nightly week after week. The joke of the opening helps enliven a routine night, and the well-worn harmonic patterns of the piece are easily traversed by professional musicians who have been there many times before. But the creative spark cannot ignite four to six hours a day, seven days a week, and this recording shows how competent professionals are able to play a good job without inspiration. Everything is in its place, but nothing exciting happens musically.

On the other hand, when the group cut *Grandpa's Spells* (*SCCJ* 9) in December 1926, it gave permanence to a classic of New Orleans–style jazz. Morton's cascading right hand is balanced at the bottom by John Lindsay's walking string bass. Johnny St. Cyr's melodic guitar playing (in contrast with the customary chordal harmonic style) is followed by New Orleans polyphony in which Kid Ory, George Mitchell, and Omer Simeon achieve an exemplary contrapuntal balance. It is in their ensemble playing that these musicians are at their best; the solos, although interesting, are on a plane considerably below that of Louis Armstrong. The solos are inhibited to the degree that this piece is carefully arranged by the composer, for in order to perform all the ensemble requirements of this complicated work, each player must devote a fair share of energy to that task. Morton's command of the keyboard is astonishing, but his style of playing was quickly being replaced by the more advanced work of a younger generation of pianists.

EARL "FATHA" HINES

Earl Kenneth "Fatha" Hines (1903–83) was born and educated in Pittsburgh. He arrived in Chicago after a tour with Lois B. Deppe's Serenaders in 1923 and played in that area and on the circuit during the early '20s, until the beginning of his association with Louis Armstrong in 1927. During the following year, Hines made a series of recordings with Armstrong that mark a major change in Armstrong's style and in the role the piano was to take in jazz ensembles. Before then, the major jazz pianists thought in terms of making full, rich orchestral sounds. Used as a solo instrument, the piano was treated as an inexpensive substitute for a band in establishments requiring live music. The left hand functioned as a rhythm section producing both the rhythm and the harmonic underpinning, and the right hand provided both the melody and the fuller ensemble sound. When used in a jazz ensemble, the piano was still treated similarly, even when its functions were reduced simply to those provided by the left hand. Hines, although certainly capable of playing in the older style, left some of the left-hand work to the drums (and bass) and began to walk that hand around on the harmonies. The major change, however, occurred in his right-hand technique, in that he allowed single-note improvisations in melodic-instrument style to predominate. In ensemble work, he looked upon the role of the pianist as equal to that of any member of the front line. Where the piano's responsibilities in group performance had been almost exclusively accompanimental, Hines developed a soloistic style of piano playing within the ensemble. The performance of *Weather Bird* (*SCCJ* 20) by Armstrong and Hines is the product of two major talents competing and cooperating successfully in a musical enterprise. Neither dominates the other, but each spurs his rival on to greater achievement. This 1928 Armstrong-Hines performance represents a slightly altered version of the original recorded by King Oliver in 1923.[67]

Weather Bird

Intro	A Trumpet & Piano	B Trumpet & Piano	B Piano solo	A Trumpet solo & Piano
4	16	16	16	16

Vamp	C Piano solo	C Trumpet & Piano solos	C Trumpet & Piano solos	Coda
4	16	16	16	16

[67] Gennett 5132.

Earl "Fatha" Hines (1903–83).

The first thirty-six measures of the piece, the introduction and the first state-ment of **A** and **B**, are played in a straightforward manner, both men hewing to the original. This procedure establishes for the listener the harmonic and melodic structure of the piece, so that the improvisations that follow are more easily perceived within the context of the basic grammar and syntax. The overall format is one of the many typical ragtime patterns, complete with introduction, first and second strain, modulatory vamp, and trio.

Hines's performance during the first statement of the second strain and during the trumpet solo, to the repeat of the first strain, demonstrates per-fectly the transformation he had effected in accompanimental piano style. Two-handed syncopated chords, walking four-beat progressions, and answering melodic passages decorate a keyboard texture that implies steady rhythm and steady harmony but in fact explicitly provides solo-piano material. Strangely, the first piano solo (the repeat of **B**) reverts to an old-fashioned barrelhouse piano style in which the left hand bounces back and forth and the right hand rolls some chords, syncopates the tune, and provides a rag-time-jazz lead. Hines plays his version of ragtime piano in the first full strain of the trio, but the two succeeding choruses, where trumpet and piano alter-nate, jostle each other, and romp in playful ecstasy, demonstrate his lead-instrument piano style.

The harmonic matching of trumpet and piano is not convincing at times, as their exuberance produces a wrong note or two. However, in jazz there is ample opportunity to make the best of chance sounds, and in measure 10 of the last full strain of the trio, Hines comes down the keyboard and pounces on a nonharmonic note that complements the sounds that preceded it in the last chorus and a half.

THE JAZZ COMMUNITY

Humor in jazz is pervasive, and the ability to laugh at others and oneself is deeply rooted in the blues tradition of black Americans. Louis Armstrong, like Fats Waller, was sometimes criticized as an "Uncle Tom" for guarding his image as an entertainer and declining to engage in political ferment. However, it has been conjectured that black musicians in the twenties wore a smiling mask that was sometimes nudged aside to reveal resentments dur-ing "their virtuoso instrumental performances, their mocking renditions of conventional lyrics, and, of course, by creating and singing 'Black and Blue.' "[68] Instrumental virtuosity was one means of demonstrating superiority in white culture, but even here black musicians had to protect their egos with humor.

[68] David A. Cayer, "Black and Blue and Black Again: Three Stages of Racial Imagery in Jazz Lyrics," *Journal of Jazz Studies*, 1 (1974), p. 53.

It was never safe to be too good or too outspoken, and special languages—both musical and verbal—reserved for intimates were necessary for personal and group survival. Bud Freeman, a white saxophonist playing in the Chicago area during the 1920s who sympathized with the plight of the black musician, explains:

> When I say the Black man's language, you have to understand that the Black man of that day [1920s] who was not educated, had to find a way to make it in the White world. He had to "yes" the White man; there were underground phrases that he had to use that the White man didn't understand.[69]

It has been convincingly demonstrated that a jazz community did in fact exist.[70] This community was not circumscribed by a geographic boundary, but instead by a definition of people with a given set of values who shared an interest in jazz at a high level of intensity and participated, to some extent, in the occupational role and ideology of the jazz musicians. The jazz community differs from other occupational groups in that

> not only do the professionals constitute a group, but their public is included in it. This is not to say, of course, that there are not cliques and inner circles of hierarchical nature within this broad social grouping, but rather that the occupational professional people and their public are set off as a relatively closely knit group which shares behaviors and the results of those behaviors in common and in contradistinction to people outside the group.[71]

Many factors contributed to the estrangement of the jazz community from society at large, but it is important to realize that the jazz musicians found acceptance within the culture of black America.

> Jazz musicians, by the middle and late 1920's, were prestigious members of the Black society. Their influence, though not institutionalized, was proportionally greater than their numbers would suggest.[72]

Dave Peyton, a leading black bandleader in Chicago at that time, served on the board of directors of the black musicians' union, Local 208, and published a weekly column in *The Chicago Defender* that he claimed was read by

[69] J. Frederick MacDonald, ed., "An Interview with Bud Freeman (5-29-74)," *Popular Music and Society*, 3 (1974), p. 332.

[70] Alan P. Merriam and Raymond W. Mack, "The Jazz Community," *Social Forces*, 38 (1960), p. 211 ff.

[71] Ibid., p. 211.

[72] John Lax, "Chicago's Black Musicians in the '20s: Portrait of an Era," *Journal of Jazz Studies*, 1 (1974), p. 109.

30,000 musicians. Peyton exercised both influence and control within the black Chicago musical establishment, and he championed education, both musical and academic, as a means to higher achievement. It is a misconception to think that the majority of successful black musicians working in Chicago were people like Louis Armstrong who had emigrated from New Orleans. One observer points out that

> a *Chicago Defender* directory of local Black groups in August, 1926, included twenty-seven bands. Only six of these could be considered New Orleans-in-Chicago groups. The rest belonged, to some extent, to the establishment. However, it is the New Orleans leaders, King Oliver, Luis Russell, and Louis Armstrong, whose names are recognized in this list. Even the leading establishment figures—Dave Peyton, Erskine Tate, Charles Elgar, Charles "Doc" Cooke, Jimmy Wade, and Sammy Stewart—are little known today.[73]

In Chicago there were four categories of musical employment: 1) cabarets catering basically to a black audience although admitting white patrons; 2) ballrooms for whites only; 3) black-oriented movie and vaudeville theaters; and 4) recording sessions. Of these, the ballrooms and theaters were dominated by the establishment bands, while the New Orleans contingent controlled the cabarets and recording sessions. Similarly, the cabaret audiences were drawn more from the "shady" side of the population, while the theater and ballroom clientele were largely respectable.[74]

In the same way that humor in blues lyrics helps salve the wounds of racial injury, humor in instrumental solos fulfills a therapeutic need for the virtuoso jazz musician. The performer laughs a lot musically, but only a percentage of the humor is good-natured. In the *Weather Bird* repartee of Hines and Armstrong, there is almost a bear-cub playfulness. The instruments roll around, scramble over each other, and do their thing in mutual trust and understanding.

When Louis Armstrong performs *Sweethearts on Parade* (*SCCJ* 21), however, it is difficult to know where the joke begins and ends. Armstrong's respect for the Lombardo society sound is in full evidence here as his Sebastian New Cotton Club Orchestra performs a composition by Guy Lombardo's brother Carmen, lead saxophonist, composer, and arranger for the Royal Canadians. The sustained, vibrato-laden chordal accompaniment and the "chunk, chunk, chunk" rhythm at the "businessman's bounce" tempo are certainly serious business for Armstrong. On the other hand, the bugle call

---

[73] Thomas J. Hennessey, "The Black Chicago Establishment 1919–1930," *Journal of Jazz Studies*, 2 (1974), p. 16.

[74] Ibid., p. 21.

that ends the parade is obviously tongue-in-cheek. The juxtaposition of the double-time jazz chorus with sweethearts politely tiptoeing arm in arm may be a joke, but it is probably an uncontrollable jazz impulse bursting forth in a pyrotechnic display. Incidentally, as the years passed, Armstrong achieved even greater technical mastery of his instrument, and here we see him climb to an E above high C (concert D) with complete ease.

WOMEN IN JAZZ

Women have played a significant role in the history of jazz from its earliest days, but the popular stereotype unfairly restricts the female contribution primarily to vocal music: the classic blues singers, the "girl vocalists" of the swing and bebop eras, and an occasional pianist. Women jazz musicians have achieved much more, but they have not found it easy to acquire full citizenship among the instrumentalists of jazz for many of the same reasons they have had to struggle for equal rights in the corporate world: Victorian notions about a woman's "place"; Puritanical views about men and women working together on the road, after hours, and in venues of pleasure and entertainment; stereotypical ideas about wind instruments for men and string instruments for "ladies"; the threat of unemployment for working males as a large outsider group attempts to gain entrance into a monopolized profession; "old boy" networks; male booking agents and club owners; hostile, cute, and ignorant music critics; and more. Therefore it is all the more remarkable that some women have been able to overcome these obstacles—and those faced as well by their male colleagues—and make major contributions throughout the history of jazz.

During the first two decades of the twentieth century, black female stage entertainers gained prominence as they worked their way throughout the black TOBA circuit (Theater Owners' Booking Association) of circuses, carnivals, tent shows, and theaters. The stars of these shows—the classic blues singers Ma Rainey, Mamie Smith, Bessie Smith, Ida Cox, Ethel Waters, Alberta Hunter, Sippie Wallace, and Victoria Spivey—have achieved almost legendary status as singers, but these women deserve credit for more than their remarkable voices and outstanding stage presentations. Many of their own compositions have entered the standard repertoire of jazz works. They employed some of the most exceptional instrumental jazz soloists of the period as their accompanists, both in their shows and on many notable early recordings—Louis Armstrong, Joe Smith, Sidney Bechet, Coleman Hawkins, Clarence Williams, James P. Johnson, Fletcher Henderson, and many others. They also paved the way for other women to enter the professional world of music. The role of these women as composers and leaders has thus far received insufficient attention in serious jazz studies.

Following on the heels of these singers, some talented female instrumentalists became active in jazz performance, beginning a continuous tradition of female accomplishment in this field. Some are little more than names now, for they apparently left no sound recordings of their work—for example, Edna Thomas, who was playing piano with Louis Armstrong at the Red Onion Cafe in New Orleans in 1919. Others entered early but recorded only at later stages of their careers—for example, Julia E. Lee, who began her career playing with her brother's band (George E. Lee) in Kansas City in 1920, but first recorded (with the Tommy Douglas Orchestra) in 1945, three and one-half decades later.[75] The year 1923 saw the recording careers of two outstanding female jazz musicians begin: Lil Hardin with King Oliver in Chicago[76] and Lovie Austin with her Serenaders, her Blues Serenaders, and her Paramount Boys, also in Chicago.[77] Although Austin's role at Paramount was as accompanist for singers Ma Rainey, Ida Cox, Alberta Hunter, and Edmonia Henderson, it is significant that she led the band and that her cornetist, Tommy Ladnier, was one of the best performers of the period. Austin was a superior musician who played piano with a strong left hand, displayed a solid harmonic sense, and kept a rock-steady rhythm during both up-tempo syncopated pieces and slow, melancholy blues. Her recordings of *Graveyard Dream Blues* with Ida Cox,[78] *Jackass Blues* with Kid Ory and Johnny Dodds,[79] and *Heebie Jeebies*[80] with Tommy Ladnier are typical of her work.

Lil Hardin is, without doubt, an unsung hero of early jazz, for although she is remembered for her accompanimental work as pianist on many of the first classic jazz recordings of King Oliver's Creole Jazz Band, the Red Onion Jazz Babies, and Louis Armstrong's Hot Five and Hot Seven, she is rarely credited with being the single most important promoter of her husband, Louis Armstrong, during his rise from obscurity to international prominence. Shortly after their marriage in 1924, she encouraged Armstrong to leave Oliver for solo spots with Ollie Powers and Fletcher Henderson, and when he returned to Chicago, she billed him as "The World's Greatest Trumpet Player" on *her* job at the Dreamland Ballroom.

She was a skillful pianist and an experienced, well-trained musician, but on most of her early recordings, her pianistic skills go undisplayed because, as she explained,

[75] *If It's Good* and *Show Me Missouri Blue*, Premium 29012.

[76] Sessions for Paramount, OKeh, and Columbia Records, and, in Richmond, Indiana, for Gennett.

[77] All for Paramount.

[78] Paramount 12044.

[79] Paramount 12361.

[80] Paramount 12283.

Lil Hardin (1898–1971).

It wasn't the style during the King Oliver days for the pianist to play many solos. . . . Sometimes I'd get the urge to run up and down the piano and make a few runs and things, and Joe [Oliver] would turn around and look at me and say, "We have a clarinet in the band."[81]

As a composer, Lil Hardin is an unrecognized master who composed some of the most interesting pieces of this period. When her works and others of the Chicago period are studied, analyzed, and compared, she may well be shown to have invented some of the characteristic Chicago sounds that were distinct from the New Orleans tradition. She was aware of the simple harmonies employed in the standard tunes of the King Oliver repertoire. When she first joined the band, she asked for the key of the first piece. As she relates she was told,

> "Key, we don't know what key. Just when you hear two knocks, start playing."
> . . . After a second I could feel what they were playing, because at that time I don't think they used over four or five chords. In fact, I'm sure they didn't.[82]

Her own compositions were far more adventurous, containing harmonies and melodic figures not common in the New Orleans repertoire. She is credited with many originals—*Skid-Dat-de-Dat, My Heart, Jazz Lips, Heah Me Talkin', Hotter than That, You're Next, Dropping Shucks, The King of the Zulus, Lonesome Blues,* and more. One of her best is *Struttin' with Some Barbecue (SCCJ* 17), whose fame has largely derived from Louis Armstrong's brilliant stoptime solo (see Transcription 2), although the composition itself is fascinating. The opening melody, after the introduction, outlines a major seventh chord, an unusual and advanced harmonic idea not stemming from the New Orleans tradition. It is important to note, too, that the seventh is stressed, it is not simply an ornamental figure.

Lil Hardin Armstrong, *Struttin' with Some Barbecue*

A♭M7

[81] Quoted in Sally Placksin, *American Women in Jazz, 1900 to the Present,* p. 60 f.
[82] Ibid., p. 59.

The harmonies, though by no means complex, display an interesting variety, asymmetrical distribution over the thirty-two-measure A A' chorus, and irregular harmonic rhythm.

Struttin' with Some Barbecue, Harmonic Rhythm

A♭						F⁷	
‖: 1	2	3	4	5	6	7	8 ‖

B♭m⁷	E♭⁷	Fm		B♭⁷		E♭⁷	
9	10	11	12	13	14	15	16 ‖

A♭				A♭⁷		D♭	
17	18	19	20	21	22	23	24 ‖

	D♭m⁷	Cm	F⁷	B♭m⁷	E♭⁷	A♭	E♭⁷
25	26	27	28	29	30	31	32 :‖

It is too early to credit Lil Hardin with any certain role in the emergence of Chicago-style jazz, but it is very late to be recognizing her significance as a jazz composer. Her role as a band leader is also virtually unknown. During the early 1930s, Hardin led two all-women bands and one all-male group, and later in the decade she returned to Chicago as the house pianist at Decca records. During this period she recorded with numerous outstanding jazz players, and she continued jobbing and recording, on various labels, until 1965. She died in 1971 while performing on stage at a Louis Armstrong memorial concert. To date, this fascinating musician and seminal jazz figure lacks a full-length musical and biographical study.

BIX BEIDERBECKE

When Louis Armstrong recorded *I Gotta Right to Sing the Blues* (*SCCJ* 22), Bix Beiderbecke had already been dead for a year and a half. Two years younger than Armstrong, he drank so heavily that he returned to his home town in 1929 to dry out. He was back in New York in 1930, but in mid-1931 he collapsed and died at the age of 28 of lobar pneumonia and cerebral edema. This musician, who has often been used as a symbol of the Jazz Age, was relatively unknown to the general public and died almost unnoticed except by a small circle of jazz associates and admirers.

Leon Bix Beiderbecke was born in Davenport, Iowa, in March 1903, into an upper middle-class family for whom music was an accepted and fostered art. He began playing the piano before he was five and began his formal study of piano at the age of seven. Beiderbecke's parents hoped that he would develop into a concert pianist. The effort was futile, for Beiderbecke was unable to learn to read music—he seems to have had a learning disability in this area. His teacher discontinued the lessons, admitting that "he couldn't teach the boy anything and that the talent was one that lay deep within."[83] Beiderbecke took up the cornet at fourteen and played it with a self-taught, unconventional fingering. Not until he joined the Paul Whiteman Orchestra in the late 1920s did he learn to read cornet music, and even then he was never expert, having attained a skill level far below the standard required of the other Whiteman musicians.

During the riverboat days, Davenport was heavily trafficked by boats that came north from Memphis, St. Louis, and New Orleans. While in high school during 1919–21, Beiderbecke began playing odd jobs and listening to Original Dixieland Jazz Band recordings. He studied the work of Nick La Rocca and was introduced to the playing of Louis Armstrong on one of the riverboats that docked at Davenport. His parents enrolled him in Lake Forest Military Academy, north of Chicago, in 1921, but he was expelled before the academic year was up. During 1921 and 1922, Beiderbecke worked occasionally around Chicago and listened frequently to King Oliver's band and the New Orleans Rhythm Kings. He joined the Wolverines in 1923, and from then until his death he developed a solo jazz-cornet style that seemed to have roots in a different musical garden. Beiderbecke played with the Wolverines, Charlie Straight's commercial orchestra, Frankie Trumbauer's ensemble, several Jean Goldkette units, the Paul Whiteman "King of Jazz" Orchestra, and possibly the Glen Gray and Dorsey brothers' bands. He was not terribly successful as an ensemble musician because of his poor music reading ability, but he quickly became the leading white cornet soloist in jazz.

While Beiderbecke was in St. Louis in 1925 with Frankie Trumbauer, he began to explore contemporary music outside the domain of jazz. His interest focused on the French impressionists, particularly Claude Debussy, and his study and practice of their sounds led him to improvisations based on expansions of conventional harmony. He used chord tones and scales that were unusual for jazz musicians at the time, sounds foreign to the genre in

[83]George Hoefer, "Bix Beiderbecke," in *The Jazz Makers*, ed. Nat Shapiro and Nat Hentoff, p. 93.

those early days of its development. He introduced flatted fifths, sixths, ninths, elevenths, thirteenths, whole-tone scales, and augmented-chord harmonies into his improvised melodic lines. Although Beiderbecke took an interest in the works of other contemporary composers—Maurice Ravel, Igor Stravinsky, Gustav Holst, Charles Tomlinson Griffes, and Edward MacDowell—it is the influence of Debussy upon his thinking that is most easily traced. Beiderbecke's piano composition *In a Mist* is patterned after the short piano sketches of Claude Debussy while incorporating some of the rhythmic activity of jazz and ragtime. The piece, which was never notated by Beiderbecke, was continually reworked in improvisatory sessions and finally recorded by him in 1927.[84]

Given his other frustrations, his inability to work with written music must have played a prominent part in the deteriorating state of his mental health. Like many of the leading ragtime composers, Beiderbecke aspired to write large compositions employing the style he loved. But his dream of composing a jazz symphony came to naught, for he was unable to put on paper the ideas he carried in his head. His problems and his limited public recognition notwithstanding, Bix Beiderbecke remains the most important white jazz musician of the 1920s because of his remarkable influence upon the playing of other jazz musicians. Beiderbecke's legacy may best be summarized thus:

> Bix was known chiefly as a cornetist with an exquisite tone and legato style of improvisation. He was probably the first white musician ever to be admired and imitated by Negro jazzmen. . . . Though often surrounded by musicians of inferior stature and by over-commercialized arrangements, notably in the Whiteman Band, Bix nevertheless left a legacy of performances unmatched in subtlety and finesse blended with a sensitive jazz feeling.[85]

When Frankie Trumbauer recorded *Ostrich Walk* (*NAJ* 3) in 1927, his cornet player, Bix Beiderbecke, was working from a familiar repertoire, the recordings of Nick La Rocca and the Original Dixieland Jazz Band he had studied as a youth. Beiderbecke's lead in the ensemble sections is impressive both for its flawless execution and its propelling rhythmic drive. His classic solo, although brief, compelled other musicians to take notice: it consists of a series of descending melodic lines with notes gracefully displaced by unexpected turns, its subtle rhythms delighting through ingenuity, virtuosity, and surprise. (See Listening Guide 3.) The piece, carefully arranged to provide the latest Chicago fashion in ensemble sound, also contains an excellent trombone solo by Bill Rank and some exciting back-to-back breaks,

[84] OKeh 40916, reissued Columbia CL 844-7.
[85] Leonard Feather, *The New Edition of the Encyclopedia of Jazz*, p. 132.

Bix Beiderbecke and the Rhythm Jugglers in 1925. (Left to right) Howdy Quicksell, banjo; Tommy Gargano, drums; Paul Mertz, piano; Don Murray, clarinet; Bix Beiderbecke, cornet; and Tommy Dorsey, trombone.

including Trumbauer's C-melody saxophone and Don Murray's clarinet.

Beiderbecke's solo work on the OKeh recording of *Riverboat Shuffle* (*SCCJ* 24)[86] displays the many characteristics for which he was justly famous: legato style, controlled tone, a lilting rhythmic treatment of eighth notes, developmental treatment of motives, and a penchant for dissonances that stress the upper partials against the simple harmonic substructure:

Riverboat Shuffle

[86] The *SCCJ* booklet has bands 4 and 5 reversed.

The asterisks mark the harmonic dissonances, and they are:

last note of the 2-measure break	major 9th
m. 1	major 6th (13th)
m. 2 and m. 6	major 7th and 9th
m. 3 and m. 7	minor 3rd against major harmony (blue 3rd)
m. 8	major 9th and minor 13th
m. 9	major 9th

It is particularly instructive to compare this *Riverboat Shuffle* solo with one he recorded at a different date:[87]

Although the solos are different, the stressed harmonic dissonances are the same. They are:

m. 2	major 6th (13th), minor 3rd against a major triad (blue 3rd), major 6th (13th), and augmented 11th
m. 3	minor 3rd against a major triad (blue 3rd)
m. 5	major 6th (13th)
m. 6	augmented 2nd (9th), major 7th, augmented 11th
m. 7	major 9th
m. 9	minor 3rd against a major triad (blue 3rd)

Beiderbecke's soft cornet quality (upper partials are less pronounced than they are in the characteristic trumpet sound) mutes the subtlety of his intonation, for he places great stress in his solo work on the expressiveness of minutely tempered intonation, a characteristic of hot jazz. The sliding harmonies of *Riverboat Shuffle* (introduction, piano break, etc.) evoke the harmonic framework characteristic of impressionist piano music, although this feature is attributable not to Bix Beiderbecke but to the composer, Hoagy Carmichael. However, it is likely that these patterns were attractive to Bei-

---

[87]Taken from Schuller, *Early Jazz*, p. 190, and transposed up a minor third.

derbecke and played some role in his selection of this piece for performance and recording.

Singin' the Blues (*SCCJ* 23) lacks the consistency of *Riverboat Shuffle*, and various flaws are apparent. The polyphony of the ensemble passage following Beiderbecke's solo includes some crude heterophony at the beginning. The Jimmy Dorsey clarinet solo is entirely devoid of inventiveness and contains a wrong note in the next-to-last measure. But certain moments in the Beiderbecke solo are exquisite. At the ninth measure, when the harmonic pattern begins a circle-of-fifths progression, Beiderbecke plays with a few of his favorite sounds and lets one dissonance melt into the next. The influence on saxophonist Lester Young of both his harmonic thinking and his "cool" sound becomes apparent when we discover that Young once carried a copy of Trumbauer's *Singin' the Blues* around in his saxophone case. Conceivably, it was Trumbauer's solo that Young admired, but just as likely it was the clean, relaxed, articulate solo work of Bix Beiderbecke.

Singin' the Blues

In the best of the Beiderbecke solos, just as in the best of the Armstrong solos, one sees a structural integrity that results from reworked motivic patterns and harmonic sounds that are individual to the players themselves. Structural unity and developmental inventiveness, while accomplished partially through conscious effort, more likely result from a subconscious interplay of stored mental images and reflexive lip-and-finger patterns. The working jazz musician recycles a finite body of musical phrases to which is added, from time to time and under the creative urging of the muses and the moment, a newly inspired sound, a clever turn of phrase, or an exciting rhythmic idea. The improvisatory techniques of most jazz musicians are almost entirely imitative, as most of the "ideas" are gathered from the plantings of the giants—the Armstrongs, the Beiderbeckes, the Mortons, and the Hineses. The phonograph recording became a teaching aid from its first introduction in 1917, and we know that jazz musicians traditionally learned their craft not only on the job but by imitating recorded solos. Bix Beiderbecke had a phonograph as early as 1918 and committed the Nick La Rocca passages to memory. The master jazz musicians, however, are able to move beyond the imitative to the creative, and as they do so, styles fluctuate and change. But for the result to have musical meaning, the notes within any particular jazz solo must be related to each other syntactically. Merely to play scales and arpeggios in the right key with the right harmonies will create little more than an extemporized embellishment, but through a process of reshaping a limited number of musical ideas within the single solo, improvisational composition takes place.

Beiderbecke's musical preoccupation with harmonic dissonances and superimposed blue thirds (see examples on pp. 196–97) is but one instance of the extemporaneous compositional process at work. As saxophonist Bud Freeman explains:

> Everybody plays something over again because you see, there are phrases that you develop . . . they become dear to you. This is the thing the critic doesn't understand. He wants you to play differently all the time. . . . The greatness of Louis was that the phrases he played were dear to him, and yet he didn't play them mechanically. He felt them.[88]

Not every jazz solo is played with the expressive quality of an Armstrong or a Beiderbecke. The first eight measures of Don Murray's clarinet solo on *Riverboat Shuffle* is a good example of a series of correct notes played mechanically. What set Beiderbecke apart was the freshness of his ideas. Even when he reworked familiar material (not only are the two *Riverboat Shuffle* solos related, but one can find strong similarities in solos performed to other compositions, for example, *Sorry*),[89] he also created new music.

Beiderbecke's solo on *Jazz Me Blues*[90] is one of his best, despite its restricted range of note values and pitch. On that same recording one hears the work of another superb musician, Adrian Rollini, a bass saxophonist who is capable of swinging in both ensemble and solo. The consistency of Rollini's solo work in *Jazz Me Blues* marks him as a leading jazz musician of the 1920s. But the bass saxophone played badly is a dangerous instrument, and one can hear on *Thou Swell*[91] a grotesque solo by Min Leibrook, a Beiderbecke sideman, and on *Ol' Man River*[92] ensemble work in which Leibrook hits many wrong notes. In spite of the brevity of his career, Beiderbecke stands apart as an important historical figure for three important reasons: the consistently high level of his performance, the innovation of his musical thought within the context of his historical framework, and the influence he had upon other jazz musicians who helped shape the course of the music they played.

[88] MacDonald, ed., "An Interview with Bud Freeman (5-29-74)," p. 336.
[89] Columbia CL-844.
[90] Ibid.
[91] Ibid.
[92] Ibid.

BOOGIE-WOOGIE

Boogie-woogie is a piano style that is characterized by an ostinato figure in the left hand that some people claim derives from an early blues style played in the barrelhouses, honky-tonks, and other places of ill repute (see *NAJ* 1 and Listening Guide 1). It has, on several occasions, made periodic reappearances in jazz as a popular fad, but very few musicians have used it to the excluson of other techniques, and it has never enjoyed long-lived success. Clarence "Pinetop" Smith, who died in a brawl in Chicago in 1929 at the age of twenty-four, is reputed to have been the pioneer who developed boogie to its most distinctive form. He recorded only twice, but *Pinetop's Boogie Woogie* was later taken up and replayed as a standard of the repertoire. Many of the influential musicians of jazz played boogie-woogie at one time or another—Count Basie, Mary Lou Williams, Fats Waller, and others—but few musicians achieved any lasting musical success with this rather limited rhythmic form. Meade Lux Lewis, who first recorded *Honky Tonk Train Blues* in 1927, combined enough musical imagination and technical skill into his performances to overcome boogie's drawbacks. His rendition of *Honky Tonk Train Blues* (*SCCJ* 31) involves an interesting combination of ternary figures with duple. A jagged hemiola results at the quarter-note and eighth-note levels of examples a and b, and the ternary grouping of eighth-notes in the right hand of example c creates a syncopated flutter with the jerky, but regular, pattern of the left hand.

Meade Lux Lewis.

It has been claimed that Jimmy Yancey, a one-time groundskeeper at the Chicago White Sox baseball park, is actually the originator of boogie-woogie, whereas Pinetop Smith, Meade Lux Lewis, Cripple Clarence Lofton, and Albert Ammons later defined the style.[93] Nevertheless, it seems to creep in and out of jazz like a panhandler cadging drinks from the doorways: not too conspicuous, not too important, but always there.

CHICAGO JAZZ

Jazz in Chicago during the 1920s slowly changed from the classic New Orleans style to a modified traditional style that is usually referred to as Chicago-style jazz. Unfortunately there is no definition that clearly differentiates this

[93] Charles Fox, *Jazz in Perspective* (London: British Broadcasting Corporation, 1969), p. 34.

music from music played in New Orleans or New York during the same period. A clearly defined line of demarcation cannot be drawn because New Orleans musicians working in Chicago played both two-beat and four-beat rhythms, used clarinet and saxophone, interchanged banjos and guitars, played pieces with introductions, vamps, and codas, and both worked out arrangements and improvised polyphonically. These characteristics and others are typical of Chicago jazz during the Roaring Twenties. The record producer and critic George Avakian writes, in the notes to his pioneering documentary jazz album, "Chicago Jazz":[94]

> The most striking aspect of Chicago style jazz is its powerful drive. The middle and end of each chorus particularly arouses in the musicians a reaction like Pepper Martin diving for home plate. They play hard, with never a let-up, but these two concentration points plus the four beats of the bar are always emphasized.
>
> Ensembles are improvised; cornet lead with the other horns rounding out the harmony and filling in, always with the rhythmic drive in mind. The rhythm section, of course, plays an important part in creating this tension, principally through the judicious use of emphases and cross rhythms by drums and banjo. Today [1940] the guitar has replaced the banjo, and this less percussive instrument has proven more effective in ensembles but not as striking for this particular purpose. . . .
>
> To further sustain this driving tension, the Chicagoans use such devices as diminuendos and crescendos in ensemble passages, coming to a sudden stop on the last beat of the sixteenth bar of a tune and picking up again on the second beat of the seventeenth, and playing out endings of a solo chorus together so as to give the next chorus a rounding send-off.
>
> One of the most-repeated adages about the peculiarities of Chicago style has always been that the Chicagoans use few notes. It is true that they seem to avoid using any more than they have to. . . .

Although some would see Chicago jazz as "A subspecies of New Orleans Jazz developed by white musicians in the Chicago area during the early 1920s,"[95] it should be remembered that Chicago had a ragtime—and perhaps jazz—tradition before the well-known New Orleans musicians arrived in the late teens. Chicago also boasts many significant and influential jazz musicians indigenous to the area and maintains a flourishing and continuous jazz history

[94] George Avakian, Notes to the record album "Chicago Jazz" (Decca Album no. 121, record nos. 18040–45).

[95] Bradford Robinson, "Chicago Jazz," *The New Grove Dictionary of Jazz*, I, p. 206.

all its own.[96] Jazz did not arrive in Chicago via the Mississippi riverboats—the Mississippi does not flow through or near Chicago. As Richard Wang points out, the New Orleans musicians "came up on the Illinois Central Railroad and got off at the Twelfth-Street Station.[97] In Chicago, musicians from widely divergent backgrounds were being attracted to jazz. One important group was the Austin Blue Friars, teenage musicians from Chicago's Austin High School who were later nicknamed the Austin High Gang: Jimmy McPartland, cornet; Frank Teschemacher, clarinet; Bud Freeman, saxophone; Dick McPartland, banjo and guitar; and Jim Lanigan, piano, formed the original group, and Lanigan switched to bass when Dave North joined the group as pianist. The drummer, Dave Tough, became a member of the gang, but he was from Oak Park and attended the Lewis Institute. Originally, they modeled their music after that of the New Orleans Rhythm Kings (NORK), and their ensemble of clarinet, cornet, tenor saxophone (and later Floyd O'Brien's trombone), and rhythm section resulted in a sound usually used to exemplify the Chicago style. Other youngsters from Chicago—Eddie Condon, the remarkable guitar and banjo player; Art Hodes, pianist; Joe Sullivan, pianist; Muggsy Spanier, a memorable cornet and plunger-mute soloist; and Mezz Mezzrow, a highly controversial clarinetist (and not much later Benny Goodman and Gene Krupa)—exerted a tremendous influence on jazz and its development. Bix Beiderbecke and Frankie Trumbauer, neither of whom were Chicagoans, played important roles in the musical life of the city during this era, and a music that is neither New Orleans nor New York was played and developed in Chicago during the 1920s.

Some of the musicians of that era were jazz musicians of consequence, who cannot be given fair treatment here for lack of space. Still, Eddie Condon; George Wettling, a leading drummer; Wingy Manone, a white, one-armed trumpet player from New Orleans; Pee Wee Russell, one of the most dexterous of all clarinet players; Mezz Mezzrow; Muggsy Spanier; Bunny Berigan; Gene Krupa; and Benny Goodman, all youngsters who would make their mark in the succeeding decade, are names of consequence in the musical environment located at the south edge of Lake Michigan. While the white musicians played the north side of Chicago, Johnny Dodds, Freddie Keppard, Lovie Austin, and Jimmy Noone, along with Louis Armstrong and Joe Oliver, worked the south side.

[96] For hints at some of the early history see John Steiner and Charles A. Sengstock, Jr., *A Survey of the "Chicago Defender" and the "Chicago Whip": Covering the Years 1909 through 1930 with Respect to the Development of Jazz Music in Chicago* (Chicago: The authors, 1966). For an outline history see Richard Wang, "Jazz in Chicago: A Historical Overview," *Black Music Research Bulletin*, v. 12, no. 2 (Fall 1990), pp. 8–11.
[97] Richard Wang, "Jazz in Chicago," p. 8.

A battered old photograph of Husk O'Hare's Wolverines with members of the Austin High Gang in 1926. (Left to right) Frank Teschemacher and Bud Freeman, saxophones, with Jim Lanigan, bass, between them; Jimmy McPartland, trumpet; Dave Tough, drums; Floyd O'Brien, trombone; Dave North, piano; and Dick McPartland, banjo.

During the 1920s, the "national" bands remained close to New York and Chicago, where the majority of the recording studios and radio stations made their headquarters and where large numbers of cabarets and dance halls provided steady employment. However, this period also spawned hundreds of "territory bands." These groups developed their own sounds, mixing elements taken from the national styles with the taste and tradition of the areas in which they worked. Regional styles flourished, and six major territories emerged: East Coast, Southeast, Midwest, Northwest, Southwest, and West Coast.[98] Southwestern bands, such as George E. Lee, Jap Allen, and Walter Page's Blue Devils, toured out of Kansas City and Oklahoma City; Oliver Cobb worked out of St. Louis; Skeets Morgan came from Alabama; and Smiley Billy Stewart traveled north from Florida. Frank "Red" Perkins, Lloyd

[98] See Thomas J. Hennessey, "From Jazz to Swing: Black Jazz Musicians and Their Music, 1917–1935," (unpublished dissertation, Northwestern University, 1973; University Microfilms no. 74-7757), pp. 121–218.

Hunter, and Ted Adams were all leaders of black bands that toured the hinterlands out of Omaha, Nebraska. An overview of the jazz activities of the late 1920s shows not a draught but a flood. Most of these lesser lights will never receive full investigation by jazz historians because their passage through history is not marked by a trail of recordings. The cumulative effect of all these musicians, sturdy members of the jazz community, undoubtedly had an impact upon the music. A few area styles did emerge, the most notable of which is from Kansas City, the result of artists such as Walter Page and Benny Moten.

Historical Recordings, 1917–29

1917		
ODJB	*Darktown Strutters' Ball*	Columbia A-2297
ODJB	*Dixieland Jazz Band One-Step*	Victor 18255
ODJB	*Livery Stable Blues*	Victor 18255
W. C. Handy	*Ole Miss Rag*	Columbia A-2420
W. C. Handy	*Livery Stable Blues*	Columbia A-2419
1918		
ODJB	*Ostrich Walk*	Victor 18457
ODJB	*Tiger Rag*	Victor 18472
1919		
Louisiana Five	*Yelping Hound Blues*	Columbia A-2742
1920		
Paul Whiteman	*Whispering*	Victor 18690
1921		
James P. Johnson	*Carolina Shout*	OKeh 4495 (*SCCJ* 13)
1922		
Mamie Smith	*Lonesome Mama Blues*	OKeh 4630
Other groups recording jazz or classic blues in 1922:		
Bailey's Lucky Seven		Gennett
Cotton Pickers		Brunswick
Johnny Dunn		Columbia
Friar's Society Orchestra		Gennett
Ladd's Black Aces		Gennett
ODJB		OKeh
Original Memphis Five		
Leona Williams and Her Dixie Band		Banner & Paramount
Edith Wilson		Columbia
		Columbia

(continued on next page)

1923		
Fletcher Henderson	*Gulf Coast Blues*	Vocalion 14636
Perry Bradford	*Daybreak Blues*	Paramount 12041
Benny Moten	*Elephant's Wobble*	OKeh 8100
New Orleans Rhythm Kings	*Wolverine Blues*	Gennett 5102
King Oliver's Creole Jazz Band	*Dippermouth Blues*	Gennett 5132 (*SCCJ* 6)

1924		
Piron's New Orleans Band	*Ghost of the Blues*	Columbia 99-D
Red Onion Jazz Babies		Gennett 5627
Fats Waller	*Cakewalking Babies*	(*SCCJ* 11)
The Wolverines	*Birmingham Blues*	OKeh 4757
	Riverboat Shuffle	Gennett 5454

1925		
Louis Armstrong	*Gut Bucket Blues*	OKeh 8261
Bix and His Rhythm Jugglers	*Davenport Blues*	Gennett 5654
Duke Ellington	*Trombone Blues*	Perfect 14514
Sonny Clay	*Jambled Blues*	Vocalion 15078
Creath's Jazzomaniacs	*King Porter Stomp*	OKeh 8210
(plus Henderson, Moten, Bailey, and many others)		

1926		
Jelly Roll Morton	*Black Bottom Stomp*	Victor 20221 (*SCCJ* 7)
Jelly Roll Morton	*Dead Man Blues*	Victor 20252 (*SCCJ* 8)
Jelly Roll Morton	*Grandpa's Spells*	Victor 20431 (*SCCJ* 9)
Fletcher Henderson	*The Stampede*	Columbia 654-D (*SCCJ* 26)
Papa Celestin	*Station Calls*	Columbia 636-D
Duke Ellington	*You've Got Those "Wanna Go Back Home Again" Blues*	Gennett 3291
Duke Ellington	*East St. Louis Toodle-Oo*	Vocalion 1064 (*SCCJ* 52)
Freddie Keppard	*Salty Dog*	Paramount 12399
Red Nichols	*Washboard Blues*	Brunswick 3407
Joe Venuti-Eddie Lang	*Stringing the Blues*	Columbia 914-D
(plus Armstrong, Moten, Oliver, Pee Wee Russell, and others)		

1927
    Bands:
        Arkansas Travelers, Louis Armstrong, Bix Beiderbecke, Charleston Chasers, Doc
        Cooke, Dixie Stompers, Johnny Dodds, Duke Ellington, Jean Goldkette, Goofus
        Five, Fletcher Henderson, Richard M. Jones, Jelly Roll Morton, Bennie Moten,
        Red Nichols, King Oliver, Red [Nichols] and Miff's [Mole] Stompers, Boyd Sen-
        ter, Jesse Stone, Frankie Trumbauer, Joe Venuti, Eddie Lang, Fats Waller, Paul
        Whiteman, Fess Williams
            Ellington (*SCCJ* 52)
            Walker (*SCCJ* 30)
            Trumbauer (*SCCJ* 23–24)
            Armstrong (*SCCJ* 15–18)

1928
    Important additions to 1927 list:
        Dorsey Brothers, Benny Goodman, McKinney's Cotton Pickers, Ben Pollack

1929
Important additions to 1928 list:
        Eddie Condon, Earl Hines, George E. Lee, Luis Russell, Pinetop Smith

6.

$\mathcal{T}$HE SWING ERA

THE GREAT DEPRESSION, JAZZ, AND POPULAR MUSIC

When the market crashed in October 1929 and fifty leading stocks plummeted almost forty points in one day, jazz in America did not come to an end. The relationship between the music and the economy had always been somewhat loose and informal; nevertheless, in the next six years, many musicians who had been regularly employed in places of entertainment were out of work. America still needed music, perhaps more than ever to lend comfort and solace, but most Americans could not afford to go out as they had in the past. They were no longer in the mood for the lively hot jazz of the carefree and extraordinarily prosperous era that immediately preceded the depression.

Popular songs and crooning prevailed, music of a dreamy, sentimental, fairytale nature that soothed white people's pain as the blues had salved black people's troubles. For example:

1929—*I'm in Seventh Heaven*
1930—*Let Me Sing and I'm Happy*
1931—*Wrap Your Troubles in Dreams*
1932—*How Deep Is the Ocean*
1933—*I've Got the World on a String*

Bands with radio contracts and those willing and able to cater to a melancholy general public weathered the financial storm and even prospered. Guy Lombardo established himself at the Roosevelt Hotel, and Paul Whiteman continued to parade an endless supply of popular singers, semiclassical arrangers and composers, vaudeville tricksters,[1] and name jazz musicians before the public. This entertainment formula earned Whiteman a regal reputation, for he almost singlehandedly dominated the popular market. Fletcher Henderson, broadcasting from the Roseland Ballroom in New York City, was a compromise figure in that he led a band of jazz musicians but strayed only rarely from the moderate path of mid-tempo, social-dance music. The leading hot-jazz musicians, such as Louis Armstrong, continued to play and record, but their broad base of support was gradually shrinking.

THE EMERGENCE OF SUBSTYLES

Between 1929 and 1935, many of the major jazz organizations crossed the Atlantic to try their luck in Europe. These trips had publicity value on this side of the ocean, and it kept some of the jazz musicians employed, as the old world was still eager to receive more hot music from the new. Armstrong ventured across during this period, as did Duke Ellington. As if commenting on the general state of big-band music in America, Ellington composed, in 1932, *It Don't Mean a Thing If It Ain't Got That Swing*.[2] Although the general public may have been only vaguely aware of the current state of jazz, the years from 1929 to 1935 produced some formidable changes in the music itself. A phenomenon was occurring that could be clearly observed from that time to the present: a multiplicity of substyles emerged and began to coexist. In the early days, ragtime, minstrel, brass band, and blues were fused, so that basically one style of jazz, albeit with individual variants, was played: hot jazz. The jazz of New Orleans, Chicago, the Southwest, and New York was essentially of one style. Gradually, throughout the 1920s, outside influences and ideas started to form new buds on the "old" plant. Where New York stride piano was initially little more than a local variant of ragtime performance, the day had finally arrived when ragtime piano players, such as Jelly Roll Morton, would coexist with swing piano players, like Fats Waller, and with a new breed, the boogie-woogie pianists, such as Pine Top Smith and Meade Lux Lewis. Before long, the hot combos of the classic jazz style would vie for jobs with the newer swing combos, groups that were still in their formative stages during these early depression years. Morton's Red Hot Peppers and Nichols's Five Hot Pennies had already mastered their craft of

[1] Whiteman's recording of *Whispering* (Victor 18690), which features a slide whistle as lead instrument, is a classic example.

[2] Brunswick 6265.

hot jazz, but the young Dorseys, Goodman, and others were learning to play with a new sound.

The swing bands had few counterparts in the early 1920s, but as some of the smaller ensembles expanded and began playing newly written compositions and special arrangements, the big band emerged toward the end of the decade (see p. 230 ff). In the music of the jazz orchestras, the most significant developments took place during the worst of the depression years. The pioneers—Duke Ellington, Fletcher Henderson, and Don Redman—were maturing in the early '30s, while some new names appeared upon the scene—perhaps the most notable of these was Glen Gray and his Casa Loma Orchestra. The musical events of this time are still an aesthetic battlefield. One commentator considers what was happening a cultural tragedy:

> The number of prosperous dance bands at the popular level multiplied, while the jazz content remained slight. At the same time, dancing the Charleston, the Black Bottom, and the Lindy was highly popular and the bands tried to oblige by playing a little hot jazz. . . . None of these large dance bands, however, could swing as a whole. The formula consisted of importing one or two "hot" soloists or "get-off" men, letting them take a chorus once in a while surrounded by acres of uninspired fellow musicians.[3]

Another observer sees things differently and views the situation as fertile and productive:

> Unnoticed at first by the general public, though impressing the musicians and jazz fans as early as 1930, were the brisk, brittle, semi-swinging big band sounds produced by the midwestern Casa Loma Orchestra. . . . Soon, not only musicians were listening to Glen Gray and the Casa Loma Orchestra. Kids, especially those in the colleges, flocked to hear the handsome-looking band that produced such mellow, musical moods, then stood around in awe as it let loose with an excitingly different-sounding big band barrage. More than any other group, the Casa Loma Orchestra set the stage for the emergence of the swing bands and eventually the blossoming of the entire big band era.[4]

Whether jazz during these years was in ascent or decline is a conjectural matter directly related to personal opinion and taste, for just as one person's religion is another's heresy, jazz was considered to have been either expanding or fragmenting. Historically, however, the issue goes beyond personal judgment. Since most, if not all, of the various schools have maintained a

---

[3] Marshall W. Stearns, *The Story of Jazz*, p. 180.
[4] George T. Simon, *The Big Bands*, p. 26 f.

continuous tradition to the present; inasmuch as the musicians considered *themselves* to be jazz artists and their own music to be jazz; and because the new music in the big-band style had roots in the past and retained the essential elements of the parent music, it is historically imperative to judge this period as one of musical development and expansion, even though fans of the earliest jazz music condemn it as less creative and exciting. The new music may have been somewhat limited, and it may have followed some musical paths for commercial rather than purely artistic reasons, but it did expand the harmonic and timbral vocabularies of jazz and it did raise the level of requisite technical mastery in performance.

Jimmy Noone (*SCCJ* 25), Jack Teagarden, Red Nichols (*SCCJ* 28), Frankie Trumbauer, Jimmy McPartland, Miff Mole, Joe Venuti, Eddie Lang, and a host of others were formidable jazz musicians who held almost universal respect within the jazz community during the early 1930s, but they, as well as many others, will receive brief or no mention in the pages that follow. By this time, the number of jazz musicians had proliferated to such an extent that, in the interest of conciseness, we must turn our attention to those masters who most strongly affected the destiny of this American music. Those who steered the course most resolutely at this time were: for hot jazz—traditionalists Louis Armstrong, King Oliver, and Jelly Roll Morton; for the establishment orchestras—Guy Lombardo and Paul Whiteman; and for the new big-band sound—Fletcher Henderson, Don Redman, Jimmie Lunceford, Bennie Moten, Glen Gray, and Duke Ellington. It was the music of the last group that led to the style called swing, and that is what we shall proceed to analyze here.

THE ARRANGER— DON REDMAN

Don Redman, alto saxophonist and arranger, joined the Fletcher Henderson band at the Roseland Ballroom in New York in 1923. Two years later, Henderson recorded a Redman arrangement of *Dippermouth Blues* called *Sugar Foot Stomp*.[5] The instrumentation called for four brasses, three reeds, and four in the rhythm section, for a total of eleven musicians. At that time, in 1925, the band concept revealed in the Redman arrangements represented only a slightly expanded version of King Oliver's New Orleans ensemble. In fact, Louis Armstrong was with the Henderson band at that time to record the hot solos. Where Oliver used two trumpets, Henderson employed three. His three reeds provided a hot jazz clarinetist in Buster Bailey, with the additional saxophones of Redman and Coleman Hawkins expanding the mid-

[5] Columbia 395-D, reissued Folkways FP 67.

The Fletcher Henderson band in 1925 consisted of (front row, left to right) Kaiser Marshall, drums; Coleman Hawkins, Buster Bailey, and Don Redman, reeds; Charlie Dixon, banjo; Fletcher Henderson, piano. (Back row, left to right) Charlie Green, trombone; Elmer Chambers, Louis Armstrong, and Howard Scott, trumpets; and Ralph Escudero, tuba.

range sonority. The four-piece rhythm section of piano, tuba, drums, and banjo was typical of the traditional jazz groups and had already crystallized as a standard grouping for hot jazz. As the years passed, the Dixieland tuba and banjo were replaced by the swing string bass and guitar.

Henderson's 1926 recording of *The Stampede*[6] (*SCCJ* 26) uses the same instrumentation that he used for *Sugar Foot Stomp*. The following year, his recording band added a second trombone for *Livery Stable Blues*.[7] This work is still strongly related to the New Orleans repertoire and style, being an arrangement of the "trad jazz" piece introduced on record in 1917 by the Original Dixieland Jazz Band. Redman's arrangement for *The Stampede* "is almost an archetype of the [swing] big band score: written passages that separate the ensemble by sections, antiphonal phrases between the sections, a written variation-on-theme . . . , solo improvisation [at designated points in the music]."[8] The piece, which was arranged by Redman, contains thirty-

[6] Columbia 654-D, reissued *SCCJ* 26.
[7] Columbia 1002-D, reissued Columbia C3L33.
[8] Martin Williams, liner notes to *SCCJ*.

The Stampede

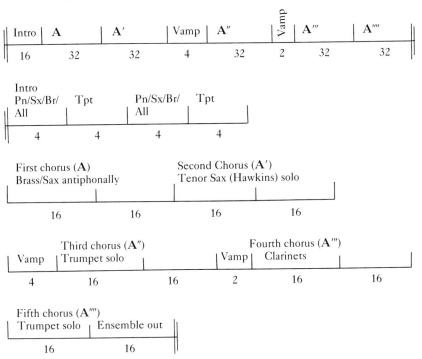

two measures divided into two sixteen-measure phrases, the first acting as an antecedent phrase with a feminine (or open) ending (I–V) and the second answering as a consequent phrase with a masculine (or closed) ending (V–I). In his score, Redman repeats the complete piece five times, but orchestrates for the entire band only the first chorus, fourth chorus, introduction, vamps, and the last half of the fifth, or final, chorus.

The musical figures played during the first chorus by the brass and saxophone sections are not unlike the riffs developed improvisationally by the Kansas City bands, but in this instance they are the inventions of the composer and arranger. To a certain degree, these riffs probably needed to be written down on paper, because the underlying chord structure of *The Stampede* is neither universally known nor commonly reused by jazz musicians, as are the chord patterns of the blues and those popular songs that formed the basis of most of the Kansas City repertoire.

Although the notes of the clarinet chorus (the fourth) differ from those used in the first chorus, they carry the same repetitious rhythmic idea exploited by Redman earlier in the piece. One fascinating aspect of the tenor-saxo-phone solo by Coleman Hawkins is his improvisatory exploration of some of these same rhythmic ideas. His solo thus relates closely to this particular piece beyond a mere melodic ornamentation over a given chordal frame-work. Note too that the trumpet solos are played in mid-range. The emerg-ing swing style calls upon the power of the instrument's center range. Another swing feature, the jagged and on-the-beat rhythms that would become a dominating feature of solos in this style, is apparent here as well.

Reed solos in swing frequently utilize arpeggiated chordal passages grouped in twos and fours so that accents fall regularly on the beat, while brass solos frequently use dotted figures with repeated notes that are rhythmically orga-nized on the beat. It seems likely that the increased musical schooling of the musicians and its concomitant technical virtuosity was brought about, and resulted from, woodshedding[9] of scales and arpeggios in the various keys. These practice habits would help account for the former characteristic. The latter, the brass solos, are not really different in kind from the majority of New Orleans–style brass solos (Bix Beiderbecke is almost unique among the brass soloists of this period, and his solos are unlike those being discussed here). The need for great volume to carry a brass solo from the back line of the band over the accompanying reeds and brass may have had something to do with the frequency of mid-range trumpet and trombone solos. Rhythmic activity and syncopation are as ever-present in swing as they were in the earlier jazz, but accentuation, in both the solos and the arrangements, falls more frequently on the beat—often on a strong beat—and becomes one of the chief characteristics of the style.

This style of arrangement does not depend upon particular personnel. If Coleman Hawkins were not available to play the tenor saxophone solo, Don Redman might just as well have played it on the alto instead. The musicians in a typical swing band using this archetypal formula arrangement are, in a sense, interchangeable—to some degree, all jazz musicians are. But here Don Redman clearly does not exploit the special talents of individual instru-mentalists, but simply leaves "blank spaces" in his arrangements where available musicians may stand up and "take a ride." His arrangements, although written for the Fletcher Henderson band, could be played by most any swing band that had sufficient personnel to cover the parts. When Redman arrange-ments were played by other bands, they sounded very much like those recorded by the Fletcher Henderson orchestra. The same is not true for the music of Duke Ellington or the head arrangements of the Bennie Moten, later the Count Basie, band.

Don Redman left the Henderson band in 1928, but Henderson continued

---

[9]"Woodshedding" refers to practicing or rehearsing in private in order to gain technical mastery of one's instrument before going into a jam session.

Fletcher Henderson's band in 1927, "The Stompingest Band in the Country." (Left to right) Henderson, Charlie Dixon, Jimmy Harrison, Jerome Pasqually, Benny Morton, Buster Bailey, June Cole, Coleman Hawkins, Kaiser Marshall, Tommy Ladnier, Joe Smith, and Russell Smith.

to employ the same-size group and the same orchestrational concepts for the next six years. In 1928, he recorded *Hop Off*[10] with three trumpets, two trombones, three reeds, piano, tuba, drums, and banjo; and in 1933 he recorded *Queer Notions*[11] with the same forces, except that a bass and guitar replaced the tuba and banjo, as they had in his band.

In the meantime, Don Redman had taken charge of the McKinney's Cotton Pickers band, and between 1928 and 1932 he recorded with a group very similar to the Fletcher Henderson orchestra. His rhythm section always had piano, drums, and banjo, and the bass part moved back and forth between tuba and string bass. Redman never exceeded three trumpets and often recorded with four reeds. Normally, there was only one trombone and it was not until 1932, when he recorded his best-known work, *Chant of the Weed*, that he augmented his trombone section to three. With this particular work, he moved from the domain of the arranger into the realm of the composer, and here, for musical reasons, he found it necessary to use a nonstandard combination.

[10] Paramount 12550, reissued Riverside RLP 12-115.
[11] Vocalion 2583, reissued Prestige 7645.

The McKinney's Cotton Pickers shown at Jean Goldkette's Greystone Ballroom, Detroit, in the late 1920s.

1928   *Cherry* (Victor 21730, reissued Victor LPV-520)
        2 trumpets, 1 trombone, 4 reeds, piano, tuba, drums, banjo
1929   *Gee, Ain't I Good to You?* (Victor 38097, reissued Victor LPV-520)
        3 trumpets, 1 trombone, 4 reeds, piano, bass, drums, banjo
1930   *Rocky Road* (Victor 22932, reissued Victor LPV-520)
        3 trumpets, 1 trombone, 3 reeds, piano, tuba, drums, banjo
1931   *Baby Won't You Please Come Home?* (Victor 22511, reissued Folkways FP 59)
        2 trumpets, 1 trombone, 3 reeds, piano, tuba, drums, banjo
1932   *Chant of the Weed* (Columbia 2675-D, reissued Columbia C3L 33)
        3 trumpets, 3 trombones, 4 reeds, piano, bass, drums, banjo

As noted earlier, in a small improvising ensemble in which the musical functions of the players are clearly defined, it is not difficult to assign roles to the various musicians and expect them to carry out their assignments with alacrity and precision. Adding another front-line instrument, such as Oliver's second trumpet, necessitates a certain increase in the amount of improvised harmony, but this is not difficult to accomplish by ear, because thirds and sixths are relatively easy to fit with the melody in this style. Therefore, an arrangement for Fletcher Henderson's 1925 band is a fairly uncomplicated matter—an additional trumpet and two reeds call for a minimum of work for the arranger. When the brasses expand to six and the reeds to four, the complexity multiplies geometrically, and more careful planning and control by the composer/arranger are necessary. But the richer harmonic and timbral possibilities compensate for the difficulties encountered. Six-way brass chords stretching from the pedal notes of the trombone (or tuba) to the upper partials of the trumpet produce richer, more resonant sounds and new chordal configurations extending into harmonics beyond the usual root, third, fifth, and seventh.

THE COMPOSER— DUKE ELLINGTON

The pioneer who scouted these new regions of musical space more than any other jazz musician of the time was Edward Kennedy "Duke" Ellington (1899–1974). Born in Washington, D.C., Ellington attended Armstrong Technical High School and played ragtime piano during his teenage years, modeling his technique on that of Washington's black pianists. In 1917 he left high school before earning his diploma and worked a variety of day jobs while breaking into the music profession at night. He played with Louis Thomas, Russell Wooding, Louis Brown, and Oliver "Doc" Perry, all local musicians with excellent reputations, and in Washington he heard many famous jazz artists—among them Luckey Roberts, Eubie Blake, Coleman Hawkins, Fletcher Henderson, and Sidney Bechet. By 1919 his own reputation was growing and he formed a band. It was then that he advertised his own jazz group, The Duke's Serenaders, in the telephone directory.[12] Soon after, through his association and study with Henry Grant, an important local musician, he developed his taste and abilities beyond ragtime.

In 1923 he left Washington for New York. After a false start with Wilbur Sweatman, he joined Elmer Snowden, whom he had met in Washington in 1920, as the pianist of Snowden's Washingtonians for an engagement at the Hollywood, a New York cabaret on Times Square. The leader played banjo and doubled soprano sax, James "Bubber" Miley played cornet and mellophone, John Anderson played trombone and trumpet, William "Sonny" Greer did drums and vocals, Otto Hardwick played saxophones and violin, Roland Smith played saxophone and bassoon, and Ellington was pianist and arranger. Here Ellington worked with musicians who later formed the nucleus of the orchestra he led for the next fifty years. Also, this ensemble provided a first sample of the instrumental variety and playing styles he would exploit in his approximately two thousand compositions. After he joined, the band played a combination of "hot" and "sweet" numbers. The group's versatility was partly attributable to the orchestral possibilities available to the young arranger through the various doubling combinations of the instrumentalists. The following year, Anderson was replaced by Charlie "Plug" Irvis, a trombonist specializing in muted techniques. More significantly, Ellington replaced

---

[12] Mark Tucker, *Ellington: The Early Years*, p. 54 f.

Snowden as leader of the band. When Ellington recorded *Choo-Choo* and *Rainy Nights*[13] in 1924, he was fronting an ensemble that closely approximates the classic jazz combo of three front-line and three rhythm instruments: trumpet, trombone, alto sax (rather than clarinet), piano, drums, and banjo. Two years later his six-member outfit had expanded to ten; for his Kentucky Club Orchestra's recording of *The Creeper*,[14] he employed the stylish Fletcher Henderson instrumentation of two trumpets, one trombone, three reeds, piano, bass, drums, and banjo. Although Ellington's personnel and instrumentation varied somewhat during this period, the orchestra remained more stable than most while following the trend of expansion. The brass and reed sections grew fuller, and the available timbral characteristics were likewise more varied.

The addition of a second bass player to the band in 1935 occurred more by accident than by design, so for the remainder of the 1930s an ensemble of six brasses, four reeds, and four rhythm players was Duke's normal working unit. In 1939 Jimmy Blanton became the regular bassist, and the piano-bass duets recorded that year displayed his artistry as well as Ellington's.[15]

Duke Ellington
Outline of Expanding Instrumental Resources*

1924   *Rainy Nights* (Blu-Disc 1002, reissued Riverside RLP 12-115)
             1 trumpet, 1 trombone, 1 reed, piano, drums, banjo
                                    [6 musicians]
1926   *The Creeper* (Vocalion 1077), reissued Folkways FP 67)
             2 trumpets, 1 trombone, 3 reeds, piano, bass, drums, banjo
                                    [10 musicians]
1928   *Hot and Bothered* (OKeh 8623, reissued Time-Life 14730)
             2 trumpets, 1 trombone, 3 reeds, piano, bass, drums, banjo, and guest guitar
                                    [11 musicians]
1930   *Rockin' in Rhythm* (OKeh 8869, reissued Time-Life 14730)
             3 trumpets, 2 trombones, 3 reeds, piano, bass, drums, banjo
                                    [12 musicians]
1932   *It Don't Mean a Thing* (Brunswick 6265, reissued Folkways FP 59)
             3 trumpets, 3 trombones, 3 reeds, piano, bass, drums, banjo
                                    [13 musicians]
1935   *Merry Go Round* (Brunswick 7440, reissued Time-Life 14730)
             3 trumpets, 3 trombones, 4 reeds, piano, 2 basses, drums, and guitar
                                    [15 musicians]

---

*To simplify, this chart does not distinguish between cornet and trumpet, valve trombone and trombone, tuba and bass, etc., and does not specify instruments on which musicians doubled, such as violin.

[13] Blu-Disc 1002. For an excellent analysis of both pieces, see Tucker, *Ellington*, pp. 140–49.
   [14] Vocalion 1077.
   [15] *Blues* and *Plucked Again* (Columbia 35322).

Edward Kennedy "Duke" Ellington (1899–1974).

The following year, Ellington recorded "Jack the Bear,"[16] a composition that exhibits the distinct solo pizzicato technique of Blanton. His performances during a much-too-brief career largely reshaped the image of the string bass in jazz from a foundation instrument restricted to work in the rhythm section to a fascinating solo instrument. This work is notable for many other reasons as well: we hear not only the supple pianistic technique of Ellington in his brief solos but also the brilliant clarinet playing of Barney Bigard, the excellent baritone saxophone solo of Harry Carney, and the now-famous solo dis-

[16]Victor 26536.

play of Joe "Tricky Sam" Nanton's plunger mute and slide work. Ellington's compositional wizardry is apparent as well in the way he employs blues form when it suits him, stretches the blues out of shape or inserts contrasting passages when the music calls for variety, and exploits a full range of orchestral timbres and dynamic levels in his orchestration.

Billy Strayhorn joined the band in 1939 as arranger and second pianist. Strayhorn not only contributed important compositions of his own but also, in a way, became Ellington's alter ego. The two developed an extremely close working relationship, and Strayhorn's uncanny understanding of Ellington's musical ideas produced a fruitful artistic atmosphere. It will still take years before scholars can separate the Ellington in Strayhorn works and the Strayhorn in Ellington.

In 1940 tenor saxophonist Ben Webster was recruited for the band, allowing for a new five-way reed voicing. In Webster, Ellington also gained a tenor soloist of extraordinary rhythmic drive, gutsy sound, and melodic invention. By 1946 the band peaked at eighteen players, but then the personnel roster began to vary, and Ellington lost the long, close, and personal contact that he had with some of his players and that he relished and utilized so brilliantly in the past.

Duke Ellington composed and arranged scores that were tailored to the special abilities of his band members, musicians whose work was intimately familiar to him. His *East St. Louis Toodle-Oo*, recorded in 1927 (*SCCJ* 52), is an early example of an orchestration designed to spotlight the special solo characteristics of specific sidemen.

East St. Louis Toodle-Oo

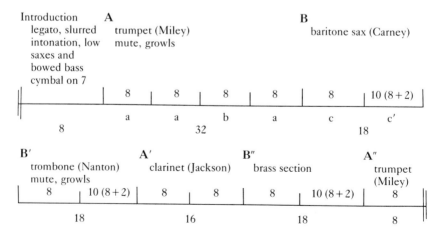

In this piece, Ellington collaborated with trumpeter Bubber Miley, whose trumpet growls, as is plainly evident, are not sounds that can be precisely notated and handed on to another trumpeter for accurate reproduction. A chord chart (music in figures that simply indicate harmonies upon which to improvise a solo) would not produce the same effect at all. For Ellington to achieve the compositional sound he envisioned for this piece, it was necessary for him to work with the performing soloists in rehearsal. We know this is a method he subsequently followed throughout his career. Once the recording existed, of course, it was possible for players in the band or elsewhere to imitate and reinterpret the established ideas. Here it is particularly instructive to listen to the two versions of the same piece recorded ten years apart, 1927 (*SCCJ* 52) and 1937 (*SCCJ* 53), and note both the similarities and the differences. To a certain extent, these compositions were created in real time rather than on paper, as is the norm for most classical Western composition—Ellington's creativity would have been hampered by his trying to use standard musical notation to express the variety of compositional ideas in this work.

As a jazz composition for big band created in 1927, the piece stands as a milestone. The irregularity of the form, the brilliant variety of orchestral timbre, the blend of arrangement and solo, and the total effect of composed music and swinging jazz are distinctive features that mark the music of Duke Ellington even in its earliest stages.

Throughout the next decade, the pioneer inexorably became the master. *Creole Rhapsody*[17] (*SCCJ* 55) of 1931 stands out as Ellington's first piece of absolute music—music without words composed solely for listening rather than for dance or social entertainment—and it gives us an indication of his growing self-awareness as a composer. In this piece, one notes the striking similarity to Gershwin's *Rhapsody in Blue*[18] and *Concerto in F*,[19] but one is also aware of significant differences: the orchestration, improvisation by the piano soloist, and improvisation by the sidemen.

Ellington was regularly employed at the Cotton Club in Harlem beginning December 4, 1927, and his band performed there for the next four years. By late 1928 his working band numbered twelve, and, as we have just observed in *East St. Louis Toodle-Oo*, Ellington began to view his orchestra as a palette of tone colors from which he might select just the right sounds to orchestrate into compositions. For him the band was not simply a fixed unit for which "a book" of arrangements was assembled; it was a magnificent instrument that might be brought to life through imagination and his per-

[17] Brunswick 6093.
[18] Recorded by the composer with Paul Whiteman in 1924, Victor 55225.
[19] Recorded by Paul Whiteman in 1928, Columbia 50139-D, 50140-D, and 7172-M.

Duke Ellington and the Cotton Club Orchestra, 1929.

sonal direction. Unlike other swing bands of the day, which essentially played a predictable format of tutti and solo passages (i.e., instruments playing ensemble choruses together or one instrument improvising a solo chorus while some or all of the others musicians play backing material), Ellington's band often played extended passages for small, unusual combinations of instruments. Sometimes, as in *Mood Indigo* (see below), Ellington used a reduced instrumentation throughout the entire work, even though his available instrumental resources were much greater. In this regard, his technique resembled the impressionist composers Claude Debussy, Maurice Ravel, and Frederick Delius, who scored for full orchestra but seldom used all the instruments at the same time, more than it did that of other jazz band leaders of the period. However, Ellington also wrote music similar to that of his jazz colleagues, the swing bandleaders, for he was a working musician required to provide dance tunes and popular song arrangements in the familiar and popular swing style.

As Gunther Schuller summarizes, Ellington wrote five categories of musical pieces during his Cotton Club "workshop period": (1) numbers for dancing; (2) jungle-style and/or production numbers for various Cotton Club *tableaux;* (3) "blue" or "mood" pieces; (4) pop tunes or ballads; and (5) independent nonfunctional instrumental compositions.[20]

A perfect example of the third category, *Mood Indigo*, shows his genius for creating distinctive orchestral blends through instrumental selection, proper scoring, and deft exploitation of microphones, mutes, and individual performance techniques. The piece was recorded on October 17, 1930.[21] Although he had available his Cotton Club "Jungle Band," numbering twelve players—three trumpets, two trombones, three reeds, banjo, string bass, drums, and piano—Ellington used but seven musicians for this composition: trumpet, trombone, clarinet, piano, string bass, drums, and banjo.[22] The distribution of trumpet, trombone and clarinet over the most interesting three of the several possible notes to be chosen from each chord is brilliantly made. Also, the distinctive sounds of the three lead instruments—Arthur Whetsol playing into a cup-muted trumpet, Joe "Tricky Sam" Nanton playing a plunger-muted trombone, and Barney Bigard playing clarinet an octave below the brass in the low *chalumeau* register of the instrument—is also unique. Ellington chose chords to accompany the slow, weaving melody—often seventh and ninth chords with chromatic alterations—parallels the twisting, chromatic tune in what later would be termed "a thickened melodic line." All these factors combine to communicate clearly the composer's musical meaning to the listener, a musical expression of a blue mood.

Ellington normally composed with ease and could do so on demand. Typical of his method, we read his own account of the origins of *Mood Indigo* (*NW* 272, II/1).

> Later that year, in the fall [of 1930], we had a six-piece recording date. [Irving] Mills never lost his liking for the original small-combo sound, even when the big band had made its mark. On this occasion, as usual, the night before was the time for me to write and think music. I already had three tunes and, while waiting for my mother to finish cooking dinner, I began to write a fourth. In fifteen minutes, I wrote the score for *Mood Indigo*. We recorded it, and that night at the Cotton Club, when it was almost time for our broadcast, Ted Husing, the announcer, asked, "Duke, what are we going to play tonight?" I

[20] Gunther Schuller, *The Swing Era: The Development of Jazz 1930–1945*, p. 48.

[21] Brunswick 4952, reissued in the *Time-Life* three-record set, "Giants of Jazz: Duke Ellington" (14730).

[22] Although Brian Rust lists seven musicians for the October 14 and 17 recording sessions (*Jazz Records 1897–1942*, 4th ed., I, p. 482), it is likely that only six performed this number. The drums are inaudible throughout the recording. Ellington's comment, "we played it on the air, six pieces out of the eleven-piece band" (Edward Kennedy Ellington, *Music Is My Mistress*, p. 79) is confusing, because his band numbered twelve, counting himself. He played piano on the *Mood Indigo* recording, so that would make six musicians plus himself.

told him about the new number, and we played it on the air, six pieces out of the eleven-piece band. The next day, wads of mail came in raving about the new tune, so Irving Mills put a lyric on it, and royalties are still coming in for my evening's work more than forty years later.[23]

Introducing his personal brand of chromatic harmonic thinking into jazz was one of Ellington's most notable accomplishments. Several writers have remarked how these sounds probably resulted from his method of scoring—notating his improvisatory explorations at the piano—rather than from studied, analytical thought. Whatever the method, his compositions are unique, communicative, and expressive, and the harmonic aspect often contributed greatly to the music's interest. This expanded harmonic vocabulary, which appears in many of his pieces, is evident in recordings of his works. One of the most striking early examples is *Sophisticated Lady*,[24] recorded in 1933 with an orchestra of fourteen: six brasses, four reeds, and four rhythm instruments. This piece, along with Redman's *Chant of the Weed*, which the Ellington band also played, stands as a landmark that guided many jazz artists in their subsequent harmonic thinking. Unlike *Mood Indigo*, however, *Sophisticated Lady* was no fifteen-minute job, as Ellington struggled for the right harmonic solution. In a radio interview for the Canadian Broadcasting Company he discussed the extraordinary amount of time it took to write the piece and referred to several different resolutions to the bridge problem (the **B** section of the **AABA** form) before settling on the one going from A♭ to G.[25]

Duke Ellington, *Sophisticated Lady*

[23] Ellington, *Music Is My Mistress*, p. 78 f.
[24] Brunswick 6600.
[25] My thanks to Professor Richard Wang for informing me about this interview in his correspondence of July 20, 1981.

Ellington's final answer was subtle and economical—four closely related chords. The first (A♭major⁷) shares three tones with the second—only one voice has to move. The second also shares three tones with the next and begins the circle-of-fifths progression A–D–G. And the third has three leading tones (E♭–D; C–B; and F♯–G) to cement the bond to the new, distantly related key of G. Simple, complex, and unusual.

During the 1930s there was some variation in the personnel of Ellington's band, but the core instrumentation remained the same: six brasses, four saxophones, and four rhythm instruments. Ellington was an outstanding businessman, and throughout these depression years in America, he kept his band together, developed as a composer, and recorded many of his most important compositions. Early in his career, his players exerted a strong influence on his musical thinking, through their skills, their joint compositions, and the inspiration of their imagination, musical invention, and personality. By the end of the decade, however, although this symbiotic relationship continued, the balance of artistic power had shifted. Ellington was clearly influencing his musicians, directing their playing, writing sounds they had never imagined—and creating musical masterpieces.

In some works we hear a level of chromaticism that at times creates bitonality and even approaches atonality, either because instruments are following their own contrapuntal paths or they are playing expanded chords, chromatically altered chords, or unusual harmonic progressions. Commonly, Ellington would score a high level of unresolved dissonance, but he had the ear to temper any exaggerated effect through creative voicing and subtle orchestration. Among his longer compositions we find many independent instrumental works of absolute music, whose goal is to communicate musical meaning to the listener. This is often accomplished by carefully relating all the parts of the piece to one another through compositional design. He achieved a high-water mark in musical craftsmanship in 1935 with *Reminiscing in Tempo*,[26] a thirteen-minute work based on one theme with thirteen variations. About this work, Gunther Schuller points out that

> nothing quite that challenging had ever been attempted in jazz composition— and with a jazz orchestra. Indeed, perhaps the most remarkable achievement of the work is the way composition and orchestra interact, and cohere in a way that was new even for Ellington—at least on such an extended scale. This is also the subtlest aspect of the work, and it is small wonder that the critics of 1935 failed to hear the thematic coherence of the work or the intimate relationship between the musical content and the orchestra for whom it was exclu-

[26] Brunswick 7546 and 7547.

The Duke and 4 Trumpets, Fall, 1959. (Left to right) Willis "Ray" Nance, William Alonzo "Cat" Anderson, John "Willie" Cook, and Eddie "Moon" Mullens.

sively written.`. . . For all its compositional craft and structural unity, it is the loveliness of its themes, its contemplative reminiscing mood, the sensuous, insinuating harmonies, the gentle warmth of its instrumental colors, that make *Reminiscing in Tempo* a memorable musical experience. It should be in the repertory of every jazz orchestra and be known to every American, for it is one of Ellington's greatest master strokes.[27]

The following year, Ellington and Barney Bigard collaborated to compose and perform a display piece for Bigard, *Clarinet Lament*. It is one of several works popularly thought of as "concertos," musical compositions for orchestra that feature a solo instrumentalist. *Clarinet Lament (Barney's Concerto)* (*NAJ* 5) proves how deftly Ellington was able to transform existing material, *Basin Street Blues*, into a unique work of art that defies further transformation (See Listening Guide 5). Although there are hundreds of recordings of *Basin Street Blues*, all of them different and yet all essentially the same, there is only the Ellington Orchestra version of *Clarinet Lament* with Bigard as soloist. Neither the orchestra nor Bigard can be satisfactorily replaced; they can be copied, but like a Michelangelo statue or a Raphael painting, the original creation is unique and truly special. The sound image represents a moment of creative inspiration at a particular instant in music's history, and as such, it becomes a part of that history.

The impact of Duke Ellington on the world of jazz is not easily measured, for in his long and prolific career he set standards in so many areas: as a composer, harmonic innovator, ensemble leader, recording artist, arranger,

[27] Gunther Schuller, *The Swing Era: The Development of Jazz 1930–1945*, pp. 75, 83. Schuller presents a detailed, insightful, and lucid analysis of *Reminiscing in Tempo*, pp. 74–83. For detailed analyses of major works from the period 1939–41, see Ken Rattenbury, *Duke Ellington, Jazz Composer*.

patron of aspiring jazz musicians, and spokesman for black Americans and their culture. The very length of his career has resulted in a corpus of Ellington compositions, arrangements, and performances that is unique and, fortunately, almost completely documented. A list of his most significant compositions, a very small percentage of his total output, must include:

1926	*East St. Louis Toodle-Oo* (collaborator, Bubber Miley)
1927	*Black and Tan Fantasy* (collaborator, B. Miley)
	Creole Love Call (collaborator, B. Miley)
1928	*The Mooche*
	Misty Mornin' (collaborator, Arthur Whetsol)
1930	*Mood Indigo* (collaborator, Barney Bigard)
1931	*Creole Rhapsody*
1932	*It Don't Mean a Thing If It Ain't Got That Swing*
	Sophisticated Lady (collaborator, Otto Hardwick)
1934	*Solitude*
1935	*In a Sentimental Mood*
	Reminiscing in Tempo
1936	*Caravan* (collaborator, Juan Tizol)
	Clarinet Lament (Barney's Concerto) (collaborator, Barney Bigard)
1937	*Diminuendo and Crescendo in Blue*
1938	*Braggin' in Brass*
	Prelude to a Kiss
1939	*Concerto for Cootie*
1940	*Ko-Ko*
	Harlem Air Shaft
	Cotton Tail
	Jack the Bear
	In a Mellotone
1941	*I Got It Bad*
	Chelsea Bridge (collaborator, Billy Strayhorn)
	Jump for Joy (musical)
1943	*Black, Brown, and Beige*
1944	*I'm Beginning to See the Light* (collaborators, Johnny Hodges and Harry James)
1947	*The Liberian Suite*
	Clothed Woman
1950	*Harlem*
	The Asphalt Jungle (film score)
1953	*Satin Doll*
1955	*Night Creature*
1956	*A Drum Is a Woman* (collaborator, B. Strayhorn)
1957	*Such Sweet Thunder* (collaborator, B. Strayhorn)
1959	*Anatomy of a Murder* (film score)
1960	*Suite Thursday*
1963	*What Color Is Virtue?* (from *My People*)
1964	*The Far East Suite* (collaborator, B. Strayhorn)
1965	*In The Beginning, God* (First Sacred Concert, Grace Cathedral, San Francisco)
1966	*La Plus Belle Africaine*
1968	*Second Sacred Concert* (St. John the Divine, New York)
1971	*New Orleans Suite*
1973	*Third Sacred Concert* (Westminster Abbey, London)

Johnny Hodges, in a 1930s photograph.

Ray Nance, violin, with (left to right) John Hardee and Gene Ammons, tenor saxophones; Harry Edison, trumpet; Max Roach, standing behind unidentified drummer; and Tiny Grimes, guitar; c. 1945.

Clark Terry, fluegelhorn, with Frank Tirro, clarinet, Numa "Pee Wee" Moore, tenor saxophone, George Duvivier, bass, and Peter Ingram, drums, at the Déja Vu Cafe in Raleigh, North Carolina, January 24, 1979.

The list of musicians who found refuge under his sympathetic, but critical and disciplined, gaze includes those who, in his band or on their own, helped shape the history of jazz in positive and creative ways. To mention but a few: the arranger Billy Strayhorn; trumpeters Bubber Miley, Arthur Whetsol, Cootie Williams, Wallace Jones, Ray Nance, Cat Anderson, and Clark Terry; trombonists Lawrence Brown, Joe Nanton, and Juan Tizol; saxophonists Johnny Hodges, Ben Webster, Harry Carney, Barney Bigard, and Paul Gonsalves; drummers Sonny Greer and Louis Bellson; and bassists Jimmy Blanton and Oscar Pettiford. He and the musicians of his orchestra maintained a symbiotic relationship of mutual interdependence that was exceedingly rare, even in the jazz world, where virtually all the music results from creative artists working collectively.

EARLY SWING BANDS

A remarkable white big band of the late twenties was led by Jean Goldkette a Frenchman who was reared in Greece and schooled in Russia. When Goldkette's Victor Recording Orchestra hit the Roseland Ballroom in 1927, members of the Fletcher Henderson band, who sat on the opposite bandstand, were struck by the imaginative arrangements, the driving rhythm, and the C-melody saxophone of Frankie Trumbauer. In the words of one of Henderson's sidemen, Rex Stewart:

> This proved to be a most humiliating experience for us, since, after all, we were supposed to be the world's greatest dance orchestra. And up pops this Johnny-come-lately white band from out in the sticks, cutting us. . . . The facts were that we simply could not compete with Jean Goldkette's Victor Recording Orchestra.[28]

An offshoot of the Jean Goldkette orchestra was a group known as the Orange Blossoms, led by Henry Biagini. From within this group, a sax player, Glen Gray (Knoblaugh), took over for the opening of a Canadian nightclub completed for the visit of the Prince of Wales to Canada in 1929. The scheduled opening never took place, but the band adopted the name of the nightclub and became the Casa Loma Orchestra; they obtained a booking at the Roseland Ballroom, and proceeded to record six sides for OKeh. Their performance was somewhat stiff, but Gene Gifford's arrangements were flashy, and the band caught the attention of the jazz world and the public. Their unique contribution to jazz took place in 1931, when the band acquired a trumpet screamer,[29] Sonny Dunham, and his sound soon became a standard part of the American big-band vocabulary. They also acquired a superb jazz clarinet player, Clarence Hutchenrider, and continued to be influential until about 1935. Their recording of *Chinatown*[30] in 1934 displays the rhythmic drive and high brass luster that placed them at the forefront of the hard-swinging jazz big bands.

About this same time, a black big band, which had been organized in

---

[28] Rex Stewart, *Jazz Masters of the Thirties*, p. 11.

[29] A trumpeter who specializes in high notes, someone with "iron chops." The big-band sound of the swing era called for higher and louder performances from the lead trumpet. Some later screamers of distinction—Cat Anderson, Conrad Gozzo, Maynard Ferguson—were also known for their endurance and accuracy.

[30] Decca 199, reissued MCA Records MCA 2-4061.

The Jimmie Lunceford big band, 1938.

Memphis in 1927 and became prominent in Buffalo in the early 1930s, made its first records for Decca. Jimmie Lunceford fronted an ensemble of exactly the same dimensions as Glen Gray's band: six brasses, four reeds, and four rhythm instruments. His recording of *Swanee River*[31] in 1935 displays the same precision and showy high brass that was a hallmark of the Casa Loma Orchestra (*NW* 217, I/2). Lunceford, too, had a talented and able arranger in Sy Oliver, and the disciplined playing characteristic of both Gray's and Lunceford's bands became as much a part of the listeners' expectations as the orchestrations themselves. Power, flash, and precision: the big bands had it, and the public loved it. The *Lunceford Special* (*SCCJ* 41)[32] recorded at the end of the decade, shows the band at its best, a prototype of the classic swing band. The driving four-beat rhythm, the up-tempo solos, the power of a final riffing chorus with a stratospheric trumpet piercing the orchestration and leading the band to an attack on the final chord—these are the hallmarks of the swing-era big-band sound.

[31] Decca 668, reissued MC Records MCA 2-4061.
[32] Columbia CS 9515, reissued in *SCCJ*.

KANSAS CITY SWING

Gray, Lunceford, Redman, and Henderson tended to move along the same path: big-band jazz versions of popular songs and music in popular-song form. Don Redman, on occasion, straddled the fence—his interest in original compositions like *Chant of the Weed* brought him closer to the road followed by Duke Ellington and his orchestra, who played not only big-band arrangements of popular tunes but also the original compositions and production numbers for the "African Jungle" of the Cotton Club. Another direction in big-band jazz was being scouted in the Southwest by Bennie Moten's Kansas City group. They were exploring the possibilities of creating arrangements for a large ensemble through improvising sections—trumpet, trombone, and saxophone—which used the blues as a base and the riff concept as the functional orchestration device. The distinctive Kansas City sound resulted not only from this type of musical arrangement but also from the creative input of its leaders and arrangers, as well as the improvising idiosyncracies of the individual musicians. Of course, musicians could be replaced, and they were, but because Kansas City trained its own instrumentalists and nourished its own talent, individual players had a greater effect on the unique character of these bands than they usually did in bands using arrangements à la Fletcher Henderson or Don Redman. For one thing, the blues tradition allowed extended solo choruses; the New York swing arrangements normally confined improvisation within narrow compositional boundaries. It should not be forgotten, however, that the big bands, like all other jazz ensembles, needed great musicians to make them come alive and swing with excitement. Regardless of the kind of jazz they made, lesser musicians always had the opposite effect. Still, the musical conception of these three jazz trends—New York, Ellington, and Kansas City—were clearly separate and resulted in music with distinctive sounds easily differentiated by educated and sensitive listeners.

The 1932 recording by Bennie Moten's band of *Moten Swing* (*SCCJ* 29) is a good example of a piece that bridges the gap between the Fletcher Henderson and the Kansas City swing styles, for it is based on popular song form, **AABA,** rather than the blues, and it embraces some other stylistic features of the New York bands as well. The chordal framework underlying the piece belongs to a composition by Walter Donaldson, *You're Driving Me Crazy (What Did I Do?)*, which was introduced by Guy Lombardo and His Royal Canadians in 1930.[33] In that same year, the work was used in the Broadway musi-

[33] Columbia 2335-D.

cal *Smiles*, sung by Adele Astaire,[34] Eddie Foy, Jr., and chorus. The pianist on this recording, William "Count" Basie, plays new chords for the opening eight-measure vamp, but from that point on, the chordal structure of the piece is identical to that of the popular song. In the **A** section, before the bridge of the second chorus, one can hear the tune of *You're Driving Me Crazy* played by the lead saxophone, but other statements of the melody do not appear in this new version.

Moten Swing
Popular-Song Form, AABA, Five Times with Four-Measure Tag

Intro 8 piano (vamp)	A 8 piano	B 8 chordal brass unison sax antiphony	A 8 piano
A sax chorus (written)	A sax chorus (original tune present)	B boogie piano guitar solo	A sax chorus
A brass riff alto-sax solo	A ditto	B piano comp alto-sax solo	A brass riff alto-sax solo
A sax chords trumpet solo	A ditto	B piano comp tenor-sax solo	A sax chords trumpet solo
A band riff unison rhythm chords	A ditto	B ditto	A ditto
tag 4			

The amount of improvisation in this work is far greater than that found in a typical arrangement by Don Redman. Not only are the complete third and fourth choruses set aside for solo with instrumental backing, but the introduction and **A** sections of the first chorus are piano solo, and the bridge of the second chorus is a piano and guitar duet of solos. The last complete chorus may well have been improvised too, for here we find the typical Kansas City big-band riff: the entire band, minus the rhythm instruments, plays

---

[34] Sister of dancer Fred Astaire, who also appeared in the musical.

rhythmically in unison a highly syncopated pattern that moves up and down together in what may be called a thickened melodic line.

Rhythm of Final-Chorus Band Riff

An interesting feature of this recording is the display of three different piano styles by Count Basie: New York stride piano throughout the first chorus, "boom-chuck" ragtime-style piano elsewhere, and boogie-woogie-style piano during the bridge of the second chorus. The one hint of the piano style he later developed, which was to become Basie's most distinguishing musical characteristic—a spare, suggestive, simple, and enticing technique—appears at the very end, two measures before the tag. On the first beat, in the middle of a pregnant pause, a single ringing piano chord is struck in the upper register.

The vitality and forward drive of the riff's rhythm for the closing chorus is the critical feature that sets Kansas City style apart from the others. Here we see it translated from blues to popular-song form, and even here it serves to wind up the piece for a final climactic moment. In Kansas City style, we often find a general formal pattern that piles riff upon riff from beginning to end, thus creating a musical pyramid effect of additive forward drive. The surge carries both the soloists and the listeners to a state of near frenzy when properly executed.[35]

The music of these big bands gradually reshaped jazz in America. The swing era, once begun, would continue to thrive well past the years of World War II. A British observer, Brian Rust, one of the most astute and knowledgeable historians of jazz, has this to say:

> One of the first records by the Basie band [Basie assumed leadership of the Moten band after Moten's death in 1935] was typical not only of the group but

[35] For more Kansas City swing, listen to Moten, *Toby* (NW 217, II/1) and Andy Kirk, *Dallas Blues* (NW 217, I/3).

of the style of some of the purely instrumental numbers that were popular at that time. It was *Doggin' Around*, [*SCCJ* 47] and it demonstrated the "riff," a phrase of just a few notes repeated in different tones by different sections of the band, sometimes as a background to a soloist or vocalist (which could be very effective), all too frequently as foreground material, which made a very monotonous effect unless used very judiciously. The amateur instrumentalists that haunted the Rhythm Clubs of those days . . . took this simple strain to their hearts and their instruments, and the programme at a Rhythm Club in the days before and in the early part of the war could hardly be complete without its performance of several dozen choruses of *Doggin' Around* by the resident band. . . . The resulting cacophony had to be heard to be believed. It was perhaps the forerunner of the present-day conception of artistic licence expressed in the inelegant phrase "doing your own thing."[36]

Count Basie's band served a catalytic role in the transition from swing to modern jazz in at least two important aspects: the expanded role and increased freedom of the soloist in the performance of each piece, and the novel tenor saxophone sound of Lester Young, which Basie highlighted as a main attraction of the band. The 1940 Basie recording of *Tickle-Toe* (*NAJ* 6) provides excellent examples of both. Of the arrangement's 140 measures, twelve may be subtracted for introduction and coda (8 + 4). Of the remaining 128 measures, 64 are solo performances, that is, one-half of the piece features the soloist rather than the arrangement. Also, the eight-measure introduction begins with four measures of solo drum and adds the bass and piano for four more measures of three-piece combo sound. (See Listening Guide 6.)

The light tone and legato tonguing technique of Lester Young's tenor saxophone style is also a pace-setting feature of this performance. In sharp contrast to the full-bodied, throaty, hot-jazz tenor sound of other key swing saxophonists, such as Coleman Hawkins, Chu Berry, and Vido Musso, Young preferred a sound more like the cornet playing of Bix Beiderbecke, a musician he much admired. Young's vibrato is smaller and slower than the norm of the swing-style tenorists, and the timbre of his tone, unique for its day, was lighter and contained fewer overtones than the sound of the other swing saxophonists. Young's sound and relaxed, laid-back approach to solo improvisation was crucial in the development of Charlie Parker's alto saxophone technique and Stan Getz's tenor saxophone playing during the next two decades. It was these younger musicians who led the way in establishing the bebop and cool schools of jazz which subsequently emerged.

[36] Brian Rust, *The Dance Bands*, p. 132.

THE "KING OF SWING"
BENNY GOODMAN

The mythical "Kingdom of Swing" was ruled by a monarch, Benny Good-man; invested with nobility, Count Basie and Duke Ellington; and peopled with subjects who blew, danced, and listened. Goodman, the "King of Swing," did not invent the style—Redman, Ellington, Moten, Henderson, and their musicians did that—but he convinced the audience, set a new standard for performance, became the spokesman for the new music, and in every way reigned as the most important and successful popular, dance, and jazz musician in America from the mid-depression years to the end of World War II.[37]

The coup had taken place in the late '20s, and Goodman only later acceded to the throne. It was no mean achievement. As one jazz scholar perceived the situation:

> Why, after so many years of being relegated to the fringes of social acceptance, jazz should have achieved the wide popularity it did is not easy to say. New York, Kansas City, Chicago, and other jazz centers, like the rest of the country, were in the midst of a great depression. Banking and finance had sunk to a new low level, industry was being bolstered by government intercession, and breadlines were a common sight in the big cities. The year before Goodman made his NBC debut, Prohibition was repealed. . . . Furthermore, musicians came cheap. . . . Working almost as if by plan, the national broadcasters piped hotel music to hundreds of thousands of people who would then flock to dance halls and theaters to hear these same bands on tour. . . . The end result was an endless multiplication of big bands.[38]

The decade from 1935 to 1945 has become known as the swing era, and no single musician did more to crystallize the style, establish the technical standards, and popularize the music than Benjamin David Goodman. His musical organization was judged by many to have been the most polished, and perhaps the best, of all the big bands of the period, a group blessed with a leader who could improvise with unfailing grace, dexterity, and imagination. Practically all by himself, Goodman revolutionized the dance-band business. As a result, he was loved, admired, and respected by millions,

---

[37] Glenn Miller overtook Benny Goodman in popularity in about 1940, and it was a closely contested battle until Miller's untimely death in 1944.

[38] Leroy Ostransky, *The Anatomy of Jazz*, p. 224 f.

including the jazz musicians themselves. When he became "King of Swing," Goodman made this music the most vital and exciting kind of social-dance music ever created in America.

Goodman was born in Chicago in 1909 and received his early training in music there. He earned himself the reputation of being a perpetual student of music and instrumental virtuosity. As a boy, he studied with classical clarinetist Franz Schoepp, who also tutored Jimmy Noone and Buster Bailey, and as late as 1949, Goodman was studying with Reginald Kell, a leading British classical clarinet soloist. In addition to hearing the early Chicago masters—Oliver, Armstrong, Keppard, Johnny and Baby Dodds, Hardin, Noone, Mares, Rappolo, and Brunies—he played, in his early years, with the Austin High Gang of Jimmy McPartland, Frank Teschemacher, Bud Freeman, and Dave Tough, as well as with Muggsy Spanier. In August 1923, at the age of fifteen, he played with Bix Beiderbecke on a riverboat gig. He began to job regularly that year and made his first recording with Ben Pollack and his Californians in September 1926. He was then eighteen years old.

Goodman's first commercial recording as leader of a group was made for Vocalion Records in 1927,[39] and the following year, Benny Goodman's Boys recorded with Jimmy McPartland and Glenn Miller.[40] By 1935, Goodman was leading his own big band. He owned a few dozen Fletcher Henderson arrangements, he had picked up the backing of jazz impresario John Hammond, and he was playing a segment of the National Biscuit Company's Saturday night three-hour dance program on NBC, "Let's Dance." While on tour with his band at the gigantic Palomar Ballroom in Los Angeles in August of that same year, his best swing arrangements stopped the crowd's dancing and pulled the people around the bandstand like ants to a honeyjar. As Goodman put it:

> After traveling three thousand miles, we finally found people who were up on what we were trying to do, prepared to take our music the way we wanted to play it. The first big roar from the crowd was one of the sweetest sounds I've ever heard in my life—and from that time on, the night kept getting bigger and bigger, as we played about every good number in our book.[41]

Benny Goodman's successes of 1934–35 marked the beginning of his flourishing musical career. He and his big band, with featured stars such as drummer Gene Krupa and vocalist Helen Ward, continued to be a peak musical attraction in America until mid-1944, when he disbanded the larger

[39] Vocalion 15705, *That's A Plenty* and *Clarinetitis.*
[40] Vocalion 15656, *A Jazz Holiday* and *Wolverine Blues.*
[41] "Benny Goodman: The Golden Age of Swing," liner notes to Victor LPT 6703.

"Spud" Murphy's 1935 arrangement of *Sweet Georgia Brown* for the Benny Goodman band, with the musicians' names penciled in (see the photograph on the next page).

Benny Goodman and his band on the Paramount lot in Hollywood, July 1936. (Left to right) Hymie Schertzer, Red Ballard, Peewee Erwin, Gene Krupa, Harry Goodman, Jess Stacy, Murray McEachern, Benny Goodman, Art Rollini, Nate Kazebier, Bill Depew, Chris Griffin, Allan Reuss, and Dick Clark. Eight of these artists are named in the score reproduced on the previous page.

When this trio—Gene Krupa, Benny Goodman, and Teddy Wilson—went on tour in the spring of 1936, racial segregation was defied for the first time on a national scale.

Part of the Goodman Sextet in performance, 1941: (left to right) Cootie Williams, trumpet; Georgie Auld, sax; Harry James, trumpet; Goodman; and Charlie Christian, guitar.

organization. At the same time that he fronted a big band, Goodman led many small combos. The trio of 1935 included Krupa and pianist Teddy Wilson. By taking Wilson with him on the road as part of the trio and as an adjunct to the band, Goodman began to break the racial taboos that separated white from black even among jazz musicians. Earlier, when the Jean Goldkette and the Fletcher Henderson orchestras played the same engagement at the Roseland Ballroom in New York, they were on separate stages and played consecutively. Although white and black musicians played together in private and informal jam sessions, integrated bands did not exist before this time. In 1936, Goodman added black vibraphonist Lionel Hampton to his trio, and the new quartet was balanced half white and half black. Occasionally, a black musician would be featured with a white band or vice versa. For example, Louis Armstrong recorded with Jimmy Dorsey in 1936,[42] and Roy Eldridge played with the Gene Krupa orchestra in the early '40s;[43] but Armstrong did not live and travel with the Dorsey band or draw a regular salary on the payroll, and Eldridge, even though a featured star of the Krupa band, suffered much indignation from the racial intolerance still prevalent in America at that time. The Goodman quartet was not a white group featuring a black star or two; it was an integrated organization of musical equals.

Beginning in 1938, Benny Goodman pursued a second, less publicized, career, that of a classical clarinetist. He recorded with the Budapest String Quartet, and, in 1939, commissioned Béla Bartók to write *Contrasts*, which

[42] Decca 949.
[43] Columbia C2L-29.

he recorded in 1940 for Columbia with violinist Joseph Szigeti.[44] He later also commissioned clarinet concertos from Aaron Copland and Paul Hindemith. The rapport between jazz and classical music was never more comfortably secure than in the talented hands of this remarkable musician. Goodman's popularity remained high over the next four decades. His stature as a leading jazz musician sent him to Europe, Asia, and South America as a jazz ambassador for the U.S. Department of State. He was awarded honorary doctorates at Harvard and Yale, and his death in 1986 occasioned worldwide tributes.

——— MUSICAL CHARACTERISTICS ———

What differentiated swing from the music that preceded it? First, the size of the bands; second, the arrangements; third, the characteristics of the solos; and, fourth, the change in the habits of the rhythm section. The first two factors have already been discussed in some detail above; now let us look into the last two, swing solos and swing rhythm-section work.

The influx of schooled musicians into the swing bands quickly increased the technical competence of the swing soloists to a higher level than it had previously been in jazz. At the same time, however, the melodic patterns tended to become fixed on standard arpeggios and scales that obviously were derived from the hours spent practicing classical etudes. Tone quality and pitch became more refined, especially among the reeds, and the bawdy and boisterous sounds of classic jazz slowly began to disappear. Trumpet solos differed little from those of classic jazz trumpeters—it was common practice to stick close to a melody and rag it by injecting a little rhythmic variety.

But reed solos were beginning to acquire a new sound. Swing was creating a breed of virtuosos who could improvise brilliantly at ever-faster tempos. As they did, they tended to arpeggiate the simple chord patterns of the swing repertoire and group notes into more or less evenly balanced units. When the brasses took their solos, it was not uncommon to hear a simple melodic riff group notes into patterns that reinforced the normal accents of a 4/4 measure rather than obscure the beat with complex syncopations and unusual rhythmic groupings. The clarinet playing of Benny Goodman is usually considered the epitome of swing clarinet-solo work, so much so that many, if not most, of the other swing reed musicians who wished to play clarinet had to copy his sound, his patterns, his speed, and his flawless execution in order just to survive in this competitive world of professional music. We can see in Goodman's solos just how these concepts were transformed into real music.

In 1939, Benny Goodman recorded *Soft Winds*[45] with a sextet also consist-

---

[44]Columbia ML 2213.
[45]Columbia 35320.

The original Goodman Quartet—(left to right) Lionel Hampton, Gene Krupa, Goodman, and Teddy Wilson—are reunited for the filming of *The Benny Goodman Story* in 1955.

ing of Lionel Hampton on vibes, Fletcher Henderson at the piano, Art Bernstein on bass, Nick Fatool on drums, and a new electric guitarist who quickly became a headliner, Charlie Christian. In 1945, a new sextet recorded *Slipped Disc*[46] with Red Norvo on vibes, Teddy Wilson on piano, Mike Bryan on guitar, Slam Stewart on bass, and Morey Feld on drums. Notice in the excerpt below that passages are either scalar or arpeggiated, and serve to outline the underlying chord structure.

Excerpts from the Goodman Solo on *Soft Winds*

[46]Columbia 36817.

Excerpts from the Goodman Solo on *Slipped Disc*

In the next excerpt, we can observe passages that reemphasize the normal accents of 4/4 meter, i.e., stress on beats one and three.

Soft Winds

Swing-style solos characteristically adhere closely to the well-known melodies of popular songs, and one sees this especially in Goodman's solo work on ballads. Good examples include his closing theme song, *Goodbye,* or his trio recording to *Body and Soul* (*SCCJ* 32). This clarinet-solo style is very closely allied to the structural notes of the original melody. It is not, in fact, improvisatory in nature, but ornamental. The compulsion to stylize the tune or provide listeners with a melody they can "hang their hats on" is one of the important musical elements of the swing style. Teddy Wilson's piano solo on the second chorus deviates somewhat from the melody, as he plays a swing solo with rapid arpeggios and regular groupings.

The swing drummers remodeled the beat of classic jazz. They still played 4/4 on the bass drum in a very insistent and pervasive pulse, but they began to "ride" the sock cymbal, or high hat, with a 2/4 pattern that set up a minor conflict of rhythmic interest.

With both feet going, four beats on the right and two beats on the left, hands were used for decorations and accents—one to "ride" the sock cymbal, as described above, and the other to lead off on whatever other equipment might be available. Chick Webb, one of the first drummers to codify the swing conventions, about 1935, used a set that was comprised of bass drum,

William "Chick" Webb (1902–39).

snare drum, high hat, hanging cymbal, and four temple blocks.[47] The complete drum set that became more or less standard from 1937 on consisted of bass drum, snare drum, tom-tom, floor tom, high hat, and two to four suspended cymbals. In this regard, drummers Gene Krupa and Dave Tough played dominant roles in stabilizing the jazz drummer's set of traps.

The traditional brass bass, in converting to the plucked double bass of the swing ensembles, still tended to play two-beat in the ragtime–classic jazz tradition during the early 1930s. Sometimes the bassists switched back and forth in their playing patterns, and occasionally they played consistent walking four-beat bass. However, using a plucked double bass provided a distinctive new sound envelope for the bands. The noisy plucking attack and the rapid decay of volume, characteristics that differ considerably from the even, sustained pitch of the blown bass tuba, gave a new lightness and liveliness of sound to the rhythm section.

The guitar players of swing chorded in 4/4, and their relentless strumming actually had much less effect on the big-band drive than the music of the banjo had on the rhythm of the classic jazz combo. Until the development

[47] George T. Simon, *Simon Says: The Sights and Sounds of the Swing Era, 1935–1955*, p. 52.

of the electric guitar, toward the middle of the swing era, the acoustic guitar could be heard only when most of the band was not playing. Its effect in the swing combos, of course, was significantly greater, and the sustaining ability of its longer and less taut strings, in contrast to the rapid decay of the banjo sound, helped establish a new characteristic sound for swing ensembles.

Nearly all these features are exposed artfully and placed on display in the fine Mel Powell composition and arrangement for the Benny Goodman Orchestra, *Mission To Moscow*, recorded in 1942 with Mel Powell at the piano (*NAJ* 7). Only the drumming in this performance differs from the typical patterns described above, but the "ride" pattern of sticks on cymbal can be clearly heard in the opening measures of Basie's *Tickle-Toe* (*NAJ* 6). For the Goodman band, drummer Howard Davies uses an almost unvarying pattern of brushes on snare drum for the entire performance. Although Powell's arrangement might serve as an exemplar for swing arrangements during the height of the big band era, it also has unique features that set it apart from and above the competition. The work is neither a twelve-measure blues nor is it in sixteen- or thirty-two-measure popular-song form. One complete chorus consists of forty-eight measures in rounded binary form, **ABA**. The entire piece is made up of sixteen-measure sections:

	Chorus I			Chorus II			Ending		
Introduction ‖	**A**	**B**	**A** ‖	**A**	**B**	**A** ‖	**A**	**A** ‖	Coda
16	16	16	16	16	16	16	16	14	16

where the last two measures of the final **A** section are cut off by the early entrance of the coda. The introduction and the coda are the same, thus rounding off the form, and they maintain a pedal-point during their first twelve measures in a key only distantly related to the tonic key of the piece. (See Listening Guide 7.)

Each **A** section is divided **aab** (4 + 4 + 8), with the **b** portion a driving stomp of saxophones against the brass. The **B** section, too, is divided **aab** (4 + 4 + 8), and the final half works its way down a circle of fifths in two-measure sequences. Only the leader has solo work in the arrangement, but Powell allows the pianist (himself, that is) to mimic Benny Goodman's solos at the ends of phrases in call-and-response patterns during the final **B** section. Goodman's first and second solos of the piece are his typical smooth, polished, and brilliant clarinet displays, but his final solo is something special. He discards his smooth legato tone and phrasing for a hot, raucous, and sharply articulated series of notes that lead perfectly to the final driving chorus of the tutti big-band finale.

When they were not playing solo, the swing pianists were gradually giving up the notion that they had to simulate the sound of an entire orchestra. We observed the transition taking place as early as 1928 and 1929, when Louis Armstrong and Earl Hines teamed up for *West End Blues* (*SCCJ* 19) and the extraordinary *Weather Bird* (*SCCJ* 20). We noted that the left hand in classic jazz had played both the bass and percussion parts, and the right hand played the harmonies as well as snatches of melody. In swing, the left hand still tended to jump back and forth, as in the old stride tradition, but the right hand played fewer chords and more single-line melodies.

VOCALISTS

Singers have been a fundamental part of jazz since its inception, and the fine line of demarcation that separates jazz vocalists from rock, blues, or folk singers is often difficult to draw with certainty. The early classic-jazz singers have already been mentioned, but there are others who gained prominence in the 1930s as jazz and its boundaries grew. Bing Crosby joined the Paul Whiteman band in 1927 and worked with it for many years. During that time he associated with many jazz artists, including Bix Beiderbecke, Frankie Trumbauer, the Dorsey brothers, Duke Ellington, and Don Redman. Crosby was the first vocalist to take advantage of the advances in electronics, and he developed the modern method of popular singing. He stopped shouting his solos into a megaphone and moved in close to the microphone to sing softly.

The Rhythm Boys—Bing Crosby, Al Rinker, and Harry Barris—reunited with Paul Whiteman several years after leaving his orchestra.

Most of his recorded vocal work is definitely in the popular idiom—he was the first "crooner"—but in 1932, he recorded *Sweet Sue* with the Paul White-man band, in which he does some scat singing with Bix Beiderbecke's licks.

Mildred Bailey, born in Tekoa, Washington, in 1907, was the first female to be a featured singer with a big band. In part because of her success, nearly every swing band from the '30s through the '50s had to have a woman vocalist. Her brother, Al Rinker, along with Bing Crosby, was one of Paul Whiteman's original "Rhythm Boys," and she joined that band in 1929. She was, incidentally, the first white female singer to be completely accepted in jazz circles. Her long career included recordings with the Dorsey brothers, Teddy Wilson, the Casa Loma Orchestra, Red Norvo (whom she married in 1933), and Benny Goodman. She combined her vocal talents with some of the leading jazz instrumentalists of the day, and her performance of *Squeeze Me*,[48] featuring Johnny Hodges, Bunny Berigan, and Teddy Wilson, is one of her best. Although her personal models were the robust voices of the early classic-blues singers, she performed in a light and high-pitched voice that was unusual among female jazz singers.

Connee Boswell, born in New Orleans in 1907, was the first white woman to bring wordless vocals (scat singing) to jazz. She had been preceded by Louis Armstrong[49] in 1926 and Adelaid Hall, with Duke Ellington, in 1927,[50] but her efforts were especially long-lasting and influential. She and her sisters helped make a seamless transition from black blues singing to the jazz / popular singing style of swing and bebop. The young Ella Fitzgerald patterned her style of singing on the familiar recorded performances of Boswell, and the close harmony, smoothly blended scat choruses of the Boswell Sisters (Connee, Martha, and Helvetia) captivated the ears of jazz musicians as well as popular audiences. Partly because they were white, partly because of their success with the Dorsey Brothers Band, but principally because of their excellent musicianship, the Boswell Sisters opened new doors for women in the profession. The Andrews Sisters, the McGuire Sisters, Kay Starr, and many others drew nourishment from the "instrumental" singing technique of the Boswells. As Jan Shapiro points out,

> The Boswell Sisters also emulated the sound of trumpets, trombones, and banjos, singing "horn riffs" (similar melodic patterns or phrases) in the middle of their songs. . . . [In] the introduction to the song *Heebie Jeebies* as sung by the Boswell Sisters . . . [one can see] vocal articulation mimicking the articulation used by jazz horn players.[51]

[48] Columbia 3CL-22.

[49] *Heebie Jeebies* (OKeh 8300) and *Hotter Than That* (1927: *SCCJ* 18).

[50] *Creole Love Call* (Victor 21137).

[51] "Connee Boswell and the Boswell Sisters: Pioneers in Vocal Jazz," *Jazz Educators Journal,* Spring 1990, p. 39.

Heebie Jeebies, as Sung by the Boswell Sisters

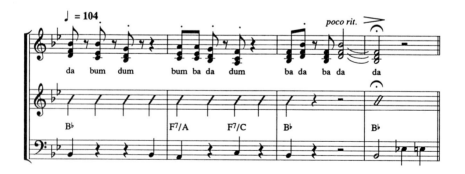

Billie "Lady Day" Holiday was born in Baltimore, Maryland, in 1915. She began singing in New York clubs in about 1930, when she was just a teenager. Her father played banjo and guitar in the Fletcher Henderson band in the early '30s, and she was "discovered" by John Hammond and Benny Goodman in 1933. The recordings for which she is most famous are those made between 1935 and the early years of the Second World War. She continued to record until the year of her death, 1959, although these last years were plagued by personal and professional problems, drug and alcohol addiction, and a noticeable decline in health. Even though her voice suffered from years of abuse, still she recorded some movingly beautiful solos in the 1950s.

Billie Holiday was never a successful blues singer, but when she accepted the popular ballad as the primary medium for her artistic expression, she created a stunning musical personality. Her recordings in 1937 of *He's Funny That Way* (*SCCJ* 35) and 1938 of *I Can't Get Started* (*NW* 95, I/1) testify to her unique vocal timbre, unfailing sense of pitch, and ability to communicate the emotion of the lyrics as though they were being sung for the first time by the person about whom and for whom they were written. The warm, intensely personal quality of her singing is an expression of herself and an indication of her professionalism and talent. Her phrasing is always gracious, her dynamics controlled, and her sensitivity to the accompanying instrumental sounds manifest, allowing for the kind of balanced interplay that characterizes real jazz. Her recordings with members of the Basie band, which she joined in 1937, are all outstanding, and the lyrical gifts of tenor saxophonist Lester Young are a perfect match for her subtle phrasing and expressive use of pitch and time. Holiday's 1941 performance of *All of Me* (*SCCJ* 36) was so influential that virtually every female vocalist who sang the number during the following decade tried to imitate her. Her artistic success was never matched by popular success, and record sales of even her most well-known songs were never outstanding. Still, the armed services radio network broadcast her work widely during the war years. As the homesick GIs of World War II listened to the young, irresistible voice of Billie Holiday offer herself in this romantic ballad, *All of Me* became, in its own way, a standard and a popular classic.

The tragedy of Billie Holiday's personal life has been endlessly recounted in print and romanticized on the screen, yet the sorrow she experienced from mistreatment of various kinds went beyond the personal. The struggle of blacks in America seeking identity and equal rights was an ever-present issue for Holiday, as it was for all black jazz musicians. She painted a terrifying picture of black bodies hanging from trees in her recording of *Strange Fruit*,[52]

[52] Commodore 526.

Billie Holiday (1915–59).

which she remade several times between April 1939 and November 1956. The stark lyrics, adapted from a poem by Lewis Allen, cry out in anguish against the horrible lynchings of blacks in America; artist that she was, Holiday never let the passion sag into melodrama.

Alcohol and narcotics affected her career, her life, and her singing, but she seemed able in her artistry to communicate a sense of hope in spite of adversity. The paradox of her youth, and that of other blacks growing up in Harlem, receives artistic expression in her 1941 recording, *God Bless the Child*,[53] in which the listener senses hope and promise on the one hand and almost insurmountable barriers on the other. Her late recordings display a longing for what might have been but no bitterness; they speak with conviction and presence, and they capture the listener's heart. *These Foolish Things* (*SCCJ* 37), recorded in 1952, and *The End of a Love Affair* (*NW* 295, I/1), from 1958, she transforms into intensely personal experiences that she shares with the listener during the moment of performance.

Another great artist, Ella Fitzgerald, brought to jazz singing the kind of virtuosity usually associated with facile instrumental technique. She was capable of singing melodic lines of a thoroughly instrumental derivation, thereby freeing herself from the strictures of precomposed popular melodies in order to engage in improvised solo journeys, much as the jazz horn players were prone to do. Where Billie Holiday compels the listener to attend to the words, Ella Fitzgerald uses words primarily as a vehicle to carry the sound of her voice. Scat singing, the use of nonsense syllables to articulate a vocal line, was fully incorporated into her technical hardware. Even some of her songs *with* words have been nonsense, e.g., "A tisket, a tasket, a green and yellow basket." Her artistry has developed more in the realms of abstract music—motive, melodic development, sequence, virtuosic flights. Born in Newport News, Virginia, in 1918, she moved to New York, where she first recorded with Chick Webb in 1935. Throughout her long career she has performed with virtually every major jazz musician—Louis Armstrong, Count Basie, Duke Ellington, Sy Oliver, Benny Carter, André Previn, and Marty Paich, to mention but a few. In 1946 she began working with Norman Granz, jazz impresario, and in the following year recorded *Robbins Nest* (*NW* 295, I/7), a light, fleeting display of vocal wizardry that goes beyond coloratura bravura to well-conceived musical creation. Her 1964 recording of *You'd Be So Nice to Come Home To* (*SCCJ* 38) is an excellent example of the way she can transform a romantic ballad into a moderately up-tempo, swinging jazz number. Without doubt Fitzgerald considers herself a member of the jazz combo or band, albeit the lead instrument: in standard format, she states the

[53] OKeh 6270.

Ella Fitzgerald.

tune and proceeds with a series of choruses. After the first chorus, she discards the melody of the pop song and improvises a melodic line—occasionally trading phrases with an instrumental soloist—by exploiting intervallic features of the tune and making full use of her range, impeccable articulation, and refined rhythmic sense. The words of the popular song are entirely incidental to her performance—they merely provide a vehicle for her articulation of the vocal sounds. Other syllables could be substituted and, indeed, often are. The Roy Eldridge solo on *I Can't Believe that You're in Love with Me* (*SCCJ* 44) is played with the same kind of inflection and articulation that characterizes most of Fitzgerald's vocal solos. If we compare her solo work with instrumental solos by well-known swing musicians, we see that her vocal lines could be played very successfully by a trumpet or alto saxophone without loss of authority and that most instrumental solo lines could be sung by this amazing artist.

ART TATUM

The absolute master of swing keyboard virtuosity was Art Tatum, a blind pianist whose total control of his instrument allowed him to execute flawlessly any musical idea he conceived. His technique was so astounding that classical giants such as Horowitz and Rubenstein are said to have made a point of visiting clubs where they might hear him play. When the young Charlie Parker traveled to New York in the late 1930s to expand his musical horizons and complete his apprenticeship, he took a job as a dishwasher in Jimmy's Chicken Shack, the club that featured Tatum at the piano—an unusual but effective classroom!

Tatum was a truly astonishing virtuoso, and the importance of this characteristic should not be minimized, but his music went far beyond a dazzling pyrotechnic display. Careful listening reveals an ingenious harmonic conception set within a framework of abrupt changes and unexpected modulations; we hear as well goal-oriented improvisations that build to their logical conclusion through a series of temporary climaxes. Throughout a performance of Tatum's we are additionally rewarded by the wit and charm that derive from a debonair tossing-off of incredibly difficult embellishments, quotations of popular songs embedded in the music, and a natural melodic grace. Tatum's 1933 recording of *Tiger Rag* (*NAJ* 4) astonished jazz musicians and public alike, and these early recordings established Tatum as the pace setter in jazz piano. (See Listening Guide 4.)

Art Tatum in January 1944, together with Tiny Grimes, guitar, and Slam Stewart, bass.

Willow Weep for Me (*SCCJ* 39) opens with Gershwinesque passages in free rhythm, measures filled with chromatic chords that luxuriously expand the original harmonies. Then a typical swing-stride bridge is inserted, which may be aesthetically out of keeping with the beginning but is not really unusual for a virtuoso display. Finally, with flawless grace and an ease that is simplicity itself, he slips in the incredibly fast arpeggios and scalar passages that leave the listener breathless.

Although Tatum's recording of *Too Marvelous for Words* (*SCCJ* 40) lacks studio-quality sound (the recording was made at a private party), it exhibits the characteristic finesse, speed, dexterity, and sound that made him the model swing pianist. It should be noted that both *Willow* and *Words* were made after swing began to decline as the predominant jazz style, in 1949 and 1956 respectively; this is but another example of the jazz phenomenon in which the latest styles coexist, comfortably or otherwise, with those developed earlier.

Art Tatum, born in Toledo, Ohio, in 1910, began his career in the 1920s and moved into club engagements and recordings in New York in 1932. His reputation grew so rapidly that he was an international figure by the mid-1930s and set London on its ear in 1938. Leonard Feather, a jazz pianist and astute critic of the art, describes Tatum's playing accurately in these words:

> Tatum's original appearance on the jazz scene in the early '30s upset all previous standards for pianists. His fantastic technique and original harmonic variations placed him far ahead of all earlier artists, eliciting the praise of Leopold Godowsky and making him the favorite jazz pianist of virtually all his contemporaries. His unequaled technique has never been abused to the point of removing him from his original jazz roots.[54]

GENE KRUPA

Around 1935, a drummer with an enormous sense of showmanship, an abundant measure of jazz "time," and a phenomenally quick technique burst on the jazz scene as part of the Benny Goodman band. Gene Krupa did more than almost anyone else to make the drums a popular solo instrument and bring the drummers of the swing era into the limelight. His recording of *Sing, Sing, Sing*,[55] performed with the Goodman band in 1937, stands as the prime example of the extended drum solo in swing. *Drum Boogie*,[56] the theme song

[54] Leonard Feather, "Arthur 'Art' Tatum," *The Encyclopedia of Jazz* (New York: Horizon Press, 1955), p. 294.
[55] Verve V-8594.
[56] Ibid.

for Krupa's own big band, formed after he left Benny Goodman in 1938, was another significant contribution to the history of jazz drumming. The most obvious characteristics of Krupa's drumming style, in addition to his facial contortions and other theatrics, were his incessant, heavy bass drum on every beat, his driving, 2/4, high-hat rhythm, and his accented, syncopated tom-toms.

Although up-tempo (i.e., fast), virtuosic tunes were an important part of the swing style, it should be remembered that ballads accounted for a large part of the swing repertoire. In this domain, the swing drummers developed another important four-beat rhythmic sound: the smart sizzle of wire brushes patting and "stirring soup" on the snare drum. The recording of the Gene Krupa band of 1941 featuring trumpeter Roy Eldridge as soloist on *Rockin' Chair* (*SCCJ* 43) illustrates how the swing drummer switches from sticks to brushes for the performance of sentimental ballads. The trumpet solo of Roy Eldridge is notable for several reasons. First, the entire piece is trumpet solo; the orchestration consists merely of a few background sounds. Second, it is obvious that the swing trumpet-solo style is not far different from that of the New Orleans solo-trumpet style. As Martin Williams points out:

> Eldridge once said that he thought he was a good trumpet soloist before he had really heard Louis Armstrong, but that when he did, he realized he hadn't been "telling a story."[57]

Armstrong was still the model and most influential trumpet player of this era as well as the previous one. His sense of melodic continuity, full-bodied sound, and powerful climactic endings carried into the solo styles of all the great swing-era trumpeters.

CHARLIE CHRISTIAN

Benny Goodman's contribution to the history of jazz must also include a role, if only a minor one, in the stylistic transition from swing to bebop. In 1939, he brought the talents of black guitarist Charlie Christian to jazz. Although Christian died tragically and prematurely in 1942, the few years he spent with Goodman brought him fame as the first modern jazz guitarist to feature single-string solos on the electric guitar, a device that later became the stock-in-trade of bebop guitarists. Charlie Christian's solo on *I Found a New Baby* (*SCCJ* 50) reveals his mastery of melodic invention and harmonic under-standing, rhythmic suppleness, and sensitivity to the unusual characteristics of the new instrument. His solo has a smooth legato character resulting from

[57]*SCCJ* liner notes.

the sustaining possibilities of the electronic instrument in combination with
a playing technique modeled upon the solo styles of the saxophone players.
During the opening clarinet chorus, we can hear the steady four-beat strumming, which matches the chordal accompaniment of the piano and the steady
push of the bass drum. Christian's solo, which follows, is totally different in
concept, in that he has transformed the instrument from a chordal rhythmic
one to one that has a melodic voice capable of sustaining a long and intricate
line. Through the effects of the electronic amplifier, Christian mellows the
tone of his instrument by cutting out the upper-partial twang of the steel-
string guitar. That his influence on subsequent guitar-playing jazz musicians
is of major proportions is all the more astounding considering the brief period
of professional activity fate allowed him.

  Born in Dallas in 1919, Charlie Christian grew up in the Southwest and
played bass and guitar in various groups around Oklahoma. John Hammond
discovered him in St. Louis and recommended him to Benny Goodman,
whom he joined in 1939. Christian later played at Minton's Playhouse in
Harlem during the first experimental bebop sessions of the early 1940s. His
ear for altered chords, running melodic lines, and electric-guitar timbre made
him the ideal exponent of bebop, the new music that was to follow and
ultimately come in conflict with swing. The legend of Charlie Christian,
which sprang up like a phoenix after his death in 1942, was based on his role
as a spiritual father of bebop, but his legacy is the stack of superb swing solos
he recorded with Benny Goodman and Lionel Hampton.

  The Benny Goodman sextet that cut *I Found a New Baby* (*SCCJ* 50) in
1941 had no weak links, as all six musicians were superb instrumentalists.
However, it was not Goodman's usual group. His standbys—Krupa, Hampton, and Wilson—were not with him for this date, and instead Count Basie
and his drummer, Jo Jones, carried the rhythm. Basie influenced Goodman's
music in more ways than simply as the pianist in his rhythm section. Basie
not only set an example with his band for all other swing ensembles, he
provided arrangements for Goodman's big band. The merger of Kansas City
style with Goodman's mainstream swing can be seen in the Count Basie–
Benny Goodman–Buck Clayton composition *Rattle and Roll*, recorded by the
Goodman band in 1946.[58] The piece is a twelve-bar blues with eight-measure introduction and ending. The first chorus, which (as might be expected)
employs clarinet lead, is followed by a sequence of twelve-measure solos and
capped by a series of ensemble-drive choruses that build up energy for the
climax at the end. Each of the last two clarinet-solo choruses is introduced
by four measures of band-ensemble playing. In the following example, one
can see the contrapuntal merger of two riffs in Basie's Kansas City style:
octave trumpets driving upward and octave saxophones turning downward.

[58] Columbia 36988.

Rattle and Roll

Benny Goodman with Count Basie's orchestra at the famous Apollo Theater in Harlem, November 1940. Basie is at the piano and Charlie Christian is on guitar.

How the blues worked their way into bebop and became the most pervasive element in jazz can be seen in the composite recording of the Benny Goodman sextet with Charlie Christian, *Blues Sequence* (from *Breakfast Feud*, *SCCJ* 51). Here, all the Christian solos display the new order and sense of freedom characteristic of bebop, within the context of a tightly structured and closely supervised swing group. The new accentuation was subtle where the old was striking; the new phrasing was extended and unbalanced, the old was regular; the new sound moved into uncharted waters, where the old exuberantly reaffirmed the faith in the long-proven precepts of swing that had so successfully driven American audiences to a pitch of near frenzy. In *Blues Sequence*, the conflict can be experienced as a cold front moving in before a storm.

COLEMAN HAWKINS

Another pivotal figure in the transition from swing to bebop was tenor saxophonist Coleman "Bean" Hawkins (1904–69). Although born and educated in Kansas, Hawkins made his name as a New York jazz musician working with Fletcher Henderson in 1923. When he left Henderson's group in the mid-'30s, he worked in Europe with Benny Carter, Django Reinhardt, and others, returning to the United States in 1939 to record *Body and Soul* (*SCCJ* 33) with his own newly formed nine-piece band. This recording, his most successful, established him as a national jazz name and served as a model of saxophone-solo playing for future generations of reed performers (see Transcription 4). The standard swing treatment of all popular songs, especially ballads, was to place the melody in prominence during the delivery of a solo, but ornament it slightly with tonal inflections, turning figures, modified rhythms, and other musical devices that stylized (or jazzed) the tune but did not obscure the melody. With great assurance, Hawkins digressed entirely from the well-known tune and leaned upon the harmonic structure to guide him in an unprecedented creative melodic effort. The result is a logical and beautiful melody in the instrumental jazz idiom, one that owes little allegiance to the popular song from which it sprung. André Hodeir sums up his analysis of Hawkins's solo thus: "On the other hand, in the second chorus of the famous improvisation . . . the only thing the theme and the variation have in common is the harmonic foundation."[59] It was customary for solo improvisation in the swing style to paraphrase the melody. The new concept demonstrated here discarded the old melody and extemporized a new one, one more idiomatic to jazz, more intimately connected with the technical capacities of the instrument and with the artistic abilities of the performer.

Body and Soul, Second Chorus, Opening of Second Phrase

A little more than two years after the recording session of *Body and Soul,* America was at war. Suddenly, millions were in uniform and traveling around the world. Farmers continued their business as usual, for America needed a steady supply of food, but many family members either joined the service or left for the cities to work in war plants.

> World War II was one of the great turning points in the history of the United States. . . . Until the Second World War [America] was regarded as an isolated, young, and relatively unimportant country by the major European powers that had shaped the destiny of the world, or at least western Europe. . . . Europeans tended to regard Americans as naive, crude, unsophisticated, and often

[59] André Hodeir, *Jazz: Its Evolution and Essence,* p. 144.

Coleman "Bean" Hawkins (1904–69), tenor sax.

vaguely comic people with little history and culture. This view was shared by many Americans, particularly musicians and other artists. . . . World War II changed the whole image of the United States. . . . At the end of the war, American troops were in almost every part of the world, having played a major role in the eventual defeat of the Germans and Japanese.[60]

Americans on the move brought their music with them, and, at that time, Coleman Hawkins was a leading soloist and exponent of jazz. Bob Thiele, owner of Signature Records, who was in the military morale department of the Coast Guard, said, "I can testify that anyone who entered a jazz night-club in 1944 would probably hear 'The Man I Love' performed at this interesting tempo [as played by Coleman Hawkins (*SCCJ* 34)] . . . It was just about the hippest thing one could do."[61] The double-time outburst over the slow chordal pattern was no Hawkins innovation; it was part of the standard repertoire of jazz-solo ideas developed twenty years earlier by Louis Armstrong. The excellence and excitement of this solo, however, captivated the ears of jazz-loving Americans and carried the name of Coleman Hawkins to the forefront of leading swing soloists. Although some of Hawkins's ideas were transitional, his style of playing was firmly rooted in the tradition popularized by the big bands and small combos of Goodman, Basie, Ellington, and Henderson. This unified style was both dominant and continuous from the early '30s through World War II.

THE BASIE BAND

Harking back to Bennie Moten's *Moten Swing* of 1932 (*SCCJ* 29) and comparing it with Count Basie's *Doggin' Around* of 1938 (*SCCJ* 47), we can hear the many musical elements they have in common. The later band is more polished, able to maintain an up-tempo beat with great ensemble precision, but it is playing scores that are virtually identical to those played in 1932. The thickened-line saxophone chorus is answered by chording brass, the rhythm section presses a metronomic four-beat pattern, and the arrangement forms a boundary within which soloists may operate.

The continuity of the Basie tradition remained unbroken well beyond World War II, and we can hear in his 1947 recording of *House Rent Boogie*[62] the instrumental blues transformed into a big-band arrangement in swing style.

[60]Charles Hamm, "Changing Patterns in Society and Music: The U.S. Since World War II," in Charles Hamm, Bruno Nettl, and Ronald Byrnside, *Contemporary Music and Music Cultures*, p. 36 f.

[61]Quoted by Martin Williams, liner notes to *SCCJ*.

[62]Victor 20-2435.

House Rent Boogie

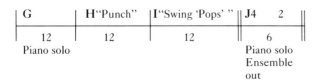

Count Basie at the piano, surrounded by Benny Carter, Charlie Barnet, and Coleman Hawkins, saxophones. Jo Jones is on the drums.

William "Count" Basie, the piano man from Red Bank, New Jersey, opened, with his band, at the Roseland Ballroom in New York in December 1936; John Hammond, Columbia Records executive and star talent scout, had arranged the engagement. Basie had worked in a nine-piece band with Buster Smith as co-leader and Walter Page on bass the year before at the Reno Club in Kansas City, but it took the "discovery" by Hammond and the date at the Roseland, opposite Woody Herman's first band, to start him on the road to recognition. Eventually, he formed a high-quality band that came to be called The Big Swing Machine. For his first band recording under his own name in January 1937, Basie had already engaged the kind of musicians that would bring his band to the forefront: in addition to Walter Page and himself, he had Buck Clayton on trumpet, Herschel Evans and Lester Young on tenor saxophones, Jo Jones on drums, and "Mr. Five by Five," Jimmy Rushing, for vocals.

In the 1940s, Basie added three key soloists to his roster—Don Byas, Illinois Jacquet, and J. J. Johnson—but the band eventually broke up for economic reasons in January 1950. The disruption was only temporary, however, and Basie fronted a variety of groups after this date in addition to his usual big band: The Count Basie Seven, featuring Clark Terry, Marshall Royal, and Wardell Gray, plus rhythm; the Count Basie Quintet / Sextet / Nonet, featuring Joe Newman, Henry Coker, Marshall Royal, Paul Quinchette, and Charlie Fowlkes, plus rhythm; and other combinations. Employing swing arrangements from some of the best hands available—Ernie Wilkins, Neal Hefti, Thad Jones, Benny Carter, and Quincy Jones, among others—he fearlessly raised the banner of swing in territories occupied by troops of the bebop, cool, progressive, and West Coast schools. His band sound always began with the forward-driving propulsion of the rhythm section. Walter Page, Jo Jones, Freddie Green, and Basie formed a rhythmic unit capable of carrying a band on its back. Page and Jones were eventually replaced, but their tradition continued. The Basie sound was always exciting, and in the words of one observer:

> Blasting ensembles taking over from a light piano solo; big brass explosions behind a moving, murmuring sax solo; a bit of light piano tinkling after a brilliant brass barrage—these dynamic devices have always been part of the excitement that the Basie band has brewed.[63]

In *Doggin' Around*, the new element was provided by a black saxophone soloist who played in a manner totally unlike that of his fellow musicians. His sound-image was neither that of the big-band member nor that of the classic jazz musician, but resembled the smooth solo lines of white cornetist Bix Beiderbecke. The qualities that characterized the playing of Lester "Prez" Young, making him unique among the saxophonists of swing, were his harmonic inflection, straight tone, and restricted timbre alongside a new, smooth-flowing melodic line.

——— LESTER YOUNG ———————————

Lester Young was born in Woodville, Mississippi, in 1909, lived in New Orleans as a young teenager, and moved with his family, while still in his teens, to Minneapolis. He toured with his father, a minstrel-show musician,

[63] George T. Simon, *The Big Bands* (New York: Macmillan, 1967), p. 87.

through Nebraska, Kansas, and the Dakotas during these formative years and adopted Frankie Trumbauer and Bix Beiderbecke as his musical idols. He worked the Midwest during the 1930s and played with Walter Page's Blue Devils and later the Bennie Moten–George Lee band. He left a small Count Basie combo briefly to replace Coleman Hawkins in the Fletcher Henderson orchestra, but he didn't stay with them very long. He was sharply criticized for lacking Hawkins's loud, resonant, and vibrato-laden tone. He rejoined Basie and remained with him until the end of 1940. He has been deemed the founding father of a new school of jazz that was eventually dubbed "cool," and he was certainly the most decisive influence on the tenor saxophonists of the late '40s and '50s, especially Stan Getz. His solo on *Doggin' Around* was, at that time, interpreted as the ultimate in understatement. The light sound and slightly accented melodic lines extracted the essence of the music, distilling the residue still further into jazz ideas of great intensity. The worship of power and drive, of virile overexuberance, was an important factor in the promulgation of swing, but amidst the most rhythmic swing band of them all, the Count Basie orchestra, Young stood out as a cool oasis on a blistering desert.

Tragically, he suffered, as did other great black jazz musicians, debilitat-

**Lester Willis "Prez" Young
(1909–59), tenor sax.**

ing wounds from the stabs of racial prejudice. From his days in the army at the end of World War II until his death in New York City in 1959, Young traveled a steadily declining road of alcoholism, nervous breakdowns, and malnutrition. In these relatively enlightened times, it is difficult to remember that during World War II, blacks were drafted into the services but were segregated into all-black units, which were never allowed to travel to the European or Pacific theaters because they were considered unfit for combat. Southern cities had separate washrooms, drinking fountains, restrooms, and even railroad platforms for black Americans, and it mattered not whether you were a soldier in the service of your country or an internationally known jazz artist. Young's role in the history of jazz was that of a pioneer, and it is terribly sad that times changed too slowly to award him, during his lifetime, the recognition he so justly deserved.

A further demonstration of the solo skill possessed by this improvisatory jazz giant may be heard in *Taxi War Dance*, recorded by Count Basie in 1939 (*SCCJ* 48), and *Lester Leaps In*, recorded by a small Basie group that same year (*SCCJ* 49). The characteristics of swing are unmistakable in the ensemble work of the other musicians, and even Young's solos (see Transcription 5) retain a tendency toward regular accentuation, arpeggiated and diatonic passages that are not harmonically adventurous, and occasional swing clichés. However, his melodic lines are constructed with an intuitive logic that invents graceful musical statements out of preceding figures and phrases. The motive is caught, reworked, and transformed. The new motive statement is once again reworked in a manner that bridges the regular phrase structure and moves, with even greater dispatch, toward the final cadence of the chorus. The strong internal logic is thus based on the notes of the solo rather than on the fixed ideas of the composer or arranger.

The seamless and effortless transition from band ensemble passages to soloist performance is captured perfectly in Young's solos on *Tickle-Toe* (*NAJ* 6). Though his sound is light and mellow and his phrasing relaxed, his articulation is characteristic of swing soloists, who place their accents on the beat rather than after the beat. Also, Young perfected the art of employing alternate fingerings for notes on his saxophone so that he might vary the sound when repeating a tone in a swinging rhythmic pattern. He employs this device sparingly in *Tickle-Toe*, but it is one of the best-remembered features of his *Lester Leaps In* solo (see Transcription 5, especially the last eight measures). Young's special attention to sound foreshadows another kind of development in jazz solo performance: the exploitation of timbral relationships as a syntactical device. This maneuver, which appears only in a nascent stage in the music of Lester Young, began to get full treatment during the 1960s when the Free Jazz explorers looked for new musical territories to conquer.

LIONEL HAMPTON

Lionel Hampton played a completely different kind of instrument and functioned entirely within the stylistic limits of swing. Yet he, too, had an incredible talent for creative melodic continuity. Born in Kentucky in 1913, he was raised in Chicago, where he played in the *Chicago Defender* Boys' Band. The *Defender*, a leading black newspaper with national circulation, carried news of jazz and dance musicians of the black community far and wide. It was an especially powerful and significant force during the '20s, when so many leading jazz musicians were based in Chicago. Still in his teens, Hampton moved to California and began playing the vibraphone, a new instrument, around 1930. From 1936 to 1940, he played with Benny Goodman, Teddy Wilson, and Gene Krupa in what quickly became the most popular small group of the era. He later fronted his own band and in 1939 recorded *When Lights Are Low* (*SCCJ* 45), arranged by alto saxophonist Benny Carter, with an all-star pick-up band. A comparison of Hampton's work on vibes with the guitar solo of Charlie Christian reveals Hampton to be a master of swing whose

Lionel Hampton, vibes.

accomplishments are measured not in innovation but in technical mastery. His execution is flawless, exciting in the clarity his precise rhythmic touch lends to his melodic improvisation. The classical regularity of his phrasing and the lucidity of his musical thought result from his dependence upon standard harmonic progressions already well developed in the swing era. This style of playing established Hampton's reputation as an equal of the other three members of the quartet—Goodman, Wilson, and Krupa—and opened the eyes of jazz percussionists to the musical potential of the vibraphone.

TERRITORY BANDS

Benny Goodman was indeed the "King of Swing," but countless other swing bands operating in the United States during the 1930s and '40s also gave royal performances. Although nationwide fame and financial rewards were possible for a band only if it established a reputation in one of the major cities, preferably New York or Chicago, there were numerous territory bands that achieved a more localized reputation. They contributed not only to the dissemination of jazz, but also to the development of the music, in subtle ways. Many of these bands are still remembered with admiration by musicians who heard them while touring on the road. Unfortunately most of these local performers never recorded, or if they did, it was for personal use only.

The blues bands of Alphonso Trent (*NW* 256, II/7–9), Troy Floyd (*NW* 256, II/4–5), Jesse Stone (*NW* 256, II/1), Lloyd Hunter (*NW* 217, II/3), and Andy Kirk (*NW* 217, I/3) were all traveling the southwest territory in the 1920s.[64] San Antonio, Texas, was a local base for territory bands, and Troy Floyd worked a band out of a San Antonio home in the late '20s and early '30s. His superb trumpeter, Don Albert, formed his own band in those early depression years and also traveled the territory well into the swing era, recording on Vocalion in 1936. Another native of the Lone Star State was Clifford "Boots" Douglas, who, between 1935 and 1938, rose to local prominence, recording blues and up-tempo pop songs with surprising frequency.

Of course, the major orchestras, like Ellington's and Cab Calloway's (*NW* 217, I/6–7), set the musical pace, but other bands, such as Jimmy Gunn's group from North Carolina and the Carolina Cottonpickers from Charleston, South Carolina, toured extensively, recorded occasionally, and brought the public enthusiastic, if somewhat less-than-polished, live hot jazz. Swing bands in America were a national phenomenon, and both white and black musicians worked at the same jobs. Business had expanded from the dancehall

[64] See Gunther Schuller, *Early Jazz*, p. 290 f., for a remarkable transcription of a chorus of *Starvation Blues* by the Jesse Stone band, the Blues Serenaders, recorded for OKeh in 1927.

and saloon to include college proms, movie theaters, local radio shows, and private parties. It has been pointed out that:

> these breakthroughs often put considerable pressure on the musicians as they bumped against the color line. Duke Ellington and Kansas City's own Benny Moten both played to white-only crowds at Kansas City's Elbion Theater. This was not an unusual situation: blacks were often denied admission or limited to Jim Crow balconies for appearances by black bands at nonblack locations. Moreover, black bands in this period often played at hotels where they could not rent a room. On prom dates, black musicians frequently had to stay at private black homes since there were no public accommodations available to them. . . . However, there was little agitation by entertainers against these restrictions. The reasons for this reticence are varied. The musicians frequently felt that their position was precarious and that protests would have a negative effect. Moreover, on the positive side, their appearances before white audiences were viewed as a way of both raising the prestige of blacks and siphoning off some white money into black pockets.[65]

Although name bands made the news during this period, local bands disseminated the style as a national phenomenon. Cities like Cleveland, Detroit, Omaha, and Dallas were important stopovers for national bands on their regional or cross-country tours, but when the luminaries were gone, local leaders—such as Red Perkins, Lloyd Hunter, Ted Adams, and Preston Love, all of Omaha—worked the clubs and played the territory on a regular basis.

Within this context, the Benny Goodman band and combos as models of musical performance and social values take on added importance. Goodman established a standard of excellence that required technical virtuosity of professional jazz artists. He applied this standard first to his own playing and then to that of the musicians he selected and rehearsed to play with him. Allowed a certain amount of freedom because of his national prestige, he was truly the first jazz artist, or musician of any genre or style, who was able to recruit others purely on the basis of job qualification rather than friendship, social environment, racial mores, or other restrictive and extraneous causes. Lionel Hampton and Teddy Wilson played so well that the American public never balked at hiring an integrated quartet and allowing them great freedom of movement. Other musicians equally talented—Roy Eldridge and Lester Young, for example—were not so fortunate, but the crack in the color barrier that Goodman effectuated was the beginning of a significant breakthrough that has had important ramifications in all aspects of American life.

[65] Thomas Joseph Hennessey, "From Jazz to Swing: Black Jazz Musicians and Their Music, 1917–1935" (unpublished dissertation, Northwestern University, 1973), p. 443 f.

THE DUKE ELLINGTON ORCHESTRA ⎯⎯⎯⎯⎯⎯⎯⎯⎯

All the while, Duke Ellington's band continued to improve. His arrangements became more sophisticated, his compositions acquired greater depth and musical meaning, and his band played with more precision than ever before. The late '30s through the early '40s were a period in which the full flowering of his genius was on display. In 1940 alone he recorded approximately seventy pieces, and many of the new compositions number among his best: *Ko-Ko, Concerto for Cootie (Do Nothin' Till You Hear from Me), Cotton Tail, Jack the Bear, Harlem Air Shaft, In a Mellotone,* and more. They are triumphs of imagination and marvels of performance virtuosity.

Ko-Ko (*SCCJ* 57) is a complicated but unpretentious big band blues, actually a minor blues, that evolved from ideas Ellington sketched for a number in his unfinished opera, *Boola.*[66] The classic formal effect of rounded binary form, **ABA,** is created when the opening baritone-saxophone sound, with heavy vibrato, recurs near the end as a quasi recapitulation. This mid-range tempo is suitable for social dancing, either as a "businessman's bounce" fox-trot or a young jazz fan's slow jitterbug. Variety occurs in the piece not through a series of captivating solo performances, though the format would certainly allow for them in a live performance, but rather through the successive display of instrumental tone color selected principally by the arranger: muted and open brass, careful saxophone scoring, the contrast between large ensemble and single instrument, and other timbral ideas.[67]

---

[66] Ken Rattenbury, *Duke Ellington, Jazz Composer,* p. 104.

[67] See Rattenbury, *Duke Ellington, Jazz Composer,* pp. 107–39, for a complete transcription of the work. Then compare Gunther Schuller's transcription in "Duke Ellington," *The New Grove Dictionary of Jazz,* p. 332 f., of mm. 71–79 (Rattenbury's measure numbers) and William W. Austin's transcription in *Music in the 20th Century,* p. 285 f, of mm. 12–17. Also note that my sense of rounded form differs from Schuller's "crescendo" or "bolero" form (*The Swing Era,* p. 116).

This is a good place to explain a key problem in jazz scholarship presented by transcriptions for analysis. Very little music can be analyzed in detail without a notated score, and in jazz, most music is preserved only on recordings. Transcribing is extremely difficult and time consuming, and can be accomplished only by highly skilled musicians with an extraordinary sense of pitch and meticulous working habits—a very select group. Many have tried their hand at transcribing Ellington's *Ko-Ko,* but few have had the nerve to venture into print. The transcriptions by three truly superlative musicians, Austin, Rattenbury, and Schuller, are fascinating to compare, for they derived their scores from a single recording—Victor 26577, of March 6, 1940. That they differ noticeably does not invalidate any of them, it simply underscores the tremendous difficulty in obtaining an "accurate" copy of sound on paper. Even when a composer's

Harlem Air Shaft (*SCCJ* 56) is a stunning combination of a New York-style swing arrangement of a piece in pop-song form, **AABA,** and the riffs of the Kansas City tradition. The "One O'Clock Jump" riff near the end gives the piece tremendous forward drive, and when the brasses open up in ensemble, the band's full power is unleashed.

Mood music began to evolve during the swing era, and *In a Mellotone* (*SCCJ* 60) epitomizes the then-current American taste for romantic dance music to accompany the dress-up occasions of ballroom dancing. The piano introduction is a standard band cliché inviting the dancers to leave their tables and move to the floor. The saxophones sneak in on a unison melody accompanied by antiphonal trombones, all of which is followed by a gentle trumpet solo with standardized band backing featuring clarinet lead. Meanwhile, the beat is never obscured by unnecessary complexities, for, in the last analysis, all this big-band music is dance music.

Ellington's recordings of March 1940 on RCA Victor mark a new phase of artistic maturity in his writing. *Jack the Bear, Morning Glory, Ko-Ko,* and *Concerto for Cootie* (*SCCJ* 58) are all prime examples of a developing compositional economy that narrows the focus of each piece and exploits fewer musical ideas in a time-limited space. Despite the growing complexity of the music, these works never lose their power of swing, their feeling of improvisational insight and momentary creation, or their sense of communication with the audience, which is drawn from the general listening public. This period, 1940–42, is considered by many experts to be the musical apex of Ellington's career, and the recording of *Jack the Bear*[68] illustrates many of the primary musical events associated with his orchestra at this time. First, and most obvious, is the solo display of Jimmy Blanton who, through his technical mastery of his instrument and remarkable musicianship, changed the role of the double bass from that of an accompanying instrument in the rhythm section to that of a solo instrument performing in its own right. Second, we

---

signed holograph exists, the notation is merely a shorthand to stimulate real sounds from performing musicians.

Rattenbury offers a complete transcription of the work, so we might use his numbering system for convenience in comparing the three. He numbers the eight-measure introduction mm. A–H, the following seven blues choruses (twelve measures each) mm. 1–84, and the coda of twelve measures that restates the introduction and adds a conclusion mm. 85–96. Austin (published 25 years ago!) gives us mm. 12–17, and Schuller mm. 71–79. Though Austin has one saxophone too few, Schuller one trumpet too many, and Rattenbury some inexact rhythms, all are excellent transcriptions that illustrate salient characteristics in Ellington's music. Critics who do not play an instrument and cannot read music have been known to condemn academics who take a scholarly interest in jazz, but those same critics can only make unsubstantiated generalities about their favorite pieces and lard their analyses of music with hyperbole.

[68] Victor 26536.

hear the solo artistry of "Tricky Sam" Nanton, who uses the plunger mute
to expand his trombone solo into a world of varied brass timbres and articulations. Third, we note excellent solos by Barney Bigard on clarinet and Harry
Carney on baritone saxophone. Bigard offers an important contrast to Goodman and other swing clarinetists, and Carney, at the time, was without peer
as a soloist on baritone saxophone. But most important of all are Ellington
and the composition itself. The piece is not more daring than some of his
earlier works, but it is economical, self-assured, balanced, and swinging.
Every passage has the composer/arranger touch—in the selection of chords,
in the combination of instruments, in the voicings and placement of tessi-
tura, in the modification of form. In its details and in its entirety, *Jack the
Bear* is an extraordinary piece.

As an example of how Ellington takes a given form, modifies it, and then
uses this modification as an important compositional element in the subsequent passages, examine the beginning.

Formal Scheme of *Jack the Bear*

mm.	Intro. 8	A 12	Trans. 4	B 32	Trans. 4	C 44 = 12 + 12 + 20	Trans. 4	A′ 16
	bass solo	piano lead with bass		clarinet solo		bari. sax + trombone + band		bass solo

After the introduction, observe that the first chorus, **A,** is a twelve-bar blues
with one important alteration—there is no move to the subdominant in the
second phrase. This idea of expanding the A♭ time frame is explored in the
next chorus, where Bigard's solo is placed above a long-lasting A♭ pedal point.
After this, we hear the other half of the idea, the regular A♭ blues, performed
four times, but once again with a modification: the last twelve-measure chorus
is cut short when the four-measure saxophone transition appears again to
connect the blues with the final chorus. This four-measure connector and
separator also serves as a ritornello in the structure, thus adding unity and
balance to the work. Finally a modified opening closes the work in a balanced, rounded form—**ABCA′.**

Jack the Bear, Final Chorus, Jimmy Blanton Solo.

In contrast to the dancelike nature of *In a Mellotone,* Ellington's *Concerto for Cootie* (*SCCJ* 58) stands apart as an exceptional work of absolute music in the jazz repertoire. Free from extramusical implications, it derives its aesthetic success or failure solely from the syntactical relationships of its musical elements. In the words of André Hodeir:

> CONCERTO FOR COOTIE is a masterpiece because what the orchestra says is the indispensable complement to what the soloist says; because nothing is out of place or superfluous in it; and because the composition thus attains unity.[69]

Hodeir goes on to point out some of the composition's unusual features: the three sections of the piece are unequal in length (excluding the introduction—30 measures, 18 measures, and 16 measures); the phrase structure is irregular (6-, 8-, and 10-measure phrases); and the composer-improviser relationship is not typical of the classical concerto (the composer's instructions, although specific, allow the soloist great latitude in interpretation). It is easy to wax eloquent on the "bouquet of sonorities" created by the soloist on his instrument, thus:

> Few records do more than the CONCERTO to make possible an appreciation how great a role sonority can play in the creation of jazz. The trumpet part is a true bouquet of sonorities. . . . He [Cootie] makes them shine forth in dazzling colors, then plunges them in the shade, plays around with them, makes them glitter or delicately tones them down; and each time what he shows us is something new. . . . It is appropriate that theme *A,* which we have already described as static, should be handled in subdued colors; that theme *B,* which is savagely

[69] *Jazz: Its Evolution and Essence,* p. 80.

harsh, should invite free use of the muted wa-wa's stridencies, which here have an extra brutality; and the lyricism of theme *C* can be fully expressed only in the upper register of the trumpet, played open.[70]

If *Concerto for Cootie* is a trumpet soloist's vehicle for timbral expression, then *Blue Serge* (*SCCJ* 61), by Duke's son, Mercer, is a similar example of the Ellington band's exploration into the realm of striking sonorities. Mercer Ellington's compositional prowess is well displayed here—the subtle harmonic shifts and the irregular phrasing are beautifully crafted. The opening phrases, played by woodwinds in the upper register, state the theme and establish the minor mode. The brasses answer to complete the six-measure introduction with chords scored to simulate the fullness and richness of an orchestral French horn section. The velvety sound of Ray Nance's glissando-filled trumpet solo follows, his tone altered with a bucket mute. The solo extends and completes the melodic phrase presented in the introduction and interprets the entire phrase through variations in timbre and pitch. The second chorus reinterprets the first with an orchestrated tutti passage that also carries a two-measure extension, but unlike the first extension, this one modulates to the relative major. During this chorus, the saxophone section does not restate the melody, which has been heard only once, but proceeds with a new phrase that serves to balance the melody. "Tricky Sam" Nanton takes his turn on the third chorus and does on trombone what Ray Nance did on trumpet—evoke in music a "blue serge" mood.

New sounds constantly follow, including that of muted trombones with a wa-wa effect. But then, a fascinating change occurs. The fourth chorus reverses the harmonic pattern of the first—I–V, I–V becomes V–I, V–I—and the harmonic idea derived from the extension of the second chorus, i.e., the change from minor to major, is used to elide this chorus with the next, Ellington's piano solo. Although the key center is intentionally ambiguous, the solo is essentially in major with a final cadence in minor. The sixth chorus, Ben Webster's brilliant tenor solo, is twelve measures divided 4 + 8. Webster starts with a four-measure passage in major that deceives the ear by seeming to modulate to a chorus in minor, but the concluding eight-measure solo has a chord pattern of its own that mixes major and minor just as skillfully as Ellington did in his piano solo. At last, the full ensemble recapitulates the original theme and chords with one last orchestral variation.

Blue Serge provides a dual function: it is music for listening, and it is eminently danceable. Still, the typical Ellington fan will not go away humming the tune. In a quite different context, Martin Williams asks the rhetorical

[70] Ibid., p. 93 f.

question, " 'Where's the melody?' or, to put it more crudely, 'What are those musicians *doing* up there?' "[71] The discussion that leads to Williams's question concerns itself with improvisation to fixed harmonic patterns and not composed songs without recognizable tunes, but the question is just as apt here. Jazz musicians began to expect more from their listeners as they began to expect more from themselves. And the same jazz pundit's answer seems valid for this situation as well:

> And so, we come back again to our question and our answer. Where's the melody? The melody is the one the player is making. Hear it well, for it probably will not exist again. And it may well be extraordinary.[72]

GLENN MILLER

Swing is and was many things, and for millions of Americans swing was the magical sound of the Glenn Miller dance band. The six years from the spring of 1939 to the night of December 15, 1944, when Glenn Miller failed to return from a military flight over the English Channel, almost became the Glenn Miller era. Everyone knew "the Miller sound," a penetrating tutti sax-section voice with lead clarinet.

Born in Clarinda, Iowa, in 1904, Miller served a typical jazz apprenticeship. He played with Boyd Senter, Ben Pollack, Paul Ash, and Red Nichols in the '20s and worked his way into the studios of New York City in the early 1930s. An extremely capable trombonist, he played with the Dorsey brothers and Ray Noble, and took up studies in music composition with Joseph Schillinger, a theoretician who applied mathematical principles to musical composition. He tried his own luck at leading a band as early as 1937, and in 1939, thanks largely to his band members and vocalists Hal McIntyre, Tex Beneke, Al Klink, Marion Hutton, and Ray Eberle, he succeeded in crashing the popular market. The danceable ballads *Moonlight Serenade* and *Sunrise Serenade*,[73] and the up-tempo swingers of *Little Brown Jug*,[74] *In the Mood*,[75] and *String of Pearls*,[76] became phenomenally popular recordings between 1939 and 1941.

During the three years immediately preceding America's entry into World

[71] Martin Williams, *Where's the Melody? A Listener's Introduction to Jazz* (New York: Pantheon Books, 1966), p. 4.
[72] Ibid., p. 13.
[73] Bluebird 10214.
[74] Bluebird 10286.
[75] Bluebird 10416.
[76] Bluebird 11382.

The Glenn Miller Band playing for the troops in England.

War II, Miller and Goodman floated on pinnacles of success and became household words around the world. Still, they were not without competition from other equally fine bands. Charlie Barnet, Bunny Berigan, Les Brown, Cab Calloway, Benny Carter, Jimmy Dorsey, Tommy Dorsey, Woody Herman, Harry James, Andy Kirk, Artie Shaw, Chick Webb, and several others were major dance-band leaders who recorded impressive sides in 1939. Suddenly, America was coming out of the depression, the market for popular music and jazz was mushrooming, and the younger musicians who had apprenticed in the guild systems of the 1930s were ready to accept the challenge of full employment. The technology of broadcasting and recording improved immeasurably, and the new quality of "canned" sound allowed music, the entertainment industry, and the media to expand at a tremendous rate. However, the seeds of discontent among the musicians themselves were beginning to thrust shoots through the well-watered soil of jazz at approximately the same time. A taste for the old hot jazz was beginning to manifest itself among those who recalled the sounds of yesteryear with fondness: blues, New Orleans, and ragtime revivals were under way. A compulsion to break free from the restrictive bonds of big-band arrangements and dance-hall entertainment attitudes was making the avant-garde jazz artists of the day question both the music they were playing and their status in society. The bebop revolution was about to erupt. In 1939, these phenomena were felt only as slight whispers on the roaring winds of swing, but Alan Lomax, Frederic Ramsey, Jr., Rudi Blesh, and Charlie Parker were all, quite independently of each other, preparing the ground for a major upheaval in what might have seemed to be an unshakable, unassailable American music. Some young musicians were beginning to pay more attention to the sounds of Lester Young and Charlie Christian than to those of Count Basie and Benny Goodman. Lomax, Ramsey, and Blesh were searching the ghettos and back alleys for authentic old-time blues musicians, ragtime piano players, and classic jazz sidemen, while Bird Parker was learning his horn and the changes.

WORLD WAR II

What was the musical effect of World War II? In general, jazz benefited in a most positive way. The Special Services units of the armed forces allowed thousands of young musicians to make music night and day where previously a relative handful of musicians were gainfully employed full-time. Nightclubs in major cities were packed with soldiers on leave, and the increased business provided many new jobs for jazz bands and combos. American armed forces took their popular music and jazz with them wherever they were stationed, via the armed-services radio system. Ironically, even the enemy propaganda agencies served to promulgate a taste for jazz by broadcasting American music in an attempt to lure the "Yanks" from their miserable foxholes, tents, and submarines to an idyllic promised land of pleasure and recreation. Tokyo Rose, the infamous voice of the Japanese airwaves, was a favorite disc jockey for the GIs in the Pacific theater. As a result of all these unusual circumstances, American jazz musicians not only proliferated and developed skills far above the norm of the prewar years, but the American public—both service personnel and citizens at home—was literally enclosed in an environment of jazz and big-band dance music. Famous musicians became national heroes as Americans took pride in everything that was American, and no town or farm was too isolated to know the names of Dorsey, Miller, Basie, Goodman, and Ellington.

Comedy and quiz shows on the radio, a favorite entertainment form of the time, had backup bands; wherever the comedian Bob Hope traveled, whether to entertain the troops at the front or to broadcast a "toothpaste show" (so called after the sponsor's product) from a studio, one could count on hearing the Les Brown Band of Renown. The music of a subculture had truly become the music of the nation, and the portion of jazz that we know as swing was a universally accepted idiom in the United States. Jazz musicians could assume a new pride in their profession. The effects of the war on this music lasted well after the close of hostilities: in 1946, one critic wrote, "The six years of the World War were years during which jazz advanced more rapidly and more impressively than in any previous period."[77]

WOMEN INSTRUMENTALISTS

Women began to make noticeable inroads into the male-dominated world of instrumental jazz during the late 1930s, and new opportunities opened up during World War II when the draft pulled many male musicians into the armed services. Two all-women orchestras stand out both for their success and renown at the time and for their technical excellence: Ina Ray Hutton and Her Melodears Orchestra, an organization that first rose to prominence before the war, and The International Sweethearts of Rhythm.

Ina Ray Hutton (1916–84) was a glamour figure, singer, and dancer who had the leadership skills to develop and sell a band in a very competitive market. She organized her first female swing band in 1934 and, promoted by Irving Mills, led one of the most popular bands of the decade. Her 1934 recording of *Wild Party*[78] is an up-tempo swing arrangement in the Fletcher Henderson style that contrasts section work with short solos, and her 1936 recording of *Truckin'*[79] is a fine demonstration of propulsive swing and technical accomplishment. The band lacked exciting soloists, but the ensemble was precise, the rhythm compelling, the solo work professional, and the overall performance convincing. The group has been labeled more a dance band or show band than a jazz band, but it had a good sense of swing which compared favorably with many of the name swing bands of the day.

The International Sweethearts of Rhythm, on the other hand, boasted some fine soloists—the tenor saxophonist Viola Burnside, the trumpeter

---

[77] Leonard Feather, "A Survey of Jazz Today," in *Esquire's 1946 Jazz Book*, ed. Paul Eduard Miller (New York: Barnes, 1946), p. 151.

[78] Stash 109.

[79] Preserved on film and released on Videocassette, *Video Film Classics: The Big Bands*, v. 105 (Indianapolis: Swingtime Video, 1954).

The International Sweethearts of Rhythm. (Top row, left to right) Ray Carter, trumpet; Marge Pettiford, saxophone; Pauline Braddy, drums; Johnnie Mae Stansbury, trumpet; Amy Garrison, saxophone; Judy Bayron, trombone; Lucille Dixon, bass; Roxanna Lucas, guitar; Johnnie Mae Rice, piano; (middle row) Helen Jones, trombone; Evelyn McGee, vocalist; Helen Saine, saxophone; (bottom row) Edna Williams, trumpet; Ina Bell Byrd, trombone; Anna Mae Winburn, leader/vocalist; Grace Bayron, saxophone; and Willie Mae Wong, saxophone.

Ernestine "Tiny" Davis, and the drummer Johnnie Mae Rice. Formed in 1939 at the Piney Woods (Mississippi) Country Life School, the band made its debut at the Howard Theater in Washington, D.C., soon after. Singer Anna Mae Winburn, who had been fronting the Lloyd Hunter Serenaders from Omaha, was the group's leader from 1941 to its dissolution in the late 1940s. Boasting excellent arrangements by Eddie Durham and Jesse Stone, the Sweethearts quickly became known as the foremost female band of the day. Among their recordings, their 1945 performances of *Galvanizing* and *Honeysuckle Rose*[80] display both their ensemble skills and their solo capacities. What they may have lacked in precision they amply supplied in power and drive.

Outside the sphere of all-women orchestras, a few female instrumentalists were able to integrate successfully into the otherwise all-male bands of the day. Some of the most notable were Valaida Snow, trumpeter with the Fletcher Henderson Orchestra, and, a little later, Billie Rogers, trumpet, and Mar-

[80] Both on Rosetta Records RR 1312.

Melba Liston, trombone, in 1978.

jorie Hyams, vibes, with the Woody Herman Band, and Melba Liston, trombone, with the Dizzy Gillespie Orchestra.

The most outstanding female instrumentalist of the day was jazz pianist Mary Lou Williams (1910–81), who recorded and performed professionally for over five decades, wrote successful arrangements for Benny Goodman, Earl Hines, Tommy Dorsey, Dizzy Gillespie, and others, brought the Andy Kirk Band to life and fame through her compositions, arrangements, performance, and musical leadership, influenced and encouraged some young originators of a new style, bebop, at a critical stage in the development of this music, wrote large compositions performed by the New York Philharmonic and danced by the Alvin Ailey American Dance Company, and received a professorial appointment at a major American university. Still, a full-length musical-biographical study of Williams is yet to be written.

Born in Atlanta in 1910, Williams grew up as a child prodigy in Pittsburgh. At twelve she sat in with McKinney's Cotton Pickers when they came to town. As a teenager, she played with Ellington's Washingtonians, she at the piano in the pit and Ellington at the keyboard when the band went on stage. At the age of fifteen she went on the road with the Seymour & Jeanette vaudeville act and, in 1929, became part of the Andy Kirk band. The group advertised itself as "The Twelve Clouds of Joy," and she was known as "The Lady Who Swings the Band." As a pianist during her early years in

Mary Lou Williams, piano (1910–81).

Sarah Vaughan.

jazz, she featured a solid left hand that could lay out a ragtime bass, stride the Kansas City swing identified with Andy Kirk's orchestra, or rock the piano in a boogie-woogie eight-to-the-bar. At the same time, her right hand was capable of virtuosic melodic flights, solid clusters of harmonic surprises, and a variety of rhythms to counterbalance the regular foundation work of the left.

Unlike many musicians in jazz, Williams was never locked into a single style. Her productive years spanned most of the history of jazz, from the early 1920s to her death in 1981. Her performance, to a large degree, kept current with the new music of the day, at least until the atonal and arhythmic explorations of the '60s set up camps she did not appreciate. A representative sample of her work during the period in which she rose to prominence, 1936–41, may be heard on "The Best of Andy Kirk."[81] *The Lady Who Swings the Band,* sung by Harry Mills, is a public relations number, but Williams's piano solo is characteristic. Her own composition, *Little Joe from Chicago,* demonstrates in a marvelous way the driving Kansas City beat and amply displays her pianistic talents.

The singers of the day must not be discounted or downplayed for, in the public eye, the successful vocalist lived in a world of stardom rarely available to the instrumentalist. Billie Holiday, Ella Fitzgerald, and Sarah Vaughan were all acknowledged masters of jazz singing in the early 1940s. Their work

[81] MCA2-4105.

varied significantly from one to the other in manner of presentation, repertoire, and tonal quality of their unique instruments, their voices. All were
superb musicians with a commanding stage presence, and each grew professionally from band musician to leader.

Where one remembers the words and presence of Billie Holiday and the
improvisational daring of Ella Fitzgerald, the listener cannot help but focus,
in the case of Sarah Vaughan (b. 1924), on the beauty of the voice itself (*NW*
271, I/2 and *NW* 295, II/1). But she was an instrumentalist, too—a good
pianist. An outstanding musician, Vaughan sang in the Mount Zion Baptist
Church choir in Newark, New Jersey, as a child and became organist at her
church at the age of twelve. After winning a talent contest in 1942 she quickly
moved to the Earl Hines band in 1943 as second pianist and singer. Billy
Eckstine, who also sang with Hines, formed a big band in 1944 which he
fronted and for which he served as lead vocalist. This group will be discussed
further in the next chapter; its female vocalist was Sarah Vaughan.

POST-WAR SWING

In the years immediately following World War II, the swing bands were
exciting musical organizations. Woody Herman, Duke Ellington, Benny
Goodman, Harry James, Tommy Dorsey, Jimmy Dorsey, Lionel Hampton,
Gene Krupa, Count Basie, Artie Shaw, Les Brown, Dizzy Gillespie, Charlie
Barnet, and Boyd Raeburn led the most impressive big bands on the market.
Concerts from Carnegie Hall and Town Hall in New York were popular;
juke boxes were doing an impressive business; and radio, movies, and dance
halls were exuding swing from every loudspeaker.

> To sum up: 1945 was another great year for jazz. You don't have to take any
> one person's word for this. Just look at the vast selection of musicians for whom
> votes were cast in this year's New Stars poll—then listen to some of their
> recorded music. It speaks very eloquently for itself. . . . 1946 will be a great
> year for jazz, just as the year before it, and the year before that. So much was
> accomplished, incredibly, during the years of war, that it's hard to conceive
> what may develop in a world at peace.[82]

The health and vitality of swing during the early postwar years, perhaps
generated by the enthusiasm of a successful war effort, gave it an impetus
that carried it safely through the 1940s and, with diminishing intensity, virtually to the end of the '50s. Other styles began to develop, and they all

[82] Feather, "A Survey of Jazz Today," pp. 161 and 163.

coexisted with swing and the revived old-time jazz. Swing remained the most popular of all the jazz styles, even though it was soon supplanted as the greatest influence in the jazz community. The effort may be summarized as follows:

> The free, spontaneous communication between the big bands and their fans was a natural culmination of the music itself. The approach of most outfits was so honest and direct that fans could recognize instinctively whether the bands were really trying or merely coasting. When a musician played an especially exciting solo, they'd cheer for it, and when the band as a whole reached especially high musical and emotional heights, it would be rewarded with enthusiastic, honest, heartfelt yelling and cheering—not the kind of hysterics evoked by a rock and roller's shaking his long tresses, but real approval for a musical job well done. . . . By 1940 there must have been close to two hundred dance orchestras, any one of which a knowing fan could identify after hearing only a few of its stylized musical measures.
>   Nothing like it had ever happened before.[83]

In sum, swing was first and foremost a big-band arranged jazz style, and the arrangers were as influential in its development as the performers themselves. Beginning in the New York-jazz band styles of the late '20s, a music with roots in the classic jazz tradition emerged and eventually became a separate and distinct musical idiom. Changes in instrumentation gave arrangers and composers new sonorities with which to work, and the guitar and string bass, which replaced the banjo and tuba, gave jazz rhythm sections an entirely different sound. A steady 4/4 rhythm with a two-beat ride was maintained by the drummers, and the rhythm section provided a more pervasive but less obtrusive rhythmic sound than that of the New Orleans combos. The softer dynamics of guitar and bass helped accelerate the catalysis.

Around 1935, the physical dimensions of swing bands increased to and then standardized at fourteen members: four rhythm instruments, five brasses, and five reeds. Frequently, arrangers would fit simple riffs for sections in unison or in a thickened melodic line to the simple chord patterns of the popular songs of the day or the blues, and ballads were as much a part of the repertoire as the up-tempo numbers commonly thought to characterize swing. Performances achieved greater precision as an influx of schooled musicians began to fill the chairs of jazz. Toward the end of the '30s, two new instruments were introduced—the electric guitar and the vibraphone—and the repertoire of possible tonal effects multiplied not only from the variety of

[83] Simon, *The Big Bands*, pp. 13 and 15.

newer instruments but also from the imaginative scoring of standard instruments in solo and combination by the arrangers.

Thomas Hennessey summarizes his excellent study with these conclusions:

> Slowly, black jazz moved from being a folk music to being a popular music. The musicians became professionals who earned their living from their music and worked hard at it. For most black jazz musicians by 1935, jazz represented a way of "making it" in American society, an upwardly mobile path to economic success, increased status and public recognition. The bonanzas of the early thirties came as a fitting climax to the efforts of the young, frequently college-trained, musicians with middle-class aspirations who had helped to transform one segment of black music from jazz to swing between 1917 and 1935.[84]

Swing also opened the doors of jazz to numerous white musicians who also began to "make it" in American society. But as we shall see, the success of the swing bands and the concomitant necessity to maintain an image eventually led to its downfall as the new bebop movement began to gain momentum in the mid-1940s.

[84]Thomas J. Hennessey, "From Jazz to Swing: Jazz Musicians and Their Music, 1917–1935" (unpublished dissertation, Northwestern University, 1973; University Microfilm No. 74-7757), p. 492 f.

$\mathcal{M}$ODERN JAZZ
THE BEBOP
REVOLUTION

ORIGINS OF A NEW STYLE

Toward the end of World War II, it became apparent that a new style of jazz was in the process of being created. A small group of musicians, seeing jazz from a different perspective, felt that big-band swing was in a rut. They felt that arrangers were not leaving enough room in their music for solo improvisation, and the style itself was harmonically empty—chord progressions were limited to triads, seventh chords, and occasional diminished and augmented chords with perhaps an added note; rhythms were too stereotyped and consisted only of formula mixtures of simple syncopations; and melodies were too tradition-bound to the four- and eight-measure phrase structure of dance music. They heard new harmonic and rhythmic implications in the famous Coleman Hawkins *Body and Soul* improvisation (*SCCJ* 33 and Transcription 4), realizing that he had constructed his melodic line as if the rhythm section were playing at twice the actual tempo of the original composition. In other words, a second level of harmonic motion and rhythmic activity was superimposed, through the addition of passing chords, upon the original structure.

These same musicians heard new sounds and new ideas in the famous Charlie Christian recordings of 1941—sessions from Monroe's Uptown House and Minton's in New York City with sidemen Thelonious Monk on piano, Kenny Clarke on drums, Don Byas on tenor saxophone, and Dizzy Gillespie on trumpet.[1] As a direct consequence of listening to these pioneer explorations of the early 1940s, a group of jazz musicians began playing a new style of music, which came to be called "bebop."[2]

The word "bebop" originated in the jazz musician's practice of vocalizing or singing instrumental melodic lines with nonsense syllables (scat singing). Bebop phrases frequently had abrupt endings with a characteristic long-short pattern on the end: ♩ ♪ ,, and this rhythm was often vocalized as "rebop" or "bebop." The name seems first to have appeared in print as the title of a tune recorded by the Dizzy Gillespie Sextet in New York in 1945.[3] A few years later, jazz musicians shortened the term to "bop."

> Of all the queer, uncommunicative, secret-society terms that jazz has surrounded itself with, few are lumpier or more misleading than "bebop." Originally a casual onomatopoeic word used to describe the continually shifting accents of the early work of Charlie Parker, Dizzy Gillespie, Kenny Clarke, and Thelonious Monk, it soon became a free-floating, generic one as well, whose tight, rude sound implied something harsh, jerky, and unattractive.[4]

Bebop developed at a period in the history of jazz when some musicians were consciously attempting to create a new elite and exclude from their number all who did not meet predetermined artistic standards. Barriers, real and artificial, were put up, not only between bebop musicians and the public at large, but between themselves and other jazz artists.[5] It is common knowledge that jazz musicians have often been held suspect by people unfamiliar with their work, and many factors estranged the jazz artists from society at large: the large proportion of black performers in a predominantly white society; the threat that jazz posed to established art music; the musicians' inverted hours of work, sleep, and recreation; and their nomadic life. It should be no surprise, then, to discover that in retaliation some jazz musicians rejected society as well. An excellent study of the jazz community concludes with the observation:

> The jazz community . . . is a social grouping drawn together by specific attitudes and behaviors which stress the differences of the musician and his public

[1] Society E-SOC 996 and Counterpoint A 5548.

[2] Also "rebop" and "bop." The etymology of the word is obscure, even though it is of recent origin. See Marshall Stearns, *The Story of Jazz*, p. 155, and André Hodeir, *Jazz: Its Evolution and Essence*, p. 110.

[3] *Salt Peanuts / Be-Bop* (Manor 5000, Regal 132).

[4] *The New Yorker*, November 7, 1959, p. 158.

[5] Portions of this chapter were taken from the author's "The Silent Theme Tradition in Jazz," *The Musical Quarterly*, 53 (1967), p. 313 ff.

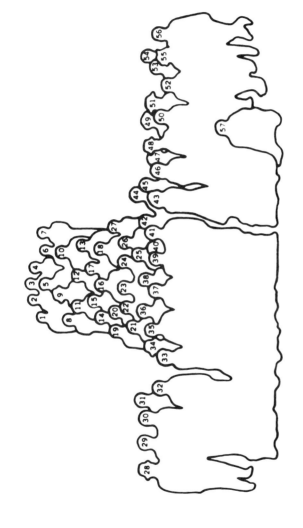

The jazz greats in the historic photograph above are numbered for ready reference: 1. Hilton Jefferson; 2. Benny Golson; 3. Art Farmer; 4. Wilbur Ware; 5. Art Blakey; 6. Chubby Jackson; 7. Johnny Griffin; 8. Dicky Wells; 9. Buck Clayton; 10. Taft Jordan; 11. Zutty Singleton; 12. Red Allen; 13. Tyree Glenn; 14. Miff Mole; 15. Sonny Greer; 16. Jay C. Higginbotham; 17. Jimmy Jones; 18. Charles Mingus; 19. Jo Jones; 20. Gene Krupa; 21. Max Kaminsky; 22. George Wettling; 23. Bud Freeman; 24. Pee Wee Russell; 25. Ernie Wilkins; 26. Buster Bailey; 27. Osie Johnson; 28. Gigi Gryce; 29. Hank Jones; 30. Eddie Locke; 31. Horace Silver; 32. Luckey Roberts; 33. Maxine Sullivan; 34. Jimmy Rushing; 35. Joe Thomas; 36. Scoville Browne; 37. Stuff Smith; 38. Bill Crump; 39. Coleman Hawkins; 40. Rudy Powell; 41. Oscar Pettiford; 42. Sahib Shihab; 43. Marian McPartland; 44. Sonny Rollins; 45. Lawrence Brown; 46. Mary Lou Williams; 47. Emmett Berry; 48. Thelonious Monk; 49. Vic Dickenson; 50. Milt Hinton; 51. Lester Young; 52. Rex Stewart; 53. J. C. Heard; 54. Gerry Mulligan; 55. Roy Eldridge; 56. Dizzy Gillespie; 57. Count Basie.

from people at large, his superiority over the layman, and the advantages to be gained from self segregation and isolation.[6]

The result, both unusual and unexpected, was that bebop musicians became disassociated from their own audience, from their own employers, from non-jazz musicians, and even from other jazz musicians. One critic writes:

> It was during the Minton's [Play House] era that men like Dizzy [Gillespie], [Kenny] Clarke, and Tadd [Dameron], finding that to a great degree they were kindred spirits, started what became in effect a clique of new musicians. It was not difficult to prevent outsiders from crashing this charmed circle. As Kenny Clarke recalls, "We'd play *Epistrophy* or *I've Got My Love To Keep Me Warm* just to keep the other guys off the stand, because we knew they couldn't make those chord changes. We kept the riff-raff out and built our clique on new chords.[7]

The most significant reason for this split was that bebop musicians were trying to raise the quality of jazz from the level of utilitarian dance music to that of a chamber art form. At the same time, they were trying to raise the status of the jazz performer from entertainer to artist. Their attempts were not immediately successful, and when their music was rejected, the bebop musicians turned inward. It was not uncommon for bebop soloists to play with their back turned toward the audience or to walk off the bandstand as soon as the solo was ended, even though the rest of the group was still playing. The bebop musicians' contempt for the public was equaled only by their disdain for people who called themselves jazz musicians but were musically incompetent by bebop standards. This attitude gave rise to a breed of person who became known as a "hipster." Of this group, Charlie Parker was the leader, the model, and the ultimate guru. His biographer writes:

> To the hipster, Bird was a living justification of their philosophy. The hipster is an underground man. He is to the Second World War what the dadaist was to the first. He is amoral, anarchistic, gentle, and overcivilized to the point of decadence. He is always ten steps ahead of the game because of his awareness, an example of which would be meeting a girl and rejecting her, because he knows they will date, hold hands, kiss, neck, pet, fornicate, perhaps marry, divorce—so why start the whole thing? He knows the hypocrisy of bureaucracy, the hatred implicit in religions—so what values are left for him?—except

[6] Alan P. Merriam and Raymond W. Mack, "The Jazz Community," *Social Forces*, 38 (1960), p. 222.

[7] Leonard Feather, *Inside Be-Bop*, p. 8.

to go through life avoiding pain, keep his emotions in check, and after that, "be cool," and look for kicks. He is looking for something that transcends all this bullshit and finds it in jazz.[8]

Technical proficiency was part of the movement, and bebop musicians did their best to belittle anyone who could not maintain the demanding pace. The jam session was the bebop musician's trial by fire. Dizzy Gillespie once told Marshall Stearns, "The modulations we manufactured were the weirdest, especially if some new cat walked in with his horn and tried to sit in with us."[9]

The transition to bebop seemed to happen overnight, but in truth, the foundations of the style were laid over a period of approximately six years, 1939–45. It might actually have taken place more quickly, but a National Federation of Musicians recording ban was imposed from August 1942, until November 1944,[10] and a major medium for the transmission of new ideas among the jazz musicians was temporarily denied them.

MUSICAL CHARACTERISTICS

By 1945, we are certain that bebop had established its stylistic independence from swing. Richard Wang analyzes a recording session of 1945 that combined musicians from both schools, swing and bebop, for performances of *Congo Blues* and *Slam, Slam Blues* (*NW* 271, I/1).[11] The jazz artists at this session were, in addition to Parker, Red Norvo, Teddy Wilson, Slam Stewart, J. C. Heard, Dizzy Gillespie, and Flip Phillips. Wang concludes:

> A comparison of the two styles reveals that: swing phrases are more uniform in length, more symmetrical in shape, and more congruent with the harmonic phrase than those of bebop; swing rhythmic patterns are less varied, more even-flowing, and less disrupted by shifting accents than those of bebop; bebop, on the other hand, is more complex, full of greater contrasts, has more rhythmic subtleties, and makes a greater and more expressive use of dissonance. The arrangement of *Congo Blues* exhibits several characteristics often found in the new style: the exotic rhythm of the introduction, the novel harmony of the interlude, and the unison riff at the end. . . . All the jazzmen discussed . . . attempted to unify their solos. . . . Only Parker, however, was successful in

[8] Robert George Reisner, *Bird: The Legend of Charlie Parker*, p. 25 f.
[9] Stearns, *The Story of Jazz*, p. 157.
[10] Robert D. Leiter, *The Musicians and Petrillo*, pp. 132–40.
[11] Comet T6-B and T7-B.

combining long-range unifying techniques with a maximum of expression, thus creating a truly great jazz solo.[12]

The importance of Charlie Parker is further dramatized by the statement of saxophonist Benny Green:

> The advent of Charlie Parker caused more violent irruptions, more bitterness, more sheer apoplectic rage than that of any jazz musician before him. Before he happened, there was no serious split down the middle of the jazz ranks. After he arrived, it was no longer sufficient to claim you were a jazz fan. . . . It was necessary to qualify the claim, to explain what kind of a jazz fan you were, to commit yourself either to the music that was pre-Charlie Parker or to the music he was playing.[13]

The musical characteristics of bebop are clearly revealed in the Dizzy Gillespie recording of *Shaw 'Nuff* (*SCCJ* 64): the characteristic introduction with "exotic" rhythm; the lightning-fast first chorus with melodic instruments playing a jagged instrumental melody in unison; the choruses of the soloists in the new style of asymmetry and rhythmic complexity; a harmonic framework that changes chords at half-note speed (at whole-note speed in the bridge section); and the unison riff at the end. Although it was Charlie Christian, Coleman Hawkins, and Lester Young, among others, who led the change to bebop, it was Charlie Parker and Dizzy Gillespie who took command and crystallized the style. Modern jazz, from its roots just before World War II to the present day, can be traced by concentrating on a careful study of the lives and music and impact of a relatively small number of dominant musicians and their associates, Charlie Parker, Dizzy Gillespie, Thelonious Monk, Miles Davis, John Coltrane, Ornette Coleman, and the Association for the Advancement of Creative Musicians (AACM). A coherent stream of development occurred in the relationships of Parker to Davis to Coltrane; Parker to Coleman to the AACM; Davis to Bill Evans, Herbie Hancock, and Wayne Shorter; and Coltrane to virtually all the jazz musicians who followed. In each of these people's lives, a stage of apprenticeship and learning is clear, a time of growth and development follows, and a period of mature artistic creation at the highest level is attained. The AACM, as distinct from the pattern of individual musicians, grew, changed, and influenced in its own unique way. But the founder of modern jazz, if one person can claim this distinction, is Charlie "Bird" Parker.

[12] Richard Wang, "Jazz Circa 1945: A Confluence of Styles," *The Musical Quarterly*, 59 (1973), p. 541 ff.

[13] Benny Green, *The Reluctant Art: Five Studies in the Growth of Jazz*, p. 159.

THE BIRD— CHARLIE PARKER

Charles Christopher Parker was born in Kansas City, Kansas, in 1920. He was raised by his mother in Kansas City, Missouri, a city that was developing its own tradition of blues-based jazz. His mother bought him an alto saxophone, but he also played baritone horn and clarinet for a brief period in high school. When he was fifteen he quit school and, that same year, played his first professional engagement. At sixteen he was married and playing with George Lee's combo. The pianist in the band gave him his first harmony lessons, and it was probably at this time that he began the heroin addiction that would plague him for the remainder of his all-too-brief life. In 1937, his apprenticeship continued with brief stints in the Jay McShann band, an organization with a solid regional reputation; Lawrence Keyes's band; and, most significantly, two bands of Buster Smith, a five-piece combo and a twelve-member group with aspirations for the road and the big time. These dreams didn't materialize, but Buster was an important influence on the young saxophonist's playing. This same year, when he was still only seventeen, saw the birth of Parker's first child, Leon Francis, and the death of his father. In many ways, Parker was typical of many male, urban-ghetto black Americans—economically disadvantaged, with little formal education, street smart, and living precariously by his wits and little else.

In 1938 he played with Harlan Leonard's band (*NW* 284, I/1–2), another group with a good local reputation, but soon he pawned his horn, rode a freight to Chicago, borrowed and pawned a clarinet, and took a bus to New York. This daring escapade was clearly the most significant step in his musical education, for although he worked only as a dishwasher, he was employed at the club where Art Tatum was the resident pianist. In 1939 he began to jam at Clark Monroe's Uptown House. Of this, Parker said:

> After I first came to New York, I played at Monroe's Uptown House. Nobody paid me much mind at first at Monroe's except Bobby Moore, one of Count Basie's trumpet players. He liked me. Everybody else was trying to get me to sound like Benny Carter.
>
> There was no scale at Monroe's. Sometimes I got forty or fifty cents a night. If business was good, I might get up to six dollars.[14]

It was in New York, as Parker explained, that the seeds of the new style took root.

[14] Nat Shapiro and Nat Hentoff, *Hear Me Talkin' to Ya*, p. 355.

Charles Christopher "Bird" or "Yardbird" Parker (1920–55).

I remember one night before Monroe's I was jamming in a chili house (Dan Wall's) on Seventh Avenue between 139th and 140th. It was December, 1939. Now I'd been getting bored with the stereotyped changes that were being used all the time at the time, and I kept thinking there's bound to be something else. I could hear it sometimes, but I couldn't play it.

Well, that night, I was working over *Cherokee*, and, as I did, I found that by using the higher intervals of a chord as a melody line and backing them with appropriately related changes, I could play the thing I'd been hearing. I came alive.[15]

On a trip back to Kansas City in 1939, Parker first met trumpeter Dizzy Gillespie, and before long they would be jamming together in Harlem. The following year, the young saxophonist rejoined the Jay McShann band and with them recorded his first solos. *Swingmatism* and *Hootie Blues*, both recorded in April 1941 in New York, show a fresh, eager apprentice hard at work as a sideman[16]; The sixteen-measure solo in *Swingmatism* displays a beautiful, light tone and competent technique. Entering on measure 15 of McShann's piano solo, Parker already demonstrates his predilection to defy regular phrase structure. His blues solo on *Hootie Blues* is in the Kansas City mode with its bouncy beat, bent pitches, flattened sounds, and cute little riff figures. One link in the interlocking network of influential musicians can be seen here, for another sideman in this band, bassist Gene Ramey, would move on to a long and varied career with Teddy Wilson, Miles Davis, Art Blakey, and many others.

During 1941 Parker jammed frequently at Monroe's in Harlem, and here a core of bebop's leading figures worked out the new style. Guitarist Charlie Christian, pianists Thelonious Monk and Bud Powell, drummers Max Roach and Kenny Clarke, and trumpeter Dizzy Gillespie were all young artists aware of their musical accomplishments and intent upon creating a new style more intricate and complex than those that had come before.

The last interesting recording from Charlie Parker's apprentice period is a 1942 version of *The Jumpin' Blues*, with Jay McShann. It is similar to the brief solos Parker had recorded the previous year. The opening phrase was later expanded by Bennie Harris into a Parker bebop standard, *Ornithology*, a title punning Parker's nickname, "Bird" or "Yardbird." In its new incarnation, *Ornithology* is separated from the blues harmonies and twelve-measure form and is molded to the chords of Morgan Lewis's *How High the Moon*.

The complete transition from Parker's swing apprenticeship to his bebop

[15] Ibid., p. 354.
[16] Decca D179236.

The Jay McShann band at the Savoy Ballroom, New York, in 1941. (Front row, left to right) McShann; Lucky Enois, guitar; Gene Ramey, bass; Walter Brown, vocalist; Bob Mabane, tenor saxophone; Charlie Parker and John Jackson, alto saxophone; Freddie Culver, tenor saxophone; Lawrence Anderson and Joe Taswell, trombone; (back row) Gus Johnson, drums; and Harold Bruce, Bernard Anderson, and Orville "Piggy" Minor, trumpet.

mastery is not fully documented because of a national recording ban enforced from 1942 to 1944 by James C. Petrillo, president of the musicians' union, in a dispute over royalties and the Music Performance Trust Fund (only patriotic efforts for the military were excepted from the ban). Parker played a short stint with Noble Sissle's band and spent almost a year playing tenor sax with Earl Hines in 1943, when he also remarried.

In September 1944 he made his first combo recordings with the Tiny Grimes Quintet. In these performances we may observe the now self-assured bebop soloist proudly displaying his wares. On *Tiny's Tempo* and *Red Cross*,[17] even as the remainder of the group pumps along in the old swing style, Bird takes flight with his characteristic openings, legato off-beat accentuations, propulsive and unpredictable melodic passages, and extended solos that blend one chorus with the next.

In 1944 Parker also worked on the road with the Billy Eckstine band, an ensemble with a remarkable personnel roster. Both Dizzy Gillespie and Fats Navarro were among the trumpets; Parker, Sonny Stitt, Gene Ammons, Dexter Gordon, and Lucky Thompson all held sax chairs; Tadd Dameron, Tommy Potter, and Art Blakey comprised the rhythm section of piano, bass, and drums; and Sarah Vaughan shared vocal duties with the leader, Eckstine. This association on the road helped cement the bond between Gillespie and Parker.

[17] Savoy MG 12001.

"DIZZY"—
JOHN BIRKS GILLESPIE

Parker's friend and musical partner, John Birks "Dizzy" Gillespie, was born in 1917 in Cheraw, South Carolina. He studied harmony and theory, took instruction on several instruments, and began working with Frank Fairfax in Philadelphia in 1935. In 1937, Gillespie replaced Roy Eldridge in the Teddy Hill band, and he later worked with Mercer Ellington, Cab Calloway, Benny Carter, Charlie Barnet, and others. When Parker and Gillespie first met in 1939, Gillespie was the senior musician—a few years older, already established, and more technically competent, in both harmonic ability and performance skill. Parker would quickly narrow the gap. Fate made an especially wise choice in teaming Gillespie with Parker, for Gillespie was perhaps the only jazz trumpeter in the world who had both a sophisticated understanding of harmonic theory and unprecedented technical virtuosity on his instrument. He was the first jazz trumpet player capable of performing up-tempo melodies in bebop style. The unison riff and long-line solos of *Shaw 'Nuff*[18] (*NW* 271, I/3, and *SCCJ* 64) prove that Dizzy Gillespie, in 1945, was a virtuoso of almost unlimited technical resources. Also, his compositions, along with those of Parker and several other young musicians, were becoming the new "standards" of the bebop style. Gillespie's *Groovin' High* (*NAJ* 8) is a typical and important example of the bebop musician's method of borrowing the chordal structure of a well-known popular song, discarding the song's melody, and creating a new jazz theme for the emerging bebop style (See Listening Guide 8).

Still, it should be noted that at the time, neither Parker nor Gillespie received widespread recognition among jazz musicians and critics for their accomplishments. For the years 1945–47, Johnny Hodges, lead altoist with the Duke Ellington orchestra, was named the outstanding saxophonist of the year by musicians and critics for the *Esquire* All-American Jazz Band, and the same group of judges selected Cootie Williams, also with Ellington, and Louis Armstrong as the outstanding jazz trumpeters of the year. The big bands were in full swing, the Dixieland revival was at work (*SCCJ* 12; recorded in 1944!), and the bebop musicians were definitely not part of the conservative musical establishment.

These outcasts developed a number of characteristics, most of which were nonmusical, that set them apart from the rest of the world: language, dress, habitat, behavior. Goatees, berets, wing-collar shirts, and drape-shape suits

[18]Guild 1002, recorded in New York, May 1945.

John Birks "Dizzy" Gillespie at Yale University, 1972.

came into vogue for the hip musician when a tuxedo or a dark-blue suit was standard garb for other musicians. Jazz performers were already on an island; bopsters built a raft and moved offshore. A noted jazz critic explained the function of jazz's special language:

> It is [the jazz musician's] language that gives him that sense of community for which he fights so hard so much of the time. But his is more than a language; it is a kind of code which gains him admittance to the secure circles of jazz, establishes him as a member of an élite, and makes it possible for him to forbid entrance to his society.[19]

The bebop musicians developed their own language, and although it was similar to the language spoken by other jazz musicians, it varied in enough detail to be useful as the password that immediately distinguished friend from foe. As soon as outsiders picked up and used reserved words, the language changed.

[19] Barry Ulanov, *A Handbook of Jazz*, p. 99.

THE MUSIC

The music of bebop, as a rule, was performed by a small jazz combo of three to six members. The standard procedure when performing without written music—and this was the norm for bebop musicians rebelling against the written arrangements of swing—was to play the melody in its entirety once (twice if a twelve-measure blues), follow it with several choruses of improvised solos to the accompaniment of the rhythm section (usually piano, bass, and drums), and repeat the melody of the first chorus to end the piece. All the while, the rhythm section maintained the structure of the piece by repeating the harmonic pattern (the changes) of a complete chorus. Even without a complete jazz combo, Don Byas took the "head chart" understood for *I Got Rhythm* and improvised a full-length jazz number to the accompaniment of Slam Stewart's bass viol (*SCCJ* 62). His one variation from the traditional pattern is his omission of the opening-melody repeat for the last chorus, where he ends with a brief tag. Carlos Wesley "Don" Byas was born in Muskogee, Oklahoma, in 1912 and became one of the best known tenor-sax performers of the mid-1940s. He won the *Esquire* Silver Award in 1946 for his outstanding playing. A jobbing musician since the 1930s, he had worked with Don Redman, Andy Kirk, Count Basie, Dizzy Gillespie, and Duke Ellington, and, as we can hear in his performance of *I Got Rhythm*, he plays with the full-voiced sound of the Hawkins school but adds the modern characteristics then being explored by the innovators, Gillespie and Parker.

With rare exceptions, the jazz performances of the 1940s and '50s were all based on this "melodic improvisation to the changes" technique. Jazz musicians, because of their frequent employment at dances, nightclubs, and parties, worked from a repertoire of popular songs, musical-comedy melodies, blues tunes, and a few jazz originals. Also, this style of employment, where musicians were called upon to produce three or four hours of improvised music five to seven days a week, led to their developing a repertoire of melodic patterns—actually a collection of instrumental finger patterns related to keys and chords—that were generally unique to the individual and were called upon as "instant ideas" for developing long-line, extemporaneous solos.[20] The better musicians did not merely repeat patterns mechanically: melodic units were modified, dropped, and added to over time so that the state of improvisation for developing jazz artists was one of flux and growth, not impoverished redundancy.

---

[20] The first in-depth study of this phenomenon has been completed using the solos of Charlie Parker as the exemplars for study. See Thomas Owens, "Charlie Parker: Techniques of Improvisation" (unpublished disseration, University of California at Los Angeles, 1974; University Microfilms no. 75-1992).

Popular ballads, such as *I Can't Get Started*, by Vernon Duke and Ira Gershwin (*SCCJ* 63), were transformed by the precepts of bebop into jazz compositions whose characteristics differed entirely from those of the original composition and yet remained related to them. When Dizzy Gillespie recorded this number in 1945 (see Transcription 6), he opened with an eight-measure introduction, played a single thirty-two-measure chorus, and closed with a four-measure tag. We can see the gradual transformation of the music to a bebop ballad by studying the opening of each **A** phrase (the form is **AABA**).

I Can't Get Started: Original Tune and Chords

The tune is regular in both its melodic construction and its harmonic framework. The first four measures are divided in half, resulting in two melodic statements that are sequential in their intervallic construction and repetitive in their rhythmic construction.

Melodic Rhythm

The harmonic rhythm of the original tune is regular: the first four measures are framed by two whole-note constructions and filled with four half-note motions.

Harmonic Rhythm

The bebop chorus regularizes the harmonic motion to steady half-note changes, the opening whole-note rhythm is changed by inserting a substitute chord, the A-minor seventh in place of the C-major triad, and changes the progression of the last two measures to a substitute chordal pattern, four descending minor-seventh chords, to fill the harmonic gap of a major third.

Altered Harmonic Rhythm

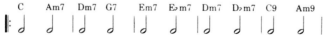

Gillespie's first statement of the ballad melody, except for the long upward flourish, is a straightforward statement of the original theme.

Gillespie's Phrase Opening: First Phrase

His opening for the second phrase totally obscures the melody, except for the last few notes,

Second Phrase

and his opening for the fourth and final phrase is elided with the ending of the bridge and rhythmically transformed.

Fourth Phrase

There is no question that Gillespie chose the notes for these structural passages with the original tune in mind and that he played these passages to allow the listener the comfort of hearing a recognized tune artfully embellished in a jazz style.

A completely different and more remarkable transformation took place in Charlie Parker's reworking of the popular song *Cherokee,* by Ray Noble. He discarded the old tune entirely and composed his new melody, *KoKo,* over the chord progression of *Cherokee.* If we compare the opening of Parker's *KoKo*

with the opening of Noble's *Cherokee*

we find that the bebop transformation is complete. No vestige of the original remains visible on the surface of the performance.[21] In a sense, the bebop musician was now composing music exclusively for other jazz artists and the popular songs, loved by the public, were being either transformed or discarded. The complex music of bebop might be categorized as "art for art's sake," and even the best of the music certainly did not have an easy appeal. Listeners were expected to be sophisticated, and dancers had no place in the audience.

> Thus with "bop," jazz met the difficulties that had bewildered the critics of new serious music ever since 1910. The best work was so complex in harmony and rhythm that it sounded at first incoherent, not only to laymen but also to professionals very close to it. Good work could no longer be discriminated with any speed or certainty from incompetent work, and incompetent workers, in all good faith, took advantage of this situation to press their claims. Some narrow-minded professionals joined impatient laymen to condemn the whole style as a product of incompetence, if not of charlatanism or madness. At the same time some supporters of the new style preferred to interpret its political or poetical purity as depending on its incomprehensibility. The controversy had a momentary publicity value. But this was soon exhausted while the bewilderment went on. The jazz community had to learn to live with it, just as did people interested in other serious new music.[22]

Significant stylistic changes were also effected by the bop rhythm section. Kenny "Klook" Clarke, who was born in Pittsburgh in 1914, first engaged in serious discussions with Dizzy Gillespie while working with the Teddy Hill band during 1939–40. Clarke worked in Minton's during the early 1940s with a combo extracted from the old Hill band. As a result of his manner of playing at that time, he is credited with being the drummer who modified the swing drum system to a new one suitable for bebop. He stopped playing bass drum on every beat, reserving it for special accentuation and rhythmic effects. He took the ride pattern off the sock cymbal and played it on a suspended cymbal so that beats two and four would not be accented; thus, he was able to use the top cymbal, later renamed the "ride cymbal," for steady rhythm.

When Gillespie recorded *52ⁿᵈ Street Theme*[23] in 1946, he was no longer

---

[21] Another example of this process can be found by comparing Parker's *Ornithology* and William Lewis, Jr.'s *How High the Moon*.

[22] William W. Austin, *Music in the 20th Century*, p. 291 f.

[23] Victor 400132.

Kenny "Klook" Clarke with Elaine Leighton.

attempting to transform well-known material from the popular-song repertory into a jazz performance, he was working with a new jazz composition in
the bebop style written by pianist / composer Thelonious Monk. Played at
breakneck speed, the melodies of the introduction and opening chorus are
striking for their angular outlines. Still, the form of the piece is nothing more
than popular-song form, **AABA,** and the harmonies are no more complex
than those found in pieces like "I Got Rhythm." The initial three solos by
young vibraphonist Milt Jackson, swing tenor player Don Byas, and electric
guitarist Bill De Arango are expertly executed and serve as a springboard for
Gillespie to demonstrate the characteristics of the bebop improvisatory style:

asymmetrical phrasing, virtuosic flights, and the stressed use of upper partials in the melodic line (pay especial attention to his choice of notes at the end of the bridge in his first solo chorus).

Formal Scheme—*52ⁿᵈ Street Theme*

	Intro.	Head	Vibes	Tenor	Guitar	Trumpet		Recap.	Coda
mm.	4	32	32	32	32	32	+32	32	2
	a'	aaba	aaba	aaba	aaba	aaba	aaba	aaba	a"
		group						group (bass on **b**)	

This recorded performance illustrates all the elements of the standard bebop combo performance: a short introduction; a few melody instruments playing the head mostly in unison (Jackson runs a parallel line on vibes); a succession of solos featuring each member of the combo; a recapitulation of the head and "out" (the group uses an "out chorus," or a new riff, at the beginning of the recapitulation but performs the original phrase of the head on the last **a** section). Throughout, the rhythm section plays the changes; the soloists "make" the changes, that is, they create fresh melodic improvisations in time with the beat and in consonance with the chords.

The work actually displays characteristics of two different styles during its solo performances—swing and bebop. Gillespie's solo is bebop, with its long, irregular phrases, its stress of upper partials or chromatic tones, and its evenness or reversal of accent in running eighth-note passages. Byas's solo is swing in the Coleman Hawkins tradition, with chordal and scalar passages frequently stressing the notes of triadic and seventh chords, regular phrasing, and eighth-note accents on the beat. Both solos are outstanding, but they are different in style and concept.

Al Haig, a leading bebop pianist who is especially respected for his rhythm-section work, demonstrates the "comping" (accompanying) style developed by Bud Powell, and Bill De Arango plays a fascinating guitar solo that begins on the turn

52ⁿᵈ Street Theme, Opening of De Arango's Solo.

in the key of C! Ray Brown, a notable successor to Jimmy Blanton, performs arco (uses the bow) for his brief but excellent solo on the bridge of the recapitulation. The drum work of J. C. Heard is especially interesting, for it combines the high hat background timekeeping developed by Jo Jones with a certain independence more in keeping with the percussion patterns pioneered by Kenny Clarke.

In 1946, Milt Jackson was a young aspiring bebop vibraphonist, and his solo displays talent, technique, and promise. A decade later, he rose to eminence in the Modern Jazz Quartet and developed a distinctive sound, a cool vibrato and mellow tone (he slowed the pulsation rate of his instrument and used softer mallets). Here, he emulates Dizzy and his other bebop models and creates an impressive solo improvisation in this style, especially on the bridge, the **b** section.

But the master of the new style is the leader, Dizzy Gillespie, as we can hear especially on his second chorus, where the meteoric rise of the trumpet line into the altissimo range and the following cascading descent gives fire to his solo. This manner of playing became a hallmark of Gillespie's bebop trumpet style.

52nd *Street Theme*

For the decade 1935–45, Fifty-second Street in midtown Manhattan was *the* street of jazz. All the inspired jazz performers worked there—Coleman Hawkins, Art Tatum, Billie Holiday, Roy Eldridge, Erroll Garner, Mary Lou Williams, Charlie Parker, Sarah Vaughan, Thelonious Monk, and, of course, Dizzy Gillespie. It was the venue for hip musicians to "sit in" with the house group and jam, and Monk in his composition displays that tradition at its best—short head, blistering tempo, and long powerful solos meant to cut his competitors down to their knees. But the tradition also implies a camaraderie of in-group musicians sharing the essence of their music and their lives.

Among the modern musicians of New York, Charlie Parker had gained his stature by 1945. He worked on and off 52nd Street with both Ben Webster and Dizzy Gillespie, and he had formed his own group at the Three Deuces, where he featured the young Miles Davis. In February of that same year he completed one of the many influential recording sessions of his lifetime. With Gillespie serving as leader, and with a rhythm section of Clyde Hart on piano, Remo Palmieri on guitar, Slam Stewart on bass, and Cozy Cole on drums, we hear in these cuts the fully mature bebop style of both Gillespie and Parker. These young artists, confident in their abilities, recorded three tunes that captured the imaginations of other jazz performers, set the standard for bebop performance, and became models for a decade of bebop creativity: *Groovin' High, Dizzy Atmosphere*, and *All the Things You Are*.[24]

[24] Musicraft 485 and 488, reissued on Rondolette A11.

THREE ASPECTS OF
THE REPERTOIRE _____

Groovin' High (*NAJ* 8) was based on the harmonic structure of a piece considered boring, maudlin, trivial, and the "epitome of square" by modern jazz musicians of the period, *Whispering* by John and Malvin Schonberger (see Listening Guide 8). The "head," or new melody, of *Groovin' High* and its relaxed performance so transformed the original that it became both a marvel to the knowledgeable listener and an insider's secret. The solos were brilliant, impossibly difficult and yet fluid. The introduction and the coda, which were startling and clever, stamped these performances as the extraordinary work of individuals from a new generation of thinkers. Even the title was encoded for the bebop community, adding to its cult value. In the 1940s, being "high," or under the influence of dope, was not part of the common language of the ordinary working-class citizen, and "grooving" was a jazz performer's synonym for both cutting a record and having sex.

The title of *Dizzy Atmosphere*, a new jazz composition with its own harmonic pattern, played on Gillespie's name and referred to the altissimo range in which he alone, among trumpeters, was able to solo brilliantly. As a composition, *Dizzy Atmosphere* would have to rate low in information value: the harmony is simple and the tune, what little there is of composed melody, is nothing more than a short, oft-repeated riff interrupted by a simple sequence figure at the bridge section. This riff evolves naturally out of the introduction and fades gracefully into the coda, and it serves as a useful vehicle to propel the soloists into their improvisatory excursions. The simple tune, however, also had an unplanned secondary value: it gave less advanced musicians an easy bebop melody that they could incorporate quickly into their performance repertoires. In the solos of this master recording, both Parker and Gillespie were sure-footed, inventive, and unique for the time. Also, Gillespie's chorus is followed by an especially interesting bass solo by Slam Stewart that is played arco (bowed, not plucked) and with which Stewart sings in parallel at the octave. Stewart developed this technique naturally and felicitously, possibly by accident, but the end result was to provide greater opportunity for melodic expressiveness on an instrument normally reserved for accompaniment and ordinarily limited to structural functions. What Stewart provides here is a particularly good example of a coherent improvisation on an instrument that is still seeking to realize more fully its soloistic potential.

The third tune from this recording session, *All the Things You Are*, was important for very different reasons. The tempo is slow and the melodic activity is nearly all restricted to ornamenting the original melody of the popular song slightly. In fact, solo improvisation is almost nonexistent—Parker's improvisation is limited to the eight measures of the bridge. But this tune was, in a way, a window to important activity of the future. Jazz musicians, to a large extent, can be identified stylistically by the repertory of pieces they choose to play. Parker and Gillespie had an unerring sense for interesting but difficult chord progressions. *All the Things You Are*, by Jerome Kern (lyrics by Oscar Hammerstein), has always been a difficult *tour de force* for improvising jazz musicians because the chord changes are rapid, varied, and far-ranging. Unlike *Dizzy Atmosphere*, which repeats a single chord for the first eight measures (A$\flat$), the second eight measures, and the last eight measures (three-fourths of the composition), *All the Things You Are* changes harmonies at the rate of one chord per measure, does not repeat the first eight measures in the same key, and ends with a twelve-measure phrase.

	m. 1	m. 2	m. 3	m. 4	m. 5	m. 6	m. 7	m. 8	m. 9	m. 10	m. 11	m. 12
A	F⁻⁷	B$\flat$⁻⁷	E$\flat$⁷	A$\flat$ maj7	D$\flat$ maj7	G⁷	Cmaj7	C⁶				
A′	C⁻⁷	F⁻⁷	B$\flat$⁷	E$\flat$ maj7	A$\flat$ maj7	D⁷	Gmaj7	G⁶				
B	A⁻⁷	D⁷	Gmaj7	G⁶	F#⁻⁷	B⁷	Emaj7	C⁺⁷				
A″	F⁻⁷	B$\flat$⁻⁷	E$\flat$⁷	A$\flat$ maj7	D$\flat$ maj7	D$\flat$⁻⁷	C⁻⁷	B°⁷	B$\flat$⁻⁷	E$\flat$⁷	A$\flat$ maj7	G⁷ C⁷

second ending: A$\flat$ maj7 ——→

Even without taking the variety of chordal configurations into account, a simple, alphabetical listing of the roots alone is impressive:

A$\flat$ A B$\flat$ B C D$\flat$ D E$\flat$ E F F# G

One can see that all twelve possible roots are used, that is, at least one chord on every scale step of the octave is called for during the performance of the piece. In other words, the improvisers must master their instruments; they must command fluency of technique in every key. This piece highlights the vision of bebop: a standard of perfection and nothing less. During this 1945 performance, no one in the band demonstrates such a level of mastery—it is a good performance of a pretty ballad. We hear little more than a clever introduction followed by the melody and chords of the original composition. But in a prophetic way, a standard was raised and placed in view at the head of the column.

The Gillespie-Parker performances of 1945 clearly defined the style and set the group of beboppers apart from their swing contemporaries. *Shaw 'Nuff* (*SCCJ* 64), recorded in New York in May of that year,[25] displays perhaps the most precise ensemble work of these two artists in addition to dazzling solos remarkable for their clarity and continuity. Al Haig, pianist for this session, made his first important appearance on this recording, and his relaxed technique, even at breakneck speed, perfectly complements the artistry of the front-line soloists.

The monumental recording session of *KoKo* (*SCCJ* 65),[26] which took place in November of that year, was followed in December by a Carnegie Hall recording of Gillespie's *Night in Tunisia*.[27] The two were at the top of their musical form and at a high point of success and influence, but Parker's drug habit was just about to get the best of him. They traveled to California to play a six-week engagement at Billy Berg's nightclub in Hollywood. Parker remained in Los Angeles to lead his own group at the Finale Club. Tragically, on July 29, 1946, heroin and alcohol caused a complete nervous breakdown, and Parker was confined for almost a half year in the Camarillo State Hospital. His recording of *Lover Man*[28] that night was one of the saddest documents in the history of jazz, for one can literally hear a great artist disintegrate as he struggles to hold his life and music together. He misses his first cue, founders around, hesitantly seems to find a path, but becomes dependent upon the others to lead him to the final cadence. He was a man destroyed.

Shortly after his release from the hospital, he appeared to have gained new life. In tribute to his recuperative stay, he recorded *Relaxin' at Camarillo* (*NW* 271, I/6),[29] with his "New Stars," Howard McGhee, trumpet; Wardell Gray, tenor sax; Dodo Marmarosa, piano; Barney Kessel, guitar; and Don Lamond, drums, and this joyful recording was, true to its title, relaxed.

—— MORE ABOUT BIRD ——

In April, he returned to New York in good health and was eagerly greeted by musicians waiting to hear him again. During the remaining years of the decade, Bird Parker flew miles above the other musicians of jazz on wings of artistic creation unequaled in his day. He had almost destroyed his career with narcotics, but upon his return to New York in the summer of 1947, he

[25] Guild 1002, reissued on *New World* 271; see also discussion above, p. 292.
[26] Savoy 597, also reissued on *NW* 271; discussed above, p. 291 f.
[27] Roulette SK 106.
[28] Dial 1002.
[29] Dial 1030.

was in complete control of himself and his music. He then produced some of his most mature, polished, and inspired work. According to Thomas Owens:

> [Charlie Parker] was the most influential player in jazz during the last ten years of his life; the musicians who imitated aspects of his syncopations, articulations, tone quality, and repertory of motives are legion. Many are themselves major jazz figures who have developed distinctive styles of their own, but who nonetheless perpetuate parts of Parker's approach to music in their own performances. . . . In addition, few other jazzmen could improvise as fluently at such rapid tempos; few others could create such ornate, well balanced, and moving solos at slow tempos; few others could play equally fine solos regardless of the environment or of the styles and abilities of the accompanying players.[30]

Parker's ability to grace the melodic line of a ballad with an airy filigree that floats above the chords like a bird coasting on a summer breeze is nowhere better demonstrated than in the first take of his recording of *Embraceable You* (see Transcription 7), dating from October 28, 1947 (*SCCJ* 67). During the first five measures of the solo, Parker develops the initial figure through sequential repetition.[31] As the solo progresses, it becomes both more florid and more rhythmically supple. All the while, snatches of the opening motive appear amidst the context of long-flowing melodic lines, but the Gershwin melody is avoided almost entirely. As Martin Williams points out, the second version (*SCCJ* 68),[32] which is slightly less distinguished than the first, is of great interest because it "not only presents a completely different improvisation, it offers a different kind of overall design."[33]

Charlie Parker the composer is indistinguishable from Charlie Parker the improvising performer. Even in compositions that bear his name, such as *Klacktoveedsedstene*, we see that the formal patterns are generally simple, the harmonic changes derive largely from standard circle-of-fifths progressions, the meter is invariably duple, and the melody is always a tonally organized tune that stretches, at most, across a twelve- to thirty-two-measure form plus introduction and coda. Some of these "composed" melodies are remarkable, and all are well-constructed riffs that are used to frame the development section of the piece—the improvisations. *Klacktoveedsedstene* (*SCCJ* 69) is a good example of a typical Charlie Parker composition. It is a thirty-two-measure composition in **AABA** (pop-song) form with an eight-measure introduction.

[30] Owens, "Charlie Parker: Techniques of Improvisation," p. 270.
[31] Transcription of the opening motive in *SCCJ* liner notes.
[32] Complete recording on *NW* 271, I/7.
[33] *SCCJ* liner notes.

Klacktoveedsedstene

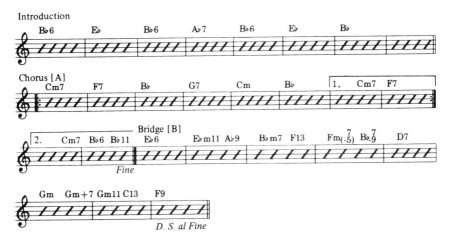

Certainly, the tune of the composition is nothing spectacular.

It is in the improviser's solo choruses that his genius shines forth, and here we see his skill demonstrated in organizing quick-tempo solos into coherent and musically sensitive phrases. The syncopation and discontinuity found in the opening of his *Klacktoveedsedstene* chorus resemble the solo ideas of Thelonious Monk, but Parker is able to organize his disconnected melodic line at an extraordinarily quick tempo. His articulation, which is always precise, serves to heighten the accentuation and syncopation of medial notes within the phrases.

Except for the omnipresent blues harmonies, no other chord progression is used more frequently in jazz throughout the 1930s, '40s, and '50s than those used by George Gershwin in *I Got Rhythm*. Charlie Parker used these same chord progressions in most of the major keys in which he improvised, and *Little Benny* (*SCCJ* 70; see Transcription 8), originally released under the title *Crazeology*, is one of the many pop-song-form compositions employing this ubiquitous progression.[34]

[34] Unfortunately, this recording of *Little Benny* (Roulette RE-105) is technically deficient. Not only was it altered by the record company to add a previous take at the end of the piece, thus destroying the standard formal structure by repeating the final unison riff too many times, but also, it was recorded on the disc at too fast a speed—the pitch is raised one half-step and the tempo is faster than it was in the actual performance.

I Got Rhythm

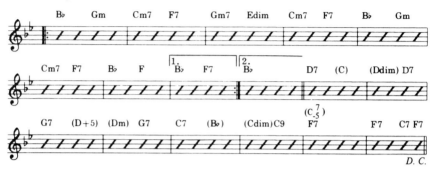

Parker was a master of the blues. In this form alone, under many different titles, he left 175 known recordings.[35] Nowhere was he more at ease, less predictable, and musically more interesting than in the middle of a twelve-measure blues chorus. *Parker's Mood* (*SCCJ* 71) and (*NW* 271, I/4), opens and closes with a flourish, and between these markers lie four improvised blues choruses: the first two by Parker (see Transcription 9), the third by John Lewis, and the last by Parker. Typically, the gamut of note values employed by Parker in his solo is large, ranging from thirty-second notes[36] to a note slightly longer than a half note.[37] Many features mark this solo as a melodic improvisation of distinction and importance, but one in particular should be singled out here as the melodic characteristic that Parker controlled better than any other musician in jazz: irregular phrasing that creates a sense of balanced asymmetry as well as an elided phrase structure. The harmonies of *Parker's Mood* move on relentlessly as they would in any other blues composition, but Parker's melodic phrases, separated clearly by rests, resemble the irregular patchwork of a crazy quilt.

The Durations of Parker's Phrasing

[35] Owens, "Charlie Parker: Techniques of Improvisation," p. 9.

[36] Groupings of five thirty-second notes to the beat in chorus 2, measure 8.

[37] Chorus 4, measure 2.

No two pieces of the fabric are alike, but all are interwoven. No one statement stands out to dominate the others, but all speak with an eloquent simplicity. A critic who knew the music of Charlie Parker well wrote:

> Charlie Parker's greatness is demonstrated by the body of his recorded art, but what made him great can be heard in even the abbreviated phrase of an individual solo. Listen, for example, only to the end of his first solo on the alternate take, initially unissued, of *Parker's Mood* on the LP *Charlie Parker Memorial* on Savoy. You will hear the soul of a giant.[38]

The late 1940s was a time of great creative activity in jazz, years of relative financial stability for jazz musicians of all credos, years of settled development for the beboppers, and a time of exploration that would soon uncover new sounds and ideas. The year 1947 was especially productive for Charlie Parker. During this twelve-month span, Parker recorded over forty different titles, some of them more than once, and many with alternate takes that would not be released to the public for years. Some pieces had been recorded earlier with other musicians, and most would become standards of the bebop repertoire. The following list of titles from 1947 includes blues, popular songs, original compositions, and tunes reworked from the changes of other compositions.

Charlie Parker Recordings in 1947

Another Hairdo	*Bongo Bop*
Bird Feathers	*Buzzy*
Bird Gets the Worm	*Carvin' the Bird*
Bird of Paradise	*Charlie's Wig*
Bird's Nest	*Chasin' the Bird*
Blow Top Blues / Hot Blues	*Cheryl*
Blue Bird	*Cheers*
Bongobeep	*Cool Blues*

[38] Ira Gitler, *Jazz Masters of the Forties*, p. 57.

Crazeology"
Dark Shadows
Dewey Square
Dexterity
Donna Lee
Don't Blame Me
Drifting on a Reed | Big Foot |
    Air Conditioned
Embraceable You
Ferd Beathers
Giant Swing
Half-Nelson
How Deep Is the Ocean
Hymn, The

Klaunstance
Klactoveedsedstene
Little Willie Leaps
Milestones
My Old Flame
Out of Nowhere
Prezology
Quasimodo
Relaxin' at Camarillo
Scrapple from the Apple
Sipping at Bell's
Stupendous
Tiger Rag
This Is Always

In spite of recognition, artistic success, and financial reward, these were years for Parker that were filled with mixed messages and confusing signals. Another marriage in 1949, to Doris Sydnor in Tijuana, Mexico, left him unsatisfied and health warnings from his doctor went unheeded. Successful engagements at the Royal Roost and Bop City helped attract a very large following, but pure blues recordings, such as *Parker's Mood,*[39] appeared at the same time as uncomfortable stylistic blends, such as *Just Friends*[40] (accompanied by strings and chorus) and *Mango Mangue*[41] (with Machito and His Orchestra). A trip to Paris as star of the International Jazz Festival was followed by a second European tour where he went on a three-day sleepless revel and temporarily disappeared to another country without warning. Finally, a club, Birdland, was opened in his honor in New York. Seemingly aware of the ironies in his life but apparently unable to cope with them successfully, Parker would eventually be banned from Birdland.

On the surface, Parker seemed to be enjoying a fulfilling life in 1950—he was playing regularly at Birdland, recording frequently, and basking in a domestic life with Chan Richardson, soon-to-be mother of his two children, Pree and Baird—but his music grew more nervous and agitated. His recording of *Leap Frog*[42] with Gillespie, Monk, Curly Russell on bass, and Buddy Rich on drums never achieved a successful take, and its ragged, too-fast performance was symptomatic: Parker was strung out. Shortly after his return from Europe, he suffered a peptic ulcer attack and had to be hospitalized. His recordings of *Tico Tico* and *La Cucuracha*[43] with his "South of the Border Orchestra" were good examples of mistaken judgment most likely brought

[39] Savoy 936.
[40] Mercury 11036.
[41] Mercury 11017.
[42] Verve MG V-8006.
[43] Verve MG V-8008.

on by an exploitative entrepreneur. An artist of Parker's stature should never have been subjected to a commercial project that had so little opportunity for creative development—a monument of poor taste. On the other hand, it was clear that Parker was periodically "out of it" during this period. In August 1951, he performed as a guest with the Woody Herman band in Kansas City and was literally unable to make the chord changes in the bridge of *Four Brothers*. In its own way, his music signaled his end.

The remaining three years of his life were tragic. At the Say When Club in Los Angeles in 1952, he was fired for insubordination. In 1953, his daughter Pree died of pneumonia, and he became extremely depressed. His disorderly state of mind was increasingly reflected in his music and his work habits. His 1953 recording of *Groovin' High*[44] displays only a shadow of the great improviser of former days. In 1954 he attempted suicide twice, the second time after he was fired from his "own" club, Birdland. A few exceptional recordings grace these last years, most notably *Confirmation*, cut in August 1953[45] (*NAJ* 10; see Listening Guide 10), but this period was generally one of quick decline and dissolution, leading to his death in Manhattan on March 23, 1955. He was given a funeral service at the Abyssinian Baptist Church on 138th Street and was subsequently flown to Kansas City for burial.

In spite of the personal tragedy of his life,

> Charlie Parker is one of the few jazzmen who can be said to have given dignity and meaning to the abused word "genius." It was his desire to devote his life to the translation of everything he saw and heard into terms of musical beauty. Though it was his inspiration, his soul and warmth that earned him an international reputation, and although he had little formal training, he was a man of amazing technical skill, a fast reader and a gifted composer-arranger. His best records were those he made with a small, informal combo, but he was proudest of the series of albums he made, starting in 1950, with a group featuring strings and woodwinds. . . .
>
> In bringing the art of improvisation to a new peak of maturity, Parker had an inestimable influence on jazz musicians regardless of what instrument they played. From the mid-'40s on, it was almost impossible for any new jazzman anywhere in the world to escape reflecting to some degree, consciously or unconsciously, a Parker influence; his work set a new standard on every level: harmonic, tonal, rhythmic and melodic.[46]

In his recordings, "Bird Lives!"

[44] Columbia JC 34831.
[45] With Al Haig, piano, Percy Heath, bass, and Max Roach, drums; Verve MG V-8005.
[46] Leonard Feather, *Encyclopedia of Jazz*, p. 376.

THE PIANISTS—TADD DAMERON, BUD POWELL, AND THELONIOUS MONK

Tadley Ewing "Tadd" Dameron, Thelonious Sphere Monk, and Earl "Bud" Powell were the three bebop pianists who influenced the development of bebop style piano technique most significantly. Although Fatha Hines and Count Basie undoubtedly prepared the way, Powell is usually credited with relieving the left hand of its rhythmic function of maintaining a steady beat, allowing it to "comp" (accompany) in a freely syncopated chordal manner. Thus, the responsibility for laying down a steady pulse was shifted to the ride pattern of the drummer's suspended cymbal and the walking quarter-note pattern of the pizzicato string bass. Just as Gillespie had played melodic solos in a style formerly thought to be reserved for saxophones, that is, rapid running melodic lines, Powell developed a piano-solo style that adopted the same characteristics for the solo melodic work of the right hand. While the right hand improvised long-line scalar solos, the left hand, by contrast, would continue to comp. Tadd Dameron played in a similar manner, but Thelonious Monk developed a personal style that avoided the difficulties of finger dexterity and that remains unique. Technical virtuosity, at least in the sense of rapid performance of scales and arpeggios, was not characteristic of his playing. Instead, he concentrated on harmonic innovation expressed in erratic rhythms and in chords and tonal clusters that were sparse, stark, and economical. Monk's greatest contribution to the bebop style was his influence on other players. He affected all kinds of instrumentalists, not only through his compositions, but also through his philosophical approach to listening for new effects and procedures and perceiving music from new perspectives. In a sense, his approach to jazz, like Anton Webern's handling of serialism and classical forms, was austere and he severely restricted his material to essential germinal ideas. His approach was in marked contrast to the overabundant, free-flowing, and often eclectic improvisations of the brilliant virtuosos.

Bud Powell's recording of *Somebody Loves Me* (*SCCJ* 74) displays two different aspects of his playing personality. The opening chorus is performed in a chordal manner, two hands basically operating in parallel motion with the melody pressed out almost entirely by the little finger of the right hand. This style of playing was later popularized by George Shearing. It is not generally thought to be bebop piano playing, but rather a semijazz, semi-commercial method of performance. However, the improvisation beginning

Earl "Bud" Powell (1924–66).

at the second chorus demonstrates why Powell was considered the leading pianist of the bebop era. The rhythmic energy and almost compulsive attack of his playing let his fingers sweep across the keyboard, mixing accents and blurring phrase structure. His impeccable touch clearly articulates the buoyant phrases, shaping them into melodic lines of continuous subtlety. The left hand follows along interjecting occasional chords, signposts to both the player and the listener of the harmonic structure that underlies the improvisation. The steady movement of the plucked string bass is quite sufficient to hold the rhythm and change the harmonies. At this medium tempo, the drummer chooses to use wire brushes on the snare rather than ride a cymbal, and the pulsating sizzle of the drum's snare presses a quiet but incessant beat upon the listener. The clarity with which all the members of this trio perform underscores the chamber-art nature of this music.[47]

Tadd Dameron's composition *Lady Bird* (*SCCJ* 76) is interesting for its simplicity, unusual design, and brevity. The composition, only sixteen measures long, is through-composed and seamless, unlike popular-song form. The harmonic rhythm moves at an erratic speed, and the chord changes, although simple, are unusual.

Lady Bird

The trumpet solo work of Fats Navarro far outshines that of the pianist and composer on this recording, but Dameron does exhibit here the fully developed bebop style of solo accompaniment. Backing chords are judiciously interspersed in a manner that guarantees harmonic certainty but leaves the air uncluttered for the soloist. Navarro died in 1950 at the age of 26. Drug addiction and tuberculosis robbed the 1950s decade of its most promising trumpet player, but not before he demonstrated possibilities for trumpet improvisation within the ranks of bebop other than those explored by Dizzy Gillespie. Navarro's playing did not totally derive from Gillespie's, as did the playing of other bebop trumpeters, and he showed that full-bodied sound, rapid notes in the middle and lower registers, and more jagged lines were also stylistically correct for bop.[48]

Thelonious Monk (1917–82) was cut from a different bolt of cloth: he was eccentric even within the community of bebop eccentrics. As a performer, he seemed not to have styled his piano technique in imitation of older masters but instead developed his own unique keyboard method. He was well known in the modern jazz community of the 1940s and '50s, beginning with his stint as house pianist at Minton's Playhouse. He worked and/or recorded

---

[47] The *SCCJ* recording of *Somebody Loves Me* does not fairly capture the excellence of Powell's creative genius or his virtuosity at the keyboard. Much better examples may be found on "The Amazing Bud Powell—Vol. 1" (Blue Note BST 81503; CD: B21K). The alternate takes of *Night in Tunisia* and *Un Poco Loco* (*NW* 271, II/1) provide insight into his imaginative explorations and overpowering virtuosity.

[48] Also hear *NW* 271, II / 3.

Tadd Dameron at the piano, Miles Davis on trumpet.

with Charlie Christian, Charlie Parker, Dizzy Gillespie, Coleman Hawkins, Cootie Williams, Don Byas, Miles Davis, John Coltrane, and a host of others, but remained relatively unknown to the general jazz public until the late 1950s. His influence on Miles Davis, Sonny Rollins, and John Coltrane was critical at that moment in jazz history, and his later imprint on the music of George Russell, Cecil Taylor, Muhal Richard Abrams, Chick Corea, Anthony Davis, and others was deep and lasting. His anachronous view of jazz melody, harmony, and rhythm, and even his percussive, angular, and dissonant piano technique, have been seminal in the thinking of younger jazz musicians, and he demonstrated clearly that the music of jazz could be interpreted and reinterpreted from different vantage points. Monk's own compositions, works stripped of excess and pared down to a compelling logic and consistency, are perhaps his greatest legacy. Many of his compositions have become jazz standards: *Round Midnight, Epistrophy, Well You Needn't, Straight No Chaser*, and *Blue Monk* are still favorites of modern jazz musicians. Yet even in Monk's piano playing, astute listeners must sense his remarkable ability to select just the right notes at just the right time.

There is, too, a deep interrelationship between Monk's piano style and his composing, the one being parallel and complementary to the other: each shows

Thelonious Sphere Monk (1917–82).

the same respect for musical logic, the same direct expression of ideas; and decoration that might occur grows out of the musical development rather than from irrelevant instrumental conventions.[49]

In his composition and performance of *Misterioso* (*SCCJ* 85), Monk transforms the blues into a melody comprised of a sequence of sixths:

Earlier in this century, Arnold Schoenberg and his two students, Alban Berg and Anton Webern, rejected traditional notions of melody and harmony and developed a new system, the tone row, with which to organize their music. In a sense, Monk was the first jazz musician to discard successfully the traditional concept of melody and the current ideas of melodic rhythm and develop his own system(s) of musical construction. The harmonies of *Misterioso* are those of the traditional blues, and the changes occur regularly. But the rhythm of the melody has little articulation—that is, the note values of the "tune" are undifferentiated and equal. It is difficult to explain how Monk, a member of the bebop clique, was able to function in a realm so totally different from that of his cohorts at a time when Dizzy Gillespie and Charlie Parker were exploring the improvisational limits of tonal melodies within the stylistic norms of bebop jazz. His doing so corroborates, in a sense, the theory that bebop musicians were questioning not only the musical and social values of the establishment, but also the musical and extramusical elements of their own society. This refreshing introspection did much to reshape jazz, and in the gregarious world of nightclub entertainers, Thelonious Monk was the embodiment of solitude and self-analysis.

In another 1948 recording, *Evidence* (*SCCJ* 86), Monk experiments with a different system of musical organization by exploring the possibility of working two separate hierarchical levels of music simultaneously. The pointillistic

[49] Max Harrison, et al., *Modern Jazz: The Essential Records*, p. 26.

layer of piano sounds is overlaid with the swing-trio sounds of Milt Jackson, John Simmons, and Shadow Wilson. As the music progresses, the two musical ideas become more unified until the piano merges with the trio and sets out on a solo that travels a traditional melodic path. Gradually, the single line of Monk's playing begins to separate into an intervallic construction again, and the vibes return partly to accept the piano's style and partly to reclaim the identity of its original sounds in the piece. Monk is working in the realm of absolute music for instruments, compositions without a tune, pieces maintaining a jazz beat and employing modern harmonic changes.

Thelonious Monk was also fascinated with rhythm, and some of his compositions take seemingly simple melodic and rhythmic figures as a point of departure for rhythmic improvisation at the piano and among members of his group. Monk's quartet recording of *Bemsha Swing* (*NAJ* 17) with Charlie Rouse on tenor rivets our attention on the metrical displacement of the opening two notes of the motive. Composed to start on the fourth beat and to continue on the "and" of beat 4 in the next measure,

Thelonious Monk, *Bemsha Swing,* Opening of Motive

Monk immediately starts imitating the saxophone on the piano in canon at an interval of one beat.

Other composers of the twentieth century, Béla Bartók, for example, might have rebarred the phrase in changing meters, thus:

Monk's rhythmic pattern is repeated four times and forms the rhythmic pattern of the entire sixteen-measure melody. The third phrase of the **AABA** song form is a simple transposition up a perfect fourth of the opening four-measure phrase. Rouse's crisp articulation, straight tone, and angular melodic style match Monk's percussive piano technique and logical improvisatory gestures during the subsequent improvisations to form a unique and intense interplay of creative musicianship. While the bass maintains a rock-solid beat throughout, the drums switch back and forth from playing time to adding an interesting rhythmic commentary of their own. (See Listening Guide 17.)

MORE ABOUT MARY LOU WILLIAMS

At the start of the bebop era, jazz pianist Mary Lou Williams was centrally involved with many of the younger figures of the new music, her New York apartment serving as a school and "crash pad" for the likes of Bud Powell, Thelonious Monk, and their compatriots. She had met Charlie Parker in Kansas City when he was still in knee pants, and she became an important supporter of the new music in New York. Her recording career to this point was prodigious, her arrangements were in demand, her compositions continued to appear regularly, and she began to take an interest in composing on a larger scale. Her first extended work, the *Zodiac Suite*,[50] contained twelve movements inspired by the astrological signs of the horoscope. It was recorded in 1945 and performed in Town Hall in 1946, and some of its movements were later scored for the New York Philharmonic Orchestra for performance in Carnegie Hall. If her career had ended there, she would already have earned a place as a major figure in American music, but she continued working as a composer, pianist, and teacher for another three decades, interrupted only by a personal and religious crisis that saw her remove herself from music from 1954 through 1957. After returning to jazz, she performed, continued to write and arrange shorter jazz works, and composed two large religious works: *Black Christ of the Andes* (1963)[51] and *Mary Lou's Mass* (1970),[52] the latter choreographed by Alvin Ailey. Shortly after her appointment as Professor of Music at Duke University, she played a two-piano concert with Cecil Taylor in New York in 1977.[53] A recording of that performance shows how two masters of opposing musical philosophies are able to accommodate each other without surrendering individual principles. Though this recording takes place long after the close of the bebop era, we can hear in her performance the sounds and values of the 1940s and '50s.

[50] Asch 620–21. Three movements recorded with the Dizzy Gillespie Orchestra at the 1957 Newport Jazz Festival are available on "Masters of the Modern Piano" (Verve VE2-2514).
[51] Saba 15062ST.
[52] Mary Records M 102.
[53] *Embraced* (Pablo Live 2620108).

Woodrow Charles "Woody" Herman and his "Band that plays the Blues." The players include Herman on the clarinet; Tommy Linehan, piano; Walter Yoder, bass; Hy White, guitar; Frank Carlson, drums; Joe Bishop, fluegelhorn.

BIG BANDS

During the mid-1940s, small-combo bebop was in its heyday. At the same time, however, two important big-band developments were occurring. On the one hand, some big bands were beginning to modify their style to allow greater freedom of improvisation by the band members and to incorporate musical developments of the bebop school into their arrangements. The most prominent band to make this change was Woody Herman's. Herman fronted a succession of bands he fondly called "Herds." With the help of arranger Ralph Burns, he remade the sound of his group into something more harmonically aggressive, especially in ballads, and more in keeping with bebop-combo sounds for the up-tempo numbers. In 1947 and 1948, the Herman Herd recorded *Four Brothers*[54] and *Early Autumn*.[55] For both these numbers, the arranger took an instrumental melody and scored it with close-harmony voicing and similar motion of saxophones in the same register. In a sense, this was an adaptation of the bebop unison riff, a modification that spread or thickened the unison melody among the members of a homogeneous section. In a more traditional manner, the brass section was required to punctuate the up-tempo number rhythmically and to decorate the extended chords

[54] Columbia 38304.
[55] Capitol 57-616.

of the ballad harmonically and timbrally. The tenor solos of Al Cohn and Zoot Sims (replacing Herbie Steward), and the baritone solo of Serge Chaloff are all in the bebop style, and the superb tenor solos of Stan Getz on both *Four Brothers* and *Early Autumn* were the beginnings of a new school in jazz, the "cool school," which would soon separate itself from the parent bebop.

On the other hand, an intentional movement toward a new style of big-band jazz was taking place on America's West Coast. Stan Kenton, Boyd Raeburn, and Earl Spencer were calling their music "progressive jazz." Of the three, Kenton was the most successful in developing the idiom and converting young musicians to his concept of big-band sound. He thought of his band as a concert orchestra and, in 1946, recorded *Concerto to End All Concertos* (a modest undertaking!).[56] The composition, which exploited the talents of tenor saxophonist Vido Musso, hardly accomplishes the stated purpose of the title. However, the expanded orchestration of five trumpets, five trombones, plus standard sax and rhythm sections; the nontraditional harmonic

The Stan Kenton expanded band, c. 1946.

changes, including frequent root-movement shifts by half step; and the frequent changes of tempo, implying concert rather than dance, captured the imagination of a large number of jazz musicians and fans. Although popular songs continued to play a major role in the repertoire of the orchestra—*April*

[56] Capitol 382.

in Paris and *Sophisticated Lady,* for example—compositions of a more abstract stripe began to appear with greater frequency *(NW* 216, I/4 and II/1). In 1947, Kenton recorded *Chorale for Brass, Piano, and Bongo*[57] (cf. Bartók, *Music for Strings, Percussion and Celesta* of 1936), *Fugue for Rhythm Section,*[58] and *Abstraction.*[59] The bebop concept of the musician as artist had definitely influenced Kenton strongly, and although bebop, progressive jazz, and swing were in a sense professional enemies, Woody Herman, Stan Kenton, and Charlie Parker had a great deal in common. *Down Beat* magazine, a trade journal for jazz musicians, established a "Music Hall of Fame," honoring those who had "contributed the most to modern American music in the Twentieth Century." In 1954, Stan Kenton was elected by the largest poll recorded to that date. Before him, only two others, Louis Armstrong and Glenn Miller, had been elected.

For a short while, bebop developed its own big-band style. In 1945, Dizzy Gillespie, now a famous musician, decided to organize a big band. A certain prestige automatically accrued to successful big-band leaders, and this, together with financial and musical considerations, led many successful combo musicians down the risky garden path. His band did not last the year, but it was reorganized in July 1946, when he recorded *Things To Come* (*NW* 271, I/5) in New York City.[60] The tempo was absolutely frantic, the performance ragged, and the philosophy clearly not that of a dance orchestra. The blinding flashes of speed that characterized the virtuosic displays of bebop musicians in small combos wreaked havoc upon the sections of the big band. Musically, the group never approached the quality produced by the combos with which Gillespie had previously worked.

Shortly thereafter, the band of Claude Thornhill, with arranger Gil Evans, played conflated solos by Charlie Parker in large ensembles. In 1947, Thornhill recorded *Anthropology*[61] and *Yardbird Suite.*[62] Entire sections played the solos in unison, and unlike Gillespie's big band, the musicians of Thornhill's band played with great precision (*NW* 284, I/8). Still, big-band bebop was a hopeless road to travel: the large organizations were too unwieldy for the style, unsuitable for the economics of small-club engagements, and unwilling to cater to the tastes of the dancing public. As a vehicle for playing to a listening audience via recordings or public concerts, the bebop big bands were filled with unrealized potential. However, the turnover in personnel,

[57] Capitol 10183.
[58] Capitol 10127.
[59] Capitol 10184.
[60] Musicraft 447.
[61] Columbia 38224.
[62] Columbia 39122.

the tendency for name musicians to want to play in smaller combos, and a lack of arrangements that were truly distinct from those of the established swing bands eliminated the big bebop bands quickly. The big-band business itself deteriorated more slowly, until the 1960s, when it almost disappeared entirely.

LOOKING BACK

Jazz was big business in the 1940s. At the beginning of the decade, the music was relatively unified around swing, and swing stood at the center of American popular music. As the years progressed, jazz divided along three main paths: swing, bebop, and a classic jazz revival. By the end of the decade, big bands were beginning to suffer economic difficulties although music, both live and recorded, remained in relatively good health. In 1940, when a reporter approached Fats Waller and asked if he could provide him with a good definition of "swing," Waller replied, "Man, if you don't know what swing is by now—don't mess with it." This self-assured attitude was repeated throughout the ranks of jazz, as the musicians were visible, working, and more respected than ever before. Benny Goodman, Glenn Miller, Duke Ellington, and Count Basie were household words.

With bebop came the first seeds of self-destruction, for only the hip were welcome. The squares, not only the general public but the majority of swing musicians as well, attacked bop's cult status, elitism, bad habits, and finally its music as well. Fletcher Henderson said in 1948, "Of all the cruelties in the world, bebop is the most phenomenal." The musical civil war cut deep, and while one party went back to its roots for sustenance, the remainder divided between swing and bop. Eventually, bop won the battle for jazz but lost the war for the large, broad, middle-class audience.

Accompanying all of this was the first intensive marketing of jazz. Norman Granz began his Jazz at the Philharmonic, later to become a series of tours, in Los Angeles in 1944. Opening at the Philharmonic Auditorium, he featured the Nat "King" Cole Trio, Benny Carter, Meade Lux Lewis, Illinois Jacquet, Nick Fatool, Barney Kessel, and others—a mixture of old, standard, and modern. At times, the audience for jazz reacted like a modern rock 'n' roll crowd. In 1940, eager fans mobbed Ella Fitzgerald and ripped away at her clothes for souvenirs. The press of people eager to buy tickets for a 1942 Benny Goodman concert in Philadelphia was so intense that a policeman's horse was killed in the rush.

The venue for jazz was changing, too. Until the 1940s, theaters and ballrooms contained most of the jazz activity of swing, but now specialized jazz clubs were opening. The most famous "Jazz Alley" of all, 52nd Street in

Manhattan, was lined with clubs filled with musicians working from dusk to dawn.

For two years, beginning August 1, 1942, records were not allowed in juke boxes or on the radio as the American Federation of Musicians attempted to preserve jobs and rights for live musicians.[63] The war provided work for musicians, but it also disrupted bands (all ten members of Red Norvo's band were drafted at once!) and gave women musicians some new opportunities. An excellent and popular women's band of the 1940s, the International Sweethearts of Rhythm, featured Vi Burnside on tenor sax and Tiny Davis on trumpet. It was the first racially integrated women's band, and it lasted for over a decade and played to primarily black audiences in theaters and ballrooms across the country. At the Howard Theater in Washington, D.C., the band set a new box office record of 35,000 patrons in one week of 1941.[64]

In a 1943 concert at Carnegie Hall, Duke Ellington premiered his *Black, Brown, and Beige,* a multisectioned composition of symphonic proportions. Where his earlier interests had led to shorter pieces of the jazz and popular varieties as well as stage works, such as his "Jungle Music" productions for the Cotton Club, his new preoccupation with formal design on a broad scale and his use of developmental compositional devices made its first significant appearance here. *Black, Brown, and Beige* marked both the apex of his creative efforts and the beginning of his compositional decline. He composed actively until his death in the early 1970s, but most musicians believe that his best mature works stem from the late 1930s and early '40s.

Drugs became a serious issue during this period, and an episode of public awareness and condemnation of jazz musicians and their habits began somewhat innocently when drummer Gene Krupa was arrested in 1943 for possession of marijuana. In 1947, Billie Holiday's arrest for heroin possession and drug addiction came right on the heels of Charlie Parker's hospitalization at Camarillo for the same reason. The gruesome reality of addiction as a significant problem in the jazz community was coming to the public's attention, and the recognition by jazz musicians themselves that lives and careers were being destroyed in this way slowly began to have a positive effect within the community.

In two substantial ways, the next decade began a year early. In 1949, Columbia released its first 33⅓-rpm long-playing records, and RCA Victor issued its first 45-rpm extended-play discs. Technology finally freed jazz

---

[63] See Scott DeVeaux, "Bebop and the Recording Industry: the 1942 AFM Recording Ban Reconsidered," *Journal of the American Musicological Society,* 41 (1988), p. 127 ff.

[64] A good sample of their music can be heard on Rosetta Records 1312, which can be ordered from Rosetta Records, 115 West 16th Street, New York, NY 10011. Also see D. Antoinette Handy, *The International Sweethearts of Rhythm.*

Gerry Mulligan (baritone sax), Thelonious Monk (piano), Shadow Wilson (drums), and Wilbur Ware (bass), cutting a side in 1957.

musicians from recording in three-minute blocks. Then, late in 1949, Miles Davis, Gil Evans, Gerry Mulligan, Lee Konitz, and a few others waxed eight sides in recording sessions that would later be known as the "Birth of the Cool." A hot decade passed into the next on a cool autumn breeze.

PROLIFERATION

OF STYLES—

FROM THE '40S

THROUGH THE '50S

OVERVIEW

At the century's halfway mark, the historical strand that linked contemporary jazz to its roots suddenly began to fray. The cohesive thread had been pulled apart in the '40s by the bebop musicians, and now every fiber was bent at a slightly different angle. Classic jazz, which had seen a new flowering because of the revival efforts of the '40s, was now competing with its forgery played by youngsters who had never seen New Orleans. The swing bands were scrambling along different musical paths in order to capture a fair portion of a diminishing market. Old-style swing—the Glenn Miller Orchestra fronted by Tex Beneke; progressive swing—the Stan Kenton Orchestra; a modified bebop swing—the Woody Herman Herd; Kansas City–style swing—Count Basie and His Orchestra; the unique swing style of Duke Ellington; and a dozen or so other big bands were feverishly touring the country and hawking their records.

Bebop suffered from the inequities of supply and demand as its imitators proliferated. The "cool school" gave rise to the "West Coast school," which, in turn, generated a competitive "East Coast hard-bop school." An Afro-Cuban element that cropped up in jazz and gave rise to many short-lived groups that capitalized on this distinctive rhythmic feature. In the struggle to gain secure economic footing while exploiting their own musical beliefs, bands and musicians strove to develop unique sounds that would identify them to their public and differentiate them from their competitors. The Billy May band worked out a saxophone-section sound with a distinctive "scoop"; the Pete Rugolo Orchestra amplified an alto flute as a lead instrumental timbre; Jimmy Giuffre developed an amplified clarinet sound that created pitch by minimally vibrating the reed beyond a mere whisper of tonal production; Chico Hamilton introduced a cello into his combo and restricted his own playing, even on up-tempo numbers, to brush-work only; Gerry Mulligan dispensed with the piano as part of the rhythm section in his West Coast quartet; and on and on. No longer was it possible for the historian to look at jazz in the '50s and discern with certainty the mainstream sound, the most influential artists, the most significant developments of the day. In fact, the term "mainstream" gave rise to yet another substyle, "third-stream" music, an attempted merger of classical compositional elements with jazz sounds and performance practices.

But what was happening in jazz was not unique, for the same tearing apart had been taking place throughout the century in literature, the visual arts, and classical music. As the scholar and aesthetician Leonard B. Meyer points out:

> The role and influence of the audience in the ebb and flow of fluctuation [of currently dominant styles] and its relationship to stylistic pluralism are more difficult to assess. One crucial characteristic of the present situation, however, does seem clear and certain: there is not now, and probably will not be, a single cohesive audience for serious art, music, and literature as, broadly speaking, there was until about 1914. Rather, there are and will continue to be a number of different audiences corresponding roughly to broad areas of the spectrum of coexisting styles.[1]

He later continues:

> Particularly in music, the conscious search for new materials, techniques, and principles of organization has led to a significant reduction in the levels of both cultural and compositional redundancy. Or, looked at from the opposite viewpoint: experimentalism has produced a marked increase in the perceptual complexity (information) which listeners are required to comprehend. It is therefore of some importance to consider the arguments for and the consequences of experimentalism in music, especially because both the temptations and the dangers of complexity are greater in music than in the other arts.[2]

[1] Leonard B. Meyer, *Music, the Arts, and Ideas*, p. 175.
[2] Ibid., p. 235.

Those members of American society who came to jazz for entertainment and relaxation were beginning to turn away from the newer forms because of the increasing levels of musical and intellectual sophistication now being demanded of them. Blithely unaware, or perhaps with premeditated disdain, the younger jazz musicians plunged into a sea of experimental complexity that had already lost the classical-music avant garde its popular audience. The fruits of these dangerous seeds did not fully ripen until the "new wave" of the 1960s, but the seeds had been planted in the '40s and were beginning to sprout in the '50s.

The first conscious experiments in jazz took place in the mid-1920s, when Bix Beiderbecke, Don Redman, and others sought to increase the vocabulary and grammar of jazz materials. Beiderbecke's work affected very few during his lifetime while Redman's produced a thoroughly marketable product. The first major step toward increased complexity and lessened redundancy was taken by the first bebop experimenters in the late '30s and early '40s. Their audiences found that they no longer had easily remembered tunes, simply understood rhythms, and well-worn harmonic patterns to guide them through the maze of a performance. The musicians, on the other hand, had to cope with a philosophy of experimentalism and increasingly complex demands of technical virtuosity. Thus, where classic jazz or swing gave rise to one or two opposing ideas, bebop opened Pandora's box and sent into the world a multiplicity of substyles, each with its own significance and none capable of overpowering all the others.

COOL JAZZ

Cool jazz pulled away first, and several musicians of the late '40s can claim some responsibility for this separation. Stan Getz, Lennie Tristano, and Miles Davis were the most instrumental in creating a sound that, in the early 1950s, was quickly labeled "cool." New York–born Stan Getz (1927–91) began playing professionally at the age of 15. A year later he was playing with Jack Teagarden, and during the next four years worked with Stan Kenton, Jimmy Dorsey, and Benny Goodman. In September 1947, he joined the new Woody Herman band and became part of the "four brothers" saxophone section: Getz, Zoot Sims, Herbie Steward, and Serge Chaloff, three tenors and a baritone saxophonist who recorded the famous *Four Brothers* that December.[3] The cool sound of Getz's saxophone playing—with few overtones and little or no vibrato—on his recording of *Early Autumn* of December 1948[4] captured the imagination of many jazz saxophonists and caused them to sep-

[3] Columbia 38304.
[4] Capitol 57–616.

Stan Getz, tenor sax (1927–91).

arate into two camps: the full-voiced, hard-bop style patterned on the sound of Coleman Hawkins and Charlie Parker, and the limpid and airy timbre patterned on Stan Getz. Getz certainly thought of himself as a bebop musician—his first recording with a group under his own leadership, made in July 1946, bore the title "Stan Getz and His Be-Bop Boys."[5] Shortly after the *Early Autumn* session,[6] Getz left the Herman band and began fronting small groups of his own. Nicknamed "The Sound," Getz was internationally recognized as the leading saxophonist of the 1950s, despite a drug problem that almost ended his career. His fully developed artistry, a judicious mixture of cool sound and phrasing with dazzling bebop technical virtuosity, is dis-

[5] Savoy MG 12114.

[6] An interesting analysis of the Getz solo may be found in Gunther Schuller, *Early Jazz*, p. 23 f.

played in his 1952 quartet recording of *Stan Getz Plays*.[7] His melodic lyricism on the ballads *'Tis Autumn* and *Stars Fell on Alabama* and his resplendent technique on the up-tempo numbers *The Way You Look Tonight* and *Lover, Come Back to Me!*[8] reveals technical mastery equal to the best work of any bebop saxophonist, and firmly established his leadership.

The Modern Jazz Quartet, well known as the MJQ, was formed in 1951 and capitalized on a growing enthusiasm for jazz among college students. They played concert music that swung gently, and they introduced into jazz many elements that were then generally foreign to the style: classical form, greater conscious attention to counterpoint, and a composed repertoire of longer works. All of its original members were "graduates" of the hard-core bop combos of the forties: John Lewis (piano), Milt Jackson (vibraphone), Percy Heath (bass), and Kenny Clarke (drums). A distinctive feature of this group's sound was the reduced frequency of the mechanical vibrato of the vibraphone. This slowing down of the pulsations of the vibe's vibrato gave the group a sound handle in keeping with the cool and quiet performance, the Brooks Brothers, Ivy League attitude, and the rising popularity of cool jazz in the 1950s. Their recording of *A Cold Wind Is Blowing*[9] was part of a score composed by John Lewis in 1959 for the science-fiction movie *Odds Against Tomorrow*, an anti-war, atom-bomb disaster film. This work takes seven minutes and thirty-one seconds, longer than the standard popular or jazz tune. It depends heavily on the timbral conflict of vibraphone and piano sonorities working against each other, inserts a modified blues format into an extended composition, melts the jazz beat in a plastic effect, and demonstrates the listener-oriented, rather than the dance-oriented, aesthetic in a modern jazz idiom of the 1950s.

In the late 1940s Dave Brubeck founded his experimental Jazz Workshop Ensemble, which recorded in 1949 under the name Dave Brubeck Octet.[10] Influenced by other West Coast jazz musicians and also by his composition studies with classical composer Darius Milhaud, he wrote arrangements for this band that reflect the chamber ensemble sound that would soon become the hallmark of cool jazz ensembles in the '50s. From 1951 to 1967 he led a quartet that achieved enormous popular success. Its altoist, Paul Desmond, produced a smooth, almost liquid, alto sound that created for this instrument an equivalent for the cool tenor sound of Stan Getz. With Paul Desmond on

---

[7] Clef Records MGC-137.

[8] For a detailed analysis of the solo on *Lover, Come Back to Me!* see the author's "Constructive Elements in Jazz Improvisation," *Journal of the American Musicological Society*, 27 (1974), p. 297 ff.

[9] United Artists UAL 4063.

[10] Fantasy 4019–20; reissued, Fantasy / Original Jazz Classics 101.

The Modern Jazz Quartet: (clockwise, from top left) Connie Kay, drums; Percy Heath, bass; Milt Jackson, vibraharp; and John Lewis, piano.

alto saxophone and various players on bass and drums, the Brubeck Quartet recorded at Oberlin College, Ohio University, and the University of Michigan, exploiting the new market for jazz as a concert form where before it had visited the campuses primarily for proms and social dancing. In 1959, the group recorded *Take Five*,[11] a jazz composition in 5/4 time, as unusual meter that is rarely, if ever, employed in jazz with any success. This recording achieved immediate and universal popularity among jazz musicians and the public, and it led the way for further explorations of metric possibilities in jazz. The Brubeck group quickly followed this recording with a work in 9/8, *Blue Rondo a la Turk*,[12] an up-tempo piece that grouped the nine eighth notes in alternations of 3/4 and 3/8.

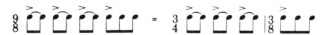

[11] Columbia 41479.
[12] Ibid.

But the leader, Brubeck, received some criticism from within the jazz community itself, because his piano style did not fit comfortably into any of the standard keyboard performance styles accepted at that time. His playing had a heavy chordal emphasis while showing a genuine interest in counterpoint. Although his complex rhythms against the patterns of the drum and bass created great momentum, one segment of the profession felt that his music did not swing. But others were impressed and were strongly affected by his ideas.

Pianists, because they can work successfully alone, often develop a personal style that is unique, even exciting, but that does not influence other pianists. When the musician is really good, as was Art Tatum, jazz musicians listened and admired, and what he created was fine. Such was the case with two other well-known pianists closely associated with jazz, Erroll Garner and George Shearing.

Garner is one of the few performers in jazz, other than the uptown New Orleans musicians of the early days, who had absolutely no formal music education and never learned to read music. Born in Pittsburgh, Pennsylvania, in 1921, he associated with two trained pianists during his youth and learned from them by ear. His early influences were Dodo Marmarosa and

Errol Garner.

Billy Strayhorn, the latter being the talented composer and arranger who collaborated with Duke Ellington during Ellington's peak years. Perhaps because he lacks musical schooling, Garner has never achieved any distinction as a combo or band musician; his fame rests entirely on his solo-piano work, performances most commonly accompanied by string bass and drums. His recording of *Frankie and Johnny (SCCJ 72)* is typical of his up-tempo piano style, and his unusual rhythmic energy is expressed by spread chords, a strumming left hand, and a right hand that is able to free itself from a lockstep rhythmic conformity with the left-hand work. Among his other distinctions, Garner was the first jazz artist to be booked by the American impresario Sol Hurok, and in 1959 he enjoyed great financial success from his own composition, *Misty*.

George Shearing also has a distinctive style as a featured solo pianist. His standard performance format, piano plus a rhythm section of bass, drums, vibes, and guitar, was distinctive not only because of the instrumentation but also because of his "locked-hands" technique, in which chords are played in both hands moving in similar or parallel motion. In fact, the effect was so startling that it was deceiving, for it disguised both the inventiveness of Shearing's extended harmonies and his interpolation of some very sophisticated counterpoint. His 1951 recording of *Over the Rainbow* is typical of his solo style: it is based on a popular song, employs extended harmonies voiced in his unusual manner, and uses a running flow of counterpoint. The music is scored with the vibraphone and guitar doubling the piano melody in a homophonic texture to which the piano left hand occasionally adds counterpoint lines.

Blind from the time of his birth in London in 1919, Shearing is one of the few jazz musicians of his era who was not born in America. His keyboard training was thorough, and he was taught to read music from Braille notation. In addition to the vast repository of jazz compositions he has committed to memory, he is capable of recalling all of Bach's *Well-Tempered Clavier* and other similar works note-perfect. In 1952, he wrote a theme song for a New York nightclub, Birdland, and his *Lullaby of Birdland* became one of the best-known jazz tunes of the 1950s.

Leonard Joseph Tristano, born in 1919 and educated in Chicago, was a blind pianist who became the leader of an informal group of progressive jazz musicians that included alto saxophonist Lee Konitz, tenor saxophonist Warne Marsh, and guitarist Billy Bauer. He was generally known as a radical thinker and outspoken critic of other contemporary jazz musicians. He explored, theoretically and in practice, the possibilities of more complex contrapuntal invention in melodic improvisation (*SCCJ* 78–79) and (*NW* 216, I/3). His alto sax player, Lee Konitz, developed a tonal conception for his instrument that was even lighter than Stan Getz's. Konitz's alto sound was virtually free of

Leonard Joseph "Lennie" Tristano (piano), with Lee Konitz (alto sax) and Charlie Mingus (bass).

vibrato except in carefully controlled situations and was so devoid of over-tones that it closely approximated the timbre of an electronically generated sine-wave tone. In 1949 and 1950, this group, with Arnold Fishkin on bass and various drummers, completed a remarkable series of recording sessions that offered some of the most advanced harmonic and contrapuntal sounds employed in jazz to that date. Some of the complexities these musicians were working with can be heard in their performance of *Tautology*, recorded in June 1949.[13] The first eight measures of the harmonic progression are not particularly unusual, but the next phrase opens with a striking series of chromatic extended chords:

Tautology

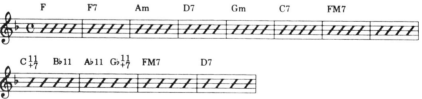

The harmonic rhythm of the chord progression is also distinctive: F chords hold measures 1, 2, 7, and 8 stable; a circle-of-fifths progression moves measures 3–6 at whole-note speed; and a sudden burst of chromatic chords slips down a whole-tone scale in root movement at half-note speed.

[13] Prestige LP 7004.

Harmonic Rhythm

The contrapuntal opening displays not only careful simultaneous linear writing, but also a melodic style that somewhat approximates serial composition. In the first three measures, the two saxophone lines, considered as a unit, use all twelve of the chromatic half-steps that fill an octave:

The incredible rapidity of the group's playing and near-perfect unison blend are truly awesome, feats of an unprecedented instrumental virtuosity. The rhythmic ideas and organization are also complex, and the last four measures of the opening riff, which are identical with measures 4–7 of the composition, play duple patterns against syncopated triplets, both within the measure and over the barline.

There is a restless alternation of tension and relaxation in this music that results partly from the extreme tempos. While listeners become uncomfortable wondering whether or not the performer will stumble, it is the compositional features that keep us off balance: asymmetry of phrase, avoidance of cliché, constantly shifting accents, and pulsating harmonic rhythm. Tristano's group moved in the direction of decreased redundancy and increased complexity.

Warne Marsh composed a work for himself and Lee Konitz which substituted a new jazz melody for that of a well-known popular song while retaining the original song's harmonic structure. *Marshmallow (NAJ* 9), to the chords of Ray Noble's *Cherokee (Indian Love Song)*, follows in the silent-theme tradition of Dizzy Gillespie's *Groovin' High* (to John and Malvin Schonberger's *Whispering*) and Charlie Parker's *KoKo* (also to *Cherokee*). *Marshmallow* is a masterpiece of shifting meters, melodic lines that emphasize upper partials, and orderly solo improvisations that maintain a sense of calm at a furious tempo. (See Listening Guide 9.) Recorded in 1949, *Marshmallow* is another prime example of the emerging cool jazz sound, with light brush work in the drums, light tone and smooth articulation in the horns, and great precision in the ensemble.

When the January 21, 1949, recording session of the Miles Davis Orchestra was reissued on a Capitol LP album,[14] the title claimed it was the "Birth of the Cool." In retrospect, however, it seems that the musicians, at that time, were not consciously trying to give birth to anything. Most of the group came from the Claude Thornhill band and were gathered primarily to test some new arrangements by Gil Evans and Gerry Mulligan. The French horn and tuba were unusual additions to a modern jazz ensemble, and the scoring for the reduced orchestration produced a new, light ensemble sonority. Unlike bebop combos, the group had too many melody instruments, and unlike the big bands, it had no homogeneous sections. Each instrument in the ensemble was unique: one each of trumpet, trombone, French horn, and tuba for a brass section; one each of alto saxophone and baritone saxophone for reeds; and one each of piano, bass, and drums for rhythm. If a saxophone-section sound was desired, brass would have to fill the mid-range pitches. One of the recordings to emerge from that session was *Boplicity* (*SCCJ* 77), a piece in which Miles Davis carries a mellow and tranquil trumpet lead over the parallel harmonies of the mixed ensemble. This music achieves a casual grace through study and design, and the pleasant, almost unobtrusive, blend marks a clear-cut reform of, if not a sharp break with, the tradition of big-band sounds of the '40s. The rhythm of the opening, with its mixture of quarter-note triplets, eighth notes grouped in three, and duple configurations, shows definite stylistic similarity to the music being created by Lennie Tristano:

Boplicity

and we should note that Tristano's alto player, Lee Konitz, was also the alto saxophonist for the Miles Davis Orchestra.

The "crosscurrent" in *Crosscurrent*, recorded by Lennie Tristano that same year (*SCCJ* 79), is the rhythmic tug that takes place between the steady 4/4 of the bass and drums and the irregular groupings of the melodic line played by the alto and tenor saxophones.

[14] Capitol T762.

Lee Konitz, who had played with the Davis and Tristano groups and the Thornhill and Kenton bands, is a central figure in the transformational sounds developing at this time.

Thelonious Monk was another jazz musician who was fascinated by the rhythmic tug-of-war that melodic motives could play with the underlying pulsation of a jazz rhythm section. In his recording of *Criss-Cross* (*SCCJ* 87), he uses a turning-figure motive to create rhythmic phrases that divide the beat into groups of four and three.

The upward leap after the turn adds interest because of the unpredictable nature of the following interval; we see here a cliché of bebop being dismembered and reorganized.

Bop was a conscious revolt against swing, but cool jazz was a development of bebop. It went its own way because some musicians found it more interesting and challenging elsewhere, but all of its leaders—Davis, Getz, Konitz, Tristano—were first thoroughly schooled in the bop tradition.

THIRD STREAM

When Davis's orchestra first recorded, at the April 1949 session, Sandy Siegelstein played French horn. At a second recording session in March 1950, Gunther Schuller came over from the Metropolitan Opera Orchestra to play French horn with the group. His dual interest in classical music and jazz eventually led to another kind of American music, a substyle labeled "third stream." Classical composition and American jazz were considered the first two streams, and the merger or blending of elements from both was taken to be the third stream. Schuller coined the term, but it was Charlie Mingus and Teo Macero who experimented successfully with incorporating avant-garde classical ideas into the ensemble work of jazz combos (*NW* 216, I/5). The Mingus recording of December 1954, *Minor Intrusion*,[15] has a simple statement of theme by the bass viol that is followed by a quasi-contrapuntal

[15] Period SPL1107, also Bethlehem BCP65.

development, with other independent lines added to the texture. At one point Macero uses quarter tones, which Bartók and other classical-music composers were incorporating into some of their works. Lee Konitz stands out as the figure linking the experiments of Charlie Mingus with the other experimental endeavors of the early 1950s. In April 1952, Konitz recorded *Precognition* and *Extrasensory Perception*[16] with the Charlie Mingus ensemble. The instrumentation of this group—alto sax, two cellos, piano, bass, and drums—and the instrumentation for the 1954 session—trumpet, clarinet and alto, tenor and baritone, cello, piano and bass, and drums—shows how the standard jazz sextet combination was being tampered with.

In 1955, Macero brought the most startling sounds to jazz by introducing studio-created electronic effects into the recording of his own composition, *Sounds of May*.[17] He altered the sounds produced by a variety of tone generators electronically and employed multirecording techniques for voice and instruments. Classical organization of form, polymeters, superimposition of various lines, and new electronic sounds are all combined in a fascinating display.

George Russell, who blended Afro-Cuban elements into jazz in the 1940s, composed large works for chamber jazz ensembles in the 1950s. His three-movement *All About Rosie* (*NAJ* 13 and Listening Guide 13) is discussed in the next chapter.

Gunther Schuller's interest in jazz brought the talents of one of America's most accomplished avant-garde composers to this music. His technical mastery of the latest compositional techniques allowed him to write a piece that truly merged two distinct sounds. In *Transformation* (*NW* 216, II/3), a rhythm section of piano, bass, drums, and guitar plus jazz instruments of saxophone, trumpet, trombone, and vibes was combined with the classical woodwinds of flute, bassoon, and French horn. Schuller attempted to maintain the integrity of the separate ensembles and their idioms while blending them to produce a musical composition characterized by a new, third sound.[18] Since jazz usually depends heavily upon improvisation, the problems facing a composer who wishes to create a marriage of jazz and classical music are enormous. Most jazz rhythms cannot be notated accurately, most classical performers have not been trained in the jazz idiom and vice versa, and the spontaneity inherent in the improvisational situation is doubly difficult to attain with complex instructions, unfamiliar harmonic sounds, and new structural frameworks. Still, the movement had validity and impact, and the third stream, along with the other prevailing jazz styles, moved on through the 1950s.

[16] Debut M101 and 103.
[17] Columbia CL 842.
[18] Columbia C2L 31.

WEST COAST JAZZ

The distinction between cool jazz and West Coast jazz is ephemeral at best. Most musicians in the early '50s categorized Stan Getz as a cool-jazz musician and Gerry Mulligan as a West Coast-jazz musician, but there was little deliberate intent on the part of the performers to separate their music into distinct styles. In fact, at the time these descriptive names came into being, the musicians were simply playing jazz, most of the white musicians having been trained in the swing big bands and most of the younger black musicians having filtered through the bebop ensembles. However, as the label "West Coast jazz" came into currency, it represented a kind of music that followed the patterns of the Davis Capitol recording sessions: arrangements for middle-sized ensembles or for smaller groups that used single instruments to represent a particular timbre (one trumpet instead of a trumpet section, one trombone instead of a trombone section). The ensemble would normally be scored for a collection of mixed instruments playing the vertical sonorities. For example, a five-tone chord might be scored, from top to bottom, for trumpet, alto saxophone, tenor saxophone, trombone, and baritone saxophone. The Dave Pell Octet used this kind of voicing, with four melody instruments (no alto sax) on *Mountain Greenery*[19] and *Mike's Peak*.[20] Shorty Rogers and His Giants employed the same technique for five lead instruments on *Popo*[21] and six winds on *Pirouette*.[22]

There was great variety in the kinds of ensembles that played in the manner of the West Coast school. Drummer Shelly Manne and pianist André Previn played crucial roles in the development of the West Coast sound and concept. After working from 1946 to 1952 with the "Progressive Jazz" band of Stan Kenton, Manne moved to Los Angeles and led a series of small groups. His mid-'50s quintet with Stu Williamson, valve trombone; Charlie Mariano or Bill Holman, saxophone; Russ Freeman, piano; and Leroy Vinnegar, bass, featured the light sound and careful arrangements of the style. The valve trombone was not new to jazz, but its use as a lead instrument in a small combo proved extremely effective for the light sounds of cool jazz. Manne's brush work and delicate stick action on the drums blended into this mix, and both contribute to the cool atmosphere of the music and swing the group. Together with pianist André Previn and bassist Leroy Vinnegar, Manne formed a trio and recorded a selection of music from Broadway musicals.

[19] Trend LP 1501.
[20] Capitol T659.
[21] Capitol 15763.
[22] Victor LPM 3137.

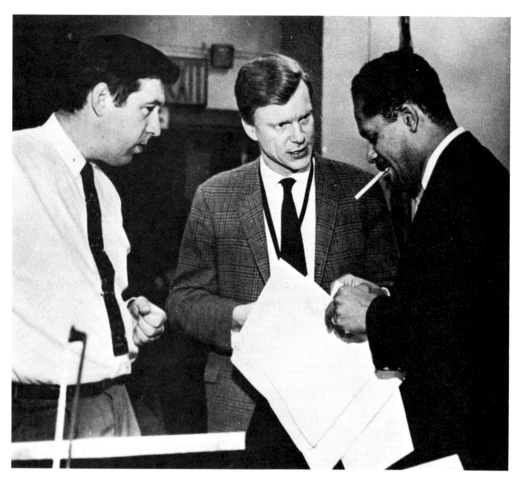

Gunther Schuller, Gerry Mulligan, and John Lewis in discussion at a recording session.

Their 1956 album, *My Fair Lady*,[23] was a near-perfect match of light, fleeting piano technique and sparkling, crisp brush work. Gerry Mulligan fronted a quartet of trumpet, baritone saxophone, string bass, and drums. The opening and closing choruses were carefully arranged, and solos were played to the implied harmonies of the walking string bass, the rhythm of bass and drums, and the occasional backing riff of the other solo instrument. Mulligan's recording of *Makin' Whoopee*[24] is an excellent example of this format, and on the flip side of the disc he adds a guest soloist, the ubiquitous Lee Konitz, who plays outstanding solos on both *I Can't Believe that You're in Love with Me* (*NAJ* 11 and Listening Guide 11) and *Lover Man*.[25] The removal of

[23] Contemporary 3527; reissued C-7527 and CD JCD-692-7527.

[24] Pacific Jazz PJLP-2.

[25] A splendid transcription of this remarkable jazz solo is available in John Mehegan, *Jazz Improvisation*, II, p. 111 ff.

a piano from the jazz quartet seems to have stirred others into action, and another West Coast experimenter, Jimmy Giuffre, tried to create jazz by exploiting the little-explored timbres of his clarinet played in novel manners and the rhythmic possibilities of a jazz performance without walking bass and riding cymbal. His 1955 recording *Tangents in Jazz*[26] removes jazz as far from the dancehall as does the third-stream music of Gunther Schuller.

West Coast jazz sold records and caught the public's attention, so, as one might expect, the musicians playing bop in New York and elsewhere tried to push their music as a competitive but superior product. These events have been viewed with a certain amount of disdain:

> Reactions to cool jazz were inevitable and, when one remembers some of the derivative claptrap and the pretentiousness produced in its name, to be wished. The reactions centered in the east, and they soon acquired the names "hard bop" and "funky." They were inevitably called "contrived" and "regressive."[27]

FUNKY AND HARD BOP

Funky jazz and hard bop had their roots in other kinds of black music current in the '50s—rhythm-and-blues and gospel—and in the '60s—soul. This hard-swinging, syncopated, blues-based jazz contrasted sharply with the carefully crafted, contrapuntal, light ensemble sounds of the cool jazz musicians. Pianists Bobby Timmons and Horace Silver, trumpeters Donald Byrd and Kenny Dorham, saxophonist Hank Mobley, and drummer Art Blakey took the lead in establishing a hard-blowing, blues-centered, duple-meter style that merged the innovations of Charlie Parker and the beboppers with the expressive traditions of the gospel singers. Later, a second generation of aggressive, technical virtuosos such as trumpeter Clifford Brown, saxophonist Sonny Rollins, and drummers Art Blakey and Max Roach took on the banner labeled hard bop or East Coast jazz and played an advanced bebop that retained the hard-cutting sound and rhythmic drive of funky jazz but added even more exaggerated up-tempo performances and a variety of formal schemes and meters. These East Coast musicians resented the lack of emotional involvement inherent in cool and West Coast jazz, so they took their stand around the banner of hot-jazz values: full-voiced instrumental sound, loud dynamics, blistering energy in the up-tempo performances, greater accentuation, and emotional fervor in the performance of ballads. Two important early examples of the funky sounds recorded in 1955 and 1956 are Horace Silver's

[26] Capitol T634.
[27] Martin Williams, "Bebop and After: A Report," in *Jazz: New Perspectives*, eds. Nat Hentoff and Albert J. McCarthy, p. 297.

The Preacher[28] (*NAJ* 12 and Listening Guide 12) and his composition *Señor Blues*.[29] They exemplify the basic simplicity of the style that underlies the much more complex playing of the solos (*SCCJ* 91).

The funky jazz and hard-bop musicians, most of whom were black, disagreed with the West Coast musicians' concept of swing, that quality of jazz performance which embodies rhythmic life and vitality. The funky players' down-to-earth rhythmic statements and full-voiced timbres were separate and distinct from the attitudes, values, and performance techniques of the cool musicians. Although the East Coast musicians were almost all black, two leading white hard-bop saxophonists were Al Cohn and Flip Phillips. The Al Cohn Quintet, which recorded *Jane Street* and *That's What You Think* in 1953,[30] used Horace Silver, Curly Russell, and Max Roach for a rhythm section—all leading bebop musicians. It was Horace Silver's piano style as much as, or more than, anyone else's playing that gave rise to the term "funky" (*NW* 271, II/6). He played a down-home blues style with strong rhythmic accentuations, producing a bouncing rhythmic sound that contrasted sharply with the light-handed, classically oriented piano styles of West Coast musicians like André Previn. Flip Phillips's recording of *Apple Honey* and *Broadway*,[31] cut in 1951, represent a continuation of the mainstream bebop tradition that was being carried on by Charlie Parker and Dizzy Gillespie.

SOMETHING OLD AND SOMETHING NEW

While cool jazz, West Coast jazz, East Coast jazz, and third-stream jazz were being played and promoted, bebop, swing, and classic jazz could be heard live or "canned" on records. An interesting detail in this complex picture was the successful style change that a few musicians were able to accomplish, an unusual, if not extraordinary, feat. As we have noted, most performers in jazz and dance work develop a musical personality which, when it has reached the level of public recognition, remains virtually unchanged throughout the remainder of the artist's career. Those who have wrought stylistic changes have either been young, and hence working without a recognizable aural personality; exceptional, in the sense that they were willing to risk their reputations for artistic reasons; or victimized by circumstance, in that their "innovations" were not new but were suddenly discovered by

[28] From "Horace Silver & the Jazz Messengers" (Blue Note BST-81518).
[29] From "Six Pieces of Silver" (Blue Note B11E-81539).
[30] Savoy XP 8123.
[31] Clef 8960.

Oscar Emmanuel Peterson, piano.

musicians, critics, and the public. A very few musicians were able to move back and forth from one style to another at will. Stan Getz recorded a hard bop–style saxophone solo when he joined the Dizzy Gillespie Quintet for a "Dizzy Gillespie-Stan Getz Sextet" session in 1953. The viciously up-tempo performance of *It Don't Mean a Thing*[32] displays all the musicians at their bebop best. Gillespie's muted trumpet flies through his repertoire of bebop licks; Oscar Peterson charges full-speed through a solo that shows him to be one of the most facile and swinging pianists in jazz; Max Roach commands a driving beat that runs the course of the work without letup; and Stan Getz wails with the group as though he had been playing with this ensemble for years. It is a remarkable recording in that it blends the talents of several musicians who did not work together regularly while it maintains great stylistic uniformity.

Bebop was teaching trumpeters to play in a new way, and the technical excellence of Dizzy Gillespie led others to follow in his stylistic footsteps. Miles Davis, one of the many musicians to work with Charlie Parker and to observe Gillespie's playing, began to travel a path of lighter sound, understatement, and lyrical melodic lines when he played with and influenced the musicians developing the West Coast tradition. Fats Navarro was a promis-

[32] Norgran EPN3.

ing successor to the bebop trumpet crown held by Gillespie, but he died in 1950, too early in his career to establish the repertoire of performances and recordings necessary to supplant the reigning monarch. Suddenly, a new name emerged: Clifford "Brownie" Brown. Born in Wilmington, Delaware, in 1930, he worked with Davis and Navarro in the late 1940s and, in the early 1950s, gained further experience with the bebop pros Tadd Dameron and Max Roach (*NW* 271, II/5). He won the *Down Beat* "new star" award in 1954. Most musicians and critics considered him the most promising youngster in jazz, someone able to inherit the mantle of Dizzy Gillespie and combine the best attributes of Davis and Navarro. His recording of *Pent-Up House* with Sonny Rollins in 1956 (*SCCJ* 96) shows him to be a thoughtful soloist who controls his instrument completely and is able to transform phrases into graceful curves brilliantly, even at demanding tempos. Just as he was being fully embraced by the jazz world as a new leader of maturity and stature, he was killed in an automobile accident on the way to a job. He died in 1956, not long after he made this recording.

Brown was able to play meaningful solos at impossible tempos, and according to legend, his technique astounded even Charlie Parker. However, it was not his speed but his rhythmic feel and unerring sense of structure that earned him a master's reputation after so short an apprenticeship. In an astute analysis of Brown's solo work on *I Can Dream, Can't I*, one authority concludes that Clifford Brown

> 1) apparently thinks at different structural levels simultaneously . . . ; 2) extracts melodic and harmonic patterns from the original piece and uses them as a means of structural development . . . ; 3) creates his own rhythmic patterns and uses them as a means of structural development . . . ; 4) creates pattern unity . . . ; [and] 7) is not thinking just in terms of playing a variation of the original piece but rather exploring and presenting the structure of the piece.[33]

Highly sophisticated accomplishments such as these are not easily achieved, even by talented art-music composers who have the opportunity to reflect on their work and gradually reshape the whole. These accomplishments were, in fact, the routine products of this extraordinary musician's performance.

With so many different things happening in the mid-1950s, it is surprising that yet another revival could take place, but it did. Suddenly, Thelonious Sphere Monk was rediscovered. For several years, in the late '40s and early '50s, Monk had suffered neglect by critics, fans, and musicians, for within

[33] Milton L. Stewart, "Structural Development in the Jazz Improvisational Technique of Clifford Brown," *Jazzforschung*, 6/7 (1974/75), p. 218.

Clifford Brown (1930–56).

the context of the '40s' musical values, Monk was an oddball, a strange musician who had little technique and couldn't keep a tune. However, the open-mindedness of the 1950s brought an awareness of the novel and experimental sounds this talented musician was creating at the piano and in his compositions. What had earlier been passed off as a lack of technical ability was now being viewed as a new way of creating musical sounds and organizing musical ideas. Monk, among others, was beginning to show jazz musicians that successful musical statements are not formulated purely in terms of rapidly moving melodic lines. His improvisation to *Bag's Groove* (*SCCJ* 89) develops a motive consisting of a harmonic crush of half steps, plays with an opening and closing harmonic interval that varies unpredictably, and spreads out the distance between successive statements so that the rhythm does not have the compulsive continuity that the old-fashioned listener had come to expect in the standard jazz solo. When working with standard repertoire tunes, for example, *Smoke Gets in Your Eyes* (*SCCJ* 88) or *I Should Care* (*SCCJ* 90), Monk approaches the music as an anatomist dissecting a cadaver rather than as a tailor clothing a body in folds that elaborate, flatter, hide, and otherwise conform to the latest wrinkles of popular taste. He picks off a fragment of the melody and sets it on its end; selects a small section of harmony and holds it up to the light; and occasionally—with a sense of satire?—throws in an arpeggio with fingers that stumble rather than glide. One critic, in reviewing some Monk recordings of 1952 and 1954, wrote:

> Perhaps because he combined advanced harmonic and rhythmic ideas with an outwardly unsensational technique, it took Monk almost two decades to win acceptance from the jazz public at large. These performances date from a period when most jazz players and the mass of listeners still regarded him merely as an eccentric. The music has a bite and aggressiveness not always present in Monk's later work, though it is only fair to point out that the scope of his talent enabled him to weather the storm. . . . It is an ironic comment . . . that players of Monk's stature should be virtually ignored at one stage of their careers only to be expected some years later to evince superhuman creativity.[34]

SONNY ROLLINS

During the 1950s, two tenor saxophonists emerged from the jazz milieu to vie for supremacy on that instrument: John Coltrane and Theodore "Sonny" Rollins. Although Coltrane held the limelight in the early years of the next decade, Rollins clearly captured the position as the most influential tenor

[34] Michael James, in Max Harrison et. al., *Modern Jazz: The Essential Records*, p. 48.

Theodore Walter "Sonny" Rollins, tenor saxophone, c. 1980.

player of the late 1950s. Born in New York City in 1930, he is generally considered a product of the Coleman Hawkins and Charlie Parker schools of jazz saxophone performance. Rollins was raised in the same immediate neighborhood with Coleman Hawkins, Thelonious Monk, and Bud Powell, and was a devoted observer of their efforts at the time bebop was gaining ground as the new voice of jazz. At the age of eighteen, he cut his first professional record with Babs Gonzales, and the next year he recorded with Bud Powell and Fats Navarro, powerful company for a nineteen-year-old musician. He traveled to Chicago in 1950 to study with drummer Ike Day, for he felt his rhythmic conception of saxophone performance could profit from instruction by a percussionist. In 1951, he recorded with Miles Davis and also cut his first recording as a group leader. The years 1951 through 1954 were extremely productive, as Rollins not only recorded with the leading jazz musicians of the era—Miles Davis, Charlie Parker (on tenor), Thelonious Monk, Horace Silver, Kenny Clarke, and the newly founded Modern Jazz Quartet—but he composed three of his best-known jazz tunes, *Oleo*, *Doxy*, and *Airegin*.

Rollins's unorthodox life style had a direct effect on his music. He periodically went into self-imposed "retirement," probably as a result of extreme self-criticism, unrealistic goals, and feelings of inadequacy. From November 1954, to November 1955, Rollins "disappeared" to Chicago where he worked as a day laborer. A second period of isolation, from August 1959, to November 1961, he spent incognito in New York, where, it is reported, he practiced his saxophone regularly at night on a bridge over the East River. Another period during which he refused to record, 1963–65, coincided with trips to Japan and India, during which he began the formal study of yoga. A fourth period of withdrawal, 1967–72, was suddenly terminated by the release of "Sonny Rollins' Next Album," which was immediately followed by professional activity.

Rollins's most significant contributions to jazz were made during the years between his first and second withdrawals. Joining the Max Roach–Clifford Brown Quintet in November 1955, Rollins was immediately acclaimed for his new technical mastery of his instrument (*NW* 271, II/5) and for his composition *Valse Hot*, the first of a rash of jazz waltzes that led to greater metric exploration by other jazz musicians. After Clifford Brown's death in 1956, Rollins's playing became somewhat erratic, but his performance on *Pent-Up House* (*SCCJ* 96) shows him in complete control of both his instrument and his musical ideas.

Rollins contributed another milestone improvisation in 1956 on *Blue Seven*[35] (*SCCJ* 97), from his "Saxophone Colossus" album. Gunther Schuller identi-

[35]Prestige LP7079.

fies this solo as an example of "real variation technique," a concept not consciously espoused by jazz musicians of the period.[36] In an astute analysis of jazz improvisation, Schuller points out that Rollins employs a melodic motive based on the interval of a tritone (augmented fourth). With this germ motive as a melodic and harmonic stimulant he improvises by employing repetition, thematic variation, diminution, motivic elision, and other compositional devices that lend great structural cohesiveness to the improvisation.

An interesting reaction to Schuller's analysis is made by another scholar, who comments:

> Though analysis reveals Rollins' right to be regarded as a serious artist, it ignores (or glosses over or attempts to explain away) many disparate elements in his musical thinking. For I believe Rollins is really a Romantic who has a sense of the "glory of the imperfect."
>
> Many of these disparate elements may be heard [elsewhere] on this LP.[37]

Indeed, this paradox in both the playing and the personality of Sonny Rollins may explain why he found it necessary on several occasions to remove himself temporarily from society in order to reassess his life and his music. Few jazz musicians are introspective by nature; Sonny Rollins was one of a growing number who constantly assessed and reassessed their own performance and that of others. This kind of thinking was gradually creating a jazz avant-garde that tried to establish a new order, attempted to expand limits, and constantly searched for better sound. Sonny Rollins, Miles Davis, Thelonious Monk, and Lennie Tristano were but four musicians who placed a positive value on musical development and change. Many of the establishment figures, technically proficient though they might be, chose to maintain their tried and true musical identities at all costs. The existence of a Glenn Miller Orchestra years after its leader's death is an obvious symptom of this characteristic. Two philosophies were at work in the jazz community, the one to preserve and the other to evolve. And in both camps, the need to survive took precedence over other considerations in driving musicians forward to their appointed tasks.

SOMETHING BORROWED

The introduction of Afro-Cuban rhythms to jazz is thought by many to be no more than a tiny ripple upon a mainstream backwater. However, most groups maintained a fair percentage of Afro-Cuban numbers in their reper-

---

[36] Gunther Schuller, "Sonny Rollins and Thematic Improvising," in *Jazz Panorama*, ed. Martin Williams (New York: Collier Books, 1964), p. 248.

[37] Lawrence Gushee, "Sonny Rollins," in *Jazz Panorama*, p. 254.

toires. Although some of this music had been around for decades—the tango was a popular dance in the '20s, the rhumba in the '30s, the conga and the samba in the '40s—it was not until the late '40s that Afro-Cuban came into prominence as a jazz idiom. Dizzy Gillespie hired a Cuban drummer, Chano Pozo, for a Town Hall concert in 1947. He impressed everyone so much that others began to think seriously about the music he played. At the end of the '30s, Machito and His Afro-Cubans were a popular band group who played in this idiom, but they touched jazz only peripherally. Stan Kenton borrowed some of Machito's drummers in 1948 for a recording of *The Peanut Vendor*,[38] which in turn seemed to influence trumpeter Shorty Rogers, who produced recordings with his orchestra in 1953 that successfully combined both elements. *Tail of an African Lobster* and *Chiquito Loco*[39] had the swing of West Coast jazz, the freedom of excellent improvising jazz musicians and an Afro-Cuban beat. An exciting combination of jazz and Afro-Cuban rhythms was recorded in 1954 by a non-jazz orchestra featuring Shorty Rogers. Perez Prado composed a score for four saxes, six trumpets, three trombones, French horn, bass, and seven drummers, a personnel roster larger than the one he maintained in his own mambo orchestra. He recruited some leading West Coast jazz musicians to complete the recording, and *Voodoo Suite*,[40] a multisectioned work, swings through its blend of chanting, drumming, and flashy instrumental sonorities and solos.

The mambo and Spanish and African drums became popular for a while in the 1950s and, like everything else in jazz, can still be found alive and well (to a greater or lesser degree) somewhere among the clubs and studios of jazz. For a few brief years, it appeared that Afro-Cuban jazz too would become a major influence, but it was just one more musical idea found at the doorstep of jazz and adopted only briefly.

MODAL JAZZ—MILES DAVIS AND KIND OF BLUE

One remarkable performer has had a professional history unlike that of most other successful musicians in the trade. Miles Davis started his career amidst the bebop musicians of the 1940s, greatly influenced the development of cool and West Coast jazz in the early '50s, explored the possibilities of jazz modality with both his small combo and a nineteen-piece studio recording orchestra in the late '50s, became part of the radical jazz movement during

[38] Capitol W569-5.
[39] Victor LPM3138.
[40] Victor EPB-1101.

the 1960s, sided with jazz/rock fusion in the '70s before his health forced his retirement, and re-emerged in the 1980s as a leader returning to older values on the one hand and exploring the new technologies of digital recording, sampling, and MIDI (music instrument digital interface) on the other. He was an enigmatic figure who represented the mystical leading edge of the jazz avant-garde. An enormous percentage of the leading jazz musicians working today have come through the ranks of his various groups or worked closely with him in one way or another. Studying his career in detail would alone give us a fairly adequate account of jazz history from the late 1940s to the present. After Armstrong, Ellington, and Parker, Miles Davis (1926–91) takes his place as the most significant and influential musician in the history of jazz.

Born in Illinois in 1926, Davis grew up in St. Louis in middle-class surroundings. He received a good education, started playing trumpet at age thirteen, and began to play professionally around St. Louis while still in high school. Clark Terry was an early influence, but a chance event in 1944 was pivotal. When Davis was a senior in high school, he went to the Riviera Club to hear the Billy Eckstine band and was asked to substitute for an ill trumpeter. That night, the band's roster included Dizzy Gillespie, Charlie Parker, Dexter Gordon, Art Blakey, and Sarah Vaughan. The event gave focus to his life. He went to New York in 1944, purportedly to study at Juilliard but actually to follow his idols. He was soon playing with Charlie Parker at the Three Deuces on 52nd Street and had a social and working relationship with Gillespie. He was playing with Bud Powell, Coleman Hawkins, and Thelonious Monk at the age of nineteen! That same year he cut his first recording with Charlie Parker's Ree Boppers, *Billie's Bounce* and *Now's the Time*,[41] at a session with Gillespie on piano, Curly Russell on bass, and Max Roach on drums. Both of these blues tunes, which still serve as standards in the jazz repertory, include outstanding choruses by Parker. Davis, on the other hand, was a novice who was struggling to master his horn as well as the style. The nineteen-year-old was overshadowed by his elders as he muffed notes and played simple choruses, but his playing with these top-of-the-line colleagues was respectable.

When Parker left for California with Gillespie shortly thereafter, Davis joined the trumpet section of Benny Carter's band, again mainly to be near his idols. Before Parker's breakdown Davis recorded with him again, this time in Hollywood. On their *Ornithology*[42] we begin to hear the lyricism that would continue to grow in the work of this young artist. Davis still muffed

[41] Savoy 573a and 573b or Savoy MG12079.
[42] Dial 1002.

Miles Davis is featured soloist with the Gil Evans Orchestra in Carnegie Hall.

notes, but his muted trumpet line was more coherent and relaxed. When Parker entered Camarillo Hospital, Davis rejoined the Billy Eckstine band in California and returned to New York.

After his release from the hospital in April 1947, Parker was back at the Three Deuces with Davis, Duke Jordan on piano, Tommy Potter on bass, and Max Roach on drums for a four-week stay that was extended "indefinitely." It was a learning experience for Davis. In his own words:

> Anything might happen when you were playing with Bird. So I learned to play what I knew and extend it upwards—a little *above* what I knew. You had to be ready for anything. . . .
>
> After we got through with that first set, Bird came up and said—again in that fake British accent—"You boys played pretty good tonight, except in a couple of places where you fell off the rhythm and missed a couple of notes." We just . . . laughed.[43]

A remarkable series of recordings followed, and one can hear that Davis, at twenty-one, was coming into his own. His performances on *Dewey Square* and *Out of Nowhere*[44] are excellent. He begins to settle into that compositional style of improvisation in mid-range that depends not on clichéd phrases or virtuosic artifice but rather on a thoughtful metamorphosis and variation of material for which he became justly famous. That year, 1947, marked the end of Miles Davis's apprentice period. He had recorded as a leader in August, and once that transformation took place, musically he never became a follower again.

[43] Miles Davis with Quincy Troupe, *Miles: The Autobiography*, p. 101 f.
[44] Dial 1019 and Dial DLP207.

That same year, Davis met Gil Evans, pianist and arranger with the Claude Thornhill Orchestra, studied some of Evans's scores for the band, and noted that Thornhill's band had woodwinds, a French horn, and a tuba. Not long after, Davis brought a nonet into the Royal Roost with Lee Konitz, alto sax; Gerry Mulligan, baritone sax; Michael Zwerin, trombone; Junior Collins, French horn; Bill Barber, tuba; John Lewis, piano; Al McKibbon, bass; and Max Roach, drums. Evans was chief arranger, and Mulligan and Evans had determined the instrumentation. Davis was the leader and guiding force, and these experiments would give birth to cool jazz.[45] The Capitol recordings of 1949 and 1950 are landmarks in the history of jazz, and *Boplicity* (SCCJ 77) is a prime example of the transformation that had taken place. The dynamic level is moderate; the tone of the horn players is light, relatively free of overtones, and carries little or no vibrato; understatement and economy of expression are prized; and extremely high or loud notes are avoided. Subtle accentuation predominates, and brushes replace the heavy stick work and "bombs" of bop drumming. Leonard Feather notes:

> In the 1960s, Davis was considered by many jazz students to be the foremost trumpeter in the field . . . [but] Davis' major contributions as soloist and as orchestral innovator were made in the 1950s. Though his performances during the '60s often reached magnificent peaks of brilliance, the historically meaningful work he has brought to jazz dates back to the Capitol band, to the later Evans collaborations, and to the combo in which Cannonball Adderley and John Coltrane were sidemen in 1957–9.[46]

The successful collaboration between Davis and Evans in 1949 obviously had its aftereffects, for in 1957 and 1958, Davis returned to the studios with Evans. Their effort, *Porgy and Bess*,[47] quickly became a popular success, and it was soon followed by similar arrangements. The concept of a jazz soloist featured with a lush orchestra background was not new—Charlie Parker, Chet Baker, and others recorded to background sounds of strings, full orchestras, and so on—but in this recording, the orchestration was both novel and perfectly suited to the style of the original music that was being scored.

---

[45] The inspiration for the sound of cool jazz playing can be traced back to Bix Beiderbecke, whose recordings were prized by Lester Young. Young served as a model for Stan Getz, Lee Konitz, and Gerry Mulligan. A remarkable recording, *Ah-Leu-Cha*, of April 1948, by Charlie Parker's All Stars with Davis and John Lewis is "cool," as is the December 1948 recording of Ralph Burns's *Early Autumn* by the Woody Herman band and Stan Getz. Change was in the air, and the Davis-Evans-Mulligan collaboration crystallized the new ideal.

[46] Leonard Feather, *The Encyclopedia of Jazz in the Sixties*, p. 105.

[47] Columbia CL 1274.

Also, Davis, the soloist, shed his normal style of solo performance and integrated his lyricism into the whole of the composition and arrangement. He played *with* the orchestra, not in spite of it, and the blend was so perfect, the sound so refreshing, that the recording became immensely popular not only with the public, but in the music world as well. *Summertime* (*SCCJ* 92) is miraculously transformed from Gershwin's classical jazz of the past into the latest music of the '50s. Evans is responsible for the inventive instrumental voicing, for the accompanying riffs scored for the lush sonorities of French horns, and for directing the ensemble in a jazz mood; Paul Chambers and Philly Joe Jones are responsible for infusing rhythmic swing into the large group; but Miles Davis brings to the session improvisations that are infused with the full richness of mature understanding. The remarkable achievement of this recording lies in Evans's giving full license to his own artistic gifts while creating ideal settings for the gem of Davis's lyricism.

Between his two monumental Gil Evans collaborations, *Birth of the Cool* and *Porgy and Bess*, Davis moved through a troubled period, both musically and personally. An exhilarating trip to Paris in 1949 with James Moody, Tadd Dameron, and Kenny Clarke provided the occasion for the musician to meet writer / philosopher Jean-Paul Sartre and artist Pablo Picasso. Davis's return to America was a disaster. He succumbed to a heroin habit that plagued him for four years, during which his name was good but his music was mediocre. *Blue Room*,[48] recorded in 1951, is unimpressive despite the quality of the sidemen Sonny Rollins, John Lewis, Percy Heath, and Roy Haynes. *The Serpent's Tooth*,[49] recorded in 1953, is better but lacks precision. Charlie Parker appears on this recording playing tenor saxophone, and his playing is sad indeed. He would be dead before two more years were to pass, and the greatness that he once possessed seems gone forever. During this period, we can identify passages on certain records that reveal the innate talent of Miles Davis, but the sustained brilliance of a master is lacking. Most of his recorded solos reflect the bebop style of the '40s rather than the new sound he grasped momentarily on the Capitol recordings. The direction of Davis's playing is as hard to follow as the direction his life was hard for him to keep in focus, yet his popularity remained strong. He had first won the *Esquire* "New Star Award" for trumpet in 1947 and tied Dizzy Gillespie for first place in the critics' poll of *Down Beat* that same year. Then he placed first in the critics' poll of *Metronome* for 1951, '52, and '53, but his success was beginning to tarnish.

Drawing on his own inner reserves, intelligence, and personal fortitude, Davis kicked his drug habit in 1954. After that, he performed two brilliant

[48] Prestige 7827.
[49] Prestige 7004.

quartet sessions for Prestige and Blue Note with Horace Silver, Art Blakey, and Percy Heath, and in this music one hears the master in charge again on *Well You Needn't*[50] and *Four*.[51] Extraordinary and historically telling sessions followed one after the other: *Walkin'*[52] with J. J. Johnson and Lucky Thompson; *Airegin, Oleo,* and *Doxy*[53] with Sonny Rollins; *Swing Spring*[54] with Thelonious Monk; and many with John Coltrane. One of the ironies for trumpeter Miles Davis, however, was his inability to develop a rock-solid lip. His recording of *Will You Still Be Mine?*[55] displays a beautiful, long-line solo, but the first time he moves up in range, he fluffs a note.

An appearance at George Wein's Newport Jazz Festival in 1955 also cemented his standing in the jazz community as the new bearer of the torch. His muted solo on Monk's *'Round Midnight* captivated the audience and, more important, the critics, and he was on his way to becoming a living legend. Despite his proven record of achievement and the beauty of his recent recordings, the critics had been hard on him of late. Of his soon-to-be-famous quintet, one critic said, "The group consisted of a trumpet player who could play only in the middle register and fluffed half his notes; an out-of-tune tenor player; a cocktail pianist; a drummer who played so loud that no one else could be heard; and a teenage bassist." So much for the critics.

Although his playing improved and he stayed clean of heroin (although he still occasionally used cocaine), his musicians had serious problems. In 1956, he recorded frequently and was playing at the Cafe Bohemia with his "classic" ensemble—John Coltrane, Red Garland, Paul Chambers, and Philly Joe Jones—a group with two soloists of genius and perhaps the best rhythm section in jazz at that time. Still, Jack Chambers would later write:

> The undercurrent for self-destruction persisted, and it was never far from the surface. . . . For most of the jazz musicians, heroin remained an occupational hazard. The Miles Davis Quintet were no exception. While Davis himself remained straight, he was all alone in that respect. . . . The addictions were taking a heavier and heavier toll on the quintet's performances, causing one or another of the musicians to be late almost every evening and sometimes to be absent for the whole night. Sometimes when they did show up, they might have been better not to.
>
> John Coltrane was suffering most conspicuously, and on several nights he spent an entire set leaning against the piano, nodding. On one such night, a

[50] Blue Note BLP5040.
[51] Prestige PRLP161.
[52] Prestige PRLP182.
[53] Prestige PRLP187.
[54] Prestige PRLP200.
[55] Prestige 7007.

major record producer sat in the audience, expecting to sign Coltrane to a contract, but he left without even approaching him when he saw his condition.[56]

Nevertheless, this ensemble was the most influential jazz group of its time. Davis was *the* musician in jazz, and his musical decisions were flawless. However, his ego often came cheek to jowl with that of other artists. There was a notorious argument with Thelonious Monk in the Prestige recording studio in 1954, and a similar estrangement with John Coltrane. Coltrane said,

> After I joined Miles in 1955 I found that he doesn't talk much and will rarely discuss his music. He is completely unpredictable; sometimes he'd walk off the stage after just a few notes, not even completing one chorus. If I asked him something about his music I never knew how he was going to take it.[57]

Coltrane left Davis for the Thelonious Monk quartet, with Wilbur Ware on bass and Shadow Wilson on drums, in late 1956, and Davis re-outfitted his band several times during the next year. He also went into the recording studio again with Gil Evans in May 1957 to record the *Miles Ahead* album. *Blues for Pablo*,[58] scored for twelve brasses, four woodwinds, bass, and drums, displays Evans's gift for scoring an impressionist palette of shimmering tone color, and Davis's extraordinary ear and lyrical gifts reshape the concept of fluegel horn sound—a full, mellow tone with an infinite variety of tonal nuance, pitch inflection, and varied articulation.

A year later Davis recorded on trumpet, with Coltrane and Julian "Cannonball" Adderley, Monk's asymmetrical *Straight, No Chaser*[59] and here Davis, the bebopper, is master of the hard, funky running line. Coltrane had been through a growth period with Monk, and his new "sheets of sound" come to the fore on this number as they do in his recording with Davis and Cannonball Adderley on Jackie McLean's *Dr. Jekyll* (*NAJ* 14). In this up-tempo blues, we can hear in Davis's solo some characteristics of the modal jazz that is about to emerge as a distinct style. Over a pizzicato bass playing long runs that obliterate a clear sense of the form, Davis employs runs that emphasize minor or modal patterns. He also experiments with timbre and pitch as he suddenly stops to distort a long note and squeeze it off the tempered pitch. He takes short motivic fragments, plays with them, and inserts them at oddly spaced intervals throughout his improvisatory narrative. Adderley and Coltrane, on the other hand, challenge each other as they trade phrases and pile

[56] Jack Chambers, *Milestones I: The Music and Times of Miles Davis to 1960*, p. 249.
[57] J. C. Thomas, *Chasin' the Trane: The Music and Mystique of John Coltrane*, p. 81.
[58] Columbia CL1041.
[59] Columbia PC9428.

layer upon layer of eighth notes into a sheets-of-sound duo. (See Listening Guide 14.) A little later, without losing his stride, Davis easily slipped back into the garb of tone poet to record *Summertime*[60] (*SCCJ* 92). All this activity was serving as a prelude to another historical turning point in jazz, *Kind of Blue*.

By the end of the 1950s, jazz was again ready for something new. The innovators were at work: Sonny Rollins was recording in meters other than 4/4; Coltrane was laying down sheets of sound; Monk was composing bare-boned, asymmetrical pieces and playing in a pointillistic style; Cecil Taylor was improvising atonal music featuring tone clusters, percussive touch, and classical forms; and Bohemian jazz musicians were mixing poetry with their music. The fermenting mixture was ripe for a vintage bottling. The theoretical framework for modal jazz had been formulated by George Russell in his book, *The Lydian Chromatic Concept of Tonal Organization for Improvisation*,[61] but it was left for Davis to lead the performers down the next important path of jazz. This he did when he went into the recording studio in March and April of 1959 with Bill Evans, John Coltrane, Cannonball Adderley, Paul Chambers, and Jimmy Cobb.

Miles Davis's "Kind of Blue" album[62] was the epitome of new expression for combo jazz in 1959. No longer were the musicians playing compositions based on a harmonic progression; instead, the structure rested on modal and scalar themes and patterns. *So What* (*SCCJ* 99) borrows the framework of popular-song form, **AABA**, but substitutes a single modal scale for a harmonic progression in each eight-measure phrase (see Transcription 12). After the rubato introduction, it is the bass that plays the melody or scale of the opening chorus. The chording by pianist Bill Evans gives the impression of harmonic changes, an illusion created by the first chord's serving as a grace to the second.[63] The historical significance of this recording is immense: Not only did the other musicians in the group—Cannonball Adderley and John Coltrane—continue to explore the implications of this session for the remainder of their careers, but the session influenced most of the younger musicians who were to establish themselves as professional jazz musicians in the 1960s. Davis's solo is spare, while those of the saxophonists overflow with a surplus of fast notes. Coltrane is a little more comfortable working in the new format than Adderley, who creates the illusion of reverting to chordal thinking in his solo by articulating triads on the diatonic degrees of the mode.

When Miles Davis first played with Charlie Parker, he was a novice jazz musician who was in over his head. He floundered occasionally but was always

---

[60] Columbia PC8085.
[61] New York: Concept Publishing, 1959.
[62] Columbia CL 1355.
[63] See the example on p. 363.

Miles Davis at the New York Jazz Festival in 1959, with John Coltrane and Cannonball Adderley in the background.

able to touch bottom, albeit on tiptoe. Through the years, he developed and matured, and by the late 1950s Davis was the most influential musician actively working in jazz.

Postwar jazz piano took a quantum jump in the late 1950s when Red Garland and Bill Evans, both pianists with the Miles Davis combos, revoiced keyboard chords by omitting the root as the lowest sounding pitch and replacing it with the seventh or the third of the chord on the bottom. Garland's 1955 and 1956 recordings with Davis[64] show the transition, and Bill Evan's 1959 work on *So What* (*SCCJ* 99) demonstrates the fully developed modern voicings.

Keyboard Voicing

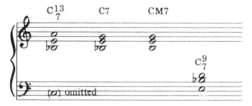

[64] Prestige LP 7007, 7014, and 7116.

In actuality, *So What* is not harmonic in the traditional sense. It is based on a D Dorian scale, a sound that earlier jazz musicians would have accompanied with a minor seventh:

Untransposed Dorian Scale

Evans, however, employs quartal harmony, chords based on fourths rather than thirds, to harmonize the modal scale and uses a sliding progression of parallel chords with roots, or modal tonic, removed from the bass to embellish the harmonic sound.

Bill Evans (1929–80).

Since that time, Bill Evans, along with Hancock, Tyner, Corea, and other modern keyboard players, has served as a prime model for jazz pianists. One of his best albums, "Interplay"[65] is one of the finest examples of combo work, but his later album "Conversations with Myself,"[66] had more impact on the jazz world. Overdubbing, before that date, had been condemned by most jazz musicians as an artificial device incapable of producing high-quality jazz. In this recording, Evans simply plays music with himself by first recording one track and successively adding others. It is his keyboard technique, best demonstrated here, that has been adopted as the standard practice for all modern keyboard musicians since.

By the end of the decade, a profusion of jazz styles assailed the unwary listener. Writing in 1961, one astute observer remarked:

> In recent years, activities in the field of jazz have increased so rapidly that the critics seem to be uneasy. A new kind of complaint appears in the columns of the commentators: "Too many unknown musicians are being recorded, too many long-playing recordings are being released, too many jazz festivals are being produced, too many jazz concerts are being staged"—and so on.
>
> A critic known for his determination to let nothing escape him finally admitted, "Man, you can't make all the scenes any more."
>
> It is true that no one human being can keep up with the Niagara of jazz recordings, concerts, and festivals, as well as the radio, night-club, and television appearances of jazz musicians. The increase in both good and bad jazz is enormous, which means, of course, that there is a lot more fine jazz than ever before.
>
> It wasn't always so.[67]

SOCIAL CAUSE AND MUSICAL EFFECT

Music and society are thought by some to be a hand-in-glove phenomenon, one the object, the other the image. Music has often been called a mirror of life, a concrete vision of the universe. A thorough intellectual grasp of music gives us both insight and understanding of the society that has produced it. The eminent historian Paul Henry Lang made the observation in the following elegant statement:

[65] Riverside RLP 445.
[66] Verve (A) 68526.
[67] Marshall W. Stearns, "What Is Happening to Jazz," in *Music 1961* (New York: Down Beat, 1961), p. 28.

Every civilization is a synthesis of man's conquest of life. Art is the ultimate symbol of this conquest, the utmost unity man can achieve. Yet the spirit of an epoch is reflected not in the arts alone, but in every field of human endeavor, from theology to engineering.[68]

He takes care to point out that no age necessarily produces a unilateral spirit, and that at any one time three elements are usually present: "the dying past, the flourishing present, and the promising future."[69] Other contemporary writers concur:

The musician's perception of the world will be conditioned by the intellectual and spiritual climate of his day and this in turn will be reflected in his style. The style of a work of art thus enables us to understand the spirit and ideals of the past.[70]

In a recent, insightful essay, "Changing Patterns in Society and Music: The U.S. Since World War II,"[71] we are told that up until the mid-1950s, American life was stable, traditional, and produced a culture with a distinct flavor. In other words, America, from the war years through 1955, had a unified spirit that exuded "obedience, trust, conformity, cooperation, discipline, of working with others for the common good—with as little friction and disagreement as possible."[72] We learn, further, that "national pride in American military and industrial accomplishments, so strong and universal during and after World War II, was gradually replaced by questions, doubts, and eventual hostility and opposition."[73] The result of this circumstance was that Americans in "every aspect of behavior—dress, speech, political and religious belief, artistic expression, personal relationships . . . [followed] their own individual desires, tastes, and needs."[74] The spirit of the age changed in the mid-1950s and alongside this change, a proliferation of musical styles occurred that is easily documented by examples from inside as well as outside the jazz idiom. The multiplicity of styles that have emerged from every corner of the music industry in America since 1955 is truly impressive—in jazz alone there was no end of experimentation taking place at the close of

[68] Paul Henry Lang, *Music in Western Civilization* (New York: W. W. Norton, 1941), p. xix.
[69] Ibid., p. xx.
[70] Beekman J. Cannon, Alvin H. Johnson, and William G. Waite, *The Art of Music* (New York: Thomas Y. Crowell, 1960), p. 3.
[71] Charles Hamm, in Charles Hamm, Bruno Nettl, and Ronald Byrnside, *Contemporary Music and Music Cultures*, chap. 2.
[72] Ibid., p. 69.
[73] Ibid., p. 61.
[74] Ibid., p. 63.

the decade. But let us look back a moment to examine the situation of the 1940s. Let us study its implications upon our concept of history, for by using jazz music of the 1940s as a case in point, we will be dealing with known quantities in both the society and its music. We shall scrutinize the events of a single year—1947—because it is equidistant between the close of World War II and the advent of cool bop.

For the moment, let us accept the thesis that in the years immediately following World War II, a feeling of unity and self-righteousness prevailed, brought about by pride in the country's achievements in science, industry, education, and, of course, its success in the war. Did this unity, harmony, and singleness of purpose extend to the kind of jazz being recorded, broadcast, and played in live performances during 1947?

On February 26, 1947, Charlie Parker recorded *Carvin' the Bird*, a bebop jazz performance; on February 28, 1947, the Stan Kenton Orchestra recorded *Collaboration*, in what was then called the progressive-jazz style; on June 10, 1947, Erroll Garner and his trio recorded *Frankie and Johnny* in a swing piano style; on September 23, 1947, Bunk Johnson and His Orchestra played Scott Joplin's *The Entertainer*, a double threat from the classic jazz and the ragtime revival; and on December 27, 1947, the Woody Herman Orchestra recorded *Four Brothers* in a modern bebop-swing style.

This diversity, in one genre only, is in reality only a portion of the sample, for Tristano was offering a precursor to cool jazz in his recording of *Coolin' Off with Ulanov* the same year that Sonny Boy Williamson and Muddy Waters were waxing some down-home blues. The Firehouse Five Plus Two were playing a newly invented Dixieland style in Hollywood, and all in all there was no genuine uniformity of jazz style in 1947.

The situation was no different in popular music. The popular songs of 1947 included the nonsense songs *Chi-Baba Chi-Baba* and *Managua, Nicaragua;* the sentimental ballads *Tenderly* and *Peg o' My Heart;* and the splendid chromatic, jazzlike composition by Sonny Burke, *Midnight Sun*, which Ronny Lang introduced on record with the Les Brown Band of Renown. That same year saw the composition of three other songs that had tremendous popular appeal: *Fifteen Tons*, a quasi-folk song; *Beyond the Sea*, a pseudo-classical song; and the *Too Fat Polka*, a freshly composed ethnic song.

Popular instrumental ensembles varied from the Harmonicats to the Dorsey brothers to the Guy Lombardo Orchestra. The *Down Beat* poll winners that year were the Stan Kenton Orchestra, the King Cole Trio, Buddy DeFranco, Benny Goodman, Johnny Hodges, Vido Musso, Harry Carney, Ziggy Elman, Bill Harris, Mel Powell, Eddie Safranski, Oscar Moore, Shelly Manne, Frank Sinatra, Buddy Stewart, Sarah Vaughan, June Christy, Sy Oliver, and the Pied Pipers—not as much variety as 1965 or 1975, but enough to make one wonder about the uniformity of American taste in 1947. Were scholars to construct a cultural history five hundred years from now on the basis of stylistic analyses of the music mentioned above, would they arrive at a picture of a unified, tradition-bound society so often suggested as characteristic of the American people in the years immediately following World War II?

On the other hand, can this diversity be explained by dividing the time period into three elements: the dying past, a flourishing present, and a promising future? Not necessarily, and certainly not easily. The death agonies of classic jazz never arrived or, possibly, death and resurrection took place simultaneously, depending on one's point of view. The tradition that was handed down to Louis Armstrong and was revived by Bunk Johnson, Sidney Bechet, and Armstrong lives in today's renewed interest in classic jazz. In fact, classic jazz has outlived the birth and maturity of many other jazz styles, including swing and cool. Some of these, if not all, continue to the present in one form or another, and none can fit easily into a tradition that represents the dying past—they are all too much alive. Although one may temporarily prosper while another waxes lean, there seems to be no real danger that any of these forms will disappear entirely. The styles of Parker, Kenton, and Herman were all thought to be the new music of their day. In jazz alone, at least three different sounds in 1947 could fit into the categories of flourishing present or promising future, and there were several others too, such as nascent cool, preliminary modal, and early Afro-Cuban.

The concept of uniformity in the American spirit seems to hinge both on the phenomenon of war and its aftereffects and on a traditional interpretation of history that generalizes about peoples and nations. The victorious nation, forcibly pulled together in a common cause, remains united for a period of time after the close of hostilities. Even if this were so—and one might consider whether the ghetto black and the suburban white identified with each other to any extent in 1947—we might wonder what this all has to do with music when we consider that

for the student of European political history, for instance, the French Revolution is an event of momentous significance, a point of hierarchic articulation; but for the historian of European music, it is a minor ripple in a style period which runs roughly from 1750 to 1827—or perhaps even to 1914. One cannot assume that history moves in a monolithic fashion.[75]

In other words, does society interact with music at all? Does social cause result in musical effect? It has been suggested that we might do well to inquire further into the question of causality:

[75] Leonard B. Meyer, *Music, the Arts and Ideas*, p. 92.

But it may yet be that the same obsession with causality that yields such a curiously one-sided history is responsible also for distortions in the narrative for which so much is sacrificed; that our categorical prejudgments affect not only the interpretation and assessment of art works, but even those matters that we take to be open to "objective," "scientific" treatment: the reading of art works and the attributions of authorship, chronology, and provenance.[76]

Indeed, in writing this history, I have omitted many people and events, emphasized certain phenomena, and made some prejudgments, all in order to achieve some semblance of a continuous narrative. On the basis of this one sample drawn from an era that is scientifically available to us, the music of any period seems to be heterogenous and to follow its own laws. It is only coincidentally related to the society in which it exists. In jazz, historical certainty is impossible, for in five hundred years, jazz may be seen as a twig floating on the stream of Western music. Or, jazz may be viewed as the stream itself, with classical art music relegated to the museum of the past. Our close proximity to the origins and development of this music has definite advantages in allowing us to to observe all the processes and products of jazz first hand. We have sufficient objectivity, in the '90s, to view the proliferation of styles in the '50s in relation to the whole picture. We can trace that decade's events and musical phenomena back to their beginnings and forward to their present incarnations. We are well removed from the personal conflicts that beset the musician who is actively involved in day-to-day performance, yet thanks to modern technology, we can document each highwater mark in the history of this highly volatile art. Further, we might say quite accurately that music is divorced from the realities of daily existence, for it is an abstraction guided by its own rules, shaped by its own creators, and understood only by the members of the society whose ears have been trained to hear it. In this sense, jazz provides us with an understanding of current history and the history of music, for it is one of the few recent phenomena that we may study in its entirety. Considered in this way, jazz may be the key to new criteria in musical and historical perception.

———— SUMMING UP THE '50S ————

East Coast, West Coast, and third stream—three names coined during the 1950s, three labels for distinct jazz sounds of the decade. The first two are misnomers. West Coast, which was essentially cool jazz in a variety of garbs, was born in New York through the music of Miles Davis and Gil Evans, or

[76] Leo Treitler, "On Historical Criticism," *The Musical Quarterly*, 53 (1967), p. 205.

in Chicago through Lennie Tristano and Lee Konitz, or on the road with Stan Getz. It gave rise to a number of prominent ensembles, among them the Dave Brubeck Quartet with Paul Desmond, the Gerry Mulligan (piano-less) Quartet with Chet Baker, the Modern Jazz Quartet, and the Dave Pell Octet. In reaction to this "white" jazz (the members of the MJQ were black), black musicians pressed on with bebop and sought musical inspiration in black roots, gospel-inflected tunes, and the hard-driving "funky" blues. Leadership came from the Jazz Messengers with Horace Silver and Art Blakey, from Clifford Brown and Sonny Rollins, and, later in the decade, the Can-nonball Adderley combo, which emphasized "soul music." In contrast to West Coast, this style of playing was called East Coast, but its advocates came from California and North Carolina as well as New York and elsewhere, and a few of its prominent soloists were white—Al Cohn and Zoot Sims, to name but two. Their music was definitely hot and swinging as contrasted with the cool and subtle arrangements of the West Coast school.

Third stream, which appeared late in the decade, resulted from the efforts of composers—only rarely performing jazz musicians—who wished to infuse improvisation and jazz techniques into notated works of the contemporary Western art tradition. At a time when composers outside jazz were struggling to develop a valid mainstream classical style for their generation, third stream appeared as a possible solution to those who believed that a synthesis of jazz's rhythmic vitality and improvisational virtuosity with the more conven-tional written techniques of formal development, orchestrational variety, serial techniques, and then-new electronic composition might stimulate a valid new course for Western art composers. Robert Graettinger's *City of Glass*, Milton Babbitt's *All Set*, Teo Macero's *Sounds of May*, Gunther Schuller's *Transformation*, and George Russell's *All About Rosie* are a few of the signifi-cant third stream compositions dating from this period.

The '50s saw the birth and phenomenal growth of the outdoor jazz festi-val. First produced in Newport, Rhode Island, by George Wein in 1954, the Newport Jazz Festival revitalized the careers of Miles Davis in 1955 and Duke Ellington in 1956. As Davis had stolen the show the year before, Paul Gonsalves exhilarated the '56 festival audience with his extended tenor solo on Duke Ellington's *Diminuendo and Crescendo in Blue*. The Jazz Spectacular succeeded indoors as well, and Norman Granz's *Jazz at the Philharmonic* led the way. The *JATP* tours succeeded not only in America but in Europe and Japan as well. In this context, jazz played its role in forcing racial issues into the open, for one of the enforced *JATP* policies was "no performances in segregated auditoriums." Colleges were especially receptive to jazz concerts, and both the Brubeck and Modern Jazz quartets were extremely popular throughout the decade. Even the State Department saw jazz as a valuable

American propaganda tool, and under its patronage, Dizzy Gillespie toured both the Middle East and Latin America. Benny Goodman and Wilbur DeParis also performed overseas tours for the State Department, and Louis Armstrong became a phenomenal idol of music fans in Europe. Television seemed to offer a new venue for jazz musicians, and Cab Calloway, Stan Getz, Dizzy Gillespie, Louis Armstrong, Thelonious Monk, and many others made appearances on the tube. The promise and expectation of regular jazz programming on television were never fulfilled.

Big bands were still glamorous during the '50s, but their days were numbered. Stan Kenton toured successfully with his Innovations in Modern Music orchestra at the start of the decade with a personnel roster of forty musicians! Such extravagance was the exception, however, as Count Basie, Woody Herman, Artie Shaw, and Benny Goodman all shed their bands for smaller ensembles. Some reorganized their big bands again later, but many, like Claude Thornhill, folded forever. The big band fever had run its course.

Serious jazz fans will mourn the senseless waste of so much talent on the altar of drugs and alcohol:

Fats Navarro	died 1950	age 26
Wardell Gray	died 1955	age 34
Charlie Parker	died 1955	age 34
Billie Holiday	died 1959	age 44
Lester Young	died 1959	age 49

As the decade closed, a young saxophonist traveled to New York and established a new avant-garde in jazz. Ornette Coleman struck the *coup de grâce* to tradition, divided the musicians and the critics once again, and devoutly pursued the Freedom Principle:

> Genuine freedom occurs when the artist can communicate most intimately with the materials, the language of his or her medium; each innovation in jazz, from the beginnings to the present, appears so that jazz artists can reveal what cannot be revealed in any other way. In today's jazz, if these innovations do not increase the artist's capacity for communication, then only Freedom, with a capital *F*, results.[77]

---

[77] John Litweiler, *The Freedom Principle: Jazz After 1958*, p. 14.

SOCIAL AND MUSICAL REVOLUTION—

THE 1960s

INTRODUCTION

The entire decade of the 1960s was a period of great turmoil throughout the world, a time of social and political turbulence in the United States, a period of war and violence abroad. Jazz musicians were among the protestors critically appraising our institutions and demanding, both with their voices and with their instruments, equal rights for all citizens, more responsible government, and, in most cases, a withdrawal of our combat troops from the Far East. They felt and expressed the tension of their era in their art, and the new jazz of the decade literally became a mirror of society, reflecting the grief, anger, frustration, and inner chaos of a people treading water in a violent sea.

America continued to send troops into Vietnam while colleges across the country were being violated by their own students—young people who at first playfully challenged society with their long hair, skinny dips, and unkempt clothes and who later captured and defaced administration buildings, burned flags and draft cards, and damned the establishment for its complacency, arrogance, and greed. During these years, a president of the United States was assassinated; his brother, the attorney general, was murdered; a great civil rights leader and Nobel laureate was shot dead; a man named X was gunned down; a wall was erected to divide a once-great city; and astronauts

walked the moon. Life was often incongruous, and many Americans ques-
tioned and reevaluated their values, wondering whether to stand and be
counted or run and hide, whether to weep and scream or get on with life.
Young Americans invented the "generation gap" and totally rejected the old
popular music of Tin Pan Alley for rock 'n' roll. Rock became the official
voice of protest and the lyrics expressed both the disgust of things present and
the hope for a new age. Large numbers of young people escaped from reality—
some by running to Canada to evade the draft and many more by entering
the world of drugs. Marijuana, LSD, speed, and other hard drugs took their
toll and left their scars. Still, by the end of the decade, much was accomplished and some real changes were evident. Blacks were integrated into the
public schools, "white only" and "separate but equal" facilities were illegal,
members of minorities were running for office and gaining political power,
and women entered the previously all-male bastions of Ivy League schools,
private clubs, and corporate offices.

   The majority of jazz musicians in America are black, and the social unrest
that simmered beneath a closed lid in the years immediately following the
Second World War boiled over in the 1960s. A musical revolution was brew-
ing in jazz at the same time that this social revolution was taking place in
America. The critical event occurred a few years earlier: on November 13,
1956, the Supreme Court ruled that segregation on buses and street cars was
unconstitutional. In the fall of 1957, the governor of Arkansas and the people
of Little Rock resisted a court order for racial integration of a public high
school. Black students were prevented from attending school by armed national
guard troops until the President of the United States ordered U.S. Army
paratroopers to Little Rock on September 24, 1957, to guard the students
and force the issue. The civil-rights movement in America had gained
momentum.

   When a black jazz saxophonist came to New York in 1959 playing an
eccentric style of improvised music that rejected traditional norms—music
that declared itself free of melodic, harmonic, and metric restraints and that
seemed to epitomize an aesthetic of anarchy and nihilism—young musicians
of the black community throughout America declared this sound "our thang."
Ornette Coleman was as much a spiritual leader as he was a musical innovator. His music carried with it a message that was interpreted by black Americans to mean freedom, love, and black beauty. Amiri Baraka (LeRoi Jones)
writes:

> Ornette Coleman's screams and rants are only musical once one understands
> the music his emotional attitude seeks to create. This attitude is real, and
> perhaps the most singularly important aspect of his music. . . . These attitudes

are continuous parts of the historical cultural biography of the Negro as it has existed and developed since there was a Negro in America, and a music that could be associated with him that did not exist anywhere else in the world. The notes *mean something;* and the something is, regardless of its stylistic considerations, part of the black psyche as it dictates the various forms of Negro culture.[1]

He continues:

The form of a Coleman solo is usually determined by the total musical shape of what he is playing, i.e., the melody, timbre, pitch and of course, the rhythm— all of these move by Ornette's singularly emotional approach to jazz, in much the same way as the older, "primitive," blues singers produced their music. . . . This *freedom* that Coleman has insisted on in his playing, has opened totally fresh areas of expression. . . . And, of course, Ornette Coleman himself, on his records, or in person, continues to excite intrepid jazz listeners all over the country by the fierceness and originality of his imagination.[2]

FREE JAZZ— ORNETTE COLEMAN

Ornette Coleman was born in Fort Worth, Texas, in 1930. At about fourteen years of age, he played with some rhythm-and-blues bands in the Fort Worth area. In 1949 he visited a friend, the cornetist Melvin Lastie in New Orleans, and accompanied Lastie to a job in nearby Baton Rouge. Coleman's personal style was, even then, individual rather than conventional—he wore long straightened hair and a beard at a time when most black males were clean shaven and wore a "razor cut." Both his playing and his appearance were put on the line. Coleman relates:

And I was sittin' there listening to the band and all of a sudden a guy came in and said some musicians wanted to meet me outside. So I went outside and there were these really big guys, six or seven of them. I said, "How you doin'?" And one of them said, "Where you from?" And I said, "Oh, I'm from Fort Worth." And they were all black guys. . . . They started using "nigger" and all this, and "You're not from Texas with your beard like that and your long hair. You must be one of those Yankee kind of niggers!" And all of a sudden a guy kicked me in my stomach and then he kicked me in the ass and I had my

---

[1] LeRoi Jones, *Black Music*, p. 15.
[2] Ibid., p. 40 f.

horn cradled in my arms and I blacked out cause blood was everywhere. . . .
They were just beating me to death. One guy took my tenor and threw it down
the street. Then Melvin and the band came out and discovered I was beat up
and they took me to the police department. The cops said, "What you doing
with that long hair?" And they started calling me nigger and they told me that
if them other niggers didn't finish me, *they were gonna.*

So I went back to Melvin's house, and I was thinking just like my mother
had told me, that the tenor was bad luck. David had an alto, and he said, "I'll
let you borrow my alto."[3]

From this anecdote we gain some insight into the society in which Coleman matured. That society would undergo a social revolution in the succeeding years, especially in the period following the appearance of his record
album "Free Jazz."

In 1954, Coleman began to get his style together in California. Two years
later he met Donald Cherry, a trumpeter of like mind and similar skills.
Coleman's first studio recordings were made on the West Coast in 1958–59,
and on *Tomorrow Is the Question,*[4] we can hear that Coleman's sound and style
are somewhat derivative, similar to those of bebop ensembles like that of
Sonny Rollins and Clifford Brown. But there is a reckless abandon, an ebul-
lience that derives from a youthful devil-may-care attitude, that hints already
of an impending break from established norms.

Lonely Woman,[5] (*SCCJ* 103), recorded in 1959, is similar in style—that is,
it is late bebop but the passion of Coleman's playing and his attention to
tone and phrasing lift this performance into the realm of the best jazz recorded
during the period. The inaccuracies of pitch and articulation in the ensemble
passages communicate an intensity and foreboding that artfully portrays the
"lonely woman." For Coleman, these are years of preparation and transition.
Change of the Century[6] (*NAJ* 16), recorded in the same year as *Lonely Woman,*
foreshadows the revolution that is about to erupt. Long solo lines, enormous
bursts of notes, and semi-unisons that gather the form together at oddly
spaced points are some of the noteworthy characteristics (see Listening Guide
16). These three works exemplify and mark the end of Coleman's first period,
the years of learning, growth, development, and change.

In 1959, Coleman attended the Lenox School of Jazz in Massachusetts,
where he interacted with John Lewis, Gunther Schuller, and other musicians

---

[3] Interview with Ornette Coleman by Jonathan Foose, November 6, 1981, quoted in Jason
Berry, et al., *Up From the Cradle: New Orleans Music Since World War II,* p. 43 ff.

[4] Contemporary 7569.

[5] Atlantic 1317.

[6] Atlantic 1327.

Ornette Coleman.

who were thoroughly grounded in the European classical traditions. This backdrop set the stage for Coleman's dramatic entrance in New York at The Five Spot in 1959. With a white plastic saxophone and a quartet of three other jazz musicians who shared his musical sympathies, he packed the house for an extended period, although he was as much the subject of scorn as of praise. Strong support came from Leonard Bernstein, Gunther Schuller, and John Lewis, who embraced his music enthusiastically; violent rejection was almost unanimous from most traditional jazz artists, who saw in his playing a negation of those musical values they had worked so hard to create and fought so long to preserve. Roy Eldridge was quoted as saying, "I listened to him high and I listened to him cold sober. I even played with him. I think he's jiving, baby. He's putting everybody on."[7] Gene Lees, who criticized the jazz critics for many unprofessional sins, looked to the Ornette Coleman situation as an illustrative example:

[The critics have a] tendency to be cowed by certain musicians of known erudition because they feel that in taking issue with them they might reveal igno-

[7] Nat Hentoff, "The Biggest Noise in Jazz," *Esquire*, March 1961, p. 82.

rance or betray inadequacy. It seems to me that this problem has found sharp focus in the case of Ornette Coleman. Coleman came to prominence largely on the say-so of John Lewis and Gunther Schuller. Both are exceptionally learned men. Their influence on criticism has been considerable. . . .

Once Lewis and Schuller had put their seal of approval on Coleman, some critics began acclaiming him vociferously: others stood neutralized, afraid of exposing themselves, afraid that Schuller and Lewis, because of their erudition, were able to see things in Coleman's music that they could not. . . .

I would take issue with Coleman's concept of perfect freedom on the grounds that it is anti-music and anti-art. Art is and always has been the ordering of the disparate and chaotic materials of life into a significant shape of expression. Freedom of Coleman's kind is *not* perfect freedom: indeed, in its way, it is perfect slavery.[8]

The strength of the reaction, in retrospect, is somewhat amusing, for Coleman's music, by the standards of the classical avant-garde musicians of the day, was neither new nor shocking. The tone row, atonality, *musique concrète*, electronic music, computer music, random composition, prepared instruments, chance performance, happenings, and even silent music were but a few of the many forays into the possibilities of musical expression being mounted by Western classical composers before 1959. But the introduction of any of these concepts into jazz had never been accomplished with any security before the thirty-year-old Coleman took his stand.

It should come as no surprise, then, that the new music of Ornette Coleman was met with strong resistance by musicians and public alike when it proclaimed its existence in New York in 1959. The miracle worth noting, however, was the speed with which this music influenced jazz and engendered a major style change. Although rock 'n' roll became the principal music of protest for young white Americans, modern jazz became the dominant sound of the Black Power social movement in this country. Today we may attribute the sweeping spread of its acceptance worldwide to its function as a voice of "young Turks" and older members of the avant-garde, to its role as anti-establishment art, to its philosophy of freedom and individuality, and, of course, to its intrinsic musical values. Free jazz became the standard, or musical flag, of people condemning oppression, the voice of minorities denouncing the bonds of tradition and institutional authority.

The musicians involved in this new music were fully aware of the profound changes that were taking place in the world and in their music at the moment the new style was being born. This extraordinary awareness, rare as

[8] Gene Lees, "The Compleat Jazz Critic," *Music 1961* (New York: Down Beat, 1961), p. 14.

it was, is in itself a measure of Coleman's accomplishment, and of his daring and fortitude. Although many of the sounds and ideas that fed the conceptual roots of Coleman's music came from elsewhere—atonality, polytonality, asymmetrical rhythm, etc.—this nourishment led Coleman to an extemporaneous outpouring of sounds and structures that jelled into a unified and consistent style. Coleman and his various ensembles produced an elegant and intricate musical fabric in a burst of artistic spontaneous combustion.

Free jazz and aleatoric, or chance, performances are similar in many essential details. Attempts to destroy feelings of structure, direction, and tonality and the introduction of elements of surprise are common to both. The main distinctions between the two usually lie in the instrumentation of the ensembles and the musical training of the performers. Free-jazz instrumentation tended to approximate that of the normal jazz group—melody instruments and rhythm section—but eventually these traditional instruments gave way to sitars, tablas, amplified thumb pianos, police whistles, electronic octave machines, psychedelic lighting, and a host of nonstandard electronic and percussion pieces of equipment. Consequently, some of the free-jazz groups have the appearance of non-jazz avant-garde ensembles.

Both kinds of performers, free jazz and aleatoric avant-garde, operate in aesthetic systems that negate formerly valid stylistic rules, rather than in rule-structured systems created for the moment that organize musical sounds toward a definitive style. One tenet of their philosophy is the rejection of style or norms. John Cage claims, "I try to arrange my composing means so that I won't have any knowledge of what might happen. . . . My purpose is to eliminate purpose."[9] In like manner, Ornette Coleman explains:

> I don't tell the members of my group what to do. I want them to play what they hear in the piece for themselves. I let everyone express himself just as he wants to. The musicians have complete freedom, and so, of course, our final results depend entirely on the musicianship, emotional make-up, and taste of the individual member.[10]

The random improviser's goal is singular novelty, and this aim results in at least two positive values: it multiplies and expands media, and it makes new and different demands on the listener's acuity of perception. Therein the music begins to demand its price, as noise and silence become relevant.

[9]Quoted by David Hamilton, "A Synoptic View of New Music," *High Fidelity*, 18 (1968), p. 56.

[10]Liner notes by Ornette Coleman, "Ornette Coleman: Change of the Century" (Atlantic 1327), 1959.

When a style exists, perceptive attention focuses on the permissible; when style is absent, all is allowable, and listeners, to function sympathetically, must try to accept all stimuli that result from the immediate situation.

It would be a gross exaggeration to say that all the music of Ornette Coleman and his group consists of random improvisation, for this certainly is not the case. His recording of *Bird Food*,[11] a blues-based composition, takes the standard twelve-measure format and forces it irregularly into the **AABA** pop-song format. Each **A** is a blues variant: after a two-measure introduction, the first **A** uses the first nine-and-one-half measures of a blues chorus; the second **A** uses eleven measures; and the last uses ten.[12]

Likewise, not all non-jazz avant-garde improvisation is random; in fact, most improvisation occurs within composed pieces with much structural integrity. Pieces that use indeterminate notation within the context of a composer- or leader-dominated score usually expect the improviser to create new music that is contextually fitting and stylistically correct, a seeming contradiction since style, in the sense of fixed norms, is not actually established. Attention to ensemble—a sensitive regard for the efforts of the other performers—is also demanded. What Coleman brought to jazz was a new set of values, not the absence of any values. To quote one informed observer:

> The album *Free Jazz*[13] is one of the monuments of his art. Coleman collected eight jazz musicians in a New York recording studio in 1964 [1960], and grouped them in two quartets: himself, Donald Cherry (trumpet), Scott La Faro (bass), and Billy Higgins (drums) in one; Eric Dolphy (bass clarinet), Freddie Hubbard (trumpet), Charlie Haden (bass), and Ed Blackwell (drums) in the other. With no rehearsal, the eight men performed a free improvisation based on no previously known tunes, no planned chord progressions, no planned structure. . . . In listening, one can notice that although the players listen to one another—an idea played by one may be picked up by others, who play it in their own style—each player, even the drummers and bass players, goes his own way rhythmically, harmonically, and structurally. To ears conditioned to traditional jazz, or traditional music of any kind, this music is chaos. To ears that can listen in other ways, it is a fascinating and exciting collage, rich in detail, that changes with each hearing, depending on which instrument or instruments one listens to most closely.[14]

[11] Atlantic 1327.

[12] See the author's transcription of *Bird Food* in "Constructive Elements in Jazz Improvisation," *Journal of the American Musicological Society*, 27 (1974), p. 293.

[13] Atlantic SD 1364. An excerpt is included in *SCCJ* 105.

[14] Charles Hamm, "Changing Patterns in Society and Music," in Charles Hamm, et al., ed., *Contemporary Music and Music Cultures*, p. 68 f.

Coleman's drift to free jazz can be seen in the transitional nature of *Lonely Woman* (*SCCJ* 103) and *Congeniality* (*SCCJ* 104). Both use a composed tune to introduce and close the piece, a framework for improvised solos; both use the bebop pattern of unison performance of the riff by lead instruments; and both still rely on an underlying pulse that is less rigid but still apparent and continuous. They both differ from bebop jazz numbers in that they omit the piano, which is unnecessary in an environment lacking chord progressions; they stretch phrase lengths into plastic shapes; and they employ improvisations that lack the goal orientation of harmonically directed solos. But discarding traditional values does not imply the casting away of all values, for the solos have motivic integrity, the ensemble adheres cohesively through timbral and rhythmic organization, and the nuances of ensemble balance are carefully maintained by the members of the organization.

The 1947 Dexter Gordon recording of *Bikini* (*SCCJ* 75) was modern for its day and exhibits the fully developed characteristics of bebop, the obvious stylistic parent of Coleman's music (*NW* 284, II/7). The 1959 Coleman recording of *Congeniality* was modern for its day but demonstrated, instead of a fully developed style, a distillation or abstraction of bebop stylistic elements that are reorganized and combined with some of the newer musical thoughts that no longer derive from jazz. *Free Jazz* (*SCCJ* 105), recorded in 1960, was the masterpiece that broke with tradition, set the standard, influenced the musicians, and truly moved jazz in a new direction. In this performance, we find improvisation on a grand scale and hear a unique sound never before employed in jazz. This effort penetrated the unknown and opened a new frontier. Periodically throughout this undulating musical voyage, the music coalesces, suggests form and direction, and then melts again into overlapping layers of pitch, timbre, and rhythm.

Coleman, the true frontiersman, was restless and seemingly driven to constant exploration. In his 1961 recording *Cross Breeding*,[15] his search for his "real" black voice caused him to return to the tenor sax, the instrument of his youth. In his quest for inspiration from African-American roots, he experiments with another timbre, the robust, full-bodied sound of the tenor. His melodic and rhythmic ideas are a natural continuation of his progress to date.

In 1965, confronted with a lack of enthusiasm for his music at home, he traveled to Europe and continued to experiment. As if suddenly aware of the ideas of John Cage, he recorded *Silence*,[16] at his "Great London Concert." Here he examines the syntactical use of an absence of sound. Passages of solo and ensemble work are interrupted by long voids, and the relationships between negative space and densely filled improvisations force the

---

[15] Atlantic 1394.
[16] Arista 1900.

listener to move up to a new level of awareness. The reaction of the London audience is interesting too—we can detect their confusion and embarrassment when they start to applaud at the wrong places.

During this phase of his career, Coleman began to spend considerable portions of his time composing works for classical ensembles. In addition to spontaneously creating new music on the band stand, he tried his hand at the drafting table with pen and manuscript paper. However, in his composition *Forms and Sounds for Wind Quintet*,[17] which was recorded in the same year as *Silence*, we hear that his writing is stiff, unnatural, and heavily dependent on repetition and repetitive ideas. He apparently was dissatisfied with this version and recorded *Forms and Sounds* again in America in 1967.[18] In this version much of the regularity and predictability of the earlier performance disappears. Still, in this new arena Coleman lacks the training and discipline of other chamber music composers writing at the time, such as Gunther Schuller, Elliott Carter, Pierre Boulez, and Leon Kirchner. Coleman's notated compositions in large form are interesting to study, for they display, from a different perspective, the vision of this creative artist. These works do not, however, stand up well beside the considerable body of chamber music composed in the 1960s. The spontaneity of the experienced improvising performer is not apparent in his composed works. One hears this in *Space Flight*[19] and *Saints and Soldiers*[20] as well; both stem from this period, and both have the same compositional problems.

For the remainder of the decade, Coleman was torn in three directions: exploiting and perfecting his established style, repeatedly searching for something new, and occasionally going back to roots for sustenance and inspiration. We hear the familiar Coleman in *Faces and Places*,[21] recorded at the Golden Circle in Stockholm. Here the jazz master is back at work in a friendly environment and the empathetic responses of the musicians creates jazz of the first quality. Similarly, in *The Garden of Souls*,[22] recorded after his return to New York in 1967, we observe the improviser at home with arco bass, free drumming, and passages of parallel fourths. Newness or unusual novelty are not present, and the sounds are satisfying, coherent, emotional. And when we hear *Broadway Blues*[23] or *Good Old Days*[24] we know that Cole-

[17] *Forms and Sounds for Wind Quintet* from "The Great London Concert" (Arista 1900).
[18] *Forms and Sounds* from "The Music of Ornette Coleman" (RCA 2982).
[19] RCA 2982.
[20] RCA 2982.
[21] Blue Note 4224.
[22] Blue Note 84287.
[23] Blue Note 84287.
[24] Blue Note 84246.

man is once again reveling in the fountainhead of jazz, the straight-ahead blues. While Coleman blows a simple riff and presses on with his characteristic rhythmic drive in *Good Old Days*, we hear his ten-year-old son, Denardo, flailing away on drums.

Coleman, the explorer, moved to brass. On *The Empty Foxhole*[25] we hear his new involvement with trumpet. His son, on drums, contributed a sometimes random element to the overall sound. Given the somewhat "random" style of the piece, this kind of drumming is not entirely inappropriate. Then Coleman, the explorer, moved to strings. On *Sound Gravitation*[26] we hear his attempts to play the violin. Although criticized at the time for his performance abilities on the violin, Coleman is bringing new textures and timbres to jazz through his unorthodox approach to the instrument. We do not hear the violin playing of a Joe Venuti or a Jean-Luc Ponty; instead, we struggle with the musician as he seeks to use the violin as a chordal, percussive, and timbral instrument rather than as a traditional melodic generator.

MUSICAL REACTIONS

Several musicians were immediately taken by the music of Ornette Coleman, but to varying degrees. John Lewis, an early defender of free jazz, recorded *Django* in 1960 with his Modern Jazz Quartet (*SCCJ* 95). Although his words of support indicate an intellectual acceptance of the new music, his recording shows a personal rejection. *Django* follows the well-trod path of his earlier recordings with the quartet, and the listener quickly feels comfortable with the circle-of-fifths progressions, the vibraphone sonorities, and the modified bebop solos.

Charles Mingus, on the other hand, absorbed the new music as a revitalizing influence (*NW* 242, II/4). His 1963 recording of *Hora Decubitus* (*SCCJ* 94) shows an interesting combination of new ideas blended with some of the oldest. The basic structural framework of the piece is the twelve-bar blues, but the sonority is atypical of mainstream jazz groups. The string-bass lead for the introduction is followed by more low-range sonorities played by the baritone saxophone. The blues begin gradually to separate at the seams, and all the while, a second ensemble sound of the remaining instruments, recorded on a separate track, builds in dynamics to effect a textural counterpoint with the first sound. Many jazz musicians were distressed at the seeming absence of beat in free jazz even when they were attracted to some of its features, for it is generally accepted that a solid beat, the jazz musician's sense of time,

[25] Blue Note 84246.
[26] Blue Note 84246.

Charles Mingus (1922–79).

was the key to swing. In *Hora Decubitus*, Mingus attempts to preserve both the beat and the blues within the context of greater freedom of sonority and solo improvisation.

The music of Cecil Taylor shows a preoccupation with complexity. His music boasts well-organized melodies; clever orchestral sonorities; a large repertoire of harmonic materials such as tone clusters, nonfunctional harmonies, and extended chords in multiple voicings; and solid formal structures that are organized on principles other than melodic or harmonic repetition. The free jazz of Ornette Coleman provided external support for the kinds of musical thinking in which Taylor was already engaged, an approach that had already crossed the borderline from jazz to the avant-garde of the university composers. On the most superficial level, the musics of Coleman and Taylor are similar—neither employs traditional melodies and harmonies—but beyond that, they are totally different. The former depends heavily on chance, the latter is carefully organized. The former has widely varying performances of the same piece, the latter polishes a singular musical idea.

Taylor's composition and performance of *Enter Evening* (*SCCJ* 101) brings European compositional thought to jazz as much as it brings the skills and habits of jazz to the workshop of the modern classical composer. Taylor has purposely removed from his jazz any ties to the world of entertainment and dancing, and created a music that can find acceptance and be understood only on a concert stage or on a recording destined for serious and well-trained listeners. At this point, we can observe that avant-garde jazz has cost working jazz musicians more than one pound of flesh: it has been intellectualized to a point where a popular market is no longer possible. The listeners for *Enter Evening* must be as musically sophisticated as the performers themselves, a somewhat Utopian dream. Jazz artists of the 1960s found it difficult, almost for the first time, to support themselves by their music. The "new thing" had opened some doors, but it was even more rapidly closing others. Milton Babbitt's outcry in "Who Cares If You Listen?"[27] was beginning to take its toll on musicians who depended on the public, rather than universities and foundations, for support.

Summarizing the year in jazz in 1963, one critic wrote:

> The disparity between the popularity of jazz on records and in person grew apace. There were more jazz records than ever, but there were fewer rooms across the country where the music could be found. In those New York clubs where jazz and only jazz had been the rule, sick comedians and folksingers now provided considerable competition, and the prospect of the hootenanny as a substitute for the jam session became a very real and dismal possibility.[28]

Some of the leading jazz musicians rejected the "new thing," and one, Stan Getz, came up with a marketable new sound that caught popular attention for several years. In 1963, he and guitarist Charlie Byrd recorded a "Jazz Samba" album,[29] and the unexpected popularity of *Desafinado* launched *bossa nova*, a new fad, onto the commercial lanes of American music. Brazilian "experts" were flown to New York for a Carnegie Hall concert, and soon cut-rate records were flooding the display racks in drug stores and grocery stores.

A CENTRAL FIGURE— JOHN COLTRANE

In the parlance of youth, John Coltrane "had it all together," yet his mastery of musical materials and his inspiring leadership were achieved only after years of bitter struggle and inner turmoil. When at the age of forty his star

[27] Milton Babbitt, "Who Cares If You Listen?" *High Fidelity*, February 1958.
[28] Stanley Dance, "The Year in Jazz," *Music Journal Anthology 1963* (1963), p. 44.
[29] Verve 8432.

finally ascended to the zenith of the profession, death swept him away. He was born in Hamlet, North Carolina, in 1926, the same year as Miles Davis, served his musical apprenticeship during the 1940s and '50s working with Eddie Vinson, Howard McGhee, Dizzy Gillespie, Earl Bostic, and Johnny Hodges, and first began playing tenor saxophone with the Miles Davis Quintet in late 1955. His performances at that time received adverse criticism, but understanding John Coltrane and his music necessarily means interpreting his work in its context—that is, the music of Miles Davis, Sonny Rollins, and Thelonious Monk, and the American social issues of the 1950s and 1960s.

Not until the end of the '50s did Coltrane acquire the stature of a giant. He was not a prodigy, his apprenticeship was slow, and his unique voice was not apparent in his youth. He jobbed and studied steadily through the 1940s and became a respected professional, but he was just one of several first-rank tenor saxophonists until he was spotlighted in the Miles Davis Quintet. Coleman Hawkins, Ben Webster, and Lester Young were the venerated establishment figures; Stan Getz, Gerry Mulligan, and Lee Konitz were the young all-stars; and Sonny Stitt and Sonny Rollins were the comers to watch. The critics viewed Rollins, not Coltrane, as the saxophonist most likely to climb the steps to Parnassus, but Rollins's personal problems affected his music in a strange and unpredictable manner. Both were extremely introspective about their work, and both had problems with drugs and alcohol, but Rollins started a pattern of "sabbaticals" during which he suddenly disappeared from public view and established his own personal retreat for practice, recuperation, and contemplation. Then just as suddenly he would return fresh and inspiring. However, Rollins stepped out of the limelight one time too many and returned to New York to discover that Coltrane, in 1958–59, had replaced him and raced ahead. "Trane" became, and would remain, the leading player of his instrument and, simultaneously, the most significant figure in jazz until his death eight years later. In 1961, when he established himself as leader of his own group and gave vent to his unique sound and compositional / improvisational concept, Coltrane was the most influential jazz artist of the period for musicians of all instruments, outdistancing even Miles Davis. Every eager young jazz musician who grew up in the 1960s or '70s and moved into prominence was a student of Coltrane in one way or another. His recordings were the new Gospel of Jazz. Many of the older players, contemporaries and seniors alike, were also influenced by his music, his commitment as an artist, his philosophy of life, and his sincere humility. His ascendancy went hand-in-glove with the powerful black Civil Rights movement of the 1960s, and his own search for musical identity and freedom of expression was stimulated by black contemporary thought about roots, equality, freedom, African traditions, mysticism, and social conscience.

Nineteen forty-seven was a significant year for John Coltrane. At the time

John Coltrane (1926–67).

he was an alto saxophonist recently returned from a stint in the navy. That year, on tour in California with the King Kolax band, he had an opportunity to meet his idol, Charlie Parker. Parker, just released from Camarillo State Hospital in January, went to the studio with Erroll Garner and recorded his *Dark Shadows* session in February. Coltrane attended, and that led to a jam session with Parker. Even though this encounter was memorable in the young saxophonist's life, Parker's overwhelming influence was innocently side-tracked that same year when Coltrane accepted a job in the new band of Eddie "Cleanhead" Vinson. Although Coltrane had worked with tenorists Bill Barron and Benny Golson, he disliked the instrument. However, the leader, Vinson, played alto and assigned Coltrane a tenor chair. Coltrane speaks of this:

> When I went with Eddie Vinson on tenor, a wider area of listening opened up for me. On alto, Bird had been my whole influence, but on tenor I found there was no one man whose ideas were so dominant as Charlie's were on alto. Therefore, I drew from all the men I heard during this period on tenor, especially Lester Young and his melodic phrasing. I found out about Coleman Hawkins later and became fascinated by his arpeggios and the way he played. I got a copy of *Body and Soul* and listened real hard. Even though I dug Pres [Young], as I grew musically, I appreciated Hawk more and more.[30]

[30] John Coltrane, quoted in J. C. Thomas, *Chasin the Trane: The Music and Mystique of John Coltrane*, p. 42.

During this period with Vinson, Coltrane was already drinking heavily; not long after, he was on drugs. Gradually, the dual habit began to destroy his life. Late in 1949, Dizzy Gillespie hired Vinson musicians as replacements in his big band, and here Coltrane made his first commercial recordings, back on alto but with no solos. Among the musicians he worked with was tenorist Paul Gonsalves, soon to become a featured soloist in the Duke Ellington Orchestra. There was also a period when Yusef Lateef played tenor with the band, and Lateef probably initiated Coltrane's investigation of Eastern religions and philosophies, a path that eventually saved him from drug addiction and led him to modal improvisation.

The next few years saw Coltrane working a hodgepodge of professional gigs: bebop with the Dizzy Gillespie Sextet; rhythm-and-blues with Gay Crosse and His Good Humor Six; and swing with Earl Bostic and Johnny Hodges. In 1954 he had to leave Hodges because of his alcohol and drug problems, and returning to Philadelphia, he discovered that his reputation had preceded him. He found little work and, at twenty-eight years of age, had recorded only twenty bars of solo work. Nineteen fifty-five stands out as the crucial year in the careers of three men: Miles Davis, Sonny Rollins, and John Coltrane.

Although well known, Davis was not working often. When he did, his tenor of choice was Rollins. Up to this time, when he toured on the road, he could bring only one musician along—the rest of the group had to be hired locally—and he chose his drummer, "Philly" Joe Jones. When Davis gained sudden prominence in 1955 at the Newport Jazz Festival, he organized a regular quintet. He, Philly Joe Jones, and Philadelphia resident Red Garland made three of the five. Rollins's drug problem had sent him into "retirement" in Chicago, so Jones and Garland talked Davis into hiring Coltrane, a fellow Philadelphian. The critics did not approve—they wanted Sonny Stitt. The public was backing the competition, the Max Roach / Clifford Brown ensemble, which Davis found doubly difficult, because not only was his music more experimental, he was having problems with his musicians. In spite of their talent they were spaced out, notoriously so. In addition to coping with his habit, Coltrane was searching for a style, dealing with a new wife, and providing for an instant family, his bride's five-year-old daughter. Musically, the combo had problems: for bebop virtuosity, Davis could not compete with Clifford Brown; Jones was a *very* loud drummer; Garland was a good accompanimental pianist but not a great soloist; the bassist, Paul Chambers, was young and inexperienced; and Coltrane did not have it all together yet. Still, the group held the seeds of greatness. Its recording of *Two Bass Hit*[31] of

[31] Columbia KC2 36278.

October 1955 and a re-recording of the same tune in 1958[32] display Coltrane's full-toned, hard bop technique spurred on by the propulsive rhythms of Jones's drums. Coltrane's 1956 solo on 'Round Midnight[33] is brilliant, a series of musical events that follow a clear path from melodic ornamentation to harmonic and modal exploration. Coltrane moves further and further afield, interspersing whole-tone and modal scales over tonal chords, scales, and arpeggios. He causes harmonic shifts by delaying or anticipating resolutions over the bass and piano patterns. He mixes irregular phrase patterns that end or begin away from cadential points. He was, at last, beginning to show his genius. That same year he challenged the competition when he recorded Oleo,[34] Sonny Rollins's own finger-twisting composition. In this performance, Garland, Chambers, and Jones prove that they were the best rhythm section in jazz as they supply supportive, swinging, and non-obtrusive piano, smooth walking bass, and beautiful brush work. The apprentice period was over.

Coltrane had proved his mastery of the music (see Transcription 11, *Blue Train*, from 1957); he needed only to master himself. He did that in 1957, when with the help of a Christian mother and Muslim wife he went cold turkey on both drugs and alcohol. Later that same year, he recorded with Thelonious Monk, whose unorthodox approach to jazz exerted profound influence. Coltrane received enough inspiration from this unique personality to effect a noticeable change in his musical thinking. He began to play more extended solos, thematically organized rather than harmonically derived and directed, and when he rejoined Davis later that year, his solo style had a new distinctive character that critics soon labeled "sheets of sound." A flurry of notes, sometimes over modal scales, an extended range, a new mastery of the upper partials of his instrument, began to draw critical acclaim and attention from fellow jazz musicians.

According to J. J. Johnson, "Since Charlie Parker, the most electrifying sound that I've heard in contemporary jazz was Coltrane playing with Monk at The Five Spot. . . . It was incredible, like Diz and Bird."[35] Monk served as a teacher who reshaped Coltrane's musical thinking, and for the first time we hear what Ira Gitler labeled sheets of sound. Coltrane began a philosophy of intense exploration, marked by a new sense of asymmetry and irregularity, and a concept of groups of notes (cluster-chordal thinking), which he learned from Monk's teaching and example. Monk's sparse accompaniment and his

[32] Columbia PC 9428.
[33] Columbia PC 8649.
[34] Prestige 7129.
[35] Reported by Ira Gitler on his liner notes for "Thelonious Monk with John Coltrane" (Jazzland [Fantasy] J946).

habit of laying out entirely during Coltrane's solos gave Coltrane the support he needed for his new exploratory style. Coltrane said, in 1960,

> Working with Monk brought me close to a musical architect of the highest order. I felt I learned from him in every way—through the senses, theoretically, technically. I would talk to Monk about musical problems and he would sit at the piano and show me the answers by playing them. I could watch him play and find out the things I wanted to know. Also, I could see a lot of things that I didn't know about at all.[36]

On his 1957 recording with Monk, *Trinkle, Tinkle*,[37] Coltrane displays brilliant saxophone improvisation, flowing technique, developmental thinking, and extended tonal sonorities with but a hint of the "sheets of sound" to come. According to McCoy Tyner, 1957 was also the year Coltrane was working out *Giant Steps* in Philadelphia, even though it wasn't recorded until 1959.

Back with Davis, Coltrane went to the studio in 1959, along with Bill Evans, Cannonball Adderley, Paul Chambers, and Jimmy Cobb for the "Kind of Blue" session. His solo on *So What* (*SCCJ* 99) displays the new improvisational freedom along modally organized lines that Coltrane was attempting. The pianist of the group, Bill Evans, writes in the liner notes of the album:

> Miles conceived these settings only hours before the recording dates and arrived with sketches which indicated to the group what was to be played. Therefore, you will hear something close to pure spontaneity in these performances. The group had never played these pieces prior to the recordings. . . . Although it is not uncommon for a jazz musician to be expected to improvise on new material at a recording session, the character of these pieces represents a particular challenge.[38]

The music and thinking of this group was to give Coltrane his first exposure to the style of playing that would characterize most of his work in the 1960s. At this time, too, he began to take an interest in the music of India, a music that is primarily melodic, devoid of harmony, and organized along principles unrelated to traditional modes of Western musical thought. In the same year, 1959, he recorded the album "Giant Steps";[39] his composition and solo on *Giant Steps* (see Transcription 10 and Listening Guide 15) became a new jazz

[36] Ibid.
[37] Ibid.
[38] Columbia GCB 60.
[39] Atlantic 5003.

John Coltrane, c. 1958.

standard, a number imitated by all the young saxophonists apprenticing in the trade (*NAJ* 15).

For performance with his own group during the '60s, Coltrane tended to select pieces with fewer chord changes. To this open framework he often attached a dense melodic covering of long improvisations, free-flowing lines, and seamless melodies. One hears the striking change in Coltrane's tone from the earlier light sound, developed probably as an altoist in imitation of Charlie Parker, to a new, more personal, full-bodied sonority, a tone that becomes hard, resonant, loud, almost brittle, and angry. Monk's spare structures on a bare stage, open support, and lack of clutter were one solution for Coltrane's growing voluminous style of melodic improvisation. McCoy Tyner's left-hand pedal points would be another.

Coltrane sensed a lack of unifying element in the free jazz of Ornette Coleman, and he found his solution to the problem in the playing of pianist McCoy Tyner and in the modal thinking developed in his earlier days with Davis and Monk. Tyner's use of pedal point in the left hand helped organize pitches around a tonal center without resorting to functional harmony and gave Coltrane's free improvisations a sense of focus that was absent in the work of his predecessors. This pedal, which resembles the sound of the drone strings of classical Indian instruments in performance, provides a pitch level around which the musical structure can be organized with both increased tension and eventual release.

His recording of *Alabama* in 1963 (*SCCJ* 102) opens with the drone and a simple statement of melodic units or patterns that will be expanded and reorganized in the measures to follow. Even the brief section in regularly measured meter holds to the scalar organization of the modal materials. The ending, which recapitulates the beginning, employs more activity in the accompaniment, to avoid the monotony of a literal repeat. Even so, *Alabama* is a relatively short number with the air of a jazz ballad; consequently, it can be viewed as a step along the road to greater freedom and more intense explorations.

"A Love Supreme,"[40] released in early 1965, was the culmination of Coltrane's thinking in this manner. *Pursuance* is a devastating orgy of furious saxophone and drum interplay. The shrill cries and blur of notes issuing from the saxophone are relentless in the chase. There is no question that the extramusical ideas stemming from the mysticism that was beginning to pervade Coltrane's thinking had its effect on the sound produced. At this point in his career, Coltrane achieved his highest public acclaim; he won simultaneously the Record of the Year award for "A Love Supreme," Jazzman of

[40] Impulse (A) S77.

the Year award, and Tenor Saxophonist of the Year award in the 1965 *Down Beat* reader's poll.

Almost immediately, however, Coltrane formed a new group, augmented by two trumpets, two alto saxophones, two more tenor saxophones, and a second bass player. *Ascension*, recorded in June 1965, is a seamless fabric of wild and turbulent instrumental and ensemble sounds ripping apart. Sheets of sound rain down in a cloudburst of incredible activity. But this total group improvisation created a music that is curiously static, for like a tragedy without comic relief, the principle of unity and variety is violated in favor of one or the other. His last recording session took place in February 1967, and suddenly, at the age of forty, he was dead. With the most intense, effective, and vibrant leader of avant-garde jazz gone, the new music floundered, lost its momentum, and began to give way.

But jazz was not dead, and different ideas took hold quickly.

OUT IN FRONT— MILES DAVIS IN THE '60S AND '70S

No jazz musician of the 1960s and early 1970s commanded more respect than trumpeter Miles Davis. Whatever he recorded became the current jazz mode, not because a worshiping fan club idolized his every movement, but because he had the gift for finding and hiring the most promising young jazz musicians for his groups and giving them a sense of musical direction and awareness that stemmed from his own current thoughts and remarkable talent. When Coleman and Coltrane were making the headlines in the early 1960s, Davis did not jump on the first available bandwagon but, instead, stepped out of the limelight temporarily to listen and ponder. He remained professionally active in the early '60s, but his efforts took the direction of solidifying the ideas of the late '50s—more recording with Gil Evans[41] and further work along the lines of the "Kind of Blue" session. *So What* and a Davis blues, *Walkin'*, were recorded and rerecorded as late as 1964.[42]

Miles Davis was literally beaten into the Black Power movement of the 1960s. On August 26, 1959, he had just finished a Voice of America broadcast from Birdland in Manhattan and walked an attractive white woman up to the street to catch a taxi. As she rode off, a white policeman walked up and told Davis to move on. Davis pointed up to the marquee and said, "I'm working

---

[41] 1961, Columbia CL 1812; and 1962, Columbia CL 2106.
[42] Columbia CL 2453.

downstairs. That's my name up there, Miles Davis." The cop answered, "I don't care where you work, I said move on! If you don't move on I'm going to arrest you." Before long, a white detective moved in, Davis was billy-clubbed, handcuffed, hauled to the hospital and the 54th Precinct station, and charged with assault, battery, and resisting arrest. As a result, he had his cabaret license revoked and could not work in New York City for a while.[43] The incident left Davis bitter and cynical, though not racist. It affected his attitude, his dress and appearance, and his music, and it seems to have stimulated his interest in things African. His was not an isolated incident. But America was about to change: in 1960, black students staged the first sit-in to integrate a lunch counter in Greensboro, North Carolina.

When Coltrane left the group in 1960, Davis tried altoist Sonny Stitt, but was dissatisfied. He settled temporarily on Hank Mobley, tenor. Their recording of *Someday My Prince Will Come*,[44] with Wynton Kelly, Paul Chambers, and Jimmy Cobb is swinging but very straight ahead, very conservative. That same year Davis first heard the music of Ornette Coleman. He admired Coleman's avoidance of clichés, but he neither liked nor trusted the music—it was too radically different from his way of thinking. He apparently sensed the need to keep up to date, and his solution was to start looking to younger musicians for inspiration.

The twenty-three-year-old pianist Herbie Hancock was added to the band in early 1963, and the rhythm section was rounded out with twenty-six-year-old bassist Ron Carter and eighteen-year-old drummer Tony Williams. Davis was now thirty-seven, and the musical personalities of these younger players affected his music radically. Hancock, although a classically trained virtuoso, was just moving through a gospel-influenced jazz style and had composed a funky rock-blues piece, *Watermelon Man*, the year before. Ron Carter was from the new school of bass virtuosi. In addition to taking on rhythm section responsibilities, he was capable of extraordinary solos in the upper register, double- and triple-stop performances, and masterful arco playing. Williams was more than a jazz drummer; he was a thoroughly modern percussionist, a young musician who sculpted sound with timbre, the variety of tonal colors available from cymbals, toms, drums, and accessories. When the group recorded at the Antibes International Jazz Festival in France in July 1963,[45] George Coleman ably held down the tenor spot, but Davis continued to search for a replacement for Coltrane. From Coleman, Davis quickly moved on to Sam Rivers and just as quickly settled on Wayne Shorter. In the Antibes recording of *Milestones* we can hear the free jazz influence in Davis's playing,

[43] Miles Davis with Quincy Troupe, *Miles: The Autobiography*, p. 238 ff.
[44] Columbia 1656.
[45] Columbia CS8983.

Miles Davis and Wayne Shorter, August 1967.

somewhat reminiscent of Don Cherry's pocket trumpet performances. With Shorter in the Quintet, however, Davis was now the leader of another classic ensemble—five instrumentalists finely attuned to each other, substantial musicians with similar musical goals and aspirations. Their 1965 album, "Live At The Plugged Nickel,"[46] lists Hancock on acoustic piano and Carter on acoustic bass—a technical differentiation between acoustic and electric instruments that signals the major change that was happening in jazz. To that point, Davis was master of "straight ahead," that is, advanced bebop, but "fusion jazz," that is, a mixture of jazz and rock, was coming on strong. That was the year, 1965, in which Coltrane recorded his "Ascension" album, but Coltrane's line of thought apparently held little interest for Davis. His ears were attuned to both bebop and the electric and electronic instruments of rock. Both his drummer, Tony Williams, and his saxophonist, Wayne Shorter, would prove to be freeing influences on their leader. Unfortunately, 1965 also marked the beginning of serious health problems that would afflict Davis for many years. His hip required an operation, and he broke a leg. Ironically, he recorded, "Miles Smiles"[47] the next year. Every piece in the

[46] Columbia C2 38266.
[47] Columbia PC2601.

album is masterful in conception and execution. With the support and influence of his younger sidemen and his recent collaborator, Gil Evans, Davis is heard as he progresses through a new phase of artistic growth and greater maturity. The elegant yet emotionally intense ballad "Circle" (*NAJ* 18) contains three striking solos, Davis's muted and reflective understatement, Shorter's lyrical essay, and Hancock's classical exploration. Each performer's personality remains distinct; still all three seem to capture the circular feeling of a sweeping Viennese waltz. (See Listening Guide 18.)

The *Miles Smiles* album, with Shorter, Hancock, Carter, and Williams, marks yet another turning point in the career of Miles Davis. As Ronald Atkins explains:

> Often a man will stagnate artistically as a result of plodding constantly through the same material, until he reaches the stage where music no longer offers a challenge.
>
> To avoid this fate, the wise leader surrounds himself with young musicians of talent and lets their ideas affect the music. Davis has always done this. . . . Once Shorter joined the Quintet, the improvisations became even freer from harmonic ties than before, and Davis's own playing took on new characteristics.[48]

While Coltrane and Coleman, and their younger exponents like Archie Shepp in New York and Roscoe Mitchell and Joseph Jarman in Chicago, were carrying the implications of free jazz to the extremes of undifferentiated novelty, Davis capitalized on the best ideas of both artists and constructed a framework of musical guideposts within each composition to satisfy the demands of tension and release. He added a dramatic intensity to the fabric of free fluctuation by imposing recognizable shapes of written melodic patterns that recur throughout the progress of extended pieces, lending a ritornello or rondo sense of unity to the long improvisations.

Then, while exploring fewer restrictions and looser structures on the one hand, Davis turned about in "Nefertiti"[49] to work with tighter organization and more disciplined ensemble interplay. Suddenly, he found the means to blend both these concepts into a unified whole. His recording "Bitches Brew"[50] had a new personnel roster of twelve musicians plus himself and a new instrumentation that included four percussionists and as many as three electric pianos. The sculptured sounds of the electronic instruments provide a

---

[48] Max Harrison, et al., *Modern Jazz: The Essential Records*, p. 90.
[49] Columbia CS 9594.
[50] Columbia GP 26.

Miles Davis, c. 1965.

structure of floating instrumental timbre underpinning the liquid instrumental solos of Shorter and Davis. The concept of rondo form, which uses a recurring musical passage or idea, gave vitality and a sense of direction to each of the pieces. The new timbres of the electronic instruments and the new rhythmic flexibility of the young musicians gave Davis one of his best opportunities to explore a variety of soloistic devices. His natural lyricism and ear for color allowed him to create sounds that mesh and contrast with the tonal fabric of the orchestra.

The music Davis recorded during the last four years of the decade is fascinating to study, for he not only made overt social statements, he explored the rapidly changing world of electronic instruments, studio recording, and engineer manipulation. In 1965, a Civil Rights march took place in Alabama; in 1966 Davis recorded "Freedom Jazz Dance."[51] In addition to the extra-musical social commentary, the solos moved one more step toward freedom: they were of no fixed length. The playing, consciously or unconsciously, reflects the free jazz influence of Ornette Coleman and John Coltrane. Davis also uses the "tape-splice" solo, which he introduced in 1965 in *Iris* on his "E.S.P." album.[52] Instead of melody, melodic fragment became the improvisational order for the day.

Nefertiti,[53] *Sorcerer,*[54] *Bitches Brew,*[55] and *Filles de Kilimanjaro,*[56] like *Freedom Jazz Dance,* were all united by "Black is Beautiful" themes. Pictures of white Americans had disappeared from Davis's album covers long ago. Now, photos of black Americans were being replaced by drawings of black Africans.

It was on his 1968 "Filles" album that Davis went electric—Hancock moved to electric piano and Carter played electric bass. However, the 1969 "In a Silent Way" album was Miles's first serious exploration into electronic jazz performance. Wayne Shorter brought Joe Zawinul, a virtuoso synthesizer player and a former associate of his in the Maynard Ferguson Orchestra, together with Davis. On this album, Davis also teamed up with English guitarist, John McLaughlin (also known as Mahavishnu), and British bass player Dave Holland. Chick Corea, who had replaced Herbie Hancock as the regular pianist of the group, was thoroughly familiar with electronic keyboards; and Hancock was invited back for the session as a third keyboardist! The last theme statement of *In a Silent Way*—a repeat of the first state-

[51] Columbia PC 9401.
[52] Columbia C1 2350.
[53] Columbia CS 9594.
[54] Columbia CS 9532.
[55] Columbia GP 26.
[56] Columbia PC 9750.

ment—was spliced on at the end, and *Shh/Peaceful,* another piece on the album, is a half-length performance stretched out double through another tape splice. Because the end result was largely a product of studio engineering, this was music that could not be performed live in a club or at a concert. This method of production radically altered the way musicians executed their music and the way listeners heard these sounds. The jazz aesthetic of live improvisation was seriously challenged here with studio-produced music. The creative responsibility for the end product was moving away from the musician and toward the audio engineer.

On his electronic masterpiece, *Bitches Brew,* Davis played his trumpet with amplification in the studio, effectively converting his acoustic trumpet into an electronic instrument. Part of the time, he apparently also used an echoplex, a device that artificially creates echo and reverberation. But the key to Davis's genius lay in his ability to inject the human element, the communication of player to listener, and his own personality into his music regardless of the external factors affecting a live performance or recording. Ian Carr sensed this crucial element when he wrote about Davis's solo on *Miles Runs the Voodoo Down:*

> His tone is more vocalized than ever—a human, crying sound. After this quiet start, he develops his ideas with swooping phrases which alternately use the blues scale and then chromaticism. He makes some death-defying forays into the upper register, and his playing is alive with slurs, smears, spaces, screams, long lines, short tense phrases. It is trumpet playing at a fantastic level, not least for the blazing feeling which he seems barely able to control.[57]

But Davis was in control—of his music, his musicians, and, for the moment, the destiny of jazz. This album, and the sidemen who worked with Davis on this recording, would have an overwhelming impact on the music of the next two decades.

THE NEW GROUPS

A key figure in jazz thought of the '60s was George Russell, a college-trained musician whose theoretical writing, *The Lydian Chromatic Concept of Tonal Organization for Improvisation,*[58] influenced countless young aspiring jazz musicians. Born in Cincinnati in 1923, Russell apprenticed as a drummer and arranger with Benny Carter and later wrote arrangements for Earl Hines

---

[57] Ian Carr, *Miles Davis: A Biography,* p. 197.
[58] New York: Concept Publishing Col, 1959.

George Russell relaxing at a recording session.

and Dizzy Gillespie. Gillespie recorded Russell's Afro-Cuban originals *Cubana be* and *Cubana bop* in 1947,[59] and these Russell charts were some of the most exploratory orchestrations the band played during that period. A few years later, the Lee Konitz Sextet with Miles Davis and Max Roach recorded two Russell originals, *Odjenar* and *Ezz-thetic*,[60] in the then-current sound of cool. By that time, Russell had already achieved stature as an arranger for Claude Thornhill, Charlie Ventura, Artie Shaw, and Buddy DeFranco, and it was at this point in his career that he completed work on his jazz treatise. In it he reexamines the traditional tonal resources of jazz and reinterprets the chromatic implications from the point of view of Lydian modality (loosely speaking, a scale made up by playing the white keys on a piano starting on F). He offered a practical demonstration of these ideas in his 1956 recording, "The Jazz Workshop,"[61] an album demonstrating a good balance between composition and improvisation.

At the Brandeis Jazz Festival in 1957, Russell presented his extended composition, *All About Rosie*, an eleven-minute work written in three sections, or movements, as a large concert piece. Scored for thirteen musicians,

[59] Victor 20-3145, reissued LPM 2398.
[60] Prestige 753 and 853, reissued Prestige 7013.
[61] Victor LPM 1372.

the instrumentation is not standard for the jazz repertoire. In addition to two trumpets and a trombone, two saxophones, and a rhythm section of piano, bass, guitar, and drums—a not unusual nonet—Russell also employs flute, bassoon, vibraphone, and French horn. This choice of instruments allows for flexible combinations of section sounds in brasses and woodwinds, distinctive solo-instrument combinations (including muted sounds), and a powerful tutti. Although *All About Rosie* is a composer-dominated score, improvisatory passages are skillfully incorporated, sometimes with a bitonal accompaniment. Only momentary pauses separate the sections (Fast—Slow—Fast), and in the recording of the third movement (*NAJ* 13) one hears a classic Bill Evans piano solo. (See Listening Guide 13.)

Russell taught at the Lenox School of Jazz and, in 1960, formed his own group, which traveled to Europe in 1964 and '65. To a certain extent, the jazz sounds of the '60s are based on his principles and for this reason, he is a key figure in the totality of a complex decade (*NW* 216 II/2 and *NW* 242, II/3).

Many of the Miles Davis's musicians moved on to form significant groups of their own. Josef Zawinul and Wayne Shorter joined forces and formed Weather Report; John McLaughlin gathered together the Mahavishnu Orchestra; Herbie Hancock, Chick Corea, and Bill Evans went their separate ways to form groups of their own. Modern jazz of the '60s and '70s was exciting and intellectual, and the younger musicians, who were not schooled in the swing bands or postwar bebop combos, were beginning to take their places as artistic leaders.

THE AACM

If jazz of the '60s was dominated by the overpowering influence of Miles Davis, John Coltrane, and Ornette Coleman, a no-less important movement was instituted early in the decade in Chicago, the Association for the Advancement of Creative Musicians, or AACM. Muhal Richard Abrams (b. 1930) was a versatile pianist who in the 1950s developed a solid reputation among Chicago's hard bop musicians. In 1961, he established an experimental band on the South Side and transformed it into an experimental school to which he invited like-minded musicians, especially young black jazz artists from the South Side, to investigate and perform music that drew nourishment from its African roots. This organization and school, the AACM, was founded in 1965 partly to fulfill creative needs and idealistic artistic goals, but also to teach and foster a principle of economic self-determination for Chicago musicians. The effort was remarkably successful in nurturing talent that would set the pace for avant-garde jazz of the '70s: Anthony Braxton,

Henry Threadgill, Jack DeJohnette, and the Art Ensemble of Chicago all grew out of the AACM.

One of Abrams's associates early in the 1960s was saxophonist Roscoe Mitchell, and from the Roscoe Mitchell Quartet—which also included Lester Bowie, trumpet; Malachi Favors, bass; and Philip Wilson, drums—evolved the Art Ensemble of Chicago, a musical-theatrical avant-garde quintet (Joseph Jarman, reeds, was added and Famoudou Don Moye replaced Wilson on percussion).

Throughout the '60s, the AACM sponsored concerts, recitals, and recordings. One of the requirements for continuing membership in the Association was the maintenance of high moral standards, and the AACM was truly a light in the ghetto wilderness. In the words of saxophonist Joseph Jarman,

> Until I had the first meeting with Richard Abrams, I was "like all the rest" of the "hip" ghetto niggers; I was cool, I took dope, I smoked pot, etc. I did not care for the life that I had been given. In having the chance to work in The Experimental Band with Richard and the other musicians there, I found the first something with meaning / reason for doing. That band and the people there was the most important thing that ever happened to me.[62]

In their first recordings, the musicians who would later become the Art Ensemble of Chicago led various small combos under their own names, and the music—collective improvisation featuring atonality, an expanded timbral palette, free jazz techniques, and, very significantly, surprise—was the most shocking in jazz. As the graffiti on south side walls proclaimed "R Thang," the music of these avant-gardists screamed their defiance at music of the establishment.

Jarman's *Non-Cognitive Aspects of the City*[63] was performed by Jarman on alto saxophone and recitation, Christopher Gaddy on piano and marimba, Charles Clark on bass, and Thurman Barker on drums. It begins with a few disjointed melodic fragments, then moves into a drum solo as prelude to the poem:

> *Non-cognitive aspects of the city*
>   *where Roy J.'s prophesies become the causes of children.*
> *Once, white black blocks of stone,*
>   *encasements of regularity.*
> *Sweet now, intellectual dada. . . .*

[62] Liner notes for "Joseph Jarman—Song For" (Delmark DL-410), released 1967.
[63] "Joseph Jarman—Song For" (Delmark DL-410).

Gone were the propulsive rhythms of jazz, the virtuoso solos, and in their stead we find reactive music, social statement, soul-searching, and isolation in both music and word. The arco bass solo is painful in its out-of-tune double stops and scratchy harmonics, but as an expression of "intellectual dada," this music was a work of art.

And on the same album,

> *SONG FOR is made of sound and silences from*
> *musical*
> *instruments, controlled by seven men; it's . . .*
>   *for itself,*
> *for love, for hate, & for the God within*
> *us*
> *all—it has no "meaning" outside of itself,*
> *the MUSIC.*

Jarman, the composer-performer-poet, was obviously trying to communicate—in spite of the expressed claim of no "meaning"—something about life and the world from the viewpoint of a young black Chicago musician of the 1960s. The album was issued in 1967, two years after the Civil Rights march in Alabama and the assassination of Malcolm X. The Rev. Dr. Martin Luther King, Jr., would be assassinated the following year. Chicago was boiling over with love, hate, anger, frustration, intellectual dada.

That same year, Lester Bowie recorded *Number 2,*[64] with Jarman, Roscoe Mitchell, and Malachi Favors. The performance begins with a huge smash on the Chinese gong, whose sound is allowed to pulsate in gradually decreasing levels of intensity until Mitchell plays a soft, slow pentatonic scale and repeats it an octave higher. Then all hell breaks loose, with a flurry of slurps, runs, police whistle, and chaos, followed by a simple-minded but out-of-tune unison passage. What is going on? As the liner notes tell us:

> Jazz, at first apart from this struggle for renewal in the Western world, has come to face these "freedoms." But there is only one true freedom for us, and that is what this music seeks. The signs of the revolution permeate most of jazz today, and in Chicago there are young musicians who, desiring freedom, are beginning to know *how* it is created.

In spite of the seemingly restricted environment of these Chicago musicians, their musical experiences had been rich, in travel, study, and record-

[64] Nessa N-1.

ings. Theirs was an intellectual and social movement as well as a musical philosophy, and the musicians branched out and proselytized in New York and Europe before the decade ran its course. They acknowledged their debt to their elders—Ornette Coleman, Cecil Taylor, John Coltrane, Rahsaan Roland Kirk, and Albert Ayler—but they were seeking their own unique identity. In one way, they were brazen and fearless, in another, insecure and fretful. These feelings were all expressed in their music.

Another free jazz scene, the Black Artists Group (BAG), formed in St. Louis in the late 1960s, modeling itself after the AACM. From its midst came three members of the World Saxophone Quartet: Oliver Lake, Julius Hemphill, and Hamiet Bluiett.

The new sounds, however, were not being met with great public acclaim. The combos were hard hit financially, but the big bands, even though they were least responsible for the state of jazz music, suffered the most. The large personnel rosters required sizable capital risks by promoters and managers. Still, the genre did not die, and a few innovations in big-band sound enlivened the jazz scene. Maynard Ferguson, who was the first screech trumpet player to play consistently in the ultrahigh range, was doing so as early as 1950 with Stan Kenton.[65] He began leading his own band in the early '50s and its eventual success was due not only to his talent but to his musicians' ability and enthusiasm and, most especially, to the quality of the arrangements produced by Al Cohn, Ernie Wilkins, Bob Brookmeyer, and Willie Maiden.

Ferguson continued touring with his band until 1965 and organized another band in the early 1970s. His performances contrasted sharply with the feats of the avant-garde musicians who were playing and recording at the time. He capitalized on his virtuosic skill as a pyrotechnic lead-trumpet player when soloistic virtuosity was being cast aside by others and he depended on the skill of young arrangers to infuse new life into traditional forms while avant-garde musicians were denigrating the concept of form. Willie Maiden was especially talented at adapting West Coast arranging principles of light ensemble sound to the forces of a standard big band. He would weave the counterpoint of saxophone-section work against the lead lines of the trumpet or trombone sections.

Ferguson kept the possibility of a big-band revival alive, for although his ideas were traditional and not particularly innovative, the sounds were fresh and the players' skills exciting. Another trumpet player, Don Ellis, formed a studio recording band that did indeed exploit new possibilities for big band: electronic instruments, studio manipulation of sound, and arrangements

---

[65] Capitol 28000–6.

Maynard Ferguson.

employing complicated meters. "Electric Bath"[66] (1967) is a dazzling exposition of studio musician virtuosity. *New Horizons* has the group playing meters of 17/8 divided into groups of 5 + 5 + 7; *Indian Lady* merely divides 5/4 into groups of 3 + 2, but the lively tempo complicates the problem and multiplies the swing. The leader improvises on a four-valve quarter-tone trumpet and in one number, *Open Beauty*, improvises in real time to his own improvisations, which are being fed back to him through a loop-delay echo chamber. The timbres of sitar, timbales, and standard instruments with their sounds distorted through reverberation amplifiers creates a new kind of avant-garde experiment within the standard framework of jazz composed and arranged for a big band.

——— ONE MORE TIME ———

The 1960s was a decade of radical change, and both free jazz and rock music symbolized and expressed that change with their anti-establishment principles, defiant attitudes, and youthful practitioners. Many problems plagued American society during these years—assassinations, riots, police-state tactics, and entrance into an unpopular war—but there were just as many great historical accomplishments—civil rights legislation, school integration, the

[66] Columbia CS 9585.

admission of women to formerly all-male colleges, and much exciting music, both inside and outside the world of jazz. There were strong reactions to the new music, both for and against, and it became apparent that most members of the jazz establishment were very conservative. But the future was not in the hands of the old, and the new music survived its years of trial by fire. Miles Davis, who loudly condemned the new music at first, gradually embraced the innovations. Charles Mingus expressed his confusion: "[Ornette's playing is] organized disorganization or playing wrong right. And it gets to you emotionally, like a drummer." Mingus quickly found his own avant-garde voice, as did George Russell, Gunther Schuller, and others. Some were right on top of the changes from the beginning, others would join the movement later.

Racism created many bitter moments for jazz musicians during these years and many of them consciously entered the world of political activism. Dave Brubeck canceled a southern jazz tour in 1960 because he would not agree to an all-white musicians' contract. Dizzy Gillespie ran for President in 1964. Gillespie "won" a mock election and proposed George Wallace, then avowed-racist governor of Alabama, as ambassador to the Congo. In 1962 the government of South Africa canceled a tour by Louis Armstrong and banned a performance of Max Roach's *Freedom Now Suite*. Only today, in the 1990s, are we seeing a significant change in South Africa's attitude toward apartheid. Strangely, Lennie Tristano claimed in 1962, "There is nothing African about jazz. Jewish cantors and gypsies sound more like it than anything from Africa." Not all protests and demonstrations were positive or responsible, either. A drunken mob of college students first rioted at the Newport Jazz Festival in 1960. A similar riot in 1969 and a worse one in 1970 forced the Newport (Rhode Island) Festival to move to New York City, where it remained and later changed its name.

Saxophonists captured center stage early in the decade. In addition to Ornette Coleman's exploits, John Coltrane left Miles Davis to start his own band, Gerry Mulligan debuted his Concert Jazz Band, Stan Getz returned to the United States after an extended stay in Denmark, and Sonny Rollins came back from another retreat to blow up a storm in New York.

Curiously, as the new jazz went truly modern, a fresh interest in the past also appeared. In 1961, Preservation Hall, a museum of living sound that features live performances by the oldest surviving members of New Orleans jazz, opened in that city. Two years later, the New Orleans Jazz Museum opened, putting on display the cornets of both King Oliver and Bix Beiderbecke. Before too long, there would be a Bix Beiderbecke museum in Davenport, Iowa, and a New York Jazz Museum in Manhattan. The Department of State and the National Endowments for the Arts and Humanities became involved in supporting jazz as a national treasure. Thelonious Monk was slated for a December 1963 cover of *Time* magazine (understandably, the publication of his picture was postponed when President John F. Kennedy was shot).

In 1965, Duke Ellington was awarded a citation from the Pulitzer Prize Committee, but there was a touch of irony in the award as he was not presented with the Pulitzer Prize for music. Jazz was not considered a sufficiently acceptable medium for so "prestigious" a prize, yet the Committee wanted to recognize Ellington in some way. That same year, he presented his *First Sacred Concert* at Grace Cathedral in San Francisco, and in 1969 he celebrated his seventieth birthday at the White House.

Artistically, the 1960s were years of growth for jazz, but they were economically difficult. The big bands all but disappeared, although a few rose once again at the end of the decade. Jazz faded from the radio, the ballrooms went out of business, Norman Granz's Jazz at the Philharmonic Tours folded, and the last 52nd Street club, the Hickory House, closed. Jazz festivals were becoming an increasingly important venue for the presentation of jazz, and their development marked the shift in jazz's status from social event to concert music. Started in the mid-'50s, the festivals slowly expanded through the '60s, and by the mid-1980s there were between seven hundred and a thousand festivals of international importance taking place annually.

1.0

CONFUSION AND FUSION—FROM THE '70S TO THE '80S

───── **INTRODUCTION** ──────────

In 1969, Sonny Rollins disappeared from public view one more time. The year before, he had spent five months meditating and studying in India, and fans assumed he was on another spiritual/musical quest. They were wrong; he was fed up and stayed away for over two years. When he reappeared in 1972 he explained, "I had got into a very disillusioned attitude by 1969, a despondent attitude. The first time I dropped out [August 1959], it was to write and study. This time it was disillusionment with the music scene."[1] Many jazz musicians were discouraged, for business was bad and there was substantial disagreement over the basic issue posed by the question, "What is jazz?" Rock 'n' roll and free jazz had attacked the mainstream music and threatened the old guard. These sounds so pervaded the music of young jazz musicians that Rollins and others foundered directionless in a turbulent sea. They had paid their dues and were ready to reap their rewards, but what they knew and what they believed in were no longer of value, or so it seemed. But one could find, in the restless turmoil of the experimental sounds produced by the younger musicians, traces of both the heritage and the future

[1] Interview with Whitney Balliett, March 15, 1972, reported in Whitney Balliett, *New York Notes: A Journal of Jazz, 1972–1975*, p. 11.

of jazz, of external influences and internal strength. By the end of the decade, the leading figures would find satisfactory and satisfying answers. But at that moment, it seemed to many that jazz would not survive.

Dexter Gordon held similar views. He chose to work in Europe and live in Copenhagen, Denmark, throughout most of the 1960s and early '70s. In 1976, he returned to the United States and explained,

> I was reading *Down Beat* one day back then [in Copenhagen] and Ira Gitler referred to me as an expatriate. That's true, you know, but at the time I hadn't really made up my mind to live there so I came back here in 1965 for about six months, mostly out on the coast. But with all the political and social strife during that time and the Beatles thing, I didn't really dig it. So I went back. . . .
>
> Copenhagen's like my home base. . . . Of course, there was no racial discrimination or anything like that. And the fact that you're an artist in Europe means something. They treat you with a lot of respect. In America, you know, they say, "Do you make any money?" If you're in the dollars, you're alright. But over there, it's an entirely different mentality.[2]

ORNETTE COLEMAN

Ornette Coleman, still a leader of the avant-garde, was struggling too. In the late '60s, jobs were few and far between. He played some dates in Europe, experimented with notation, performed on various instruments, and recorded with different ensembles, but his music was not accepted by most critics or by the general public. His attitude, like that of Rollins, was one of hopeless dejection. Both the old guard and the avant-garde were in a state of shock. Coleman said,

> I don't feel healthy about the performing world anymore at all. I think it's an egotistical world; it's about clothes and money, not about music. I'd like to get out of it, but I don't have the financial situation to do so. . . . I don't want to be a puppet and be told what to do and what not to do.[3]

He was bewildered and perhaps frightened, but in his confusion he did not recognize the illusion of failure at a time of success. What he lacked was what he decried most: money, public recognition, and the trappings that come with steady work. What he had, in spite of his troubles, was respect,

---

[2] From an interview with Chuck Berg, "Dexter Gordon: Making His Great Leap Forward," reprinted in *Down Beat*, September 1989, p. 83.

[3] Quoted in John Litweiler, *The Freedom Principle*, p. 53.

for himself and for his music. An important cadre of influential musicians put his music and his beliefs under careful study, and soon a whole generation of younger musicians would, along with Coleman himself, chart the course of jazz during the remainder of the decade. Before long, the fusion of jazz and rock would solve his artistic and financial dilemma. His time did come. Prime Time, a band he organized in 1975, would move Coleman to center stage in the electronic arena.

Coleman had already brought significant changes to the traditional norms of jazz. The pianoless double quartet of the "Free Jazz" recording session revealed a truly viable artistic solution to the restraints of harmony, melody, rhythm, and conventional timbre. Technically, his music changed:

1. **Melody.** The solo instrumental line was freed from chord patterns, liberated from melodic segments, and dissociated from the beat. The tonal range for each instrument was expansive, and the melodic intervals, although normally close, were sometimes large and disjunct.

2. **Harmony.** The harmonic substructure was discarded in every traditional sense. The harmony of free jazz was simply the composite of the resulting vertical complex of pitches in combination with the flow of the lowest sounding pitch. Functional harmony, that is, tonal organization and goal-oriented harmonic resolution, was destroyed.

3. **Form.** The form of any piece, solo, or section of a free jazz work was primarily the resultant form that the mind of the performer and the ear of the listener imposed upon the flow of sounds. As suggested by Gestalt psychology, relationships are perceived, connections are made, gaps are filled by listeners in response to their own experiences and expectations. The cognitive groupings are different for each listener and are imposed upon the performance as listeners focus their attention on their own choices of sounds and actions.

4. **Texture.** Where earlier jazz had an orchestral standard, that is, layers of sound organized by the style, by the ensemble musicians, or by the arranger, free jazz sought an amorphous mix of varying densities.

5. **Timbre.** Jazz has always sought instrumental sounds that were unique to the individual player and were capable of emotional expression, but free jazz expanded the instrumental effects used by standard instruments and incorporated non-traditional instruments as well in varying combinations. The employment of intentional squeaks and the use of pocket trumpet, police whistle, tam-tam, and bass clarinet are examples that occur in well-known performances.

6.   **Rhythm.** The standard jazz concept of regular, metronomic "time" was replaced by simultaneously occurring layers of beats, meters, tempos, and rhythmic groupings that need not coincide at structural points.

7.   **Improvisation.** Collective improvisation, which was a standard feature in classic jazz, replaced solo improvisation in free jazz, but collective improvisation was redefined. Where earlier collective improvisation required tones to come together in some stylistic order, free collective improvisation was simply a series of actions and reactions by the musicians in no predetermined framework. As a result, the role and importance of the soloist were minimized.

Having accomplished this unbelievable feat almost single-handedly nearly ten years before, Coleman continued to search for new ideas and the next great masterpiece. As the new decade started, he was still probing for more satisfying results. In 1971, he recorded *What Reason Could I Give?*[4] which combined the sound of a woman's voice in the texture of an instrumental ensemble. The voice was not used as an independent solo voice, in the sense of a jazz singer accompanied by a band, but was incorporated into the complex of sounds as a distinct instrumental color. However, the orchestration was often simple-minded, with everyone playing in parallel. The ensemble was sloppy: attacks were not executed together, the balance was poor, and the intonation was less-than-good. In his free jazz style, Coleman could avoid considerations of ensemble—it was everyone for himself. In these orchestrated works, the absence of ensemble reduced whatever potential the piece may have had.

A more successful example of a similar experiment can be heard in *Science Fiction*, from the album of the same name. While the instruments either raced at break-neck speed or plodded along, as the bowed bass sometimes did, a male voice penetrated the cloud of sound and brought focus and meaning to the listener. Much of what Coleman had been experimenting with during the '60s coalesced here into a work of artistic integrity.

Still unfulfilled and dissatisfied with a decade of experimentation and performance, Coleman returned to the drafting table to compose an orchestral work in twenty-one movements. In 1972 he completed a score for the London Symphony Orchestra, *Skies of America*, which was recorded under the baton of David Measham.[5] Where Coleman was able to amplify musical ideas into extended works in live performance through his improvisatory skills, he seemed unable to accomplish the same on paper. His composition for orches-

[4]Columbia 31061.
[5]Columbia 31562.

tra shows little of the expansive musical thought that his improvising jazz combos display. The first movement is bombastic and repetitive; the sixth movement, "Sounds of Sculpture," is simple, redundant, and lacking in excitement. Throughout the symphonic work, there is no large form, no extended movement. Not one among the twenty-one movements of the composition is more than a short piece, and the relationship of each to the whole composition is not convincing. As a symphonic composer Coleman was out of his element. A statement of his at the time reveals the nature of his probing—his musical principles were in seeming conflict with some of the basic tenets of free jazz.

> The orchestration [is] based on a theory book called The Harmolodic Theory which uses melody, harmony, and the instrumentation of movement of forms. . . . The writing is applied to harmolodic modulation meaning to modulate in range without changing keys. There are eight themes and a harmolodic movement for each theme.

Harmolodic theory depends on structure and rules, free jazz denigrates the value of restriction. Equally important, his concerns are not all musical. He continues,

> The skies of America have had more changes to occur under them in this century than any other country: assassinations, political wars, gangster wars, racial wars, space races, women's rights, sex, drugs and the death of god, all for the betterment of the American people. . . . Why, where and what is the purpose of a country that has the essence of mankind and the blessing of the skies?[6]

During the next few years the influence of rock and jazz-rock fusion styles gradually shaped his thinking. In 1975 he formed his commanding electric band, Prime Time, which first appeared in France as a quintet of sax, two electric guitars, electric bass, and drums, but often added a second drummer and later a second bass. In this ensemble, Coleman had a vehicle to integrate his improvisatory powers within his new conceptual framework, which he called "harmolodic theory." His lyrical gifts shine on *Sex Spy* from the album "Soapsuds"[7] from 1977. With this group Coleman would move into the 1980s as a leading voice in the avant-garde once again. And his musical success would be matched with financial reward as well.

[6] Liner notes by Ornette Coleman for "Skies of America," ibid.
[7] Artists House 6.

MILES DAVIS AGAIN

Miles Davis continued to be an innovator in the 1970s, but his attitude about the state of jazz at the end of the '60s was little different from that of Coleman or Rollins. He said,

> Nineteen sixty-nine was the year rock and funk were selling like hotcakes and all this was put on display at Woodstock. There were over 400,000 people at the concert. That many people at a concert makes everybody go crazy, and especially people who make records. The only thing on their minds is, How can we sell records to that many people all the time? . . . And jazz music seemed to be withering on the vine, in record sales and live performances. It was the first time in a long time that I didn't sell out crowds everywhere I played. In Europe I always had sellouts, but in the United States, we played to a lot of half-empty clubs in 1969. That told me something.[8]

What it apparently told Davis was that he should take his music to where the people were and educate them. He went, and started to rebuild a new audience. Not long after the "Bitches Brew" recording, he agreed to open for the Grateful Dead at a concert at the Fillmore in San Francisco. The enormity of this gesture should not be minimized. Davis opened (that is, he was not the main attraction) for a rock group, and he played to about 5,000 spacy, young white hippies! It was not a one-night stand. He continued to do this at Fillmore East in New York and elsewhere. Soon he moved to top billing and had a new audience listening to his music, and he learned both from his audience and from the rock musicians with whom he associated.

Davis had already expanded artistically into the world of electronic music and studio-controlled events through his associations with young musicians and his recordings of "In a Silent Way" and "Bitches Brew." After his Fillmore experience he gained momentum to forge ahead. He recorded frequently at the beginning of the '70s with sterling young soloists, many of whom would go their separate ways as leaders: John McLaughlin, Chick Corea, Herbie Hancock, Keith Jarrett, Steve Grossman, Wayne Shorter, Joe Zawinul, Ron Carter, and others. He also took an interest in the music of Karlheinz Stockhausen, a German pioneer in classical electronic music and open forms. Although not a commercial success, one of Davis's most interesting albums of the period dates from 1972, "On the Corner."[9] The record

---

[8] Miles Davis with Quincy Troupe, *Miles Davis*, p. 297.
[9] Columbia KC 31906.

is an unusual combination of New York street music, Eastern drones, African and South American rhythms, electronic jazz both in and out of time, and a gradual but continuous series of musical transformations. Davis played amplified trumpet with a wah-wah, a device giving the instrument some of the color and effects of the electric guitar, and for long periods during the recording he did not play at all. Jazz fans, buying the album to hear the sound of their beloved hero on trumpet or fluegelhorn were sadly disappointed; they probably could not hear him playing at all, for his modified trumpet was blended almost inconspicuously into the mix. Jazz critics did not know how to react, for the blend had gone beyond the collective improvisation principles of free jazz. But a growing body of young fans who had been weaned on long tracks of instrumental rock were finding a new fascination in his music. Davis, on the other hand, was growing musically, consciously incorporating characteristics he admired or was curious about in the music of Stockhausen, Ornette Coleman, the English composer Paul Buckmaster, and funk musicians Sly Stone and James Brown. Davis's "On the Corner" band is an unorthodox combination: five rhythm players (two drummers, two percussionists, and a tabla, or Indian drum, player); three keyboards; three plucked string instruments (guitar, bass guitar, and sitar, an Indian instrument); two reeds (soprano sax and bass clarinet); and trumpet. As Davis described this recording, "The music was about spacing, about free association of musical ideas to a core kind of rhythm and vamps of the bass line."[10] Surely, Davis was reassessing his own music, and music in general. On this recording, perhaps for the first time in his career, he was content to be part of the background. Strangely, despite the large number of outstanding percussionists playing on the album, the rhythmic complexity is minimal, resulting in a relatively homogeneous blend. In one regard, this music resembled free jazz in that it sounds different on each rehearing. The collective ensemble sound and the absence of distinct solos leaves the organization of material largely to the listener. It is music that says, "Here I am. Take what you want. Come again and take something else." "On the Corner" was a radical experiment, and it helped shape Davis's thinking for the years ahead.

Unfortunately, Davis's health took a serious turn for the worse, and his recording activity virtually stopped in 1973 and '74. Cocaine addiction became a serious problem; a gallbladder operation was followed by an auto accident and two broken ankles; a hip was not functioning well; a stomach ulcer required surgery; nodes were removed from his larynx. Davis's style of living had finally caught up with him. For almost six years, from 1975 to 1980, he became a recluse and for over four of those years he did not play his trumpet once. Domestic problems also plagued him, and he went to jail for non-support in

[10] Davis and Troupe, *Miles Davis*, p. 322.

1978. His disappearance from public view was so complete that many jazz fans thought he was dying or indeed had died, before he once again broke his drug habit. By then, a new decade had begun.

CECIL TAYLOR

Some of the most influential jazz musicians of the '70s were the keyboard players, and many led their own groups. Cecil Taylor, who never enjoyed a large following in either America or Europe, set an important example for those wise enough to listen carefully to his music. He opened another world of artistic possibilities, successfully incorporating many ideas and sounds from "classical" avant-garde composition into his own unique jazz style. Taylor represented a totally uncompromising stance in jazz, the position that musical values and human expression must both generate and determine musical outcome. His sound concept was sparse and economical, and the net effect of his music was more like that of classical chamber music than that of traditional jazz ensemble sounds. The music he performed and composed was never trivial, and it demanded the utmost in listener concentration.

The foundations of Cecil Taylor's musical thinking rested, like the foundations of jazz itself, upon the bedrock of music from Europe, Africa, and America, a blend of advanced Western musical thought (Stravinsky, the serialists, and Lennie Tristano) and advanced African-American musical thought (Ellington and Monk). It was also based on a rejection of both the electronic European contingent represented by Stockhausen and the free form advocates of jazz represented by Ornette Coleman. Taylor's music depended on structure, organization, and developmental processes, and it required human expression through instrumental performance and improvisation. Taylor was a pianist, not a keyboard player. A resonant, acoustical instrument was vital to his performance, and the sound of acoustical, not electric or electronic, instruments were part of his conceptual framework. In his compositions, musical statements were related logically, but the vocabulary of organized units goes beyond melody and harmony to theme groups, timbres, rhythmic units, and gestures.

Taylor was an extraordinary pianist, a player of sensitive touch, astounding virtuosity, and sometimes demonic fire. He often overlaid atonal sounds and tone clusters upon a tonal substructure. The characteristics of his distinctive musical style could be observed as early as the '50s (*e.g.*, *Song*[11]), and it became more daring during the '60s (*e.g.*, *Cell Walk for Celeste*[12] or *Enter Evening* [*SCCJ* 101]). Not until the 1970s did the significance of his musical

[11] Recorded in 1955 on Transition and reissued on Blue Note LA458-H2.
[12] Recorded in 1961, Candid 9034.

Mary Lou Williams and Cecil Taylor at Carnegie Hall, April 17, 1977.

presence become obvious, and during this decade he gained recognition from academic as well as performance circles. Beginning in 1970, Taylor taught black music history and aesthetics in college, first at the University of Wisconsin–Madison and later at Antioch College in Ohio. These teaching appointments were followed by a Guggenheim Fellowship and, later in the decade, an honorary doctorate from the New England Conservatory of Music and a performance at the White House. He often found his teaching experiences unsatisfying, but his new level of recognition helped him project his music to a wide and influential audience. In 1974, his album "Silent Tongues"[13] was named "Jazz Album of the Year" by *Down Beat* magazine's international critics.

During the '70s, Taylor recorded brilliant solo piano works and, in 1977, played a strange *Embraced* concert of two pianos with swing/bebop pianist Mary Lou Williams at Carnegie Hall. He also displayed his genius as composer/director/performer with performances and recordings of his ensemble, the Cecil Taylor Unit, a combo of changing personnel. In 1978, the Unit, then consisting of Jimmy Lyons on alto saxophone, Raphé Malik on trumpet, Ramsey Ameen on violin, Sirone on bass, and Ronald Shannon Jackson on drums, recorded *Idut* (*NW* 201, I/1), a piece of volcanic activity that builds

[13] Arista 1005.

on an ensemble sound similar to that explored in 1918 by Igor Stravinsky in *L'Histoire du soldat*. But unlike Stravinsky, Taylor called on his players to take compositional elements and, through improvisation, fuse them together freely into a polyphonic collage that assembles and reassembles, dances and struggles, runs and relaxes. If the three compositions of the album—*Idut*, *Serdab*, and *Holiday en masque*—which run to a total performance time of almost one hour (57′ 54″), are taken together as one complete composition, the listener has the equivalent of a large-scale work of symphonic proportions. The hierarchic relationship among the parts is strong, the balance of fast-slow-fast (quasi sonata allegro–song form–rondo) is satisfying, and the developmental scheme of the parts is convincing. What then differentiates this work as jazz and not "classical" concert music? Very little. It is an excellent work in both spheres, and one has to accept improvisation, trap drum set and saxophone, jazz training, and African-American roots as sufficient evidence for its inclusion in the corpus of works called jazz. It is an outstanding composition / improvisation regardless of its categorization.

THE KEYBOARD PLAYERS— BILL EVANS, HERBIE HANCOCK, CHICK COREA, KEITH JARRETT, JOE ZAWINUL

Five of the keyboard players who passed through the Miles Davis band in the late '60s became major figures and trend setters on their own during the '70s: Bill Evans, Herbie Hancock, Chick Corea, Keith Jarrett, and Joe Zawinul. The influence of Bill Evans went far beyond the contributions he made with the Miles Davis combos, and during the '70s he acquired, through his presence and personality, the aspect of a guru—thoughtful, gentle, introspective, caring. When he played, especially as a soloist, he almost seemed to become one with the instrument. The image of his body, curved over the keyboard, listening intently to every aspect of the sound his fingers released from the strings of the piano, became a symbol to many jazz artists seeking beauty in a Romantic but completely unpretentious quest. His contributions during this last decade of his life were in many ways a summation of his career, a further expression of the perfected post-bebop style that he championed—great lyricism, flowing swing, meticulous attention to chord choice and voicing, expressive touch, and a disdain for ostentatious display. Yet even in recapitulation, one performance was never just a repeat of another. In 1972 Evans recorded one of his most unusual albums, a collaborative effort with composer George Russell. *Living Time*[14] is a composition in eight sections for jazz orchestra and Evans. Compositional attention is focused on delicate and unusual timbres bathed in Afro-Cuban rhythms. The swirling sounds require our close attention just to perceive the remarkable variety and infinite detail found in combinations of triangle, flute, fluegel horns, drums, keyboards, and more. The spotlight of attention is not directed at Evans, the gifted soloist, but on the music of Evans and Russell, the collaborating composers. Of course, there are moments when the great keyboardist rises above the forest of sound, as in Events IV and VIII, but the net effect is as much one of performers listening to each other as it is of musicians playing for an audience.

In 1975, Bill Evans was invited to the Montreux Jazz Festival for the third time, and his duo performances there, recorded with bassist Eddie Gomez, are clear encapsulations of his solo style—light, precise, thoughtful, and lyrical. Every cut of "Montreux III,"[15] recorded live before the festival audience, is a distillation of Evans the soloist at his mature best. The waltz tempo *Driftin'*, composed by gifted pianist Dan Haerle, glides along effortlessly; *Elsa* is an especially interesting study of Evans's left-hand technique. Beneath the flowing solo lines of the right hand, the left injects sliding modal implications and a fascinating variety of rhythmic groupings and punctuations. All in all, Evans's playing during the 1970s represented a codification and fulfillment of a mature master's concept of sound.

In contrast, the younger group of keyboard artists affiliated with Miles Davis seemed more interested in exploring the new jazz/rock possibilities. Herbie Hancock, who left Davis to form his own group in 1968, achieved commercial success in 1973 with his band and his album "Headhunters."[16] Like Davis, Hancock found a new audience with younger listeners attuned to rock. It is easy to see how a number like *Chameleon*, with its relentless but catchy ostinato, would have a popular appeal. The "gulping" sound envelope of the electronic bass, the vibrant rhythms of percussion and electronic instruments, and the simple band riffs make for excellent dance music. Similarly, in his well-known composition *Watermelon Man*, we can hear the playful aspects of jazz in full flower. And *Sly*, an obvious reference in both title and sound to the music of gospel / funk hero Sly Stone, offered real competition by jazz musicians to the commercial music makers of the pop music arena.

Following his success with "Headhunters," Hancock regrouped with his old friends, trumpeter Freddie Hubbard, saxophonist Wayne Shorter, bassist

[14] Columbia KC 31490.
[15] Fantasy F-9510.
[16] Columbia KC 32731.

Herbie Hancock listening to a playback during a recording session.

Ron Carter, and drummer Tony Williams for a recording in 1976 and a 1977 tour with his band V.S.O.P. For the musicians it was a return to "pure jazz," a reversion to acoustic jazz. After years of immersion in electronic sound, these players brought the old acoustical standard—albeit with modern ideas— to over 100,000 paying listeners. On the 1977 album, "V.S.O.P.: The Quintet,"[17] the cuts are long and the solos extended. Often the chord patterns for the solos are the slow-changing shifts of modal jazz, but the heads of the pieces are reminiscent of old-fashioned bebop. In this return to mainstream jazz, a meld of hard bop and modal jazz, Freddie Hubbard proves himself a competent successor for the trumpet mantle of Clifford Brown. His playing is crisp and facile, his ideas quick and engaging. Wayne Shorter delivers solos that explore the tonal possibilities of both soprano and tenor saxophones while following the older melodic-developmental solo patterns. None of the players seem restrained by the acoustic framework of the performances. They retain their own modern personae, making the presentation of "V.S.O.P." an artistic balance of old-fashioned acoustic and new-fangled exploratory modern jazz.

When Chick Corea left the Davis entourage, he formed a free jazz trio, later a quartet, called Circle, with Anthony Braxton on reeds, Dave Holland

[17] Columbia C2 34976.

Chick Corea.

on bass, and Barry Altschul on drums. With this ensemble, he tried his hand at free improvisation and found it unsatisfying. In 1971, he formed his first Return to Forever combo, which was in a sense diametrically opposed to free jazz principles. Lush harmonies, long-line melodies, Romantic vocal lines, Latin rhythms, and a brilliant manipulation of electrical, electronic, and acoustic timbres highlight a fascinating jazz/rock fusion sound. Return to Forever's 1976 "Romantic Warrior" album[18] with Stanley Clarke playing various bass instruments and percussion, Lenny White on drums, and Al DiMeola on guitars and percussion shows Corea's concern for, and mastery of, electronic instrumental sounds. On one album alone, he plays acoustic piano, Fender Rhodes (electric piano), an assortment of electronic keyboards and synthesizers, electric organ, and some percussion instruments. In a way, it is almost an orgy of virtuosity at the expense of continuous musical thought. The music tends to be eclectic, sometimes maudlin, often disconnected, but always fun. Fun was something many jazz musicians overlooked or ignored during the 1960s.

Corea's impish musical nature was on display as well in his 1975 album "The Leprechaun,"[19] and it seemed that he, along with Hancock and others, was searching for a way to bring pleasure through jazz to the average music consumer. The *Imp's Welcome* is a riot of electronically generated double-reed flourishes in and out of tempered tuning; *Pixieland Rag* is a cute keyboard piece that could easily appear in a youngster's recital; and the *Lep-*

[18] Columbia PC 34076.
[19] Polydor PD 6062.

rechaun's Dream borrows some movie music from Walt Disney, concert sounds of a classical string quartet, and just about everything else. The soul-wrenching cries of free jazz, the tortuous paths of advanced bebop, and all those cerebral forms of music that seemed to have led jazz to artistic heights and financial bankruptcy were dispossessed, at least temporarily, in favor of fun and the search for a people's music.

Without question, however, Chick Corea's sensitive, gifted artistry was functioning at the same time. He played more than easy-listening music and music for athletic dancing. In a more serious but still thoroughly accessible vein, his composition *Crystal Silence*,[20] which he recorded in 1972 with premier vibraphonist Gary Burton, stands out as a jazz classic, a performance that surrenders nothing of value and still delights the ear with musical and extramusical sensations. Reflecting the title of the piece, the instruments of both Corea and Burton sparkle in the sunlight of harmony. The piano becomes an orchestra of delightful sounds, the vibraphone a network of scintillating vibrations. After the difficulties of the '60s and the uncertain future of jazz at the start of the '70s, these jazz musicians were building a road to better days through a new romanticism, a return to the "old-fashioned" concept of musical beauty.

Keith Jarrett, in spite of his outstanding work with Miles Davis and with his own band, will be remembered best (and deserves special attention) for his solo concerts, unusual one-person displays that he first tried in 1972. His solo recitals consisted of two improvisations on acoustic piano lasting a half-hour or longer. The performances were Lisztian in both nature and scope, and like Liszt he attracted an extremely large and devoted following, especially in Europe. After initial forays into the world of electronic keyboards at the end of the '60s, Jarrett renounced electric or electronic keyboard instruments in 1971. He declared himself a pianist and, in part through the enormous popularity of his solo concerts, led the movement to revive acoustic jazz. It was not really a revival, since acoustic bands never disappeared from the scene entirely, but at the time, the trend-setters were so overwhelmingly encrusted with waffle-stack speakers that it was difficult to hear anything else for miles around, or so it seemed.

Jarrett actually used two formats in his solo performances: the traditional piece for clubs, consisting of head, improvisation, and recapitulation, and the open-ended improvisation for solo concerts. An excellent example of the former is preserved on the title track of his 1972 album *"Facing You."*[21] We hear the initial statement of a long-note theme over a complex rhythmic accompaniment. The ensuing improvisation expands and varies the motivic

[20] Polydor ECM 1024 ST.
[21] Polydor ECM 1017 ST.

Keith Jarrett.

ideas from the exposition. The ending, instead of simply restating the theme, assumes the garb of a coda through a slowing of tempo and a decompression of rhythmic activity. Jarrett's concert in Cologne, Germany, in January 1975 is also preserved on record,[22] but the second half of the performance stretches over three sides of two LP albums. Along with other Romantic characteristics, the notion of grandiose dimension had become a value in itself in jazz, and the length of the second improvisation—41 minutes, 18 seconds—exceeded the mechanical possibilities of one side of a 12-inch, 33⅓-rpm record. The first half of the concert, which takes 26 minutes, 15 seconds, is uninterrupted on the recording. In it Jarrett followed the classical pattern of theme and variation, simple to complex. His opening statement has four phrases, all in the hypodorian mode. The first is built on four notes:

Facing You

Structural Notes, First Phrase   Opening Melody

the second restates the first four and adds two more notes of the scale:

[22] "The Köln Concert" (Polydor ECM 1064/65).

the third changes range, for contrast, and adds the final two notes of the modal scale:

and the last rounds out the phrase by returning to a form of the original motive. The cut concludes on an appropriate modal final:

Slowly and logically during this performance, Jarrett moves further and further afield, first in diatonic and later in chromatic digressions. He lays down ostinatos, invents new melodies, escapes into pianistic fantasies, and creates a continuous musical journey through fields of consonance.

Not all students of the period saw the work of Evans, Hancock, Corea, and Jarrett in a positive light. John Litweiler, the most perceptive historian of free jazz and its outspoken advocate, interpreted the music of these artists during this period as an escape from the battlefield of reality. He observed:

> Some of the spirit left his [Bill Evans's] music by the 1960s as he adopted a most distinctive touch, delicate as butterfly wings. This unique delicacy was excellent camouflage for Evans's unremarkable melodic conception . . . and limited rhythmic range. . . .
>
> The eclectic Herbie Hancock, with his vague kind of impressionism . . . turned to fusion music and became a leading seventies money-maker. . . . Sometimes Hancock sings, too, but into a voice-distorting device rather than a microphone, in order to keep emotion at a distance. . . .
>
> Corea led several combos named Return to Forever, which moved from Latin-edged, West Coast-ish postbop to loud jazz-rock fusion and then back. The appeal of his music is its optimism; his very popular *Light as a Feather* is modest in every way. . . .
>
> In Jarrett's music the most obvious manifestations of pure sensation are the length of his ostinatos and his autoerotic groans, sighs, grunts, and moans as he leaps from his chair to thrust his pelvis at the keyboard while he plays. . . . Except for insane or intoxicated people, life is not a series of inspired impulses; no moment is ever preceded or succeeded by any equally intense experience. So Jarrett's very creativity is pathetically fleeting.[23]

The passionate struggle that first separated bebop and swing musicians in the 1940s, seriously divided mainstream jazz musicians from avant-garde

[23] John Litweiler, *The Freedom Principle*, pp. 231–34.

players in the '60s, and then nurtured adversarial attitudes that divided camps in the '70s, was unquestionably reflected in Litweiler's opinion in the '80s. The problem is still not resolved today: for example, few jazz musicians share Litweiler's views concerning the quality and importance of Bill Evans's playing, and we must keep in mind that it is the musicians, not the critics, who create the music about which the critics write. Gene Lees, editor and publisher of *Jazzletter*, wrote:

> In 1984, growing curious about the actual status of various pianists with other pianists, I did a survey of the sixty-odd well-known pianists who subscribed to the *Jazzletter*. The forty-seven respondents included pianists such as Alan Broadbent, Dave Brubeck, Kenny Drew, Dave Frishberg, Dizzy Gillespie, Roger Kellaway, Junior Mance, Nat Pierce, and Billy Taylor. I asked them to name, in no particular order, five pianists in three categories: those they considered the "best," those they thought the most influential, and their personal favorites. The results were startling.
>
> As best, Art Tatum garnered 36 votes, Bill Evans 33, and Oscar Peterson 27. As most influential, Tatum 32, Bill 30, Bud Powell 24. Among personal favorites, Bill won: Bill 25, Tatum 22, Oscar 19.[24]

Perhaps if Lees had polled Cecil Taylor, Muhal Richard Abrams, McCoy Tyner, and Anthony Davis, the results might have been different. Or perhaps not. In fact, they may have been included in the poll. The point is that there was struggle and disagreement, not that there is here a right or wrong, a better or worse. The camps and the opposing points of view are historical fact.

———— WEATHER REPORT ————

The first ensemble that completely mastered synthetic sound for the production of jazz masterworks was Weather Report. Led by keyboardist Joe Zawinul and saxophonist Wayne Shorter, the group, originally a quintet, successfully combined the collective improvisation principles of free jazz with the sonorities and techniques of jazz/rock fusion. In their 1971 first album, "Weather Report,"[25] we can hear brilliant solos appearing from a background of continuously changing textures. Joe Zawinul's synthetic creations display a combination of state-of-the-art technology and state-of-the-art virtuosity. His ear for sound was attuned to the complex mixes emanating from the European electronic music studios, and his performing and compositional

---

[24] Gene Lees, *Meet Me at Jim & Andy's*, p. 169.
[25] Columbia PC 30661.

Weather Report in 1976: (left to right) Wayne Shorter, soprano and tenor saxophone; Alejandro Neciosup Acuna, congas and percussion; Jaco Pastorius, Fender bass; Joe Zawinul, keyboards; and Chester Thompson, drums.

instincts for jazz were developed through his associations with Cannonball Adderley, Maynard Ferguson, and Miles Davis. *In a Silent Way* and *Pharaoh's Dance* were two of his important earlier compositions, and now, together with Shorter and bassist Miroslav Vitous, who also composed for the first album, he had an opportunity to sculpt sound, drive the ensemble, and improvise freely. Philosophically he, too, was trying to reestablish an audience. On the liner notes for the album, he is quoted as saying, "We're trying to make music happen for the people. Unless you try to open people's minds you'll never know what they are really like."[26] *Tears* (*NAJ* 19) washes the listener in a luxurious shower of electronic sounds separated by curtains of lyrical soprano sax, wordless voice, and varied percussion figures. The work is an integrated gestalt of timbre, gesture, time, and motion. Weather Report has discarded improvisation in the traditional sense as completely as Ornette Coleman threw off the restraints of harmony, melody, and form, but the work is indeed an improvised jazz composition. It draws its sustenance from roots sunk into jazz, rock, and classical soils. (See Listening Guide 19.)

Milky Way is almost pure electronics, *Seventh Arrow* is a combination of relentless jazz/rock drive pushing fragmented solos, timbral searches, and playful gestures, and *Orange Lady* is a ballad of other-worldly character.

[26] Ibid.

Ensemble members created a balance of synchronized and asynchronous movement as some played in time while others phased in and out. The group was original, expressive, and pathbreaking. They followed this first success with a similar venture, "I Sing the Body Electric,"[27] and one can sense on many of the cuts an increasing interest in the sound picture and improvisational style of Near-Eastern music. A real affinity with the free jazz creations of Ornette Coleman and the Association for the Advancement of Creative Musicians is also discernible throughout the album, but especially in the last cut, *Directions*.

Except for Zawinul and Shorter, the personnel of Weather Report varied; in 1976 the ensemble recorded *Heavy Weather*[28] with electric bassist Jaco Pastorius. Although the group had moved further along the road toward a heavy metal rock sound, one group of jazz musicians—the bassists—were captivated by the album. Pastorius brought the fretless electric bass, which combines the acoustical qualities of an amplified electric instrument with the touch and pitch sensitivity of the acoustic bass, to a new level of artistic excellence. His virtuosity, which propelled the band and captured the imagination of electric bassists, also won the respect of acoustic bass players. His imaginative solos, remarkable intonation, and unbelievable finger speed made him an overnight hero. He is on display throughout this album, and he plays at the top of his form on the final cut, *Havona*.

THE MAHAVISHNU ORCHESTRA

Another creation of the '70s was the Mahavishnu Orchestra, an electric ensemble titled after the spiritual name that its founder, John McLaughlin, was given by his guru, Sri Chinmoy. The band built its shrine to volume by stacking piles of equipment on the stage, turning up the gain controls to full, and exploding in rhythmically complex fusions of Indian/jazz/rock music. If on a dynamic scale measured from absolute silence to atomic explosion, the jazz music of Bill Evans or Keith Jarrett might have registered near the threshold of audibility, the Mahavishnu Orchestra would easily have straddled the threshold of pain. Their recordings will never capture the visceral sensation of their live performances, where the sympathetic vibrations of floor and walls literally moved the audience and pressed the music into its pores.

With keyboardist Jan Hammer, violinist Jerry Goodman, and drummer Billy Cobham, McLaughlin formed the group in 1971 and recorded, that

[27] Columbia KC 31352.
[28] Columbia KC 34418.

Mahavishnu John McLaughlin.

same year, "Inner Mounting Flame."[29] With phase shifter and wah-wah distortions of incredibly fast rock-guitar solos, McLaughlin led the band in numbers based on ostinatos, some of which used unusual, and difficult, divisions of time, such as meters accented in irregular patterns that add up to 7, 11, 14, or 17. Often, the tempos would be extremely fast, as in *Vital Transformation* or *Awakening*, but the group also created lovely slow, meditative, quasi-Indian ballads, such as *You Know You Know*. Important advancements in microphone technology and miniaturization allowed the violin to return to jazz with a new voice, and Jerry Goodman led the way, followed by Jean-Luc Ponty, John Blake, Noel Pointer, and Michal Urbaniak, thus proving the instrument to be an effective ensemble and solo instrument for both rock and fusion-jazz ensembles.

THE AACM AND THE ART ENSEMBLE OF CHICAGO

The AACM was still influential and continued to be active during the '70s. Its founder, Muhal Richard Abrams, and its first-generation "graduates"— the Art Ensemble of Chicago, Anthony Braxton, Henry Threadgill, and others—recorded frequently, concertized, and played club dates to survive. The

[29] Columbia KC 31067.

The Art Ensemble of Chicago: (left to right) Don Moye, Joseph Jarman, Lester Bowie, Malachi Favors, and Roscoe Mitchell.

reception of their music in Europe was strong and growing, but the presentation of their music and ideas in America tended to get shunted into experimental quarters rather than the mainstage, where it might have become more widely accepted. However, the principles of their philosophy influenced all modern styles and infiltrated all but the most conservative groups.

Abrams, in his solo keyboard performances, was highly proficient, but his tendency toward eclecticism failed to cement a style or present a single message. In his 1975 recording "Sightsong,"[30] the seven tracks feature a host of ideas: *W.W.*—a post bebop sound with a bitonal, or "wrong-chord," accompaniment; *J.G.*—almost straight-ahead bebop; *Sightsong*—a romantic ballad; *Two over One*—a rhythmic exploration of 12/8 metrical possibilities; and so on. In 1976 he moved to New York, but his presence in the Chicago-based AACM continued to be felt.

The most exciting group of musicians to emanate from the AACM was the Art Ensemble of Chicago—Roscoe Mitchell, Lester Bowie, Malachi Favors, and Joseph Jarman—which organized as a drummerless quartet for performances in Paris in 1969. During the ensemble's eighteen-month expatriation, they added percussionist Don Moye and returned to this country

[30] Black Saint BSR 0003.

with European critical acclaim, with a track record of broadcasts, recordings, and government-sponsored tours, and with substantial popular admiration. In significant ways, their recordings do not do justice to their creations, for their performances were combinations of costume, choreography, stage settings of unusual instruments, music, poetry, noise, and an element of surprise that can only appear in rapport with a live audience. Several members performed in traditional African dress, and some added face paint. Instruments used by the Ensemble varied over time, but racks of bells, dozens of drums (some African, some American), nose flutes, whistles, bells, and countless percussion objects made appearances and were incorporated into their music. African and African-American themes predominated in their work, and intense, serious effort was effectively counterbalanced by injections of delightful humor. Their 1973 album, "Fanfare for the Warriors,"[31] is an excellent sampling of their music and styles, but it preserves only an echo, the audio portion, of their live concerts. *Illistrum* depends on surprise or shock and is unified by its poetry; *Barnyard Scuffel Shuffel* moves from slow piano (with guest artist Muhal Richard Abrams) to chaos to rhythm-and-blues;

Muhal Richard Abrams.

and *Nonaah* is a symphony of honks and bleats. From a purely musical point of view, the title track, *Fanfare for the Warriors,* is the most interesting, for many imaginative ideas are developed over an ostinato, but the phrase "purely musical" misses the point in evaluating the Art Ensemble's offerings. Abstract

[31] Atlantic 90046-1.

music criticism is far too Western in philosophy for a music that is participative and experiential, a facet of living that goes beyond the intellectual and
the auditory. It is also telling to observe how the recording was accomplished, for its making demonstrates another variety of studio production in
the '70s. Every afternoon for three days, the musicians gathered in the studio
and recorded all seven pieces. When they had finished, they selected their
choices of the best versions of each tune and gathered them into an album.
Given the nature of the style, three renditions of the same piece on three
different days could have been radically different. Also, in contrast to the
"cut and splice," studio-engineered recordings that were beginning to reach
the market at the time, these recordings were unaltered, continuous takes
of each piece. The recording studio played an active, ever-changing role in
jazz during the '70s.

In contrast to the self-generating music of the Art Ensemble of Chicago,
the music of Anthony Braxton, also a fledgling from the AACM nest, was
highly cerebral and tightly organized, calling for improvisatory statements
within a carefully demarcated framework. Also, the spontaneous bursts of
free improvisation necessarily required avant-garde techniques, such as multiphonics, pointillistic lines, and timbral explorations. Braxton first came to
public notice in 1970 as a member of Chick Corea's combo Circle, and when
Corea disbanded the ensemble in 1971, Braxton assumed leadership of his
own quartet with the other former Circle members, Kenny Wheeler on trum-

Anthony Braxton.

pet, Dave Holland on bass, and Barry Altschul on percussion. Braxton recorded at the Montreux Jazz Festival in 1975.[32] His composition on side 1, cut 1, whose title is represented by the following design,

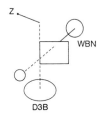

begins with a carefully assembled opening of percussion, muted trumpet, arco bass, and a variety of reed lines and jells into a work that compares favorably with the best compositions of the avant-garde "university composers"—a tightly organized, pointillistic, thin-textured piece. As the work unfolds, it gradually transforms as it moves into a section with traditional jazz rhythm and solos. But Braxton's solo goes further and further afield, until it reached a frenzy of notes flying in all directions. The bass and trumpet follow with their own statements, and the piece ends on a unison bebop riff. Where the Art Ensemble of Chicago found its inspiration in things African, the Anthony Braxton Quartet was gaining sustenance from a blend of free jazz and European compositional thought.

Shortly after this concert, Braxton reformed his group, with trombonist George Lewis replacing Wheeler. His composition[33] on side 2, cut 2,

$$C\text{-}M = B05$$
$$\mid$$
$$7$$

recorded in Berlin in 1976, is an amazing display of collective improvisation within a composer-dominated composition. George Lewis, also from the AACM, was a young virtuoso with ears and sympathies especially attuned to this style, and the rapport between his instrument and those of the other three members of the ensemble is artistically gratifying and persuasive.

REHEARSAL AND RECORDING BANDS

Although work opportunities increased consistently throughout the 1970s for soloists and combos, big bands struggled to make a comeback. At the start of the decade, most of the well-known orchestras were defunct, and the

[32] "The Montreux/Berlin Concerts" (Arista AL 5002).
[33] Ibid.

surviving few were more a living music museum than a medium of contemporary expression. Many large cities had rehearsal bands that met at, or through, the local musicians' union hall. Their rosters were often filled by young, highly skilled players whose training had been garnered in the lab bands of the colleges and universities from which they graduated rather than in the clubs, cabarets, and dance halls that traditionally had served as jazz musicians' training grounds. Occasionally, musicians would be brought into the studio as a recording band to perform a particular set of arrangements for an album, and some of the efforts were outstanding, for example, the Don Ellis Orchestra's "Tears of Joy" album[34] in 1971 and Bill Watrous and the Manhattan Wildlife Refuge album of 1975, "The Tiger of San Pedro"[35]). Don Ellis and his group continued to explore purely musical ideas in an attempt to revitalize the big-band concept. Their instrumentation is one of their most significant features. The leader plays quarter-tone trumpet and four-valve fluegel horn, two high-brass instruments with nondiatonic pitch possibilities, the former producing a strident sound and the latter a mellow sound; the brass section employs three trumpets, a French horn, and three bass instruments—two trombones and a tuba; the woodwind section comprises four players who make great use of doubling on single reeds, double reeds, and flutes, all amplified; a string quartet plays amplified instruments; and a four-member rhythm section of piano, bass, drums, and conga also controls amplified piano, electric piano, ring modulator, pianette, and clavinette. The composers and orchestrators apparently took a certain amount of inspiration from Near Eastern folk music and arranged scores in meters that grouped subdivisions of 5, 7, 9, 11, . . . 25, 27, and 33. It is in part the virtuosity of the orchestra that gives the album its significance, for although these meters and electronic sounds were used by others, the group, like the Mahavishnu Orchestra, demonstrates its easy ability to use these devices and even improvise in a stylistically satisfying manner within new and complex contexts.

Only a few of the larger organizations—those with a regular membership of a dozen or more players—lasted more than a few dates, except for show bands (e.g., Doc Severinsen's *Johnny Carson Show* Orchestra), nostalgia bands (e.g., Mercer Ellington and the Duke Ellington Orchestra), college stage bands (although amateur, some were outstanding), and rehearsal bands. Three of the best professional rehearsal bands—the Gil Evans Orchestra, the Gerry Mulligan Concert Jazz Band, and the Thad Jones / Mel Lewis Jazz Orchestra—kept the fire alive with new charts, weekly local performances, and occasional concerts and recordings. In this way, these bands kept the intellectual ferment and fervor for big band jazz alive.

While jazz groups in the 1970s were almost exclusively led by men, one

[34] Columbia G 30927.
[35] Columbia PC 33701.

The Thad Jones / Mel Lewis Jazz Orchestra at Shelly's Manne Hole in Los Angeles, c. 1974, with Jones leading and Lewis on drums.

excellent band was run by a woman, Toshiko Akiyoshi. A gifted pianist and arranger whose career started in Japan in the '50s and continued successfully on the East Coast of the United States in the '60s, Akiyoshi founded a rehearsal band in Los Angeles in 1973 with her husband, saxophonist/flutist Lew Tabackin. In this organization she had a medium with which she might explore her considerable compositional talents. At first her music with this orchestra was similar to the traditional big band sounds of the past, but she also brought some of the logic and sonorities of her native Far Eastern music to this combination. Although most of the tracks on her 1974–75 album "Long Yellow Road"[36] are still fixed along traditional lines, *Children in the Temple Ground* achieves success in integrating Japanese traditional singing together with Asian bell and flute sounds into the big band format. Throughout the album one hears interesting echoes of the big band past—thickened-voice sectional writing, answering riffs, interjected solos—and some innovations—surpris-

[36] RCA JPL1-1350.

Lew Tabackin and Toshiko Akiyoshi.

ing changes of tempo, unusual combinations of instruments, and a mixture of tonal and modal harmonies. The players are studio musicians of the highest caliber, the ensemble is precise, and the rhythm swings well.

THE DECADE IN REVIEW

Much of the jazz of the 1970s was played by musicians surrounded by stacks of speakers amplified by solid-state electronics capable of vibrating the floor of an amphitheater. They played on instruments that were electric or electronic: electric pianos, keyboard and analog synthesizers, electric guitars and basses, microphoned standard instruments, fuzz boxes, wah-wah pedals, ring modulators, exotic percussion instruments, African and Indian musical devices, and, as always, the voice. It was a decade of transition, experimentation, and consolidation, a period when young musicians developed the virtuoso techniques necessary to perform on the state-of-the-art inventions in live performance. Formerly, synthesizers were studio instruments that could be used only to create sound in a piecemeal manner—recorded snippets of tape that would later be joined laboriously into complete compositions. Now Herbie Hancock, Joe Zawinul, and other keyboard players commanded entire repertoires of synthesized sounds that they could call upon freely during a performance to accompany others or to use for their own solo jazz improvisations. There was much chaff during the decade, but the winnowed grain was substantial in quality and quantity, and many of the recorded performances have entered the standard repertoire.

All was not pleasant during these years, and although black America moved relentlessly toward equal rights, it was a painful, incremental struggle. In 1960, Max Roach declared public support for the sit-in demonstrations by black students in the South and wrote *We Insist! Freedom Now Suite*,[37] which opens with Abbey Lincoln singing about the "Driva' Man" who patrols the roads for runaway slaves and ends with "All Africa" and "Tears for Johannesburg." In 1971, Archie Shepp recorded an album, "Things Have Got To

Abbey Lincoln, c. 1970.   Archie Shepp.

Change,"[38] as his personal expression of political and musical philosophies. His poignant cry of "Give me my money!" communicates vividly the condition of blacks in American society at the time, and his music reaches out to his African roots. He combined the lessons he learned from his associations with John Coltrane and Cecil Taylor with his impressions of African-derived patterns and applied them both in musical commentaries on contemporary American social problems: *Money Blues*, *Dr. King, the Peaceful Warrior*, and *Things Have Got to Change*. In his own way, he used the jazz idiom as the country folksinger used the blues, "to tell it like it is" and to relieve the pressures of a difficult daily life through a catharsis of expression.

[37] Candid CJM 8002.
[38] Impulse AS 9212.

Many factors outside the music itself helped shape the history of jazz, including racial struggles in America, social interactions between musicians and the general public, and an explosive growth in technology, which affected musical instruments as well as concert and recording techniques. Also many musical forces operated on the changing picture of this art form, such as shifting tastes in popular music, developments in classical theory and composition, and a heightened interest in chamber music. The resulting jazz developed naturally according to the tastes, sensitivities, opportunities, and abilities of the individual jazz musicians. A key factor in the music of this period was the growing awareness of the musics, philosophies, and values of the newly emerging third-world countries. The search by American jazz musicians for extraterritorial inspiration frequently extended to India. The first importations of these ideas seemed ephemeral, probably done as much for the publicity value as for genuine musical reasons. Eventually, jazz musicians traveled to India to study, not simply to tour, and the increasing popularity of transcendental meditation among college students gave rise to an increased knowledge of Far-Eastern ways, both aesthetic and musical. The lasting effect on jazz may have been minimal, but at the time, some jazz musicians took these matters seriously. In 1967, Paul Horn, a young saxophonist, recorded his "Cosmic Consciousness" album[39] in Kashmir. He is the only jazz musician in the quartet; the other three are native Kashmiri musicians who play sitar, tabla, dilruba, and tamboura. Horn himself restricts his performance to alto flute, and the musical designs created by the quartet are interesting, although they may well not be considered jazz.

Horn continued to follow his own musical path through the '70s, and the exotic beauty of the Far East as well as the loveliness of the natural world proved inspirational to him. His 1978 recording, "Plenty of Horn,"[40] mixes the sounds of the East—*House of Horn, Siddhartha,* and *The Golden Princess*—with more current sounds of American jazz—*Willow Weep for Me* and *Give Me the Simple Life.*

The importance of Africa and its musical traditions on black American jazz musicians took on new significance. Africa no longer represented simply the roots, now it was the source of rhythms, melodic ideas, and extramusical inspiration for much modern jazz. Pianist McCoy Tyner, in 1972, recorded his album "Sahara,"[41] and on the cover we see pictured the modern musician seated amidst the rubble of urban renewal with a koto (a Japanese zither) on his lap. The intended comparison of the distant Saharan sands and the urban trashscape is further qualified by the titles of the composition's five parts:

---

[39] World Pacific WP-1445.
[40] Impulse IA-9356 / 2.
[41] Milestone MSP 9039.

McCoy Tyner.

Ebony Queen, *A Prayer for My Family*, *Valley of Life*, *Rebirth*, and *Sahara*. The music of Tyner, on acoustic piano, remains in the style he developed earlier with John Coltrane, but the other members of the quartet provide rhythmic and tonal effects that occasionally add a layer of impressionistic, neo-African sounds.

Herbie Hancock is one of the most facile and adept improvisers of electronic keyboard sounds. His 1972 album, "Crossings,"[42] is a remarkable demonstration of sculptured electronic sounds in a jazz context. Although the music is as close to absolute music as jazz can get, the seeming importance of Africa to the musicians becomes obvious when one reads the listing of their names: Mwandishi Herbie Hancock, Mganga Eddie Henderson, Pepo Mtoto Julian Priester, Jabali Billy Hart, Mwile Benny Maupin, and Mchezaji Buster Williams. Two additional musicians play Moog synthesizer and congas, and five voices are blended into the total mix.

Although the 1970s drew strength from the leadership of the older masters Miles Davis and Ornette Coleman, the decade also saw the death of many other revered artists: from the first generation, Louis Armstrong, Kid Ory, and Duke Ellington; from the second generation, Eddie Condon, Johnny Hodges, and Gene Krupa; from the third generation, Erroll Garner and Charles Mingus; and many more—Stan Kenton, Paul Desmond, Don Byas, Paul Gonsalves, Cannonball Adderley, and Lennie Tristano, to name but a few.

[42] Warner Brothers BS 2617.

Suddenly, the profession became aware of its own mortality, for virtually none of the first generation were left, while the second was approaching extinction. Like it or not, certain aspects of jazz became historical, and during this decade the first serious efforts were made at establishing repertory groups—ensembles dedicated to recreating the classic performances of jazz and preserving earlier performance techniques and improvisational styles. Chuck Israels founded the National Jazz Ensemble in 1973, George Wein the New York Jazz Repertory Company in 1974, and others followed suit. Similarly, traditional New Orleans–style jazz moved from the shack of neglect to the house of revival. Jazz history and jazz appreciation courses started to become a regular feature in college curricula across the land, all the more remarkable for the rapidity of the subject's acceptance into a formerly hostile environment.

Ronnie Roullier directing a rehearsal of the New York Jazz Repertory Orchestra for its inaugural concert at Town Hall, September 1974.

In addition to the innovations that occurred in the major recording studios, artist-produced recording companies emerged to satisfy the musicians' need for artistic control over repertoire and to provide recording opportunities for non-commercial artistic ventures. These new labels held only a minuscule fraction of the record market at first, but they allowed the dissemination of avant-garde music among the relatively closed community of jazz musicians. They thus became a significant vehicle for the spread of new ideas, and they often helped establish the reputations of young, unknown artists who recorded first on these smaller labels. The sale and distribution of these recordings at concerts and festivals, especially in Europe, proved to be a useful method of entering a market formerly monopolized by major labels.

Guitarists gained new stature during the decade through their vital role in fusion jazz. John McLaughlin, Pat Metheny, John Abercrombie, John Scofield, and others were no longer ensemble musicians, as most acoustic guitar players had been before, but soloists. The role of pianists changed too, and most became "keyboardists." Technology and jazz moved hand in hand throughout the period. Finally, jazz truly became a world phenomenon during the decade. With its long history in North America, England, and Europe established, jazz saw native-born artists, festivals, and markets begin to appear in Africa, South America, Australia, the Former Soviet lands, and the Far East. The '70s started poorly but ended in fine fettle; they proved to be years of consolidation, transition, and growth.

11

A PLURALITY OF STYLES— THROUGH THE '80S AND INTO THE '90S

INTRODUCTION

One clear indication of a thriving art form is disagreement, a climate where creative intellectuals might dispute the merits of, say, serialism versus neo-classicism, where performers might argue, through their music, the primacy of human emotions and acoustical instruments over objective logic or digital sampling, and where critics might dispute the superiority of spontaneous, free expression as against the artifice of composition or tradition. Ultimately it is never a question of right and wrong. One side is not pure, the other tainted; both are simply interpreting the world through different lenses. Both see a unique distortion of reality, and each may lay claim to its own span of the historical continuum. Every artist strives to interpret and influence the world and reveal a personal vision of contemporary thought in the *speculum musicae*, music's mirror. One set of values may temporarily gain sway over another but only for a while, until it too is toppled and replaced by a newer "truth," which temporarily negates the values the former espoused with such fervor and certainty. Jazz in the '80s was no exception.

Jazz did not lack for activity during this decade—it was a hotbed of conflicting styles, clashing critical opinions, and unprecedented technical changes. These ten years witnessed a wholesale increase of "young" players (born after the Second World War) among the musicians acquiring critical acclaim, and they saw recording companies promoting the new music and artists with competitive furor while reissuing shelves of jazz classics with equal determination. The '80s glimpsed the Congress of the United States formally declaring jazz a national treasure and, in at least one notable example, they saw youth and age reverse roles. Wynton Marsalis, the youngster of impeccable artistic credentials, gentlemanly demeanor, and the highest musical standards, led a conservative movement in jazz which praised tradition and condemned the influence of pop, rock, and fusion. At the same time, sexagenarian Miles Davis, a trendy international figure for forty years, returned to the performing world and continued to probe the funky frontiers of electric, electronic, and studio fusion. Critic Francis Davis was less than sanguine about the health of the art form at mid-decade:

> Things are tough all over in the 1980s, but especially so for jazz, a music long ago banished to the no man's land between popular culture and fine art, where it figures to remain so long as its mongrel beginnings are held against it by those in high places. It's no longer honorable to exist on the fringes, which leaves jazz musicians out in the cold, in this decade of the homeless and *Lifestyles of the Rich and Famous*. . . . What little jazz one hears on the radio has paid too dear a cost to get there, and too few alternative concert venues have materialized to replace the jazz nightclubs that padlocked their doors in the '60s and '70s.[1]

But critic James Lincoln Collier, at approximately the same time, interpreted the same events in a totally different light and with almost opposite conclusions:

> The 1970s saw a substantial improvement in the fortunes of jazz in the U.S.A. By the end of the decade there were as many jazz clubs operating as there had been in the good times of the 1920s and the 1950s. . . .
>
> The precise cause of the rising interest in jazz is difficult to pinpoint. . . . In part it was the result of . . . jazz grants from public and private foundations, . . . reviews of jazz performances in the press, . . . courses in jazz in universities, and the like. In part it was related to the more widespread acceptance of Blacks in white society. In part it had to do with the respectability jazz had

---

[1] Francis Davis, *In the Moment: Jazz in the 1980s*, p. ix.

achieved. And, of course, in part the virtues of the music itself were responsible for its new popularity.[2]

If you were the kind of jazz fan during the '80s who believed that the "best" jazz could be found only in newly created virtuosic solo improvisations within a structure of changing chords in measured time by a recognized master, you might have chosen, for example, a live concert by the Gerry Mulligan Orchestra or a new combo recording by this trend setter of the '50s.[3] Mulligan, like Sonny Rollins or Dexter Gordon, was as close as the local record store for new issues and reissues and only as far away as a New York club or an international jazz festival for a live performance. If your taste ran to the swing sounds of the '30s, you would still have been able to attend a performance of Benny Goodman leading an orchestra playing the old Fletcher Henderson charts, or been able to purchase his new recordings of that same traditional style, or buy reissues of his now-famous old recordings, or acquire new compact discs of old recordings previously unreleased.[4] The variety, availability, and sheer quantity of jazz in the 1980s was extraordinary.

Traditional jazz buffs might have traveled to New Orleans to hear Pete Fountain or to Colorado Springs to hear Doc Cheatham. In many locales they might have chosen to attend a "Trad Jazz Festival" to hear the Louisiana Repertory Jazz Band or the Galvanized Jazz Band, ensembles of "younger" musicians recreating the jazz sounds of an earlier era. If, on the other hand, you were of a mind to reject improvisation as the key element of black musical expression, you may have preferred to attend concerts or buy records of African-American jazz composers such as Anthony Davis and his ensemble, Episteme.[5] Davis believes in

> a different concept of playing, which involved the idea of composing, rather than improvisation, being of central importance in the ongoing development of black music. . . . We're in a new period, and some people are confused by what they're hearing, because the music is developing chiefly in the area of composition, not in terms of what people have been taught to listen for—new directions in improvisation.[6]

Unlike the early '70s, the '80s were not years of crisis, they were years of intense activity and healthy ferment. Jazz was at its creative best, proud

---

[2] James Lincoln Collier, "Jazz," *The New Grove Dictionary of Jazz*, I, p. 605.

[3] Gerry Mulligan and His Orchestra, "Walk on the Water" (DRG Records SL 5194); or Gerry Mulligan, "Little Big Horn" (GRP Records A-1003).

[4] A continuing series of Benny Goodman releases sponsored by the Music Library of Yale University: vol. 1 (Music Masters CIJ 20142), vol. 2 (Music Masters CIJ 60156); etc.

[5] Gramavision GR 8101.

[6] Francis Davis, *In the Moment*, p. 6.

musicians vying with each other in essentially constructive rivalries. Jazz, in many ways, fulfilled Leonard B. Meyer's prophesy of 1967:

> What the proposed hypothesis, then, envisages is the persistence over a considerable period of time of a fluctuating stasis—a steady-state in which an indefinite number of styles and idioms, techniques and movements, will coexist in each of the arts. There will be no central, common practice in the arts, no stylistic "victory." In music, for instance, tonal and non-tonal styles, aleatoric and serialized techniques, electronic and improvised means will all continue to be employed. . . .
>
> Though new methods and directions may be developed in any or in all of the arts, these will not displace existing styles. The new will simply be additions to the already existing spectrum of styles. Interaction and accommodation among different traditions of music, art, or literature may from time to time produce hybrid combinations or composites, but the possibility of radical innovation seems very remote. . . . the abrupt juxtaposition of markedly unlike styles—perhaps from different epochs and traditions—within a single work may not be uncommon.[7]

All of this was proven true of jazz in the '80s.

——— FUSION AND MILES DAVIS ———

Miles Davis was a living bridge of jazz styles from the 1940s to the 1990s. His role with Charlie Parker and his leadership in cool jazz, modal jazz, free improvisation, and fusion jazz kept him at the forefront of modern jazz in every era since the early days of bebop. During the last years of the 1970s, his health forced a retirement, but after four years of reclusive behavior and musical paralysis, Davis astounded the jazz world in 1980 with a comeback. His first efforts were disappointing, for during his illness he had lost his lip, his endurance, and the keen edge that a brilliant improviser constantly hones.

In 1980 he went into the studio with various combinations of musicians on guitars, keyboards, synthesizers, soprano sax, bass, drums, percussion, and vocals, and recorded his first comeback album, which was not released until 1981, "The Man with the Horn."[8] None of the tracks were high-quality jazz, despite the wizardry of studio splicing, re-recording, overdubbing, omissions, and insertions, but the session got Davis playing again with some of the musicians he would use in the future. His working group included Bill Evans on saxophone (not to be confused with the pianist Bill Evans,

[7] Leonard B. Meyer, *Music, the Arts, and Ideas*, p. 172.
[8] Columbia PC 36790.

who died in 1980), Al Foster on drums, and Marcus Miller on Fender bass.

Davis took his group on the road in 1981, first to Boston, then to the Kool Jazz Festival in New York City, and finally to Tokyo. In spite of continuing health problems, he immersed himself in his music and not only regained his old mastery over instrument, repertoire, and musicians, but set out on new exploratory quests. It is fascinating to compare the recording of *Back Seat Betty* from the 1980 album with the recording of the same tune from his next album, recorded live in 1981 and released the following year.[9] During the performance of the earlier recording, Davis's efforts were tentative, brief, unsure. The only interesting solo on the cut is that of Bill Evans on soprano sax. On the second album, Davis takes command. In his solo, he first explores minute pitch and timbre variations, then moves on to play with rhythmic figures and continues into an ever-expanding barrage of sound over an extended range. Finally, he removes his mute, foregoes distortion techniques, and plays on his open horn, dramatically accelerating the speed of the notes.

This fusion band picked up where Davis left off in the '70s and laid the groundwork for him to begin exploring sound again, that is, probing into a variety of tonal characteristics and adjustments to pitch in various combinations and with a variety of rhythmic formats. Adding to the drum work of Al Foster, Mino Cinelu, a second percussionist, contributed a carpet of complex, semi-independent rhythms. We can hear his special talents displayed well on *Fast Track*.[10] This album won a Grammy award for the best jazz album of 1982, and Davis was named Jazz Musician of the Year by *Jazz Forum* in 1983. Miles Davis was back in full force and was beginning to influence another generation of young jazz musicians.

In 1984 Davis traveled to Denmark to receive the Sonning Music Prize; he returned there in 1985 to record "Aura,"[11] an album composed by Palle Mikkeborg. Inspired by his perception of Davis's ability to paint in tone, Mikkeborg composed a ten-movement suite in a serial style based on ten pitches. These ten pitches were drawn from the letters of Davis's name, and they were used both as a chord (ten notes together) and as a melodic subject. For the performance, Davis was joined by two of his regular compatriots— John McLaughlin on guitar and Vincent Wilburn (Davis's nephew) on electric drums—and a large European recording band of five trumpets/ fluegelhorns, four trombones and tuba, five saxophones/woodwinds, three keyboards, two basses, three drums/percussion, oboe, harp, and vocals. Once again, Davis surrounded himself with electronic sounds and acoustic combinations, a conglomerate of composition and improvisation, mixtures of steady

[9] "We Want Miles" (Columbia C2 38005).
[10] Ibid.
[11] Columbia CTX 45332.

rhythms and irregular groupings, old formulas and free responses. In his own way, he was spearheading the attack.

That same year, he also recorded "You're Under Arrest,"[12] and although the music was similar to much of the funky fusion-jazz he played most of the time, the social and biographical message was less than subtle. The work of John McLaughlin and John Scofield on guitars was a stylistic model for jazz/rock guitar playing. The synthesizer work of Robert Irving, III, was state-of-the-art. From the mix recorded on the album, it is difficult to distinguish between the more jazzlike drumming of Al Foster and the more rocklike drumming of Vince Wilburn, but Davis was about to terminate his longtime association with Foster. Davis's interests were moving ever closer to synthetic sound and funk.

In 1985, he ended a thirty-year affiliation with Columbia Records, and although Columbia continued to issue new recordings by Davis from archive material, his next innovation came on the Warner Brothers label. He chose not to use his working band in the studio for his 1986 recording of the album "Tutu,"[13] named after Bishop Desmond Tutu of South Africa. The title of another track, *Full Nelson*, was a pun that honored the South African political prisoner Nelson Mandela and alluded to *Half Nelson*, a piece Davis composed when he was playing with Charlie Parker. Both "You're Under Arrest" and "Tutu" were conceived and produced at a time when Davis was once again strongly feeling the anguish of black people.

> That's where the concept for "You're Under Arrest" came from: being locked up for being a part of a street scene, being locked up politically. Being subjected to the looming horror of a nuclear holocaust—plus being locked up in a spiritual way.[14]

Beyond the social message of *Tutu*, *Full Nelson*, and *Don't Lose Your Mind*, the musical production of the album broke new ground. Digital technology allowed musicians in the studio to achieve new levels of isolation, independence, and corrective surgery. Marcus Miller composed most of the music, and together with Jason Miles, a synthesizer programmer, began to assemble the music one part at a time. As a first step, Miller recorded several tracks of synthesized sound alone, without Davis's presence. Miller and executive producer Tommy LiPuma worked through the night recording layers of synthesized bass drum, percussion instruments, and then keyboard sounds. Davis came to the studio the following day, listened to the prerecorded background

[12] Columbia FC 40023.
[13] Warner Brothers W2 25490.
[14] Davis with Troupe, *Miles Davis*, p. 362.

sounds, recorded and re-recorded solos to be added and mastered to the former, and left. Then Miller and Davis worked and reworked the music. After they were done, additional players were called to the studio to add tracks: Michal Urbaniak on electric violin, Adam Holzman on synthesizer, Omar Hakim on drums and percussion, and others. Eventually the studio technicians completed the work. Still, though the album gleams with remarkable technology, it is not entirely original. The title track is strongly reminiscent of the Gil Evans orchestrations for Davis's earlier recording of *Porgy and Bess*, except that on this album the band is synthesized and unreal.

On his 1989 release, "Amandla,"[15] Davis also made both political and musical statements. The word "amandla" means "freedom" in Zulu, one of the languages of black South Africa, and some of the rhythms employed were Davis's interpretation of Zouk, a music played in the West Indies. But this music is a conglomerate—jazz, rock, Zouk, acoustic, synthetic, electric, electronic, digital, analog, composed, improvised. These sounds could not have been produced in the 1970s; the thoughts expressed here are tightly bound to the events of the day.

Even after he passed his sixty-fifth birthday, Davis continued to seek inspiration and artistic renewal from exotic quarters, from advanced technology, and from associations with youth. He explained:

> When I hear jazz musicians today playing all those same licks we used to play so long ago, I feel sad for them. . . . Most people my age like old, stuffy furniture. I like the new Memphis style of sleek high tech stuff, a lot of it coming from Italy. Bold colors and long, sleek, spare lines. I don't like a lot of clutter. . . .
>
> I love challenges and new things; they reenergize me. But music has always been healing for me, and spiritual. . . . I'm still learning every day.[16]

Miles Davis died of a stroke on September 28, 1991.

NEOCLASSICISM AND MODERN BEBOP

No informed listener would mistake Stravinsky's Symphony in C or a Hindemith piano concerto for a work by Mozart, even though both twentieth-century composers drew their inspiration, their sense of formal design, and some of their compositional principles from the music of Mozart, Haydn,

---

[15] Warner Brothers 9 25873-4.
[16] Davis with Troupe, *Miles Davis*, p. 391.

and other composers of the classical era. Igor Stravinsky, Paul Hindemith, Sergei Prokofiev, Arthur Honegger, William Schuman, and many other composers of this century wrote music in a style categorized as "neoclassical," that is, music composed with balanced forms, clearly perceptible thematic processes, opening statements, cadential formulas, tonal relationships, motivic developmental techniques, and so on. But, the forms were not the same, the harmonic speed was not a perfect match, the key relationships and chordal structures were not equivalent. The principles of composition, however, were derived from those of the eighteenth century, as was the quest for beauty in music, but the detailed substance of these modern works was twentieth-century music that could not have been composed at any earlier time.

A similar movement occurred in jazz during the 1980s, and no informed listener would mistake the music of Wynton Marsalis or Freddie Hubbard for the bebop of Dizzy Gillespie or Fats Navarro. With deference to and respect for the major accomplishments of older jazz masters, and in reaction to the increasing rock influences in jazz on the one hand and the formlessness and eclecticism of free jazz on the other, a group of talented young musicians ushered in a style of jazz that we might refer to as "modern bebop" or "post-modern bebop," a contemporary neoclassical jazz style of the 1980s. Unlike the bebop of Charlie Parker, Dizzy Gillespie, and other avant-garde jazz musicians of the late 1940s, modern bebop often uses expanded tonalities, modal and timbral improvisation, forms other than "pop song" and blues, and other devices either not present or little used in the '40s, but the principles of modern bebop are based on those developed by the bebop masters. The music has a perceivable formal structure, the improvisations relate directly to that structure, the element of craftsmanship is held in the highest regard, and beauty of tone, elegance of melody, and importance of message are inherent in the value system of the music. As Gary Giddins writes under the heading "Jazz Turns Neoclassical,"

> As I see it, the avant-garde has been studiously aligning itself with mainstream jazz for some time. The resurgence of jazz means in large measure the resurgence of swing, melody, and beauty, as well as other vintage jazz qualities such as virtuosity, wit, and structure—not that they've ever been entirely absent. If jazz, like other fine arts, had to be relearned in a period of avant-garde extremism, it has long since—and with a vengeance—turned neoclassical. Musicians weaned on the free jazz of the '60s now sift '20s' classicism, '30s' swing, '40s' bop, and '50s' soul for repertoire and expressive wisdom. They are, in effect, going home again.[17]

[17] Gary Giddins, *Rhythm-a-ning*, p. xi f.

WYNTON MARSALIS

The artist who championed neoclassicism in jazz in the early 1980s was trumpeter Wynton Marsalis. Marsalis's spectacular rise during this period overshadowed even Miles Davis's 1981 comeback. Born in New Orleans in 1961, the son of jazz pianist and teacher Ellis Marsalis, he studied both classical music and jazz, performed the Haydn Trumpet Concerto with the New Orleans Philharmonic Orchestra at age fourteen, attended the Berkshire Music Center at Tanglewood at seventeen (where he was cited as the outstanding brass player of the season), enrolled at the Juilliard School at eighteen, and was playing and recording with Art Blakey's Jazz Messengers at nineteen. In 1981, he toured with Herbie Hancock's V.S.O.P. II, and the following year he formed his own band with his brother, tenor saxophonist Branford Marsalis. At the 1982 Kool Jazz Festival in New York he won public and critical accolades. In 1983 two of his recordings were issued, one classical and the other jazz, and both won Grammys in 1984. He was now 23 years old.

Wynton Marsalis's first recording with Blakey and the Jazz Messengers in 1980[18] already displayed his spellbinding technique. As a sample from his apprentice years, the recording demonstrates his straight-ahead approach to improvisation—play the changes and keep the beat—that stem from his education in the traditions of jazz, especially bebop and hard bop. His 1981 recording, "Wynton Marsalis,"[19] is his first as leader, and his duets with Branford on his composition *Hesitation* generate excitement through the fluid exchange of ideas that pass back and forth between the brothers.

His second album as leader, "Think of One,"[20] was issued concurrently with his recording of classical trumpet concertos,[21] and it is fascinating to compare the different standards by which the two performances are judged. In the classical recording there is a universally accepted standard of tone quality and an insistence on accuracy of pitch. Also, clean articulation, correct ornamentation, appropriate musical phrasing, "authentic" interpretation (as the composer and tradition dictate), and other factors mandate the limits of a performance and restrict the freedom of the artist to interject much personality. Every trumpeter who approaches the Haydn Concerto, for example, is confronted with thousands, perhaps hundreds of thousands, of previous performances of exactly the same notes, and the judgment of bad,

---

[18] "Recorded Live at Bubba's" (Who's Who in Jazz D21S-72209).

[19] Columbia FC-37574.

[20] Columbia FC-38641.

[21] Franz Joseph Haydn, Johann Nepomuk Hummel, and Leopold Mozart (Columbia IM-37846).

mediocre, good, or excellent is based on some absolute standard (which, of course, is never absolute) of correctness and conformity. Though he has since foresaken classical performance, Marsalis was able to place his 1982 recital of a classical masterwork among those in a long history of trumpet virtuoso performances and recordings of the *Urtext*, or "authentic score," and come away with international honors and a prize.

For his performances on "Think of One," Marsalis was judged by entirely different standards: freshness of ideas during improvisation, response to the improvisatory gestures of his group, ability to surprise the listener, skill at generating a feeling of swing, and a range of considerations not applicable to a concerto performance. Even those elements that exist in both genres are dissimilar: good tone quality is vital, but in jazz it should be unique, varied, non-standard, mixed with growls, muted sounds, bends, squeezed notes, and whatever will make it expressive; virtuosity is essential, but one note rather than another, or a slurry of ten notes one time and eight crisp notes the next, can all be correct and advantageous, or wrong and disastrous,

Wynton Marsalis.

depending on context, tempo, the moment, and the artist. In other words, Marsalis the jazz trumpeter had a different musical persona from Marsalis the classical trumpeter, yet Marsalis the performer was able in the same year to garner international acclaim and prizes in both realms. With such truly astounding credentials, Marsalis immediately became a spokesman and model for his style of jazz performance, and modern bebop became a driving force for the rest of the decade.

In 1985, Branford Marsalis left the band to join the first group founded by the British rock star Sting, and Wynton continued with a quartet. In December 1986 Wynton recorded "Live at Blues Alley"[22] with pianist Marcus Roberts, acoustic bass player Robert Leslie Hurst, III, and Jeff "Tain" Watts on drums. The instrumentation of the band and the repertoire chosen for the album demonstrate clearly the neoclassical approach Marsalis espouses. The band is an acoustic quartet with standard rhythm section of piano, bass, and drums (the jazz equivalent of classical chamber instrumentations for trio sonata, piano quartet, or mixed quartet and a combo that was omnipresent during the bebop era). The tunes are a combination of standards—*Just Friends, Cherokee, Autumn Leaves*—and originals with formal design, tonality, and commonly understood performance expectations—*Knozz-Moe-King* (one long version and three "interludes"), *Juan, Delfeayo's Dilemma*. The album is the recorded equivalent of an evening's work at a club, and the performances, although all good, vary in quality, approach, and function.

Delfeayo's Dilemma (NAJ 20) is a Wynton Marsalis original, and the head of the tune, with its sawtooth angularity, is certain to eliminate second-rate trumpet players from its performance. Marsalis, the virtuoso, traverses the pattern as easily as most trumpeters play a scale. Driven on by Watts's powerful drumming in the Elvin Jones tradition and by the piano playing of Roberts in patterns that do not merely accompany but respond actively to the trumpet's improvisations, Marsalis plays a long continuous solo that gradually builds to a logical and natural climax. Roberts is a virtuoso in his own right, and his piano solo coheres well in a scheme of expanding ideas. The details of this performance differ in some ways from those found in most traditional bebop but the general principles of acoustic instruments performing an exposition and recapitulation and improvising to a harmonic scheme form the basis of this work. Thus for all its newness, the piece is neoclassical in its resurrection of classical bebop principles. (See Listening Guide 20.)

Juan is blues with a humorous twist that is useful for entertaining a live audience. It is also part of a long tradition of humor in jazz. *Knozz-Moe-King* is a concert piece much like a Baroque toccata, a full-winded display to impress

[22] Columbia G2K-40675.

Wynton Marsalis.

the audience, get the music started, and loosen up the fingers and the instruments. *Do You Know What it Means to Miss New Orleans?* is an expressive and tender ballad that not only changes pace, quiets the listeners, and sets an entirely different mood, but serves as a vehicle to display the mature expression of which this young musician is capable. Marsalis's playing is tender, relaxed, soulful, and elegant. But as a model of the neoclassic in jazz, *Autumn Leaves* stands out. A popular standard by Johnny Mercer, it has been sung, played, and orchestrated ad infinitum, to the point, in fact, that all educated jazz listeners know the harmonic and melodic sequences. Thus, it is ripe for a post-modern change. Through the first statement of the theme, time—in the sense of steady beat and single meter—comes and goes. The players mix groups of twos and threes, and they speed up and slow down. During the second statement, time not only continues to fade and return as a cohesive factor, but it is stretched and squeezed further as the tune is distorted. During the first solo chorus, harmonic progression is still noticeable, but during the second chorus of the trumpet improvisation, chords become static and attention is focused on rhythm as rhythmic development replaces melodic improvisation. Just before he leaves the limelight, Marsalis muffs a couple of notes as he slowly sequences up and around, but that too is part of the aesthetic of live performance. Many outstanding musicians will not let a studio technician clean up errors; instead, they strive and polish in the hope of one day achieving the perfect performance in real time.

The pianist in *Autumn Leaves*, in his accompanying and his solo performance, thinks and reacts the way Marsalis does. At times the bass is a harmonic instrument while at other times it creates lines, sounds, and rhythms that drift freely but always match the work of the other players. The drummer in this session, no longer principally a timekeeper, is not free—his role is to react, put glue in the holes, lead tempo changes, and straighten the alignment. Were this a bebop performance, the soloist would invent to the changes, the bass would lay down those changes, the drummer would keep time and drop bombs, and the piano would comp, albeit with syncopation, in time. In a neoclassical interpretation, the norm of a bebop performance is present in the listener's ear to set a standard by which the inventiveness, precision, and beauty of the new performance might be judged. To signal a bass solo, the piano clears the air with the harmonic progression of the last eight measures of the model. The bass player, too, ranges over his instrument, choosing a double-plucking rhythm as a motive for invention; he leaves the harmony, but not the time. Then the trumpet returns for a combination solo/recapitulation of theme, and a standard, simple ("Sears Roebuck") ending draws the piece to a close.

Wynton Marsalis has taught the jazz world that newness is not a be-all and end-all. By exciting listeners, musicians, and non-players alike with a music that looks back to tradition rather than to other worlds (Africa, the Far East), other cultures (pop and rock), or technology (digital sampling, MIDI, computers, and synthesizers), Marsalis has reenergized an entire segment of the jazz community and attracted a new, young audience that was returning, in other ways too, to more conservative values. Were he a less phenomenal musician, or less of a gentleman or intellectual, he might not have succeeded. But his talent, training, personal qualities, and fortuitous moves initiated and fortified a 1980s jazz style rich with old values—modern bebop. In his words,

> Jazz music really teaches you what it is to live in a democracy. . . . The whole negotiation of the rights of individuals with responsibility to the group, that is the greatest beauty of jazz music as a mythic entity. The myth of jazz teaches you what it is to be an American. Just as a spiritual mythology has gods and heroes, the gods of the jazz mythology are Duke Ellington and Louis Armstrong.[23]

The strength and importance of philosophical principles at the core of neoclassical jazz can be seen in a similar statement by Marcus Roberts, pianist with Wynton Marsalis since 1985 and leader in 1988 of his own recording group. On the liner notes to his own album, "The Truth Is Spoken Here,"[24] Roberts is quoted as saying:

> American music organizes human experiences and emotions into a language which describes the lofty ideals of humanity, and is very indicative of the democratic conception upon which this country was founded.

OTHER NEOCLASSICISTS

Tradition and enduring values are obviously central to the frame of mind of these musicians and to their playing as well. The music recorded on this album, however, hardly ventures beyond the limits of bebop. In the performances of the Monk and Ellington tunes, Roberts's group might even be considered a repertory band rather than a neoclassic jazz ensemble.

Not so with the music of Terence Blanchard and Donald Harrison. Their principles are rooted in the past but their ears are tuned to the present. On their album "Black Pearl,"[25] recorded in 1988, there are few if any compromises. All the tunes are original except *Somewhere* by Leonard Bernstein, and

---

[23] Quoted by Dave Helland, "Wynton: Prophet in Standard Time," *Down Beat*, September 1990, p. 18.
[24] BMG 3051-2-N.
[25] Columbia CK 44216.

Terence Blanchard (left) with film producer/director Spike Lee on the set of Lee's "Malcolm X."

the performers exhibit high standards of precision, beauty of tone, and creativity in solo improvisation. The opening track, *Selim Sivad,* is an excellent example of a composition whose formal structure, tonality, and harmonic pattern fit no other existing structure precisely. It uses an **AAB** form, somewhat like the blues, but the chord patterns are unusual, the phrase lengths are different, and the **B** section is set in a different meter. In the same manner, *Ninth Ward Strut* is similar to some of the Charlie Parker / Dizzy Gillespie introductions, but the ostinato becomes the main organizing principle, getting a cadential demarcation at the end of each chorus. These young musicians, brilliant technicians on their instruments, are thoughtful and inventive creators who are exploring as they mature. The music becomes eclectic, at times, as the influences of Coltrane and some of the free jazz musicians appear in the solo improvisations, but it is clear that this music is pegged to formal design, acoustic sounds, and developmental improvisation.

These same features are apparent as well when Branford Marsalis leads

Branford Marsalis on the set of NBC's *Tonight* show.

his own group. "Random Abstract,"[26] recorded in 1987, is neoclassical on some of the tracks, bebop on the others. *Steep's Time*, the outstanding cut on the album, seems to draw inspiration from two sources: drum solo numbers that were common in the swing days of Louis Bellson and Gene Krupa and the modal jazz days of Wayne Shorter with Miles Davis. Whereas the line between eighteenth-century classical and twentieth-century neoclassical is easy to draw stylistically, the lines between any of the modern jazz styles tend to be fuzzy. The same players cross over from one group to the next, only a few years separate one set of ideas from another, and a distant view of the 1980s is not yet possible. Still, a large core of young jazz musicians have jumped on neither the fusion nor the free jazz bandwagons. They play old standards, not as learning exercises but as new music. They struggle for new ideas and an individual musical voice just as their predecessors did. They have captivated a large, informed, and basically young audience, and they show no sign of wavering in their determination to hold jazz to its historic principles.

Two other leading voices in the neoclassic movement of the '80s are trumpeter Freddie Hubbard and the collective voice of the World Saxophone Quartet (*SCCJ* 106). Hubbard, Wynton Marsalis, and Terence Blanchard, successively, played with Art Blakey and the Jazz Messengers, and the influence of that hard bop ensemble on the development of modern bebop is easy to hear. On the other hand, the members of the World Saxophone Quartet have strong ties to BAG, the Black Artists Group of St. Louis, a prime mover of free jazz in the early '70s and certainly an unexpected source of renewal for neoclassical music. But, like the AACM, BAG taught a respect for tradition, and the four saxophonists proved their understanding of the past by creating innovative and unique styles of both modern swing and modern bebop. Freddie Hubbard and the members of the saxophone quartet—Hamiet Bluiett, baritone, Julius Hemphill and Oliver Lake, altos, and David Murray, tenor (replaced in 1986 by John Stubblefield)—are versatile musicians who cross over from one style to another when different recording and performing activities become available. Hubbard, along with pianist Chick Corea, tenor saxophonist Joe Henderson, bassist Stanley Clarke, and drummer Lenny White, can be heard in a swinging version of modern bebop, "The Griffith Park Collection,"[27] and in an unusual mixture of fusion jazz with a large orchestra, "Ride Like the Wind,"[28] both recorded in 1981. The members of the World Saxophone Quartet, in similar fashion, display an

[26] Columbia CK 44055.
[27] Elektra E1-60025.
[28] Elektra E1-60029.

The World Saxophone Quartet: (left to right) Arthur Blythe, David Murray, Hamiet Bluiett, and Oliver Lake.

even more remarkable versatility of styles. On their 1981 recording "Live in Zurich,"[29] the first cut, *Hattie Wall*, is modern swing with a mambo beat; the second, *Funny Paper*, modern bebop; the third, *Touchic*, a "classical" French saxophone quartet piece that might have been written by Poulenc; and the fourth, *My First Winter*, a composition reminiscent of Ralph Burns's composition for Woody Herman, *Early Autumn*. Their awareness of their own neoclassicism is made apparent in Leonard Feather's album liner notes:

> Speaking of *Funny Paper*, Hemphill comments that this work is "an application of bebop tendencies." True, bop elements are discernible, yet it is inescapably true that the main thrust derives from concepts developed almost four decades later.[30]

Their 1985 "Live at Brooklyn Academy of Music" recording,[31] which displays their neoclassic wares to excellent advantage, also includes a masterpiece of free jazz improvisation/composition, *Great Peace*. Among the interworkings of free melodies in shifting rhythms across atonal space, we can note a beauty of sound and a coherence that are exceptional in this style.

[29] Black Saint BSR 0077.
[30] Ibid.
[31] Black Saint BSR 0096.

FREE JAZZ OF THE '80S— GEORGE LEWIS

Some of the younger musicians, however, would simply not be restrained—
they are the "young Turks" of jazz, *les enfants terribles*. One such artist is
trombonist George Lewis. A "graduate" of the AACM and a graduate, in
philosophy, of Yale University, Lewis draws nourishment from the experience of sound itself. In his music he is unmanageable, mischievous, and
impudent, but he forces us to think seriously while listening. From 1971 to
1975, as a member of the AACM, he toured and recorded with Anthony
Braxton and Count Basie, musicians of two different worlds: avant-garde free
jazz and Kansas City swing. In 1976 he recorded "The George Lewis Solo
Trombone Record,"[32] an unusual experiment in multiphonics, overdubbing,
mute and slide effects, time distortions, and jazz. Two years later he recorded
Charon,[33] and he had begun using an electronically modified trombone as
well as some homemade electronic instruments. Since these Canadian and
Italian labels were not readily available in the United States, his fame in
Europe rose dramatically before he was even recognized in America. But the
members of the AACM circle and their close associates knew both his music
and his capabilities. *Charon*, a tone poem that somberly portrays the funereal
boatman of the river Styx, is a major composition of the period, incorporating
the advanced compositional thought usually associated with university composers. Douglas Ewart, on bass clarinet, creates an interesting study of tones,
squeaks, and wails in excellent harmony with the eerie composition itself.

   From 1978 to 1981, Lewis worked on *Atlantic*, a composition for four
trombones, homemade filters, and various electronics, most of them hand-
crafted. In jazz, as elsewhere, faddish labels are invented to categorize similar objects or sounds. About this time, New Wave jazz was filtering back to
this country from avant-garde European record labels, so in order to have
something "new," New Wave was followed by Next Wave. *Atlantic* is the
closest thing to "No Wave" jazz that one can imagine. A work lasting almost
an hour, it employs a continuous drone of one bass pitch that is relieved only
by indistinct sounds that resemble whale and dolphin communication. Is it
jazz? Is it composition? Is it music? Emphatically yes, but with values different from the norms of classical music and jazz, and with a sense of time more
closely resembling geological ages than beats in a measure. It is an improvising jazz thinker's probe into the world opened by composers like Stockhausen and Cage and the many contributors to *Source* magazine. A 1981 record

---

[32] Sackville 3012.
[33] Black Saint BSR 0026.

George Lewis.

release by Lewis, "Chicago Slow Dance,"[34] is anything but slow in comparison with *Atlantic*.

During the early 1980s, Lewis served as director of the Kitchen, an avant-garde cultural center in New York. Through his work there and his presence as a performer, Lewis was influential in shaping radical thought about jazz and composition throughout the decade. Although his compositional interests tended to distance him somewhat from jazz, he continued to perform with Anthony Braxton, Anthony Davis (in the ensemble Episteme), and Henry Threadgill. Today he is a professor of computer music at the University of California, San Diego.

The founding father of free jazz, Ornette Coleman, concerned himself during the '80s with fusion, free improvisation, and harmolodic bebop, and his 1985 album, "Opening the Caravan of Dreams,"[35] is a tour de force. His band of two guitarists, two bass players, and two drummers provides the free jazz soloist an electric, fusion environment without the restrictions of rock harmony or rhythm. The six performances contrast markedly with each other, demonstrating the broad range of approaches Coleman employs to construct his music. The opening number, *To Know What to Know*, uses a simple ostinato and a street dance rhythm to generate steam; the second cut, *Harmolodic Bebop*, furiously runs in all directions at all speeds until it finally closes with a complicated riff; *Sex Spy* is a funky number in strict 4/4 that repeats a two-measure bass pattern endlessly. Throughout the album, whistles, cowbells, and various percussion instruments punctuate the fabric of sound, sometimes rhythmically, sometimes to give direction, and often only because the player was moved to play at that point. *See Through* is especially interesting as a study in timbres, trills, and seamless passages of transparent sound. That same year, Coleman recorded with guitarist Pat Metheny, bassist Charlie Haden, and drummers Jack DeJohnette and Denardo Coleman. Their joint album, "Song X,"[36] is remarkably different from the "Prime Time" recording in both precision and discipline. Metheny apparently imposed some of his stricter musical values on Coleman's free expression, and the result is one of fine ensemble work and eloquent solo improvisation, especially in the title track, *Song X*. The opening unison riff is as fast or complex as any in free jazz, but Coleman and Metheny play a unison that is exceptionally precise and in-tune for this style. The extended work, *Endangered Species*, contains a nebulous cloud of musical chaos that relates like a surrealistic vision back to the first free jazz sounds of 1960. The album, "Song X," is an important document.

[34] Lovely Music VR 1101.
[35] Caravan of Dreams Productions CDP 85001.
[36] Geffen 9 24096-2.

Pat Metheny.

After demonstrating both his understanding of free jazz in the "Song X" album and his sympathy for it, Metheny turns right around in 1987 with his Pat Metheny Group album, "ᔆᵀᴵᴸᴸlife(talking),"[37] to record "New Age" music, a quiet, pacific, contemplative sound related to natural habitat and environmental concerns. Carefully orchestrated with lush, tonal harmonies, the music employs gentle Latin rhythms and soft melodic passages with delicate shadings of volume. It is hard to imagine that the guitarist on this album is the same musician jamming freely with Ornette Coleman in "Song X." Hearing Metheny plays solos in "ᔆᵀᴵᴸᴸlife(talking)," one marvels at his virtuosity but finds it difficult to reconcile his musical philosophies. This dichotomy is typical of music in the '80s: many of the best musicians can, and do, play expertly in many styles.

Much New Age music is little more than elevator music, background sounds designed to inconspicuously accompany other activities, but some fine jazz musicians, most notably saxophonist Paul Winter,[38] have found a natural habitat for both their music and their environmental concerns. However, labels can be deceptive, and the music of one free jazz powerhouse, soprano

[37] Geffen M2G 24145.
[38] "Concert for the Earth" (Living Music 0005) or "Canyon" (Living Music LM 0006).

saxophonist Steve Lacy, is often found in the New Age section of record stores. Lacy is as radical a free jazz exponent as anyone who was working during the '80s. His 1989 album "Anthem"[39] is certainly not elevator music. Employing a combination of free improvisation, classical composition, and poetry, he created exciting and appropriate sounds to help celebrate the two hundredth anniversary of the French Revolution. His music combines many of the elements first explored by Thelonious Monk, Cecil Taylor, and Ornette Coleman, and within his sixteen-minute track, *Prelude and Anthem*, one finds a French translation of a Russian poem that celebrates not only the French Revolution but the American pioneer, Thelonious Monk: *Le Crépuscule de la liberté* (The twilight of liberty).

Oregon, a notable jazz chamber ensemble that developed in the 1970s, grew out of a combination of current musical elements: minimalist devices (drone or ostinato bass and recurring melodic patterns), complex harmonies, ethnic music based on different melodic and rhythmic schemes, serial composition, and the sensitive interaction of classical chamber ensembles. Originally a part of the Paul Winter Consort, this quartet of Paul McCandless (double reeds and bass clarinet), Ralph Towner (upper brasses, piano, and acoustic guitar), Collin Walcott, replaced after his death in 1984 by Trilok Gurtu (Eastern and Western percussion), and Glen Moore (violin, bass, flute, and piano) formed their own improvisation group, which, without the standard jazz tonal and metrical norms, set out to create music through collective improvisation, just as the classic jazz combos did at the start of the century. Oregon's similarity in approach to the Art Ensemble of Chicago is striking. In addition to collective improvisation, the musicians use dozens of instruments in a single performance, although their tone picture is not based primarily on strong African roots and results in entirely different colors and hues. Their albums "Oregon" (1983)[40] and with Gurtu, "Ecotopia" (with Gurtu, 1988)[41] display a characteristic oboe lead, smooth improvisatory interplay, and a world-culture approach to music making.

JAZZ COMPOSITION IN THE 1980S—ANTHONY DAVIS

A significant composer of the 1980s is Anthony Davis, a pianist whose views about composition and the development of black music were cited earlier in this chapter. For most of his career, Davis has mixed his composing and performing activities in about equal portions. While still a college student,

[39] Novus 3079-4-N.
[40] ECM 811711-1.
[41] ECM 833120-1.

Anthony Davis.

he was a founding member of the free jazz group Advent, which included trombonist George Lewis, and he later played in trumpeter Leo Smith's New Dalta Ahkri band and violinist Leroy Jenkins's trio. Lewis, Smith, and Jenkins all had connections with the AACM, so even though Davis was never formally a part of this Chicago-based group, his musical philosophy was strongly influenced by the association members' mode of thinking. In 1978 he worked with flutist James Newton and three years later formed his ensemble, Episteme, as a performance medium for his music. His 1978 quartet recording "Song for the Old World,"[42] with Jay Hoggard on vibes, Mark Helias on bass, and Edward Blackwell on drums, demonstrates the broad scope of his interests, influences, and abilities. *Behind the Rock*, for solo piano, is a virtuosic display of avant-garde piano with its clustered motives, plucked and muted strings, and attention to timbral effects. Rhythm is a prime organizing factor in most of Davis's music, and "Song for the Old World" employs rhythmic units in irregular meters to propel the Asian and African thematic materials. The ensemble of the quartet is exceptional, and even at this early stage in Davis's career, one notices the composer's attention to detail. The remaining four cuts of this album all display stylistic differences, what one

[42] India Navigation IN 1036.

might expect from a young, inquiring mind: *African Ballad* reminds one of the MJQ, *59* of Thelonious Monk (another strong influence on Davis's thinking), *An Anthem for the Generation that Died* of the bebop musicians it commemorates, and *Andrew* of good old funk. In addition to the free-jazz philosophy of the AACM, the most obvious influences one detects in this music are the compositional method of Monk, the orchestral and compositional ideas of Ellington, and the piano work of Bud Powell and Cecil Taylor. The music at this developmental stage in his career is impressive, especially as a display of skill and talent. Overall, the album is somewhat eclectic and not unified enough to present a coherent, individual musical identity. However, Davis soon organized his growing artistic abilities and was able to communicate a powerful vision of musical expression in his compositions of the 1980s.

Fascinated with Balinese gamelan music and the wayang shadow puppet theater, Davis composed a series of pieces titled "Wayang." It is fascinating to compare two recorded versions of *Wayang IV*, the first a solo piano recording of 1980[43] and the second an orchestration recorded in 1981.[44] *Under the Double Moon (Wayang IV)* is moody, and Davis uses the piano in the solo version like an orchestra, creating effects with the pedal, contrasting percussive finger technique with a delicate, brushing sound, and laying melodic-rhythmic motives over an integrating ostinato. In the fully orchestrated version, in which Mark Helias conducts and Davis plays piano, the sections are more clearly formalized and divided, the contrasting instrumental solos are more varied, and the object of attention, at any one time, is more limited and focused. The full ensemble, Episteme, employs three strings (violin, cello, and bass), one woodwind player (doubling flute, piccolo, and bass clarinet), one brass (trombone), three percussionists (drums, gongs, cymbals, and a variety of tuned instruments—vibes, marimba, etc.), and piano. It is a tightly controlled work in which free improvisation is closely monitored most of the time by the composer's instructions and restrictions. It is tonal music with a strong interest in Asian and African musical ideas. And it is a work that clearly could not exist without the nourishment of jazz.

In 1984, Davis composed an opera, *X*, based on the life of Malcolm X, the martyred black leader. Davis's brother, Christopher, compiled information from many sources, including *The Autobiography of Malcolm X*, and wrote the story for the opera; his cousin, Thulani Davis, wrote the libretto. Composed for and developed with the Philadelphia workshop of the American Music Theater Festival, a portion of *X* received a first public performance in

---

[43] "Lady of the Mirrors" (India Navigation IN 1047).
[44] "Episteme" (Gramavision GR 8101).

Scene from Anthony Davis's opera X, performed by the New York City Opera, September 1986.

Philadelphia in 1984. The opera was given a fully staged, orchestrated, full-length premiere there in 1985 and a much-heralded New York premiere at the New York City Opera in 1986. *X* was a musical, dramatic, and critical success. The music underscores the raw emotions of the libretto and expresses, in non-verbal terms, the several complex transformations that contributed to the formation of the adult Malcolm X, a charismatic, powerful, feared, respected, and often scorned leader. Davis prefers now that his music not be classified as jazz, but jazz is overtly present in the opera in more than name and inspiration. It can be heard in styles ranging from tailgate trombone to Coltrane-like sheets of sound.[45] The opera is a monumental achievement by Davis in that the music has in no way cheapened or diminished the soul and spirit of the historical figure (an ever-present danger in musical/dramatic works). Instead, the music has aggressively propelled the martyr's message—about life in America, black identity, and self-sufficiency—through yet another voice. *X* is a masterpiece of twentieth-century art music; it is also a monument in the history of jazz.

Davis continues his dual life of composer/teacher and jazz performer, occasionally playing or recording as a jazz pianist. He did so in 1988 as a sideman for a recording with trombonist Ray Anderson.[46] However, his prin-

---

[45] A commercial recording is not yet available.
[46] "Blues Bred in the Bone" (Gramavision R2 79445).

cipal mission is composition, and his recent creation, *Ghost Factory,* is an impressive work for his performance unit Episteme. The composition draws unity from motivic ideas and their development, and it achieves variety by relying upon an extensive catalogue of instrumental effects and compositional devices.[47] Though the regular concertgoer would recognize little in the performance that sounded like jazz, the work fits smoothly into the evolving continuum of Davis's music. He has not wavered in his artistic beliefs, and this recent music is but another affirmation of his unshakable credo about contemporary music of African-Americans. Writing in 1980, he said,

> I consider myself fortunate to be a part of a long and vital tradition of com-poser-pianists in creative music. From Scott Joplin to Cow-Cow Davenport, to Jelly Roll Morton, James P. Johnson, Duke Ellington, Fats Waller, Thelonious Monk, Bud Powell, and Cecil Taylor, this is a tradition which has always been at the fulcrum of change and evolution in our music.
>
> I believe that today is a pivotal time for our music. There has been a gradual shift from the pre-eminence of the performer, the player, to what I believe is the natural ascendance of the composer. This change has met with great resis-tance, not only from critics, but from my fellow musicians. I think this is the underlying problem when one hears about these "dangerous classical influ-ences." As a composer, I feel free to draw from any influence, Black, Brown, or Beige, Asian, European, or African. In a sense, this freedom can only be realized through the composition, through the Musical Idea.[48]

POSTMODERNISM AND JAZZ— JANE IRA BLOOM

Postmodern composers are, in a way, reactionaries, for by definition they create in a style that responds to events of the past. Sometimes the reaction is negative, but it can be tangential or even positive. One characteristic com-mon to postmodern music, however, is the conscious incorporation of sub-stantive issues from the surrounding culture into the mix of experimental devices, unusual sounds, and traditional elements to generate an artwork that consciously "makes a statement." In some of her work, soprano saxo-phonist Jane Ira Bloom is a postmodern jazz musician. Her performance career blends music, dance, electronics, and current phenomena into works of art. Recently commissioned by N.A.S.A. to compose music inspired by the star-

[47] Private recording of a concert at Sprague Hall, New Haven, Connecticut, October 19, 1990.

[48] Liner notes for "Lady of the Mirrors" (India Navigation IN 1047).

Jane Ira Bloom.

burst liftoffs at Cape Kennedy, she formed sound into musical structures that seem to pulsate, bend, weave, twist, and dance. On stage her performance is a form of dance, for the notes she plays and the tones she generates are partially made by the physical motion of her instrument around the microphone. With a saxophone that is connected to an electronic synthesizer, a unique instrument built for her by an engineer and operated partly by foot pedals, she and the machine are able to manipulate the notes played on her saxophone, sometimes directly and sometimes indirectly through the signals received from the microphone, which is sensitive to the Doppler effect created by her moving saxophone. In performance, Jane Ira Bloom reacts in real time with her fellow musicians and in real time with the electronic gadgetry of this age. The result is music with spirit, spontaneity, and great creativity. On her album "Modern Drama,"[49] we need to listen only to *The Race,* a track dedicated to the race driver Shirley Muldowney, to realize that the opening swirl of sound, the layers of sound upon sound, the high-speed chase of saxophone after piano after drum, and the fluid harmonies are evocations of today's genius, this decade's technology, this generation's concerns. It is like the past in neither substance nor nature, but it is music, it is jazz, it is a postmodern sound art.

NEW SOUNDS, NEW WAVE, NEW AGE, AND GOOD OLD-FASHIONED JAZZ

The most obvious feature of jazz in the 1980s was its extensive stylistic diversification, and one of the most powerful external forces pressing the music for change during this decade was technology. New instruments affected jazz beginning in the 1960s, most notably when Miles Davis recorded "In a Silent Way" in 1969. Directed by the sound of the instruments, the music formed integrated sound structures rather than series of solo improvisations. The novelty of three electric keyboards and electric guitar inspired these musicians and the younger jazz musicians who listened. Soon, the keyboard work of Joe Zawinul with Weather Report and the guitar work of John McLaughlin of the Mahavishnu Orchestra would forever change the way young musicians approached these instruments. The same was true of electric bass, when Jaco Pastorius recorded *Heavy Weather* with Weather Report in 1976. When Jan Hammer played synthesizer with the Mahavishnu Orchestra during the '70s, he demonstrated the new capabilities and suggested the enormous possibilities available with keyboard synthesizers. But in spite of

[49]Columbia FC 40755.

the tremendous improvements in sound and the reductions in size and weight that the new machines offered, these instruments were still analog machines, that is, synthesizers limited in possibilities to sounds generated by oscillators. And like it or not, a sine-wave generator produces a bland, inflexible sound in comparison with the variety of wave forms available from a complete complement of acoustical instruments.

The 1980s made available digital recorders, digital synthesizers, digital samplers, MIDI (musical instrument digital interface), and laser technology for CDs (compact discs). All these played an active role in the history of jazz.

During the five decades from World War II to the present, the music industry moved from 78-rpm records to 45-rpm extended-play records to 33⅓-rpm records to cassettes and finally to CDs, each stage lengthening the recording time available and improving the reproduced sound quality. During that same period, musicians altered sound (Pierre Schaeffer's *musique concrète* in 1948) and synthesized sound (the electronic music studios at the universities of Illinois and Michigan, 1958; Columbia-Princeton, 1959; and Yale, 1960), and scientists advanced the technology of these sound machines and their first cousins, computers, from tubes to solid state to chips and modules. For jazz musicians, a studio recording once meant a three-minute performance with no alterations possible. Group sound was picked up by a few microphones for monaural recording and playback. Eventually two-track recording replaced single track, overdubbing became possible, two tracks moved to four and eventually thirty-two, and sound isolation in the studio picked up by better, directional, individual microphones allowed players to lay track upon track and clean up mistakes virtually note by note.

Digital recording freezes the recorded waveforms as numbers, so splicing could be eliminated and background static lowered below the threshhold of hearing. It also brought sampling, that is, recording a small sample of sound from an instrument, voice, choir, or anything, and generating an entire range of notes from low to high that match the original sample. From that point on, electronic instruments could approximate closely the sound of real instruments and could also generate new sounds that could previously not even be imagined. MIDI allowed computers and musical instruments to communicate back and forth and to "stack" boxes of sound tracks, each track of compact disc quality. (In other words, you fill up a module—or black box—with digitally encoded sound tracks, then fill up further boxes and hook them together. You can stack and access the modules almost without limit.) Only a small fraction of the potential capabilities of these instruments was utilized by the jazz musicians of the '80s, but without question the novelty items of one generation will become the standard and even outdated hardware of the next.

One of the fascinating experiments during the '80s entailed real-time interactive performance between musician and computer. MIDI made possible a machine that could, upon hearing music or receiving signals from a performer, play its own parts, improvise, and react as another partner in a combo or jazz band. On the down side of the ledger, MIDI and digital sampling also made possible the replacement of live musicians by one keyboard player and a machine, especially in musical theater pits and movie and television studios.

Jazz has just begun to open up to the creative possibilities brought about by the latest technology, and it certainly will continue to do so in the future, but it has, at the same time, reacted with a conservative backlash, a return to the old sounds and the old values. For example, in 1983, Markus Stockhausen (trumpet and synthesizer), Michael Daugherty (piano, synthesizer, and percussion), and Simon Stockhausen (saxophone and synthesizer) recorded "The Next Wave"[50] and effectively utilized some of these interactive techniques in jazz performance, and in 1989, the young saxophonist Christopher Hollyday returned to the sounds of Charlie Parker and Dizzy Gillespie in his "Christopher Hollyday" debut album.[51] Should one forge ahead or return to fundamentals? Excellent musicians are looking back—Eddie Daniels, "Memos from Paradise (1987–88)";[52] Scott Hamilton, "The Right Time" (1987);[53] Frank Morgan, "A Lonesome Thing" (1990);[54]—and excellent musicians are probing in new directions, striving for innovation—the Steve Coleman Group, "Motherland Pulse" (1985);[55] Jane Ira Bloom, "Modern Drama" (1987);[56] John Zorn, "Spy vs Spy" (1988).[57]

RAY ANDERSON

One of the most interesting young musicians in jazz is trombonist Ray Anderson, and his albums cross all musical borders, sometimes several at the same time. His music defies stylistic classification. Writing in 1980, he tells us:

> *Don't call it new*
> *Don't call it old*
> *Out/in, avant/derriere*

[50] "The Next Wave," recorded in Europe for private use only.
[51] BMG 3055-2-N.
[52] GRP GRD-9561.
[53] Concord CCD-4311.
[54] Antilles 422-848 213-2.
[55] JMT 852 001 834 401-2.
[56] Columbia FC 40755.
[57] Elektra 9 60844-2.

Ray Anderson.

Don't chain it with "freedom"
or insist that it be "ethnic"
Don't categorize, conceptualize,
 hypothesize or listen with your eyes,
Don't worry if it's up, down
 front, back, "swing" "rock"
 "blues" "bop" "classical"
 or even "art."

Study the history and
 acknowledge the source
But remember, it all comes
from the heart and
 Please Please Please

 Listen[58]

The critics listened, and *Down Beat*'s Critics Poll named him the number one trombonist five years in a row, 1987–91. Respecting his wishes (and taking the easy way out), we will offer no style categorizations for this young

---

[58] From the album cover of "Harrisburg Half Life" (Moers Music 01074).

phenomenon, but we should note that he played with Anthony Braxton beginning in 1977,[59] formed a jazz trio with Mark Helias (bass) and Gerry Hemingway (drums and vibes) in 1978,[60] formed his own group, Slickaphonics, soon after,[61] and constantly surprises us with old, new, borrowed, and blue.[62]

TODAY AND TOMORROW

Jazz of the 1980s seems to have separated into four main substyles: fusion jazz, neoclassic jazz, free jazz, and composed jazz. In most cases the lines of demarcation are not clear, and many musicians move back and forth between and among styles with surprising frequency. Some styles are closer in sound to popular music and others are nearer contemporary "classical" composition, but each has its modus operandi, its advocates, and its detractors. In addition to these four principal substyles, other musical modes also claim their places in the sun.

Rock 'n' roll, technology, developing nations, and American societal changes have all played their part in the history of jazz during the last three decades. New means and new ideas became available to young improvising musicians, and it is likely that jazz will continue to proliferate, for a time at least, in a somewhat disorderly manner. The determinant remains, as it always has, in the talents of the individual musicians. Because of the variety of exponents who now crowd the field, we are led to expect that jazz will follow no set line of development for some years to come but will, instead, separate into distinct parts of a pluralistic musical world.

Jazz is more than a historical style, it is a living music that will continue to change, speak for the people, and reflect both humanity and technology. As one aspect of the total picture of world history, it is a new idiom created by obscure African-American musicians after the Civil War, and it is unlike other contemporary Western music in that it relies heavily upon improvisation for its creation, performance, and reconstruction. It is documented chiefly through phonograph recordings, but since most of its past lies within living memory, its musicians, critics, and audiences are able to tell us much about it. As time proceeds, the heroes and heroines of jazz will be enshrined, the lasting monuments of this art form will be preserved in places of honor, and our understanding and appreciation of the past will of necessity be modified by the music yet to come.

[59] "Performance 1979" (hat ART 1984).
[60] "OAHSPE" (Auricle AUR-2).
[61] Blue Heron BLU 705-1 D.
[62] "It Just So Happens" (1987; ENJA 5037); "Wishbone" (1991; Gramavision R2 79454).

APPENDICES

$\mathcal{L}$ ISTENING
GUIDES

Robert Johnson

I Believe I'll Dust My Broom

Music and Lyrics: Robert Johnson
Recorded: San Antonio, Texas, November 23, 1936
Original Issue: Vocalian 03475, matrix SA 2581-1
Performer: Robert Johnson, guitar and voice

Johnson sings and plays a standardized three-line blues stanza of a repeated first line and a rhyming second line (**aab**) to music in a twelve-measure repeated harmonic form (**ABC**):

Each measure of the music has its own chord, with embellishments:

measure:	1	2	3	4	5	6	7	8	9	10	11	12
words:	a				a				b			
music:	A				B				C			
harmony:	I	I	I	I	IV	IV	I	I	V	IV	I	I

Normally, each verse or stanza of the blues is unique and is performed in an endless string: **ABCDEFG . . ..** However, in the blues *I Believe I'll Dust My Broom*, Johnson repeats the first verse as the next-to-last verse and creates a feeling of recapitulation and close, a standard practice in jazz. Also, within each four-measure phrase, Johnson employs a call-and-response pattern: two measures of lyrics followed by two measures of instrumental fill. During the singing, Johnson accompanies the text with a boogie-woogie pattern, eight eighth-notes to the bar

$$|\,\music\,|\,\music\,|$$

played unevenly

$$|\,\music\,|\text{ or }|\,\music\,|$$

He does this on the low strings of the guitar,

and then plays a triplet-pattern response on the high strings of the instrument.

The listener will also note that despite the steady beat, Johnson drops beats during one verse and adds extra beats in another, a practice common in solo blues performances. Although probably unintentional, it adds an interesting shift of accent to the regularly recurring pattern.

With a two-measure introduction, the overall form is:

I Believe I'll Dust My Broom

I

I'm gon' get up in the mornin',
   I believe I'll dust my broom;
I'm gon' get up in the mornin',
   I believe I'll dust my broom;
Girlfriend, the black man you been lovin',
   girlfriend, can get my room.

II

I'm gon' write a letter,
   telephone every town I know;
I'm gon' write a letter,
   telephone every town I know;
If I can't find her in West Helena,
   She must be in East Monroe, I know.

III

I don't want no woman
   wants every downtown man she meet;
I don't want no woman

wants every downtown man she meet;
She's a no good doney,
* they shouldn't 'low her on the street.*

IV

I believe,
* I believe I'll go back home;*
I believe,
* I believe I'll go back home;*
You can mistreat me here, babe,
* but you can't when I go home.*

V

And I'm gettin' up in the mornin',
* I believe I'll dust my broom;*
I'm gettin' up in the mornin',
* I believe I'll dust my broom;*
Girlfriend, the black man you been lovin',
* girlfriend, can get my room.*

VI

I'm 'on' call up Chiney,
* see is my good girl over there;*
I'm gon' call up China,
* see is my good girl over there;*
If I can't find her on Philippine's Island,
* she must be in Ethiopia somewhere.*

Louis Armstrong and His Hot Five

Cornet Chop Suey

Music: Louis Armstrong
Recorded: Chicago, February 26, 1926
Original Issue: OKeh 8320, matrix 9535-A
Performers: Louis Armstrong, cornet
Johnny Dodds, clarinet
Kid Ory, trombone
Lil Hardin Armstrong, piano
Johnny St. Cyr, banjo

This classic recording by Louis Armstrong of his own composition, *Cornet Chop Suey*, features a superlative display of the master's instrumental virtuosity. Reissued countless times since its first appearance, this recording has long served as a model for aspiring trumpeters to copy. The ensemble, without bass or drums in the rhythm section, relies on the banjo and piano to "keep time." Lil Hardin's piano solo, although a characteristic, better-than-competent solo-piano rendition of the work, exhibits little improvisation. Louis Armstrong's stop-time chorus, on the other hand, is remarkable for both its invention and its virtuosity, traits for which Armstrong was unequaled in his day. The freedom and driving swing of his lead cornet playing in the ensemble sections give these passages a feeling of solo improvisation as well.

The form of the piece is typical of many from the New Orleans repertoire and is similar to the first half of many brass band marches (the portion before the change of key). In this case, we hear an introduction, a first and second strain, the second strain repeated, a *dal segno* (repeat of **A** and **B**), a coda, and out. However, the *dal segno* is not a simple repeat but an Armstrong solo on the first chorus and a collective improvisation on the second. With classically good instincts, Armstrong balances the pyrotechnics of his solo introduction with a similar solo at the coda, and the group concludes on a single chord.

Formal Outline

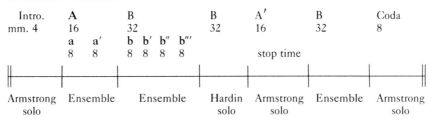

	Intro.	A	B		B	A′	B	Coda
mm. 4		16	32		32	16	32	8

a a′ b b′ b″ b‴
8 8 8 8 8 8

stop time

Armstrong solo   Ensemble   Ensemble   Hardin solo   Armstrong solo   Ensemble   Armstrong solo

Introduction

Melody A

Melody B

Frankie Trumbauer and His Orchestra

Ostrich Walk

Music: The Original Dixieland Jazz Band
Arranger: Bill Challis
Recorded: New York, May 9, 1927
Original Issue: OKeh 40822, matrix 81071-B
Performers: Bix Beiderbecke, cornet
Frankie Trumbauer, C-melody saxophone
Bill Rank, trombone
Doc Ryker, alto saxophone
Don Murray, clarinet, baritone saxophone
Itzy Riskin, piano
Eddie Lang, guitar
Chauncey Morehouse, drums

Both the influence of the New Orleans musicians and the characteristics of the new Chicago-style jazz can be heard on this Beiderbecke and Trumbauer rendition of *Ostrich Walk*. The composition comes from the repertoire of the Original Dixieland Jazz Band. The form is taken from that of the concert and marching band repertoire of an earlier day: introduction, first and second strains (with a repeat of the first), vamp (a short connecting passage to a new key), third and fourth strains (with a repeat of the third), a *da capo* (back to the beginning for the introduction and first two strains), and a coda. The new elements in the music include the arrangement itself, for the ensemble passages are scored by a new figure in jazz, the arranger. Among the arranger's contributions that we hear are the saxophones having a *soli* chorus of their own (several musicians playing passage work together, *soli* [plural] as opposed to *solo* [singular]); the ensemble performing a group crescendo; and the introduction and ending being scored rather than improvised. But the fame of this work is not due to the arrangement, which is more typical than extraordinary, but to the cornet playing of Bix Beiderbecke. His sound is

10*

new and his solo style unique. In his easy, relaxed, almost velvety cornet tone and his quasi-legato style, he blends a coolness with the hot syncopations and the pressing urgency of the piece. The squeezed and delicately bent pitches that interrupt his solo at measures 11 and 12 are a sound uniquely his own. His choice of notes to complement a chord, his relaxed eighth notes, and his phrasing, which disguises the regular phrasing of the piece, are characteristics of his playing that later influenced many younger musicians.

Trumbauer is a fine soloist in his own right but gets little opportunity to display his skills in this piece. However, the trombone work of Bill Rank is first rate, and the brief solo passages where four connected one-measure solos are played one after the other (saxophone, cornet, trombone, and clarinet) are also interesting highlights of this recording.

Formal Scheme

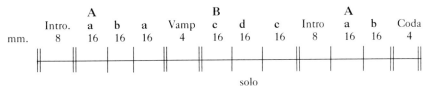

Bix Beiderbecke solo

Art Tatum

Tiger Rag

Music: Nick La Rocca
Recorded: New York, March 21, 1933
Original Issue: Brunswick 6543, matrix B-13164-A
Performer: Art Tatum, piano

Once again, the influence of the New Orleans musicians can be traced in later styles. Art Tatum, a master of swing piano, reinterprets *Tiger Rag*, a composition that stems from the repertoire of the Original Dixieland Jazz Band. Tatum's awesome technical command of his instrument strikes most listeners immediately, but the progress of his musical invention throughout a performance is equally interesting and finally more significant. We hear in the slow introduction the parallel seventh chords so characteristic of French impressionism. The effect is one of disguise and contrast that leaves the listener unprepared for the breathtaking first chorus. Throughout the performance there are abrupt changes of tempo and mood, circuitous harmonic diversions, and always unbelievably good passage work. The left hand shows its own independence and invention—in the passage accompanied only by a left-hand trill; in incredibly fast and accurate left-hand stride leaps; and in showers of ascending and descending scales, sometimes joined by the right hand and sometimes not.

Tatum was first taught music at a school for the blind. Although his later education did not match those of conservatory-trained concert artists, his lifelong interest in the classical piano repertoire clearly had a strong influence on his jazz playing. He had an extraordinary breadth of conception, an even tone and delicate touch, an interest in exploring the full range of the instrument, and an unerring sense of direction during performance. *Tiger Rag* was for him a standard show piece that became set in its format. On this recording, it is possible that all the improvisation was developed during earlier years and that what we hear is the accurate performance of a composition. Still, the genesis of this performance was improvisation, its style is swing, it is a classic of the jazz repertoire, and its execution is exhilarating. Compare the simplicity of the original with the marvelous elaboration of the 1933 recording.

Formal Scheme

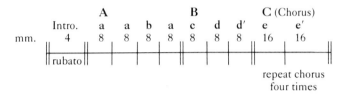

Tiger Rag

Duke Ellington and His Famous Orchestra

Clarinet Lament (Barney's Concerto)

Music: Barney Bigard and Duke Ellington
Arranger: Duke Ellington
Recorded: Chicago, February 27, 1936
Original Issue: Brunswick 7650, matrix B-18736-1 (Col. C-6059)
Performers: Duke Ellington, piano
Arthur Whetsol, Cootie Williams, trumpets
Rex Stewart, cornet
Joe Nanton, Lawrence Brown, trombones
Juan Tizol, valve trombone
Barney Bigard, clarinet
Johnny Hodges, clarinet, soprano and alto saxophones
Harry Carney, clarinet, alto and baritone saxophones
Fred Guy, guitar
Hayes Alvis, bass
Sonny Greer, drums

Most experts agree that 1932–42 were the most creative years in Ellington's long and illustrious career. In the mid-1930s, Ellington began composing a series of works designed to feature the talents of individual performers in his band, not just as a small part of the total composition but as the focus around which the work was composed. The first of the "concertos" was *Clarinet Lament*, written for Barney Bigard. Bigard was a New Orleans jazz musician taken on by Ellington when the band needed to expand for the Cotton Club. He already had performed and recorded with King Oliver, Johnny Dodds, Jelly Roll Morton, and Louis Armstrong. His playing with Ellington, while demonstrating a style that is truly individual, retains traits of the New Orleans sound. On *Clarinet Lament*, we can enjoy his long glissandos, elegant phrasing, and smooth legato runs as he delivers, over all the registers, that warm New Orleans tone and fast vibrato.

Bigard and Ellington collaborated to write *Clarinet Lament,* and its arrangement is based on an altered version of the chord structure of *Basin Street Blues.* The striking, three-layered introduction is begun by Bigard and followed by Rex Stewart on cornet and Juan Tizol on valve trombone. It is bitonal, in E♭ and A♭, and remains so when measured time begins and the band enters (the bass plays a simple pattern modulating to E♭, D–F–E♭).

Introduction

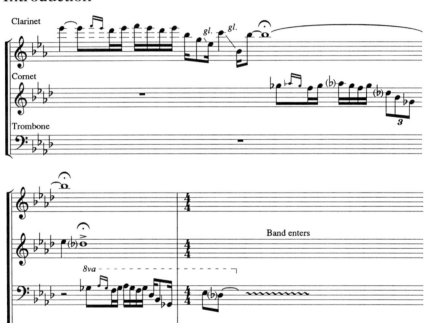

The first solo chorus for clarinet is a regular twelve-measure E♭ blues. This is immediately followed by a second solo chorus, in thirty-two-measure popular-song form, and it is here that the arrangement employs the *Basin Street* harmonies. A bridge is newly composed for the b section, and the familiar harmonies return.

Basin Street progression in A♭

| A♭ | C⁷ | F⁷ | F⁷ | B♭⁷ | E♭⁷ | A♭ B^dim | B♭^m7 E♭⁷ |

The third solo chorus balances the first. It too is in the key of E♭ and extends to twelve measures, but it is not a blues. Ellington cleverly adapted harmonies similar to *Basin Street* and used them in a three-phrase final solo chorus. The band adds a brief closing cadence.

Formal Scheme

	Intro.	I	Trans.	II	III	Coda
mm.	[1]+8	12	2	32	12	2
		blues		aaba	4+4+4	
		E♭		A♭	E♭	

Count Basie and His Orchestra

Tickle-Toe

Music: Lester Young
Arranger: Andy Gibson
Recorded: New York, March 19, 1940
Original Issue: Columbia 35521, matrix 26656-1
Performers: Count Basie, piano
　　　　　　Buck Clayton, Ed Lewis, Harry Edison, Al Killian,
　　　　　　　trumpets
　　　　　　Dicky Wells, Vic Dickenson, Dan Minor, trombones
　　　　　　Earl Warren, alto saxophone
　　　　　　Jack Washington, alto and baritone saxophones
　　　　　　Buddy Tate, Lester Young, tenor saxophones
　　　　　　Fred Green, guitar
　　　　　　Walter Page, bass
　　　　　　Jo Jones, drums

Unlike the composer-dominated orchestra of Duke Ellington, the Count Basie big band relied on common forms, predictable arrangements, improvised section riffs, powerfully swinging section work, and featured soloists from throughout the band. Where Ellington's orchestra was unique, Basie's was a model for many orchestras and defined big band jazz from the Kansas City point of view. In so doing, he and his musicians paved the way for greater soloistic freedom in this idiom.

The heart of Basie's band is not the arrangement but the rhythm section, consisting of Basie, Walter Page, Jo Jones, and Freddie Green. Jones is usually credited with transferring the basic pulse of the band from the bass drum to the sound of sticks on the high hat cymbal; Green is a rock-steady rhythm guitar player; Page lays down a sure-footed harmonic foundation with an equally rock-steady beat; and Basie punctuates. Though he apprenticed in the stride style of Fats Waller and James P. Johnson and played it capably, Basie abandoned the showy display of leaping hands and racing fingers for the lean, economical, and bouyant style we hear in this performance.

Many outstanding soloists are associated with the Basie bands of the late 1930s and '40s—Herschel Evans, Buck Clayton, Harry Edison, and Vic Dickenson, to name a few—but none had a more profound effect on the next generation of jazz musicians than Lester Young. In opposition to the "hot" saxophone style of Coleman Hawkins and Herschel Evans, Young's light, wistful, restrained, and gently effervescent sound influenced, in a significant way, the playing of Charlie Parker, Stan Getz, Miles Davis, and countless others.

Tickle-Toe is a deceptive composition, in that its apparent simplicity camouflages a sophisticated harmonic scheme. The thirty-two measure piece is divided in two, **A A′**, and each half is similarly subdivided into **a a′**. The minor opening and the emphasis on subdominant harmonies leads us to expect a minor blues (the first four measures are in D♭ minor and the second four in E♭ minor with a return to D♭). It is all a ruse, for the piece then moves down another fifth (a new subdominant) and continues on a varied harmonic journey to return to where it began.

Tickle-Toe

Formal Scheme

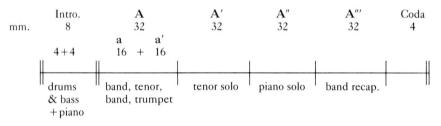

	Intro.	**A**		**A′**	**A″**	**A‴**	Coda
mm.	8	32		32	32	32	4
		a	a′				
	4+4	16 +	16				
	drums & bass + piano	band, tenor, band, trumpet		tenor solo	piano solo	band recap.	

Benny Goodman and His Orchestra

Mission to Moscow

Music: Mel Powell
Arranger: Mel Powell
Recorded: New York, July 30, 1942
Original Issue: Columbia 36680, matrix CO-33070-1
Performers: Benny Goodman, clarinet
Jimmy Maxwell, Lawrence Stearns, Tony Faso, trumpets
Lou McGarity, Charlie Castaldo, trombones
Hymie Schertzer, Clint Neagley, alto saxophones
Jon Walton, Leonard Sims, tenor saxophones
Bob Poland, baritone saxophone
Mel Powell, piano
Dave Barbour, guitar
Cliff Hill, bass
Howard Davies, drums

This recording has an interesting sidelight. Because of a dispute between the American Federation of Musicians and the record companies, the union's president, James C. Petrillo, imposed a commercial recording ban beginning August 1, 1942, that would last twenty-seven months, until November 1944. Goodman hurried into the studio for one final session, and *Mission to Moscow* was his final cut that day.

Unlike the Count Basie big band, the Benny Goodman orchestra was primarily a vehicle to deliver snappy arrangements in perfect order and to spotlight the superb virtuosity of its leader. In this case, the composer-arranger partly steals the show. In 1942, Mel Powell, one of the most extraordinary American musicians of this last half century, was a gifted nineteen-year-old pianist. He joined the band as a replacement for Johnny Guarnieri in May 1941 and immediately started doing arrangements for a June recording date. *Mission to Moscow* demonstrates his mastery of the arranger's craft.

The sixteen-measure introduction (and coda) is in the wrong key—that is, it is in D major (with a B pedal!), which is only distantly related to B♭ major, the key of the first chorus. The transition is fascinating to observe:

Mission to Moscow, Introduction

The first chorus has three parts, the first a saxophone unison melody,

Mission to Moscow, Melody A

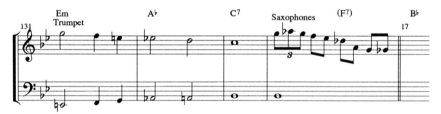

the second a stomping, driving riff supported by brass punctuations,

Mission to Moscow, Riff and Backing Rhythm
Formal Scheme

and the third a bridge, in which the clarinet takes the lead. The formal scheme of the entire work is based on an **ABA** formula where one complete chorus is forty-eight measures long (3 × 16) and each section is divided in half. The last chorus omits the bridge section, repeats the opening melody, and goes directly to the coda, which repeats the introduction except for the final chords.

Formal Scheme

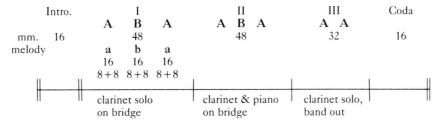

Goodman solo

Dizzy Gillespie Sextet

Groovin' High

Music: Dizzy Gillespie
Recorded: New York, February 29, 1945
Original Issue: Guild 1001 (Musicraft 485), matrix G554
Performers: Dizzy Gillespie, trumpet
Charlie Parker, alto saxophone
Remo Palmieri, guitar
Clyde Hart, piano
Slam Stewart, bass
Harold West, drums

Groovin' High is a superb example of the bebop musician's ability to transform a well-known popular song, *Whispering*, by Malvin and John Schonberger, into a complicated work of jazz art music. When Paul Whiteman recorded *Whispering* in 1920, it sold over two million copies and remained popular through many subsequent recordings well into the 1950s. *Whispering* is divided into two sections that are almost identical melodically and harmonically, differing only in the presence of a first and second ending. The same is true of *Groovin' High*. However, Gillespie borrowed only the harmonies, altered them but slightly, and wrote a new melody for the head.

Whispering, chord progression (above)
Groovin' High, chord progression (below)

(First eight measures)

E♭	E♭	Adim⁷	Adim⁷	E♭	E♭	C⁷		C⁷	
E♭	E♭	Am⁷ D⁷	Am⁷ D⁷	E♭	E♭	Gm⁷	C⁷	Gm⁷	C⁷

Gillespie's new melody divides regularly into four-measure phrases and sequences through the harmonic levels, as did the original. But Gillespie did not stop there—he worked out a composition that includes a six-measure introduction that obscures the key,

24*

Groovin' High, Introduction

he clipped the last two measures of the head and inserted transitional passages,

Head

he put the head in one key, E♭, and the first solo chorus in another, D♭,

Charlie Parker Solo

Slam Stewart Solo

Voice, one octave higher
Bass, sounds one octave lower

he returned to the original key for his solo and for the remainder of the piece, and he added a coda that proceeds in half-time.

All the solos are outstanding, but they are exceptionally brief—one-half chorus each. Parker's and Gillespie's solos became classics overnight, to be liberally copied and imitated by hundreds of jazz musicians. On the other hand, Slam Stewart's solo is uniquely his own. While playing the solo with a bow, he sang the identical part two octaves higher than the sound of his bass. Very few musicians copied this technique, which became a hallmark for this splendid bass player.

Formal Scheme

Intro.	Head	Transition	Alto Sax solo	Bass solo	Transition	Trumpet solo	Guitar solo	Coda
	a a′		Intro. a	a′		Intro. a	a′	
6	16 + 14	4	2 + 16	14	3	4 + 16	14	8

|| || | | | | | | | | || ||

| | | | Parker | Stewart | | Gillespie | Palmieri | |

Lee Konitz / Warne Marsh Quintet

Marshmallow

Music: Warne Marsh
Recorded: New York, June 28, 1949
Original Issue: Prestige 7004, matrix PRLP-7004-B
Performers: Lee Konitz, alto saxophone
    Warne Marsh, tenor saxophone
    Sal Mosca, piano
    Arnold Fishkin, bass
    Denzil Best, drums

Marshmallow is a masterpiece of melodic writing, a new jazz composition based on the chord pattern of the 1938 popular song by Ray Noble, *Cherokee (Indian Love Song)*.

Cherokee (Indian Love Song)

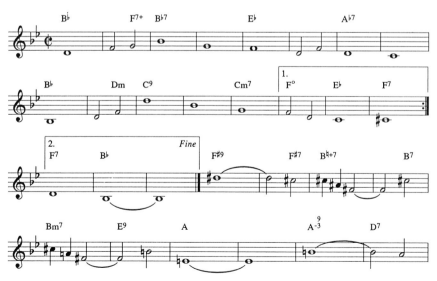

29*

The original is in the standard popular-song form, **AABA,** as is *Marshmallow,* but notice the one-beat displacement on the return to **A** after the bridge, the basic 3/2 meter of the new tune against the 4/4 construction of the model, the 3/8 pattern (through melodic contour) of the notes that begin the bridge,

Marshmallow, Bridge

and the first phrase of six measures, which subdivides into beat groups 6 + 4 + 4 + 4 + 6.

The musicians, strongly influenced by Lennie Tristano and Gil Evans, are pioneers in cool jazz. The straight and pure horn tone, the relegation of brushes on drums to background pulsations, the intellectual (as opposed to spontaneous) approach to composition and improvisation, and the moderate dynamic level are some of the characteristics of the cool jazz style that are exemplified here. The virtuosity of the two saxophonists is breathtaking: their intonation is pure and their articulation so exact that the two instruments in unison sound like one, until they choose to separate on distinct melodic paths.

Formal Scheme

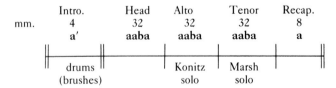

mm.	Intro. 4 a′	Head 32 aaba	Alto 32 aaba	Tenor 32 aaba	Recap. 8 a
	drums (brushes)		Konitz solo	Marsh solo	

Marshmallow

Charlie Parker and His Quartet

Confirmation

> **Music:** Charlie Parker
> **Recorded:** New York, August 4, 1953
> **Original Issue:** Clef MG C-157
> **Performers:** Charlie Parker, alto saxophone
>   Al Haig, piano
>   Percy Heath, bass
>   Max Roach, drums

Recorded as early as 1945, *Confirmation* stands as one of Charlie Parker's finest compositions, a magical transformation of popular-song form into an asymmetrical melodic challenge. The first phrase twists back and forth upon itself rather than leave the confined space of a tenth. With turning ornaments adding a baroque filigree, the syncopations constantly place and displace accents and beats. But with Parker, it is rarely the melody that captures the imagination but the improvisation. *Confirmation*, recorded late in Parker's life just before failing health would end his recording career, proceeds from start to finish with an unerring sense of logic. Unlike many of his earlier solos, which employ clever quotes from other sources, this improvisation develops—through sequence, displacement, alteration, but never exact repetition—motivic ideas that emerge during the progress of the solo.

Al Haig, who accompanied Dizzy Gillespie on his 1946 recording of *52nd Street Theme,* is present at this session. His solo is graceful and complements Parker's. Max Roach plays conservatively most of the time, but his short solo in the last chorus exemplifies the aggressive and virtuosic solo technique of which he is capable.

Formal Scheme

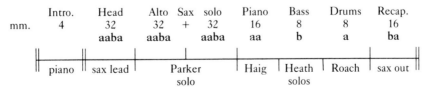

	Intro.	Head	Alto	Sax	solo	Piano	Bass	Drums	Recap.
mm.	4	32	32	+	32	16	8	8	16
		aaba	aaba		aaba	aa	b	a	ba

piano ‖ sax lead | Parker solo | Haig | Heath solos | Roach | sax out ‖

Confirmation

The Gerry Mulligan Quartet with Lee Konitz

I Can't Believe that You're in Love with Me

Music: C. Gaskill and Jimmy McHugh
Recorded: Los Angeles, June 10, 1953
Original Issue: World Pacific PJM-406
Performers: Gerry Mulligan, baritone saxophone
Chet Baker, trumpet
Joe Mondragon, bass
Larry Bunker, drums
Lee Konitz, alto saxophone

In a number of ways, Gerry Mulligan set the style for modern jazz in the 1950s, especially as it came to be played on the West Coast. Like Mel Powell, he displayed his talents for orchestration early and contributed arrangements to Johnny Warrington at the age of seventeen and Gene Krupa when he was only nineteen. His charts for Claude Thornhill and Miles Davis in the late 1940s (he was still in his early 20s) were a part of the "birth of the cool," and the various ensembles he led, especially his pianoless quartet, were models of innovation and relaxed swing. As a baritone saxophonist, he was, and is, without peer. Following in the footsteps of Harry Carney and Serge Chaloff, Mulligan firmly established the baritone saxophone as a solo instrument and not just a bass member of the woodwind ensemble.

A pianoless jazz quartet of two melody and two rhythm instruments opens up the tonal space of the ensemble, lightens the sound, and opens routes of great flexibility for the improvising soloist; it also creates unique and fascinating problems for the composer-arranger. Although the bass alone can carry the beat and imply the harmonies, space must be filled for the listener, so at least one horn player must be performing all the time. The only exception to this rule occurs during bass and drum solos, and they cannot carry the arrangement for long. Also, in a decade that requires chromatic harmonies in every modern style, the second player (the first being the one playing melody or blowing a solo) must play exactly the right harmonic note, again, all the time. Mulligan had a miraculous ear for hearing harmony and an uncanny sense of how to progress melodically from one structural note to another. Without a piano to fill in the changes, the baritone saxophone had to supply or imply everything else with great contrapuntal skill. The ensemble becomes a concert ensemble, much like a string quartet, that is no longer well suited for accompanying a three- or four-hour dance, as there is no piano to relieve the horns.

This particular recording is fascinating for another reason: it includes a guest soloist from a different "class" of the "cool school." Mulligan's concept of cool, swinging jazz followed the mainstream tradition of Lester Young, Charlie Parker, Gil Evans, and the like. Konitz's concept of the same general style developed from the *avant-garde* ideas of Lennie Tristano. It is fascinating to compare the light, relaxed, and swinging solos of Mulligan and Baker with the intense, angular, and asymmetric lines and sound of Konitz. The contrast is especially noticeable if we compare the choice of rhythms and pitches that open Baker's solo with those at the beginning of Konitz's.

Openings of Trumpet and Alto Saxophone Solos

Opening of Baritone Saxophone Solo

Where the bass is critical in the ensemble and provides both the harmony and rhythm of the changes, the drum's role has been diminished and is restricted to an ephemeral background pulsation. The structure of the performance adheres to a straightforward popular-song form, followed by solos and a recapitulation. The bass plays solo for the introduction and during the bridge section of the recapitulation.

Formal Scheme

mm.	Intro. 4 a'	Head 32 aaba	Baritone 32 aaba	Trumpet 32 aaba	Alto 32 aaba	Recap. 32 aaba
	bass	Ensemble	Mulligan	Baker	Konitz	bass solo on bridge

I Can't Believe that You're in Love with Me

The Horace Silver Quintet

The Preacher

Music: Horace Silver
Recorded: Hackensack, New Jersey, February 6, 1955
Original Issue: Blue Note BLP-5062
Performers: Horace Silver, piano
Hank Mobley, tenor saxophone
Kenny Dorham, trumpet
Doug Watkins, bass
Art Blakey, drums

The Jazz Messengers was a cooperative hard-bop ensemble formed by Art Blakey and Horace Silver in 1953. Not all black jazz musicians were pleased with the direction in which jazz seemed to be heading at that time. Cool jazz innovations and third-stream music was regarded by some as too "white" and intellectual, and some black jazz artists wanted to plant their feet even more firmly in the musical traditions of their own heritage—blues, gospel, rhythm-and-blues, and the straight line of development from classic jazz to bebop. Horace Silver was a leader in the creation of, or return to, funky jazz—hard-playing, free-swinging, blues-based jazz. Of his many compositions, none became more popular in the jazz world and outside than *The Preacher*, and few pieces had a more lasting effect. With *I've Been Working on the Railroad* harmonies (I–I^7–IV–I–$II_{\sharp 3}^{7}$–V^7), and with Blakey's insistent back-beat accents, Dorham's loud and wailing hard-bop trumpet,

Beginning of Dorham Solo

39*

and Mobley's full-voiced tenor,

Beginning of Mobley Solo

Silver created a work that defined "funky." It swings, it's simple, it's fun, and it's "down home." With his riffing, rollicking, two-fisted style, Silver leads the way in this new black, reactionary music.

The head and recapitulation are in an old-fashioned, two-beat style, but Doug Watkins slips into walking, four-beat patterns when he backs the solos. With its emphasis on the subdominant and its repetition of a simple melodic phrase, *The Preacher* gives the impression of being a blues. In spite of the riffs, the style, and the sound, it is not. The tune is laid out over sixteen measures with four-measure phrases in an **AA′A″B** pattern.

Formal Scheme

mm.	Head	Trumpet	Tenor	Piano	Riff	Recap.
	16×2	16×2	16×2	16×2	16×2	16×2
	a a′a″b	a a′a″b	a a′a″b	a a′a″b	a a′a″b	a a′a″b
	Ensemble	Dorham	Mobley	Silver	ensemble	ensemble

The Preacher

George Russell

All About Rosie, Third Movement

Music: George Russell
Recorded: Waltham, Massachusetts, June 10, 1957
Original Issue: Columbia WL-127
Performers: Robert DiDomenica, flute
Hal McKusick, alto saxophone
John LaPorta, tenor saxophone
Manuel Zegler, bassoon
Jim Buffington, French Horn
Louis Mucci, Art Farmer, trumpets
Jimmy Knepper, trombone
Teddy Charles, vibes
Bill Evans, piano
Barry Galbraith, guitar
Teddy Somer, drums
Joe Benjamin, bass

All About Rosie is an example from the "Third Stream," the musical tributary that draws its substance from two primary sources, classical art music and jazz, and intentionally blends them together. Most of the third-stream repertoire is composer-dominated concert music; this piece is a large work in three movements. It incorporates jazz elements of instrumentation, performance practice, harmonic schemes, and improvisation. It also uses non-jazz elements of instrumentation (flute, French horn, bassoon), large-scale form, and developmental schemes. Like many classical concertos, it is in three movements—fast, slow, fast—and like some modern concertos, it features the orchestra and many soloists from the orchestra (e.g., Béla Bartók, *Concerto for Orchestra*).

All three movements of *All About Rosie* are based on the tune of a traditional black children's song-game, *Rosie, Little Rosie,*

Rosie, Little Rosie

Ros - ie, lit - tle Ros - ie__

and the first two movements are entirely notated, that is, there is no improvisation in the instrumental solos. The third movement gives *ad lib* solos to several instrumentalists, and in this performance, Bill Evans improvised one of the most brilliant and famous solos in the jazz piano repertoire. The three movements, all in D minor, are tightly unified by the motive and by the harmonic scheme. The final movement recapitulates the opening of the first movement (in a kind of cyclical form) and then burns to a meteoric close in C major. A broad overview of form reveals this plan:

I Fast (♩=240) II Slow (♩=66) III (♩=120)
Dm→C Dm→Dm Dm→C

or **ABA'**. The third movement also subdivides **ABA'** with an exposition, improvisations, and recapitulation:

A B A'

A B A'
Expo. Imp. Recap.

The exposition has an introduction (sticks on crown of cymbal) followed by a brass statement of theme and then transitional and developmental passages. Within the exposition there are six subsections of 16, 12, 16, 32, 8, and 11 measures each, all in 4/4 time. In the middle portion of the movement, the improvisations are all in popular-song form, aaba. The harmonic pattern of the repeated thirty-two-measure unit is:

Harmonic Scheme for Improvisations

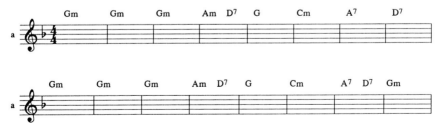

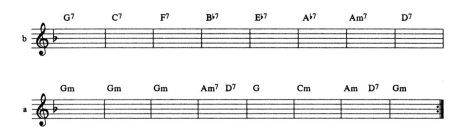

Bill Evans takes four full choruses of thirty-two measures each, with the band entering to accompany his final chorus. Evans's first chorus is backed by the cymbal only, the bass and drums play stop-time to accompany his second chorus, and the walking-bass pattern begins the third chorus. Russell backs the other solos with band and intersperses band articulations among the solos. After the piano solo, the band enters; after the alto saxophone, trumpet, and vibraphone solos, the band returns; and during the last half of the tenor saxophone solo, the band enters again. This time, Russell elides the last two measures of the solo chorus with the opening of the recapitulation, and the full ensemble plays to the end.

Formal Scheme of the Third Movement

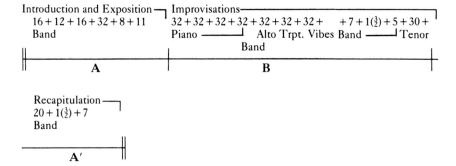

Miles Davis Sextet

Dr. Jekyll

Music: Jackie McLean
Recorded: New York, April 3, 1958
Original Issue: Columbia CL1193
Performers: Miles Davis, trumpet
             Julian "Cannonball" Adderley, alto saxophone
             John Coltrane, tenor saxophone
             Red Garland, piano
             Paul Chambers, bass
             Philly Joe Jones, drums

This 1958 sextet is one of Miles Davis's classic bands. As we can hear on this recording, Adderley and Coltrane stimulate, challenge, and complement each other into solos of raw power and great inspiration. The rhythm section is equal to the front line, and the players hold tough on the most demanding up-tempo tunes. Davis, who never established a reputation as a dazzling improviser at fast tempos, plays brilliantly on this number. Not only does he play the head with clarity and invent interesting running, hard-bop lines in his solo, he experiments with intervals, timbre, and pitch, squeezing long A♭s into sculptured shapes. His solo is not merely a succession of notes—even at this fast tempo he creates a tapestry of sounds.

The performances of Coltrane and Adderley are truly amazing. For twelve choruses they play follow-the-leader, alternating solos. Each picks up on the ideas just played by the other and forges ahead with an almost seamless connection to the preceding section. Paul Chambers takes to the bow for his solo and plays seven worthy melodic choruses. Throughout, Philly Joe Jones punctuates, drives, and syncopates in the background, and just before the end of the piece he performs a powerful solo of his own. Only the piano is left out of the spotlight.

Jackie McLean's angular composition is a blues with minor subdominant and dominant harmonies. At times, the opening F major is lowered to F minor (when Davis plays a descending riff after the bass solo). The piece was performed in a straightforward presentation of head, solos, and recapitulation of the head. Davis signals the end by returning with a minor riff and another short solo. The drum solo sets up the recapitulation, and the band takes it out.

Formal Scheme of *Dr. Jekyll*

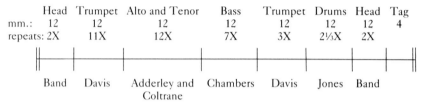

	Head	Trumpet	Alto and Tenor	Bass	Trumpet	Drums	Head	Tag
mm.:	12	12	12	12	12	12	12	4
repeats:	2X	11X	12X	7X	3X	2⅓X	2X	
	Band	Davis	Adderley and Coltrane	Chambers	Davis	Jones	Band	

Dr. Jekyll

John Coltrane Quartet

Giant Steps

> **Music:** John Coltrane
> **Recorded:** New York, May 4, 1959
> **Original Issue:** Atlantic LP1311
> **Performers:** John Coltrane, tenor saxophone
> Tommy Flanagan, piano
> Paul Chambers, bass
> Art Taylor, drums

No saxophonist after Charlie Parker has been more admired or imitated than John Coltrane, and no Coltrane composition has had a more lasting effect than *Giant Steps*. At a time in the history of jazz when harmonic rhythm was slowing down under increasing pressure from the developments in modal theory and practice, Coltrane recorded his *Giant Steps*, in which the chords fly by relentlessly. Performed at a blistering tempo, the sixteen-measure structure is filled with twenty-six chords, almost two per measure. Further, the chords do not progress in the most familiar patterns (the circle of fifths, I–IV–V–I, I–VI–II–V–I, etc.), and they require harmonic improvisation on nine of the twelve possible root positions—B, C♯, D, E♭, F, F♯, G, A, B♭ (all the notes of the twelve-tone scale except the augmented triad C–E–G♯).

The melody of the head has an interesting rhythmic pattern that intentionally disguises the phrase ending and that, through elision, overlaps patterns of two, three, and four measures. The first phrase might stop at the end of measure 3, or perhaps at the end of measure 4. But measure 4 sounds like a pickup to measure 5, which continues on to measure 7, or 8, or 9. The two-measure units overlap, or fit between, the normal cadential points in a sixteen-measure piece. Harmonic sequences are obvious, and they establish the logic of the harmonic progressions (measures 1–3 and 5–7, and all the two-measure units). One interpretation of the phrasing divides the sixteen measures 3 + 4 + 2 + 2 + 2 + 2 + 1.

Giant Steps

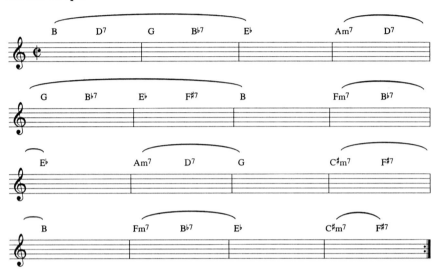

A complete transcription of the head and Coltrane solo can be found in Transcription 10. Though Coltrane plays an incredibly large number of notes per second, this solo is not an example of his "sheets of sound," where a downpour of notes creates an effect. In *Giant Steps*, Coltrane is "playing the changes," that is, he is improvising to the harmonies in such a way that his scales and arpeggios coincide, moment by moment, with the underlying harmonic structure of the composition.

Formal Scheme of *Giant Steps*

	Head	Tenor Solo	Piano Solo	Tenor Solo	Head	Tag
mm.	16	16	16	16	16	4
repeats:	2X	11X	4X	2X	2X	

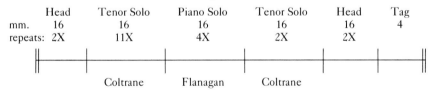

| | Coltrane | Flanagan | Coltrane | | |

Ornette Coleman Quartet

Change of the Century

Music: Ornette Coleman
Recorded: New York, October 8–9, 1959
Original Issue: Atlantic LP1327
Performers: Ornette Coleman, alto saxophone
Donald Cherry, pocket trumpet
Charlie Haden, bass
Billy Higgins, drums

On the liner notes of the original issue album, Ornette Coleman is quoted as saying:

> When our group plays, before we start out to play, we do not have any idea what the end result will be. Each player is free to contribute what he feels in the music at any given moment. . . . CHANGE OF THE CENTURY expresses our feeling that we have to make breaks with a lot of jazz's recent past. . . . We want to incorporate more musical materials and theoretical ideas—from the classical world, as well as jazz and folk—into our work to create a broader base for the new music we are creating.

Like Gerry Mulligan, Coleman dispenses with piano in his quartet, but for entirely different reasons. Here it would be superfluous, for the piece has no harmonic structure. Certainly the quartet worked out and coordinated melodic and rhythmic phrases to be used at the beginning and end of the composition, but this performance is essentially a combination of four free-floating musical lines (alto, trumpet, bass, and drums) playing independently but reacting to each other. Tonality is not an essential feature—the musicians may or may not play in a key, and this tonal center may or may not be the same as that employed by any of the other members of the ensemble. The soloists have no set chorus structure for solos; they may begin when they choose, play as long as they please, and explore ideas in whatever manner or by whatever standards they select. One may play fast while another plays slowly; one may seek atonal sounds or timbral squeaks while another resorts to clichés and eclecticism. The artistic success or failure of the result depends on the talent and virtuosity of the players and their sensitivity and response to the others in the group. Most important, the success of a composition also depends on the experience, mindset, and perceptual acuity of the listeners. The audience must be able to organize these sounds into meaningful patterns and interpret the musical and extramusical symbols contained in the sounds they hear.

A Loose Guide to the Formal Scheme of *Change of the Century*

A (head) **B′** and **B″** (solos) **A′** (recapitulation)

Head **A**	Alto Solo **B′**	Trumpet Solo **B″**	Recapitulation **A′**
running, trilling melody; arco bass on pedal point; free drums	some free, some sequence; occasional tonal patterns; pizz. and arco bass; drums play time	contrasts of high and low, fast and slow; walking bass; at end, tpt. plays material from head	running, trilling melody; abrupt stop

Thelonious Monk Quartet

Bemsha Swing

Music: Thelonious Monk
Recorded: Tokyo, May 21, 1963
Original Issue: Columbia C2 38510
Performers: Thelonious Monk, piano
Charlie Rouse, tenor saxophone
Butch Warren, bass
Frankie Dunlop, drums

Although Monk's major contributions to jazz as a performer and composer were made in the 1940s and '50s, it was not until Columbia Records took him under contract in the early '60s that he began to achieve widespread public acclaim. During this period he re-recorded many of his earlier compositions and worked regularly with one of the most compatible sidemen of his career, tenor saxophonist Charlie Rouse. Rouse's bouncy articulations, clear sound, and swing phrasing seem to complement perfectly the percussive touch, angular melodic lines, and erratic syncopations of Monk's performance and composition.

First recorded ten years earlier with Miles Davis (Prestige 7109), *Bemsha Swing* is almost a minimalist composition. Within the limits of the style, it reduces the compositional elements to a bare minimum: one four-measure phrase repeated four times (once on the subdominant level), six chords on four roots (C C^7 Dm^7 F G^7 and Gm^7), and **aaba** form. Even the rhythm of all the phrases is exactly identical. The tune is a sparse, gap-fill melody, that is, an interval is established by the first two notes of the melody and the root note of the harmony,

and the gap is filled artistically to close the void. In this case, the descent is direct, with no melodic excursions and a minimum of rhythmic digressions, and just before arriving, it cleverly avoids the second step with a turn around the leading tone.

Both solos are playful, bouncing from one area to the next, but Monk's is especially interesting in his preference for the "cracks" between many of the keys (i.e., he strikes two adjacent notes at one time) to the tempered intonation of one note or the other.

Formal Scheme of *Bemsha Swing*

	Intro.	Head	Tenor Sax solo	Piano solo	Head
mm.	4	16	16	16	16
repeats:		2X	4X	5X	2X
		aaba	aaba	aaba	aaba
			Rouse	Monk	

Bemsha Swing

*The composition's original bass line is notated as above, and is available in sheet music from Second Floor Music, 130 West 28th Street, New York, NY 10001.

Miles Davis Quintet

Circle

Music: Miles Davis
Recorded: New York, October 24, 1966
Original Issue: Columbia PC 9401
Performers: Miles Davis, trumpet (muted)
           Wayne Shorter, tenor saxophone
           Herbie Hancock, piano
           Ron Carter, bass
           Tony Williams, drums

Circle is a complex waltz whose form has some elastic elements, that is, during a solo, a phrase might be collapsed or stretched a few extra measures at will without doing harm to the whole. However, certain structural harmonies signal the soloist and the listener, and guide the flow of the music. There are two phrases in this composition, the first of ten measures and the second of eight to twenty measures or more. The main features of the first phrase are the harmonic opening on D minor, a transitory middle, and a rise to C (usually major).

Circle, First Phrase

The chords of the middle four measures may vary, but they usually follow the pattern of Example 1.

The second phrase, in its first statement of this performance, is twelve measures long, and it too has three main features: a rising pattern beginning

(G–G♯–A) that falls to F, a middle section that cadences on D, and a final two measures that provide a turn-around (E–A) to the beginning (D). In this manner, the piece circles over and over, each complete pattern slightly different from the previous one.

Circle, Second Phrase

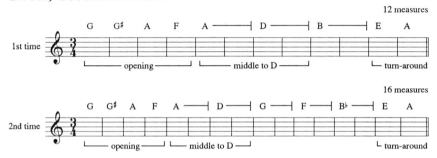

To obscure the form even further, Wayne Shorter begins his tenor solo immediately after Davis ends his in the middle of the second phrase. When Hancock begins his solo, he and Shorter elide the middle section of the second phrase (with its cadence on D) with the opening of the first phrase (also on D).

In jazz, as in all music, the message is not the complexity of form or harmony but the emotion and meaning conveyed to the listener by musical and extra-musical means. *Circle* is an intense, introspective work played by performers who passionately feel what they play. It is what they do with the notes within the constraints of the piece and the style that gives pleasure and satisfaction to the listener and makes this one of the great performances of the decade.

Circle

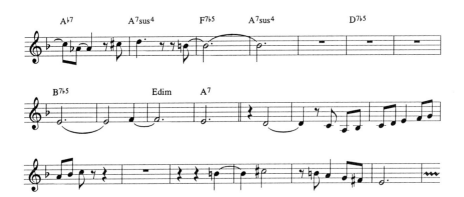

Formal Scheme of *Circle*

		A	B
Chord		10	12
	Davis - - - - -►		
		10	16
		10	10 + 10
			Shorter - - - - -►
		10	16
		10	8
		10	12
	Hancock - - - - -►		
		10	16
		10	20
		10	8
		10	8 + 20 + 2 + 16
	Davis - - - - -►		(D pedal point)

Weather Report

Tears

Music: Wayne Shorter
Recorded: New York, 1971
Original Issue: Columbia PC 30661
Performers: Joe Zawinul, keyboards
Wayne Shorter, soprano saxophone
Miroslav Vitous, bass
Alphonze Mouzon, drums
Airto Moreiro, percussion

Jazz/Rock/Fusion had no more eloquent representative than Weather Report, a group founded on the principle of collective improvisation within a context of the latest electronic wizardry. In *Tears*, we may observe that the traditional soloist and accompanist have been replaced by five equal partners sharing the lead, supplying the counterpoints, and contributing timbres and rhythms as the music dictates. The sound of Weather Report resulted primarily from the extraordinary advances in musical technology during the 1970s—new and improved electric and electronic instruments, smaller and more powerful synthesizers, better microphones, and sixteen- and thirty-two-track studios. Also, the profound changes in our jazz and popular music cultures—free jazz, rock 'n' roll, soul, and world music—had their effect.

Tears is neither a notated composition nor a "head and improvisations" structure, but a sequence of musical events following the presentation of initial sounds and, perhaps, a motive. Although strongly influenced by the thinking of musicians from the free jazz movement, the sounds of Weather Report remain remarkably consonant. In addition to incorporating electronic sounds, the group paints a tonal portrait that derives from the older jazz tradition of harmonic improvisation, taking into account the players' preference and respect for accurate pitch, beautiful and even tone, motivic development, and unity over variety.

Tears unfolds one musical gesture after another. There are no formal introductions, expositions, developments, and the like. There is instead a related series of motives, sounds, rhythms, and ideas. The piece opens "out of time," that is, the drums and percussion are not keeping time but sculpting percussive sounds. The electronic keyboard establishes a tonality and the soprano saxophone intones a motive. From that point to the conclusion, the piece is one undulating wave of sound following another.

Sketch of *Tears*

Wynton Marsalis Quartet

Delfeayo's Dilemma

Music: Wynton Marsalis
Recorded: Washington, D.C., December 19–20, 1986
Original Issue: Columbia G2K-40675
Performers: Wynton Marsalis, trumpet
Marcus Roberts, piano
Robert Leslie Hurst, III, bass
Jeff "Tain" Watts, drums

Wynton Marsalis is a virtuoso of the first rank, but the significance of his playing extends far beyond the bravura technique, beautiful tone, total control, and flawless intonation that first amazes and then awes his listeners. He has brought to jazz, and to each performance, a return to principles espoused in past decades: acoustic playing, harmonic and modal improvisation, thematic development, and rhythmic swing. Against a jazz environment influenced strongly by rock 'n' roll, New Age romanticism, Free Jazz principles, electronic and digital innovations, and studio productions, Marsalis has demonstrated, better than any of his contemporaries, that the neoclassical approach of live performance on standard instruments in tonal frameworks not only provides a viable option for jazz musicians but also leaves room for growth and expansion.

Delfeayo's Dilemma is performed in the traditional manner—a head followed by a series of improvisations and ending with a recapitulation of the beginning. The instrumental performance is rooted in the perfection of technique and the employment of traditional playing methods: a trumpet approach related to that of Louis Armstrong and Clifford Brown, piano playing with elements of Bud Powell and Thelonious Monk, drumming with the strong influence of Art Blakey and Elvin Jones, and bass performance that respects the principles of Jimmy Blanton and Ron Carter. Here, the group and individual sounds spring from the players' inspiration and invention, near-perfect execution, and the eclectic combination of qualities derived from sounds of the past.

Although the quartet performs head, solos, and recapitulation, Marcus

Roberts on piano is not content to back the trumpet solo and stay out of the way. Instead, he solos in the background, builds on motives played by Marsalis, and challenges his partner to greater risk-taking. The same is true of "Tain" Watts, whose powerhouse drumming constantly pushes his colleagues while filling all the voids with patterns of his own. The melody of the "tune" is built on fourths and fifths, and so are the harmonies.

Patterns of Fourths and Fifths

Unlike the standard formal patterns based on four- and eight-measure phrases (twelve-bar blues; sixteen- and thirty-two measure popular-song form), this head repeats after twenty-seven measures and is subdivided 5 + 6 + 16:

The change from 4/3 to 3/2 with measures staying equal provides an exciting rhythmic effect (hemiola with syncopation) in the first statement of the theme. The head has four distinct sections, abcd. The first, containing the opening motive, Example 1, is five measures long; the second is the six-measure piano improvisation; the third follows; and the last, the final six measures of the second statement, serves as a closing motive. The improvisations, which take place over shifting modal harmonies, exhibit great freedom of form and length.

Delfeayo's Dilemma

Formal Scheme of *Delfeayo's Dilemma*

	Head	Trumpet solo	Piano solo	Head
mm.	27			27
repeats:	2X			2X
	abcd	3 min. 45 sec.	3 min. 40 sec.	**abcd**
		Marsalis	Roberts	

TRANSCRIPTIONS

S.O.L. Blues, Louis Armstrong Solo (*SCCJ* 15)

Struttin' with Some Barbecue, Louis Armstrong Solo (*SCCJ* 17)

63*

West End Blues, Louis Armstrong Solo (*SCCJ* 19)

Body and Soul, Coleman Hawkins Solo (*SCCJ* 33)

Lester Leaps In, Head and Lester Young Solo (*SCCJ* 49)

68*

I Can't Get Started, Dizzy Gillespie Solo (*SCCJ* 63)

Embraceable You, Charlie Parker Solo (*SCCJ* 67)

Little Benny, Head and Charlie Parker Solo (*SCCJ* 70)

Parker's Mood, Introduction and Charlie Parker Solo
(*SCCJ* 71)

Giant Steps, Head and John Coltrane Solo (*NAJ* 15)

Chords ut supra

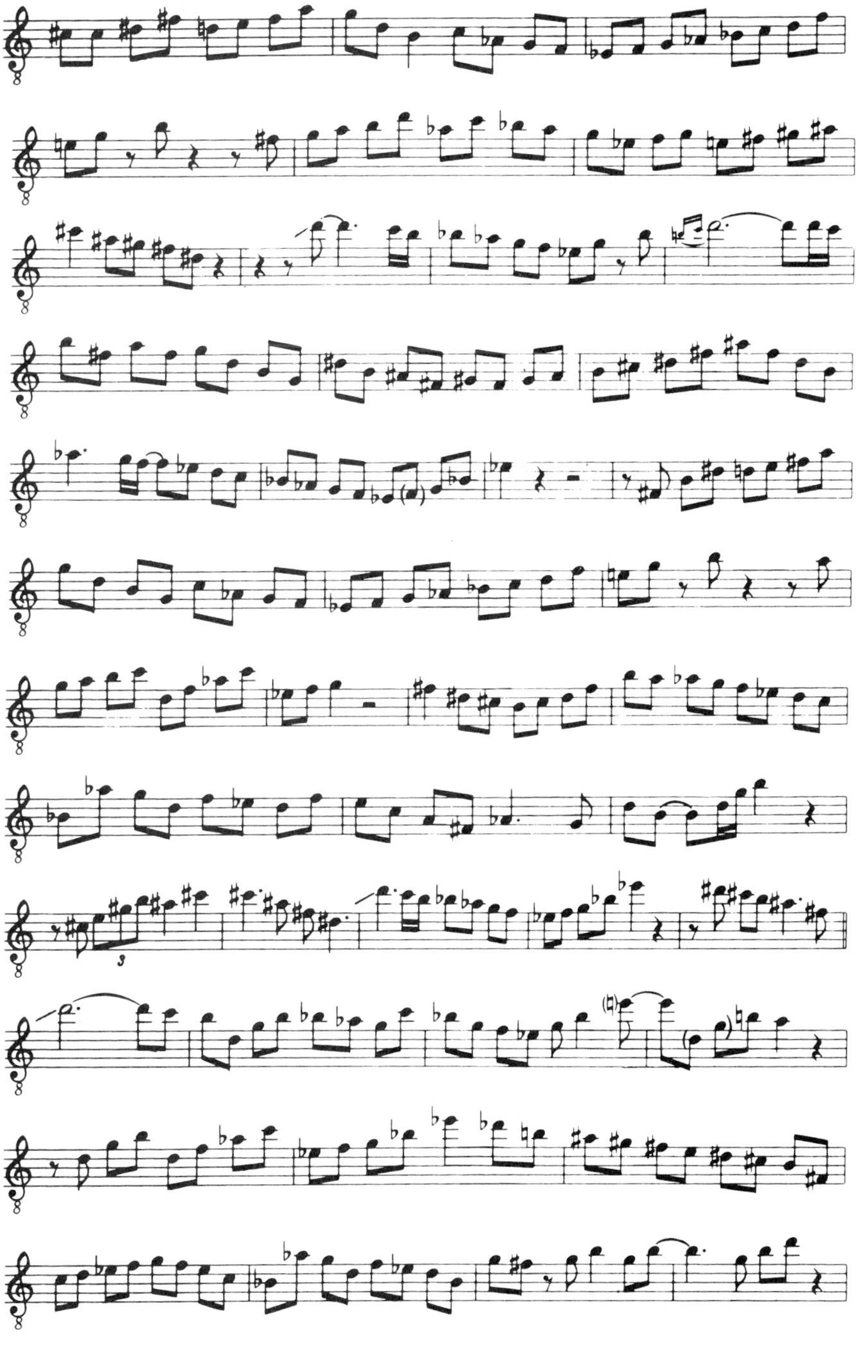

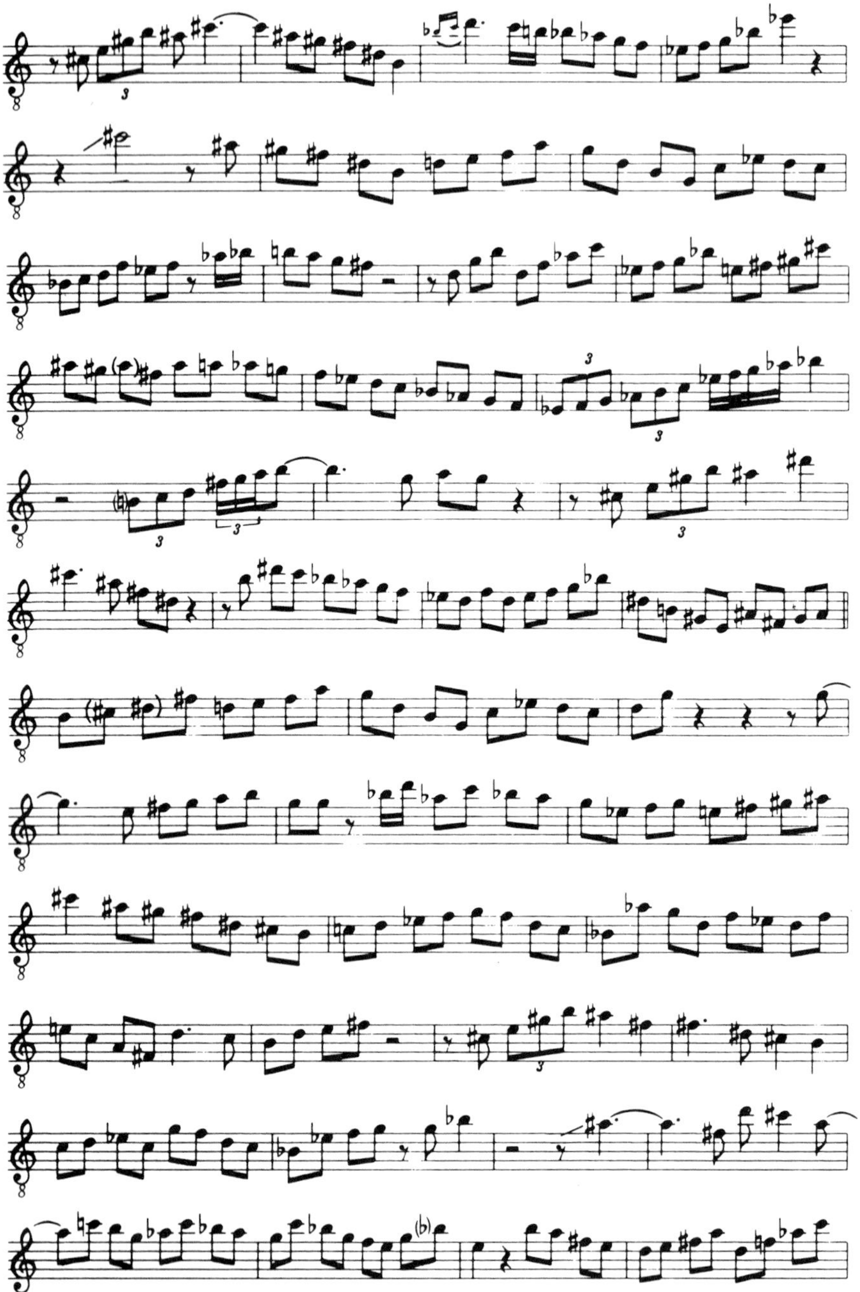

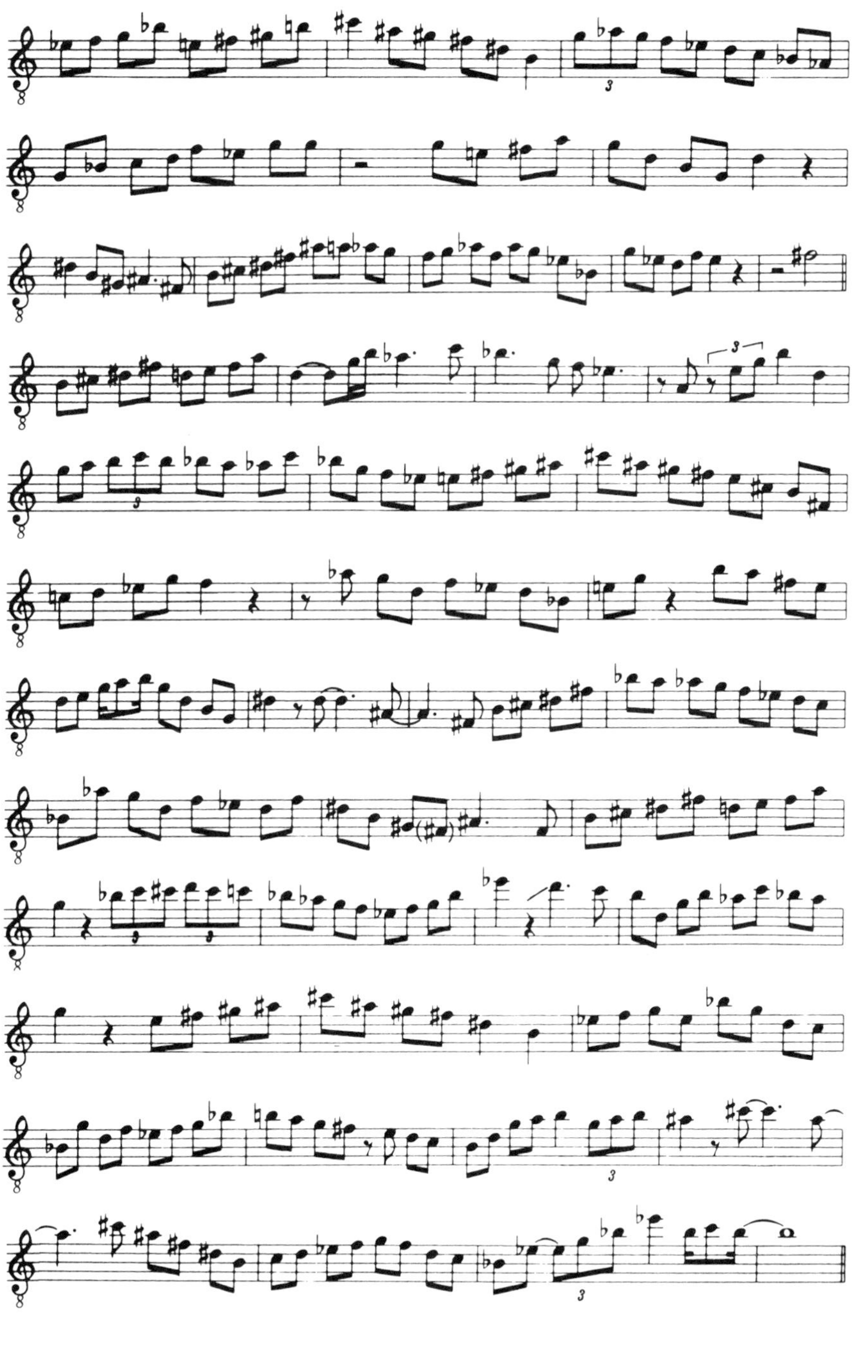

Piano solo

Blue Train, Head and John Coltrane Solo (Blue Note
45-1691; Reissued BST 89903)

So What, Miles Davis Solo (*SCCJ* 99)

SYNOPTIC TABLE

The following chronology is designed to place the history of jazz in a historical context and help the reader view it as a living tradition within the framework of other cultural and sociological events.

	JAZZ	ART, LITERATURE, AND CONCERT MUSIC	HISTORY AND SCIENCE
1893	Scott Joplin plays at World's Columbian Exposition in Chicago.	Verdi, *Falstaff*. Tchaikovsky, Sixth Symphony. Dvořák, *New World Symphony*.	Edison builds the first movie studio in America.
1894		Mark Twain, *Tom Sawyer Abroad* Debussy, *Prélude à l'aprés-midi d'un faune*.	
1895		Bates, *America, the Beautiful*.	Congress passes income-tax law; declared unconstitutional. Roentgen discovers X-rays.
1896		MacDowell, *Indian Suite*. Puccini, *La bohème*. Hogan, *All Coons Look Alike to Me*.	
1897		Sousa, *The Stars and Stripes Forever*.	Klondike gold rush begins. Queen Victoria's Diamond Jubilee.

	JAZZ	ART, LITERATURE, AND CONCERT MUSIC	HISTORY AND SCIENCE
1898		R. Strauss, *Ein Heldenleben*. Rostand, *Cyrano de Bergerac*.	Spanish-American War. U.S. annexes Hawaiian Islands. Trans-Mississippi-Omaha Exhibition.
1899	Joplin, *Maple Leaf Rag*. Buddy Bolden playing in New Orleans. Eubie Blake playing in Baltimore.	Schoenberg, *Verklärte Nacht*.	U.S. announces Open Door Policy.
1900		Philadelphia Orchestra founded.	Marines help terminate Boxer Rebellion. U.S. population 76,303,387.
1901		Shaw, *Caesar and Cleopatra*.	Pan-American Exposition in Buffalo. Marconi transmits telegraph signal across Atlantic. Planck develops quantum theory. President McKinley assassinated.
1902	Year in which Jelly Roll Morton claims to have invented jazz.	Mascagni tours U.S. with own opera company.	Curies discover radium.
1903		Yeats lectures in U.S.	Wright brothers' first successful airplane flight.
1904		Puccini, *Madama Butterfly*. Rolland, *Jean Christophe*.	St. Louis Exposition. American occupation of Panama Canal and construction of Canal begins.
1905		Debussy, *La Mer*.	Freud founds psychoanalysis. Ty Cobb joins Detroit Tigers.
1906		Sinclair, *The Jungle*. Scriabin concertizes in U.S.	San Francisco earthquake and fire.
1907	Buddy Bolden committed to mental institution. Scott Joplin moves to New York.	R. Strauss's *Salome* opens in New York and creates scandal.	U.S. endures twentieth depression since 1790.
1908		Bartók, First String Quartet.	Automobile manufacture passes 50,000 mark. Peary sails for Arctic.

	JAZZ	ART, LITERATURE, AND CONCERT MUSIC	HISTORY AND SCIENCE
1909		Schoenberg, Piano Pieces, Op. 11. Wright, Robie House in Chicago.	Peary reaches the North Pole.
1910	Papa Celestine Orchestra at Tuxedo Dance Hall in New Orleans. James Reese Europe organizes Clef Club in New York.	Ravel, *Daphnis et Chloé*. Stravinsky, *The Firebird*.	Halley's Comet reappears. U.S. population 93,402,151.
1911	Joplin's *Treemonisha* performed in New York.	Mahler, *Lied von der Erde*.	Amundsen reaches South Pole.
1912	King Oliver joins Olympia Orchestra under A. J. Piron. Freddie Keppard takes New Orleans group to Los Angeles. W. C. Handy writes *Memphis Blues*.	Schoenberg, *Pierrot Lunaire*. Duchamp, *Nude Descending a Staircase*.	*Titanic* sinks after striking an iceberg.
1913	Word "jazz" first appears in print.	Lawrence, *Sons and Lovers*. Webern, Six Orchestral Pieces. Stravinsky, *Sacre du printemps*.	60-floor Woolworth Building completed, tallest in the world.
1914	Handy writes *St. Louis Blues*.	Vaughan Williams, *London Symphony*.	World War I begins in Europe. Panama Canal opens.
1915	King Oliver forms band in New Orleans, Bechet on clarinet. Morton publishes *Jelly Roll Blues*. Tom Brown's New Orleans Jazz Band to Chicago.	Ives, *Concord Sonata*.	Einstein, General Theory of Relativity.
1916	Handy, *Beale Street Blues*.	Diaghilev's Ballet Russe at Metropoliton Opera House.	Bolshevik Revolution in Russia. Liner *Sussex* torpedoed.
1917	Storyville area of New Orleans closed. Original Dixieland Jazz Band records in New York. Frisco Jazz Band records on cylinder.	Jascha Heifetz, at 16, has Carnegie Hall debut.	U.S. enters World War I.

	JAZZ	ART, LITERATURE, AND CONCERT MUSIC	HISTORY AND SCIENCE
1918	King Oliver leaves New Orleans for Chicago. Louisiana Five record in New York.	Cather, *My Antonia*. Spengler, *Decline of the West*.	End of World War I.
1919	Original Dixieland Jazz Band in London. Will Marion Cook's American Syncopated Orchestra in London and Paris. Ansermet praises artistry of Bechet.	Mencken, *The American Language*.	President Wilson collapses. Race riots in Chicago. First Atlantic airplane crossing.
1920	First blues recording, *Crazy Blues*, by Mamie Smith.	Lewis, *Main Street*.	First commercial radio broadcast. U.S. goes dry—prohibition. U.S. population 105,710,620.
1921	James P. Johnson records *Harlem Strut* and *Carolina Shout*. New Orleans Rhythm Kings at Chicago's Friar's Inn.	Picasso, *Three Musicians*.	First Miss America bathing-beauty contest.
1922	Armstrong joins Oliver in Creole Jazz Band in Chicago. Kid Ory records in Los Angeles with Spikes's Seven Pods of Pepper Orchestra. Coleman Hawkins records with Mamie Smith and her band. Fats Waller records *Birmingham Blues*.	Schoenberg, *Method of Composing with Twelve Tones*. Eliot, *The Waste Land*. Joyce, *Ulysses*.	Tomb of King Tutankhamen opened. Episcopal Bishops eliminate word "obey" from marriage ceremony. Babe Ruth becomes an outfielder.
1923	Jelly Roll Morton's first recording session. Fletcher Henderson forms 10-piece band, joined by Coleman Hawkins. Ellington returns to New York. Bessie Smith records *Downhearted Blues*.	Lon Chaney in *The Hunchback of Notre Dame*.	5,000 speakeasies in New York alone.

	JAZZ	ART, LITERATURE, AND CONCERT MUSIC	HISTORY AND SCIENCE
1924	Armstrong joins Henderson in New York. First Wolverine Orchestra recordings with Beiderbecke.	Gershwin, *Rhapsody in Blue.* Mann, *Magic Mountain.* Kafka, *The Trial.*	Stalin becomes dictator of Russia.
1925	Armstrong's first recordings as a leader. Ellington's first recordings as a leader.	Berg, *Wozzeck.* Fitzgerald, *The Great Gatsby.*	Columbia and Victor issue first electrical recordings.
1926	First Jelly Roll Morton's Red Hot Peppers recordings.	First talking motion picture. Hemingway, *The Sun Also Rises.* Toscanini guest conductor of New York Philharmonic.	Brigadier General Billy Mitchell court-martialed.
1927	Armstrong Hot Seven recordings. Earl Hines joins Armstrong. Ellington opens 5-year engagement at Cotton Club in New York, including national radio broadcasts.	Sandburg, *American Songbag.*	Lindbergh solos across the Atlantic. First Oscar awarded. Babe Ruth hits 60 home runs. Columbia Broadcasting System inaugurated.
1928	Count Basie joins Walter Page's Blue Devils. Pinetop Smith records *Pinetop's Boogie Woogie.* Johnny Hodges joins Ellington. Bechet joins Noble Sissle in Paris.	Weill, *Threepenny Opera.* First radio broadcast of the New York Philharmonic. Lawrence, *Lady Chatterley's Lover.* Gershwin, *An American in Paris.* Al Jolson in *The Jazz Singer*, first feature film with sound.	106 radio stations across the U.S.
1929	Fats Waller writes *Black and Blue.*	Faulkner, *The Sound and the Fury.* Hoagy Carmichael, *Stardust.*	Stock market crash: New York Stock Exchange closed for three days. St. Valentine's Day Massacre in Chicago.
1930	Ellington makes first hit recording, *Mood Indigo.*	Stravinsky, *Symphony of Psalms.* Frost, *Collected Poems.*	U.S. population 122,775,046. Thirty lynchings during year.

	JAZZ	ART, LITERATURE, AND CONCERT MUSIC	HISTORY AND SCIENCE
1931	Don Redman forms own big band. Ellington records *Creole Rhapsody*.	Stokowski performs Berg's *Wozzeck* in Philadelphia and New York.	Japan invades Manchuria. *Star-Spangled Banner* declared national anthem. Empire State Building opens, tallest in the world.
1932	Armstrong visits Europe.	Folger Shakespeare Memorial Library dedicated.	Lindbergh's son kidnapped. Olympic Games in Los Angeles.
1933	Ellington, *Sophisticated Lady*. Billie Holiday records with Benny Goodman and His Orchestra. Ellington and band tour Europe.	Schoenberg comes to U.S. to teach at Malkin Conservatory.	Franklin D. Roosevelt becomes President of the U.S. Adolph Hitler becomes Chancellor of Germany.
1934	Benny Goodman starts "Let's Dance" series on network radio. Jimmie Lunceford records extensively.	Virgil Thomson, *Four Saints in Three Acts*, with all-black cast. Howard Hanson, *Merry Mount*.	Dust storms and drought in Midwest. Hitler becomes "Führer."
1935	Count Basie forms own band. Dizzy Gillespie replaces Roy Eldridge in Teddy Hill Band. Goodman tours California; Palomar Ballroom success. Tommy Dorsey starts own swing band.	Gershwin, *Porgy and Bess*. Eliot, *Murder in the Cathedral*. Berg, Violin Concerto.	Italy invades Ethiopia. W.P.A. established. First night games in baseball.
1936	Woody Herman forms own band. First Lester Young dates with Count Basie combo.	Eugene O'Neill awarded Nobel Prize for literature.	Spanish Civil War. Mussolini completes Ethiopian campaign.
1937	Charlie Parker joins Jay McShann Band. Gillespie tours France and England with Hill Band. Andy Kirk's Kansas City Band in New York with Mary Lou Williams. Goodman records *Sing, Sing, Sing*.	Orff, *Carmina Burana*. Berg, *Lulu*. Picasso, *Guernica*. Hindemith settles in U.S. Toscanini appointed director of NBC Symphony Orchestra.	Japan invades China. Nylon patented.

	JAZZ	ART, LITERATURE, AND CONCERT MUSIC	HISTORY AND SCIENCE
1938	First Goodman Carnegie Hall concert. First John Hammond "Spirituals to Swing" concert at Carnegie Hall. Ella Fitzgerald records *A-Tisket a-Tasket* with Chick Webb.	Thomas Mann settles in U.S. Society for the Preservation and Encouragement of Barbershop Quartet Singing in America founded.	Cellulose-acetate-based magnetic tape used for music recording. Bobby Feller strikes out 18 batters in one game.
1939	Parker goes to New York, plays at Monroe's Uptown House. Charlie Christian joins Goodman. Coleman Hawkins records *Body and Soul.* Billie Holiday records *Strange Fruit.*	Bartók, Sixth String Quartet. Prokofiev, *Alexander Nevsky.* Roy Harris, Third Symphony. Joyce, *Finnegans Wake.* Steinbeck, *Grapes of Wrath.* Sandburg, *Abraham Lincoln: The War Years.*	World War II breaks out in Europe. International Exposition in San Francisco. New York World's Fair.
1940	Parker's first recordings with McShann. Ellington records *Concerto for Cootie.* Harry James forms own band; hires Frank Sinatra.	Hemingway, *For Whom the Bell Tolls.* Milhaud settles in America.	Roosevelt elected to third term. U.S. population 131,669,275.
1941	Stan Kenton's Band opens at Rendezvous Ballroom in Balboa, California. Gil Evans joins Claude Thornhill Orchestra.	National Gallery of Art opens.	Japanese bomb Pearl Harbor; U.S. enters war. Joe DiMaggio hits safely in 56 straight games.
1942	Max Roach joins Parker at Monroe's. Bunk Johnson cuts first New Orleans revival records. Swing bands become service bands. RCA sprays first gold disc—Glenn Miller's *Chattanooga Choo-Choo.*	All-black performance of *Aïda* at Chicago Lyric Opera.	Recording ban begins. American Federation of Musicians strike against record companies. United Nations Alliance. Congress of Racial Equality founded.
1943	Parker, Gillespie, and Vaughan with Earl Hines Band. Ellington's first Carnegie Hall Concert—*Black, Brown, and Beige.*	Chagall, *Crucifixion.*	Mussolini resigns. Women's Army Corp initiated. 30,000 Sinatra fans riot at Paramount Theater in New York.

	JAZZ	ART, LITERATURE, AND CONCERT MUSIC	HISTORY AND SCIENCE
1944	Norman Granz presents first "Jazz at the Philharmonic" concert. Thelonious Monk, *Round Midnight.*	Copland, *Appalachian Spring.*	Roosevelt elected to fourth term. Recording ban ends.
1945	Gillespie tours his first big band. Parker and Gillespie record *Shaw 'Nuff, Hot House.* Woody Herman tours first Herd.	Britten, *Peter Grimes.*	Surrender of Germany. Atomic bombs dropped on Japan.
1946	Parker records *Ornithology* and *Confirmation.* Stravinsky writes *Ebony Concerto* for Woody Herman and his band.		Nuremberg war trials begin.
1947	Herman's second Herd records *Four Brothers.* Ellington, *Deep South Suite.* Gillespie plays John Lewis's *Toccata for Trumpet and Orchestra* at Carnegie Hall.	Williams, *A Streetcar Named Desire.* Charles Ives awarded Pulitzer Prize for Third Symphony (composed 1911!).	Marshall Plan put into operation. Independence of India from British Empire.
1948	Stan Getz records *Early Autumn.* Stan Kenton begins concert series at Hollywood Bowl. Armstrong at jazz festival in Nice, France.	Cage, *Sonatas and Interludes for Prepared Piano.*	Columbia introduces first commercial 33⅓-rpm 12″ record. First telecast of a major American symphony orchestra.
1949	Lennie Tristano and Lee Konitz record *Marshmallow* and *Subconscious-Lee.* Miles Davis records "Birth of the Cool." George Shearing organizes quintet. Dave Brubeck records a trio and an octet.	Orwell, 1984. Albert Schweitzer visits U.S.	Communist government in China.
1950	Paul Desmond joins Dave Brubeck. Basie organizes septet. Kenton organizes 40-piece Innovations in Modern Music Orchestra. Herman begins his third Herd.	Heyerdahl, *Kon-Tiki: Across the Pacific by Raft.*	Beginning of the Korean War. Hydrogen-bomb development approved. U.S. population 150,697,361.

	JAZZ	ART, LITERATURE, AND CONCERT MUSIC	HISTORY AND SCIENCE
1951	Louis Bellson joins Ellington. Kenton records Graettinger's *City of Glass*. Brubeck forms quartet with Paul Desmond.	Menotti, *Amahl and the Night Visitors*. Boulez, *Polyphonie X*.	Formation of NATO.
1952	Gerry Mulligan organizes quartet without piano. Modern Jazz Quartet records *Vendome* and *La Ronde*. Granz takes "Jazz at the Philharmonic" to Europe.	Columbia University electronic studio founded. Hemingway, *The Old Man and the Sea*.	Hydrogen bomb exploded in the Marshall Islands.
1953	Miles Davis records *Walkin'*.	Stockhausen, *Kontra-Punkte*. Stravinsky, *Rake's Progress*. Baldwin, *Go Tell It on the Mountain*.	Eisenhower inaugurated President. End of Korean War. McCarthy reigns as chair of Senate Permanent Investigating Committee.
1954	J. J. Johnson and Kai Winding organize trombone-duo-lead quartet. First Newport Jazz Festival. Blues singer Joe Williams joins Basie. Sonny Rollins records *Airegin* and *Oleo*.	Gershwin's *Porgy and Bess*, with black company, sent on worldwide State Department tour.	Vietnam War begins. Supreme Court rules racial segregation in public schools unconstitutional. First atom-powered submarine.
1955	Parker dies. John Coltrane joins Miles Davis Quintet. Clifford Brown records *Joy Spring*. Teo Macero incorporates electronic music techniques in *Sounds of May*.	Boulez, *Le Marteau sans maître*.	Salk perfects polio vaccine. NBC telecasts in "compatible color."
1956	Jazz as international exchange: Gillespie to Middle East; Kenton to England; Heath to U.S.; Goodman to Far East. Horace Silver forms quartet and records *Opus De Funk*. Clifford Brown dies in auto accident.	Bernstein, *Candide*. Schuman, *New England Triptych*.	Russian tanks invade Hungary. Grace Kelly marries Prince Rainier III of Monaco. Don Larsen pitches first World Series no-hitter.

	JAZZ	ART, LITERATURE, AND CONCERT MUSIC	HISTORY AND SCIENCE
1957	John Coltrane records "Blue Train" album. Brandeis University Festival of the Arts Jazz Concert with commissioned works by Mingus, Giuffre, Schuller, Babbitt, Shapero.	Bernstein, *West Side Story*.	Gov. Faubus calls out National Guard to prevent desegregation of Little Rock public schools. First Sputnik orbited.
1958	First Ornette Coleman recording. Davis and Gil Evans collaborate on "Porgy and Bess" album.	Barber and Menotti, *Vanessa*. Pasternak, *Dr. Zhivago*.	First stereo records issued. Nautilus cruises under North Pole.
1959	Coleman records "Shape of Jazz to Come" and "Change of the Century." Davis records "Kind of Blue" with J. Adderley, Coltrane, and B. Evans. Coltrane records "Giant Steps" album.	Barzun, *House of Intellect*. Frank Lloyd Wright, Guggenheim Museum.	Alaska and Hawaii become 49th and 50th states. Castro overthrows Batista government in Cuba.
1960	Riot at the Newport Jazz Festival. Ornette Coleman Double Quartet records "Free Jazz."	Boulez, *Pli selon pli*. Pinter, *The Caretaker*.	Recording studios begin to use multitrack tape recorders. Black students in Greensboro, N.C. stage sit-down demonstration against segregated lunch counters. U.S. population 179,323,175.
1961	Eric Dolphy and John Coltrane collaborate.	Carter, *Double Concerto*. Penderecki, *Threnody for the Victims of Hiroshima*. "Art of Assemblage" show at Museum of Modern Art.	Berlin Wall erected. First manned space flights. Maris hits 61 home runs.
1962	Archie Shepp leaves Cecil Taylor and forms Shepp-Dixon Quartet.	Britten, *War Requiem*. Albee; *Who's Afraid of Virginia Woolf?* Lincoln Center for the Performing Arts opens.	Cuban missile crisis. Vatican Council II convenes.

	JAZZ	ART, LITERATURE, AND CONCERT MUSIC	HISTORY AND SCIENCE
1963	Coltrane's *Alabama* a reaction to racial tension in South. Mingus records *Hora Decubitus.* Bill Evans records "Conversations With Myself."	Carson, *Silent Spring.*	President Kennedy assassinated. Increasing U.S. involvement in Vietnam.
1964	Coltrane and Tyner in "A Love Supreme" session.	Bellow, *Herzog.*	U.S. Civil Rights Bill passed. Martin Luther King awarded Nobel peace prize.
1965	Coltrane, *Ascension.* Coleman reemerges in New York with trio.	*Autobiography of Malcolm X.* First performance of Ives's Fourth Symphony.	Civil Rights march in Alabama. Malcolm X assassinated.
1966	Cecil Taylor records "Looking Ahead."	Pinter, *The Homecoming.* Barber, *Antony and Cleopatra.*	First space walk.
1967	Davis, Shorter, Hancock, Carter, and Williams record "Nefertiti." Coltrane dies.	The Beatles, *Sergeant Pepper's Lonely Hearts Club Band.*	Israeli-Arab Six Day War. First successful heart transplant.
1968	Jazz Composers' Orchestra, a cooperative, forms and records.	Davies, *Eight Songs for a Mad King.*	Assassinations of Martin Luther King, Jr., and Robert Kennedy. Antiwar protests in U.S. U.S.S.R. invades Czechoslovakia.
1969	Don Cherry in Paris, records *Mu.* Davis, "Bitches Brew." Art Ensemble of Chicago moves to Paris.	Roth, *Portnoy's Complaint.* Puzo, *The Godfather.*	Men walk on moon. Lottery system established for draft.
1970	London Jazz Composers Orchestra formed. Coleman, "Ornette Lives at Prince Street."	Toffler, *Future Shock.* Segal, *Love Story.* Crumb, *Ancient Voices of Children.*	Voting age lowered to 18. U.S. intervention in Cambodia. First synthesis of a gene.
1971	Shepp, *Things Have Got To Change.* Armstrong dies.	Blatty, *The Exorcist.*	First quadraphonic discs. Indo-Pakistan War. Independence of Bangladesh.

	JAZZ	ART, LITERATURE, AND CONCERT MUSIC	HISTORY AND SCIENCE
1972	Weather Report, *I Sing The Body Electric.* Joplin complete works published. Davis, *On The Corner.*		Nixon visits Communist China and U.S.S.R. Israeli athletes murdered at Munich Olympics.
1973	Eubie Blake, at 90, releases three albums. Goodman, Krupa, Hampton, and Stewart at Newport Jazz Festival.	Vonnegut, *Breakfast of Champions.*	Watergate Affair begins. Vietnam peace agreement signed.
1974	Ellington dies. National Jazz Ensemble and New York Jazz Repertory Company perform in New York.	Benchley, *Jaws.* Solzhenitsyn, *Gulag Archipelago.* Britten, *Death in Venice.*	Nixon resigns U.S. Presidency in disgrace.
1975	Bill Watrous, Manhattan Wildlife Refuge. Cecil Taylor attracts overflow audiences at New York's Five Spot. Coleman forms Prime Time.	Bellow, *Humboldt's Gift.* Doctorow, *Ragtime.* Joplin's *Treemonisha* has Broadway run. Dance Theater of Harlem founded.	Apollo-Soyuz project, U.S.-U.S.S.R. cooperative space venture. Vietnam War concluded.
1976	Weather Report, *Heavy Weather.* Dexter Gordon returns to U.S.	Haley, *Roots.* "Concert of the Century" to renovate Carnegie Hall—Menuhin, Rostropovich, Bernstein, Horowitz, and Stern. Copyright reform.	Concorde supersonic jet service. Viking 1 lands on Mars. Ordination of women approved by Episcopal Church.
1977	Cecil Taylor and Mary Lou Williams in "Embraced" Concert at Carnegie Hall. V.S.O.P. Tour.	*Star Wars* and *Close Encounters of the Third Kind* released.	Reported development of neutron bomb. First National Women's Conference.
1978		Congress awards Marian Anderson a gold medal. *Ain't Misbehavin'* revived.	Hannah H. Gray, first woman university president. Margaret A. Brewer, first woman Marine Corp general. Mass suicide in Guyana.
1979	Charles Mingus dies.	Musical *Grease* achieves record for longest run. First major art theft at Metropolitan Museum of Art.	Nuclear near-disaster at Three Mile Island. U.S.S.R. invades Afghanistan. Iranian Islamic revolutionaries take U.S. hostages.

	JAZZ	ART, LITERATURE, AND CONCERT MUSIC	HISTORY AND SCIENCE
1980		Baryshnikov becomes director of American Ballet Theater. Digitally recorded LP records widely marketed.	Mt. St. Helens volcano erupts. Over 100,000 refugees escape to U.S. from Cuba.
1981	Davis returns to jazz, records "Man with the Horn." Mary Lou Williams dies.	*Nicholas Nickleby* opens on Broadway. Maya Lin, 21, wins competition for Vietnam War Memorial.	President Reagan shot by John W. Hinckley, Jr. Sandra Day O'Connor becomes first woman Supreme Court justice. Maiden flight of space shuttle Columbia.
1982	Wynton Marsalis a hit at Kool Jazz Festival.	New York's Joffrey Ballet becomes part-year resident company in Los Angeles.	U.S. Marines sent to Beirut as peacekeeping force.
1983		100th anniversary of Metropolitan Opera Company. "The Vatican Collections" exhibit in New York.	U.S. invades Grenada. 250,000 march on Washington to commemorate 1963 civil rights march. Cabbage Patch Doll craze.
1984	Anthony Davis's opera, *X*, opens in Philadelphia.	Television Academy Hall of Fame established. Michael Jackson's *Thriller* album tops 20,000,000 sales.	School Prayer Amendment rejected by Supreme Court. World Court claims jurisdiction in Nicaragua vs. U.S.A.
1985	Coleman records "Opening the Caravan of Dreams." Branford Marsalis joins Sting.	Compact discs widely marketed. Metropolitan Opera announces cancellation of national tour after 1986.	Liner *Achille Lauro* hijacked. Leaded gasoline banned. *Titanic* wreck found.
1986	Miles Davis records "Tutu."	Central Ballet of China performs in U.S. Robert Penn Warren first U.S. Poet Laureate. Carnegie Hall reopens after $50,000,000 renovation.	Reagan and Gorbachev appear together on Soviet television. U.S. air strike against Libya. Beginning of Iran-Contra affair.
1987	Jane Ira Bloom records "Modern Drama."	National Museum of African Art opens as part of Smithsonian. Van Gogh's *Irises* purchased for $53,900,000.	Reagan and Gorbachev sign first treaty to reduce nuclear arsenals. October 19 stock market crash of 508 points.

	JAZZ	ART, LITERATURE, AND CONCERT MUSIC	HISTORY AND SCIENCE
1988	Terence Blanchard and Donald Harrison record "Black Pearl."	Live/animated film, *Who Framed Roger Rabbit*.	Soviet troops withdraw from Afghanistan. Harvard patents genetically altered mouse.
1989	Davis records "Amandla."		
1990			Berlin Wall comes down.
1991	Deaths of Miles Davis and Stan Getz.		Soviet Union dissolves.

ANNOTATED BIBLIOGRAPHY

The following highly selective bibliography contains only a few of the many thousands of published items that are now available to help the serious student of jazz learn more about this fascinating subject. More complete bibliographies are available, and many are listed below, but this compilation should be particularly useful to readers of this book, in that it 1) emphasizes but is not limited to books in English; 2) organizes material by subject; 3) includes items on African music, other American music, and related subjects not often found in jazz bibliographies; and 4) omits writings that have not proven particularly useful in the preparation of this study.

GENERAL BIBLIOGRAPHY

Because of their excellence, usefulness, and availability, the following items are listed both here and in their proper places in the bibliography. These books can be found in many college and community libraries, and serious jazz enthusiasts will want to possess their own copies.

1. Kernfeld, Barry, ed. *The New Grove Dictionary of Jazz.* 2 vols. London & New York: Macmillan Press, 1988. The first comprehensive jazz encyclopedia, *"JazzGrove"* was prepared by an international team of scholars and musicians.

2. Schuller, Gunther. *Early Jazz: Its Roots and Musical Development.* New York: Oxford University Press, 1968.

———. *The Swing Era: The Development of Jazz, 1930–1945.* New York: Oxford University Press, 1989. The first two books of a projected three-volume study by a musician and jazz scholar of the highest credentials.

3. Rust, Brian. *Jazz Records, 1897–1942.* 2 vols. 4th ed. New Rochelle, NY: Arlington House, 1978. The standard reference work for jazz 78-rpm records. Lists personnel, dates, matrix numbers, and alternate issue numbers, and contains indices of artists and song titles.

4. Jepsen, Jorgen Grunnet. *Jazz Records, 1942–196[9]: A Discography.* 8 vols. in 11. Holte and

Copenhagen, Denmark: K. E. Knudsen, 1963–70. Does for LPs what Rust does for 78s.

5.   Feather, Leonard. *The New Edition of the Encyclopedia of Jazz*. New York: Horizon Press, 1962. Reprinted, 1984. Individual biographies, photographs, and essays on the history and sociology of jazz. Long the standard reference work on the musicians and still useful for those not included in *JazzGrove*.

———. *The Encyclopedia of Jazz in the Sixties*. New York: Horizon Press, 1967. Supplement to the above.

———, and Ira Gitler. *The Encyclopedia of Jazz in the Seventies*. New York: Horizon Press, 1976. Reprinted, New York: Da Capo Press, 1992. A continuation of the series.

DICTIONARIES AND ENCYCLOPEDIAS

American Society of Composers, Authors and Publishers. *The ASCAP Biographical Dictionary of Composers, Authors and Publishers*. 4th ed. New York: Bowker, 1980. Brief biographies of ASCAP members and an index of publisher members.

Bogaert, Karel. *Blues Lexicon*. Antwerp: Standaard Uitgeverij, 1971. Accurate biographies and brief discographies of American blues musicians. In Dutch.

Carles, Philippe, André Clergeat, and Jean-Louis Comolli. *Dictionnaire du jazz*. Paris: Robert Laffont, 1988. A fine compendium, excellent coverage of modern musicians. In French.

Carr, Ian, Digby Fairweather, and Brian Priestley. *Jazz: The Essential Companion*. New York: Prentice-Hall, 1988. A one-volume jazz encyclopedia written by three British jazz musicians. Up-to-date biographies and definitions of many jazz terms.

Case, Brian, and Stan Britt. *The Harmony Illustrated Encyclopedia of Jazz*. 3rd ed. New York: Harmony Books, 1986. Beautifully written by two British jazz musicians, the concise biographies are insightful, interesting, and well illustrated. Paperback and inexpensive.

Charters, Samuel B. *Jazz: New Orleans, 1885–1963*. Rev. ed. New York: Oak Publications, 1963. Reprinted, New York: Da Capo Press, 1983. An index to the black musicians of New Orleans, divided by period, with biographies, information on groups, and short textual surveys. Useful discography.

Chilton, John. *Who's Who of Jazz: Storyville to Swing Street*. 4th ed. New York: Da Capo Press, 1985. Brief biographies of over 1,000 jazz musicians.

Claghorn, Charles E. *Biographical Dictionary of Jazz*. Englewood Cliffs, NJ: Prentice-Hall, 1982. In addition to brief biographies of over 3,400 musicians, contains a useful index of jazz groups.

Clayton, Peter, and Peter Gammond. *Jazz A–Z*. Enfield, Middlesex: Guinness Superlatives, 1986. Listing of musicians, works, and recordings. Interesting British emphasis.

Eckland, K. O. *Jazz West, 1945–1985: The A–Z Guide to West Coast Jazz Music*. Carmel-by-the-Sea, CA: Cypress, 1986. A specialized jazz dictionary.

Ewen, David. *American Composers: A Biographical Dictionary*. New York: G. P. Putnam's Sons, 1982. Useful biographical resource, but primarily concerned with composers working outside the field of jazz.

———. *Popular American Composers, from Revolutionary Times to the Present*. New York: H. W. Wilson, 1962. First supplement, 1972. Guide to important composers with an index of songs.

Feather, Leonard. *The New Edition of the Encyclopedia of Jazz*. New York: Horizon Press, 1962. Reprinted, 1984. Individual biographies, photographs, essays on the history and sociology of jazz. Long the standard reference work on the musicians and still useful for those not included in *JazzGrove*.

———. *The Encyclopedia of Jazz in the Sixties*. New York: Horizon Press, 1967. Supplement to the above.

————, and Ira Gitler. *The Encyclopedia of Jazz in the Seventies*. New York: Horizon Press, 1976. Reprinted, New York: Da Capo Press, 1992. A continuation of the series.

Gammond, Peter. *The Oxford Companion to Popular Music*. New York: Oxford University Press, 1991. Listing of works and recordings of principal composers, terms, and song titles, with a British emphasis.

Gold, Robert S. *A Jazz Lexicon*. New York: Knopf, 1964. A dictionary of jazz-world terms, with sociological emphasis.

Hitchcock, H. Wiley, ed. *The New Grove Dictionary of American Music*. 4 vols. London & New York: Macmillan Press, 1986. The current standard reference work, *"AmeriGrove"* contains entries by the leading scholars in the field.

Kernfeld, Barry, ed. *The New Grove Dictionary of Jazz*. 2 vols. London & New York: Macmillan Press, 1988. The first comprehensive jazz encyclopedia, *"JazzGrove"* was prepared by an international team of scholars and musicians.

Kinkle, Roger D. *The Complete Encyclopedia of Popular Music and Jazz 1900–1950*. New Rochelle, NY: Arlington House, 1974. Detailed study, in four volumes: music year by year, 1900–50, biographies with lists of compositions and recordings, and exhaustive indices.

Laade, Wolfgang. *Jazz-Lexikon*. Stuttgart: G. Hatze, 1953. A useful jazz dictionary in German.

Ortiz Oderigo, Nestor R. *Diccionario del Jazz*. Buenos Aires: Ricordi Americana, 1959. Terms and phrases associated with jazz and its history. In Spanish.

Panassié, Hugues, and Madeleine Gautier. *Dictionnaire du jazz*. 3rd ed. Paris: Albin Michel, 1987. (A translation of the first edition appeared as *Guide to Jazz*. Boston: Houghton Mifflin, 1956.) Entries for individuals, bands, song titles, and terms.

Rice, Edward Le Roy. *Monarchs of Minstrelsy from "Daddy" Rice to Date*. New York: Kenny, 1911. Chronologically arranged biographies of the leaders of nineteenth-century American minstrelsy.

Rose, Al, and Edmond Souchon. *New Orleans Jazz: A Family Album*. 3rd ed. Baton Rouge, LA: Louisiana State University Press, 1984. Copiously illustrated, with brief entries on people, places, and bands of New Orleans.

Roxon, Lillian. *Lillian Roxon's Rock Encyclopedia*. rev. ed., compiled by Ed Naha. New York: Grosset & Dunlap, 1978. Short sketches of individuals and groups, with discographies.

Southern, Eileen. *Biographical Dictionary of Afro-American and African Musicians*. Westport, CT: Greenwood Press, 1982. An excellent reference work prepared by a leading scholar of African-American music.

Stambler, Irwin. *Encyclopedia of Pop, Rock, and Soul*. rev. ed. New York: St. Martin's Press, 1989. Critical biographies of individuals and groups, with some entries for terms and shows.

————, and Grelun Landon. *Encyclopedia of Folk, Country, and Western Music*. 2nd ed. New York: St. Martin's Press, 1984. Similar to the above.

Ténot, Frank. *Dictionnaire du jazz. Les dictionnaires de L'homme du XXᵉ Siècle*. Paris: Larousse, 1967. A typical "Larousse," with brief biographies and term entries.

Testoni, Gian Carlo, et al. *Enciclopedia del Jazz*. 2nd ed. Milan: Messaggerie Musicali, 1954. Extended textual surveys on the art and history of jazz, brief biographies, and detailed discographies of jazz recordings issued in Italy, 1920–52.

HISTORIES AND CHRONOLOGIES

Austin, William W. *Music in the 20th Century from Debussy through Stravinsky*. New York: W. W. Norton, 1966. Excellent general survey of Western art music, with two chapters devoted to jazz. An extensive annotated bibliography.

Berendt, Joachim Ernest. *The Jazz Book: From Ragtime to Fusion and Beyond*. Westport, CT: L. Hill, 1982. Perceptive and well considered survey from the European viewpoint.

Berry, Mary Frances, and John Blassingame. *Long Memory: The Black Experience in America*. New

York: Oxford University Press, 1982. An insightful, sensitive, and scholarly history of African Americans. Although music receives little space, this book is an outstanding source for understanding the background and circumstances of black Americans.

Blesh, Rudi. *Shining Trumpets, a History of Jazz*. 2nd ed. London: Cassel, 1958. Reprinted, New York: Da Capo Press, 1975. A pioneering work of major importance to jazz historiography.

Charters, Samuel B., and Leonard Kunstadt. *Jazz: A History of the New York Scene*. New York: Da Capo Press, 1981. Detailed treatment of the 1920–62 period, including the big bands.

Collier, James Lincoln. *The Making of Jazz: A Comprehensive History*. Boston: Houghton Mifflin, 1978. An interesting book that is often criticized for being highly opinionated. Nonetheless, the work of a good scholar and writer.

———. *The Reception of Jazz in America: A New View*. Brooklyn: Institute for Studies in American Music, 1988. A controversial and much-criticized study of early jazz and swing which presents an unorthodox view of the public's attitude toward jazz during those years.

Crowther, Bruce, and Mike Pinfold. *The Jazz Singers: From Ragtime to the New Wave*. New York: Blandford Press, 1986. Clear presentation, good critical judgments, and attention to the lyrics make this brief book an excellent survey of jazz singing.

Dauer, Alfons M. *Der Jazz: seine Ursprünge und seine Entwicklung*. Kassel: E. Röth, 1958. Particularly valuable for the copious transcribed examples of African music and early jazz.

Dexter, Dave. *Jazz Cavalcade: The Inside Story of Jazz*. New York: Da Capo Press, 1977. Pleasant reading, but a superficial treatment.

Feather, Leonard G. *The Book of Jazz: From Then till Now*. Rev. ed. New York: Dell, 1976. Sections on sources, instruments, sounds, and performers, the nature and future of jazz. In addition to being an outstanding critic and writer, Feather is a fine jazz musician as well.

Finkelstein, Sidney W. *Jazz: A People's Music*. New York: Citadel Press, 1948. Reprinted, New York: International Publishers, 1988. Analytical survey up to the beginning of the bop era, with a Marxist political orientation.

Gioia, Ted. *The Imperfect Art: Reflections on Jazz and Modern Culture*. New York: Oxford University Press, 1988. Philosophical essays that relate phenomena in jazz to critical thought in other areas of the arts and society in general. Very well done.

Goffin, Robert. *Jazz from the Congo to the Metropolitan*. New York: Doubleday, Doran & Co., 1944. Reprinted, New York: Da Capo Press, 1975. A classic book; excellent insights into the music of early jazz.

Gourse, Leslie. *Louis' Children: American Jazz Singers*. New York: Morrow, 1984. A loving, personal account of the great jazz vocalists. Sometimes inaccurate but always interesting reading.

Gridley, Mark C. *Jazz Styles: History and Analysis*. 3rd ed. Englewood Cliffs, NJ: Prentice-Hall, 1988. The coverage of modern jazz is especially perceptive and informative.

Hamm, Charles. *Music in the New World*. New York: W. W. Norton, 1983. Comprehensive history of American music by an outstanding scholar.

Harris, Rex. *Jazz*. 5th ed. Harmondsworth, England: Penguin Books, 1957. Superseded, but good on the origins and traditional styles of jazz.

Hentoff, Nat, and Albert J. McCarthy, eds. *Jazz: New Perspectives on the History of Jazz by Twelve of the World's Foremost Jazz Critics and Scholars*. New York: Rinehart, 1959. The subtitle is accurate. All the chapters are excellent; those by Steiner, Driggs, and Schuller help fill serious gaps in the literature.

Hitchcock, H. Wiley. *Music in the United States: A Historical Introduction*. 3rd ed. Englewood Cliffs, NJ: Prentice-Hall, 1988. Fine one-volume survey of American music. Complete, up-to-date, authoritative, and well documented.

Hobson, Wilder. *American Jazz Music*. New York: W. W. Norton, 1939. Reprinted, New York: Da Capo, 1976. Written at the height of the swing period, important for its observations at that date.

Hodeir, André. *Jazz: Its Evolution and Essence*. New York: Grove Press, 1956. Reprinted, New York: Da Capo Press, 1975. A major work of analysis and criticism with emphasis on the modern jazz style of the '40s and early '50s.

————. *Toward Jazz*. New York: Grove Press, 1962. Reprinted, New York: Da Capo Press, 1976. A respected critic's views at a stylistic turning point in the history of jazz.

Keepnews, Orrin, and Bill Grauer, Jr. *A Pictorial History of Jazz: People and Places from New Orleans to Modern Jazz*. New ed. New York: Crown Publishers, 1966. Reprinted, New York: Bonanza Books, 1981. Outstanding collection of photographs.

Leonard, Neil. *Jazz and the White Americans: The Acceptance of a New Art Form*. Chicago: University of Chicago Press, 1962. Reprinted, 1970. Significant study with strong sociological emphasis. Should compare views with James Lincoln Collier, "The Faking of Jazz," *New Republic* (November 18, 1985), pp. 33–40.

Longstreet, Stephen. *The Real Jazz, Old and New*. Baton Rouge: Louisiana State University Press, 1956. Highly individualistic survey of traditional styles, with many factual errors.

Newton, Francis. *The Jazz Scene*. New York: Monthly Review Press, 1960. Reprinted, New York: Da Capo Press, 1975. Particularly good on the sociological and cultural aspects of jazz.

Ogren, Kathy J. *The Jazz Revolution: Twenties America and the Meaning of Jazz*. New York: Oxford University Press, 1989. Sociological study of jazz during a crucial decade.

Osgood, Henry Osborne. *So This Is Jazz?* Boston: Little, Brown, and Co., 1926. Reprinted, New York: Da Capo Press, 1978. Strange view, by today's standards, but gives a vivid, contemporary picture of a white critic's perceptions in the early 1920s.

Ostransky, Leroy. *The Anatomy of Jazz*. Seattle: University of Washington Press, 1960. Reprinted, Westport, CT: Greenwood Press, 1973. Analytical study of jazz as a phenomenon within the general history of music. Written just before the Free Jazz revolution.

————. *Jazz City: The Impact of Our Cities on the Development of Jazz*. Englewood Cliffs, NJ: Prentice-Hall, 1978. Interesting view of jazz as an urban phenomenon.

Polillo, Arrigo. *Jazz: A Guide to Its History*. London: P. Hamlyn, 1969. A superficial work whose most interesting portions deal with modern musicians.

Sargeant, Winthrop. *Jazz, Hot and Hybrid*. New York: Arrow Editions, 1938. Reprinted, New York: Da Capo Press, 1975. Penetrating insights into early jazz, with good musical examples.

Schuller, Gunther. *Early Jazz: Its Roots and Musical Development*. New York: Oxford University Press, 1968. Significant contribution to the history of the pre-1930 period.

————. *The Swing Era: The Development of Jazz, 1930–1945*. New York: Oxford University Press, 1989. A continuation of *Early Jazz*, the second in a projected three-volume history. Outstanding musical analyses.

Southern, Eileen. *The Music of Black Americans: A History*. 2nd ed. New York: W. W. Norton, 1983. Excellently documented history of all aspects of African-American music from the African heritage to the present.

————, comp. & ed. *Readings in Black American Music*. 2nd ed. New York: W. W. Norton, 1983. A companion volume to Southern's history.

Stearns, Marshall Winslow, and Jean Stearns. *Jazz Dance: The Story of American Vernacular Dance*. New York: Macmillan, 1968. Reprinted, New York: Schirmer Books, 1979. The first serious study of the dance that accompanied the music of jazz throughout its formative years.

Stearns, Marshall W. *The Story of Jazz*. New York: Oxford University Press, 1958. Reprinted, 1970. Scholarly and well-documented comprehensive history. The 1970 edition contains an expanded bibliography and a syllabus of lectures on the history of jazz.

Tanner, Paul Ora Warren. "A Technical Analysis of the Development of Jazz." Unpublished thesis, University of California at Los Angeles, 1962. Technical analyses of jazz music from various periods.

————, and Maurice Gerow. *A Study of Jazz*. 5th ed. Dubuque, IA: W. C. Brown, 1984. A practical jazz appreciation text with constructed musical examples. Little reliance on the work of other writers.

Ulanov, Barry. *A Handbook of Jazz*. New York: Viking Press, 1957. Contains essays on the history and cultural context of jazz, with very brief biographies.

————. *A History of Jazz in America*. New York: Viking Press, 1952. Well balanced study from origins to bebop; now superseded.

BIBLIOGRAPHIES

Adkins, Cecil, and Alis Dickinson, eds. *Doctoral Dissertations in Musicology*. Philadelphia: American Musicological Society, 1990. Lists many excellent dissertations in jazz, African-American music, and American music in general that have been completed in recent years. Arranged by subject category.

Allen, Daniel. *Bibliography of Discographies. Vol. 2, Jazz*. New York: R. R. Bowker, 1981. Alphabetized by subject and then by author within each subcategory. Also contains an index.

Carl Gregor, Herzog zu Mecklenburg. *International Jazz Bibliography: Jazz Books from 1919 to 1968*. Strasbourg, France: Heitz, 1969. Extensive listing, without annotations. 2 Supplements: Graz, Austria: Universal Edition, 1971 and 1975.

Colvig, Richard. "Black Music," *Choice* (November, 1969), p. 1169 ff. Annotated selection of English-language monographs.

Cooper, David Edwin. *International Bibliography of Discographies*. Littleton, CO: Libraries Unlimited, 1975. Approximately one-third of the volume is devoted to jazz and blues, with sections on genres and individual performers.

De Lerma, Dominique-René. *Bibliography of Black Music*. 4 vols. Westport, CT: Greenwood Press, 1981–84. A reference work by one of America's finest scholars of African-American Music.

Epstein, Dena J. "Slave Music in the United States before 1860: A Survey of Sources," *Notes*, 20 (1963), pp. 195–212 and 377–90. An extensive description and synoptic "preliminary report" of contemporary accounts.

Floyd, Samuel A., Jr., and Marsha J. Reisser. *Black Music Biography: An Annotated Bibliography*. White Plains, NY: Kraus International Publications, 1987. Useful starting point for biographical studies.

———. *Black Music in the United States: An Annotated Bibliography of Selected Reference and Research Materials*. Millwood, NY: Kraus International Publications, 1983. Invaluable listing of specialized reference materials.

Gillis, Frank, and Alan P. Merriam. *Ethnomusicology and Folk Music: An International Bibliography of Dissertations and Theses*. Middletown, CT: Wesleyan University Press, 1966. Includes both master's theses and doctoral dissertations.

Handy, William Christopher. *Negro Authors and Composers of the United States*. New York: Handy Brothers Music Co., c. 1936. A short list, but of great historical interest.

Hefele, Bernhard. *Jazz Bibliography: International Literature on Jazz, Blues, Spirituals, Gospel and Ragtime Music with a Selected List of Works on the Social and Cultural Background from the Beginning to the Present*. Munich: Saur, 1981. The introductory material is in both English and German. Lists many items useful for the study of jazz in Europe. Includes an index.

Hippenmeyer, Jean Roland. *Jazz sur films; ou, 55 années de rapports jazz-cinéma vus à travers plus de 800 films tournés entre 1917 et 1972*. Yverdon: Éditions de la Thièle, 1973. Introductory essay on the appearance of jazz in motion pictures, with a detailed 1917–72 filmography and analytical indices.

International Repertory of Music Literature. *RILM Abstracts*. New York: RILM, 1967–. A most useful guides to books, articles, and reviews. Surveys the world-wide literature on all fields of music, including jazz. Abstracts in English. Issued quarterly, several years' time lag, but invaluable nonetheless.

Jackson, Richard. *United States Music: Sources of Bibliography and Collective Biography*. Brooklyn, NY: Institute for Studies in American Music, 1973. Well annotated. A section on "Blues, Ragtime, and Jazz."

Kennington, Donald. *The Literature of Jazz: A Critical Guide*. 2nd ed., revised. Chicago: American Library Association, 1980. Eight surveys by category, each followed by an annotated bibliography. One chapter discusses and lists jazz periodicals. Useful book, available in paperback.

Markewich, Reese. *The Definitive Bibliography of Harmonically Sophisticated Tonal Music.* Riverdale, NY: Markewich, 1970. A pompously titled but modest accomplishment.

————. *Jazz Publicity II: Newly Revised and Expanded Bibliography of Names and Address of Hundreds of International Jazz Critics and Magazines.* Riverdale, NY: Markewich, 1974. Now outdated, but an interesting list nonetheless.

————. *The New Expanded Bibliography of Jazz Compositions Based on the Chord Progression of Standard Tunes.* Riverdale, NY: Markewich, 1974. Listing of standard tunes by title, with indications of composers, publishers, significant recordings, and original appearances.

Mead, Rita H. *Doctoral Dissertations in American Music: A Classified Bibliography.* Brooklyn, NY: Institute for Studies in American Music, 1974. Useful because it picks up items from fields not covered in Adkins and Dickinson.

Meadows, Eddie S. *Jazz Reference and Research Materials: A Bibliography.* New York: Garland Publishing, 1981. A useful list with interesting critical annotations.

Merriam, Alan P., and Robert J. Brenford. *A Bibliography of Jazz.* Philadelphia: American Folklore Society, 1954. Reprinted, New York: Da Capo, 1970. A comprehensive bibliography of books and journal articles. Contains a separate listing of 113 jazz-oriented magazines.

Nettl, Bruno. *Reference Materials in Ethnomusicology.* 2nd ed. Detroit: Information Coordinators, 1967. Survey of major reference works, organized by topic.

Reisner, Robert George. *The Literature of Jazz: A Selective Bibliography.* New York: New York Public Library, 1959. Now outdated, but still useful. A checklist of books (including fiction) and magazine articles. Includes a list of jazz journals.

Schatz, Walter, ed. *Directory of Afro-American Resources.* New York: R. Bowker, 1970. A catalogue of primary sources organized by states. Includes a subject index and a bibliography.

Skowronski, JoAnn. *Black Music in America: A Bibliography.* Metuchen, NJ: Scarecrow, 1981. Jazz included as part of a larger survey.

Southern, Eileen. *Biographical Dictionary of Afro-American Musicians.* Westport, CT: Greenwood Press, 1982. Accurate short biographies. Each individual history has its own bibliographical and discographical references. General bibliography at the end of the volume.

Southern, Eileen, and Josephine Wright. *African-American Traditions in Song, Sermon, Tale, and Dance, 1600s–1920: An Annotated Bibliography of Literature, Collections, and Artwork.* New York: Greenwood Press, 1990.

Szwed, John F., and Roger D. Abrahams. *Afro-American Folk Culture: An Annotated Bibliography of Materials from North, Central, and South America, and the West Indies.* Philadelphia: Institute for the Study of Human Issues, 1978.

DISCOGRAPHIES

Bruyninckx, Walter. *60 Years of Recorded Jazz, 1917–1967.* Mechelen, Belgium: Bruyninckx, 1978–82. An excellent discography, but not readily available. Supplements are extending the survey into the 1980s.

Delaunay, Charles. *New Hot Discography: The Standard Dictionary of Recorded Jazz.* New York: Criterion, 1963. Originally published in France in 1936 as *Hot Discography*, this work laid the foundation for modern jazz discography. It is still particularly valuable for the earlier decades of jazz recording.

Dixon, Robert M. W., and John Godrich. *Blues & Gospel Records 1902–1943.* 3rd ed. Chigwell, Essex, England: Storyville, 1982. The standard discography for 78s.

Harris, Rex, and Brian Rust. *Recorded Jazz: A Critical Guide.* Harmondsworth, England: Penguin, 1958. A critical discography of the pre-1957 recordings of traditional jazz only.

Harris, Steve. *Jazz on Compact Disc: A Critical Guide to the Best Recordings.* New York: Harmony Books, 1987. Arranged alphabetically by artist or group, the book rates the albums (1–3 stars) for both performance and quality of recording. Interesting short introduction to the manufacture of compact discs.

Harrison, Max, et al. *Modern Jazz: The Essential Records.* London: Aquarius Books, 1975. Extensive historical, analytical, and critical discussions of 200 jazz recordings of "permanent worth."

Jason, David A. *Recorded Ragtime 1897–1958*. Hamden, CT: Archon, 1973. International discography.

Jepsen, Jorgen Grunnet. *Jazz Records, 1942–196[9]: A Discography*. 8 vols. in 11. Holte and Copenhagen, Denmark: K. E. Knudsen, 1963–70. Does for LP records what Rust does for 78s.

Kernfeld, Barry, ed. *The Blackwell Guide to Recorded Jazz*. Cambridge: Blackwell, 1991. An up-to-date selection of available jazz recordings by the editor of *JazzGrove* and six other experts. A comprehensive and historical listing of issues on CD, LP, and cassette. Excellent personnel rosters and critical notes.

Leadbitter, Mike, and Neil Slaven. *Blues Records 1943–1970: A Selective Discography*. 2 vols. London: Record Information Service, 1987– . A selective and critical guide to a vast field. Only volume 1, A–L, has appeared to date.

Leder, Jan. *Women in Jazz: A Discography of Instrumentalists, 1913–1968*. Westport, CT: Greenwood Press, 1985. The first thorough survey of this subject. Well done and accurate. Unlike Rust, does not have a tunes index.

Lyons, Len. *The 101 Best Jazz Albums: A History of Jazz on Records*. New York: Morrow, 1980. An extremely good selection, with interesting accompanying notes.

McCarthy, Albert J., et al. *Jazz on Record: A Critical Guide to the First 50 Years, 1917–1967*. London: Hanover Books, 1968. Selective listing with criticism, biography, and discography.

Raben, Eric. *A Discography of Free Jazz*. Copenhagen: JazzMedia Aps, 1969. A specialized discography covering the first decade of this style.

Rust, Brian. *Jazz Records, 1897–1942*. 2 vols. 4th ed. New Rochelle, NY: Arlington House, 1978. The standard reference work for jazz 78-rpm recordings. Lists personnel, dates, matrix numbers, and alternate issue numbers; contains indices of artists and song titles. Rust's companion discographies, *The American Dance Band Discography, 1917–1942* (New Rochelle, NY: Arlington House, 1976) and *The Complete Entertainment Discography, from the Mid-1890s to 1942* (New Rochelle, NY: Arlington House, 1973), are also excellent and extremely useful.

Stagg, Tom, and Charlie Crump. *New Orleans, The Revival: A Tape and Discography of Negro Traditional Jazz Recorded in New Orleans or by New Orleans Bands 1937–1972*. Dublin: Bashall Cabes, 1973. A guide to issued and unissued recordings, with a special section on religious recordings.

Swenson, John, ed. *The Rolling Stone Jazz Record Guide*. New York: Random House / Rolling Stone Press, 1985. One of the most useful discographies in print for record librarians or individuals who wish to purchase and build a basic jazz record collection. Over 4,000 albums are listed, provided with commentary, and rated (1–5 stars). Of little value to the serious collector or scholar, however, as personnel, matrix numbers, accurate dates, etc., are not included.

Wante, Stephen, and Walter De Block. *V-Disc Catalogue*. Antwerp: De Block, 1954. A guide to noncommercial recordings made for use by the armed services.

Wilson, John Steuart. *The Collector's Jazz: Modern*. Philadelphia: Lippincott, 1959. A critical discography of LPs, arranged by group or individual artist. In view of its publication date, "modern jazz" means primarily bebop.

———. *The Collector's Jazz: Traditional and Swing*. Philadelphia: Lippincott, 1958. A good, critical list.

In addition to the discographies recommended above, there are many jazz discographies compiled and written by dedicated amateurs without institutional funding, on specialized subjects, the pet projects of the individual compiler. Although these works are too numerous to list here, some are of extraordinarily high quality, for example, D. Russell Connor and Warren W. Hicks, *BG on the Record* (New York: Arlington House, 1973), and Walter C. Allen, *Hendersonia:*

The Music of Fletcher Henderson and His Musicians (Highland Park, NJ: Walter C. Allen, 1974). Many *JazzGrove* subject articles include listings of specialized discographies. Also, Walter Bruyninckx is publishing a series of discographies differentiated by style: traditional jazz, swing, modern jazz, etc.

A very interesting history of the jazz recording industry is Brian Priestley, *Jazz on Record: A History* (London: Elm Tree Books, 1988). Pages 188–201 contain a guide to those recordings referred to in the text. I can also recommend Ronald Clifford Foreman's, "Jazz and Race Records, 1920–1932" (Ph.D. dissertation, University of Illinois, 1968).

——— INDICES OF MUSIC ———

Armitage, Andrew D. (continued by Dean Tudor). *Annual Index to Popular Music Record Reviews.* Metuchen, NJ: Scarecrow Press, 1973–. Locating guide to reviews, grouped by genres with appendices of selected books and significant journal articles in the field.

Burton, Jack. *The Blue Book of Tin Pan Alley.* Watkins Glen, NY: Century House, 1962; expanded new ed., 2 vols., 1962–65. Textual surveys and biographies, with detailed song listings of major popular composers, arranged chronologically, 1776–1965.

———. *The Index of American Popular Music.* Watkins Glen, NY: Century House, 1957. Extensively cross-referenced guide to songs in anthologies.

Chipman, John H. *Index to Top-Hit Tunes, 1900–1950.* Boston: B. Humphries, 1962. Alphabetical title index of America's most popular songs, with composers, authors, publishers, and dates indicated.

Ewen, David. *American Popular Songs: From the Revolutionary War to the Present.* New York: Random House, 1966. Brief, informative entries on over 3,600 songs.

Mattfeld, Julius. *Variety Music Cavalcade, 1620–1969: A Chronology of Vocal and Instrumental Music Popular in the United States.* 3rd ed. Englewood Cliffs, NJ: Prentice-Hall, 1971. Chronological bibliography, with annual surveys of cultural and historical events.

Shapiro, Nat. *Popular Music: An Annotated Index of American Popular Songs.* New York: Adrian Press, 1964–. The eight published volumes cover the years 1920–79, with detailed information on the original appearance of songs in all popular fields.

——— PERIODICALS ———

American Music. The quarterly journal of the Sonneck Society. Well researched articles by leading scholars of American music.

Billboard Magazine. Directed to popular-music industry, with marketing data, news releases, book reviews, personnel notices.

The Black Perspective in Music. Addressed to a general audience interested in black studies. Occasional worthwhile articles about black jazz musicians.

The Black Scholar. Concerns itself with major political and cultural issues affecting black America.

Down Beat. Trade journal for American jazz musicians. News and analysis of the music world, especially jazz, with special review sections for records and live performances.

Ethnomusicology. International, interdisciplinary scholarly journal with current bibliographies, discographies, and reviews.

IAJE Journal [International Association of Jazz Educators]. Principally useful to music instructors who direct school jazz-lab bands. Good theoretical articles and reviews.

Jazz Journal. Leading British jazz periodical containing articles and reviews by noted authorities.

Jazz Magazine. French publication (in French) of real merit. Informative articles and reviews.

Jazz-Podium. Principal German jazz periodical with newsstand trade. Interesting news, features, and reviews.

Jazzforschung / Jazz Research. Journal of the International Society for Jazz Research. Authoritative, scholarly, generally well written. Articles and reviews in English as well as German.
Journal of Jazz Studies. Scholarly papers on musical, historical, and social aspects of jazz.
Journal of Popular Culture. Deals with all aspects of contemporary popular culture.
Living Blues. Contemporary and historical coverage of the black American blues tradition.
Mecca: The Magazine of Traditional Jazz. Newsletter for New Orleans traditional-jazz enthusiasts.
Metronome. A trade journal for the entertainment business. An important record for the swing era.
Record Research. Important source for recording information and statistics.
Rolling Stone. Covers contemporary pop music, films, social issues, and lifestyles. Has become a trade journal for rock musicians.

INDICES TO PERIODICAL LITERATURE

(Especially useful for locating material in non-jazz and non-music periodicals.)
Music Article Guide. Philadelphia, 1966–. Author-title-subject index to c. 150 American periodicals, including some house organs and trade journals, with brief annotations.
The Music Index. Detroit: Information Coordinators, 1949–. International index of c. 300 journals, scholarly and popular, by author and subject. Also available on CD-ROM.
New York Times Index. New York, 1913–. Careful subject index to this most important American newspaper, with brief synopses of articles. An earlier index, covering 1851–58, 1860, and 1863–1905, is available on microfilm.
Readers' Guide to Periodical Literature, 1900–. New York: Wilson, 1905–. Full dictionary catalogue index, with entries under author, subject, and title where appropriate, of general and popular U.S. periodicals with a selection of nontechnical magazines from specific subject fields.
RILM Abstracts of Music Literature. New York, International RILM Center, 1967–. Abstracts, indexed by computer, of all significant literature of music (books, articles, essays, reviews, dissertations, etc.) that have appeared since January 1967. Five-year cumulative indices. Also available on CD-ROM.

JAZZ ARCHIVES

Arkansas Arts Center, Little Rock, AR (John D. Reed Collection of American Jazz).
Detroit Public Library, Music Division, Detroit, MI.
Emory University, Atlanta, GA.
Fisk University, Nashville, TN (Scott Joplin).
Free Library of Philadelphia, Philadelphia, PA (Harvey Huston Jazz Library).
Indiana University, Bloomington, IN (Archives of Traditional Music).
Library of Congress, Music Division, Washington, DC.
New Orleans Jazz Museum, New Orleans, LA.
New York Jazz Museum, New York, NY.
New York Public Library, Harlem Branch, New York, NY (Schomburg Collection of Negro Literature and History).
New York Public Library, Lincoln Center, New York, NY (Rogers and Hammerstein Archive of Recorded Sound).
North Texas State University, Denton, TX.
Rutgers University, Newark, NJ (Institute of Jazz Studies).
The Smithsonian Institution, Division of Performing Arts, Washington, DC.

Tulane University Library, New Orleans, LA (William Ransom Hogan Jazz Archive).
University of California at Los Angeles, Los Angeles, CA (John Edwards Memorial Foundation).
Williams College, Williamstown, MA (Paul Whiteman).
Yale University, New Haven, CT (Benny Goodman, Stanley Dance, and James Weldon Johnson Collections; also Oral History American Music Archive—Duke Ellington Project.)

———— AFRICAN MUSIC ————

Abraham, Roger D., and John F. Schwed, ed. *Discovering Afro-America*. Leiden, Netherlands: Brill, 1975.
Allen, William Francis, et al. *Slave Songs of the United States*. Westport, CT: Oak Publications, 1965.
Bebey, Francis. *African Music: A People's Art*. New York: Lawrence Hill, 1975.
Berry, Mary Frances, and John Blassingame. *Long Memory: The Black Experience in America*. New York: Oxford University Press, 1982.
Blacking, John. "Some Notes on a Theory of African Rhythm Advanced by Erich von Hornbostel," *Journal of the African Music Society*, 1 (1955), pp. 12–20.
Blassingame, John W. *The Slave Community: Plantation Life in the Antebellum South*. Rev. and enl. New York: Oxford University Press, 1979.
Borneman, Ernest. "Black Light and White Shadow," *Jazzforschung*, 2 (1970), pp. 24–92.
Brandel, Rose. *The Music of Central Africa*. The Hague: Martinus Nijhoff, 1961.
Courlander, Harold. *Negro Folk Music, U.S.A*. New York: Columbia University Press, 1963.
De Lerma, Dominique-René. *Reflections on Afro-American Music*. Kent, Ohio: Kent State University Press, 1973.
Dundes, Alan, ed. *Mother Wit from the Laughing Barrel: Readings in the Interpretation of Afro-American Folklore*. Englewood Cliffs, NJ: Prentice-Hall, 1972. Reprinted, New York: Garland, 1981.
Epstein, Dena J. "African Music in British and French America," *The Musical Quarterly*, 59 (1973), pp. 61–91.
————. "Slave Music in the United States Before 1860: A Survey of Sources," *Notes*, 20 (1963), pp. 195–212, 377–90.
————. *Sinful Tunes and Spirituals: Black Folk Music to the Civil War*. Urbana: University of Illinois Press, 1977.
Gates, Henry Louis, Jr. *The Signifying Monkey: A Theory of Afro-American Literary Criticism*. New York: Oxford University Press, 1988.
Graham, Ronnie. *The Da Capo Guide to Contemporary African Music*. New York: Da Capo, 1988.
Herskovits, Melville J. *The Myth of the Negro Past*. New York: Harper & Bros., 1941. Reprinted, Boston: Beacon Press, 1958, 1970.
Howard, Joseph H. *Drums in the Americas*. New York: Oak, 1967.
Ita, Bassey. *Jazz in Nigeria: An Outline Cultural History*. Lagos, Nigeria: Radical House, 1984.
Johnson, James Peter. *Bibliographic Guide to the Study of Afro-American Music*. Washington, DC: Howard University Libraries, 1973.
Jones, A. M. *Africa and Indonesia: The Evidence of the Xylophone and Other Musical and Cultural Factors*. Leiden, Netherlands: Brill, 1971.
————. *Studies in African Music*. London: Oxford University Press, 1959.
Kaufman, Fredrick. *African Roots of Jazz*. Sherman Oaks, CA: Alfred Publishing Co., 1979.
King, Anthony. *Yoruba Sacred Music from Ekiti*. Ibadan, Nigeria: Ibadan University Press, 1961.
Krehbiel, Henry Edward. *Afro-American Folksongs*. New York: G. Schirmer, 1914. Reprinted, New York: Frederick Ungar, 1962.
Levine, Lawrence W. *Black Culture and Black Consciousness: Afro-American Folk Thought from Slavery to Freedom*. New York: Oxford University Press, 1977.

List, George, and Juan Orrego Salas. *Music in the Americas*. Bloomington: Indiana University Research Center in Anthropology, Folklore, and Linguistics, 1967.
Locke, Alain LeRoy. *The Negro and His Music*. New York: Arno Press, 1969.
Lovell, John. *Black Song: The Forge and the Flame*. New York: Macmillan, 1972.
Lucas, John. "Rhythms of Negro Music and Negro Poetry." Unpublished thesis, University of Minnesota, 1945.
Mason, Bernard Sterling. *Drums, Tomtoms and Rattles: Primitive Percussion Instruments for Modern Use*. New York: Dover, 1974.
Nathan, Hans. *Dan Emmett and the Rise of Early Negro Minstrelsy*. Norman: University of Oklahoma Press, 1962.
Nettl, Bruno. *Folk and Traditional Music of the Western Continents*. Englewood Cliffs, NJ: Prentice-Hall, 1973.
———. *Music in Primitive Culture*. Cambridge: Harvard University Press, 1956.
Nikiprowetzky, Tolia. *Trois Aspects de la musique Africaine: Mauritanie, Senegal, Niger*. Paris: Office de Cooperation Radiophonique, 1967.
Nketia, J. H. Kwabena. *African Gods and Music*. Legon: University of Ghana, 1970.
———. *African Music in Ghana*. Evanston: Northwestern University Press, 1963.
———. *The Music of Africa*. New York: W. W. Norton, 1974.
Patterson, Lindsay. *The Negro in Music and Art*. New York: United Publishers Co., 1970.
Roach, Hildred. *Black American Music, Past and Present: Pan-African Composers Thenceforth and Now*, 2nd ed. Malabar, FL: Krieger, 1991.
Roberts, John Storm. *Black Music of Two Worlds*. New York: Praeger, 1972.
Rublowsky, John. *Black Music in America*. New York: Basic Books, 1971.
Southern, Eileen. *The Music of Black Americans: A History*. New York: W. W. Norton, 1971.
Standifer, James A., and Barbara Reeder. *Source Book of African and Afro-American Materials for Music Educators*. Washington, DC: Contemporary Music Project, 1972.
Tallmadge, William H. *Afro-American Music*. Rev. ed. Buffalo: State University College, 1969.
Tracey, Hugh, et al. *Codification of African Music and Textbook Project: A Primer of Practical Suggestions for Field Research*. Roodepoort, South Africa: International Library of African Music, 1969.
Trotter, James M. *Music and Some Highly Musical People*. Boston: Lee and Shepard, 1881. Reprinted, New York: Johnson Reprint, 1968.
Varley, Douglas H. *African Native Music, An Annotated Bibliography*. London: Dawsons of Pall Mall, 1970.
Wachsmann, Klaus P., ed. *Essays on Music and History in Africa*. Evanston: Northwestern University Press, 1971.
Walton, Ortiz M. *Music: Black, White and Blue*. New York: Morrow, 1972.
Warren, Fred, with Lee Warren. *The Music of Africa: An Introduction*. Englewood Cliffs, NJ: Prentice-Hall, 1970.
Waterman, Richard A. " 'Hot' Rhythm in Negro Music," *Journal of the American Musicological Society*, 1 (1948), pp. 24–37.
———. "African Influence on the Music of the Americas," in *Acculturation in the Americas*, ed. Sol Tax. Chicago: University of Chicago Press, 1952.
Williams, Raymond. *The African Drum*. Highland Park, MI: Highland Park College Press, 1973.

MUSIC OF THE U.S. IN THE LATE NINETEENTH CENTURY

Austin, William W. *"Susanna," "Jeanie," and "The Old Folks at Home": The Songs of Stephen C. Foster from His Time to Ours*. New York: Macmillan, 1975.
Blassingame, John W. *Black New Orleans: 1860–1880* Chicago: University of Chicago Press, 1973.

Blum, Daniel. *A Pictorial Treasury of Opera in America*. New York: Greenberg, 1954.
Chase, Gilbert. *America's Music from the Pilgrims to the Present*. Rev. 3rd ed. Urbana: University of Illinois Press, 1987.
Cron, Theodore O., and Burt Goldblatt. *Portrait of Carnegie Hall*. New York: Macmillan, 1966.
Elson, Louis Charles. *The History of American Music*. New York: Macmillan, 1904. Reprinted, New York: B. Franklin, 1971.
Erskine, John. *The Philharmonic-Symphony Society of New York: Its First Hundred Years*. New York: Macmillan, 1943.
Ewen, David. *History of Popular Music*. New York: Barnes & Noble, 1961.
———. *Panorama of American Popular Music*. Englewood Cliffs, NJ: Prentice-Hall, 1957.
Filby, P. William. *Star-Spangled Books: Books, Sheet Music, Newspapers, Manuscripts, and Persons Associated with the Star-Spangled Banner*. Baltimore: Maryland Historical Society, 1972.
Goldman, Richard Franko. *The Wind Band*. Boston: Allyn & Bacon, 1961.
Howard, John Tasker. *Stephen Foster, America's Troubador*. Rev. ed. New York: Crowell, 1953.
Howe, M. A. DeWolfe. *The Boston Symphony Orchestra 1881–1931*. Boston: Houghton Mifflin, 1931.
Isaacs, Edith. *The Negro in the American Theatre*. New York: Theatre Arts, 1947.
Jackson, George Pullen. *White Spirituals in the Southern Uplands*. Chapel Hill: University of North Carolina Press, 1933.
Kmen, Henry A. *Music in New Orleans: The Formative Years 1791–1841*. Baton Rouge: Louisiana State University Press, 1966.
Lang, Paul Henry. *One Hundred Years of Music in America*. New York: G. Schirmer, 1961.
Lengyel, Cornel. *A San Francisco Songster 1849–1939*. San Francisco: W.P.A. History of Music Project, 1939.
Mattfeld, Julius. *A Hundred Years of Grand Opera in New York*. New York: New York Public Library, 1927.
Morris, Berenice Robinson. *American Popular Music: The Growing Years, 1800–1900*. New York: F. Watts, 1972.
Mueller, John. *The American Symphony Orchestra*. Bloomington: Indiana University Press, 1951.
Niles, John J. "Shout, Coon, Shout!" *The Musical Quarterly*, 16 (1930), pp. 516–30.
Pearsall, Ronald. *Victorian Sheet Music Covers*. Detroit: Gale Research, 1972.
Revett, Marion S. *A Minstrel Town*. New York: Pageant Press, 1955.
Rich, Arthur. *Lowell Mason*. Chapel Hill: University of North Carolina Press, 1946.
Sablosky, Irving L. *American Music*. Chicago: University of Chicago Press, 1969.
Schwartz, H. W. *Bands of America*. Garden City, NY: Doubleday, 1957.
Southern, Eileen. *The Music of Black Americans: A History*. 2nd ed. New York: W. W. Norton, 1983.
Spaeth, Sigmund Gottfried. *A History of Popular Music in America*. New York: Random House, 1948.
Stevenson, Robert. *Protestant Church Music in America*. New York: W. W. Norton, 1966.
Stoutamire, Albert. *Music of the Old South: Colony to Confederacy*. Rutherford, NJ: Fairleigh Dickinson University Press, 1972.
Swoboda, Henry. *The American Symphony Orchestra*. New York: Basic Books, 1967.
Upton, William Treat. *Art-Song in America*. Boston: Oliver Ditson, 1930; Supplement, 1938.
Wittke, Carl. *Tambo and Bones*. Durham, NC: Duke University Press, 1930.

RAGTIME

Berlin, Edward A. *Ragtime: A Musical and Cultural History*. Berkeley: University of California Press, 1980.
Blesh, Rudi, ed. *Classic Piano Rags*. New York: Dover, 1973.
———, and Harriet Janis. *They All Played Ragtime*. 4th ed. New York: Oak Publications, 1971.

Dapogny, James. *Ferdinand "Jelly Roll" Morton: The Collected Piano Music.* New York: G. Schirmer; Washington, DC: Smithsonian Institution Press, 1982.

Floyd, Samuel A., Jr., and Marsha J. Reisser. "The Sources and Resources of Classic Ragtime Music," *Black Music Research Journal,* vol. 4 (1984), pp. 22–59.

Gammond, Peter. *Scott Joplin and the Ragtime Era.* New York: St. Martin's Press, 1975.

Hazze, John Edward, ed. *Ragtime: Its History, Composers, and Music.* New York: Schirmer Books, 1985.

Joplin, Scott. *The Collected Works of Scott Joplin.* Ed. Vera Brodsky Lawrence. 2 vols. New York: New York Public Library, 1971.

———. *Scott Joplin, King of Ragtime.* Comp. Albert Gamse. Carlstadt, NJ: Lewis Music, 1972.

Lomax, Alan. *Mister Jelly Roll: The Fortunes of Jelly Roll Morton, New Orleans Creole and "Inventor of Jazz."* 2nd ed. Berkeley: University of California Press, 1973.

Morath, Max, comp. *100 Ragtime Classics.* Denver: Donn Print Co., 1963.

Schafer, William J., and Johannes Riedel. *The Art of Ragtime.* Baton Rouge: Louisiana State University Press, 1973.

——— THE BLUES ————————————

Albertson, Chris. *Bessie.* New York: Stein and Day, 1972.

Bradford, Perry. *Born with the Blues: Perry Bradford's Own Story.* Westport, CT: Hyperion Press, 1973.

Broonzy, William "Big Bill." *Big Bill Blues: Big Bill Broonzy's Story as Told to Yannick Bruynoghe.* Rev. ed. New York: Oak, 1964.

Charters, Samuel. *The Bluesmen: The Story and the Music of the Men Who Made the Blues.* New York: Oak Publications, 1967. Reprinted under title, *The Blues Makers,* New York: Da Capo Press, 1991.

———. *The Country Blues.* New York: Rinehart, 1959.

———. *The Legacy of the Blues.* New York: Da Capo, 1977.

———. *The Life, the Times, the Songs of Country Joe and the Fish.* New York: Ryerson Music, 1971.

———. *The Poetry of the Blues.* New York: Oak Publications, 1963.

———. *Robert Johnson.* New York: Oak Publications, 1973.

———. *Sweet as the Showers of Rain: The Bluesmen.* New York: Oak Publications, 1977. Reprinted under title, *The Blues Makers,* New York: Da Capo Press, 1991.

Cone, James H. *The Spirituals and the Blues: An Interpretation.* New York: Seabury Press, 1972. Reprinted, Westport, CT: Greenwood Press, 1980.

Evans, David. *Big Road Blues.* Berkeley: University of California Press, 1982.

Fahey, John. *Charley Patton.* London: Studio Vista, 1970.

Ferris, William. *Blues from the Delta: An Illustrated Documentary on the Music and Musicians of the Mississippi Delta.* Garden City, NY: Anchor Press / Doubleday, 1978. Reprinted, New York: Da Capo Press, 1984.

Garvin, Richard M., and Edmond G. Addeo. *The Midnight Special: The Legend of Leadbelly.* New York: Bernard Gale, 1971.

Grossman, Stefan, et al. *Country Blues Songbook.* New York: Oak Publications, 1973.

Handy, William Christopher, ed. *Blues: An Anthology.* New York: A. and C. Boni, 1926. Several rev. eds.

———. *Father of the Blues: An Autobiography.* New York: Macmillan, 1941. Reprinted, New York: Da Capo Press, 1985.

Harrison, Daphne Duval. *Black Pearls: Blues Queens of the 1920s.* New Brunswick, NJ: Rutgers University Press, 1988.

Jackson, Bruce. *Wake Up Dead Man: Afro-American Worksongs from Texas Prisons.* Cambridge: Harvard University Press, 1972.

Knaack, Twila. *Ethel Waters: I Touched a Sparrow.* Waco, TX: Word Books, 1978.

Leadbitter, Mike. *Delta Country Blues*. Bexhill-on-Sea, Sussex, England: Blues Unlimited, 1968.
———. *Nothing but the Blues*. Westport, CT: Hyperion, 1973.
Lehman, Theo. *Blues and Trouble*. Berlin: Henschelverlag, 1966.
Malone, Bill C. *Country Music U.S.A.: A Fifty-Year History*. Austin: University of Texas Press, 1968.
Mann, Woody. *Six Black Guitarists*. New York: Oak Publications, 1973.
Mitchell, George. *Blow My Blues Away*. Baton Rouge: Louisiana State University Press, 1971.
Moore, Carman. *Somebody's Angel Child: The Story of Bessie Smith*. New York: Crowell, 1969.
Murray, Albert. *Stomping the Blues*. New York: McGraw-Hill, 1976.
Napier, Simon A. *Back Woods Blues*. Bexhill-on-Sea, Sussex, England: Blues Unlimited, 1968.
Neff, Robert, and Anthony Connor. *Blues*. Boston: David R. Godine, 1975.
Oakley, Giles. *The Devil's Music: A History of the Blues*. New York: Harcourt Brace Jovanovich, 1976.
Oliver, Paul. *Aspects of the Blues Tradition*. Westport, CT: Hyperion Press, 1973.
———. *Bessie Smith*. London: Cassell, 1959.
———. *Blues Fell This Morning: The Meaning of the Blues*. 2nd ed. Cambridge; New York: Cambridge University Press, 1990.
———. *Conversation with the Blues*. New York: Horizon, 1965.
———. *Savannah Syncopators: African Retentions in the Blues*. New York: Stein and Day, 1970.
———. *The Story of the Blues*. New York: Barrie, 1969.
Oster, Harry. *Living Country Blues*. Detroit: Folklore Assoc., 1969.
Russell, Tony. *Blacks, Whites and Blues: Negro and White Folk Traditions*. New York: Stein and Day, 1970.
Sackheim, Eric. *The Blues Line: A Collection of Blues Lyrics*. New York: Grossman, 1969.
Stewart-Baxter, Derrick. *Ma Rainey and the Classic Blues Singers*. New York: Stein and Day, 1970.
Waters, Ethel. *His Eye Is on the Sparrow: An Autobiography*. Garden City, NY: Doubleday, 1951. Reprinted, Westport, CT: Greenwood Press, 1978.

—— EARLY JAZZ ————————————

Allen, Walter C. *King Joe Oliver*. London: Sidgwick and Jackson, 1958.
Armstrong, Louis. *Louis Armstrong—A Self-Portrait: The Interview by Richard Maryman*. New York: Eakins Press, 1971.
———. *Satchmo: My Life in New Orleans*. New York: Prentice-Hall, 1954.
———. *Swing That Music*. New York: Longmans, Green, and Co., 1936.
Balliett, Whitney. *Jelly Roll, Jabbo, and Fats: 19 Portraits in Jazz*. New York: Oxford University Press, 1983.
Bechet, Sidney. *Treat It Gentle: An Autobiography*. New York: Hill and Wang, 1960. Reprinted, New York: Da Capo Press, 1975.
Becker, Howard Saul. "The Professional Dance Musician in Chicago." Unpublished thesis, University of Chicago, 1949.
Berton, Ralph. *Remembering Bix: A Memoir of the Jazz Age*. New York: Harper and Row, 1974.
Blesh, Rudi. *Shining Trumpets: A History of Jazz*. 2nd ed. New York: Knopf, 1958. Reprinted, New York: Da Capo Press, 1975.
Brown, Scott E. *James P. Johnson: A Case of Mistaken Identity*. Metuchen, NJ: Scarecrow Press, 1986. Includes a James P. Johnson Discography, 1917–50, by Robert Hilbert.
Brunn, Harry O. *The Story of the Original Dixieland Jazz Band*. Baton Rouge: Louisiana State University Press, 1960. Reprinted, New York: Da Capo Press, 1977.
Buerkle, Jack V., and Danny Barker. *Bourbon Street Black: The New Orleans Black Jazzman*. New York: Oxford University Press, 1973.
Charters, Samuel, and Leonard Kunstadt. *Jazz: A History of the New York Scene*. Garden City, NY: Doubleday, 1962. Reprinted, New York: Da Capo Press, 1984.

Chilton, John, and Max Jones. *Louis: The Louis Armstrong Story 1900–1971*. Boston: Little, Brown, 1971.

Collier, James Lincoln. *Louis Armstrong: An American Genius*. New York: Oxford University Press, 1983.

Condon, Eddie. *Treasury of Jazz*. New York: Dial Press, 1956.

———. *We Called It Music*. New York: H. Holt, 1947. Reprinted, New York: Da Capo Press, 1992.

Crawford, Ralston. *Music in the Street: Photographs of New Orleans*. New Orleans: Historic New Orleans Collection, 1983.

Dauer, Alfons M. *Der Jazz: Seine Ursprünge und seine Entwicklung*. Kassel: E. Röth Verlag, 1958.

DeLong, Thomas A. *Pops: Paul Whiteman, King of Jazz*. Piscataway, NJ: New Century Publishers, 1983.

Driggs, Frank, and Harris Lewine. *Black Beauty, White Heat: A Pictorial History of Classic Jazz, 1920–1950*. New York: W. Morrow, 1982.

Engel, Carl. "Jazz: A Musical Discussion," in *Backgrounds of Book Reviewing*, ed. H. S. Mallory, pp. 343–51. Ann Arbor: G. Wahr, 1923.

Foster, George Murphy. *Pops Foster: The Autobiography of a New Orleans Jazzman, as Told to Tom Stoddard*. Berkeley: University of California Press, 1971.

Fountain, Pete. *A Closer Walk: The Pete Fountain Story*. Chicago: Regnery, 1972.

Gara, Larry. *The Baby Dodds Story*. Los Angeles: Contemporary, 1959.

Giddins, Gary. *Satchmo*. New York: Doubleday, 1988.

Goffin, Robert. *Aux Frontières du jazz*. Paris: Éditions du Sagittaire, 1932.

———. *Horn of Plenty: The Story of Louis Armstrong*. New York: Allen, Towne and Heath, 1947. Reprinted, New York: Da Capo Press, 1977.

———. *Jazz from the Congo to the Metropolitan*. Garden City, NY: Doubleday, 1944.

———. *La Nouvelle-Orléans*. New York: Éditions de la Maison française, 1946.

Hadlock, Richard. *Jazz Masters of the Twenties*. New York: Macmillan, 1965.

Handy, William Christopher. *Father of the Blues: An Autobiography*. New York: Macmillan, 1941. Reprinted, New York: Da Capo Press, 1985.

Hennessey, Thomas Joseph. "From Jazz to Swing: Jazz Musicians and Their Music, 1917–1935." Unpublished dissertation, Northwestern University, 1973. University Microfilm No. 74-7757.

James, Burnett. *Bix Beiderbecke*. New York: Barnes, 1959.

Johnson, Grady. *The Five Pennies: The Biography of Jazz Band Leader Red Nichols*. New York: Dell, 1959.

Jones, Max, and John Chilton. *Louis: The Louis Armstrong Story*. Boston: Little, Brown, 1971.

Kaminsky, Max. *My Life in Jazz*. New York: Harper and Row, 1963.

Lambert, George Edmund. *Johnny Dodds*. New York: Barnes, 1961.

Lomax, Alan. *Mister Jelly Roll: The Fortunes of Jelly Roll Morton, New Orleans Creole and "Inventor" of Jazz*. 2nd ed. Berkeley: University of California Press, 1973.

Longstreet, Stephen. *Sportin' House: A History of the New Orleans Sinners and the Birth of Jazz*. Los Angeles: Sherbourne Press, 1965.

McCarthy, Albert J. *Louis Armstrong*. New York: Barnes, 1959.

McComb, David G. *Houston: The Bayou City*. Austin: University of Texas, 1969.

Manone, Wingy, and Paul Vandervoort II. *Trumpet on the Wing*. New York: Doubleday, 1948.

Merriam, Alan P., and Fradley H. Garner, "Jazz—The Word," *Ethnomusicology*, 12 (1968), pp. 373–96.

Mezzrow, Milton, and Bernard Wolfe. *Really The Blues*. New York: Random House, 1946.

Mordden, Ethan. *That Jazz! An Idiosyncratic Social History of the American Twenties*. New York: Putnam's Sons, 1978.

Ogren, Kathy J. *The Jazz Revolution: Twenties America and the Meaning of Jazz*. New York: New York: Oxford University Press, 1989.

Oliver, Paul. *Savannah Syncopators: African Retentions in the Blues*. New York: Stein and Day, 1970.

————. *Songsters and Saints: Vocal Traditions on Race Records.* Cambridge, England: Cambridge University Press, 1984.

Olsson, Bengt. *Memphis Blues and Jug Bands.* London: Studio Vista, 1970.

Osgood, Henry Osborne. *So This Is Jazz.* Boston: Little, Brown, 1926. Reprinted, New York: Da Capo Press, 1978.

Panassié, Hugues. *Hot Jazz: The Guide to Swing Music.* New York: M. Witmark, 1936.

————. *Louis Armstrong.* New York: C. Scribner's Sons, 1971.

Pyke, Launcelot Allen. "Jazz, 1920–1927." Unpublished dissertation, University of Iowa, 1962. University Microfilm No. 62-4988.

Ramsey, Frederic. *Been Here and Gone.* New Brunswick: Rutgers University Press, 1960.

————. *Jazzmen.* New York: Harcourt, Brace, 1939. Reprinted, 1977.

Rose, Al. *Eubie Blake.* New York: Schirmer Books, 1979.

————. *I Remember Jazz: Six Decades Among the Great Jazzmen.* Baton Rouge: Louisiana State University Press, 1987.

Schafer, William J. "Thoughts on Jazz Historiography: 'Buddy Bolden's Blues' versus 'Buddy Bottley's Balloon,' " *Journal of Jazz Studies,* 2 (1974), pp. 3–14.

Schuller, Gunther. *Early Jazz: Its Roots and Musical Development.* New York: Oxford University Press, 1968.

Smith, Jay D., and Len Guttridge. *Jack Teagarden: The Story of a Jazz Maverick.* London: Cassell, 1960. Reprinted, New York: Da Capo Press, 1976.

Smith, Willie. *Music on My Mind: The Memoirs of an American Pianist.* Garden City, NY: Doubleday, 1964. Reprinted, New York: Da Capo Press, 1975.

Souchon, Edmond. "King Oliver: A Very Personal Memoir," in *Jazz Panorama,* ed. Martin T. Williams, pp. 21–30. New York: Crowell-Collier Press, 1964. Reprinted, New York: Da Capo Press, 1979.

Stearns, Marshall W. *The Story of Jazz.* New York: Oxford University Press, 1957. Reprinted with expanded bibliography and syllabus, 1970.

Sudhalter, Richard M. *Bix: Man and Legend.* New Rochelle, NY: Arlington House, 1974.

Trolle, Frank H. *James P. Johnson: Father of Stride Piano.* The Netherlands: Micrography, 1981.

Wareing, Charles H., and George Garlick. *Bugles for Beiderbecke.* London: Sidgwick and Jackson, 1958.

SWING

Baron, Stanley. *Benny: King of Swing.* New York: William Morrow, 1979.

Basie, William "Count," with Albert Murray. *Good Morning Blues: The Autobiography of Count Basie.* New York: Random House, 1985.

Carmichael, Hoagy. *The Stardust Road.* New York: Rinehart, 1946. Reprinted, New York: Greenwood Press, 1969.

Chilton, John. *Billie's Blues: The Billie Holiday Story 1933–1959.* New York: Stein and Day, 1975.

Collier, James Lincoln. *Duke Ellington.* New York: Oxford University Press, 1987.

Connor, D. Russell, and Warren W. Hicks. *BG on the Record: A Bio-Discography of Benny Goodman.* New Rochelle, NY: Arlington House, 1969.

Crowther, Bruce, et al. *The Big Band Years.* New York: Facts on File Publications, 1988.

Dance, Stanley. *The World of Count Basie.* New York: Charles Scribner's Sons, 1980.

————. *The World of Duke Ellington.* New York: Charles Scribner's Sons, 1970.

————. *The World of Earl Hines.* New York: Charles Scribner's Sons, 1977. Reprinted, New York: Da Capo Press, 1983.

DeVeaux, Scott Knowles. "Jazz in Transition: Coleman Hawkins and Howard McGhee, 1935–1945." Unpublished dissertation, Berkeley, University of California, 1985.

Driggs, Franklin S. "Kansas City and the Southwest," in *Jazz,* ed. Nat Hentoff and Albert J. McCarthy, pp. 189–230. New York: Rinehart, 1959.

Ellington, Edward Kennedy "Duke." *Music Is My Mistress*. Garden City, NY: Doubleday, 1973. Reprinted, New York: Da Capo Press, 1976.

Fernett, Gene. *Swing Out: Great Negro Dance Bands*. Midland, MI: Pendell, 1970.

———. *A Thousand Golden Horns: The Exciting Age of America's Greatest Dance Bands*. Midland, MI: Pendell, 1966.

Flower, John. *Moonlight Serenade: A Bio-Discography of the Glenn Miller Civilian Band*. New Rochelle, NY: Arlington House, 1972.

Fox, Charles. *Fats Waller*. New York: Barnes, 1961.

Frankenstein, Alfred V. *Syncopating Saxophones*. Chicago: R. O. Ballon, 1925.

Gammond, Peter. *Duke Ellington: His Life and Music*. New York: Roy Publishers, 1958. Reprinted, New York: Da Capo Press, 1977.

———, and Raymond Horricks. *Big Bands*. Cambridge: P. Stephens, 1981.

Goodman, Benny. *The Kingdom of Swing*. New York: Stackpole Sons, 1939. Reprinted, New York: F. Ungar, 1961.

Haskins, Jim. *The Cotton Club*. New York: Random House, 1977.

Horricks, Raymond. *Count Basie and His Orchestra, Its Music and Its Musicians*. New York: Citadel Press, 1957.

———. *These Jazzmen of Our Time*. London: Gollancz, 1959.

Jewell, Derek. *Duke: A Portrait of Duke Ellington*. New York: W. W. Norton, 1977.

Kirkeby, Ed. *Ain't Misbehavin': The Story of Fats Waller*. New York: Dodd, Mead, 1966.

Lambert, George Edmund. *Duke Ellington*. New York: Barnes, 1959.

McCarthy, Albert J. *Big Band Jazz*. New York: Putnam, 1974.

———. *The Dance Band Era: The Dancing Decades from Ragtime to Swing; 1910–1950*. Philadelphia: Chilton Book, 1971.

Machlin, Paul S. *Stride: The Music of Fats Waller*. Boston: Twayne Publishers, 1985.

Montgomery, Elizabeth Rider. *Duke Ellington: King of Jazz*. Champaign, IL: Garrard Publishing Co., 1972.

Morgenstern, Dan, and Jack Bradley, eds. *Count Basie and His Bands*. New York: New York Jazz Museum, 1975.

Panassié, Hugues. *Douze années de jazz (1927–1938): Souvenirs*. Paris: Corréa, 1946.

Porter, Lewis. *Lester Young*. Boston: G. K. Hall, 1985.

———. "Some Problems in Jazz Research," *Black Music Journal*, vol. 8, no. 2 (Fall 1988).

Rattenbury, Ken. *Duke Ellington: Jazz Composer*. New Haven, CT: Yale University Press, 1990.

Rosenkrantz, Timme. *Swing Photo Album 1939*. London: Scorpion, 1964.

Russell, Ross. *Jazz Style in Kansas City and the Southwest*. Berkeley: University of California Press, 1971.

Rust, Brian. *The Dance Bands*. London: Ian Allan, 1972.

Sanford, Herb. *Tommy and Jimmy: The Dorsey Years*. New Rochelle, NY: Arlington House, 1972.

Schuller, Gunther. *The Swing Era: The Development of Jazz, 1930–1945*. New York: Oxford University Press, 1989.

Simon, George Thomas. *The Big Bands*. Rev. enl. ed. New York: Macmillan, 1974.

———. *Simon Says: The Sights and Sounds of the Swing Era, 1935–1955*. New Rochelle, NY: Arlington House, 1971.

Stewart, Rex William. *Jazz Masters of the Thirties*. New York: Macmillan, 1972.

Tucker, Mark. *Ellington: The Early Years*. Urbana, IL: University of Illinois Press, 1991.

Ulanov, Barry. *Duke Ellington*. New York: Creative Age, 1946. Reprinted, New York: Da Capo Press, 1975.

Walker, Leo. *The Wonderful Era of the Great Dance Bands*. Berkeley: Howell-North, 1964.

Wells, Dicky, and Stanley Dance. *The Night People: Reminiscences of a Jazzman*. Boston: Crescendo Publishing Co., 1971.

MODERN JAZZ

Baker, David N., ed. *New Perspectives on Jazz: Report on a National Conference Held at Wingspread . . . 1986*. Washington, DC: Smithsonian Institution Press, 1990.

Balliett, Whitney. *Improvising: Sixteen Jazz Musicians and Their Art*. New York: Oxford University Press, 1977.

———. *New York Notes: A Journal of Jazz, 1972–1975*. Boston: Houghton Mifflin, 1976.

Berry, Jason, et al. *Up from the Cradle of Jazz: New Orleans Music Since World War II*. Athens, GA: University of Georgia Press, 1986.

Blancq, Charles. *Sonny Rollins: A Journey of a Jazzman*. Boston: Twayne Publishers, 1983.

Budds, Michael J. *Jazz in the Sixties: The Expansion of Musical Resources and Techniques*. Iowa City: University of Iowa Press, 1978.

Cane, Giampiero. *Canto nero: Il free jazz degli anni Sessanta*. Rimini, Italy: Guaraldi, 1973.

Carr, Ian. *Miles Davis: A Biography*. New York: William Morrow, 1982.

Chambers, Jack. *Milestones I: The Music and Times of Miles Davis to 1960*. Toronto: University of Toronto Press, 1983.

———. *Milestones II: The Music and Times of Miles Davis Since 1960*. Toronto: University of Toronto Press, 1985.

Cole, Bill. *John Coltrane*. New York: Schirmer Books, 1976.

———. *Miles Davis: A Musical Biography*. New York: William Morrow, 1974.

Coryell, Julie, and Laura Friedman. *Jazz-Rock Fusion: The People—The Music*. New York: Dell, 1978.

Dance, Stanley F., ed. *Jazz Era: The Forties*. London: Jazz Book Club, 1962.

Davis, Francis. *In The Moment: Jazz in the 1980s*. New York: Oxford University Press, 1986.

Davis, Miles, with Quincy Troupe. *Miles: The Autobiography*. New York: Simon and Schuster, 1989.

Feather, Leonard. *Inside Be-Bop*. Reissued as *Inside Jazz*. New York: J. J. Robbins, 1949.

———. *Jazz: An Exciting Story of Jazz Today*. Los Angeles: Trend Books, 1958.

———. *The Passion For Jazz*. New York: Horizon Press, 1980.

———. *The Pleasures of Jazz: Leading Performers on Their Lives, Their Music, Their Contemporaries*. New York: Horizon Press, 1976.

Feigin, Leo, ed. *Russian Jazz: New Identity*. London: Quartet Books, 1985.

Giddins, Gary. *Celebrating Bird: The Triumph of Charlie Parker*. New York: Beech Tree Books, 1987.

———. *Rhythm-a-ning: Jazz Tradition and Innovation in the 80s*. New York: Oxford University Press, 1985.

———. *Riding on a Blue Note: Jazz and American Popular Music*. New York: Oxford University Press, 1981.

Gitler, Ira. *Jazz Masters of the Forties*. New York: Macmillan, 1966.

———. *Swing to Bop: An Oral History of the Transition in Jazz in the 1940s*. New York: Oxford University Press, 1985.

Godbolt, Jim. *A History of Jazz in Britain, 1919–1950*. London: Quartet Books, 1984.

Goldberg, Joe. *Jazz Masters of the Fifties*. New York: Macmillan, 1965.

Goldblatt, Burt. *Newport Jazz Festival: The Illustrated History*. New York: Dial Press, 1977.

Green, Benny. *The Reluctant Art: Five Studies in the Growth of Jazz*. New York: Da Capo, 1976.

Harrison, Max. *Charlie Parker*. London: Cassel, 1960.

Hellhund, Herbert. *Cool Jazz: Grundzuge seiner Entstehung und Entwicklung*. Mainz: Schott, 1985.

Horricks, Raymond. *Gerry Mulligan's Ark*. London: Apollo, 1986.

Ita, Bassey. *Jazz in Nigeria: an Outline Cultural History*. Lagos: Radical House, 1984.

James, Michael. *Dizzy Gillespie*. New York: Barnes, 1959.

———. *Miles Davis*. New York: Barnes, 1961.

Jost, Ekkehard. *Europas Jazz, 1960–1980*. Frankfurt-am-Main: Fischer Taschenbuch, 1982.

———. *Free Jazz*. Graz, Austria: Universal Edition, 1974.

———. *Sozialgeschichte des Jazz in den USA*. Frankfurt-am-Main: Fischer Taschenbuch, 1982.

Kernfeld, Barry. "Adderley, Coltrane, and Davis at the Twilight of Bebop: The Search for Melodic Coherence (1958–59)." Unpublished dissertation, Cornell University, 1981.

Klinkowitz, Jerome. *Listen, Gerry Mulligan: An Aural Narrative in Jazz*. New York: Schirmer, 1991.

Kofsky, Frank. *Black Nationalism and the Revolution in Music*. New York: Pathfinder Press, 1970.

Larkin, Philip. *All What Jazz: A Record Diary 1961–1968*. New York: St. Martin's Press, 1970.

Leiter, Robert D. *The Musicians and Petrillo*. New York: Bookman Assoc., 1953.

Litweiler, John. *The Freedom Principle: Jazz After 1958*. New York: William Morrow, 1984.

McRae, Barry. *The Jazz Cataclysm*. South Brunswick, NY: Barnes, 1967.

Merriam, Alan P., and Raymond W. Mack. "The Jazz Community," *Social Forces*, 38 (1960), pp. 211–22.

Morgan, Alun, and Raymond Horricks. *Modern Jazz: A Survey of Developments Since 1939*. London: Gollancz, 1956. Reprinted, Westport, CT: Greenwood Press, 1977.

Morgenstern, Dan, et al. *Bird & Diz: A Bibliography*. New York: New York Jazz Museum, 1973.

Owens, Thomas. "Charlie Parker: Techniques of Improvisation." Unpublished dissertation, University of California at Los Angeles, 1974. University Microfilms, no. 75-1992.

Porter, Lewis. "John Coltrane's Music of 1960 through 1967: Jazz Improvisation as Composition." Unpublished dissertation, Brandeis University, 1983. University Microfilms, no. 22-1985.

Reisner, Robert George. *Bird: The Legend of Charlie Parker*. New York: Citadel Press, 1962. Reprinted, New York: Da Capo Press, 1975.

———. *The Jazz Titans, including "The Parlance of Hip."* Garden City, NY: Doubleday, 1960. Reprinted, New York: Da Capo Press, 1977.

Russell, Ross. *Bird Lives: The High Life and Hard Times of Charlie Parker*. New York: Charterhouse, 1973.

Shaw, Arnold. *The Street That Never Slept*. New York: Coward, McCann, and Geoghegan, 1971.

Spellman, A. B. *Black Music: Four Lives in the Bebop Business*. New York: Schocken Books, 1970.

Starr, S. Frederick. *Red and Hot: The Fate of Jazz in the Soviet Union, 1917–1980*. New York: Oxford University Press, 1983.

Stokes, W. Royal. *The Jazz Scene: An Informal History from New Orleans to 1990*. New York: Oxford University Press, 1991.

Taylor, Billy. *Jazz Piano: A Jazz History*. Dubuque, IA: W. C. Brown, 1983.

Thomas, J. C. *Chasin' The Trane: The Music and Mystique of John Coltrane*. New York: Doubleday, 1975. Reprinted, New York: Da Capo, 1976.

Wilson, John Steuart. *Jazz: The Transition Years, 1940–1960*. New York: Appleton-Century-Crofts, 1966.

WOMEN IN JAZZ

Dahl, Linda. *Stormy Weather: The Music and Lives of a Century of Jazzwomen*. New York: Pantheon Books, 1984.

Handy, D. Antoinette. *Black Women in American Bands and Orchestras*. Metuchen, NJ: Scarecrow Press, 1981.

———. *The International Sweethearts of Rhythm*. Metuchen, NJ: Scarecrow Press, 1983.

Leder, Jan. *Women in Jazz: A Discography of Instrumentalists, 1913–1968*. Westport, CT: Greenwood Press, 1985.

Lindemann, Carolynn A., comp. *Women Composers of Ragtime*. Bryn Mawr, PA: Theodore Presser, 1985.

Placksin, Sally. *American Women in Jazz, 1900 to the Present: Their Words, Lives, and Music*. New York: Seaview Books, 1982.

Unterbrink, Mary. *Jazz Women at the Keyboard*. Jefferson, NC: McFarland, 1983.

MISCELLANEOUS— LITERATURE, PHILOSOPHY, INTERVIEWS, ROCK, GOSPEL, RECORDINGS, ETC.

Amram, David. *Vibrations: The Adventures and Musical Times of David Amram*. New York: Macmillan, 1968.

Balliett, Whitney. *Dinosaurs in the Morning*. Philadelphia: Lippincott, 1962.

———. *Ecstasy at the Onion*. Indianapolis: Bobbs-Merrill, 1971.

———. *The Sound of Surprise*. New York: Dutton, 1969.

———. *Such Sweet Thunder*. Indianapolis: Bobbs-Merrill, 1966.

Baraka, Imamu Amiri. *Black Music*. New York: W. Morrow, 1967. Reprinted, Westport, CT: Greenwood Press, 1980.

———. "The 'Blues Aesthetic' and the 'Black Aesthetic': Aesthetics as the Continuing Political History of a Culture," *Black Music Research Journal*, vol. 11, no. 2 (Fall 1991), pp. 101–10.

———. *Blues People: Negro Music in White America*. New York: W. Morrow, 1963. Reprinted, Westport, CT: Greenwood Press, 1980.

———. *Home: Social Essays*. New York: W. Morrow, 1966.

Bart, Teddy. *Inside Music City, U.S.A*. Nashville: Aurora, 1970.

Batten, Joe. *Joe Batten's Book: The Story of Sound Recording*. London: Rockliff, 1956.

Belz, Carl. *The Story of Rock*. 2nd ed. New York: Oxford University Press, 1972.

Blesh, Rudi. *Combo, U.S.A.: Eight Lives in Jazz*. Philadelphia: Chilton, 1971. Reprinted, New York: Da Capo Press, 1979.

Broadcast Music, Inc. *Five Decades of Rhythm and Blues*. New York: Broadcast Music, Inc., 1969.

Brown, H. Rap. *Die Nigger, Die*. New York: Dial Press, 1969.

Carr, Roy, et al. *Hip, Hipsters, Jazz, and the Beat Generation*. London: Faber and Faber, 1986.

Chew, V. K. *Talking Machines, 1877–1914: Some Aspects of the Early History of the Gramophone*. London: Her Majesty's Stationery Office, 1967.

Cohn, Nik. *Rock from the Beginning*. New York: Stein and Day, 1969.

Dalton, David. *Janis*. New York: Simon & Schuster, 1971.

———, ed. *The Rolling Stones: The First Twenty Years*. New York: A. A. Knopf, 1981.

Daufouy, Philippe, and Jean-Pierre Sarton. *Pop Music / Rock*. Paris: Éditions Champ Libre, 1972.

Davis, Francis. *Outcats: Jazz Composers, Instrumentalists, and Singers*. New York: Oxford University Press, 1990.

Denisoff, R. Serge. *Sing a Song of Social Significance*. 2nd ed. Bowling Green, OH: Bowling Green State University Popular Press, 1983.

———, and Richard A. Peterson, comp. *The Sounds of Social Change: Studies in Popular Culture*. Chicago: Rand McNally, 1972.

De Toledano, Ralph. *Frontiers of Jazz*. 2nd ed. New York: F. Ungar, 1962.

Dexter, Dave, Jr. *Jazz Cavalcade*. New York: Criterion, 1946. Reprinted, New York: Da Capo Press, 1977.

Dillard, J. L. *Black English: Its History and Usage in the United States*. New York: Random House, 1972.

Eisen, Jonathan, ed. *The Age of Rock, Sounds of the American Cultural Revolution: A Reader*. New York: Random House, 1969.

Ellison, Ralph. *Invisible Man*. New York: Vintage Books, 1947.

———. *Shadow and Act*. New York: Random House, 1964.

Erlich, Lillian. *What Jazz Is All About*. New York: J. Messner, 1962.

Ewen, David. *The Life and Death of Tin Pan Alley*. New York: Funk and Wagnalls, 1964.

Feather, Leonard. *From Satchmo to Miles*. New York: Stein and Day, 1972.
————. *The Jazz Years: Earwitness to an Era*. New York: Da Capo Press, 1987.
————. *The Passion for Jazz*. New York: Horizon Press, 1980. Reprinted, New York: Da Capo Press, 1990.
————, and Jack Tracy. *Laughter from the Hip*. New York: Horizon Press, 1963.
Friedwald, Will. *Jazz Singers: America's Great Voices from Bessie Smith to Bebop and Beyond*. New York: C. Scribner's Sons, 1990.
Gabree, John. *The World of Rock*. Greenwich, CT: Fawcett, 1968.
Gamble, Peter, and Peter Symes. *Focus on Jazz*. New York: St. Martin's Press, 1988.
Gammond, Peter. *Fourteen Miles on a Clear Night: An Irreverent Book about Jazz Records*. London: Owen, 1966. Reprinted, Westport, CT: Greenwood Press, 1978.
Gant, Roland. *World in a Jug*. New York: Vanguard, 1960.
Garland, Phyl. *The Sound of Soul*. Chicago: Regnery, 1969.
Gelatt, Roland. *The Fabulous Phonograph, 1877–1977*. 2nd rev. ed. New York: MacMillan, 1977.
Gillett, Charlie. *The Sound of the City: The Rise of Rock and Roll*. New York: Outerbridge & Dienstfrey, 1970.
Gioia, Ted. *The Imperfect Art: Reflections on Jazz and Modern Culture*. New York: Oxford University Press, 1988.
Gleason, Ralph J. *Celebrating the Duke and Louis, Bessie, Billie, Bird, Carmen, Miles, Dizzy, and Other Heroes*. Boston: Little, Brown, 1975.
————. *Jam Session: An Anthology of Jazz*. New York: Putnam, 1958.
Gold, Robert S. *Jazz Talk*. Indianapolis: Bobbs-Merrill, 1975.
Goldberg, Isaac. *Tin Pan Alley: A Chronicle of the American Popular Music Racket*. New York: John Day, 1930.
Grime, Kitty. *Jazz Voices*. London: Quartet Books, 1983.
Gunther, Helmut. *Jazz Dance: Geschichte, Theorie, Praxis*. Berlin: Henschelverlag, 1980.
Guralnick, Peter. *Feel Like Going Home: Portraits in Blues & Rock 'n' Roll*. New York: Outerbridge & Dienstfrey, 1971.
Guthrie, Woody. *Bound For Glory*. Garden City, NY: Doubleday, 1943. Reprinted, New York: Dutton, 1970.
Haas, Robert Bartlett, comp. *William Grant Still and the Fusion of Cultures in American Music*. Los Angeles: Black Sparrow Press, 1972.
Hamm, Charles. *Yesterdays: Popular Song in America*. New York: W. W. Norton, 1979.
————, et al. *Contemporary Music and Music Cultures*. Englewood Cliffs, NJ: Prentice-Hall, 1975.
Henthoff, Nat. *Jazz Country*. New York: Harper and Row, 1965.
————. *The Jazz Life*. New York: Dial Press, 1961.
————. *Journey Into Jazz*. New York: Coward-McCann, 1968.
————, and Albert J. McCarthy, eds. *Jazz: New Perspectives on the History of Jazz*. New York: Rinehart, 1959. Reprinted, New York: Da Capo Press, 1974.
Hippenmeyer, Jean Roland. *Le Jazz en Suisse, 1930–1970*. Yverdon: Éditions de la Thièle, 1971.
Hirsch, Paul. *The Structure of the Popular Music Industry*. Ann Arbor: Institute for Social Research, University of Michigan, 1969.
Hodeir, André. *Toward Jazz*. New York: Grove Press, 1962. Reprinted, New York: Da Capo Press, 1976.
————. *The Worlds of Jazz*. New York: Grove Press, 1972.
Jablonski, Edward. *From Sweet and Swing to Rock 'n' Roll*. New York: F. Ungar, 1961.
Jones, LeRoi. *See* Baraka, Imamu Amiri.
Jones, Max. *Talking Jazz*. New York: W. W. Norton, 1988.
Keil, Charles. *Urban Blues*. Chicago: University of Chicago Press, 1966. Reprinted, 1991.
Kofsky, Frank. *Black Nationalism and the Revolution in Music*. New York: Pathfinder Press, 1970.
Lange, Horst Heinz. *Jazz in Deutschland*. Berlin: Colloquium Verlag, 1966.
Lees, Gene. *Meet Me at Jim & Andy's: Jazz Musicians and Their World*. New York: Oxford University Press, 1988.
Leonard, Neil. *Jazz: Myth and Religion*. New York: Oxford University Press, 1987.

Lydon, Michael. *Rock Folk: Portraits from the Rock 'n' Roll Pantheon.* New York: Dial Press, 1971.

McCable, Peter, and Robert D. Schonfeld. *Apple to the Core: The Unmaking of the Beatles.* New York: Pocket Books, 1972.

McGregor, Craig, comp. *Bob Dylan.* New York: Morrow, 1972.

Marcus, Greil, comp. *Rock and Roll Will Stand.* Boston: Beacon Press, 1969.

Mellers, Wilfrid Howard. *The Twilight of the Gods: The Beatles in Retrospect.* London: Faber, 1974.

Meyer, Leonard B. *Music, The Arts, and Ideas: Patterns and Predictions in Twentieth-Century Culture.* Chicago: University of Chicago Press, 1967.

Millar, Bill. *The Drifters: The Rise and Fall of the Black Vocal Group.* New York: Macmillan, 1972.

Mingus, Charles. *Beneath the Underdog.* New York: Knopf, 1971.

Moore, MacDonald Smith. *Yankee Blues: Musical Culture and American Identity.* Bloomington: Indiana University Press, 1985.

Morse, David. *Motown and the Arrival of Black Music.* London: Studio Vista, 1971.

Nanry, Charles, comp. *American Music: From Storyville to Woodstock.* New Brunswick, NJ: Transaction Books, 1972.

Orloff, Katherine. *Rock 'n' Roll Woman.* Los Angeles: Nash, 1974.

Pleasants, Henry. *Death of a Music? The Decline of the European Tradition and the Rise of Jazz.* London: Gollancz, 1961.

———. *Serious Music and All That Jazz.* New York: Simon and Schuster, 1969.

Price, Steven. *Old as the Hills: The Story of Bluegrass Music.* New York: Viking, 1975.

Read, Oliver, and Walter L. Welch. *From Tin Foil to Stereo.* 2nd ed. Indianapolis: Sams, 1976.

Redd, Lawrence N. *Rock Is Rhythm and Blues (The Impact of the Mass Media).* East Lansing: Michigan State University Press, 1974.

Rivelli, Pauline, comp. *The Rock Giants.* New York: World Publishing Co., 1970.

Roach, Max, et al. "On Black Music," *The Black Scholar,* 3 (1972).

Rockmore, Noel. *Preservation Hall Portraits.* Baton Rouge: Louisiana State University Press, 1968.

Ruff, Willie. *A Call To Assembly: The Autobiography of a Musical Storyteller.* New York: Viking, 1991.

Scaduto, Anthony. *Bob Dylan.* New York: Grosset & Dunlap, 1972.

Shapiro, Nat, and Nat Henthoff. *The Jazz Makers.* New York: Rinehart, 1957. Reprinted, Westport, CT: Greenwood Press, 1975.

———, eds. *Hear Me Talkin' To Ya.* New York: Rinehart, 1955. Reprinted, New York: Dover, 1966.

Shaw, Arnold. *Honkers and Shouters: The Golden Years of Rhythm & Blues.* New York: Macmillan, 1978.

———. *The Rock Revolution.* New York: Crowell-Collier, 1969.

Shaw, Artie. *I Love You, I Hate You, Drop Dead.* New York: Fleet, 1965.

———. *The Trouble with Cinderella.* New York: Farrar, Straus & Young, 1952. Reprinted, New York: Da Capo Press, 1979.

Sidran, Ben. *Black Talk.* New York: Holt, Rinehart & Winston, 1971. Reprinted, New York: Da Capo Press, 1981.

Simmons, Herbert. *Man Walking On Eggshells.* Boston: Houghton Mifflin, 1962.

Simon, George T. *The Feeling of Jazz.* New York: Simon and Schuster, 1961.

Sinclair, John, and Robert Levin. *Music and Politics.* New York: World Publishing Co., 1971.

Smith, W. O. *Sideman: The Long Gig of W. O. Smith.* Nashville: Rutledge Hill Press, 1991.

Somma, Robert, ed. *No One Waved Good-Bye: A Casualty Report of Rock and Roll.* New York: Outerbridge & Dienstfrey, 1971.

Stambler, Irwin, and Grelun Landon. *Golden Guitars: The Story of Country Music.* New York: Four Winds Press, 1971.

Stokes, W. Royal. *The Jazz Scene.* Oxford University Press, 1991.

Sumner, John Daniel. *Gospel Music Is My Life.* Nashville: Impact Books, 1971.

Terkel, Studs. *Giants of Jazz.* Rev. ed. New York: Crowell, 1975.

Tormé, Mel. *The Other Side of the Rainbow.* New York: Morrow, 1970.

Traill, Sinclair. *Concerning Jazz*. London: Faber and Faber, 1957.

Vallée, Rudy. *Vagabond Dreams Come True*. New York: Dutton, 1930.

Walley, David. *No Commercial Potential: The Saga of Frank Zappa, Then and Now*. Rev. ed. New York: E. P. Dutton, 1980.

Whiteman, Paul. *How to Be a Bandleader*. New York: R. M. McBrice, 1948.

———, and Mary Margaret McBride. *Jazz*. New York: J. H. Sears, 1926.

Wilder, Alec. *American Popular Song: The Great Innovators, 1900–1950*. New York: Oxford University Press, 1972.

Wilmer, Valerie. *Jazz People*. Indianapolis: Bobbs-Merrill, 1970.

Wise, Herbert H., ed. *Professional Rock and Roll*. New York: Collier Books, 1967.

Yorke, Ritche. *Axes, Chops and Hot Licks: The Canadian Rock Music Scene*. Edmonton: M. G. Hurtig, 1971.

Zinsser, William. *Willie and Dwike: An American Profile*. New York: Harper & Row, 1984.

SELECTED

DISCOGRAPHY

The following list was compiled as an aid for jazz enthusiasts who wish to invest in a few recorded treasures that will bring a lifetime of listening enjoyment and satisfaction. Veteran jazzophiles may pass over these pages quickly, as they probably already own a collection of jazz recordings and have luxuriated in far more performances than these few CDs, discs, and cassettes provide. When these longtime members of the jazz community are ready to expand their holdings, they would best refer to the extensive discographies by other authors that are cited in the bibliography of discographies (p. 117* ff.).

Newcomers to this music, however, must begin somewhere. They have already been introduced to the three anthologies frequently cited throughout the text: the *Norton Anthology of Jazz*, the *Smithsonian Collection of Classic Jazz*, and the jazz items in the New World Records *Anthology of American Music*. Having sampled these choice selections, they will surely want to start their own collections, and there are two likely approaches: (1) acquire recordings of specific jazz artists comprehensively, and (2) build a general jazz collection from a core list of major artists and significant performances. Toward that end, I recommend the following titles, all of which are currently available and guaranteed to contain excellent music. Even though these hundred-plus albums hardly do justice to the subject, they represent a sizable investment at today's record prices. Still, the lasting reward of intense listening pleasure will certainly compensate many times over for the initial expenditures.

The albums are listed in approximate chronological order. Most items are available on compact disc. The others are labeled (C) for cassette or (LP) for long-playing record.

1.	*The Beauty of the Blues: Roots N' Blues*	Columbia CK-47465
2.	Scott Joplin: *The Original Rags, 1896–1904*	Zeta ZET-726
3.	*The Roots of Robert Johnson*	Yazoo C-1073 (C)
4.	Robert Johnson: *The Complete Recordings*	Columbia C2K-46222
5.	*Cylinder Jazz* [1913–1927]	Saydisc CDSDL-334
6.	*Jazz, Vol. 3: New Orleans*	Folkways 2803 (LP)
7.	*Louis Armstrong and His Hot Five*	Columbia CK-44049
8.	Louis Armstrong: *The Hot Fives and Hot Sevens*	Columbia CK-44253

9.	*The Legendary Sidney Bechet, 1932–41*	Bluebird 6590-2-RB
10.	*Jelly Roll Morton and His Red Hot Peppers*	Bluebird 6588-2-RB
11.	Bessie Smith: *Empress of the Blues*	Columbia C2K-47091
12.	Bix Beiderbecke: *At the Jazz Band Ball*	Columbia C2K-46175
13.	*Fletcher Henderson, 1927–31*	Classics 572
14.	*The Jazz Arranger, Vol. 1, 1928–40*	Columbia CK-45143
15.	James P. Johnson: *Carolina Shout*	Biograph BCD-105
16.	*Earl "Fatha" Hines, 1928–32*	Classics 595
17.	*The Definitive Fats Waller*	Stash ST-CD-528
18.	*The Jazz Singers*	Prestige 5P-24113 (C)
19.	*The Jazz Age: New York in the Twenties*	Bluebird 3136-2-RB
20.	*The 1930s: The Big Bands*	Columbia C2K-40651
21.	Duke Ellington: *The Blanton-Webster Band*	Bluebird 5659-2-RB
22.	*The Ellington Suites*	Fantasy OJCCD-446-2
23.	Duke Ellington: *The Yale Concert*	Fantasy OJCCD-664-2
24.	Count Basie: *The Golden Years, Vol. 2*	EPM FDC-5510
25.	Count Basie: *April in Paris*	Verve 825575-2
26.	Benny Goodman: *Carnegie Hall Jazz Concert*	Columbia C2K-40244
27.	*Jimmy Lunceford, 1937–39*	Classics 520
28.	Coleman Hawkins: *Body and Soul*	Bluebird 5717-2-RB
29.	*The Best of Lester Young*	Pablo 2405-420
30.	*The Big Three* [Hawkins, Young, Webster]	Signature AK-40950
31.	Johnny Hodges: *Caravan*	Prestige PCD-24013
32.	Charlie Christian: *Solo Flight*	VJC 1021-2
33.	Art Tatum: *Piano Starts Here*	Columbia PCT-9655E (C)
34.	*The Blues Piano Artistry of Meade Lux Lewis*	Fantasy OJCCD-1759-2
35.	*The Essence of Billie Holiday*	Columbia C2K-47917
36.	Billie Holiday: *God Bless the Child*	Columbia C2K-30782
37.	*Jazz, Vol. 4: The Jazz Singers*	Folkways 2804 (LP)
38.	*Ladies Sing the Blues*	Bella Musica BMCD-89940
39.	*Boogie Woogie Blues*	Biograph 115
40.	Dizzy Gillespie: *The Legendary Big Band Concerts*	Vogue VG-655612
41.	Dizzy Gillespie: *Shaw 'Nuff*	Musicraft MVSCD-53
42.	*Tadd Dameron & His Orchestra*	Fantasy OJCCD-055-2
43.	Dexter Gordon: *Our Man in Paris*	Blue Note B21Y-46394
44.	Fats Navarro: *Fat Girl*	Savoy Jazz 2-SJL-2216 (LP)
45.	*The Amazing Bud Powell*, Vol. 1	Blue Note B21Y-81503
46.	Charlie Parker: *Early Bird*	Pair PDC2-1242
47.	*Bird: The Savoy Master Takes*	Vogue 2-660508
48.	*Jazz at Massey Hall*	Fantasy OJCCD-044-2
49.	Woody Herman: *Early Autumn*	Bluebird 07863-61062-2
50.	Stan Kenton: *18 Original Big Band Recordings*	Hindsight HCD-407
51.	*Greatest Jazz Concert Ever*	Prestige 2-24024 (LP)
52.	*The Best of Sarah Vaughan*	Pablo PACD-2405-416-2
53.	Ella Fitzgerald: *The Rogers and Hart Songbook*	Verve 821579-2
54.	Lennie Tristano: *Wow*	Jazz Records JR-9-CD
55.	Miles Davis: *Birth of the Cool*	Blue Note C21Y-92862
56.	*The Best of the Gerry Mulligan Quartet with Chet Baker*	Pacific Jazz B21Y-95481
57.	*The Best of Stan Getz*	Roulette Jazz B21Y-98144
58.	*Diz and Getz*	Verve 835559-2
59.	*Clifford Brown and Max Roach*	EmArcy 814645

60.	Sun Ra Arkestra: *Jazz in Silhouette*	Evidence ECD-22012
61.	Sonny Rollins: *Saxophone Colossus*	Fantasy OJCCD-291-2
62.	John Coltrane: *Blue Trane*	Blue Note B21Y-46095
63.	John Coltrane: *Giant Steps*	Atlantic 1311-2
64.	Miles Davis: *Walkin'*	Fantasy OJCCD-213-2
65.	Mary Lou Williams / Jutta Hipp: *First Ladies of Jazz*	Savoy Jazz ZDS-1202
66.	Miles Davis: *'Round About Midnight*	Columbia CK-40610
67.	Marian McPartland: *At the Hickory House*	Savoy Jazz ZDS-4404
68.	Horace Silver: *Six Pieces of Silver*	Blue Note B21Y-81539
69.	Modern Jazz Quartet: *Django*	Fantasy OJCCD-057-2
70.	Dave Brubeck: *Time Out*	Columbia CK-40585
71.	Thelonious Monk: *5 by Monk by 5*	Fantasy OJCCD-362-2
72.	Oscar Peterson: *Live at the Blue Note*	Telarc CD-83304
73.	Lee Konitz: *Subconscious-Lee*	Fantasy OJC-5186 (C)
74.	George Russell: *Stratus Seekers*	Fantasy OJCCD-365-2
75.	Charles Mingus: *Mingus Ah Um*	Columbia CK-40648
76.	Miles Davis: *Kind of Blue*	Columbia CK-40579
77.	Miles Davis: *Porgy and Bess*	Columbia CK-40647
78.	Ornette Coleman: *The Shape of Jazz to Come*	Atlantic 1317-2
79.	Ornette Coleman: *Free Jazz*	Atlantic 1364-2
80.	John Coltrane: *A Love Supreme*	MCA MCAD-5660
81.	*The Major Works of John Coltrane*	GRP GRD2-113
82.	Miles Davis: *Filles de Kilimanjaro*	Columbia CK-46116
83.	Miles Davis: *In a Silent Way*	Columbia CK-40580
84.	Cecil Taylor: *Unit Structures*	Blue Note B21Y-84237
85.	Archie Shepp: *Fire Music*	MCA MCAD-39121
86.	Bill Evans: *The Complete Riverside Recordings*	Riverside RCD-018-2
87.	Roscoe Mitchell: *Sound*	Delmark 408 (LP)
88.	Don Ellis: *How Time Passes*	Candid CCD-79004
89.	*Best of Maynard Ferguson*	Columbia CK-36361
90.	Weather Report: *I Sing the Body Electric*	Columbia CK-46107
91.	The Mahavishnu Orchestra: *The Inner Mounting Flame*	Columbia CK-31067
92.	Art Ensemble of Chicago: *Live at Mandel Hall*	Delmark DE-432
93.	Chick Corea and Gary Burton: *Crystal Silence*	ECM 831331-2
94.	Return to Forever: *Romantic Warrior*	Columbia CK-46109
95.	Miles Davis: *Bitches Brew*	Columbia C2K-40577
96.	V.S.O.P.: *The Quintet*	Columbia CGK-34976
97.	Hank Mobley: *Straight No Filter*	Blue Note B21Y-84435
98.	Rahsaan Roland Kirk: *Case of the 3-Sided Dream in Color*	Atlantic 1674.2
99.	Pharoah Sanders: *Moon Child*	Timeless CDSJP-326
100.	Bill Watrous: *Bone-Ified*	GNP Crescendo GNPD-2211
101.	Wynton Marsalis: *Live at Blues Alley*	Columbia G2K-40675
102.	*Take 6*	Reprise W2-25670
103.	Prime Time: *Opening the Caravan of Dreams*	Caravan of Dreams CDP85001 (LP)
104.	George Lewis: *Solo Trombone Record*	Sackville 3012 (LP)
105.	Henry Butler: *Orleans Inspiration*	Windham Hill Jazz WD-0112
106.	Yosuke Yamashita: *Sakura*	Antilles 422 849 141-2
107.	Chick Corea: *Eye of the Beholder*	GRP GRD-9564
108.	*Diane Schuur and The Count Basie Orchestra*	GRP GRD-9550
109.	World Saxophone Quartet: *Metamorphosis*	Elektra 79258-2
110.	Gerry Mulligan: *Little Big Horn*	GRP GRD-9503

111.	Ray Anderson: *Wishbone*	Gramavision R21S-79454
112.	Art Ensemble of Chicago: *Urban Bushmen*	ECM 829394-2
113.	Steve Coleman Group: *Motherland Pulse*	JMT 834401-2
114.	John Zorn: *Spy vs. Spy*	Elektra / Musician 60844-2
115.	*Jazz Women: A Feminist Retrospective*	Stash ST 109 (LP)
116.	Jane Ira Bloom: *Mighty Lights*	Enja R21Y-79662
117.	Pat Metheny & Ornette Coleman: *Song X*	Geffen 9 24096-2
118.	Henry Threadgill: *Easily Slip into Another World*	BMG 3025-2
119.	Donald Harrison / Terence Blanchard: *Black Pearl*	Columbia CK 44216
120.	Miles Davis: *Tutu*	Warner Bros. W2 25490
121.	Randy Sandke: *New York Stories*	Stash ST-C-264 (C)
122.	Steve Turre: *Fire and Ice*	Stash ST-CD-7
123.	Barbara Thompson: *Songs from the Center of the Earth*	Black Sun 15014-2
124.	Anthony Davis: *Variations in Dream-Time*	India Navigation IN-1056

INDICES TO THE
RECORD COLLECTIONS

INDEX I

Integrated File of the Norton Anthology of Jazz, the New World Records Anthology of American Music, and the Smithsonian Collections of Classic Jazz

(Alphabetical Order and Locator Numbers)

ARTIST, LEADER, OR GROUP	WORK	YEAR	NAJ NO.	NW NO.	SIDE/BAND	SCCJ NO.
Ace, Johnny and the Beale Streeters	Clock, The	1952		249	I/2	
Adams, Faye (w. Joe Morris and His Orchestra)	Shake a Hand	1953		249	I/4	
Allen, Henry and Coleman Hawkins	Sister Kate	1933		250	I/4	
American Quartet	Let's All Be Americans Now	1917		222	I/3	
Ammons, Albert	Bass Goin' Crazy	1939		259	II/2	
Ammons, Albert	Boogie Woogie Stomp	1936		259	II/1	
Ammons, Albert and Pete Johnson	Cuttin' the Boogie	1941		259	II/8	
Armstrong, Joe and Group A	Kneebone	1800s		278	I/2	
Armstrong, Joe and Group A	Pay Me	1800s		278	II/7	
Armstrong, Louis and Earl Hines	Weather Bird	1928				20.
Armstrong, Louis and His Orchestra	I Double Dare You	1938		274	II/1	
Armstrong, Louis and His Orchestra	I Gotta Right to Sing the Blues	1933				22.
Armstrong, Louis and His Orchestra	Sweethearts on Parade	1930				21.
Armstrong, Louis and His Orchestra	Big Butter and Egg Man	1926				14.
Armstrong, Louis, Hot Five	Cornet Chop Suey	1926	2			
Armstrong, Louis, Hot Five	Hotter Than That	1927				18.
Armstrong, Louis, Hot Five	Struttin' with Some Barbecue	1927				17.
Armstrong, Louis, Hot Five	West End Blues	1928				19.
Armstrong, Louis, Hot Seven	Potato Head Blues	1927				16.
Armstrong, Louis, Hot Seven	S.O.L. Blues	1927				15.
Ashley, Tom C. and Guinn Foster	Haunted Road Blues	1931		245	II/5	
Askew, Alec	Emmaline, Take Your Time	1800s*		252	I/7	
Bakari-Badji	Field Song from Senegal	1800s		252	I/1	
Baker, Kenny	I Left My Heart at the Stage Door Canteen	1942		222	II/5	
Basie, Count and His Orchestra	Doggin' Around	1938				47.
Basie, Count and His Orchestra	Every Tub	1938		274	I/1	

*Recordings dated "1800s" are recent recordings of pre-1900 traditional music.

Artist	Title	Year		Page	Vol./No.	No.
Basie, Count and His Orchestra	Jive at Five	1939		274	II/9	48.
Basie, Count and His Orchestra	Taxi War Dance	1939				
Basie, Count and His Orchestra	Tickle-Toe	1940				49.
Basie, Count, Kansas City Seven	Lester Leaps In	1939		222	I/4	
Bayes, Nora	Over There	1917				12.
Bechet, Sidney, Blue Note Jazz Men	Blue Horizon	1944	6	274	I/4	
Berry, Chuck	What Is this Thing Called Love?	1941		249	I/6	
Bigard, Barney	Maybelle	1955		250	II/7	
Blackwell, Francis "Scrapper"	Tapioca	1940		290	II/3	
Blake, Blind	Blue Night Blues	1934		235	I/2	
Blake, Eubie	Southern Rag	1927		260	I/6	
Blake, Eubie	Baltimore Buzz; In Honeysuckle Time	1921		260	I/4	
Blake, Eubie	Bandana Days	1922		260	I/3	
Blake, Eubie	Love Will Find a Way	1921		260	I/1	
Blake, Eubie and Shuffle Along Orchestra	I'm Just Wild about Harry	1921		216	II/5	
Blake, Ran and Jeanne Lee	Laura	1961		259	I/1	
Blythe, Jimmy	Chicago Stomp	1924		259	I/2	
Blythe, Jimmy	Mr. Freddie Blues	1926		290	I/2	
Bolling, Pillie	Brownskin Woman	1930		249	II/9	
Bonds, Gary U. S.	New Orleans	1960		222	II/2	
Bonney, Betty (w. Les Brown)	He's 1-A in the Army and He's 1-A in My Heart	1941		217	II/2	
Boots and His Buddies	Blues of Avalon	1937		235	II/5	
Boyd, Bill and His Cowboy Ramblers	Barn Dance Rag	1935		269	II/8	
Bradford, Perry, Jazz Phools	I Ain't Gonna Play No Second Fiddle	1925		261	II/1	
Bradshaw, Tiny and His Orchestra	Well, Oh Well	1950		271	II/5	
Brown, Clifford and Max Roach	What Is this Thing Called Love?	1956		261	II/5	
Brown, Ruth	Mama, He Treats Your Daughter Mean	1953		290	I/5	
Buck Mountain Band	Yodeling Blues	1929		275	I/5	
Byard, Jaki	Diane's Melody	1960		275	I/4	
Byard, Jaki	II, V, I	1960		250	II/4	
Byas, Don and Slam Stewart	I Got Rhythm	1945		217	I/6	62.
Caceres, Emilio	What's the Use?	1937				
Calloway, Cab (w. Dizzy Gillespie)	Pickin' the Cabbage	1940				

133*

ARTIST, LEADER, OR GROUP	WORK	YEAR	NAJ NO.	NW NO.	SIDE/BAND	SCCJ NO.
Calloway, Cab (w. Milt Hinton)	Ebony Silhouette	1941		217	I/7	
Candy and Coco	China Boy	1934		250	I/5	
Carpenter, John Alden	Krazy Kat	1921		228	I/1	
Carter, Benny, and His Orchestra	Pardon Me, Pretty Baby	1937		274	I/5	
Carter, Betty	Can't We Be Friends?	1955		295	II/4	
Carter, Betty	Moonlight in Vermont	1955		295	II/2	
Carter, Betty	Thou Swell	1955		295	II/3	
Casa Loma Orchestra	Casa Loma Stomp	1930		217	I/2	
Chaloff, Serge	Body and Soul	1955		275	I/6	
Charles, Ray and the Raelets	I'm Movin' On	1959		249	II/7	
Chicago Loopers (Beiderbecke & Trumbauer)	Three Blind Mice	1927		274	II/3	
Chocolate Dandies (w. Benny Carter)	That's How I Feel Today	1929		256	I/4	
Chocolate Dandies (w. Eldridge & Carter)	I Can't Believe that You're in Love with Me	1940				44.
Chocolate Dandies (w. Hawkins & Carter)	Bugle Call Rag	1930		274	II/5	
Clark, Dee	At My Front Door	1960		249	II/6	
Clarke, Kenny and His 52nd Street Boys	Royal Roost	1946		284	II/6	
Clovers, The	One Mint Julep	1951		261	II/3	
Coasters, The	What About Us?	1959		249	II/8	
Cole, Nat "King"	Straighten Up and Fly Right	1943		261	I/4	
Coleman, Ornette, Double Quartet	Free Jazz [excerpt]	1960				105.
Coleman, Ornette, Quartet	Change of the Century	1959	16			
Coleman, Ornette, Quartet	Congeniality	1959				104.
Coleman, Ornette, Quartet	Lonely Woman	1959				103.
Coltrane, John	Alabama	1963				102.
Coltrane, John	Giant Steps	1959	15			
Connor, Chris	Love	1960		295	II/6	
Connor, Chris	Misty	1959		295	II/5	
Counce, Curtis (w. Hope and Land)	Into the Orbit	1958		275	I/2	
Counce, Curtis (w. Hope and Land)	Race for Space	1958		275	I/3	
Crenshaw, Rev. and Congregation	Lining Hymn and Prayer	1800s		252	II/2	
Dallas String Band	Dallas Rag	1928		235	I/1	
Dameron, Tadd and Fats Navarro	Jahbero	1948		271	II/3	76.
Dameron, Tadd, Sextet	Lady Bird	1948				

Artist	Title	Year		Page		
Dandridge, Putney (w. Chu Berry)	Chasing Shadows	1935		250	I/8	
Davenport, Cow Cow	Atlanta Rag	1929		235	I/5	
Davis, John and Group A	Carrie Belle	1800s		278	II/8	
Davis, John and Group A	Live Humble	1800s		278	I/4	
Davis, John and Group A	Read 'Em, John	1800s		278	I/7	
Davis, John and Group B	Moses	1800s		278	I/1	
Davis, John and Group B	Raggy Levy	1800s		278	II/2	
Davis, John and Group C	Beulah Land	1800s			I/8	
Davis, Miles and His Orchestra	Boplicity	1949				77.
Davis, Miles, Gil Evans Orchestra	Summertime	1958				92.
Davis, Miles, Quartet	Circle	1966	18			
Davis, Miles, Sextet	Dr. Jekyll	1958	14			
Davis, Miles, Sextet	So What	1959				99.
Davis, Rev. Gary	Maple Leaf Rag	1964		235	I/8	
Dickerson, Carroll (w. Armstrong & Hines)	Symphonic Raps	1928		256	I/2	
Dodds, Baby, Trio	Wolverine Blues	1946		274	II/6	
Dodds, Johnny, Black Bottom Stompers	Melancholy	1927		274	I/2	
Domino, Fats	I Can't Go On	1955		249	I/8	
Dudley, John	Po' Boy Blues	1800s		252	I/2	
Dunn, Johnny, Original Jazz Hounds	Bugle Blues	1921		269	II/5	
Dunn, Johnny and His Jazz Band	Dunn's Cornet Blues	1924		269	II/6	
Eckstine, Billy	Good Jelly Blues	1944		284	I/6	
Ellington, Duke	Clothed Woman, The	1947		216	I/2	
Ellington, Duke	Mood Indigo	1930		272	II/1	
Ellington, Duke and His Famous Orchestra	Blue Serge	1941				
Ellington, Duke and His Famous Orchestra	Clarinet Lament (Barney's Concerto)	1936	5			61.
Ellington, Duke and His Famous Orchestra	Concerto for Cootie	1940				58.
Ellington, Duke and His Famous Orchestra	Cotton Tail	1940				59.
Ellington, Duke and His Famous Orchestra	Creole Rhapsody	1931				55.
Ellington, Duke and His Famous Orchestra	Diminuendo and Crescendo in Blue	1937				54.
Ellington, Duke and His Famous Orchestra	In a Mellotone	1940				60.
Ellington, Duke and His Famous Orchestra	Ko-Ko	1940				57.
Ellington, Duke and His Famous Orchestra	New East St. Louis Toodle-O, The	1937				53.
Ellington, Duke and His Orchestra	East St. Louis Toodle-Oo	1927				52.

ARTIST, LEADER, OR GROUP	WORK	YEAR	NAJ NO.	NW NO.	SIDE/BAND	SCC/ NO.
Ellington, Duke and His Orchestra	Harlem Air Shaft	1940		274	II/8	56.
Ellington, Duke and Jimmy Blanton	Pitter Panther Patter	1940		260	II/5	
Europe, James Reese (w. Noble Sissle)	How Ya' Gonna Keep 'Em Down on the Farm	1919				
Europe, James Reese (w. Noble Sissle)	Mirandy	1919		260	II/4	
Europe, James Reese (w. Noble Sissle)	On Patrol in No Man's Land	1919		260	II/6	
Europe, James Reese, Hell Fighters	Clarinet Marmalade	1919		269	I/4	
Europe, James Reese, Hell Fighters	Memphis Blues	1919		269	I/3	
Europe, James Reese, Society Orchestra	Castle House Rag	1914		269	I/1	
Europe, James Reese, Society Orchestra	Castle Walk	1914		269	I/2	100.
Evans, Bill, Trio	Blue in Green	1959				
Fairfield Four, The	Tree of Level [Tree of Lebanon]	1950		224	I/4	
Famous Blue Jay Singers, The	Canaan Land	1947		224	I/2	
Farmer, Art and Benny Golson	Blues March	1960		242	II/1	
Fitzgerald, Ella	Robbins Nest	1947		295	I/7	38.
Fitzgerald, Ella	You'd Be so Nice to Come Home to	1964				
Five Breezes, The	My Buddy Blues	1940		290	II/8	
Flatt, Lester and Earl Scruggs	Randy Lynn Rag	1960s		235	II/8	
Floyd, Troy, Plaza Hotel Orchestra	Dreamland Blues Part I	1929		256	II/4	
Floyd, Troy, Plaza Hotel Orchestra	Dreamland Blues Part II	1929		256	II/5	
Ford, Ricky	Aerolinos	1977		204	II/3	
Ford, Ricky	Blues Peru	1977		204	I/3	
Ford, Ricky	Dexter	1977		204	I/4	
Ford, Ricky	Loxodonta Africana	1977		204	I/1	
Ford, Ricky	My Romance	1977		204	II/1	
Ford, Ricky	One Up One Down	1977		204	II/2	
Ford, Ricky	Ucil	1977		204	I/2	
Forrest, City Joe	You Gotta Cut that Out	1800s		252	II/8	
Forrest, Helen	My Guy's Come Back	1946		222	II/9	
Fuller, Blind Boy	Piccolo Rag	1938		235	I/4	
Gant, Cecil	I Wonder	1945		261	I/5	
Garner, Erroll	Fantasy on Frankie and Johnny	1947				
Gary, Leroy	Mama Lucy	1800s		252	I/9	
Gershwin, George	Someone to Watch Over Me	1926		272	I/5	72.

ARTIST, LEADER, OR GROUP	WORK	YEAR	NAJ NO.	NW NO.	SIDE/BAND	SCCJ NO.
Holiday, Billie	End of a Love Affair, The	1958		295	II/8	
Holiday, Billie	I Can't Get Started	1938		295	I/1	
Holiday, Billie and Eddie Heywood	All of Me	1941				36.
Holiday, Billie and Her Orchestra	He's Funny That Way	1937				35.
Holiday, Billie and Her Orchestra	These Foolish Things	1952				37.
Holly, Buddy and the Crickets	That'll Be the Day	1957		249	II/2	
Holman, Libby	Moanin' Low	1929		215	I/7	
Hopkins, Lightnin'	Hello, Central	1950		261	II/2	
Howard, Bob (w. Teddy Bunn)	Beale Street Mama	1938		250	II/6	
Hudson, Hattie	Doggone My Good Luck	1927		290	I/6	
Hunter, Lloyd, Serenaders	Sensational Mood	1931		217	II/3	
Hyman, Dick and His Dance Orchestra	Chinatown, My Chinatown	1920a†		293	II/3	13.
Hyman, Dick and His Dance Orchestra	Kansas City Blues	1920a		293	II/5	
Hyman, Dick and His Dance Orchestra	Ma Ragtime Baby	1920a		293	II/2	
Hyman, Dick and His Dance Orchestra	Sweet Man	1920a		293	II/6	
Hyman, Dick and His Dance Orchestra	Waltzing the Blues	1920a		293	II/6	
Jazz Messengers	Nica's Dream	1956		242	I/3	
Johnson Boys, The	Violin Blues	1928		290	I/3	
Johnson, Bunk	Entertainer, The	1947		235	I/7	
Johnson, Charlie, Paradise Orchestra	Boy in the Boat, The	1928		256	I/3	
Johnson, James P.	Carolina Shout	1921			I/3	
Johnson, James P.	What Is this Thing Called Love?	1930		274	I/3	
Johnson, Pete	Blues on the Downbeat	1940		259	II/6	
Johnson, Pete	Climbin' and Screamin'	1939		259	II/5	
Johnson, Pete	Kaycee on My Mind	1940		259	II/7	
Johnson, Robert	Hellhound on My Trail	1937				
Johnson, Robert	I Believe I'll Dust My Broom	1936	1			3.
Jolson, Al	Hello Central! Give Me No Man's Land	1918		222	I/5	
Jolson, Al	I've Got My Captain Working for Me	1919		222	I/7	
Jolson, Al	Mr. Radio Man (Tell My Mammy)	1924		233	II/2	
Jones, Bessie	Beggin' the Blues	1800s		252	II/5	
Jones, Bessie and Group A	Buzzard Lope, The	1800s		278	II/1	

†The group dated "1920a" are recent recordings of 1920s dances.

Artist	Title	Year	Page	Vol/Track
Jones, Bessie and Group A	O Death	1800s	278	I/6
Jones, Bessie and Group B	Sheep, Sheep, Don't You Know	1800s	278	I/3
Jones, Bessie and Group C	Reg'lar, Reg'lar, Rollin' Under	1800s	278	II/6
Jones, Bessie and Group C	See Aunt Dinah	1800s	278	II/4
Jones, Bessie and Group C	Titanic, The	1800s	278	II/10
Jones, Spike	Der Fuehrer's Face	1942	222	II/1
Joplin, Scott	Maple Leaf Rag	1916	261	I/6
Jordan, Louis	Choo Choo Ch'Boogie	1946	216	II/1
Kenton, Stan	Egdon Heath	1954	216	I/4
Kenton, Stan	Mirage	1950	269	I/6
Keppard, Freddie, Jazz Cardinals	Stock Yard Strut	1926	224	I/1
Kings of Harmony, The	God Shall Wipe All Tears Away	1946	250	II/9
Kirby, John	Bugler's Dilemma	1941	217	I/3
Kirk, Andy (w. Mary Lou Williams)	Dallas Blues	1930	242	I/2
Konitz, Lee and Warne Marsh	Donna Lee	1955		
Konitz, Lee and Warne Marsh, Sextet	Marshmallow	1949		
Krupa, Gene and His Orchestra	Rockin' Chair	1941		
Kyser, Kay	Praise the Lord and Pass the Ammunition	1942	222	II/8
Lacy, Steve	Introspection	1960	275	II/2
Lacy, Steve	Louise	1960	275	II/1
Lawrence, Elliot	Elevation	1949	284	I/4
Lawrence, Elliot	Five O'Clock Shadow	1946	284	I/5
Lee, George E., Kansas City Orchestra	Ruff Stuffing	1929	256	II/6
Leonard, Harlan	A-La-Bridges	1940	284	I/1
Leonard, Harlan	Dameron Stomp	1940	284	I/2
Lewis, Jerry Lee	Good Golly Miss Molly	1962	249	II/3
Lewis, John	Piazza Navona	1960	216	II/4
Lewis, Meade "Lux"	Honky Tonk Train	1935	259	I/6
Lewis, Meade "Lux"	Honky Tonk Train Blues	1937		
Lewis, Meade "Lux"	Mr. Freddie Blues	1936	259	I/8
Lewis, Meade "Lux"	Yancey Special	1936	259	I/7
Lincoln, Abbey	When Malindy Sings	1961	295	II/7
Little Richard	Every Hour	1951	249	I/9
Little, Booker, Sextet	Strength and Sanity	1961	275	II/4
Little, Booker, Sextet	We Speak	1961	275	II/3
Long, Johnny (w. Patti Dugan)	No Love, No Nothin'	1943	222	II/7

ARTIST, LEADER, OR GROUP	WORK	YEAR	NAJ NO.	NW NO.	SIDE/BAND	SCCJ NO.
Louisiana Sugar Babes	Willow Tree	1928		256	I/7	41.
Lunceford, Jimmy and His Orchestra	Lunceford Special	1939				42.
Lunceford, Jimmy and His Orchestra	Organ Grinder's Swing	1936				
Marmarosa, Dodo	Mellow Mood	1946		284	II/5	
Marsala, Joe	Clarinet Marmalade	1937		250	II/5	
Marsalis, Wynton	Delfeayo's Dilemma	1986	20			
McClennan, Tommy	Deep Blue Sea Blues	1941		290	II/6	
McDowell, Fred	Death Comes A-Creepin' in My Room	1800s		252	II/3	
McDowell, Fred and Miles Pratcher	Old Original Blues	1800s		252	I/5	
McDowell, Fred and Pratcher and Davis	Goin' Down to the Races	1800s		252	II/7	
McTell, Blind Willie	Kill It Kid	1949		235	I/6	
Miller, Flournoy and Aubrey Lyles	The Fight (dialogue)	1924		260	II/2	
Miller, Leroy and Prisoners	Berta, Berta	1800s		252	I/4	
Mills Blue Rhythm Band	Jammin' for the Jackpot	1937		217	I/8	
Mingus, Charles	Eclipse	1953		216	I/5	
Mingus, Charles	Original Faubus Fables	1960		242	II/4	
Mingus, Charles and His Orchestra	Hora Decubitus	1963				94.
Mingus, Charles, Quintet	Haitian Fight Song	1957				93.
Modern Jazz Quartet	Django	1960				95.
Modern Jazz Quartet	Woody'n You	1956		242	I/1	
Monarch Jazz Quartet of Norfolk	What's the Matter Now?	1929		290	I/4	
Monk, Thelonious	Bag's Groove	1954				89.
Monk, Thelonious	I Should Care	1957				90.
Monk, Thelonious	Misterioso	1948		271	II/4	85.
Monk, Thelonious, Quartet	Bemsha Swing	1964	17			
Monk, Thelonious, Quartet	Evidence	1948				86.
Monk, Thelonious, Quintet	Criss-Cross	1951				87.
Monk, Thelonious, Quintet	Smoke Gets in Your Eyes	1954				88.
Montgomery, J. Neal and Orchestra	Atlanta Low Down	1929		217	II/5	
Montgomery, J. Neal and Orchestra	Auburn Avenue Stomp	1929		217	II/6	
Montgomery, Wes, Quartet	West Coast Blues [abridged]	1960				98.
Mooney, Joe	I Can't Get Up the Nerve	1947		284	II/4	
Mooney, Joe	Tea for Two	1946		284	II/3	
Moore, Grant and the Black Devils	Original Dixieland One-Step	1931		217	II/4	

Morgan, Sam, Jazz Band	Bogulousa Strut	1927		269	II/1	10.
Morgan, Sam, Jazz Band	Steppin' on the Gas	1927		269	II/2	2.
Morrison, Henry and Group A	Ain't I Right	1800s		278	II/3	7.
Morrison, Henry and Group B	Laz'rus	1800s		278	II/9	8.
Morton, Jelly Roll	King Porter Stomp	1939				9.
Morton, Jelly Roll	Maple Leaf Rag	1938				29.
Morton, Jelly Roll, Red Hot Peppers	Black Bottom Stomp	1926				
Morton, Jelly Roll, Red Hot Peppers	Dead Man Blues	1926				
Morton, Jelly Roll, Red Hot Peppers	Grandpa's Spells	1926				
Moten, Bennie, Kansas City Orchestra	Moten Swing	1932		217	II/1	
Moten, Bennie, Kansas City Orchestra	Toby	1932				
Mulligan, Gerry, with Lee Konitz	I Can't Believe that You're in Love with Me	1953	11			
New Brown Chapel, Memphis, Congregation	Church-House Moan	1800s		252	II/4	28.
New Orleans Rhythm Kings	She's Cryin' for Me	1925		269	II/4	
Nichols, Herbie	'S Wonderful	1952		275	I/1	
Nichols, Red and His Five Pennies	Dinah	1929				
Nichols, Red and Miff Mole's Stompers	Slippin' Around	1927		274	II/7	25.
Noone, Jimmy, Apex Club Orchestra	Four or Five Times	1928		274	I/6	
Noone, Jimmy, Apex Club Orchestra	I Know that You Know	1928		250	I/7	
Norvo, Red	I Got Rhythm	1936		271	I/1	
Norvo, Red (w. Parker and Gillespie)	Congo Blues	1945				
Norvo, Red and Stan Getz	Body and Soul [excerpt]	1947		290	I/8	80.
O'Connor, George	Nigger Blues	1916	10			
Oliver, King, Creole Jazz Band	Dippermouth Blues	1923		269	I/7	6.
Ory, Edward "Kid," Sunshine Orchestra	Ory's Creole Trombone	1922		269	I/8	
Ory, Edward "Kid," Sunshine Orchestra	Society Blues	1922		256	II/2	
Page, Walter, Blue Devils	Blue Devil Blues	1929		256	II/3	
Page, Walter, Blue Devils	There's a Squabblin'	1929				
Parker, Charlie	Confirmation	1953		271	I/7	68.
Parker, Charlie	Embraceable You	1947		271	I/8	65.
Parker, Charlie	KoKo	1945		271	I/4	71.
Parker, Charlie	Parker's Mood	1948		271	I/6	66.
Parker, Charlie	Relaxin' at Camarillo	1947				67.
Parker, Charlie, Jazz at the Philharmonic	Lady, Be Good	1946				
Parker, Charlie, Quintet	Embraceable You (take #1) excerpt	1947				

141*

ARTIST, LEADER, OR GROUP	WORK	YEAR	NAJ NO.	NW NO.	SIDE/BAND	SCC/NO.
Parker, Charlie, Quintet	Klactoveedsedstene	1947				69.
Parker, Charlie, Sextet	Little Benny (Crazeology) [1 & 4]	1947				70.
Peerless Quartet	My Dream of the Big Parade	1926		222	I/8	
Piron, Armand J., New Orleans Orchestra	West Indies Blues	1923		269	II/3	
Poplin, China	Sumter Rag/Steel Guitar Rag	1962		235	II/6	
Powell, Bud	Un Poco Loco	1951		271	II/2	
Powell, Bud, Trio	Night in Tunisia	1951				73.
Powell, Bud, Trio	Somebody Loves Me	1947				74.
Powell, John	Rhapsody N'egre	1918		228	II/2	
Pratcher, Miles and Bob Pratcher	Buttermilk	1800s		252	I/8	
Pratcher, Miles and Bob Pratcher	I'm Gonna Live Anyhow Until I Die	1800s		252	I/10	
Price, Lloyd	Mailman Blues	1958		249	I/7	
Prima, Louis (w. Pee Wee Russell)	In a Little Gypsy Tearoom	1935		250	II/1	
Proctor, Willis and Group A	Daniel	1800s		278	I/5	
Proctor, Willis and Group A	Walk, Billy Abbot	1800s		278	II/5	
Quillian, Rufus and Ben Quillian	Keep it Clean	1930		290	II/2	46.
Quintet of the Hot Club of France	Dinah	1934				
Rachell, Yank and Sonny Boy Williamson	Peach Tree Blues	1941		290	I/1	
Ratcliff, Henry	Louisiana	1800s		252	I/1	
Ravens, The	Give Me a Simple Prayer	1956		261	I/9	11.
Red Onion Jazz Babies (w. Armstrong & Bechet)	Cake Walking Babies from Home	1924				
Reisman, Leo (w. Bubber Miley)	What Is This Thing Called Love?	1930		256	I/8	
Roberta Martin Singers, The	Yield Not to Temptation	1947		224	I/5	
Robertson, Dick	Goodbye, Mama	1941		222	II/6	
Robertson, Dick	We Did It Before and We Can Do It Again	1941		222	II/4	
Robinson, Bill "Bojangles" (w. D. Redman)	Doin' the New Low-Down	1932		215	I/6	
Roland, Walter	House Lady Blues	1933		290	II/4	
Rollini, Adrian	Bugle Call Rag	1937		250	II/2	
Rollins, Sonny	Now's the Time	1964		242	II/2	

Artist	Title	Year		Page	Side	
Rollins, Sonny, Plus Four	Pent-Up House [abridged]	1956		295	I/2	96.
Rollins, Sonny, Quartet	Blue 7	1956				97.
Rushing, Jimmy (w. Count Basie)	I Left My Baby	1939				
Russell, George	All About Rosie (Third Movement)	1957	13			
Russell, George	Concerto for Billy the Kid	1956		216	II/2	
	War Gewesen	1960		242	II/3	
Saunders, Gertrude	Daddy, Won't You Please Come Home	1921		260	I/5	
	I'm Craving for That Kind of Love	1921		260	II/1	
Schuller, Gunther	Transformation	1957		216	II/3	
Shannon Four	There's a Vacant Chair in Every Home Tonight	1918		222	I/6	
Shirelles, The	I Met Him on a Sunday	1958		249	II/5	
Silhouettes, The	Get a Job	1957		249	II/1	
Silver, Horace	Stop Time	1954		271	II/6	
Silver, Horace, Quintet	Moon Rays	1958				
Silver, Horace, Quintet	Preacher, The	1955				
Sissle, Noble and Orchestra	Gee, I'm Glad That I'm From Dixie	1920	12	260	II/3	91.
Sissle, Noble and Sizzling Syncopators	Baltimore Buzz	1921		260	II/7	
Sissle, Noble and Sizzling Syncopators	In Honeysuckle Time	1921		260	I/2	
Six Brown Brothers	Down Home Rag	1915		269	I/5	
Smith, Bessie	Lost Your Head Blues	1926				5.
Smith, Bessie	St. Louis Blues	1925				4.
Smith, Clara	Let's Get Loose	1929		290	I/7	
Smith, Clarence "Pinetop"	Jump Steady Blues	1929		259	I/5	
Smith, Clarence "Pinetop"	Pinetop's Boogie Woogie	1928		259	I/4	
Smith, Jabbo and His Rhythm Aces	Sweet and Low Blues	1929		256	I/5	
Smith, Jabbo and His Rhythm Aces	Till Times Get Better	1929		256	I/6	
Smith, Stuff (w. Jonah Jones)	Knock, Knock	1936		250	I/9	
Smith, Willie Me Ford	Give Me Wings	1950s		224	I/7	
Soul Stirrers, The	Walk Around	1944		224	I/3	
Sousa Band, The John Philip	Creole Belles	1912		282	I/2	
Sousa Band, The John Philip	Trombone Sneeze	1902		282	I/7	
South, Eddie	Hejre Kati	1931		250	I/3	

ARTIST, LEADER, OR GROUP	WORK	YEAR	NAJ NO.	NW NO.	SIDE/BAND	SCC/ NO.
Spooney Five	Chinese Rag	1929		235	II/4	
Stone, Jesse, Blues Serenaders	Starvation Blues	1927		256	II/1	
Stuart, Herbert	When the Lusitania Went Down	1915		222	I/1	
Tangle Eye	Katie Left Memphis	1800s		252	I/3	
Tangle Eye	No More, My Lord	1800s		252	II/1	
Tanner, Gid and His Skillet Lickers	Hawkins Rag	1934		235	II/2	
Tarlton, Jimmie	Mexican Rag	1930		235	II/1	
Tate, Erskine (w. Louis Armstrong)	Static Strut	1926		256	I/1	
Tatum, Art	Tiger Rag	1933	4			40.
Tatum, Art	Too Marvelous for Words	1955				39.
Tatum, Art	Willow Weep for Me	1949				
Taylor, Cecil	Holiday en Masque	1978		201	II/1	
Taylor, Cecil	Idut	1978		201	I/1	
Taylor, Cecil	Serdab	1978		201	I/2	101.
Taylor, Cecil, Unit	Enter Evening	1966				
Tharpe, Rosetta and Katie Bell Nubin	Daniel in the Lion's Den	1949		224	I/6	
Thomas, Hersal	Suitcase Blues	1925		259	I/3	
Thornhill, Claude	Donna Lee	1947		284	I/8	
Thornton, Willie Mae "Big Mama"	Hound Dog	1952		261	II/4	
Til, Sonny and the Orioles	Crying in the Chapel	1953		261	II/6	
Travis, Merle	Cannon Ball Rag/Bugle Call Rag	1960s		235	II/7	
Trent, Alphonso and His Orchestra	After You've Gone	1930		256	II/8	
Trent, Alphonso and His Orchestra	Black and Blue Rhapsody	1928		256	II/7	
Trent, Alphonso and His Orchestra	I've Found a New Baby	1933		256	II/9	
Tristano, Lennie	Yesterdays	1949		216	I/3	
Tristano, Lennie, Quintet	Crosscurrent	1949				79.
Tristano, Lennie, Quintet	Subconscious Lee	1949	3			78.
Trumbauer, Frankie and His Orchestra	Ostrich Walk	1927				24.
Trumbauer, Frankie and His Orchestra	Riverboat Shuffle	1927				23.
Trumbauer, Frankie and His Orchestra	Singin' the Blues	1927				
Turner, Joe	Careless Love	1940		295	I/4	
Turner, Joe	Piney Brown Blues	1940		295	I/3	
Turner, Joe	Shake, Rattle and Roll	1954		249	I/1	
Turner, Joe and Pete Johnson	Roll 'Em Pete	1938		261	I/2	
Tyus, Charles and Effie Tyus	Dad's Ole Mule	1931		290	II/1	
Underwood, Sugar	Dew Drop Alley	1927		235	I/3	

Norton Anthology of Jazz

NAJ	ARTIST, LEADER, OR GROUP	WORK	DATE
1	Robert Johnson	*I Believe I'll Dust My Broom*	1936
2	Louis Armstrong and His Hot Five	*Cornet Chop Suey*	1926
3	Frankie Trumbauer and His Orchestra	*Ostrich Walk*	1927
4	Art Tatum	*Tiger Rag*	1933
5	Duke Ellington and His Famous Orchestra	*Clarinet Lament (Barney's Concerto)*	1936
6	Count Basie and His Orchestra	*Tickle-Toe*	1940
7	Benny Goodman and His Orchestra	*Mission to Moscow*	1942
8	Dizzy Gillespie Orchestra (Septet)	*Groovin' High*	1945
9	Lee Konitz and Warne Marsh (Sextet)	*Marshmallow*	1949
10	Charlie Parker Quartet	*Confirmation*	1953
11	Gerry Mulligan Quartet with Lee Konitz	*I Can't Believe that You're in Love with Me*	1953
12	Horace Silver Quintet	*The Preacher*	1955
13	George Russell (Brandeis Festival Orchestra)	*All About Rosie (Third Movement)*	1957
14	Miles Davis Sextet	*Dr. Jekyll*	1958
15	John Coltrane Quartet	*Giant Steps*	1959
16	Ornette Coleman Quartet	*Change of the Century*	1959
17	Thelonious Monk Quartet	*Bemsha Swing*	1964
18	Miles Davis Quintet	*Circle*	1966
19	Weather Report	*Tears*	1971
20	Wynton Marsalis Quartet	*Delfeayo's Dilemma*	1986

Smithsonian Collections of Classic Jazz

(Alphabetical Order and Locator Numbers)

SCCJ NO.	ARTIST, LEADER, OR GROUP	WORK
20	Armstrong, Louis and Earl Hines	*Weather Bird*
22	Armstrong, Louis and His Orchestra	*I Gotta Right to Sing the Blues*
21	Armstrong, Louis and His Orchestra	*Sweethearts on Parade*
14	Armstrong, Louis, Hot Five	*Big Butter and Egg Man*
18	Armstrong, Louis, Hot Five	*Hotter than That*
17	Armstrong, Louis, Hot Five	*Struttin' with Some Barbecue*
19	Armstrong, Louis, Hot Five	*West End Blues*
16	Armstrong, Louis, Hot Seven	*Potato Head Blues*
15	Armstrong, Louis, Hot Seven	*S.O.L. Blues*
47	Basie, Count and His Orchestra	*Doggin' Around*
48	Basie, Count and His Orchestra	*Taxi War Dance*
49	Basie, Count, Kansas City Seven	*Lester Leaps In*
12	Bechet, Sidney, Blue Note Jazz Men	*Blue Horizon*
62	Byas, Don and Slam Stewart	*I Got Rhythm*
44	Chocolate Dandies (w. Eldridge & Carter)	*I Can't Believe that You're in Love with Me*
105	Coleman, Ornette, Double Quartet	*Free Jazz* [*excerpt*]
104	Coleman, Ornette, Quartet	*Congeniality*
103	Coleman, Ornette, Quartet	*Lonely Woman*
102	Coltrane, John	*Alabama*
76	Dameron, Tadd, Sextet	*Lady Bird*
77	Davis, Miles and His Orchestra	*Boplicity*
92	Davis, Miles, Gil Evans Orchestra	*Summertime*
99	Davis, Miles, Sextet	*So What*
61	Ellington, Duke and His Famous Orchestra	*Blue Serge*
58	Ellington, Duke and His Famous Orchestra	*Concerto for Cootie*
59	Ellington, Duke and His Famous Orchestra	*Cotton Tail*
55	Ellington, Duke and His Famous Orchestra	*Creole Rhapsody*
54	Ellington, Duke and His Famous Orchestra	*Diminuendo and Crescendo in Blue*
60	Ellington, Duke and His Famous Orchestra	*In a Mellotone*
57	Ellington, Duke and His Famous Orchestra	*Ko-Ko*
53	Ellington, Duke and His Famous Orchestra	*The New East St. Louis Toodle-O*
52	Ellington, Duke and His Orchestra	*East St. Louis Toodle-Oo*
56	Ellington, Duke and His Orchestra	*Harlem Air Shaft*
100	Evans, Bill, Trio	*Blue in Green*
38	Fitzgerald, Ella	*You'd Be so Nice to Come Home to*

SCCJ NO.	ARTIST, LEADER, OR GROUP	WORK
72	Garner, Erroll	*Fantasy on Frankie and Johnny*
64	Gillespie, Dizzy, All Star Quintette	*Shaw 'Nuff*
63	Gillespie, Dizzy, Sextet	*I Can't Get Started*
51	Goodman, Benny (w. Christian & Basie)	*Breakfast Feud* [*composite*]
50	Goodman, Benny (w. Christian & Basie)	*I Found a New Baby*
32	Goodman, Benny, Trio	*Body and Soul*
75	Gordon, Dexter, Quartet	*Bikini*
45	Hampton, Lionel and His Orchestra	*When Lights Are Low*
33	Hawkins, Coleman and His Orchestra	*Body and Soul*
34	Hawkins, Coleman, Quartet	*The Man I Love*
26	Henderson, Fletcher and His Orchestra	*The Stampede*
27	Henderson, Fletcher and His Orchestra	*Wrappin' It Up*
36	Holiday, Billie and Eddie Heywood	*All of Me*
35	Holiday, Billie and Her Orchestra	*He's Funny That Way*
37	Holiday, Billie and Her Orchestra	*These Foolish Things*
13	Johnson, James P.	*Carolina Shout*
3	Johnson, Robert	*Hellhound on My Trail*
1	Joplin, Scott	*Maple Leaf Rag*
43	Krupa, Gene and His Orchestra	*Rockin' Chair*
31	Lewis, Meade "Lux"	*Honky Tonk Train Blues*
41	Lunceford, Jimmie and His Orchestra	*Lunceford Special*
42	Lunceford, Jimmie and His Orchestra	*Organ Grinder's Swing*
94	Mingus, Charles and His Orchestra	*Hora Decubitus*
93	Mingus, Charles, Quintet	*Haitian Fight Song*
95	Modern Jazz Quartet	*Django*
89	Monk, Thelonious	*Bag's Groove*
90	Monk, Thelonious	*I Should Care*
85	Monk, Thelonious	*Misterioso*
86	Monk, Thelonious, Quartet	*Evidence*
87	Monk, Thelonious, Quintet	*Criss-Cross*
88	Monk, Thelonious, Quintet	*Smoke Gets in Your Eyes*
98	Montgomery, Wes, Quartet	*West Coast Blues* [*abridged*]
10	Morton, Jelly Roll	*King Porter Stomp*
2	Morton, Jelly Roll	*Maple Leaf Rag*
7	Morton, Jelly Roll, Red Hot Peppers	*Black Bottom Stomp*
8	Morton, Jelly Roll, Red Hot Peppers	*Dead Man Blues*
9	Morton, Jelly Roll, Red Hot Peppers	*Grandpa's Spells*
29	Moten, Bennie, Kansas City Orchestra	*Moten Swing*
28	Nichols, Red and His Five Pennies	*Dinah*

SCCJ NO.	ARTIST, LEADER, OR GROUP	WORK
25	Noone, Jimmie, Apex Club Orchestra	*Four or Five Times*
80	Norvo, Red and Stan Getz	*Body and Soul* [*excerpt*]
6	Oliver, King, Creole Jazz Band	*Dippermouth Blues*
71	Parker, Charlie, All Stars	*Parker's Mood*
66	Parker, Charlie, Jazz At The Philharmonic	*Lady, Be Good*
67	Parker, Charlie, Quintet	*Embraceable You (take #1) excerpt*
68	Parker, Charlie, Quintet	*Embraceable You (take #2) excerpt*
69	Parker, Charlie, Quintet	*Klactoveedsedstene*
65	Parker, Charlie, Re-Boppers	*KoKo*
70	Parker, Charlie, Sextet	*Little Benny (Crazeology* [*1 & 4*]*)*
73	Powell, Bud, Trio	*Night in Tunisia*
74	Powell, Bud, Trio	*Sombody Loves Me*
46	Quintet of the Hot Club of France	*Dinah*
11	Red Onion Jazz Babies	*Cake Walking Babies from Home*
96	Rollins, Sonny, Plus Four	*Pent-Up House* [*abridged*]
97	Rollins, Sonny, Quartet	*Blue 7*
91	Silver, Horace, Quintet	*Moon Rays*
5	Smith, Bessie	*Lost Your Head Blues*
4	Smith, Bessie	*St. Louis Blues*
40	Tatum, Art	*Too Marvelous for Words*
39	Tatum, Art	*Willow Weep for Me*
101	Taylor, Cecil, Unit	*Enter Evening*
79	Tristano, Lennie, Quintet	*Crosscurrent*
78	Tristano, Lennie, Quintet	*Subconscious Lee*
24	Trumbauer, Frankie and His Orchestra	*Riverboat Shuffle*
23	Trumbauer, Frankie and His Orchestra	*Singin' the Blues*
84	Vaughan, Sarah	*Ain't No Use*
81	Vaughan, Sarah	*All Alone*
83	Vaughan, Sarah	*Dancing in the Dark*
82	Vaughan, Sarah	*My Funny Valentine*
30	Waller, Fats	*I Ain't Got Nobody (1927)*
30a	Waller, Fats	*I Ain't Got Nobody (1937)*
106	World Saxophone Quartet	*Steppin'*

Smithsonian Collections of Classic Jazz

(Series Order and Locator Numbers)

SCCJ NO.	ARTIST, LEADER, OR GROUP	WORK	SCCJ	SCCJ REV., LP	SCCJ REV., CASS.	SCCJ REV., CD
1	Joplin, Scott	Maple Leaf Rag	I/1	I/1	A/1	I/1
2	Morton, Jelly Roll	Maple Leaf Rag	I/2	I/2	A/2	I/2
3	Johnson, Robert	Hellhound on My Trail	I/3	—	—	—
4	Smith, Bessie	St. Louis Blues	I/4	I/3	A/3	I/3
5	Smith, Bessie	Lost Your Head Blues	I/5	I/4	A/4	I/4
6	Oliver, King, Creole Jazz Band	Dippermouth Blues	I/6 (OKeh)	I/5 (Gen.)	A/5 (Gen.)	I/5 (Gen.)
7	Morton, Jelly Roll, Red Hot Peppers	Black Bottom Stomp	II/1	I/6	A/6	I/6
8	Morton, Jelly Roll, Red Hot Peppers	Dead Man Blues	I/8	I/7	A/7	I/7
9	Morton, Jelly Roll, Red Hot Peppers	Grandpa's Spells	I/7	I/8	A/8	I/8
10	Morton, Jelly Roll	King Porter Stomp	—	I/9	A/9	I/9
11	Red Onion Jazz Babies	Cake Walking Babies from Home	II/2	II/1	A/10	I/10
12	Bechet, Sidney, Blue Note Jazz Men	Blue Horizon	II/3	II/2	A/11	I/11
13	Johnson, James P.	Carolina Shout	II/4	II/3	A/12	I/12
14	Armstrong, Louis, Hot Five	Big Butter and Egg Man	—	II/4	A/13	I/13
15	Armstrong, Louis, Hot Seven	S.O.L. Blues	II/6	—	—	—
16	Armstrong, Louis, Hot Seven	Potato Head Blues	II/7	II/5	B/1	I/14
17	Armstrong, Louis, Hot Five	Struttin' with Some Barbecue	II/5	II/6	B/2	I/15
18	Armstrong, Louis, Hot Five	Hotter than That	II/8	II/7	B/3	I/16
19	Armstrong, Louis, Hot Five	West End Blues	II/9	II/8	B/4	I/17
20	Armstrong, Louis and Earl Hines	Weather Bird	III/1	III/1	B/5	I/18
21	Armstrong, Louis and His Orchestra	Sweethearts on Parade	III/2	III/2	B/6	I/19
22	Armstrong, Louis and His Orchestra	I Gotta Right to Sing the Blues	III/3	III/3	B/7	I/20
23	Trumbauer, Frankie and His Orchestra	Singin' the Blues	III/5	III/4	B/8	I/21
24	Trumbauer, Frankie and His Orchestra	Riverboat Shuffle	III/4	III/5	B/9	I/22

No.	Performer	Title				
25	Noone, Jimmie, Apex Club Orchestra	*Four or Five Times*	—	III/6	B/10	I/23
26	Henderson, Fletcher and His Orchestra	*The Stampede*	III/6	III/7	B/11	II/1
27	Henderson, Fletcher and His Orchestra	*Wrappin' It Up*	III/7	III/8	B/12	II/2
28	Nichols, Red and His Five Pennies	*Dinah*	—	III/9	C/1	II/3
29	Moten, Bennie, Kansas City Orchestra	*Moten Swing*	III/8	IV/1	C/2	II/4
30	Waller, Fats	*I Ain't Got Nobody (1927)*	IV/1	—	—	—
30a	Waller, Fats	*I Ain't Got Nobody (1937)*	—	IV/2	C/3	II/5
31	Lewis, Meade "Lux"	*Honky Tonk Train Blues*	IV/2	IV/3	C/4	II/6
32	Goodman, Benny, Trio	*Body and Soul*	IV/3	IV/4	C/5	II/7
33	Hawkins, Coleman and His Orchestra	*Body and Soul*	IV/4	IV/5	C/6	II/8
34	Hawkins, Coleman, Quartet	*The Man I Love*	IV/5	IV/6	C/7	II/9
35	Holiday, Billie and Her Orchestra	*He's Funny That Way*	IV/6	IV/7	C/8	II/10
36	Holiday, Billie and Eddie Heywood	*All of Me*	IV/7	—	—	II/11
37	Holiday, Billie and Her Orchestra	*These Foolish Things*	—	IV/8	C/9	II/12
38	Fitzgerald, Ella	*You'd Be so Nice to Come Home to*	IV/8	V/1	C/10	II/13
39	Tatum, Art	*Willow Weep for Me*	V/1	V/2	C/11	II/14
40	Tatum, Art	*Too Marvelous for Words*	V/2	V/3	C/12	—
41	Lunceford, Jimmie and His Orchestra	*Lunceford Special*	V/3	—	—	II/15
42	Lunceford, Jimmie and His Orchestra	*Organ Grinder's Swing*	—	V/4	C/13	II/16
43	Krupa, Gene and His Orchestra	*Rockin' Chair*	V/4	V/5	D/1	II/17
44	Chocolate Dandies (w. Eldridge & Carter)	*I Can't Believe that You're in Love with Me*	V/5	V/6	D/2	II/18
45	Hampton, Lionel and His Orchestra	*When Lights Are Low*	V/6	V/7	D/3	II/19
46	Quintet of the Hot Club of France	*Dinah*	—	V/8	D/4	II/20
47	Basie, Count and His Orchestra	*Doggin' Around*	V/7	V/9	D/5	II/21
48	Basie, Count and His Orchestra	*Taxi War Dance*	V/8	VI/1	D/6	II/22
49	Basie, Count, Kansas City Seven	*Lester Leaps In*	VI/1	VI/2	D/7	II/23
50	Goodman, Benny (w. Christian & Basie)	*I Found a New Baby*	VI/2	VI/3	D/8	II/24
51	Goodman, Benny (w. Christian & Basie)	*Breakfast Feud* [composite]	VI/3	VI/4	D/9	

SCCJ NO.	ARTIST, LEADER, OR GROUP	WORK	SCCJ	SCCJ REV., LP	SCCJ REV., CASS.	SCCJ REV., CD
52	Ellington, Duke and His Orchestra	East St. Louis Toodle-Oo	VI/4	VI/5	D/10	III/1
53	Ellington, Duke and His Famous Orchestra	The New East St. Louis Toodle-O	VI/5	VI/6	D/11	III/2
54	Ellington, Duke and His Famous Orchestra	Diminuendo and Crescendo in Blue	—	VI/7	D/12	III/3
55	Ellington, Duke and His Famous Orchestra	Creole Rhapsody	VI/6	—	—	—
56	Ellington, Duke and His Famous Orchestra	Harlem Air Shaft	VI/7	—	—	—
57	Ellington, Duke and His Famous Orchestra	Ko-Ko	VII/2	VI/8	D/13	III/4
58	Ellington, Duke and His Famous Orchestra	Concerto for Cootie	VI/8	VII/1	E/1	III/5
59	Ellington, Duke and His Famous Orchestra	Cotton Tail	—	VII/2	E/2	III/6
60	Ellington, Duke and His Famous Orchestra	In a Mellotone	VII/1	VII/3	E/3	III/7
61	Ellington, Duke and His Famous Orchestra	Blue Serge	VII/3	VII/4	E/4	III/8
62	Byas, Don and Slam Stewart	I Got Rhythm	VII/4	VII/5	E/5	III/9
63	Gillespie, Dizzy, Sextet	I Can't Get Started	VII/5	VII/6	E/6	III/10
64	Gillespie, Dizzy, All Star Quintette	Shaw 'Nuff	VII/6	VII/7	E/7	III/11
65	Parker, Charlie, Re-Boppers	KoKo	VII/7	VII/8	E/8	III/12
66	Parker, Charlie, Jazz At the Philharmonic	Lady, Be Good	—	VIII/1	E/9	III/13
67	Parker, Charlie, Quintet	Embraceable You (take #1) excerpt	VII/8	VIII/2	E/10	III/14
68	Parker, Charlie, Quintet	Embraceable You (take #2) excerpt	VII/9	VIII/3	E/11	III/15
69	Parker, Charlie, Quintet	Klactoveedsedstene	VIII/1	VIII/4	E/12	III/16
70	Parker, Charlie, Sextet	Little Benny (Crazeology [1 & 4])	VIII/2	VIII/5	F/1	III/17 & 18
71	Parker, Charlie, All Stars	Parker's Mood	VIII/3	VIII/6	F/2	III/19
72	Garner, Erroll	Fantasy on Frankie and Johnny	VIII/4	VIII/7	F/3	III/20
73	Powell, Bud, Trio	Night in Tunisia	—	VIII/8	F/4	III/21
74	Powell, Bud, Trio	Somebody Loves Me	IX/5	—	—	—
75	Gordon, Dexter, Quartet	Bikini	IX/3	IX/1	F/5	III/22

76	Dameron, Tadd, Sextet	Lady Bird	—	IX/2	F/6	III/23
77	Davis, Miles and His Orchestra	Boplicity	IX/1	IX/3	F/7	IV/1
78	Tristano, Lennie, Quintet	Subconscious Lee	—	IX/4	F/8	IV/2
79	Tristano, Lennie, Quintet	Crosscurrent	VIII/8	—	—	—
80	Norvo, Red and Stan Getz	Body and Soul [excerpt]	—	IX/5	F/9	IV/3
81	Vaughan, Sarah	All Alone	—	IX/6	F/10	IV/4
82	Vaughan, Sarah	My Funny Valentine	VIII/6	IX/7	F/11	IV/5
83	Vaughan, Sarah	Dancing in the Dark	VIII/7	—	—	—
84	Vaughan, Sarah	Ain't No Use	IX/4	X/1	G/1	IV/6
85	Monk, Thelonious, Quartet	Misterioso	IX/6	X/2	G/2	IV/7
86	Monk, Thelonious, Quartet	Evidence	IX/5	X/3	G/3	IV/8
87	Monk, Thelonious, Quintet	Criss-Cross	IX/7	—	—	—
88	Monk, Thelonious, Quintet	Smoke Gets in Your Eyes	X/1	X/4	G/4	IV/9
89	Monk, Thelonious	Bag's Groove	IX/8	X/5	G/5	IV/10
90	Monk, Thelonious	I Should Care	—	X/6	G/6	IV/11
91	Silver, Horace, Quintet	Moon Rays	X/2	XI/1	G/7	IV/12
92	Davis, Miles, Gil Evans Orchestra	Summertime	—	XI/2	G/8	IV/13
93	Mingus, Charles, Quintet	Haitian Fight Song	X/5	—	—	—
94	Mingus, Charles and His Orchestra	Hora Decubitus	X/4	XI/3	H/1	IV/14
95	Modern Jazz Quartet	Django	XI/1	XI/4	H/2	IV/15
96	Rollins, Sonny, Plus Four	Pent-Up House [abridged]	X/3	XII/1	H/3	V/1
97	Rollins, Sonny, Quartet	Blue 7	—	XII/2	H/4	V/2
98	Montgomery, Wes, Quartet	West Coast Blues [abridged]	XI/3	XII/3	H/5	V/3
99	Davis, Miles, Sextet	So What	—	XIII/1	I/1	V/4
100	Evans, Bill, Trio	Blue in Green	XI/2	XIII/2	I/2	V/5
101	Taylor, Cecil, Unit	Enter Evening	XII/4	XIII/3	I/3	V/6
102	Coltrane, John	Alabama	XII/1	XIII/4	I/4	V/7
103	Coleman, Ornette, Quartet	Lonely Woman	XII/2	XIV/1	J/1	V/8
104	Coleman, Ornette, Quartet	Congeniality	XII/3	XIV/2	J/2	V/9
105	Coleman, Ornette, Double Quartet	Free Jazz [excerpt]	—	XIV/3	J/3	V/10
106	World Saxophone Quartet	Steppin'				

Integrated File of the Norton Anthology of Jazz, the New World Records Anthology of American Music, and the Smithsonian Collections of Classic Jazz

(Chronological Order)

YEAR	ARTIST, LEADER, OR GROUP	WORK	NAJ NO.	NW NO.	SIDE/BAND	SCC/ NO.
1800s*	Armstrong, Joe and Group A	Kneebone		278	I/2	
1800s	Armstrong, Joe and Group A	Pay Me		278	II/7	
1800s	Askew, Alec	Emmaline, Take Your Time		252	I/7	
1800s	Bakari-Badji	Field Song from Senegal		252	I/1	
1800s	Crenshaw, Rev. and Congregation	Lining Hymn and Prayer		252	II/2	
1800s	Davis, John and Group A	Carrie Belle		278	II/8	
1800s	Davis, John and Group A	Live Humble		278	I/4	
1800s	Davis, John and Group A	Read 'Em, John		278	I/7	
1800s	Davis, John and Group B	Moses		278	I/1	
1800s	Davis, John and Group B	Raggy Levy		278	II/2	
1800s	Davis, John and Group C	Beulah Land		278	I/8	
1800s	Dudley, John	Po' Boy Blues		252	I/2	
1800s	Forrest City Joe	You Gotta Cut that Out		252	II/8	
1800s	Gary, Leroy	Mama Lucy		252	I/9	
1800s	Hemphill, Rose and Fred McDowell	Rolled and Tumbled		252	II/6	
1800s	Jones, Bessie	Beggin' the Blues		252	II/5	
1800s	Jones, Bessie and Group A	Buzzard Lope, The		278	II/1	
1800s	Jones, Bessie and Group A	O Death		278	I/6	
1800s	Jones, Bessie and Group B	Sheep, Sheep, Don't You Know		278	I/3	
1800s	Jones, Bessie, and Group C	Reg'lar, Reg'lar, Rollin' Under		278	II/6	
1800s	Jones, Bessie and Group C	See Aunt Dinah		278	II/4	
1800s	Jones, Bessie and Group C	Titanic, The		278	II/10	
1800s	McDowell, Fred	Death Comes A-Creepin' In My Room		252	II/3	
1800s	McDowell, Fred and Miles Pratcher	Old Original Blues		252	I/5	
1800s	McDowell, Fred and Pratcher and Davis	Goin' Down to the Races		252	II/7	

*The first group (1800s) are recent recordings of pre-1900 traditional music.

Year	Artist	Title	Page	Ref
1800s	Miller, Leroy and Prisoners	Berta, Berta	252	I/4
1800s	Morrison, Henry and Group A	Ain't I Right	278	II/3
1800s	Morrison, Henry and Group B	Laz'rus	278	II/9
1800s	New Brown Chapel, Memphis, Congregation	Church-House Moan	252	II/4
1800s	Pratcher, Miles and Bob Pratcher	Buttermilk	252	I/8
1800s	Pratcher, Miles and Bob Pratcher	I'm Gonna Live Anyhow Until I Die	252	I/10
1800s	Proctor, Willis and Group A	Daniel	278	I/5
1800s	Proctor, Willis and Group A	Walk, Billy Abbot	278	II/5
1800s	Ratcliff, Henry	Louisiana	252	I/1
1800s	Tangle Eye	Katie Left Memphis	252	I/3
1800s	Tangle Eye	No More, My Lord	252	II/1
1800s	Young, Ed and Lonnie Young	Jim and John	252	I/6
1902	Sousa Band, The John Philip	Trombone Sneeze	282	I/7
1906	Gilbert, Henry F.	Dance in Place Congo, The	228	I/2
1912	Sousa Band, The John Philip	Creole Belles	282	I/2
1914	Europe, James Reese, Society Orchestra	Castle House Rag	269	I/1
1914	Europe, James Reese, Society Orchestra	Castle Walk	269	I/2
1915	Six Brown Brothers	Down Home Rag	269	I/5
1915	Stuart, Herbert	When the Lusitania Went Down	222	I/1
1916	Harvey, Morton	I Didn't Raise My Boy to Be a Soldier	222	I/2
1916	Joplin, Scott	Maple Leaf Rag	290	I/8
1916	O'Connor, George	Nigger Blues	222	I/3
1917	American Quartet	Let's All Be Americans Now	222	I/4
1917	Bayes, Nora	Over There	222	I/5
1918	Jolson, Al	Hello Central! Give Me No Man's Land	228	II/2
1918	Powell, John	Rhapsody Nègre	222	I/6
1918	Shannon Four	There's a Vacant Chair in Every Home Tonight		
1919	Europe, James Reese, Hell Fighters	Clarinet Marmalade	269	I/4
1919	Europe, James Reese, Hell Fighters	Memphis Blues	269	I/3
1919	Europe, James Reese (w. Noble Sissle)	How Ya' Gonna Keep 'Em Down on the Farm	260	II/5
1919	Europe, James Reese (w. Noble Sissle)	Mirandy	260	II/4

1.

YEAR	ARTIST, LEADER, OR GROUP	WORK	NAJ NO.	NW NO.	SIDE/BAND	SCC/NO.
1919	Europe, James Reese (w. Noble Sissle)	On Patrol in No Man's Land		260	II/6	
1919	Jolson, Al	I've Got My Captain Working for Me		222	I/7	
1919	Williams, Bert	Everybody Wants a Key to My Cellar		233	I/8	
1920	Sissle, Noble and Orchestra	Gee, I'm Glad that I'm From Dixie		260	II/3	
1920a†	Hyman, Dick and His Dance Orchestra	Chinatown, My Chinatown		293	II/3	
1920a	Hyman, Dick and His Dance Orchestra	Kansas City Blues		293	II/5	
1920a	Hyman, Dick and His Dance Orchestra	Ma Ragtime Baby		293	II/2	
1920a	Hyman, Dick and His Dance Orchestra	Sweet Man		293	II/6	
1920a	Hyman, Dick and His Dance Orchestra	Waltzing the Blues		293	II/6	
1921	Blake, Eubie	Baltimore Buzz; In Honeysuckle Time		260	I/6	
1921	Blake, Eubie	Love Will Find a Way		260	I/3	
1921	Blake, Eubie and Shuffle Along Orchestra	I'm Just Wild about Harry		260	I/1	
1921	Carpenter, John Alden	Krazy Kat		228	I/1	
1921	Dunn, Johnny, Original Jazz Hounds	Bugle Blues		269	II/5	
1921	Johnson, James P.	Carolina Shout				13.
1921	Saunders, Gertrude	Daddy, Won't You Please Come Home		260	I/5	
1921	Saunders, Gertrude	I'm Craving for that Kind of Love		260	II/1	
1921	Sissle, Noble and Sizzling Syncopators	Baltimore Buzz		260	II/7	
1921	Sissle, Noble and Sizzling Syncopators	In Honeysuckle Time		260	I/2	
1921	Whiteman, Paul	Gypsy Blues		260	I/7	
1922	Blake, Eubie	Bandana Days		260	I/4	
1922	Ory, Edward "Kid," Sunshine Orchestra	Ory's Creole Trombone		269	I/7	
1922	Ory, Edward "Kid," Sunshine Orchestra	Society Blues		269	I/8	

† The group "1920a" are recent recordings of 1920s dances.

Year	Artist	Title	Page	Rec.	No.
1922	Whiteman, Paul	I'll Build a Stairway to Paradise	215	I/4	6.
1923	Oliver, King, Creole Jazz Band	Dippermouth Blues	269	II/3	
1923	Piron, Armand J., New Orleans Orchestra	West Indies Blues			
1923	Williams, Clarence, Blue Five	Old Fashioned Love	269	II/7	
1924	Blythe, Jimmy	Chicago Stomp	259	I/1	
1924	Dunn, Johnny and His Jazz Band	Dunn's Cornet Blues	269	II/6	
1924	Jolson, Al	Mr. Radio Man (Tell My Mammy)	233	II/2	
1924	Miller, Flournoy and Aubrey Lyles	The Fight (dialogue)	260	II/2	
1924	Red Onion Jazz Babies (w. Armstrong & Bechet)	Cake Walking Babies from Home			11.
1925	Bradford, Perry, Jazz Phools	I Ain't Gonna Play No Second Fiddle	269	II/8	
1925	New Orleans Rhythm Kings	She's Cryin' for Me	269	II/4	4.
1925	Smith, Bessie	St. Louis Blues	259	I/3	
1925	Thomas, Hersal	Suitcase Blues			14.
1926	Armstrong, Louis, Hot Five	Big Butter and Egg Man	259	I/2	
1926	Armstrong, Louis, Hot Five	Cornet Chop Suey	272	I/5	
1926	Blythe, Jimmy	Mr. Freddie Blues			
1926	Gershwin, George	Someone to Watch Over Me			
1926	Henderson, Fletcher and His Orchestra	The Stampede	269	I/6	26.
1926	Keppard, Freddie, Jazz Cardinals	Stock Yard Strut			
1926	Morton, Jelly Roll, Red Hot Peppers	Black Bottom Stomp			7.
1926	Morton, Jelly Roll, Red Hot Peppers	Dead Man Blues			8.
1926	Morton, Jelly Roll, Red Hot Peppers	Grandpa's Spells			9.
1926	Peerless Quartet	My Dream of the Big Parade	222	I/8	
1926	Smith, Bessie	Lost Your Head Blues			
1926	Tate, Erskine (w. Louis Armstrong)	Static Strut	256	I/1	5.
1927	Armstrong, Louis, Hot Five	Hotter than That			
1927	Armstrong, Louis, Hot Five	Struttin' with Some Barbecue			
1927	Armstrong, Louis, Hot Seven	Potato Head Blues			18.
1927	Armstrong, Louis, Hot Seven	S.O.L. Blues	235	I/2	17.
1927	Blake, Blind	Southern Rag	274	II/3	16.
1927	Chicago Loopers (w. Beiderbecke & Trumbauer)	Three Blind Mice			15.
1927	Dodds, Johnny, Black Bottom Stompers	Melancholy	274	I/2	

2

YEAR	ARTIST, LEADER, OR GROUP	WORK	NAJ NO.	NW NO.	SIDE/BAND	SCCJ NO.
1927	Ellington, Duke and His Orchestra	East St. Louis Toodle-Oo		290	I/6	52.
1927	Hudson, Hattie	Doggone My Good Luck		269	II/1	
1927	Morgan, Sam, Jazz Band	Bogulousa Strut		269	II/2	
1927	Morgan, Sam, Jazz Band	Steppin' on the Gas		269		
1927	Nichols, Red and Miff Mole's Stompers	Slippin' Around		274	II/7	
1927	Stone, Jesse, Blues Serenaders	Starvation Blues	3	256		
1927	Trumbauer, Frankie and His Orchestra	Ostrich Walk			II/1	
1927	Trumbauer, Frankie and His Orchestra	Riverboat Shuffle				24.
1927	Trumbauer, Frankie and His Orchestra	Singin' the Blues				23.
1927	Underwood, Sugar	Dew Drop Alley		235	I/3	
1927	Waller, Fats	I Ain't Got Nobody				30.
1928	Armstrong, Louis and Earl Hines	Weather Bird				20.
1928	Armstrong, Louis, Hot Five	West End Blues				19.
1928	Dallas String Band	Dallas Rag		235	I/1	
1928	Dickerson, Carroll (w. Armstrong & Hines)	Symphonic Raps		256	I/2	
1928	Johnson Boys, The	Violin Blues		290	I/3	
1928	Johnson, Charlie, Paradise Orchestra	Boy in the Boat, The		256	I/3	
1928	Louisiana Sugar Babes	Willow Tree		256	I/7	
1928	Noone, Jimmy, Apex Club Orchestra	Four or Five Times				25.
1928	Noone, Jimmy, Apex Club Orchestra	I Know that You Know		274	I/6	
1928	Smith, Clarence "Pinetop"	Pinetop's Boogie Woogie		259	I/4	
1928	Trent, Alphonso and His Orchestra	Black and Blue Rhapsody		256	II/7	
1928	Venuti, Joe	My Honey's Loving Arms		250	I/1	
1929	Buck Mountain Band	Yodeling Blues		290	I/5	
1929	Chocolate Dandies (w. Benny Carter)	That's How I Feel Today		256	I/4	
1929	Davenport, Cow Cow	Atlanta Rag		235	I/5	
1929	Floyd, Troy, Plaza Hotel Orchestra	Dreamland Blues Part I		256	II/4	
1929	Floyd, Troy, Plaza Hotel Orchestra	Dreamland Blues Part II		256	II/5	
1929	Holman, Libby	Moanin' Low		215	I/7	
1929	Lee, George E., Kansas City Orchestra	Ruff Scuffling		256	II/6	

YEAR	ARTIST, LEADER, OR GROUP	WORK	NAJ NO.	NW NO.	SIDE/BAND	SCCJ NO.
1931	Webb, Chick (w. Benny Carter)	Heebie Jeebies		217	I/5	
1932	Hines, Earl	Love Me Tonight		274	II/4	29.
1932	Moten, Bennie, Kansas City Orchestra	Moten Swing				
1932	Moten, Bennie, Kansas City Orchestra	Toby		217	II/1	
1932	Robinson, Bill "Bojangles" (w. D. Redman)	Doin' the New Low-Down		215	I/6	
1933	Allen, Henry and Coleman Hawkins	Sister Kate				
1933	Armstrong, Louis and His Orchestra	I Gotta Right to Sing the Blues		250	I/4	22.
1933	Roland, Walter	House Lady Blues		290	II/4	
1933	Tatum, Art	Tiger Rag	4			
1933	Trent, Alphonso and His Orchestra	I've Found a New Baby		256	II/9	
1934	Blackwell, Francis "Scrapper"	Blue Night Blues		290	II/3	
1934	Candy and Coco	China Boy		250	I/5	
1934	Harvey, Roy and Jess Johnson	Guitar Rag		235	II/3	
1934	Henderson, Fletcher and His Orchestra	Wrappin' It Up		217	I/4	27.
1934	Hines, Earl and His Orchestra	Madhouse				
1934	Quintet of the Hot Club of France	Dinah		235	II/2	46.
1934	Tanner, Gid and His Skillet Lickers	Hawkins Rag		235	II/5	
1935	Boyd, Bill and His Cowboy Ramblers	Barn Dance Rag		250	I/8	
1935	Dandridge, Putney (w. Chu Berry)	Chasing Shadows		250	I/6	
1935	Gifford, Gene (w. Bunny Berrigan)	Squareface		259	I/6	
1935	Goodman, Benny, Trio	Body and Soul		250	II/1	32.
1935	Lewis, Meade "Lux"	Honky Tonk Train		259	II/1	
1935	Prima, Louis (w. Pee Wee Russell)	In A Little Gypsy Tearoom				
1936	Ammons, Albert	Boogie Woogie Stomp				
1936	Ellington, Duke and His Famous Orchestra	Clarinet Lament (Barney's Concerto)	5			
1936	Johnson, Robert	I Believe I'll Dust My Broom	1			
1936	Lewis, Meade "Lux"	Mr. Freddie Blues		259	I/8	
1936	Lewis, Meade "Lux"	Yancey Special		259	I/7	
1936	Lunceford, Jimmy and His Orchestra	Organ Grinder's Swing				
1936	Norvo, Red	I Got Rhythm		250	I/7	42.

160*

Year	Artist	Title			
1936	Smith, Stuff (w. Jonah Jones)	Knock, Knock	250	I/9	54.
1937	Boots and His Buddies	Blues of Avalon	217	II/2	
1937	Caceres, Emilio	What's the Use?	250	II/4	
1937	Carter, Benny and His Orchestra	Pardon Me, Pretty Baby	274	I/5	
1937	Ellington, Duke and His Famous Orchestra	Diminuendo and Crescendo in Blue			53.
1937	Ellington, Duke and His Famous Orchestra	The New East St. Louis Toodle-O			
1937	Harlem Hamfats	I'm Cuttin' Out	290	II/5	
1937	Hayes, Edgar (w. Kenny Clarke)	Caravan	217	I/1	35.
1937	Holiday, Billie and Her Orchestra	He's Funny that Way			3.
1937	Johnson, Robert	Hellhound on My Trail			31.
1937	Lewis, Meade "Lux"	Honky Tonk Train Blues			
1937	Marsala, Joe	Clarinet Marmalade	250	II/5	
1937	Mills Blue Rhythm Band	Jammin' for the Jackpot	217	I/8	30a.
1937	Rollini, Adrian	Bugle Call Rag	250	II/2	
1937	Waller, Fats	I Ain't Got Nobody			
1938	Armstrong, Louis and His Orchestra	I Double Dare You	274	II/1	47.
1938	Basie, Count and His Orchestra	Doggin' Around			
1938	Basie, Count and His Orchestra	Every Tub	274	I/1	
1938	Fuller, Blind Boy	Piccolo Rag	235	I/4	
1938	Holiday, Billie	I Can't Get Started	295	I/1	
1938	Howard, Bob (w. Teddy Bunn)	Beale Street Mama	250	II/6	
1938	Morton, Jelly Roll	Maple Leaf Rag			2.
1938	Turner, Joe and Pete Johnson	Roll 'Em Pete	261	I/2	
1938	Wilson, Teddy (w. Hackett and Hodges)	Jungle Love	250	II/3	
1939	Ammons, Albert	Bass Goin' Crazy			
1939	Basie, Count and His Orchestra	Jive at Five	259	II/2	48.
1939	Basie, Count and His Orchestra	Taxi War Dance	274	II/9	49.
1939	Basie, Count, Kansas City Seven	Lester Leaps In			45.
1939	Hampton, Lionel and His Orchestra	When Lights Are Low			
1939	Handy, William Christopher	Loveless Love			
1939	Hawkins, Coleman and His Orchestra	Body and Soul	272	I/3	33.
1939	Johnson, Pete	Climbin' and Screamin'	274	I/8	
1939	Lunceford, Jimmy and His Orchestra	Lunceford Special	259	II/5	41.
1939	Morton, Jelly Roll	King Porter Stomp			10.

YEAR	ARTIST, LEADER, OR GROUP	WORK	NAJ NO.	NW NO.	SIDE/BAND	SCCJ NO.
1939	Rushing, Jimmy (w. Count Basie)	I Left My Baby		295	I/2	
1939	Waller, Thomas "Fats"	Honeysuckle Rose		272	I/7	
1939	Watson, Leo	It's the Tune that Counts		295	I/6	
1939	Watson, Leo	Ja-Da		295	I/5	
1939	Yancey, Jimmy	Mellow Blues, The		259	II/3	
1939	Yancey, Jimmy	Tell 'Em About Me		259	II/4	
1940	Basie, Count and His Orchestra	Tickle-Toe	6			
1940	Bigard, Barney	Tapioca		250	II/7	
1940	Calloway, Cab (w. Dizzy Gillespie)	Pickin' the Cabbage		217	I/6	
1940	Chocolate Dandies (w. Eldridge & Carter)	I Can't Believe that You're in Love with Me				44.
1940	Ellington, Duke and His Famous Orchestra	Concerto for Cootie				58.
1940	Ellington, Duke and His Famous Orchestra	Cotton Tail				59.
1940	Ellington, Duke and His Famous Orchestra	In a Mellotone				60.
1940	Ellington, Duke and His Famous Orchestra	Ko-Ko				57.
1940	Ellington, Duke and His Orchestra	Harlem Air Shaft				56.
1940	Ellington, Duke and Jimmy Blanton	Pitter Panther Patter		274	II/8	
1940	Five Breezes, The	My Buddy Blues		290	II/8	
1940	Goodman, Benny, (w. Christian & Basie)	Breakfast Feud [composite]				51.
1940	Johnson, Pete	Blues on the Downbeat		259	II/6	
1940	Johnson, Pete	Kaycee on My Mind		259	II/7	
1940	Leonard, Harlan	A-La-Bridges		284	I/1	
1940	Leonard, Harlan	Dameron Stomp		284	I/2	
1940	Turner, Joe	Careless Love		295	I/4	
1940	Turner, Joe	Piney Brown Blues		295	I/3	
1940	Williams, Mary Lou, Six Men and a Girl	Zonky		284	II/2	
1941	Ammons, Albert and Pete Johnson	Cuttin' the Boogie		259	II/8	
1941	Bechet, Sidney	What Is this Thing Called Love?		274	I/4	
1941	Bonney, Betty (w. Les Brown)	He's 1-A in the Army and He's 1-A in My Heart		222	II/2	

Year	Artist	Title	p.	Disc	No.
1941	Calloway, Cab (w. Milt Hinton)	Ebony Silhouette	217	I/7	61.
1941	Ellington, Duke and His Famous Orchestra	Blue Serge	261	I/3	50.
1941	Golden Gate Quartet	Sun Didn't Shine, The	274	I/7	36.
1941	Goodman, Benny (w. Christian & Basie)	I Found a New Baby	274	II/2	43.
1941	Hodges, Johnny and His Orchestra	Passion Flower	250	II/9	
1941	Holiday, Billie and Eddie Heywood	All of Me	290	II/6	
1941	Kirby, John	Bugler's Dilemma	290	I/1	
1941	Krupa, Gene and His Orchestra	Rockin' Chair	222	II/6	
1941	McClennan, Tommy	Deep Blue Sea Blues	222	II/4	
1941	Rachell, Yank and Sonny Boy Williamson	Peach Tree Blues	250	II/8	
1941	Robertson, Dick	Goodbye, Mama	222	II/5	
1941	Robertson, Dick	We Did it Before and We Can Do it Again	222	II/3	
1941	Williams, Cootie	Blues in My Condition	261	I/1	
1942	Baker, Kenny	I Left My Heart at the Stage Door Canteen	222	II/1	
1942	Golden Gate Quartet	Stalin Wasn't Stallin'	222	II/8	
1942	Goodman, Benny and His Orchestra	Mission to Moscow	290	II/7	
1942	Hampton, Lionel	Flying Home	261	I/4	34.
1942	Jones, Spike	Der Fuehrer's Face			12.
1942	Kyser, Kay	Praise the Lord and Pass the Ammunition			
1942	Williamson, Sonny Boy	Love Me, Baby			
1943	Cole, Nat "King"	Straighten Up and Fly Right			
1943	Hawkins, Coleman, Quartet	Man I Love, The			
1944	Long, Johnny (w. Patti Dugan)	No Love, No Nothin'			
1944	Bechet, Sidney, Blue Note Jazz Men	Blue Horizon			
1944	Eckstine, Billy	Good Jelly Blues	222	II/7	
1944	Heywood, Eddie, Jr.	Begin the Beguine	284	I/6	
1944	Soul Stirrers, The	Walk Around	298	II/3	
1944	Webster, Ben	Perdido	224	I/3	
1945	Byas, Don and Slam Stewart	I Got Rhythm	284	II/1	
1945	Gant, Cecil	I Wonder	261	I/5	62.
1945	Gillespie, Dizzy and Charlie Parker	Shaw 'Nuff	271	I/3	64.

7

YEAR	ARTIST, LEADER, OR GROUP	WORK	NAJ NO.	NW NO.	SIDE/BAND	SCCJ NO.
1945	Gillespie, Dizzy, Sextet	Groovin' High	8	271	I/1	63.
1945	Gillespie, Dizzy, Sextet	I Can't Get Started		271	I/8	
1945	Norvo, Red (w. Parker and Gillespie)	Congo Blues		295	I/8	
1945	Parker, Charlie	KoKo		284	II/6	65.
1945	Washington, Dinah	Blowtop Blues				
1946	Clarke, Kenny and His 52nd Street Boys	Royal Roost				
1946	Dodds, Baby, Trio	Wolverine Blues		274	II/6	
1946	Forrest, Helen	My Guy's Come Back		222	II/9	
1946	Gillespie, Dizzy and His Orchestra	Things to Come		271	I/5	
1946	Herman, Woody	Summer Sequence (Parts 1, 2, 3)		216	I/1	
1946	Jordan, Louis	Choo Choo Ch' Boogie		261	I/6	
1946	Kings of Harmony, The	God Shall Wipe all Tears Away		224	I/1	
1946	Lawrence, Elliot	Five O'Clock Shadow		284	I/5	
1946	Marmarosa, Dodo	Mellow Mood		284	II/5	
1946	Mooney, Joe	Tea for Two		284	II/3	
1946	Parker, Charlie, Jazz At The Philharmonic	Lady, Be Good				66.
1946	Vaughan, Sarah (w. Tadd Dameron)	You're Not the Kind		271	I/2	
1946	Wilson, Gerald	Saint, The		284	I/3	
1947	Ellington, Duke	Clothed Woman, The		216	I/2	
1947	Famous Blue Jay Singers, The	Canaan Land		224	I/2	
1947	Fitzgerald, Ella	Robbins Nest		295	I/7	
1947	Garner, Erroll	Fantasy on Frankie and Johnny				72.
1947	Gordon, Dexter and Wardell Gray	The Chase (Parts 1 & 2)		284	II/7	75.
1947	Gordon, Dexter, Quartet	Bikini				
1947	Hampton, Lionel	Mingus Fingers		284	I/7	
1947	Harris, Wynoonie "Blues"	Good Rockin' Tonight		261	I/8	
1947	Johnson, Bunk	Entertainer, The		235	I/7	
1947	Mooney, Joe	I Can't Get up the Nerve				
1947	Norvo, Red and Stan Getz	Body and Soul [excerpt]		284	II/4	80.
1947	Parker, Charlie	Embraceable You		271	I/7	68.
1947	Parker, Charlie	Relaxin' at Camarillo		271	I/6	
1947	Parker, Charlie, Quintet	Embraceable You (take #1) excerpt				67.
1947	Parker, Charlie, Quintet	Klactoveedsedstene				69.

Year	Artist	Title			
1947	Parker, Charlie, Sextet	Little Benny (Crazeology [1 & 4])	224	I/5	70.
1947	Powell, Bud, Trio	Somebody Loves Me	284	I/8	74.
1947	Roberta Martin Singers, The	Yield Not to Temptation	261	I/7	
1947	Thornhill, Claude	Donna Lee	271	II/3	
1947	Walker, T-Bone	Call it Stormy Monday			
1948	Dameron, Tadd and Fats Navarro	Jahbero			76.
1948	Dameron, Tadd, Sextet	Lady Bird	271	II/1	
1948	Herman, Woody	Lemon Drop	271	II/4	85.
1948	Monk, Thelonious	Misterioso			86.
1948	Monk, Thelonious, Quartet	Evidence	271	I/4	71.
1948	Parker, Charlie	Parker's Mood			77.
1949	Davis, Miles and His Orchestra	Boplicity			
1949	Konitz, Lee and Warne Marsh, Sextet	Marshmallow	284	I/4	
1949	Lawrence, Elliot	Elevation	235	I/6	
1949	McTell, Blind Willie	Kill it Kid			
1949	Tatum, Art	Willow Weep for Me	224	I/6	39.
1949	Tharpe, Rosetta and Katie Bell Nubin	Daniel in the Lion's Den			
1949	Tristano, Lennie	Yesterdays	216	I/3	
1949	Tristano, Lennie, Quintet	Crosscurrent			79.
1949	Tristano, Lennie, Quintet	Subconscious Lee			78.
1950	Bradshaw, Tiny and His Orchestra	Well, Oh Well	261	II/1	
1950	Fairfield Four, The	Tree of Level [Tree of Lebanon]	224	I/4	
1950	Hopkins, Lightnin'	Hello, Central	261	II/2	
1950s	Kenton, Stan	Mirage	216	I/4	
1951	Smith, Willie Me Ford	Give Me Wings	224	I/7	
1951	Clovers, The	One Mint Julep	261	II/3	
1951	Little Richard	Every Hour	249	I/9	
1951	Monk, Thelonious, Quintet	Criss-Cross			87.
1951	Powell, Bud	Un Poco Loco	271	II/2	
1952	Powell, Bud, Trio	Night in Tunisia			73.
1952	Ace, Johnny and the Beale Streeters	Clock, The	249	I/2	
1952	Holiday, Billie and Her Orchestra	These Foolish Things			
1952	Nichols, Herbie	'S Wonderful	275	I/1	37.
1952	Thornton, Willie Mae "Big Mama"	Hound Dog	261	II/4	
1952	Waters, Muddy	Hoochie Coochie Man	261	II/7	
1953	Adams, Faye (w. Joe Morris and His Orchestra)	Shake a Hand	249	I/4	

YEAR	ARTIST, LEADER, OR GROUP	WORK	NAJ NO.	NW NO.	SIDE/BAND	SCCJ NO.
1953	Brown, Ruth	Mama, He Treats Your Daughter Mean		261	II/5	
1953	Mingus, Charles	Eclipse	11	216	I/5	
1953	Mulligan, Gerry, Quartet with Konitz	I Can't Believe that You're in Love with Me				
1953	Parker, Charlie, Quartet	Confirmation	10	261	II/6	
1953	Til, Sonny and the Orioles	Crying in the Chapel		249	I/3	
1953	Ward, Billy and His Dominoes	Have Mercy, Baby		216	II/1	89.
1954	Kenton, Stan	Egdon Heath				88.
1954	Monk, Thelonious	Bag's Groove		271	II/6	
1954	Monk, Thelonious, Quintet	Smoke Gets in Your Eyes		249	I/1	
1954	Silver, Horace	Stop Time		249	I/6	
1954	Turner, Joe	Shake, Rattle and Roll		295	II/4	
1955	Berry, Chuck	Maybellene		295	II/2	
1955	Carter, Betty	Can't We Be Friends?		295	II/3	
1955	Carter, Betty	Moonlight in Vermont		275	I/6	
1955	Carter, Betty	Thou Swell		249	I/8	
1955	Chaloff, Serge	Body and Soul		249	I/5	
1955	Domino, Fats	I Can't Go On		242	I/2	
1955	Haley, Bill and the Comets	See You Later, Alligator				
1955	Konitz, Lee and Warne Marsh	Donna Lee				
1955	Silver, Horace, Quintet	Preacher, The	12			
1955	Tatum, Art	Too Marvelous for Words				40.
1956	Brown, Clifford and Max Roach	What Is this Thing Called Love?		271	II/5	
1956	Jazz Messengers	Nica's Dream		242	I/3	
1956	Modern Jazz Quartet	Woody'n You		242	I/1	
1956	Ravens, The	Give Me a Simple Prayer		261	I/9	
1956	Rollins, Sonny, Plus Four	Pent-Up House [abridged]				96.
1956	Rollins, Sonny, Quartet	Blue 7				97.
1956	Russell, George	Concerto for Billy The Kid		216	II/2	83.
1956	Vaughan, Sarah	Dancing in the Dark				
1957	Holly, Buddy and the Crickets	That'll Be the Day				
1957	Mingus, Charles, Quintet	Haitian Fight Song		249	II/2	93.
1957	Monk, Thelonious	I Should Care	13			90.
1957	Russell, George (Brandeis Festival Orchestra)	All about Rosie (Third Movement)				

Year	Artist	Title		Track	Page	
1957	Schuller, Gunther	Transformation		II/3	216	
1957	Silhouettes, The	Get a Job		II/1	249	
1957	Wilson, Jackie	Reet Petite		II/4	249	
1958	Counce, Curtis (w. Hope and Land)	Into the Orbit		I/2	275	
1958	Counce, Curtis (w. Hope and Land)	Race for Space		I/3	275	
1958	Davis, Miles, Gil Evans Orchestra	Summertime	14			92.
1958	Davis, Miles, Sextet	Dr. Jekyll				
1958	Holiday, Billie	End of a Love Affair, The		II/8	295	
1958	Price, Lloyd	Mailman Blues		I/7	249	
1958	Shirelles, The	I Met Him on a Sunday		II/5	249	
1958	Silver, Horace, Quintet	Moon Rays				91.
1959	Charles, Ray and the Raelets	I'm Movin' On		II/7	249	
1959	Coasters, The	What About Us?		II/8	249	
1959	Coleman, Ornette, Quartet	Change of the Century	16			104.
1959	Coleman, Ornette, Quartet	Congeniality				103.
1959	Coleman, Ornette, Quartet	Lonely Woman				
1959	Coltrane, John, Quartet	Giant Steps	15			
1959	Connor, Chris	Misty		II/5	295	
1959	Davis, Miles, Sextet	So What				99.
1959	Evans, Bill, Trio	Blue in Green				100.
1960	Bonds, Gary U. S.	New Orleans		II/9	249	
1960	Byard, Jaki	Diane's Melody		I/5	275	
1960	Byard, Jaki	II, V, I		I/4	275	
1960	Clark, Dee	At My Front Door		II/6	249	
1960	Coleman, Ornette, Double Quartet	Free Jazz [excerpt]				105.
1960	Connor, Chris	Love		II/6	295	
1960	Farmer, Art and Benny Golson	Blues March		II/1	242	
1960	Lacy, Steve	Introspection		II/2	275	
1960	Lacy, Steve	Louise		II/1	275	
1960	Lewis, John	Piazza Navona		II/4	216	
1960	Mingus, Charles	Original Faubus Fables		II/4	242	
1960	Modern Jazz Quartet	Django				
1960	Montgomery, Wes, Quartet	West Coast Blues [bridged]				95.
1960	Russell, George	War Gewesen				98.
1960s	Flatt, Lester and Earl Scruggs	Randy Lynn Rag		II/3	242	
1960s	Travis, Merle	Cannon Ball Rag/Bugle Call Rag		II/8	235	
1960s	Vaughan, Sarah	Key Largo		II/7	235	
				II/1	295	

YEAR	ARTIST, LEADER, OR GROUP	WORK	NAJ NO.	NW NO.	SIDE/BAND	SCCJ NO.
1961	Blake, Ran and Jeanne Lee	Laura		216	II/5	
1961	Lincoln, Abbey	When Malindy Sings		295	II/7	
1961	Little, Booker, Sextet	Strength and Sanity		275	II/4	
1961	Little, Booker, Sextet	We Speak		275	II/3	
1961	Vaughan, Sarah	Ain't No Use				84.
1962	Lewis, Jerry Lee	Good Golly Miss Molly		249	II/3	
1962	Poplin, China	Sumter Rag/Steel Guitar Rag		235	II/6	
1963	Coltrane, John	Alabama				102.
1963	Mingus, Charles and His Orchestra	Hora Decubitus				94.
1964	Davis, Rev. Gary	Maple Leaf Rag		235	I/8	
1964	Fitzgerald, Ella	You'd Be so Nice to Come Home to				38.
1964	Monk, Thelonious, Quartet	Bemsha Swing	17			
1964	Rollins, Sonny	Now's the Time		242	II/2	
1966	Davis, Miles, Quintet	Circle	18			101.
1966	Taylor, Cecil, Unit	Enter Evening				81.
1967	Vaughan, Sarah	All Alone				
1970s	Williams, Marion	They Led My Lord Away		224	I/8	
1971	Weather Report	Tears	19			82.
1973	Vaughan, Sarah	My Funny Valentine				
1977	Ford, Ricky	Aerolinos		204	II/3	
1977	Ford, Ricky	Blues Peru		204	I/3	
1977	Ford, Ricky	Dexter		204	I/4	
1977	Ford, Ricky	Loxodonta Africana		204	I/1	
1977	Ford, Ricky	My Romance		204	II/1	
1977	Ford, Ricky	One Up One Down		204	II/2	
1977	Ford, Ricky	Ucil		204	I/2	
1978	Taylor, Cecil	Holiday en Masque		201	II/1	
1978	Taylor, Cecil	Idut		201	I/1	
1978	Taylor, Cecil	Serdab		201	I/2	
1981	World Saxophone Quartet	Steppin'				
1986	Marsalis, Wynton, Quartet	Delfeayo's Dilemma	20			106.

GLOSSARY

back line: the rhythm section in a jazz ensemble, usually consisting of drums, bass (string or brass), and a chordal instrument such as piano, banjo, or guitar.

bebop (bop, rebop): a style that evolved in the early 1940s, characterized by asymmetrical phrases, ornate melodic lines with much solo improvisation, complex rhythmic patterns, and more novel and dissonant harmonies than those used in the swing style of the preceding decade.

blue notes: the lowered third, fifth, and seventh degrees of the major scale, which, in blues and jazz performances, vary in intonation and fall somewhere between the normal major and minor tempered scale intervals.

blues: a type of vocal or instrumental music, usually patterned in twelve-measure stanzas of three four-measure phrases over simple tonic, dominant, and subdominant harmonies, incorporating flexible rhythmic patterns over a steady 4/4 pulse, and, in its vocal form, lyrics dealing with social protest or sexual themes.

boogie-woogie: a piano blues style of the 1920s and '30s characterized by a left-hand ostinato figure underlying a rhythmically freer right hand.

bop: *see* bebop.

bottleneck guitar: when an ordinary guitar is tuned so that the open strings sound a chord (e.g., E–G–C–G–C–E) instead of the regular tuning in fourths plus a third (E–A–D–G–B–E), then it may be played for simple blues accompaniment by stopping all the strings at the same fret position with a straight edge, rather than by using complex fingering. A closed pocket knife, clasped between two fingers, is often used to play the instrument in this manner, but a bottleneck, broken off an ordinary soda bottle and worn over the middle finger of the left hand, will also work. Hence, the term "bottleneck

guitar" was applied to this combination of tuning and method of performance.

break: a short instrumental bridge between phrases in a vocal line, probably deriving
from African call-and-response performance patterns.

cakewalk: a dance characterized by syncopated rhythms, popular in American minstrel shows.

chorus: in jazz performance, the refrain of a popular song (or its harmonic outline),
usually repeated over and over by different members of the ensemble.

classic blues (city blues): a type of blues usually performed by female singers
accompanied by jazz band or piano, with lyrics relating to sexual or social
and racial problems.

classic jazz: the music that originated in the southern part of the United States in
the late nineteenth century, which came to be characterized by: 1) group
and solo improvisation; 2) rhythm sections in ensembles; 3) steady, underlying pulse to which syncopated melodies and rhythmic patterns are added;
4) reliance on popular-song form and blues form; 5) tonal harmonic organization often using blue notes; 6) vocal and instrumental timbral features
such as vibrato, glissando, etc.; 7) a performer or performer-composer aesthetic rather than a composer-centered orientation. Classic jazz has also been
referred to as Dixieland and New Orleans jazz.

classic ragtime: the ragtime school represented chiefly by Scott Joplin, James Scott,
and Joseph Lamb.

comp: to accompany.

concert pitch: for a transposing instrument, the pitch sounded, rather than the pitch
notated. Thus for a B♭ clarinet, written C is concert B♭.

cool jazz: an early 1950s development of the bebop style, combining the technical
virtuosity of bebop with a new timbral quality—usually heard in the sax—
using few overtones and little or no vibrato.

coon song: a type of song, popular in the 1880s, in syncopated ragtime style, often
with lyrics that reflected the white American stereotypes of black Americans.

country blues (rural blues, Southern blues): a type of blues usually performed by
a male singer accompanying himself on a simple instrument such as banjo
or guitar, and dealing with topics affecting the lives of country blacks, often
with implicit sexual references.

Dixieland jazz: *see* classic jazz.

East Coast hard-bop school: a 1950s style formed as a reaction to cool and West
Coast jazz, incorporating full-voiced instrumental sound, loud dynamics,
and emotional, energetic performances.

ensemble "out": the last full chorus in a jazz piece, usually played by the entire ensemble.

free jazz: performances that negate stylistic rules that were formerly valid, by attempting to destroy feelings of structure, direction, and tonality while introducing random improvisation and nontraditional instruments such as sitars, amplified thumb pianos, police whistles, etc.

front line: the melodic instruments of a traditional jazz ensemble, usually consisting of clarinet, cornet, and trombone.

funky: a term used to describe the rhythmic style of East Coast hard-bop jazz, with strong accentuations and a bouncing rhythmic style.

head arrangement: a piece of music that is not written down but is worked out in rehearsals and duplicated as exactly as possible in subsequent performances.

high hat (sock cymbal): a pedal-operated pair of cymbals in which the bottom part is stationary and the top part is moved up and down by the pedal.

jig: an early Midwestern term for ragtime, as in jig band, jig piano.

lick: a riff, a musical idea, a break.

Mickey ending: a term that jazz musicians use to refer disparagingly to a rhythmic cliché often used by commercial bands, such as Guy Lombardo and His Royal Canadians, to signal the end of a dance number. The rhythm is identical to that used in Mickey Mouse cartoon music (hence the term).

minstrel show: a type of American entertainment popular in the nineteenth century, in which whites dressed as blacks and performed songs in a stylized black-American dialect, written mostly by white composers.

New Orleans–style jazz: *see* classic jazz.

patting juba: clapping hands, stamping feet, and slapping thighs in syncopated, polyrhythmic patterns, a practice performed by American slaves to produce dance accompaniment.

progressive jazz: a mid-1940s development of the big-band style using expanded orchestration, nontraditional harmonic changes, and frequent changes of tempo, implying concert rather than dance music.

ragtime: a style popular in the first two decades of the twentieth century characterized by a nonsyncopated bass in duple meter underlying a syncopated treble melody; functional, diatonic harmonies stressing tonic, dominant, subdominant, and applied dominants in major keys; and compounded song-form structures with sixteen- or thirty-two-measure periods and shorter introductions, vamps, and codas.

rebop: *see* bebop.

ride: to concentrate on playing with virtuosity; to improvise.

ride cymbal: a single cymbal, usually mounted on the rim of the bass drum and hit with a stick.

riff: a repeated musical phrase, usually short, used as a background for a soloist or a theme for a final chorus. Also, an instrumental blues melody.

rip: upward glissando.

rural blues: *see* country blues.

scat singing: an instrumental solo performed by the voice to vocables, or nonsense syllables.

sideman: a member of a jazz band or swing orchestra.

skiffle band: a novelty orchestra that depends largely on showmanship, slapstick, and extramusical effects for audience appeal.

sock cymbal: *see* high hat.

song form: a design consisting of a section (usually eight measures long) that is repeated and then returns following a contrasting section (usually the same length as the initial section): **AABA.**

Southern blues: *see* country blues.

stomp: the process of repeating a rhythmic figure in the melodic line in a riff pattern, leading to polyphonic accentuation that produces a strong rhythmic momentum within the improvising polyphony.

stoptime: the process of playing a regular, but discontinuous, rhythm, most often a staccato chord played on the first beat of every measure or every other measure. It is usually employed as a background effect for an instrumental solo, and derives from a common accompaniment pattern used to support tap dancing.

stride: a piano style characterized by use of the left hand in a downbeat-upbeat pattern (oom-pah, oom-pah rhythm), in which beats one and three (in 4/4) are heavily accented single notes, octaves, or tenths, and beats two and four are unaccented triads.

swing: a style popular from around 1930 to 1945, characterized by arrangements for large ensembles (big bands), with written passages that separate the ensembles by sections in antiphonal writing and solo improvisations at designated points in the score, a lightened rhythm section led by the string bass keeping a regular accentuation on the beat, melodic patterns based on scales and arpeggios, and a generally refined dance-band sound.

tailgate trombone: a New Orleans style of trombone playing, so called from the customary location of the trombonist on a horse-drawn parade cart. Because of the freedom of movement necessary to operate a trombone slide, the open tailgate was the preferred seat of most trombonists.

third-stream music: a term coined by Gunther Schuller to denote the merger of jazz and classical styles.

trap drums: the entire set of percussion instruments, including bass drum, snare drum, cowbell, woodblock, etc.

up-tempo: fast.

urban blues: a blues style in which the vocalist is accompanied by a swing-style band—and later, by electric guitar and amplified sax—and sings of love, sex, and society's impact on and meaning for black Americans.

vamp: a short connecting passage, usually four or eight measures long, that joins, usually by modulation, two sections of music lying at different harmonic levels. When no modulation occurs, a simple chord pattern is repeated as a "filler" between sections.

West Coast jazz: a 1950s style characterized by performance in middle-sized or smaller ensembles using single instruments rather than groups (e.g., one trumpet rather than a trumpet section) playing in a style virtually indistinguishable from cool jazz.

woodshed: to practice or rehearse in private in order to gain technical mastery of one's instrument before going into a jam session.

COPYRIGHT
ACKNOWLEDGMENTS

Photographs reproduced in this volume have been supplied by the following, whose courtesy is gratefully acknowledged:

INDEX

Starred page numbers refer to the back section of the book. Boldface page numbers indicate the main discussions of persons and subjects. Boldface italic page numbers signify illustrations. An "n" is appended to the page number when the reference appears only in the footnotes.